WHO WAS WHO IN THE
CONFEDERACY

WHO WAS WHO IN THE
CONFEDERACY

A comprehensive, illustrated biographical reference to more than
1,000 of the principal Confederacy participants in the Civil War

by
Stewart Sifakis

Facts On File
New York • Oxford

PHOTO CREDITS

AC	Author's collection	LC	Library of Congress
B&L	Battles and Leaders of the Civil War	NA	National Archives
Harper's	*Harper's Weekly*	NPS	National Park Service
Leslie's	*Frank Leslie's Illustrated Newspaper*	SI	Smithsonian Institution

Who Was Who in the Confederacy

Copyright © 1988 by Stewart Sifakis

Originally published with *Who Was Who in the Confederacy* as *Who Was Who in the Civil War.*

Facts On File, Inc.
460 Park Avenue South
New York, New York 10016

Library of Congress Cataloging-in-Publication Data

Sifakis, Stewart.
    Who was who in the Confederacy / by Stewart Sifakis.
       p. cm.
    Excerpted from the author's Who was who in the Civil War.
    Bibliography: p.
    Includes index.
    ISBN 0-8160-2204-6
    1. United States—History—Civil War, 1861-1865—Biography-
-Dictionaries. 2. Generals—Southern States—Biography-
-Dictionaries. 3. Confederate States of America—Biography-
-Dictionaries. 4. Confederate States of America. Army—Biography-
-Dictionaries.   I. Sifakis, Stewart. Who was who in the Civil War.
II. Title.
F467.S54   1989
973.7′45′0922—dc20   89-35004
                                                              CIP

Who Was Who in the Union 0-8160-2203-8
Who Was Who in the Confederacy 0-8160-2204-6
Two-volume set 0-8160-2202-X

British CIP data available on request

Printed in the United States of America

10 9 8 7 6 5 4 3 2 1

CONTENTS

For my parents

INTRODUCTION

It has been estimated that for every day since the end of the American Civil War one book, magazine or newspaper article has appeared dealing with some aspect of that fratricidal struggle. Why has interest been so extensive and enduring?

Most probably, because it was an all-American fight. Before and after the war the North and South were one common country. In fact, the war was the key factor in forming the two sections into a true nation. The relatively rapid cooling off of animosities is remarkable. Ex-Confederate generals, such as Joe Wheeler and M. Caldwell Butler, wore Federal blue as general officers in the Spanish-American War—alongside their former opponents. Other ex-Confederates were serving in the U.S. Congress as early as the 1870s. Well into the 20th century there were joint reunions of Union and Confederate veterans—most notably at Gettysburg, Pennsylvania.

In recent times it has been perfectly natural for Northerners to share in the admiration of the accomplishments of Robert E. Lee, "Stonewall" Jackson, Nathan B. Forrest or Jeb Stuart. The differences in nomenclature used to identify the Civil War—War of the Rebellion, War for Southern Independence, War of Secession, War of the Northern Aggression, and The Late Unpleasantness—have taken on an almost whimsical ring, while still identifying a speaker's attitude regarding the conflict.

But what of America's other wars? To a large extent, because of a matter of scale, they have not sparked the same level of interest as the Civil War. Great Britain did not use her full resources to oppose the American Revolution; and the American army itself was constantly dissolving and there were few Colonial successes to report. Furthermore, the Colonies themselves were not fully behind the Revolution. Modern estimates indicate that only one-third of the population of the 13 Colonies were for independence. Another third were either actively or passively loyal to the crown. The balance just wanted to be left alone.

Like the Revolution, the War of 1812 sported few American battlefield successes and was fought with a lack of enthusiasm on both sides. The American army was composed mostly of short-term militia, and tended to melt away when the immediate danger had passed. In Europe the War was considered a sideshow in the conflict against Napoleon. Accordingly, Great Britain invested a minimum of her resources in the conflict on the western side of the Atlantic.

The Mexican War was fought against an enemy that most Americans felt was racially inferior and that it was only natural they should defeat easily. Actually, this conflict should be studied more closely by Civil War scholars since many of the senior Union and Confederate officers received their education in combat south of the Rio Grande.

The Spanish-American War, like the Mexican War, was fought against an "inferior" enemy and thus lacks the spark to kindle widespread interest. To a certain extent the same can be said of the various Indian wars.

World War I was for the United States only a brief conflict. While the European continent was convulsed in mutual genocide for years, Americans actively entered the conflict only in the final months.

World War II is the closest rival to the Civil War in the level of literature and public interest it has spawned. But it will probably never take over from the Civil War since America was only one of many actors in the global struggle.

The Korean War lacks interest on a wide scale since it ended in a draw. While the Vietnam War was an out and out debacle.

Another key factor in the continuing fascination with the War Between the States is its amazing cost. In four years of war over 600,000 lives were lost, North and South. To put this figure in perspective, when one puts America's losses in all of its other wars together, it is not until well into the Vietnam War that the losses in the Civil War are exceeded.

No large portion of the United States has ever felt the destruction wrought by a foreign, occupying power. Only the Confederacy has suffered such devastation and that at the hands of other Americans.

The Civil War marks a turning point in the history of the American republic. Not only did it forge a united nation but it also facilitated the Industrial Revolution that made the United

States a world power and leader by the early 20th century. New industries and inventions placed in operation during the Civil War, and expanded afterwards, prepared the nation for its role in the next century's world wars. Also, the release of so many men from the opposing armies, so soon after Appomattox, provided the manpower that led to the rapid conquest of the West and the establishment of a truly transcontinental power, with interests beyond both the Atlantic and Pacific oceans.

Furthermore, the Civil War was a war of innovation. The extensive use of longer-range rifles and artillery drastically altered battlefield tactics. Trench warfare became extensive. Railroads were used tactically and strategically for the first time; railroad artillery came into use. Aerial observation and fire-control of artillery came into being in the first years of the war. Telegraphic communications were used extensively. Land and water mines (they called them torpedoes) were devised, as were primitive hand grenades. Ironclad vessels fought each other for the first time. The first sinking of a warship by a submarine occurred. The first Congressional Medals of Honor were awarded. Breech-loading carbines, rifles and cannon were brought into battlefield use. Repeating carbines and rifles began to make their debut, and some primitive machine guns were developed. Both North and South introduced a national military draft for the first time in American history. The Union introduced the first federal income tax. And the war led to the first assassination of a president of the United States.

Many ask: If so much has been written on the Civil War, is there really a need for more? The answer is an emphatic yes. There are many aspects of the conflict that have been covered only superficially and require more in-depth research. But for such research a bedrock of reference works is essential. That is where *Who Was Who In The Confederacy* comes in.

To date, there are encyclopedic biographies dealing collectively with Confederate generals, West Point graduates, regular army officers, volunteer officers from certain states, medical officers, Confederate congressmen and civilian appointees in the regular army. Some of these were published in the last century and are hard to locate today. There is no one, current source available covering the full range of personalities who made—and fought—the Civil War for the South.

In any collective biography the major difficulty is the establishment of selection criteria. For this work I have tried to include those persons who most affected the conflict. At the same time I have attempted to strike a reasonable balance between military and civilian, and heroes and rogues.

Among the nearly 1,000 entries I have included those political leaders who had the most impact on prewar and wartime policy matters. Thus the presidential and vice presidential candidates in 1860 are treated as well as several prewar U.S. presidents. For the Congress I have included most senators and those members of the lower houses who either served as committee chairmen or were particularly noted for their legislative activities, such as William P. Miles. All of the state governors—e.g., Joe Brown—are covered.

Other political activists—such as secessionist Edmund Ruffin and Southern Unionist John A. Gilmer—are included.

Of course, in dealing with any war most of the coverage is going to be devoted to the military. Accordingly, I have included all of those 425 officers generally recognized as having attained one of the four grades of general. In addition I have treated most of those who were, then or later, generally referred to as having been general officers but for whom there is no official confirmation of their appointments, such as George P. Harrison, Jr. Militia officers who actually served at the front—like M. Jeff Thompson—are included. Also, those officers promoted to brigadier or major general by General E. Kirby Smith in the cut-off Trans-Mississippi Department—e.g., Alexander W. Terrell.

In selecting officers below the grade of brigadier general, I have included those lower-ranking officers who led forces larger than a regiment for a lengthy period or in major actions. Also included are junior officers—like John Pelham—who were particularly distinguished in leading smaller units. Officers and men who took part in important raids (Jesse C. McNeill) are treated.

Other combatants include: naval personnel, such as Franklin Buchanan; scouts and spies, such as Longstreet's Harrison; and Marine Corps officers, such as Lloyd J. Beall.

Among the noncombatants at the front were: the journalists, such as Peter W. Alexander; the artist-correspondents, such as Conrad W. Chapman; the surgeons, such as Hunter H. McGuire; and the nurses, such as Sally L. Tompkins.

On the diplomatic front many ambassadors from the South (John Slidell) and from abroad (Henri Mercier) are included. Foreign leaders such as Napoleon III and Queen Victoria are treated.

In addition, all members of the Confederate cabinet are covered.

This work concentrates on the characters' actions during the Civil War, giving researchers the basic career data of the participants. Thus pre- and postwar activities are only briefly sketched. Of course, when an individual played a role in bringing about secession and the war, much more attention is given to his prewar actions.

In the biographies of those military officers who led units larger than regiments, it should be noted that armies and departments frequently operated as one organization with the same commander. Thus Robert E. Lee commanded the Department of Northern Virginia as well as the Army of Tennessee. Where confusion may occur both titles are given for clarity.

In the list or organizations led by an individual, the dates of command are often only approximate due to the lack of adequate records. Those records in existence may indicate several different dates for an officer's assumption or relinquishment of command. These dates might be the actual date of physical assumption, the date on which he issues the order announcing his assumption of command, the date he was assigned by a local commander to duty, and/or the date that this was confirmed by the War Department. Due to the difficulties of travel, it was not uncommon for an officer to take a matter of weeks in reporting to a new assignment. I have always tried to determine the date closest to actual assumption but this was frequently not possible. This has led to some overlapping of dates of assignment. Another cause of such overlapping are actual cases of duplicate assignments. Often an officer would command a field brigade and a geographical district simultaneously. Also, in times of limited activity a brigade commander would be in charge of the division while still retaining his normal command.

A

ADAMS, Daniel Weisiger (1821-1872)

Wounded three times during the Civil War, Confederate General Daniel W. Adams spent the last several months of the war in district commands. The Kentucky lawyer had practiced in both Mississippi and Louisiana before the war. In a not-uncommon antebellum occurrence, he was acquitted of murder in the duelling death of a newspaper editor who Adams felt had slighted his father. At the outbreak of the secession crisis, Adams became part of a three-man board charged with preparing for war. His later assignments included: lieutenant colonel, 1st Louisiana Regulars (1861); colonel, 1st Louisiana Regulars (October 30, 1861); commanding 2nd Brigade, 2nd Corps, 2nd Grand Division, Army of the Mississippi (March 9-29, 1862); commanding 1st (Gladden's) Brigade, 2nd (Withers') Division, 2nd Corps, Army of the Mississippi (April 6, 1862); brigadier general, CSA (May 23, 1862); commanding 2nd Brigade, 2nd (Anderson's) Division, Left Wing, Army of the Mississippi (August 13-November 20, 1862); commanding 2nd Brigade, Anderson's-Breckinridge's Division, Hardee's Corps, Army of Tennessee (November 20-December 31, 1862 and early 1863-May 1863); commanding brigade, Breckinridge's Division, Department of the West (ca. May 31-July 1863); commanding brigade, Breckinridge's Division, Department of Mississippi and East Louisiana (July-August 25, 1863); commanding brigade, Breckinridge's Division, Hill's Corps, Army of Tennessee (August 28-September 20, 1863); commanding District of Central and North Alabama, Department of Alabama, Mississippi and East Louisiana (ca. August-September 24, 1864); commanding District of Central Alabama, Department of Alabama, Mississippi and East Louisiana (September 24, 1864-March 11, 1865); and commanding District of Alabama, Department of Alabama, Mississippi and East Louisiana (March 11-May 4, 1865). Initially stationed at Pensacola, he and his regiment were part of the Confederate buildup before Shiloh at Corinth, Miss. During the battle's first day he took command of the brigade when Adley H. Gladden was killed in front of the Hornet's Nest.

Shortly thereafter Adams also fell with a wound that cost him an eye. Promoted to brigadier general, he returned to command a brigade at Perryville, and he was again wounded at Murfreesboro on the last day of 1862. Returning to duty early the next year, he led a brigade under Joseph E. Johnston during the siege of Jackson. Rejoining Bragg's army in northern Georgia, he was wounded for the third time on the second day at Chickamauga and was also taken prisoner. It appears that the Confederate authorities were reluctant to have him exchanged—possibly due to the number of wounds he had sustained—and he was not freed from his parole until the middle of 1864. At that time he was assigned to a series of district commands in Alabama and then spent the final days of the war in command of the entire state except for the Mobile area. He took part in the feeble defense against Wilson's raid through Alabama and Georgia. Included in Richard Taylor's surrender on May 4, 1865, he resumed his practice.

ADAMS, John (1825-1864)

In the suicidal Confederate attack at Franklin, John Adams became one of six generals to sustain a fatal wound in that battle. The native Tennesseean and West Pointer (1846) had won a brevet with the dragoons in the Mexican War. Following frontier duty he resigned as a captain in the 1st Dragoons on May 31, 1861. Joining the Confederacy, his assignments included: captain, Cavalry (May 27, 1861); colonel, Cavalry (May 1862); brigadier general, CSA (December 29, 1862); commanding 4th Military District, Department of Mississippi and East Louisiana (ca. January-June 1863); commanding Tilghman's (old) Brigade, Loring's Division, Department of the West (June-July 1863); commanding brigade, Loring's Division, Department of Mississippi and East Louisiana (July 1863-January 28, 1864); commanding brigade, Loring's Division, Department of Alabama, Mississippi and East Louisiana (January 28-May 1864); and commanding brigade, Loring's Division, Polk's (Army of Mississippi)-Stewart's Corps, Army of Tennessee (May-November 30, 1864). After service at

Memphis he was promoted to command of the deceased Lloyd Tilghman's brigade during the operations around Vicksburg under Joseph E. Johnston. He took part in the defense of Jackson, Miss., and later faced Sherman's Meridian campaign. Going with Leonidas Polk to Mississippi, he served through the Atlanta Campaign and then went on the invasion of middle Tennessee. Once wounded at Franklin, he continued on until repeatedly struck on the very works of the enemy.

ADAMS, William Wirt (1819-1888)

Generally known simply as Wirt Adams, this Kentuckian refused Jefferson Davis' tender of a cabinet postal portfolio and instead rose to the rank of brigadier general in the Confederate cavalry. Adams had fought in Texas before becoming a Mississippi plantation owner, banker, and state legislator. His military assignments included: colonel, Adams' Mississippi Cavalry Regiment (October 15, 1861); brigadier general, CSA (September 25, 1863); commanding Logan's (old) Brigade, Jackson's Division, Lee's Cavalry Corps, Department of Mississippi and East Louisiana (ca. November 21, 1863-January 28, 1864); and commanding in the Department of Alabama, Mississippi, and East Louisiana: same brigade, Jackson's Division, Lee's Corps (January 28-ca. May 4, 1864); cavalry division (May-August 1864); District North of Homochitto (August-November 6, 1864); District of Northern Mississippi, District of Mississippi and East Louisiana (November 6-mid November 1864); Northern Sub-District, District of Mississippi and East Louisiana (mid-November 1864-January 1865); Sub-District of Southwest Mississippi and East Louisiana, District of Mississippi and East Louisiana (January-February 3, 1865); also the district (January 31-February 3, 1865); District South Mississippi and East Louisiana, District of Mississippi and East Louisiana (February 3-18, 1865); and brigade, Chalmers' Division, Forrest's Cavalry corps (February 18-May 4, 1865). Before his promotion to brigadier general, he led his regiment at Iuka and Corinth and during Grant's drive into central Mississippi. He also tangled with Grierson's raiders and fought at Vicksburg and with Joseph E. Johnston at Jackson. Thereafter he held a number of district commands and ended the war with Nathan Bedford Forrest, facing Wilson's raid at Selma. After the war he was a public official until killed in a personal encounter with a journalist.

AKIN, Warren (1811-1877)

When many in the Confederate Congress became disillusioned with the leadership of Jefferson Davis in the latter stages of the war, Davis still had at least one hero-worshipping representative—Congressman Warren Akin of Georgia's 10th District. A native Georgian, Akin had been a lawyer, sometime Methodist minister, a trustee of Emory University, presidential elector in 1840, and a member of the Nashville convention of the Southern States in 1850. In 1859 he was defeated by Governor Joseph E. Brown when running as a Constitutional Unionist to become chief executive of Georgia. For the first two years of the Civil War he served in the lower house of the state legislature and, although a freshman, was given the position of speaker. In the fall elections in 1863 he was elected to the Second Congress on a platform of full support of the Davis Administration. The threatened 10th District appreciated this position after the peace resolutions of his predecessor, Augustus R. Wright. Taking his seat in May 1864, he was appointed to the Committee on Claims. Although his district was shortly overrun by Sherman's armies, his faith in Davis was never shaken and an interview with the president early in 1865 reconfirmed his position. Akin proposed an unsuccessful amendment to the law that had made Lee general in chief; he wanted to prevent any lessening of the President's powers. Following the collapse of the Confederacy, he resumed the practice of law. (Wiley, Bell I., ed., *Letters of Warren Akin*)

ALCORN, James Lusk (1816-1894)

A plantation owner and lawyer, James Lusk Alcorn was an active Whig politician whose political associations earned him a position in the Mississippi military structure at the outbreak of the war. He served in the state legislature's lower and upper houses and failed in an attempt for a seat in congress. Attending the 1861 state convention he opposed secession but signed the ordinance in the end. In return the convention named him a brigadier general in the state army. By the fall of 1861 he was serving under General S.B. Buckner in Kentucky, and on October 2 he was assigned command of a district around Hopkinsville. In December and January he commanded, again in Kentucky, a force of three regiments of 60-day state troops known as the "Army of Mississippi." His troops were raw and were not counted on for much by the authorities. After leaving the service, he returned home to the Yazoo country of Mississippi. Here, during the Vicksburg Campaign, he provided information to Confederate military leaders about Union troop movements. After the war he served part of a term as governor before resigning to join the U.S. Senate in 1871; he had been refused his seat in 1865. He retired in 1877. (Pereyra, Lillian A., *James Lusk Alcorn, Persistent Whig*)

ALEXANDER, Edward Porter (1835-1910)

The most capable artillerist in the Army of Northern Virginia, E. Porter Alexander, was a West Point graduate, third in the 1857 class, with four years engineering experience. The second lieutenant resigned on May 1, 1861, to join the Confederacy where his assignments included: captain, Engineers (June 3, 1861); lieutenant colonel, Artillery (December 1861); colonel, Artillery (December 1862); commanding Lee's (old) Battalion, Reserve Artillery, 1st Corps, Army of Northern Virginia (November 7, 1862-July 1863); commanding artillery battalion, 1st Corps, same army (July-September 9, 1863); commanding artillery battalion, Longstreet's Corps, Army of Tennessee (September 19-November 5, 1863); commanding Artillery, Department of East Tennessee (November 5, 1863-April 7, 1864); brigadier general, CSA (February 26, 1864); and commanding Artillery, 1st Corps, Army of Northern Virginia (April 12-June 1864 and August 1864-April 9, 1865). Drawing upon his service with Albert J. Myer, he headed Beauregard's signal corps and at 1st Bull Run warned Colonel N.G. Evans (by signals) that his flank was about to be turned. As chief of ordnance after the battle he also was involved with signals, new weapons, engineering, reconnaissance, supply, training gun crews, and organizing a secret service. He witnessed the fighting at Gaines' Mill from a balloon and was transferred from ordnance duty to command an artillery battalion in time for Fredericksburg. His placement of the guns facilitated the easy repulse of the enemy. He fought again at Chancellorsville, and at Gettysburg he supervised the bombardment preceding Pickett's Charge, in effect supplanting Colonel J.B. Walton. Arriving too late for the battle of Chickamauga, he served as Longstreet's artillery chief in the Knoxville Campaign and back in Virginia, seeing action at Spotsylvania, Cold Harbor, and Petersburg. In June, he was wounded by a sharpshooter during the latter battle and was absent part of the summer. He then commanded the artillery on the north side of the James around Richmond for the remainder of the siege. After his surrender at Appomattox he was active in education and railroading and wrote a highly respected work, *Military Memoirs of a Confederate*. (Klein, Maury, *Edward Porter Alexander*)

ALEXANDER, Peter Wellington (1824-1886)

In at least one battle Southern reporter Peter W. Alexander crossed the vague line between reporter and military observer or scout. A native of Georgia, he had practiced law and journalism before the Civil War. His journalistic credits during the Civil War included the *Atlanta Confederacy, Columbus Sun,* and *Mobile Advertiser and Register.* Although he had been a staunch Unionist delegate to the state secessionist convention, he passed on information from his frontline observations to the Confederate high command at 1st Bull Run and was rewarded with the honorary title of colonel. Also present at Antietam, he became a friend and supporter of Confederate General Robert Toombs who resigned shortly after the battle because he felt he had been passed over for promotion. This may have contributed to Alexander's later writings, which were highly critical of the direction the government was taking, and his support for states' rights principles within the Confederacy. After the war he resumed the practice of law. (Andrews, J. Cutler, *The South Reports the Civil War*)

ALGER, Cyrus (1781-1856)

Although he died half a decade before the Civil War began, Cyrus Alger had a tremendous influence on how it was fought. Entering the iron foundry business, Alger eventually became an expert in artillery and much of his business's time was spent in filling government contracts. In 1834 his plant manufactured the first U.S.-made rifled cannon. Tackling the problems of the old-style wooden fuses for explosive shells, in the 1840s he invented a bronze model fuse that included several safety features. His innovation permitted the Navy to use its preferred method of firing, skipping the shell along the water and against its target, with a much lower percentage of duds when fuses were snuffed out by sea water. A safety plug allowed the already

charged shells to be stacked on deck during an action. These improvements allowed for a much greater rate of fire, with the ability to actually roll shells into enemy coastal fortifications as was effected at Battery Wagner in Charleston Harbor. Alger never patented his process due to the War Department's fear that it would be appropriated by potential enemies. The Confederates immediately adopted it at the outbreak of the war.

ALLEN, Henry Watkins (1820-1866)

As Louisiana's last wartime governor, Henry W. Allen proved to be a highly effective leader. Born in Virginia, he fought in the war for the independence of Texas and then entered upon the practice of law. Following a journey to Europe he was elected to the Louisiana legislature and upon the outbreak of the Civil War joined the Confederate army. His assignments included: lieutenant colonel, 4th Louisiana (May 25, 1861); colonel, 4th Louisiana (March 1862); commanding 2nd Brigade, 2nd Division, District of the Mississippi, Department #2 (August 1862); and brigadier general, CSA (August 19, 1863). After service at Ship Island and Jackson, Mississippi, he was wounded in the face at Shiloh. In charge of a brigade, he was again wounded, this time in the leg, at Baton Rouge. During his lengthy recovery he was promoted to brigadier general and on November 2, 1863, he was elected governor of his adopted state. As the state's chief executive he organized exports to Mexico for needed goods. Leaving office on June 2, 1865, he went to Mexico where he ran an English-language newspaper until his death. (Dorsey, Sarah A., *Recollections of Henry Watkins Allen, Brigadier General Confederate States Army, Ex-Governor of Louisiana* and Cassidy, Vincent H., *Henry Watkins Allen of Louisiana*)

ALLEN, William Wirt (1835-1894)

William W. Allen may have been born in New York City, but he was raised to become an Alabama planter and eventually became a Confederate major general of cavalry. His assignments included: first lieutenant, Company A, 1st Alabama Cavalry (1861); major, 1st Alabama Cavalry (March 18, 1862); colonel, 1st Alabama Cavalry (ca. July 11, 1862); brigadier general CSA (February 26, 1864); commanding brigade, Kelly's Division, Wheeler's Cavalry Corps, Army of Tennessee (spring 1864); commanding John T. Morgan's (old) Brigade, Martin's Division, Wheeler's Cavalry Corps, Army of Tennessee (ca. May-December 5, 1864); commanding division, Wheeler's Cavalry Corps, Army of Tennessee (ca. December 5, 1864-April 26, 1865); and major general, CSA (March 4, 1865). After serving as a subaltern in the Montgomery Mounted Rifles for a number of months he fought as a field officer at Shiloh and during the Corinth siege. Promoted to colonel, he was wounded at both Perryville and Murfreesboro. Not returning to field duty for a lengthy period, he was named brigadier general and assigned to a brigade under Joseph Wheeler. For the balance of the war he served under Wheeler as a brigade and division commander in the Atlanta, Savanah and Carolinas campaigns. After surrendering with Joseph E. Johnston, Allen engaged in planting and railroading, and also served as state adjutant general and as a U.S. marshal.

ALLISON, Alexander (?-?)

The lesser-known partner in the firm of Kurz and Allison, Alexander Allison had been a Chicago engraver when in 1880 he joined Kurz's lithograph business. Over the next two decades the firm produced scores of lithographs depicting various aspects of American life. However, their most famous work was a series of 36 chromolithographs of major Civil War battles. These somewhat less than realistic prints—showing perfectly uniformed men in well-dressed battle lines—are noted for their use of color, with as many as 10 being used in each print. Unfortunately the originals are now extremely rare. The firm closed its doors in 1903. (*Battles of the Civil War 1861-1865: The Complete Kurz & Allison Prints*)

ANDERSON, Charles D. (1829-1901)

As the man who surrendered Fort Gaines in Mobile Bay, Charles D. Anderson came in for a great deal of criticism from his superiors. He dropped out of West Point after two years of study but eight years later was commissioned directly into the 4th Artillery. The South Carolina-born and Texas-raised first lieutenant resigned his commission on April 1, 1861, and offered his services to the Confederacy. Shortly after the Battle of Shiloh, on May 8, 1862, he was appointed colonel, 21st Alabama. A few months later the regiment was sent to the defense of Mobile where it served for the rest of the war. On August 7, 1864, he was commanding Fort Gaines, guarding the harbor. After a naval bombardment he raised the white flag. There were charges that his post was defended inadequately. The city itself held out until the very end of the war. He is sometimes confused with brigadier general Charles David Anderson of the Georgia Militia.

ANDERSON, Charles David (1827-1901)

Although wounded and forced to give up his commission, Charles David Anderson nevertheless found himself leading combat troops as the war ground on. His Confederate service included: captain, Company C, 6th Georgia (May 27, 1861); major, 6th Georgia (September 17, 1862); lieutenant colonel, 6th Georgia (May 15, 1863); colonel, 2nd Georgia Militia (early 1864); brigadier general, Georgia Militia (mid-summer 1864); and commanding 3rd Brigade, 1st Division, Georgia Militia (mid-summer-November 22, 1864). The 6th saw service at Yorktown, Williamsburg, Seven Pines, the Seven Days, Antietam, Fredericksburg, and Chancellorsville. The regiment subsequently went to South Carolina but he was forced by his wounds to resign on January 20, 1864. Commissioned into the state militia, he served during the latter stages of the Atlanta Campaign and was promoted to brigade command during the siege. With Hood's army off to Tennessee, the militia tried to delay Sherman's drive through Georgia. In the only major infantry action of the campaign, Anderson was wounded at Griswoldville. He served in the state legislature for

the final months of the war. He is sometimes confused with Colonel Charles D. Anderson of the 21st Alabama who served mostly at Mobile and who surrendered Fort Gaines.

ANDERSON, George Burgwyn (1831-1862)

Although George B. Anderson effectively commanded a brigade for nine months, he was not recognized and promoted to brigadier until June 1862. The West Pointer (1852) had resigned his first lieutenant's commission in the 2nd Dragoons on April 25, 1861, to join the South. His assignments there included: colonel, 4th North Carolina (May 16, 1861); commanding Garrison at Manassas, 1st Corps, Army of the Potomac (October 14-22, 1861); commanding Garrison at Manassas, Potomac District, Department of Northern Virginia (October 22, 1861-March 25, 1862); commanding brigade, D.H. Hill's Division, same department (April 2-6, 1862); commanding Featherston's (old) Brigade, D.H. Hill's Division, Army of Northern Virginia (May-July 1 and July-September 17, 1862); and brigadier general, CSA (June 9, 1862). Until the evacuation of the Manassas lines he was in charge of the garrison and then of the brigade organized from it until relieved by General C.S. Winder. A few days later he was briefly back in command, but commanded only his regiment at Williamsburg. He directed the brigade at Seven Pines and a short time later was promoted to its permanent leadership. In the last of the Seven Days battles, Malvern Hill, he was wounded but returned in time to aid in the defense of the gaps in South Mountain during the Maryland invasion. Three days later, at Antietam, he was wounded in the foot. Carried back to North Carolina, he died on October 16 after amputation of the foot. (Freeman, Douglas S., *Lee's Lieutenants*)

ANDERSON, George Thomas (1824-1901)

Nicknamed "Tige," George T. Anderson was in command of a brigade for half a year before he received his Confederate general's wreath. A lieutenant of Georgia cavalry during the Mexican War, he received a captain's commission in the regular cavalry in 1855. He resigned three years later but when the Civil War broke out he went with his native Georgia. His assignments included: colonel, 11th Georgia (July 2, 1861); commanding S. Jones' Brigade, G.W. Smith's Division, Potomac District, Department of Northern Virginia (January 10-February 17, 1862); commanding D.R. Jones' Brigade, D.R. Jones' Division, Magruder's Command, same department (May-July 3, 1862); commanding D.R. Jones' Brigade, D.R. Jones' Division, 1st Corps, Army of Northern Virginia (July-October 27, 1862); commanding same brigade, Hood's-Field's Division, same corps and army (October 27, 1862-February 25, 1863; May-July 2, 1863; April 12, 1864-January 1865; and March-April 9, 1865); brigadier general, CSA (November 1, 1862); commanding brigade, Hood's Division, in the Department of Virginia and North Carolina (February 25-April 1, 1863) and in the Department of Southern Virginia (April 1-May 1863); commanding brigade, 1st Military District of South Carolina, Department of South Carolina, Georgia and Florida (September 1863); commanding brigade, Hood's Division, Longstreet's Corps, Army of Tennessee (October 5-November 5, 1863); and commanding brigade, Hood's-Field's Division, Department of East Tennessee (November 5, 1863-April 12, 1864). Too late for the fighting at 1st Bull Run, he saw action at Yorktown and, in command of the brigade, at the Seven Days, 2nd Bull Run, Turner's Gap, Antietam, and Fredericksburg. After service with Longstreet in southeastern Virginia he was wounded on the second day at Gettysburg. Recovering, he was detached to the Charleston area when Longstreet's Corps went to Georgia. He rejoined the corps after Chickamauga. After the Knoxville Campaign the corps rejoined Lee, and Anderson saw heavy action at the Wilderness, Spotsylvania, and Cold Harbor. After serving through the Richmond-Petersburg siege he surrendered with Lee at Appomattox. He was subsequently police chief in Atlanta and in Anniston, Alabama. (Freeman, Douglas S., *Lee's Lieutenants*)

ANDERSON, James Patton (1822-1872)

Briefly serving in the Provisional Confederate Congress, J. Patton Anderson resigned after only one session, joined the army and rose to the rank of major general. Born in Tennessee, he was a doctor in Mississippi when the Mexican War broke out. In that conflict he was lieutenant colonel of the 2nd Mississippi Rifles Battalion. He was then, successively, a Mississippi state legislator, U.S. marshal in Washington Territory, territorial delegate from the territory to Congress, and a resident of Florida. Attending the state secession convention, he was named to the Montgomery body and served on the committees on Military Affairs and Public Lands before resigning on April 8, 1861. During his brief tenure his main interest was in maritime matters. His military assignments included: colonel, 1st Florida (April 5, 1861); brigadier general, CSA (February 10, 1862); commanding brigade, Ruggles' Division, 2nd Corps, Army of the Mississippi (March 29-June 1862); commanding the division (June 1862); commanding brigade, 2nd Corps, Army of the Mississippi (June-July 1862); commanding division, Army of the Mississippi (July-August 15, 1862); commanding division, Left Wing, Army of the Mississippi (August 15-November 20, 1862); commanding division, Hardee's Corps, Army of Tennessee (November 20-December 1862); commanding brigade, Withers'-Hindman's Division, Polk's Corps, Army of Tennessee (December 1862-September 20, 1863); commanding Hindman's Division, Polk's-Breckinridge's-Hindman's Corps, Army of Tennessee (September 20, 1863-January 1864); major general, CSA (February 17, 1864); commanding District of Florida, Department of South Carolina, Georgia and Florida (March 4-August 3, 1864); commanding Hindman's (old) Division, Lee's Corps, Army of Tennessee (July 29-September 1, 1864); and commanding Taliaferro's (old) Division, Stewart's Corps, Army of Tennessee (April 9-26, 1865). His initial service came at Pensacola and then, promoted to brigadier general, as a brigade commander at Shiloh. He led a division at Perryville and a brigade again at Murfreesboro. On the second day at Chickamauga he succeeded the wounded Thomas C. Hindman

in division command. Early in 1864 he was assigned to district command in Florida but was ordered to rejoin the Army of Tennessee during the Atlanta Campaign; he fought at Ezra Church and, until wounded, at Jonesboro. He did not rejoin the army until the Carolinas Campaign was virtually concluded. At that time he was given command of a division of troops drawn from the coastal defenses of South Carolina. Surrendering with Joseph E. Johnston at Durham Station, he became a tax official and ran a farming journal.

ANDERSON, Joseph Reid (1813-1892)

A Confederate brigadier early in the war, Joseph Anderson was more important in his civilian capacity as head of the Tredegar Works in Richmond, where he became the "Krupp of the Confederacy." In August 1861, the West Point graduate (1836) was made a major of artillery, after resigning from a year's service as a lieutenant of engineers and artillery. For two decades he had been the superintendent of the iron works; as a major he was assigned to continue his work there. However on September 3, 1861, he was appointed brigadier general, CSA, and assigned to field duty in North Carolina. His commands included: District of the Cape Fear, Department of North Carolina (October 5, 1861-March 19, 1862); the department (March 19-24, 1862); brigade, A.P. Hill's Division, Army of Northern Virginia (May 27-June 30 and early July 1862); and temporarily the division, Longstreet's Command, Army of Northern Virginia (July 13-19, 1862). After service in North Carolina, Anderson brought a brigade of Georgians to Virginia and took command of the force facing McDowell's command at Fredericksburg during April and May 1862. During the Seven Days he led his brigade at Beaver Dam Creek, Gaines' Mill and Frayser's Farm where he was wounded. Returning in July he took over command of A.P. Hill's Division while that officer was under arrest but resigned effective July 19, 1862, to return to the iron works. For almost three years, until the fall of Richmond, he provided arms for the men in the field. The federal government returned the confiscated plant to him in 1867 and he ran it until his death. (Dew, Charles B., *Ironmaker to the Confederacy: Joseph R. Anderson and the Tredegar Iron Works*)

ANDERSON, Richard Heron (1821-1879)

"Fighting Dick" Anderson served throughout the career of the Army of Northern Virginia only to be relieved of duty the day before the Appomattox surrender. A West Pointer (1842) from South Carolina, he was a veteran of the Mexican War and resigned a captaincy in the 2nd Dragoons on March 3, 1861, to join the South. His services included: major, Infantry (March 16, 1861); colonel, 1st South Carolina Regulars (early 1861); commanding Charleston Harbor (May 27-August 1861); brigadier general, CSA (July 19, 1861); commanding D.R. Jones' (old S.C.) Brigade, Longstreet's Division (in Potomac District until March), Department of Northern Virginia (February 15-May 31; June 1-29; and July 1-14, 1862); commanding the division (May 31-June 1 and June 29-July 1, 1862); major general, CSA (July 14, 1862); commanding Huger's (old) Division, 1st (3rd after May 30, 1863) Corps,

Army of Northern Virginia (July 14-September 17, 1862 and November 1862-May 7, 1864); commanding 1st Corps, same army (May 7-October 19, 1864); lieutenant general, CSA (May 31, 1864); and commanding 4th Corps, same army (October 19, 1864-April 8, 1865). After commanding his regiment at the bombardment of Fort Sumter and, after Beauregard's departure, the Confederate forces in the harbor, he was transferred to western Florida where he was wounded in the October 9, 1861, attack at Santa Rosa Island. His connection with what was to become Lee's army began when he was assigned to a brigade on the Manassas lines on February 15, 1862. He led either a portion or all of the division at Williamsburg, Seven Pines, and during the latter stages of the Seven Days Battles. Promoted and given Huger's old command from Norfolk, he fought at 2nd Bull Run, Crampton's Gap, and was wounded at Antietam. Returning to duty he was lightly engaged at Fredericksburg but played a key role at Chancellorsville. With the reorganization of the army after Stonewall Jackson's death, his division was transferred to the newly created 3rd Corps. He fought at Gettysburg and the Wilderness after which he was given command of the wounded Longstreet's 1st Corps. He won the dramatic race from the Wilderness to Spotsylvania and went on to fight at North Anna, Cold Harbor, and near Richmond during the Petersburg operations. In the late summer of 1864 he was detached with part of his corps to reinforce Early in the Shenandoah but was soon recalled. Upon Longstreet's return he was given charge of a new corps, which he directed through the remainder of the siege. His command was virtually destroyed at Sayler's Creek and the day before Appomattox he was sent home by Lee since he had no command. After the war he was impoverished but declined a position in the Egyptian Khedive's army, preferring to stick with his Reconstruction-troubled state. (Walker, C. Irvine, *The Life of Lieutenant General R.H. Anderson*)

ANDERSON, Robert Houstoun (1835-1888)

Despite the fact that his entire service in the old army was with the infantry, Georgia West Pointer (1857) Robert H. Anderson earned the three stars and wreath of a Confederate brigadier general with mounted troops. Serving in the Pacific Northwest, he resigned as a second lieutenant with the 9th Infantry on May 17, 1861, and tendered his services to the South. His assignments included: first lieutenant, Artillery (March 6, 1861); major and assistant adjutant general (September 1861); major, 1st Georgia Sharpshooters Battalion (June 20, 1862); colonel, 5th Georgia Cavalry (January 20, 1863); commanding Allen's (old) Brigade, Kelly's Division, Wheeler's Cavalry Corps, Army of Tennessee (ca. May-September 1864); brigadier general, CSA (July 20, 1864); and commanding brigade, Allen's Division, Wheeler's Cavalry Corps, Army of Tennessee (ca. January 2-April 26, 1865). His early service came as a staff officer with William H.T. Walker on the coast of South Carolina and Georgia before he transferred to a sharpshooters unit that continued to serve in the same area. Finally at the head of a mounted regiment, he joined the Army of Tennessee, seeing action through most of the Atlanta Campaign. He then participated, under Joseph Wheeler, in the efforts to stop

Sherman during the March to the Sea and through the Carolinas. After the war he was the police chief of his native Savannah.

ANDERSON, Samuel Read (1804-1883)

Virginia-born and a former Kentucky resident, Tennessean Samuel Anderson had been lieutenant colonel of the 1st Tennessee during the Mexican War and a bank cashier and postmaster in Nashville before being called upon to serve as one of the two state major generals on May 9, 1861. Exactly two months later, with the Tennessee troops transferred to Confederate service, Anderson accepted the rank of brigadier general for those forces. On August 5 he was assigned to command a brigade of Tennessee troops in western Virginia; as a part of Lee's Army of the Northwest, he took part in the first battle planned by that general. In this action at Cheat Mountain, Anderson led his men into position, as directed, behind the Union position. However, some of the other troops failed to complete their assignments and the attack fizzled out before it fairly got started. That winter Anderson's brigade accompanied the Army of the Northwest to join Stonewall Jackson's Romney Campaign. Although the expedition took the town, it failed to destroy the Union forces there. On February 24, 1862, Anderson was ordered to proceed with two of his regiments to Manassas and join Johnston's army. Anderson's brigade, reinforced by another regiment from Tennessee, was assigned to G.W. Smith's Division, Department of Northern Virginia. Anderson went with his brigade when the army was moved to the Peninsula, but on May 10, 1862, he resigned due to ill health. On November 19, 1864, Anderson was reappointed a brigadier general (to rank from November 7) and assigned to duty with the conscript bureau in Alabama where he was responsible for the Tennessee operations of that agency. He became a Nashville businessman after the war. (Freeman, Douglas S., *R. E. Lee*)

ANDERSON, William (1840-1864)

A graduate of the William C. Quantrill school of bushwhacking, "Bloody Bill" Anderson went off on his own hook to perpetrate some of the most brutal actions of the Civil War. When the Kansas City prison for women—which was being used to confine Southern sympathizers—collapsed, one of Anderson's sisters was killed and another crippled. With a band from Clay County, Missouri, Anderson joined up with Quantrill in time for the sacking of Lawrence, Kansas. Displaying an aptitude for cold-blooded killing, he became a first lieutenant in the guerrilla band early in 1864. A short time later he refused to serve under Quantrill after one of his men was shot for killing a farmer. Anderson and most of his men rode off for their own depradations north of the Missouri River and joined in Price's invasion of Missouri. That September 27 he perpetrated the infamous Centralia massacre in which he captured a train and killed the crew and 24 unarmed soldiers on furlough. Civilians trying to hide their valuables were also slain. When three companies of the 39th Missouri and a detachment of the 1st Iowa Cavalry set out in pursuit, they were ambushed. Out of 147 men, 116 were killed, two were wounded and six more were unaccounted for. A month later, on October 26, 1864, Anderson was killed in an assault on a militia company near Richmond, Missouri. He was decapitated and the trophy mounted on a telegraph pole. Anderson had a lasting impact on the West—he had given Jesse James his initiation in blood. (Hale, D.R., *They called Him Bloody Bill*)

ANDREWS, Richard Snowden (1830-1903)

Baltimore architect turned artillery commander, R. Snowden Andrews was told that his abdominal wound from a shell was certain to prove fatal, but he defied the experts. Although born in the nation's capital, he decided to offer his services to the South but not until he had obtained technical information on the organizing of a battery from the U.S. government. His assignments included: captain, 1st Maryland Battery (May 29, 1861); major, Artillery (July 15, 1862); commanding Artillery Battalion, Jackson's (old) Division, Jackson's Command, Army of Northern Virginia (July-August 9, 1862); lieutenant colonel, Artillery (April 4, 1863); commanding Artillery Battalion, Early's Division, 2nd Corps, Army of Northern Virginia (April 16-June 2, 1863); and commanding Artillery Battalion, Johnson's Division, 2nd Corps, Army of Northern Virginia (June 2-15, 1863). After serving in the blockade of the Potomac early in the war, he took part in the Seven Days Battles and was slightly wounded. Given command of a battalion, he distinguished himself at Cedar Mountain but was nearly cut in two by an enemy shell. Considered a hopeless case, he was left on the field with an old doctor friend who expected him to die. By the middle of October 1862 he was fit enough to perform ordnance duty. The next spring he rejoined Lee's army for Chancellorsville. In the early stages of the Gettysburg Campaign, he fought at 2nd Winchester and was again wounded the next day at Stephenson's Depot. In January 1864 he was dispatched to Europe to purchase much-needed ordnance supplies. He returned to Baltimore at the war's close. Despite his wounds, he died a natural death. (Wise, Jennings C., *The Long Arm of Lee*)

ARCHER, James Jay (1817-1864)

A lawyer and Mexican War veteran, James Archer resigned his captain's commission in the regular army on March 14, 1861, to receive the same rank in the Confederate service two days later. Although a Marylander, Archer was appointed colonel, 5th Texas, a regiment organized in Richmond from independent companies, on October 2, 1861. He commanded his regiment, and sometimes the brigade, at the batteries at Evansport along the Potomac and on the Peninsula in the actions at Eltham's Landing and Seven Pines. He was promoted brigadier general, CSA, June 3, 1862, and given command of Hatton's old brigade of Alabama, Georgia, and Tennessee troops (that officer having been killed at Seven Pines). The Georgians were eventually transferred out and replaced by more Alabamians, but the brigade became known as the Tennessee Brigade. Archer's commands in the Army of Northern Virginia included: Tennessee Brigade, A.P. Hill's Division (June 3-July

1862); Tennessee Brigade, A.P. Hill's Division, Jackson's Corps (July 27, 1862-May 30, 1863); Tennessee Brigade, Heth's Division, A.P. Hill's Corps (May 30-July 1, 1863); and Archer's and Walker's Brigades, Heth's Division, A.P. Hill's Corps (August 19-October 24, 1864). Commanding his brigade, Archer took part in actions at Beaver Dam Creek, Gaines' Mill, Frayser's Farm, Cedar Mountain, 2nd Bull Run, the capture of Harpers Ferry, Antietam, Fredericksburg, and Chancellorsville. On the first day at Gettysburg he was picked up by an Irishman from the Union's Iron Brigade, becoming the first general captured from the Army of Northern Virginia since Lee took command. While imprisoned at Johnson's Island, Ohio, Archer let the Confederate War Department know through a paroled prisoner that the guards could be overwhelmed but the Southerners would have no way of getting off the island. On June 21, 1864, Archer was ordered sent to Charleston Harbor to be placed under Confederate fire in retaliation for southern treatment of prisoners. Later exchanged, Archer was ordered to the Army of Tennessee for duty on August 9, 1864, but he was redirected to the Army of Northern Virginia 10 days later. He was assigned command of his own as well as Walker's Brigades, which had been temporarily consolidated. Suffering from the effects of his imprisonment and the rigors of the Petersburg trenches, including the battle of Peebles' Farm, Archer died on October 24, 1864. (Freeman, Douglas S., *Lee's Lieutenants*)

James J. Archer, victim of Union prison camps. (NA)

ARMISTEAD, Lewis Addison (1817-1863)

Lewis A. Armistead nearly scuttled his military career when he broke a plate over the head of fellow cadet Jubal A. Early and was expelled from West Point. He was, however, commissioned directly into the infantry in 1839 and served in the Mexican War, being wounded at Chapultepec and earning two brevets. He resigned his captaincy on May 26, 1861, and headed back east to offer his services to the Confederacy. His assignments included: major, Infantry (from March 16, 1861); colonel, 57th Virginia (September 23, 1861); brigadier general, CSA (April 1, 1862); commanding brigade, Department of Norfolk (ca. April 1-12, 1862); commanding brigade, Huger's Division, Department of Northern Virginia (April 12-July 1862); commanding brigade, Anderson's Division, 1st Corps, Army of Northern Virginia (July-September 17, 1862); and commanding brigade, Pickett's Division, in 1st Corps, Army of Northern Virginia (October 1862-February 25, 1863 and May-July 3, 1863), in the Department of Virginia and North Carolina (February 25-April 1, 1863), and in the Department of Southern Virginia (April 1-May 1863). After serving in western Virginia, he was given command of a brigade in the Norfolk area and later served with it on the Peninsula, seeing action at Seven Pines and in the Seven Days. He fought at 2nd Bull Run and Antietam, where he was wounded. After being lightly engaged at Fredericksburg, he went to southeastern Virginia, his home state, with Longstreet. Returning for the invasion of Pennsylvania, he fell mortally wounded among the guns of Cushing's Battery during Pickett's Charge at Gettysburg. He died two days later in Union hands. (Freeman, Douglas S., *Lee's Lieutenants*)

ARMSTRONG, Frank Crawford (1835-1909)

The only general officer in the Civil War who managed to fight on both sides, Frank C. Armstrong fought at 1st Bull Run before switching sides and becoming a Confederate brigadier general. Born in the Indian Territory—the son of an Indian agent—he received his appointment to the regular army from Texas and was named a second lieutenant in the 2nd Dragoons. His Civil War assignments, on both sides, included: first lieutenant, 2nd Dragoons (since March 9, 1859); captain, 2nd Dragoons (June 6, 1861); captain, 2nd Cavalry (designation change August 3, 1861—resignation accepted August 13); volunteer aide-de-camp (early August 1861); lieutenant and assistant adjutant general (1861); colonel, 3rd Louisiana (ca. May 26, 1862); acting brigadier general, CSA (July 7, 1862); commanding Cavalry Brigade, Price's Corps, Army of West Tennessee, Department #2 (September-October 1862); commanding brigade, Jackson's Division, Cavalry Corps, Department of Mississippi and East Louisiana (January-February 1863); commanding brigade, Forrest's Cavalry Division, Army of Tennessee (spring-September 1863); brigadier general, CSA (April 23, 1863, to rank from January 20); commanding division, Forrest's Cavalry Corps, Army of Tennessee (September-October 1863); commanding division, Wheeler's Cavalry Corps, Army of Tennessee (October 1863-March 5, 1864); commanding brigade, Jackson's Cavalry Division, Department

of Alabama, Mississippi, and East Louisiana (spring-May 4, 1864); commanding brigade, Jackson's Cavalry Division, Polk's-Stewart's Corps (Army of Mississippi), Army of Tennessee (May 4-July 26, 1864); commanding brigade, Jackson's Cavalry Division, Army of Tennessee (July 26, 1864-February 18, 1865); and commanding brigade, Chalmers' Division, Forrest's Cavalry Corps, Department of Alabama, Mississippi, and East Louisiana (February 18-May 4, 1865). Having accepted a regular army captaincy in June he led the one company of his regiment present, K, at 1st Bull Run and performed well. However, the next month he served as a volunteer aide to Benjamin McCulloch at Wilson's Creek. Three days later his resignation from the old army was accepted without any recriminations for his having fought against it. He was still on McCulloch's staff when that general was killed at Pea Ridge. Soon thereafter he was elected colonel of the 3rd Louisiana in place of the promoted Louis Hebért. That summer he was given charge of all of Sterling Prince's cavalry as an acting brigadier, having served well in the Corinth siege. Formally promoted, he was given a brigade under Forrest and fought in the Tullahoma and Chickamauga campaigns. When Forrest was ordered to west Tennessee, Armstrong and his division were assigned to Wheeler's corps and served at Knoxville. After a brief stint back in Mississippi he returned to Georgia, leading a brigade throughout the Atlanta Campaign and into middle Tennessee with Hood. In the last months he led a brigade against Wilson's raid. Following the war he held numerous government posts.

ARMSTRONG, Sir William George (Baron Armstrong of Cragside) (1810-1900)

Most field artillery in the Civil War was of the muzzle-loading variety but some breechloaders, like that designed by Sir William George Armstrong, were tried by both sides. An English inventor of considerable renown, he became involved in military equipment during the Crimean War, when he designed submarine mines. In 1855 he developed a three-inch, 10-pound rifled breechloading cannon that was eventually adopted by the British military. Running a private company, he sold samples to the Union government during the Civil War and a few were run through the blockade to the Confederates. But, the technology being new, there were problems with the new ordnance. The breechblocks had a tendency not to fit in place properly. In 1863 he went out of business when the British army returned to the old-fashioned muzzleloaders. He kept on working and in 1880 developed an improved model that was adopted by the armed services. He continued his engineering pursuits until his death.

ARNOLD, Samuel Bland (1834-1906)

The last survivor of the eight conspirators tried in May and June 1865 for killing Lincoln, Samuel B. Arnold had actually withdrawn from the plot a month before the assassination. A school friend of John Wilkes Booth and fellow conspirator Michael O'Laughlin, he had grown up in Baltimore before joining the Confederate army. After returning to Baltimore, when

Samuel Arnold, Lincoln kidnap conspirator. (NA)

Booth told him of the plot to kidnap the president and smuggle him to Richmond, he thought his friend was mad. But although he thought there was little chance of success, he went along with the scheme until March 1865 when he informed Booth of his withdrawal until they should receive definite authority from Richmond. Arnold then secured a job as a supply clerk at Fortress Monroe. He was arrested there on April 17, 1865, and confined with the others aboard a monitor. Taken to the arsenal penitentiary, he sat through the one-sided trial presided over by General Lew Wallace. He admitted that he had been involved in the kidnapping caper, but denied any connection with the assassination. On June 30 he was found guilty and sentenced to life. Sent to Dry Tortugas, he survived a yellow fever epidemic and was pardoned in 1869 by Andrew Johnson.

ALLEN, E.J.

See: *Pinkerton, Allan*

ASHBY, Turner (1828-1862)

Although he was one of the South's early war heroes, as the ideal of a chivalrous cavalryman, Turner Ashby's control of his troopers, and his intelligence gathering, left much to be desired. Raising a company of cavalry at the time of John Brown's Raid, the Shenandoah Valley planter and politician arrived too late to take part in Brown's capture. Again reporting at Harpers Ferry, in early 1861, he offered his services to the Confederacy. His assignments included: captain, Virginia

cavalry company (spring 1861); lieutenant colonel, 7th Virginia Cavalry (ca. June 25, 1861); colonel, 7th Virginia Cavalry (ca. October 1861); commanding cavalry, Valley District, Department of Northern Virginia (ca. October 1861-April 1862); commanding Cavalry, Jackson's Division, Valley District, Department of Northern Virginia (April 1862-June 2, 1862); brigadier general, CSA (May 23, 1862); and commanding Cavalry, Valley District, Department of Northern Virginia (June 2-6, 1862). Serving at Harpers Ferry, usually commanding a mixed force of cavalry and infantry, he quickly became known for his daring escapades, including his undercover intelligence gathering trip to Chambersburg, Pennsylvania. During the 1st Manassas Campaign he teamed up with Jeb Stuart to deceive Union General Patterson into believing that Johnston's army was still in the Shenandoah Valley. Remaining in the Valley, he joined Jackson in the fall of 1861 when that officer took over command of the Valley District. But by a misleading report of enemy strength he brought about the Confederate attack on Kernstown and the resulting defeat. Ashby rarely had all 21 of his companies under his immediate control, and those detached companies were often ill-led, causing demoralization in the ranks. Jackson tried to divide up Ashby's command but was forced to revoke the order when faced with the latter's resignation. Ashby went on to fight through the rest of the Valley Campaign and was promoted to brigadier general by the War Department without the recommendation of Jackson. On June 2 the district commander gave Ashby command of the full cavalry force of the enlarged Valley army. Four days later the newly-named general was killed in a minor action at Harrisonburg, Virginia. (Bushong, Millard K., *General Turner Ashby and Stonewall's Valley Campaign*)

ASHCRAFT, Thomas (1786-1866)

The Civil War left businessman-scientist Thomas Ashcraft a broken man and he died a year after the Confederacy's collapse. Born in North Carolina and South Carolina-raised, he lived in Georgia until he removed to Alabama as a farmer in 1836. There he also gained a reputation as something of an inventor, designing a threshing machine and a cotton press. Associated with the Selma Iron Works, he naturally came into the Confederate war effort. He served as a consultant for the War Department and gave it the plans for a torpedo—now called a mine—he had patented. He was also active in the manufacturing of material for uniforms for the field armies. He retired to Clay County, Alabama, after Appomattox.

ASHE, Thomas Samuel (1812-1887)

It was not until Lincoln made his April 1861 call for troops, including a quota from North Carolina, that Thomas S. Ashe, a lawyer, planter, and former legislator, changed from a Unionist to a secessionist. He attended the state's secession convention, and, the following November, was elected to the First Regular Confederate Congress, taking his seat in February 1862. A firm believer in the rights of persons and states, he made his principal legislative efforts in an attempt to constrict the powers of the national government. However he did support those war measures that he felt were essential. In 1863 the 7th District, in south-central North Carolina, rejected him in favor of a peace candidate. Out of office with the adjournment of the First Congress in February 1864, Ashe set his sights on the Senate seat of Edwin G. Read, whom he defeated in the December election. However, the South was defeated before he could take his seat. After the war he served two terms in the U.S. Congress and was a justice of the North Carolina supreme court.

ASHE, William Sheppard (ca. 1813-1862)

A North Carolina planter and attorney—who rarely practiced—William S. Ashe had earned a reputation for building up the state's railroads and so served the Confederacy as director of rail transport, from Richmond to New Orleans. He had served in Congress for a number of years but did not let his secessionist sentiments interfere with his efforts to obtain internal improvements for his state. An opponent of rail lines from western North Carolina to South Carolina's Charleston, he was a prime mover in the construction of east-west communications within his own state. For the last eight years of his life he was president of the Wilmington and Weldon Railroad. Appointed major and later colonel in the Confederate army, he directed rail operations during the early part of the war. He was injured on September 14, 1862, when the hand-car he was using was struck by a train while he was en route to visit a wounded son. He died three days later. At the time he was trying to organize his own unit for the army.

ATKINS, John DeWitt Clinton (1825-1908)

A native Tennesseean, John D.C. Atkins studied law and then immediately entered politics; he had already served in both houses of the state legislature and in the U.S. Congress when the Civil War began. Entering the military service, he was appointed lieutenant colonel, 5th Tennessee (May 20, 1861), before resigning his commission later in the year to become a representative to the Provisional Congress, where he served on the Committee on Military Affairs. In this position he began his policy of supporting almost anything to staff and equip the military forces. He carried this policy through into the First and Second Congresses in which he represented the 9th District in the northwestern corner of the state. In the First Congress he served on the Committee on Post Offices and Post Roads; in the Second on the Committees on Commerce, Foreign Affairs, and on Ordnance and Ordnance Stores. He was, despite his support for the military, a troublesome congressman for the administration. On domestic and foreign affairs matters he was frequently in opposition. After the overrunning of his home district by Union troops in early 1862, he wanted to launch an investigation into the conduct of General Albert S. Johnston in the disaster. Following Reconstruction he served a decade in the U.S. Congress and was commissioner of Indian affairs from 1885 to 1888. The remainder of his time was spent in farming.

ATKINSON, Edmund Nathan (1834-1884)

Putting his Georgia Military Institute education to use for the Confederacy, Edmund Atkinson nevertheless wound up his Civil War career in the hands of the enemy for the second time. He entered the army of the Confederacy during the first year of the war and his assignments included: first lieutenant and adjutant, 26th Georgia (1861); colonel, 26th Georgia (May 9, 1862); commanding Lawton's Brigade, Ewell's Division, 2nd Corps, Army of Northern Virginia (fall 1862-December 13, 1862); and commanding Evans' Brigade, Gordon's Division, Valley District, Department of Northern Virginia (July 9-September 1864). At the regiment's reorganization in the spring of 1862, he was elected to command the regiment and he led it in the Seven Days Battles. He took over brigade command after Antietam, replacing the wounded General Lawton. In this position he was wounded and captured at Fredericksburg. Following his exchange, he led his regiment at Gettysburg, Mine Run, the Wilderness, Spotsylvania, and Cold Harbor. Taking part in Early's advance on Washington, he took over command of the brigade when General Clement A. Evans was wounded at Monocacy. Evans had been Atkinson's junior when he was promoted to general. Evans returned in September and Atkinson resumed command of his regiment for 3rd Winchester. At Fisher's Hill the latter was captured for a second time and this time was not released until three months after Lee's surrender.

ATZERODT, George A. (1835-1865)

The fact that he had lost the nerve to carry out his assignment, from John Wilkes Booth, to kill Vice President Andrew Johnson did not save George A. Atzerodt from hanging. Born in Germany, he immigrated to the United States and became a carriage maker in Port Tobacco, Maryland. During the Civil War he aided the Confederacy by smuggling mail and couriers and possibly some supplies across nearby Pope's Creek and the

George Atzerodt failed to kill his target, Vice President Andrew Johnson. (NA)

Potomac River. He became involved with Booth in unsuccessful attempts to kidnap Lincoln and spirit him off to Richmond. When the Confederate capital fell and the plan was changed to murder, Atzerodt remained an active conspirator. He was supposed to kill Andrew Johnson at the Kirkwood House while Lincoln was at Ford's Theater. After riding to Ford's, he saw the presidential carriage outside and headed for his assignment. But instead of carrying it out he went into a bar and waited until he got word that Booth had carried out his part of the plan. He then panicked and fled on his own. On April 20, 1865, a detachment from the 1st Delaware Cavalry captured him near Rockville, Maryland. He was confined aboard a monitor, then tried by the military commission under Lew Wallace. Sentenced to the gallows on June 30, 1865, he was hanged on July 7.

AUTON, Lawrence W.

See: *Williams, William Orton*

AVERY, Clarke Mouton (1819-1864)

North Carolinian Clarke M. Avery spent almost half of his Confederate career as a prisoner of war. His assignments included: captain, Company C, 1st North Carolina Volunteers (April 25, 1861); lieutenant colonel, 33rd North Carolina (September 20, 1861); and colonel, 33rd North Carolina (January 17, 1862). After participating in the Battle of Big Bethel, his company was mustered out and he became the field officer of a new regiment. In the Confederate debacle in New Bern in March 1862 he was taken prisoner and not released until October 1863. Upon his release, he rejoined his regiment and commanded it until he was wounded at Spotsylvania on May 12, 1864. He lingered until June 18, but some accounts list him as having been killed at the Wilderness on May 6.

AVERY, Isaac Erwin (1828-1863)

A farmer and railroader, Isaac Avery was one of those able Confederate officers who did not live long enough to wear a general's wreath. He became captain of Company E, 6th North Carolina State Troops, when that regiment was organized on May 16, 1861. His later assignments included: lieutenant colonel, 6th

North Carolina (June 1, 1862); colonel, 6th North Carolina (June 11, 1862): and commanding Hoke's North Carolina Brigade, Early's Division, Jackson's-Ewell's Second Corps, Army of Northern Virginia (May 4-July 2, 1863). During the Seven Days Battles he led his regiment at Gaines' Mill and Malvern Hill, where he was wounded. He returned to field duty in time to assume command of Hoke's Brigade after that officer was wounded at Chancellorsville. At the 2nd Battle of Winchester, Avery led the brigade but it was not actively engaged. On the first day at Gettysburg, the brigade advanced on the extreme left of the Confederate line of battle and in conjunction with Hays' Louisianans swung around Barlow's Knoll and smashed into Coster's Union Brigade, capturing two Napoleon cannons and driving them back into the town. The next evening the two brigades stormed East Cemetary Hill, but were driven back when support failed to arrive, resulting in the loss of many men, including Colonel Avery who was mortally wounded and died the next day. Avery's command was known for the high level of discipline and drill, and he had been recommended for promotion by Pender, Hood, Law, and Early.

AYER, Lewis Malone (1821-1895)

Although he demanded a vigorous prosecution of the war, if Lewis M. Ayer had had his conservative way on financial matters the Confederacy's military effort would have been scuttled. A South Carolina lawyer and militia general, Ayer was elected to the U.S. Congress in 1860 but instead attended the state's secession convention and urged the disruption of the Union. Elected to the First Confederate Congress, he took his seat in February 1862 and served on the committees on Quartermaster's and Commissary Departments and on Ordnance and Ordnance Stores. In the Second Congress he moved to the Committee on Commerce. He was also chairman of the Committee on the War Tax where his shortsightedness was apparent in proposals to cancel the tax in kind, on grounds of states' rights and constitutional questions. And yet he demanded that the war continue and opposed peace negotiations. After the war he was a cotton merchant; Baptist minister in Texas, Tennessee, and South Carolina; and a professor at a private military institute.

B

BAGBY, Arthur Pendleton (1833-1921)

After the fall of Vicksburg, the Trans-Mississippi Department was cut off from regular communications with Richmond, and its commander, General E.K. Smith, was forced to resort to the appointment of general officers without complying with the legal requirement that the president make such appointments. One Texas officer, Arthur P. Bagby, received two such promotions. He had graduated from West Point in 1852 and served for one year in the 8th Infantry before resigning. The Alabama-born ex-officer offered his services to his adopted state of Texas upon the start of hostilities. His assignments in the Trans-Mississippi Department included: lieutenant colonel, 7th Texas Cavalry (1861); colonel, 7th Texas Cavalry (1862); commanding brigade, Green's Cavalry Division, District of West Louisiana (ca. March 17-summer 1864); brigadier general, CSA by Smith (April 13 to rank from March 17, 1864); commanding 4th Texas Cavalry Brigade, 2nd Texas Cavalry Division, 1st Corps (summer 1864-early 1865); commanding cavalry division, 1st Corps (early 1865-May 26, 1865); and major general, CSA by Smith (May 16 to rank from May 10, 1865). His first service was in Sibley's New Mexico Campaign where he saw action at Valverde. He continued on the frontier until March 1864 when his command was ordered to western Louisiana to help stop Banks' Red River Campaign. For the rest of the war he served there and in Arkansas. After the department's surrender he resumed his law practice.

BAGBY, George William (1828-1883)

Briefly a Lynchburg physician, George W. Bagby, after dabbling in journalism with a few articles for the *Lynchburg Virginian*, served as the editor of the *Southern Literary Messenger* in Richmond during most of the Civil War. Joining the Confederate army, he was soon found to be unfit for the field and, after a stint on Beauregard's staff as a clerk, he returned to literary pursuits. From his Richmond post he served as a correspondent in the nation's capital for numerous Southern publications. Following his departure from the *Messenger* he was an associate editor for the *Richmond Whig* until the close of the war. After a journalistic career in New York came to an end due to failing eyesight, he returned to the Old Dominion to take up the lecture circuit on which he was highly popular. For almost a decade he was the state librarian and wrote numerous short works. (King, Joseph Leonard, *Dr. William Bagby, a Study of Virginian Literature, 1850-1880*)

BAKER, Alpheus (1828-1891)

Serving throughout the war in the western theater, Alpheus Baker of Alabama appears to have been a general without a command in the very final days of the Confederacy. The South Carolina-born attorney's military assignments included: private, Eufaula Rifles (January 1861); captain, Company B, 1st Alabama (January 1861); colonel, 1st Alabama, Tennessee and Mississippi or 4th Confederate (December 27, 1861); colonel, 54th Alabama (October 9, 1862); brigadier general, CSA (March 5, 1864); commanding Moore's (old) Brigade, Stewart's-Clayton's Division, Hood's-Lee's Corps, Army of Tennessee (March 19-September 1864); commanding some brigade, District of the Gulf, Department of Alabama, Mississippi and East Louisiana (September-October 1864); commanding brigade, Liddell's Division, District of the Gulf, Department of Alabama, Mississippi and East Louisiana (October 1864-early 1865); and commanding brigade, Clayton's Division, Lee's Corps, Army of Tennessee (March 16-April 9, 1865). The month before his company was disbanded upon the expiration of its one-year term of enlistment Baker was named colonel of a regiment composed of companies from three states. While commanding this he was captured at Island #10 and not exchanged until September 1862. The regiment was then reorganized, and Baker was transferred to an Alabama regiment with which he was wounded at Champion Hill while serving in William W. Loring's division (which was thereafter cut off from the rest of the army, which subsequently surrendered at Vicksburg). Promoted to brigadier general, he led a brigade through the Atlanta campaign—being wounded at Ezra Church—and then served several months near Mobile. Rejoining the main western army, he fought at Bentonville but in the subsequent reorganization and consolidation of brigades he appears to have become a supernumerary officer. In the postwar years he returned to his law practice.

BAKER, Cullen M. (1838-1869)

A deserter from both the Union and Confederate armies Cullen M. Baker became the head of a band of "Confederate" irregulars which terrorized much of Texas and Arkansas during and after the Civil War. Conscription into the Confederate army provided him with a refuge from an Arkansas murder case but he soon deserted, killed two Union soldiers and again found sanctuary by enlisting in the Northern army. He deserted again to join the irregulars—actually bandits preying on farmers—and continue the vicious ways he had practiced since at least 1855. With the war over he saw no reason to stop and by 1868 Arkansas Governor Clayton Powell, a former Union general, had put a $1000 reward on his head. Late that year he kidnapped a crippled teacher named Thomas Orr whom a girl had chosen over Baker, and hung him from a tree. Although Orr survived, this event destroyed the good reputation he had locally for fighting Union troops and black police. A posse caught up with him on January 7, 1869, and Orr shot and killed him.

BAKER, James McNair (1821-1892)

In November 1861, after a closely contested election requiring 41 ballots, the Florida legislature appointed a former Unionist lawyer and judge to a two-year term in the Confederate Senate. He was James M. Baker, a transplanted North Carolinian. In 1863 he was unanimously reelected to a six-year term. He served on the Committees on Claims; Commerce (First Congress only); Engrossment and Enrollment (First Congress only); Naval Affairs; Post Offices and Post Roads; Public Buildings; and Public Lands, which he chaired during the Second Congress. Baker was primarily concerned with the administrative organization of the new nation. Although a supporter of the war policies, he felt that many of the measures taken were unduly affecting the economic life of much of the South. This view may have been influenced by the fact that throughout the war only a small portion of Florida was occupied or threatened by Union troops. Baker returned to the practice of law after the war, but was removed from the state supreme court during Reconstruction. Eventually receiving a judgeship, he held it for almost a decade until his retirement in 1890.

BAKER, John A. (?-?)

A resident of New Hanover County, North Carolina, John Baker's career during the Civil War made him *persona non grata* in the South after the war. The governor appointed Baker a first lieutenant in the "Wilmington Light Artillery," which was designated Company E, 1st North Carolina Artillery, on May 16, 1861. He resigned that commission on April 9, 1862,

and was promoted captain and aide-de-camp to General S.G. French. On September 3, 1862, he was again promoted, this time to colonel and given command of a group of independent cavalry companies that became the 3rd North Carolina Cavalry. Although his regiment was not serving together as a unit, Baker did take part in the fighting at White Hall, near Kingston, North Carolina, in mid-December 1862 and was slightly wounded there. After a year of service in North Carolina and southeastern Virginia, Baker and his regiment joined the Army of Northern Virginia on May 26, 1864. It was immediately involved in an almost daily series of cavalry fights on the Hanover Town Road, at Haw's Shop, Hanover Court House, Ashland, and near Meadows Bridge. During Grant's move from Cold Harbor to Petersburg, Baker and his men fought at White Oak Swamp, Malvern Hill and Harrison's Landing. In a fight along the Weldon Railroad, at Davis' Farm on June 21, 1864, Baker was captured. Part of the 600 rebel prisoners sent to Charleston Harbor to be placed under Southern fire in retaliation for Confederate treatment of Union captives, Baker did something that angered his fellow soldiers. When in September 1864, an exchange of prisoners seemed possible, Secretary of War James Seddon wrote that charges had been preferred against Colonel Baker and he did not wish there to be any furlough or indulgence shown him and that he should be sent to Richmond for appropriate measures. Seddon further wrote, "This last matter had best be preserved secret, as any intimation to him might probably cause him to remain with the enemy." The exchange never came off. In March 1865 Baker took the oath of allegiance to the U.S. government and was released on the 6th. Whatever the secret matter was, it was loathsome enough in the South that Baker fled to the West Indies and apparently never returned.

BAKER, Laurence Simmons (1830-1907)

A veteran of the Army of Northern Virginia's cavalry operations, Laurence S. Baker was wounded before he received formal notification of his promotion to brigadier and was never able to rejoin the unit. An 1851 graduate of West Point, he had served a decade in the Regiment of Mounted Rifles before resigning a first lieutenant's commission on May 10, 1861. His Confederate assignments included: lieutenant colonel, 1st North Carolina Cavalry (May 16, 1861); colonel, 1st North Carolina Cavalry (March 1, 1862); commanding Hampton's Brigade, Cavalry Division, Army of Northern Virginia (July 3-August 1, 1863); brigadier general, CSA (July 23, 1863); commanding 2nd Military District, Department of North Carolina (June 9, 1864-February 1865 but detached in Georgia November-December 1864); commanding 1st Brigade North Carolina Junior Reserves, Hoke's Division, Hardee's Corps (March-April 9, 1865); and commanding same brigade, Hoke's Division, Hardee's Corps, Army of Tennessee (April 1865). As a regimental commander he fought at the Seven Days, Antietam, Fredericksburg, and Gettysburg where he succeeded the wounded Hampton. Four weeks later he was himself wounded and after a long recovery was made a district commander in his native North Carolina. He was sent at the head of a brigade to aid in the unsuccessful defense of Savannah but then returned to his district. Commanding some reserves he fought at Bentonville but was absent at the time of the surrender. He was a farmer and a railroad employee after the war. (Freeman, Douglas S., *Lee's Lieutenants*)

BALDWIN, William Edwin (1827-1864)

Having twice survived capture, Mississippi bookseller William E. Baldwin rose to the rank of brigadier general in the Confederate army only to die in a riding accident. The South Carolina native had entered the state militia in his adopted state. His assignments included: lieutenant, Columbus Riflemen (since 1849); captain, Company K, 14th Mississippi (spring 1861); colonel, 14th Mississippi (spring 1861); commanding 2nd Brigade, 2nd (Buckner's Division, Central Army of Kentucky, Department #2 (October 28, 1861-February 9, 1862); commanding 2nd Brigade, Buckner's Division, Fort Donelson, Central Army of Kentucky, Department #2 (February 9-16, 1862); brigadier general, CSA, (September 19, 1862); commanding Lee's (old) Brigade, Smith's Division, 2nd Military District, Department of Mississippi and East Louisiana (April 1863); commanding brigade, Smith's Division, Department of Mississippi and East Louisiana (April-July 4, 1863); commanding brigade, Forney's Division, Department of Mississippi and East Louisiana (November-December 1863); commanding brigade, Walker's Division, Hardee's Corps, Army of Tennessee (December 1863-January 1864); and commanding brigade, Department of the Gulf (January-February 19, 1864). After serving at Pensacola and in central Kentucky, he was captured while commanding a brigade at Fort Donelson. Exchanged in August 1862, he was captured again at Vicksburg when that place fell to Grant. Again freed from parole he led his brigade in Mississippi, northern Georgia and around Mobile. A fluke riding accident near Dog River Factory, Alabama, proved fatal on February, 19, 1864.

BARKSDALE, Ethelbert (1824-1893)

One of Jefferson Davis' most influential supporters in the Confederate Congress was the representative from Mississippi's 6th District, Ethelbert Barksdale. A journalist, Barksdale was an editor by the time he was 21. He diffused his Democratic views through the pages of the *Yazoo City Democrat*, *Jackson Mississippian*, and the *Jackson Clarion*. A delegate to the 1860 Democratic convention and a supporter of John C. Breckinridge in the presidential race, Barksdale declared that he would become a secessionist if Lincoln were elected. Named to the First Confederate Congress, he soon became known as a powerful debater and an introducer of controversial bills supporting the Davis Administration. He even favored the institution of martial law. Having gained the support of Robert E. Lee in the final months of the war, Barksdale pushed through the bill to arm the slaves. Returning to journalism after the war, Barksdale was active in ending carpetbag rule in Mississippi. In the 1800s he served two terms in the U.S. Congress. Ethelbert's brother, General William Barksdale, was killed at Gettysburg.

BARKSDALE, William (1821-1863)

The brother of Confederate Congressman Ethelbert Barksdale, William Barksdale died as a Southern brigadier at Gettysburg. Born in Tennessee he moved to Mississippi to practice law and later edited the pro-slavery *Columbus Democrat*. After taking part in the Mexican War as an assistant commissary of subsistence for the volunteers with the rank of captain, he soon entered Congress as a states' rights representative. He resigned with the secession of his state and in March 1861 became quartermaster general of the state's forces. When he transferred to Confederate service his assignments included: colonel, 13th Mississippi (May 1861); commanding Griffith's (old) Brigade, Magruder's Division, Magruder's Command, Army of Northern Virginia (June 29-July 1862); commanding same brigade, McLaws' Division, 1st Corps, same army (July 1862-July 2, 1863); and brigadier general, CSA (August 12, 1862). He led his regiment at 1st Bull Run, Yorktown, and in the Seven Days. In the latter he succeeded to brigade command upon the death of General Richard Griffith at Savage Station. After service in the Maryland Campaign he particularly distinguished himself in the early stages at Fredericksburg. His brigade, along with other units, delayed the crossing of the Union troops by firing upon the engineers attempting to lay pontoon bridges. Despite artillery barrages that nearly leveled the town, Barksdale and his men fought on until forced out by a Union amphibious landing. His brigade was part of the force that defended Marye's Heights at Fredericksburg during the

Confederate General William Barksdale. (Harpers)

Battle of Chancellorsville. He was mortally wounded in the attack on the second day at Gettysburg, and died the next day. (Freeman, Douglas S., *Lee's Lieutenants*)

BARNEY, Joseph Nicholson (?-?)

A veteran of 16 years in the United States Navy, Lieutenant Joseph N. Barney resigned his commission in June 1861 in order to join the Confederacy. Commissioned a lieutenant in that service, he commanded the *Jamestown* during the battle between the *Monitor* and the *Virginia* in Hampton Roads in March 1862. The next month he took part in the successful capture of three Union transports under the guns of the *Monitor*. After taking part in the action at Drewry's Bluff he was named to the rank of commander and commanded the *Harriet Lane* after it was captured at Galveston at the beginning of 1863. He then briefly commanded the cruiser *Florida* off the coast of France in the winter of 1863-64 but was forced to relinquish command due to ill health.

BARNWELL, Robert Woodward (1801-1882)

A lifelong states' rights advocate, Robert W. Barnwell had a distinguished record before he began his career in the Confederate Congress. Born into the plantation society of South Carolina, Barnwell received his degree from Harvard summa cum laude. After serving in the state house, he served two terms in the U.S. Congress and was involved in the nullification crisis of 1832 on the side of his state. He spent half a dozen years as president of the South Carolina College. After nine years of retirement on his plantation, he succeeded to Calhoun's seat in the Senate but again went into retirement in 1853. He was a member of the South Carolina secession convention, a state commissioner to President Buchanan and temporary chairman of the Montgomery convention, which eventually became the Provisional Confederate Congress. Backing Davis for president, Barnwell turned down the state department portfolio and remained in the Congress. He was elected to a Senate seat for both regular congresses. Considered an ardent supporter of the Confederate president, Barnwell from the chair of the Committee on Finance actually often opposed the administration on fiscal matters. The Davis administration, however, usually got its way with Barnwell on military affairs. He opposed the establishment of the position of general in chief since it would weaken the executive's power. Financially ruined by the war, Barnwell was connected with the University of South Carolina until his death, except for a period of four years when he was removed by black and carpetbag rule.

BARRINGER, Rufus (1821-1895)

After serving for two years as captain, Rufus Barringer rose to brigadier in less than a year. A native North Carolina lawyer and politician, he had misgivings about secession but enlisted anyway. His assignments included: captain, Company F, 1st North Carolina Cavalry (May 16, 1861); major, 1st North Carolina Cavalry (May 16, 1861); major, 1st North Carolina

Cavalry (August 26, 1863); lieutenant colonel, 1st North Carolina Cavalry (October 17, 1863); lieutenant colonel, 4th North Carolina Cavalry (temporarily assigned January 1864); brigadier general, CSA (June 1, 1864); and commanding Gordon's (old) Brigade, W.H.F. Lee's Division, Cavalry Corps, Army of Northern Virginia (June 4, 1864-April 3, 1865). As a company commander, he served at the Seven Days, Antietam, Fredericksburg, and Brandy Station, where he was severely wounded. After Gettysburg his rapid rise began. He served through the Bristoe and Mine Run campaigns and in January 1864 was transferred to the temporary command of the 4th North Carolina Cavalry. This unit was transferred out of the brigade and Barringer continued to serve with it in the Department of North Carolina and Southern Virginia until the death of General Gordon prompted his promotion and assignment to the old brigade. He led the unit through the Petersburg operations and in the Appomattox Campaign in which it was virtually destroyed. Barringer was captured at Namozine Church on April 3, 1865, and was not released until July. Active in Republican politics, he supported Reconstruction after the war.

BARRON, Samuel (1809-1888)

At the outbreak of the Civil War the chief of the Union navy's Bureau of Detail resigned his commission and offered his services to his native Virginia. A veteran of over 40 years at sea, Barron was commissioned commander CSN, on June 10, 1861. His first assignment was to take charge of all naval defenses on the coasts of Virginia and North Carolina. Arriving at Fort Hatteras a day after the bombardment of that position had begun, he was requested by the army commander to take over the general direction of the defense since the fort's armament was comprised of naval ordnance. However, the next day, August 29, Barron was forced to surrender the position to the overwhelming Union fleet. Exchanged after 11 months of confinement, he again commanded the naval forces in Virginia until sent to England as a captain, where he secured the *Stonewall* and *Georgia* for the Confederacy. Moving his Confederate operations to Paris, he continued procurement operations for the navy. Following the war, he went into retirement in Virginia. (Scharf, J. Thomas, *History of the Confederate States Navy*)

BARRY, John Decatur (1839-1867)

By the time that he got his temporary appointment as a Confederate brigadier John D. Barry had been wounded and, as his predecessor was ready to return to duty, his short-lived appointment was cancelled. After graduating from the University of North Carolina, Barry entered the service of his native North Carolina at the outbreak of the conflict. His assignments included: private, Company I, 8th North Carolina Volunteers (April 15, 1861); private, Company I, 18th North Carolina State Troops (a change of designation on November 14, 1861); captain, Company I, 18th North Carolina (April 24, 1862); major, 18th North Carolina (November 11, 1862); colonel, 18th North Carolina (May 27 to rank from May 3, 1863); commanding Lane's Brigade, Wilcox's Division, 3rd Corps, Army of Northern Virginia (June 2-July 2, 1864 and February-March 1865); and temporarily brigadier general, CSA (August 3, 1864). As he steadily rose in rank, his regiment saw action at the Seven Days, Cedar Mountain, 2nd Bull Run, Chantilly, Harpers Ferry, Antietam, Fredericksburg, and Chancellorsville. He led the regiment at Gettysburg, including Pickett's Charge. Directing his men through the Overland Campaign, he succeeded the wounded General Lane in command of the brigade, but he was wounded a month later on the Petersburg lines. His temporary brigadier's appointment came through while he was recuperating but was cancelled when Lane was able to return to duty first. Returning to his regiment in February 1865, as colonel, he was in temporary brigade command at the end of the month. Wounds or illness seem to have forced him from the field before the retreat to Appomattox; he returned from the war to run a Wilmington newspaper. In poor health, he died two years after the war.

BARRY, William Taylor Sullivan (1821-1868)

An extreme secessionist politician and plantation owner, William T.S. Barry took his fight for the South from the halls of political institutions to the battlefield and ended his Confederate career as a regimental commander. The Mississippi-born Barry was a Yale graduate, lawyer, state legislator, U.S. Congressman, and speaker in the Mississippi state house. He participated in the Southern walkout at the Democratic convention in Charleston. Barry then chaired the convention that took Mississippi out of the Union. Sent to the Provisional Confederate Congress, Barry was soon known for presenting extreme measures for consideration. For example, he favored the reopening of the African slave trade and wanted to constitutionally ban any Confederate state from abolishing slavery without the approval of the remainder. At the close of the Provisional Congress, Barry decided to enter the army. His assignments included: colonel, 35th Mississippi (spring 1862); commanding Sears' Brigade, French's Division, Army of Mississippi (May 1864); and commanding Sears' Brigade, French's Division, Stewart's Corps, Army of Tennessee (July-August 1864). He led his regiment at Corinth, Chickasaw Bluffs, and in the Vicksburg siege, where, in reply to an inquiry from his brigade commander, he stated that his men were in no condition to evacuate the city in the face of the enemy. Two days later the army surrendered. Paroled immediately, he was exchanged by the end of the year and served in the Atlanta Campaign, sometimes in command of a brigade, and suffered a wound. The regiment went on to the Tennessee invasion and then to Mobile where Barry was captured again. He returned to the legal profession for his few remaining years.

BARTON, Seth Maxwell (1829-1900)

Virginian Seth M. Barton had a great deal of difficulty in pleasing his divisional commanders in the latter half of the war. A West Pointer (1849), he was a veteran of a dozen years in the infantry when he resigned his captain's commission on June 11, 1861, to offer his services to the South. His assignments included: captain, Infantry (June 1861); lieutenant colonel, 3rd Arkansas (July 1861); brigadier general, CSA (March 11, 1862); commanding brigade, Department of East Tennessee (March-June 1862); commanding brigade, Stevenson's Division, same department (June-November 20, 1862); commanding brigade, Stevenson's Division, 2nd Military District, Department of Mississippi and East Louisiana (December 18, 1862-April 1863); commanding brigade, Stevenson's Division, same department (May-July 4, 1863); commanding Armistead's (old) Brigade, Department of North Carolina (October 4, 1863-February 1864); commanding same brigade (in Ransom's Division in May), Department of Richmond (February-May 11, 1864); commanding another brigade (in Lee's Division from March), Department of Richmond (September-December 1864 and January-April 2, 1865); and commanding brigade, G. W. C. Lee's Division, Army of Northern Virginia (April 2-6, 1865). After serving in the Cheat Mountain Campaign he was Stonewall Jackson's engineer during the Romney Campaign. Sent to East Tennessee, he commanded a brigade until Stevenson's Division was sent to Mississippi, where he was captured at Vicksburg. Exchanged on July 13, 1863, he was eventually given command of the late Lewis Armistead's Brigade, which was then serving with Pickett in North Carolina. In the January 1864 attack on New Bern he was accused of slowness in advancing, resulting in the Confederate failure. To avoid further conflict with Pickett, his brigade was transferred to Richmond. In May 1864 he came under General Ransom's control during the fighting at Drewry's Bluff and was again found wanting. He was relieved on May 11, 1864, but his request for a court of inquiry was never acted upon. Interestingly enough, the regimental commanders petitioned for his return to brigade command. Finally in September 1864, he was given command of another brigade with which he served until the fall of Richmond. In the retreat to Appomattox he was captured at Sayler's Creek on April 6, 1865. He was not released until July 1865. (Freeman, Douglas S., *Lee's Lieutenants*)

BARTOW, Francis Stebbins (1816-1861)

Although his only military experience was five years as a militia captain, lawyer Francis Bartow became Georgia's first martyr of the Civil War. As a Whig and later a member of the Know-Nothings, Bartow was a prominent local politician, although he had been defeated for a seat in Congress. As captain of the Oglethorpe Light Infantry, Bartow took part in the capture of Fort McAllister at the time of the secession of Georgia. As a member of the secession convention he was named to the Confederate Provisional Congress where he chaired the Committee on Military Affairs. When the second session adjourned, Bartow's company volunteered for service for the term of the war. Bartow's assignments included: captain, Company B, 8th Georgia (May 21, 1861); colonel, 8th Georgia (June 1, 1861); and commanding 2nd Brigade, Army of the Shenandoah (June-July 21, 1861). After service in the Valley, Bartow led part of his brigade, along with the rest of Johnston's army, to join

Francis S. Bartow, 1st Bull Run victim. (NA)

Beauregard along Bull Run. Here, on July 21, 1861, the partial brigade was part of the force that tried to stop the Union movement to turn the left flank. After fighting north of the Warrenton Turnpike, the remnants of his command were rallying on Henry House Hill when Bartow was killed. In Georgia he was popularly acclaimed a brigadier general, although never appointed to that rank, and was considered a martyr to the cause. (Freeman, Douglas S., *Lee's Lieutenants*)

BATE, William Brimage (1826-1905)

A division commander in the last year of the war, Tennesseean William B. Bate appears to have been without a command when the Confederate Army of Tennessee surrendered. In a varied prewar career he was a steamboatman, journalist, first lieutenant in the 3rd Tennessee during the Mexican War, lawyer, and state legislator. His Confederate assignments included: colonel, 2nd Tennessee (May 6, 1861); brigadier general, CSA (October 3, 1862); commanding Rains' (old) brigade, McCown's-Stewart's Division, Polk's Corps, Army of Tennessee (March 12-May 25, 1863); commanding brigade, Stewart's Division, Hardee's-Hill's-Breckinridge's Corps, Army of Tennessee (June 6-September 1 and October 1-November 12, 1863); commanding brigade, Stewart's Division, Buckner's Corps, Army of Tennessee (September 1-October 1, 1863); commanding Breckinridge's Division,

Breckinridge's-Hindman's-Hood's Corps, Army of Tennessee (November 12, 1863-February 20, 1864); commanding division, Hardee's-Cheatham's Corps, Army of Tennessee (February 20-August 1864 and September 1864-April 9, 1865); and major general, CSA (February 23, 1864). In command of his regiment, which was sometimes designated the 2nd Confederate, he served in northern Virginia in the vicinity of Aquia Creek and was present at 1st Bull Run before being ordered to East Tennessee. Heading further west he was severely wounded at Shiloh and during his recovery was promoted to brigadier general. He recovered in time to command a brigade during the Tullahoma and Chickamauga compaigns. He led a division at Chattanooga and was promoted to major general just before the Atlanta Campaign. Leading his division he fought at Franklin and Nashville and then in the Carolinas. However, upon the April 9, 1865, reorganization and consolidation of the army he was left without a command. It does appear that he was included in the surrender at Durham Station. Having been wounded three times in the course of the war, he resumed his practice. During the war he had turned down the governorship but in 1882 he was elected and later served in the U.S. Senate.

BATTLE, Cullen Andrews (1829-1905)

When General Lee found a newly appointed brigadier, E.A. O'Neal, failing the grade, he canceled his appointment and in his place Cullen A. Battle was promoted. A Georgia-born Alabama lawyer active in politics, he was a lieutenant colonel in a militia regiment even before the secession of his adopted state. His assignments for the Confederacy included: major, 3rd Alabama (April 28, 1861); lieutenant colonel, 3rd Alabama (July 31, 1861); colonel, 3rd Alabama (May 31, 1862); commanding Rodes' (old) Brigade, Rodes' Division, 2nd Corps, Army of Northern Virginia (July 1863-June 13, 1864); brigadier general, CSA (August 20, 1863); and commanding brigade, Rodes' Division, Valley District, Department of Northern Virginia (June 13-October 19, 1864). After service in the Norfolk area, the regiment moved to the Peninsula and Battle fought at Seven Pines. Missing the Seven Days Battles, he fought again in the Maryland Campaign at South Mountain and Antietam. After falling from his horse, he relinquished command of his regiment the day before Chancellorsville started. Briefly in command the next day, he suffered further damage when his horse jumped a ditch; Battle had to go off duty. Returning to duty just in time for the Gettysburg Campaign, he attached his regiment to Ramseur's Brigade when his own brigade, then under O'Neal, became disorganized on the first day of the battle. Later that month he replaced O'Neal and led the brigade at the Wilderness, Spotsylvania, and Cold Harbor. As part of Early's campaign, he fought at Monocacy and reached the suburbs of Washington. Back in the Valley, he was at 3rd Winchester and Fisher's Hill, and fell wounded at Cedar Creek. He was unable to return to duty before the close of hostilities. Returning to the law, he was refused a seat in Congress and instead became mayor of New Bern. He was also a newspaper editor in New Bern, North Carolina. (Freeman, Douglas S., *Lee's Lieutenants*)

BAYLOR, George Wythe (ca. 1832-1916)

Failure to gain a promotion in the Confederate army was often considered grounds for personal violence among officers. Such was the case with George W. Baylor. Born into a military family on the frontier, Baylor had become a famed Indian fighter and secessionist by the outbreak of the Civil War. Joining the army early in 1861 he was commissioned lieutenant, 2nd Texas Cavalry, and took part in the Arizona Campaign before being detailed as aide-de-camp to General A.S. Johnston. Serving in the battle of Shiloh he lost his commander and joined Beauregard's staff. Given command of the 2nd Texas Cavalry, Arizona Brigade, with the rank of colonel, he distinguished himself in the battles of Mansfield and Pleasant Hill. Under consideration for promotion to a general's wreath, Baylor became disgusted with the failure of his division commander, John A. Wharton, to act in the matter. Then late in 1864 his regiment was dismounted and assigned to an infantry division. By this time the unit was back in Texas. Running into Wharton on a Houston street on April 6, 1865, Baylor had a heated discussion with his former commander. When the pair met again at General Magruder's headquarters a short while later, Wharton called Baylor a liar. A slap in the face followed. Baylor fired his pistol; the general fell dead. After the war Baylor served for two decades in the Texas Rangers and then in the state legislature. He regretted the death of Wharton, for which he was never tried, until his own death.

BAYLOR, John Robert (1822-1894)

One of the more varied of Confederate careers was that of John R. Baylor of Texas who served as a lieutenant colonel of cavalry, governor of the Arizona Territory, private soldier, and finally as congressman. Born in Kentucky, Baylor moved to Texas at the age of 17 and became an Indian fighter, but his hatred of the Indians led him into difficulties with the Richmond authorities during the Civil War. He served briefly in the state legislature until appointed as an Indian agent, but was then removed from this position because of his extreme views. However he urged and obtained the removal of Indians to the Indian Territory, now Oklahoma. In December 1860 he organized the famous "buffalo hunt" for rebel military operations. He was present at General Twiggs' surrender in May 1861. As lieutenant colonel, 2nd Texas Mounted Rifles, he led a force of about 250 men from El Paso into the New Mexico Territory. On July 25, 1861, he won the battle of Mesilla and in the next two days took Fort Fillmore and captured 11 Union companies without firing a shot. On August 1, 1861, Baylor proclaimed himself governor of the provisional Confederate Territory of Arizona, the southern part of what is now Arizona and New Mexico. This action was formally recognized by the Confederate government on February 14, 1862, but his proposals to launch a war of extermination against the Indians forced his removal later in the year. While back in Texas, he participated in the capture of Galveston at the start of 1863. In the fall he was elected to the Second Confederate Congress from Texas' 5th District. In Richmond he supported extreme measures in the prosecution of the war but tried to restrict the powers of Jefferson Davis. He

was a consistent opponent of a negotiated settlement of the conflict. Appropriately he served on the Committee on Indian Affairs and also on the Committee on Patents. Following the Confederacy's defeat, Baylor practiced law in San Antonio. (Thompson, Jerry Don, *Colonel John Robert Baylor: Texas Indian Fighter and Confederate Soldier*)

BAYLOR, William Smith Hanger (1831-1862)

The unusually high mortality rate among commanders of the famed Stonewall Brigade claimed William S.H. Baylor before he could be promoted to the appropriate rank of brigadier general. A lawyer and commonwealth attorney in his native Shenandoah Valley, he became captain of a militia company, the West August Guards, in the late 1850s. His Civil War assignments included: captain, Company L, 5th Virginia (April 1861); major, 5th Virginia (May 28, 1861); colonel, 5th Virginia (April 21, 1862); and commanding Stonewall Brigade, Jackson's (old) Division, Jackson's Corps, Army of Northern Virginia (ca. August 20-August 30, 1862). Serving with his regiment, and at times as Jackson's inspector general, he took part in the battles of 1st Bull Run and Kernstown. With the reorganization of the regiment in the spring of 1862 he was named its new commander with the support of all the regimental officers. His popularity with his fellow officers was to earn him yet another promotion, one he would not live to see. Distinguishing himself in the Valley Campaign of 1862, leading a charge on foot after his horse was shot out from under him at Winchester, he went on to further glory in the Seven Days battles. Moving north to face Pope's Union army, he fought at Cedar Mountain and upon the recommendation of all the field officers of the brigade he was placed in charge of Jackson's old command. In the defense of the railroad cut at 2nd Bull Run, Baylor distinguished himself for three days but in the final stages of the last day he picked up the fallen colors of the 33rd Virginia and led a counterattack. He was struck down by an enemy volley—and so denied a general's wreath. (Robertson, James I., Jr., *The Stonewall Brigade*)

BEALE, Richard Lee Turberville (1819-1893)

Throughout the war, Richard L.T. Beale followed W.H.F. Lee through the cavalry battles of the Army of Northern Virginia and up the ladder of command. A Virginia lawyer, he served one term each in the U.S. Congress and the state senate. His military assignments included: first lieutenant, Lee's Light Horse (May 1861); captain, Lee's Light Horse (July 1861); major, 9th Virginia Cavalry (January 1862); lieutenant colonel, 9th Virginia Cavalry (April 28, 1862); colonel, 9th Virginia Cavalry (October 18, 1862); commanding Chambliss' (old) Brigade, W.H.F. Lee's Division, Cavalry Corps, Army of Northern Virginia (October 1864-April 9, 1865); and brigadier general, CSA (February 6 to rank from January 6, 1865). After service along the Rappahannock, he moved to the Peninsula and saw action in the Seven Days. Later combat occurred at 2nd Bull Run, Antietam, Fredericksburg, and facing Stoneman's raid during the Chancellorsville Campaign. He led the regiment with Stuart around the Union army and at Gettysburg. Wounded in September 1863 he was out of action for several months but returned for the Overland and Petersburg campaigns. He succeeded to the command of the brigade, which had once been "Rooney" Lee's, in October during the siege. Not promoted until early the next year, he was one of only two cavalry generals who surrendered at Appomattox. He resumed the practice of law and sat in the congress of a reunited nation. (Freeman, Douglas S., *Lee's Lieutenants* and Beale, Richard Lee Turberville, *History of the Ninth Virginia Cavalry*)

BEALL, John Yates (1835-1865)

One of the greatest Confederate adventurers, John Y. Beall gave his life for his new country in the waning days of the Civil War. The Virginia native had studied law but never practiced and instead became a country gentleman. Early in the Civil War he enlisted in Company G, 2nd Virginia, as a private. With the Stonewall Brigade he fought at 1st Bull Run. On October 16, 1861, his infantry career came to an end with a bullet wound in the lung. He then turned to a scheme to release Confederate prisoners held at Johnson's Island, Ohio (in Lake Erie) from a Canadian base. Instead he was appointed an acting master in the Confederate navy and was assigned to raiding activities in Chesapeake Bay, at which he was highly successful. However on November 1, 1863, he and his band were captured and confined in Fort McHenry as pirates. Union hostages were named and Beall and his men were exchanged on May 5, 1864. He then went to Canada again and gained approval for his plan, now enlarged to encompass the capture of the only Union warship on the Great Lakes, the *USS Michigan*. Seizing the lake steamer *Philo Parsons*, he was closing in on his quarry when his crew mutinied due to the lack of a planned signal from shore (the agent there had been arrested as a spy). Beall then attempted to rescue prisoners being transported by rail in New York, but was captured on December 16, 1864, while attending to one of his party who had fallen asleep within a few hundred yards of the Canadian border. This man later testified against Beall, and the Confederate spy went to the gallows on February 24, 1865.

BEALL, Lloyd James (?-1887)

The one and only commandant of the Confederate Marine Corps was West Pointer (1830) Lloyd J. Beall. Born in Rhode Island, he had received his appointment to the military academy from Maryland. Initially posted to the infantry, he transferred to the dragoons and finally, in 1844, to the paymaster's department. On April 22, 1861, he resigned his commission as major and paymaster and joined the Confederate cause. Initially appointed an army colonel, he was transferred to the navy on May 23, 1861, and named colonel and commandant of the infant marine corps. It was only of regimental size, but was scattered from Virginia to Texas and served both ashore and afloat. Throughout the war Beall was forced to struggle with a shortage of funds and supplies that were slowed by the blockade. The corps was con-

sidered one of the best Confederate units in existence. After Appomattox Beall retired to his Richmond home where most of the corps' records that had survived the war were destroyed in a fire.

BEALL, William Nelson Rector (1825-1883)

Captured at Port Hudson, Kentucky-born West Pointer (1848) William N.R. Beall was paroled by the Union authorities to act as a Confederate agent in charge of supplying Southern prisoners of war. He had received his appointment to the military academy from Arkansas and upon his graduation was posted to the infantry. Transferred to the cavalry in 1855, virtually his entire service was on the western frontier. Resigning as a captain in the 1st Cavalry on August 20, 1861, his Confederate assignments included: captain, Cavalry (March 16, 1861); brigadier general, CSA (April 11, 1862); commanding 2nd District, Department of Southern Mississippi and East Louisiana (June 26-July 2, 1862); commanding 3rd Military District, Department of Mississippi and East Louisiana (October 21-December 27, 1862 and May 6-11, 1863); and commanding brigade, 3rd Military District, Department of Mississippi and East Louisiana (December 27, 1862-July 8, 1863). Following service in Arkansas and at Corinth, Mississippi, he was assigned to duty at Port Hudson where he commanded a brigade until the city's surrender on July 8, 1863. Imprisoned on Johnson's Island, Ohio, he was freed and given an office in New York City in 1864. This arrangement came to an end on August 2, 1865, when he was formally released. After the war he was in business in St. Louis.

William N.R. Beall, prisoner at Port Hudson. (NA)

BEAUREGARD, Pierre Gustave Toutant (1818-1893)

The services of "The Hero of Fort Sumter," Pierre G.T. Beauregard, were not utilized to their fullest due to bad blood between the Confederate general and Jefferson Davis. The native Louisianan had graduated second in the 1838 class at West Point. There he had become a great admirer of Napoleon and was nicknamed "The Little Napoleon." Posted to the artillery, he was transferred to the engineers a week later. As a staff officer with Winfield Scott in Mexico he won two brevets and was wounded at both Churubusco and Chapultepec. In the interwar years he was engaged in clearing the Mississippi River of obstructions. In 1861 he served the shortest term ever—January 23-28—as superintendent at West Point. Southern leanings probably resulted in his prompt removal. On February 20, 1861, he resigned his captaincy in the engineers and offered his services to the South. His Confederate assignments included: brigadier general, CSA (March 1, 1861); commanding Charleston Harbor (March 3-May 27, 1861); commanding Alexandria Line (June 2-20, 1861); commanding Army of the Potomac (June 20-July 20, 1861); commanding 1st Corps, Army of the Potomac (July 20-October 22, 1861); general, CSA (August 31, 1861 to rank from July 21); commanding Potomac District, Department of Northern Virginia (October 22, 1861-January 29, 1862); commanding Army of the Mississippi (March 17-29 and April 6-May 7, 1862); second in command, Army of the Mississippi and Department #2 (March 29-April 6, 1862); commanding the department (April 6-June 17, 1862); commanding Department of South Carolina, Georgia and Florida (August 29, 1862-April 20, 1864); commanding Department of North Carolina and Southern Virginia (April 22-ca. September 23, 1864); commanding Military Division of the West (October 17, 1864-March 16, 1865); and second in command, Army of Tennessee (March 16-April 26, 1865). Placed in charge of the South Carolina troops in Charleston Harbor, he won the nearly bloodless victory at Fort Sumter. "The Little Creole" was hailed throughout the South. Ordered to Virginia, he commanded the forces opposite Washington and created the Confederate Army of the Potomac. Reinforced by Joseph E. Johnston and his Army of the Shenandoah, Beauregard was reduced to corps command under Johnston the day before 1st Bull Run. However, during the battle Beauregard, being familiar with the field, exercised tactical command while Johnston forwarded troops to the threatened left. Both officers later claimed that they could have taken the Union capital if they had been properly supplied with rations for their men. This was one of Beauregard's first conflicts with Davis. Nonetheless he was named a full general from the date of the battle and early in 1862 was sent to the West as Albert Sidney Johnston's second in command. Utilizing Napoleonic style, he drafted the attack orders for Shiloh and took command when Johnston was mortally wounded on the first day of the battle. On the evening of the first day he let victory slip through his fingers by calling off the attacks. Controversy over his decision has raged to this day. The next day he was driven from the field by Grant's and Buell's combined armies. He was eventually forced to evacuate Corinth, Mississippi—his supply base—in

P.G.T. Beauregard, "The Little Napoleon." (NA)

the face of Henry W. Halleck's overwhelming force. Shortly after that he went on sick leave without gaining Davis' permission; he was permanently relieved of his army and departmental commands on June 27, 1862, by special direction of the president. Two months later he returned to the scene of his earlier triumph as commander along the Southern coast from the North Carolina-South Carolina line to the tip of Florida. He held this command for over a year and a half and was engaged in the determined defense of Charleston against naval and ground forces. Ordered north, he took command in North Carolina and southern Virginia while Lee faced Grant in northern Virginia. Gradually the two forces were pushed together in an awkward command arrangement. Beauregard managed to bottle up Benjamin F. Butler in the Bermuda Hundred lines after defeating him at Drewry's Bluff. This was Beauregard's finest performance of the war. At this point he started making grandiose proposals for defeating both Butler and Grant and invading the North by taking a large part of Lee's army with him. This resulted in lengthy correspondence between the two commanders and the Richmond authorities. Beauregard also managed to thwart the early Union attempts to take Petersburg while Lee was still north of the James River. With the siege of the city under way, he continued to serve under Lee until September 1864 when he was assigned to overall command in the West with John B. Hood's Army of Tennessee and Richard Taylor's Department of Alabama, Mississippi and East Louisiana under him. With no forces under his immediate command he was powerless in trying to stop Sherman's March to the

Sea. In the final days of the war he was again second in command to Joseph E. Johnston, this time in North Carolina. Following the capitulation he returned to New Orleans and refused high rank in the Egyptian and Rumanian armies. Engaged in railroading, his reputation was tarnished by his association with the Louisiana Lottery as a supervisor. For a time he was Louisiana's adjutant general, and he engaged in historical writing including his *A Commentary on the Campaign and Battle of Manassas*. (Williams, T. Harry, *P.G.T. Beauregard, Napoleon in Gray*)

BECKHAM, Robert Franklin (1837-1864)

In the battle of Franklin, General John B. Hood's chief of artillery, Robert F. Beckham, became one of the senior Confederate officers to lose his life in that disastrous fight. A West Pointer (1859) and sixth in his class, the Virginian resigned his commission as a brevet second lieutenant in the topographical engineers on May 3, 1861. His Confederate assignments included: lieutenant, Artillery (to date from March 16, 1861); captain, Jeff Davis Artillery (March 31, 1862; declined); major, Artillery (August 30, 1862); commanding Horse Artillery Battalion, Cavalry Division (Corps from September 9), Army of Northern Virginia (April 8, 1863-February 16, 1864); colonel, Artillery (early 1864); commanding Artillery, 2nd Corps, Army of Tennessee (July 24-November 30, 1864). Attached to the Culpeper (Virginia) Artillery, he commanded the battery at 1st Bull Run. On January 14, 1862, he was assigned to ordnance duty on the staff of General G.W. Smith. In this position he played a key role in the Battle of Seven Pines. He continued on staff duty until given command of the cavalry's artillery in the spring of 1863. He commanded the guns at Brandy Station and Gettysburg. Then in the winter of 1863-1864, he was promoted and transferred to the West. He commanded the artillery of Hood's Corps until that officer took over command of the Army of Tennessee. At that time Beckham became the army's chief artillerist. In these two positions he served throughout the Atlanta Campaign and later in the invasion of Tennessee. Mortally wounded at Franklin, he died on December 5, 1864. (Wise, Jennings C., *The Long Arm of Lee*)

BEE, Barnard Elliott (1824-1861)

The man who gave "Stonewall" Jackson his immortal nickname, was Barnard Bee, but it is not known for certain whether it was meant as a compliment or an insult. A native of South Carolina, Bee graduated from West Point in 1845 and served in the infantry in Mexico, being wounded at Cerro Gordo, and fought against Indians and bandits, until he resigned his captain's commission on March 3, 1861. Joining the Confederacy, his assignments included: major, Infantry (March 1861); colonel (spring 1861); brigadier general CSA (June 17, 1861). Ordered to the Valley, Bee led his brigade, along with Johnston's army, to Beauregard's line on Bull Run. With the Union flank attack on July 21, Bee moved his men north of the Warrenton Turnpike and held back the Union force, in conjunction with Bartow's and Evans' commands, while reinforcements were sent to bolster the Confederate left.

Falling back to Henry House Hill, Bee saw General T. J. Jackson's Virginia Brigade, a little to his rear, in line of battle and not yet engaged. Bee called out to his men, "There is Jackson, standing like a stone wall. Let us determine to die here, and we will conquer. Follow me." A dispute has arisen as to whether Bee was, in fact, knocking Jackson for not coming to his support. The answer will never be known since Bee fell mortally wounded moments later. He died the next day but Jackson and his brigade were thereafter known as "Stonewall." (Freeman, Douglas S., *Lee's Lieutenants*)

Barnard E. Bee, the man who nicknamed Jackson "Stonewall." (B&L)

BEE, Hamilton Prioleau (1822-1897)

Serving entirely beyond the Mississippi, Texas legislator Hamilton P. Bee consequently saw only limited action as a Confederate brigadier general. The South Carolina native—and brother of Barnard E. Bee—had moved with his family to Texas. During the Mexican War he served as a second lieutenant in both the Texas Rangers and Bell's regiment of Texas volunteers. His Civil War assignments included: brigadier general, Texas Militia (1861); brigadier general, CSA (March 6, 1862 to rank from the 4th); commanding Sub-District of the Rio Grande, Department of Texas (April 24-May 26, 1862); and commanding in the Trans-Mississippi Department: Sub-District of the Rio Grande (May 26, 1862-June 1863); Western Sub-District of Texas, District of Texas, New Mexico and Arizona (June 1863-March 16, 1864); also 1st Division, District of Texas, New Mexico and Arizona (December 15, 1863-March 16, 1864); brigade, Green's Cavalry Division, District of West Louisiana (March 16-spring 1864); division, Cavalry Corps (February-April 1864); and brigade, Maxey's Division, District of Texas, New Mexico and Arizona (April-May 26, 1865). Early in the war, from his station at Brownsville, Texas, he supervised smuggling operations via Mexico. His first major field service came during the Red River Campaign in which some of his superiors criticized him. In the final months of the war he was back in Texas serving with both infantry and cavalry. For a number of years he was in exile in Mexico.

BEERS, Fannie A. (?-?)

Although born in the North, Fannie A. Beers served throughout the Civil War in Confederate hospitals, in both major theaters of the conflict. Marrying into a Louisiana family in the 1850s, she settled in New Orleans and was visiting her mother in New York when the war broke out. She refugeed to Richmond where she was persuaded to join the nursing staff, since her husband had already enlisted in the army. She later followed him to the western theater and at the close of the war chose to remain with her charges until the Union troops took over the hospital at Newnan, Georgia. In the late 1880s and early 1890s she published her *Memories*, which is the only known source on her life. It is full of anecdotes but very sketchy on her personal life.

BELL, Caspar Wistar (1819-1898)

Due to the fact that his 3rd District in Missouri almost immediately fell into Union hands, Confederate Congressman Caspar W. Bell was never really elected to his position by his district's residents. A prominent lawyer with no political experience, he was named by the secessionist portion of the state legislature to represent them in Richmond. In the Provisional Congress he served on the Committees on Public Lands and on Territories. In the First Regular Congress his committee assignments were in the Medical Department, in Military Affairs, and as chairman of Patents. A close friend of Senator Henry Foote, Bell was not a friend of the Davis administration and constantly tried to limit the executive's power. He voted to override vetoes and was opposed to the suspension of the writ of habeas corpus, but he supported measures to further the Confederate cause in the military and financial fields. During his time in Richmond he wrote Missouri-related articles for the *Richmond Examiner*. In a May 1864 election among Missouri refugees and soldiers Bell lost his seat. Taking up his law practice again, he remained in Virginia until 1867, then returned home. Although referred to as a "general" after the war, he had in fact never been such. In early 1861 he had briefly served as an adjutant-general in the Missouri State Guard.

BELL, Hiram Parks (1827-1907)

Georgian Hiram P. Bell was never a supporter of secession, and so he became one of the most obstructionist members of the Second Confederate Congress. A teacher and lawyer, Bell entered politics as a Unionist delegate to the Georgia secession convention in 1861. But with secession a reality, he proceeded to Tennessee to urge that state to join in the movement. In October 1861 he was elected to the Georgia senate but resigned to become lieutenant colonel, 43rd Georgia. He fought and was wounded at Chickasaw Bayou in December 1862. During the siege of Vicksburg he was again wounded, this time severely enough to incapacitate him for further service; he resigned his commission. In October 1863 he was elected to the Second Regular Congress as the representative of the 9th District, in Georgia's northeastern corner. Bell later claimed that he took his seat in May 1864 with the determination to force the government to open peace negotiations. He served on the Committees on Elections, Patents, and Post Offices and Post Roads. He wanted to end the policy of impressment of supplies and eliminate the inequalities of existing tax policies. He tried to facilitate the payment of claims against the government. With only a month until the final adjournment of the Confederate Congress, Bell left Richmond to look after the safety of his family. Resuming his law practice, Bell was active in Democratic politics and served two terms in the U.S. Congress in the 1870s. Around the turn of the century he served in both houses of the Georgia legislature.

BELL, John (1797-1869)

In a forlorn attempt to prevent the Civil War he saw coming, Tennesseean John Bell ran for president in 1860 on the Constitutional Union ticket. A prominent Nashville attorney, he had served a term in the state senate and 14 years in Congress. Originally a Jacksonian, he split with them and became a leader of the Whig Party. He served a few weeks as Harrison's secretary of war in 1841 and then went into semi-retirement for six years. Elected to the U.S. Senate, he was recognized as a conservative Southerner. Himself a large slave owner, he had no love for the abolitionists but cautioned for moderation on the part of the South. He supported the right of petition, even on the sensitive issue that he would have preferred to see simply go away. He believed that Congress could, constitutionally, ban slavery in the territories but nevertheless thought it to be unwise policy. He voted against the admission of Kansas under the pro-slavery

Lecompton Constitution. His actions were sharply criticized in the South but recognized in the North as those of moderation. With the death of the Whig Party Bell shifted around for some new alliance, even with moderate Republicans. In 1860 a group composed mostly of old Whigs nominated Bell for the presidency. Bell and his running mate, Edward Everett, ran on a platform of upholding the constitution, the union, and the laws. They carried only Tennessee, Kentucky, and Virginia. Once it became obvious that the North was going to use troops to preserve the Union, Bell reluctantly advised Tennessee to ally itself with the Confederacy to fight against suppression. A broken man, he lived through the fall of the Confederacy, his career over. (Parks, Joseph Howard, *John Bell of Tennessee*)

BELL, Tyree Harris (1815-1902)

When Kentucky planter Tyree H. Bell became a supernumerary officer he eventually was given command of a mounted brigade, under the famous Nathan Bedford Forrest, for the balance of the war. His assignments included: captain, Company G (later A), 12th Tennessee (June 4, 1861); lieutenant colonel, 12th Tennessee (June 1861); colonel, 12th Tennessee (May 1862); colonel, 12th and 22nd Tennessee Consolidated (June 17, 1862); commanding independent brigade, Forrest's Cavalry Corps, Department of Mississippi and East Louisiana (January 25-28, 1864); commanding independent brigade, Forrest's Cavalry Corps, Department of Alabama, Mississippi and East Louisiana (January 28-ca. February 1864); commanding brigade, Buford's Division, Forrest's Cavalry Corps, Department of Alabama, Mississippi and East Louisiana (ca. February 1864-May 4, 1865); and brigadier general, CSA (February 28, 1865). Entering the service at the head of the New Bern Blues, he was soon made a lieutenant colonel and commanded the regiment at Belmont and Shiloh. At the regiment's reorganization in May 1862 he was named colonel, but the unit was so depleted that it was permanently merged with the 22nd Tennessee. Bell retained command of the unit and led it in the operations about Corinth, Mississippi, and at Richmond, Kentucky. A field consolidation was then ordered on October 30, 1862, with the 47th Tennessee, and in the following spring Bell was determined to be an excess officer. Eventually given a mounted brigade, he fought at Fort Pillow, Brice's Crossroads, Tupelo, and against Andrew J. Smith in August 1864—all under Forrest. In addition he participated in a number of raids and took part as a brigadier general in the defense against Wilson's raid through Alabama and Georgia. In the postwar years he was a farmer in California.

BELO, Alfred Horatio (1839-1901)

A former student at the University of North Carolina, Alfred Belo served in the Confederate infantry where he not only fought Yankees but also other Confederates, for the honor of the regiment. He was named captain, Company D, 21st North Carolina, on May 22, 1861, and fought at 1st Bull Run. In April 1862 he was defeated at the reorganization of the company and on November 1, 1862, he was made captain and assistant

quartermaster, 55th North Carolina. Promoted to major, he was present at the action at Fort Huger during the siege of Suffolk by Longstreet's Confederates. On April 19, 1863, a force of Union troops attacked the garrison and captured some five guns and 137 men. There was much dispute over which of the defenders were responsible. Captains Terrell and Cussons, of General Law's staff, made a report which questioned the North Carolinians' bravery. Colonel Connally, the 55th's commander, after determining the source of the allegations, proposed to the officers of the regiment that they demand satisfaction and, if it were not given, challenge the offending officers to a duel, with each of the 55th's officers taking their turn until they were all dead or the Alabamians altered their statements. After Lieutenant Colonel Smith refused to take part on moral grounds, Major Belo joined Colonel Connally in making the challenge. Belo and Cussons accordingly faced each other with Mississippi rifles; at the first discharge Cussons' hat was hit. At the second Belo was nicked in the neck. While they were reloading the dispute was settled verbally between Connally and Terrell. Belo fought at Gettysburg, where he was severely wounded, and at the Wilderness, Spotsylvania, and Cold Harbor, where he was again wounded. He was made lieutenant colonel on July 3, 1863. After the war he joined a newspaper in Texas. (Freeman, Douglas S., *Lee's Lieutenants*)

BENBOW, Henry Laurens (1829-1907)

A South Carolina planter, Henry L. Benbow entered the Confederate army as a private and rose to the rank of colonel and temporary brigade command. His assignments included: private, Hampton Legion (1861); captain, Company I, 23rd South Carolina (November 15, 1861); colonel, 23rd South Carolina (April 16, 1862); and temporarily commanding Evans' Brigade, 1st Military District, Department of South Carolina, Georgia and Florida (summer and fall 1863). When one examines the service record of Colonel Benbow, it becomes obvious why the brigade became known as the "Tramp Brigade," since the unit served in most major theaters of the war. After service at 1st Bull Run, he received a commission in the 23rd on the South Carolina coast. Sent to join Lee in Virginia, he was wounded at 2nd Bull Run and missed the Maryland Campaign. He served again in the Charleston area before the brigade was dispatched to Mississippi in a futile effort to relieve besieged Vicksburg. He then took part in the defense of Charleston in the summer of 1863. At this point the brigade commander, Evans, was having constant problems with his superiors and the brigade was suffering. There were charges of lax discipline and near mutiny among the men. With Evans frequently suspended from command or assigned to other duties, Benbow was often left in command. A new brigade commander, Stephen Elliott, Jr., took Benbow and the 23rd to the defense of Petersburg. During the siege Benbow was wounded. At Five Forks he was again wounded and this time captured. He was not released until two months after Lee's surrender. He was a planter after the war.

BENJAMIN, Judah Philip (1811-1884)

Born in St. Croix, the Virgin Islands, Judah Benjamin resigned from the U.S. Senate in order to serve his state of Louisiana and the Confederacy. The lawyer and former state legislator was appointed attorney general in the provisional cabinet of Jefferson Davis, whom he had once challenged to a duel. On February 25, 1861, Benjamin entered upon the duties of the first of three portfolios he was to hold in the rebel nation. After a successful few months as attorney general, he took over the War Department from Leroy Walker, on September 17, 1861. Holding this position during the disastrous winter of 1861-62, he was blamed for the Confederate defeats in North Carolina, Kentucky, and Tennessee. The Congress called for his removal, and his friend Davis was forced to replace him. But on the same day, March 18, 1862, Davis appointed him secretary of state, a move that upset many of Davis' numerous critics. In this post Benjamin displayed the attributes that earned him the sobriquet "The Brains of the Confederacy." During his tenure he was instrumental in obtaining foreign loans for the government but failed as head of the diplomatic efforts to obtain recognition from European states. At the collapse of the Confederacy, Benjamin fled via Florida and in small boats to the West Indies and eventually reached England where he became Queen's Counsel. Upon his retirement in 1883, he was given a farewell banquet by the Bar of England. He died in Paris the next year. (Butler, Pierce, *Judah P. Benjamin*, and Meade, Robert D., *Judah P. Benjamin, Confederate Statesman*)

BENNING, Henry Lewis (1814-1875)

Nicknamed "Rock," Henry L. Benning proved to be one of the more capable brigadiers of Lee's army. A Georgia lawyer and justice of the state supreme court, he entered the military at the outbreak of the Civil War. His assignments included: colonel, 17th Georgia (August 15, 1861); commanding Toombs' Brigade, D.R. Jones' Division, 1st Corps, Army of Northern Virginia (July-August 30 and September 17-October 27, 1862); commanding same brigade, Hood's-Field's Division, same corps and army (October 27, 1862-February 25, 1863; May-September 9, 1863; April 12-May 6, 1864; October 1864-February 1865; and March-April 9, 1865); commanding brigade, Hood's Division, in the Department of Virginia and North Carolina (February 25-April 1, 1863) and in the Department of Southern Virginia (April 1-May 1863); brigadier general, CSA (April 23 to rank from January 17, 1863); commanding brigade, Hood's Division, Longstreet's Corps, Army of Tennessee (September 19-November 5, 1863); and commanding brigade, Hood's-Field's Division, Department of East Tennessee (November 5, 1863-April 12, 1864). After serving in the Seven Days he commanded the brigade in part of the fighting at 2nd Bull Run and Antietam. He became the permanent commander after Fredericksburg, when General Toombs resigned, and led the brigade through the rest of the war. He went with Longstreet to southeastern Virginia and saw action later at Gettysburg, Chickamauga, Knoxville and the Wilderness. In the latter he was severely wounded. Returning to duty in October he was present for most of the remainder of

the Petersburg Campaign. Surrendered and paroled at Appomattox, he rebuilt his lucrative law practice. (Freeman, Douglas S., *Lee's Lieutenants*)

BENTON, Samuel (1820-1864)

A nephew of Thomas Hart Benton, Samuel Benton did not receive his commission as a brigadier general in the Confederate army until he had already been mortally wounded. Born in Tennessee, he was a lawyer and state legislator in Mississippi. After serving as a delegate to the state's secession convention he joined the army where his assignments included: captain, 9th Mississippi (1861); colonel, 37th Mississippi (April 19, 1862); colonel, 34th Mississippi (designation change ca. May 1864); commanding Walthall's (old) Brigade, Hindman's Division, Hood's Corps, Army of Tennessee (June-July 22, 1864); and brigadier general CSA (July 26, 1864). After serving in the Tullahoma Campaign at the head of his regiment he missed the fighting at Chickamauga and Chattanooga. During the beginning of the Atlanta Campaign he was in charge of the 24th and 27th Mississippi regiments. On May 11, 1864, he returned to his own regiment but took charge of the brigade the next month. After fighting at Peach Tree Creek he took part in the Confederate attacks in the battle of Atlanta proper on July 22, 1864. There he was wounded in the foot and chest. The limb was amputated but he died in a hospital on July 28th. He had been promoted two days earlier.

BEST, Emory F. (ca. 1840-?)

Detailed with his regiment to guard an important position in Jackson's rear at the battle of Chancellorsville, Emory F. Best saved scarcely more than himself and the regimental colors. He had entered Confederate service in the war's first year and his assignments included: lieutenant, Company C, 23rd Georgia (August 31, 1861); major, 23rd Georgia (same date); lieutenant colonel, 23rd Georgia (August 16, 1862); and colonel, 23rd Georgia (November 25, 1862). After serving at Williamsburg and Seven Pines, he commanded the regiment in the Seven Days Battles. When his colonel was killed at Antietam, he took over command, only to fall severely wounded shortly thereafter. Taken prisoner at some time after this, he was exchanged in early December 1862. When Jackson made his famous flank march at Chancellorsville, Best and the 23rd were detached from Colquitt's Brigade and left at the Catharine Furnace to protect the column's rear. A Union attack on his position resulted in the capture of almost the entire unit. For this failure he was arrested and dismissed from the service by order of a court-martial on December 23, 1863.

BICKLEY, George Washington Layfayette (1823-1867)

A thorough scoundrel before the Civil War, George W.L. Bickley became a Copperhead but was never able to do the Union much harm. Having posed as a doctor and abandoned one wife and child and the child of a previous marriage, the Virginia-born schemer tried to regain control of an organization, the Knights of the Golden Circle, which he had formed before the war. Its original purpose, when established in 1857, was to launch a filibustering expedition into northern Mexico. With the outbreak of hostilities the southern wing of the organization faded away and "Major General" Bickley, being in the South at the time, lost control of the northern wing. After almost two years of trying to raise Confederate units, and apparently having worn out his welcome with the authorities, he escaped to the North. Requesting to return to his home in Cincinnati, he was tailed and arrested when he went to Indiana instead. Recognized as the founder of the secret Copperhead organization, he was confined from July 17, 1863, until October 14, 1865. His Knights continued to function throughout the war under a series of names and leaders. Bickley died shortly after the war.

BLACKBURN, Luke Pryor (1816-1887)

One of the more shady episodes of the Civil War was the alleged plot of Dr. Luke Blackburn to infect the Union war machine with yellow fever. Before the war, Blackburn was well known for his work in the lower Mississippi Valley fighting the almost yearly outbreak of the dreaded disease. During the Civil War he served as a Confederate agent in Canada. When in the spring of 1864 yellow fever broke out in Bermuda, so the story goes, Blackburn was sent by the rebel government to gather infected clothing from the victims for shipment to the North. For his services aiding local doctors in the epidemic he was actually praised by the British authorities. But first word of the "plot" surfaced on April 14, 1865, and there was outrage both in the North and South. More detailed testimony was given by Godfrey Joseph Hyams, considered by many to be a less than totally reliable source. The Union informer had reported that at Blackburn's direction he had passed the infected trunks on to various parts of the North. One of these trunks was delivered to New Bern, North Carolina, where an epidemic broke out at the regimental hospital of the 9th Vermont. In October 1865 Blackburn was acquitted in a Canadian court, on the grounds that there was no evidence of the trunks having been in that country. There was no further action against him. Returning to medicine in Louisville, he became popular enough for the state to elect him governor. As for the plot itself, it may well have existed but modern knowledge shows that it could not have succeeded because yellow fever is transmitted by mosquitoes. Germ warfare would have to wait.

BLACKFORD, Eugene (1839-1908)

The effect of a continuous campaign over a long series of months upon a previously distinguished officer is exemplified by the case of Major Eugene Blackford of Alabama. He entered the army at the outbreak of the war and his assignments included: captain, Company K, 5th Alabama (May 15, 1861), and major, 5th Alabama (July 17, 1862). His unit served through 1st Bull Run, Williamsburg, Seven Pines, the Seven Days, Antietam, Fredericksburg, Chancellorsville, and Gettysburg. At least during the latter two engagements he commanded a specially organized battalion of sharpshooters drawn from the various

units of Rodes', later O'Neal's, Brigade. In these actions he was praised by his superiors. But in the spring of 1864 Grant launched his relentless drive on Richmond. The 5th saw action at the Wilderness, Spotsylvania, North Anna, and Cold Harbor before being detached with Early to the Shenandoah Valley. A long series of actions followed including Monocacy, 3rd Winchester, Fisher's Hill, and Cedar Creek. In the latter action he failed to live up to the duties of an officer and was hauled before a court-martial, charged with misconduct in the face of the enemy. He was found guilty and dismissed from the service. However, he was reinstated in February 1865 upon the urging of senior and junior officers.

BLACKFORD, William Willis (1831-1905)

One of the few officers to leave Jeb Stuart's original staff, not as a result of enemy fire, was William W. Blackford, his engineer. An engineer by profession, he helped raise a company of cavalry at the beginning of the war. His assignments in the Confederate army included: lieutenant, 1st Virginia Cavalry (May 14, 1861); captain, Engineers (May 26, 1862); major, 1st Confederate Engineers (January 19, 1864); and lieutenant colonel, 1st Confederate Engineers (April 1, 1864). Reporting with his company to Harpers Ferry, he soon came to the attention of Jeb Stuart who detailed him as an aide in July 1861. He remained with Stuart, becoming his engineering officer, until January 1864 and saw action at 1st Bull Run, the Seven Days, Antietam, Fredericksburg, Chancellorsville, Brandy Station, and Gettysburg. With the formation of regular engineering units, he was promoted to major and assigned to the first such unit, ending his service with Stuart. Organizing the new unit, he took part in the Petersburg and Appomattox campaigns and surrendered at the latter place. Returning to civilian life, he wrote his famous memoirs. (Blackford, William W., *War Years With Jeb Stuart*)

BLANCHARD, Albert Gallatin (1810-1891)

Massachusetts-born Confederate Albert G. Blanchard was not happy with his lot in the Southern military. A West Pointer (1829) and 11-year infantry veteran, he took time out from civilian pursuits to serve as a captain of volunteers and a major of regulars during the Mexican War. In peacetime he was in education, business, railroading, and engineering in New Orleans. His Civil War assignments included: colonel, 1st Louisiana (early 1861); commanding brigade, Department of Norfolk (May 1861-April 12, 1862); brigadier general, CSA (September 21, 1861); commanding 3rd Brigade, Huger's Division, Department of Northern Virginia (April 12-June 1862); and commanding brigade of South Carolina Reserves, McLaws' Division, Department of South Carolina, Georgia and Florida or Hardee's Corps (February-April 9, 1865). Following the fall of Norfolk, he led his brigade over to the Peninsula and was at Seven Pines, where the performance of the division was questionable. Sent to northern Louisiana on conscript duty a few days later, he was soon found to be incompetent by General Richard Taylor. He was blamed for allowing Grant's army to land on the Louisiana bank of the Mississippi, unchecked in the advance on Vicksburg. He had virtually no troops under his charge, still being on conscript duty. Asking for relief from this assignment to get back to the field, he was inactive until the War Department found work for him with the South Carolina Reserves, a brigade of which he led in the Carolinas Campaign until he apparently lost his post in the consolidating of Johnston's forces. He was a surveyor after the war.

BLAND, Elbert (ca. 1822-1863)

During the Civil War Elbert Bland faced hostile fire from both a fellow officer and the enemy, but it was the latter that proved fatal. A native South Carolinian, he had received his medical training in New York before being named as an assistant surgeon in the Palmetto (South Carolina) Regiment during the Mexican War. He then resumed his medical practice until the secession of his state. His Civil War assignments included: surgeon, 1st South Carolina, PACS (ca. January 7, 1861); first lieutenant, Company A, 7th South Carolina (early 1861); captain, Company A, 7th South Carolina (April 15, 1861); and lieutenant colonel, 7th South Carolina (May 14, 1862). After taking part in the battle of 1st Bull Run he became embroiled in a dispute with the regiment's major, Emmett Seibels. That winter it developed into a duel but neither party was killed. Seibels lost his election for colonel the following May but Bland became lieutenant colonel. Moving to the Peninsula, Bland saw action at Williamsburg and in the Seven Days Battles where he was wounded at Savage Station. He rejoined the regiment in time to command it at Fredericksburg where he was slightly wounded. He commanded the regiment at Chancellorsville and one wing of it at Gettysburg. Going west with Longstreet, he was killed on the second day of the Battle of Chickamauga while again in command of the 7th. (Dickert, D. Augustus, *History of Kershaw's Brigade*)

BLEDSOE, Albert Taylor (1809-1877)

At the end of the Civil War former Assistant Secretary of War for the Confederacy Albert T. Bledsoe was researching a constitutional defense of secession at the British Museum. The native Kentuckian was a total Southerner and never let his faith in the cause waver. He graduated from West Point in 1830 but, after two years of frontier duty as a brevet second lieutenant in the 7th Infantry, he submitted his resignation and became a college professor and lawyer. In 1856 he published a defense of Southern life entitled *An Essay on Liberty and Slavery*. In 1861 he was named the chief of the Bureau of War in the Confederate War Department and then became the assistant secretary of war. He held the latter post until October 1, 1862, and the next year he set sail for London to do his research. Returning to the re-United States in 1866, he found Jefferson Davis imprisoned and wrote *Is Davis a Traitor; Or, Was Secession a Constitutional Right*. It is sometimes credited with having halted an indictment for treason. The following year he began editing the quarterly *Southern Review* in Baltimore. Through that organ he continued to promote the South until his death.

BOCOCK, Thomas Stanhope (1815-1891)

After he lost out to a compromise candidate for the speakership of the U.S. House of Representatives in the famous 1859-60 stalemate, Thomas S. Bocock of Virginia served as the speaker of the Confederate House of Representatives for over three years. After a career as a lawyer, Bocock began his 14 years in the U.S. Congress in 1847, being much of the time chairman of the Committee on Naval Affairs. Representing Virginia's 5th District, which was spared the depredations of the Union forces until the very end of the Civil War, Bocock served in the Provisional Congress and both of the regular congresses. Serving as speaker in the regular congresses, Bocock held himself aloof from debate as was the custom of the U.S. Congress. Nevertheless, the record does indicate that he generally supported the administration, but not until the end of the war was he willing to support the sacrifices that were really necessary for victory. Losing confidence in the cabinet, he led the Virginia delegation before Davis, expressing their disatisfaction. This resulted in Secretary of War Seddon's resignation. Following the war Bocock was active in law and Virginia politics.

BOGGS, William Robertson (1829-1911)

As a Confederate general, West Pointer (1853) William R. Boggs of Georgia never held a field command. For the first year after his graduation he was posted to the topographical engineers, then transferred to the ordnance service. Resigning as a first lieutenant on February 1, 1861, he joined the Confederacy and his assignments included: captain, Engineers (February 1861); chief of engineers and artillery, Pensacola (1861); chief engineer of Georgia (December 21, 1861); brigadier general, CSA (November 4, 1862); and chief of staff, Trans-Mississippi Department (ca. March 7, 1863-May 26, 1865). After serving as Bragg's artillery and engineering chief he resigned his Confederate commission on December 21, 1861, in order to accept the position of chief engineer with the state of Georgia. He held that position for about a year before reentering the Confederate service as a brigadier general. He then served the balance of the war as E. Kirby Smith's staff chief west of the Mississippi. After the war he was a civil engineer and professor. He also wrote his reminiscences. (Boggs, William Robertson, *Military Reminiscences of General William R. Boggs*)

BONDURANT, James William (?-?)

Although he had distinguished himself in some of the early actions of the war, and had earned promotions thereby, James W. Bondurant's later career is rather obscure. A native Virginian, he entered the Confederate service from Alabama. His assignments included: sergeant, Jeff Davis Artillery (July 23, 1861); lieutenant, Jeff Davis Artillery (January 28, 1862); captain, Jeff Davis Artillery (early 1862); major, Artillery (May 8, 1862); chief of artillery, Department of North Carolina (May-July, 1863); and chief of artillery, 2nd Corps, Army of Tennessee (July 1863-March 1864). In command of his battery he distinguished himself at Seven Pines and went on to fight with the Army of Northern Virginia in the Seven Days Battles and at Antietam and Fredericksburg. He joined his old division commander, D.H. Hill, in southern Virginia and North Carolina, serving as his artillery chief. When Hill was promoted and sent to the Army of Tennessee, Bondurant became head of his corps' artillery. He held this post under a series of commanders until early 1864. In September of that year he was assigned to duty at Andersonville, Georgia, and was apparently with Hill, back in the Carolinas, at the war's end.

BONHAM, Milledge Luke (1813-1890)

Although not a West Pointer, South Carolina lawyer Milledge Bonham did have some military experience commanding a company of volunteers in the Seminole War and a regular regiment in Mexico. After serving in the U.S. House of Representatives from 1857-60, Bonham was sent to Mississippi by the state legislature to obtain the cooperation of that state in the secession winter of 1860-61. As a major general of state volunteers, from February 1861, Bonham was placed in charge of Morris Island in Charleston Harbor on April 15, 1861, two days after the fall of Fort Sumter. His later assignments included: brigadier general, CSA (April 23, 1861); commanding Alexandria Line (May 21-31, 1861); commanding a South Carolina brigade, Alexandria Line (May 31-June 20, 1861); commanding same brigade, Army of the Potomac (June 20-October 22, 1861); and

Milledge L. Bonham, Confederate general, congressman, governor, and again general. (NA)

commanding same brigade, in Longstreet's Division (October 22-November 9, 1861) and in Van Dorn's Division (November 9, 1861-January 29, 1862), Potomac District, Department of Northern Virginia. Going to Virginia in May 1861, Bonham superseded Colonel Cocke in command of the Alexandria Line and was in general command of the area when the fight at Fairfax Court House took place. Superseded after 10 days by General Beauregard, he commanded his brigade at 1st Bull Run and until January 29, 1862, when, slighted over seniority matters, he resigned. Bonham won a seat in the Confederate House where he served on the Ways and Means Committee, then resigned on January 17, 1863, to become governor of his state. He served in that office for two years, until reappointed brigadier general, on February 16, 1865. He commanded a cavalry brigade under Johnston in the Carolinas Campaign. After the surrender he resumed the life of a lawyer and planter. (Freeman, Douglas S., *Lee's Lieutenants*)

BOOTH, John Wilkes (1838-1865)

When the fall of Richmond aborted his plan to kidnap Abraham Lincoln and take him to the Confederate capital for a prisoner exchange, noted actor John Wilkes Booth changed his plot to murder. Born into a Maryland stage family that included his father, Junius Brutus Booth, and his brother, Edwin Booth, he did not achieve the acting success that he thought he deserved. Although his family tended to support the Union, his sympathies were entirely with the South and, while he didn't enter the military service, he wanted to strike a blow for his "country." He apparently planned to kidnap the president-elect before the 1861 inauguration but failed when the travel plans were altered secretly. Late in the war he plotted with several others to capture Lincoln and spirit him off to Richmond. Several times the band went into action but for one reason or another never succeeded. With the collapse of the Confederacy, Booth realized that the kidnapping would serve no purpose. His new scheme called for simultaneous attacks on Lincoln, Andrew Johnson, cabinet members, and General Grant. On the night of April 14, 1865, Booth, having made arrangements earlier, entered the President's box at Ford's Theater and shot Lincoln in the back of the head. Major Henry Rathbone, who was a guest of the president, was wounded with a knife by the actor/assassin. Booth then jumped from the box but caught his leg in the decorative flags draped around the ledge and broke his leg landing on the stage. Despite attempts to stop him, notably that of Joseph B. Stewart, he managed to escape the theater. He crossed the Navy Yard Bridge after informing Sergeant Silas Cobb, the guard, who he was and that he had been unavoidably detained in the city. He met up with fellow conspirator David E. Herold who escorted him through his flight. He stopped at the farm of Dr. Samuel A. Mudd to have his leg set and then with the help of numerous people along the way, he made it to Virginia and across the Rappahannock River. But here his luck ran out and he was cornered at the farm of Richard H. Garrett near Port Royal. Trapped in the tobacco shed by a cavalry detachment under the direction of detectives Everton J. Conger and Luther B. Baker,

Actor-turned-assassin John Wilkes Booth. (NA)

Flag and Seal; Indian Affairs; Ordnance and Ordnance Stores; Printing; and Rules and Officers. When Congress was not in session he served on the staff of Stonewall Jackson, becoming a sort of public, and congressional, relations officer. In this latter capacity he helped smooth over the Loring-Jackson feud and save Jackson's services for the South. Boteler failed to gain reelection to the Second Congress; he served as an aide to Jeb Stuart. Holding several political appointments in the post-war years, Boteler spent much of his time writing historical articles.

BOTTS, John Minor (1802-1869)

His long-known Unionist views made John Minor Botts a marked man when martial law was declared in the Richmond area. A Virginia lawyer and politician, he was a consistent opponent of John C. Calhoun and the disunionist Southern portion of the Democratic Party. He also opposed the abolitionists who were, in his view, giving the secessionists a weapon. Recognizing secession as an established fact, he tried to get the U.S. Constitution amended to accept it. Retiring to his farm he continued to speak out; the day after martial law was declared for the vicinity of the Confederate capital, March 1, 1862, he was arrested. His confinement lasted eight weeks, until a new secretary of war released him on parole. Moving to Culpeper County he was offered a nomination for the U.S. Senate from the wartime Unionist government. This he declined but after the war Botts was for a time presiding officer of the Republican Party in Virginia. He withdrew from politics for the last two years of his life.

he refused to surrender. The troopers were under the direct command of Lieutenant Edward P. Doherty. Herold surrendered but Booth remained stubborn. After the shed had been torched, a shot rang out and Booth fell mortally wounded. Whether it was suicide or a shot from Sergeant Boston Corbett has never been determined. The only other part of the conspiracy that was carried out was the attack on Secretary of State William H. Seward by Lewis T. Powell.

BOTELER, Alexander Robinson (1815-1892)

As the representative of Virginia's 10th District to the Provisional and First Regular Confederate Congresses, Alexander R. Boteler lost about half of his district to the new state of West Virginia when it was recognized by the U.S. Congress. An opponent of secession, farmer Boteler served two years in Congress before the state of Virginia seceded early in his second term. He was then named to the Provisional Confederate Congress and was barely reelected in late 1861. During his term of service, Boteler proved to be a supporter of the Davis administration; he served on the Committees on Buildings;

Virginia Unionist John Minor Botts. (NA)

BOTTS, Lawson (1825-1862)

When one looks at the pitiful remnant, 210 men, of the Stonewall Brigade when it surrendered at Appomattox, it becomes obvious that the unit had suffered tremendously during the conflict. The senior commanders were not exempt from the slaughter, as is evidenced by the case of Lawson Botts, one of the regimental commanders. A lawyer in Charlestown, now in West Virginia, he was appointed by the court to defend John Brown in his 1859 trial. During this time he also became captain of the Botts Greys, one of the many local companies raised following the raid on Harpers Ferry. With the outbreak of the Civil War the unit joined the Confederate army and Botts' assignments included: captain, Company G, 2nd Virginia (April 18, 1861); major, 2nd Virginia (June 12, 1861); lieutenant colonel, 2nd Virginia (September 11, 1861); and colonel, 2nd Virginia (to date from June 27, 1862). Having fought at 1st Bull Run, Kernstown, and the Shenandoah Valley Campaign, he took over command of the regiment upon the death of Colonel Allen at Gaines Mill and led it through the rest of the Seven Days Battles. After fighting at Cedar Mountain, Botts and the 2nd took part in the famed "stand up" fight with what later became known as the Iron Brigade, at Groveton—the start of 2nd Bull Run. During the conflict he was shot in the head but lingered about two weeks before dying on September 11, 1862. (Robertson, James I., Jr., *The Stonewall Brigade*)

BOUDINOT, Elias Cornelius (1835-1890)

Although only a non-voting representative to the Confederate Congress, Elias C. Boudinot was probably the most effective legislator his Indian constituency had in Richmond. Half-white and half-Cherokee, Boudinot had been a railroad engineer and Arkansas lawyer before the outbreak of the Civil War. He used his journalistic talents to further Democratic politics and attended the Arkansas secession convention. Returning home he served in the 1st Cherokee Mounted Rifles, seeing action at Oak Hills and Pea Ridge as a major. Appointed by his tribe, he took his seat in the First Regular Congress on October 9, 1862. He was made a non-voting member of the Committee on Indian Affairs. He frequently proposed and endorsed bills and amendments that would have an impact upon his people. Following the Confederacy's collapse, he was instrumental in regularizing Cherokee relations with the United States. Subsequently he practiced law in Arkansas and engaged in agricultural pursuits.

BOWEN, John Stevens (1830-1863)

Appointed to a Confederate major generalcy during the Vicksburg siege, Georgian West Pointer (1853) John S. Bowen did not long survive the surrender. Serving mostly on the frontier with the Regiment of Mounted Riflemen after his graduation, he resigned as a second lieutenant in 1856 to become an architect in St. Louis. His Confederate assignments included: captain, Missouri State Guard (early 1861); colonel, 1st Missouri (June 11, 1861); commanding 4th Division, 1st Geographical Division, Department #2 (October 24-

December 1861); commanding brigade, Central Army of Kentucky, Department #2 (January-February 1862); commanding brigade, 3rd (Pillow's) Division, Central Army of Kentucky, Department #2 (February-March 29, 1862); brigadier general, CSA (March 14, 1862); commanding brigade, Reserve Corps, Army of the Mississippi (March 29-April 6, 1862); commanding Green's (old) Brigade, Maury's Division, 2nd Military District, Department of Mississippi and East Louisiana (January 22-April 1863); commanding the division (April 17-April 1863); commanding division, Department of Mississippi and East Louisiana (April-July 4, 1863); and major general, CSA (May 25, 1863). After serving at Camp Jackson as Daniel M. Frost's chief of staff and being captured and released, he raised a volunteer regiment, which he took to central Kentucky. There he commanded at times a division or brigade and then moved to Corinth, Mississippi, for the pre-Shiloh buildup. Leading his brigade in that battle he was severely wounded. When he recovered he took over a brigade in the vicinity of Vicksburg and was soon promoted to brigadier general. During the Vicksburg Campaign he directed a division until the surrender on July 4, 1863. Paroled the same day, he died nine days later at Raymond, Mississippi, from the effects of the siege and while still a paroled prisoner of war.

BOWLES, Pinckney Downie (1835-1920)

South Carolinian Pinckney D. Bowles entered the Confederate army from Alabama. His assignments included: captain, Company E, 4th Alabama (April 1, 1861); major, 4th Alabama (August 22, 1862); lieutenant colonel, 4th Alabama (September 30, 1862); colonel, 4th Alabama (October 3, 1862); and commanding Law's Brigade, Field's Division, 1st Corps, Army of Northern Virginia (ca. June 3-September 1864). Commanding his company, the "Conscript Guards," he participated in the Battle of 1st Bull Run and in the Seven Days. While he was a field-grade officer, the regiment fought at 2nd Bull Run, Antietam, Fredericksburg, in southeastern Virginia, Gettysburg, Chickamauga, Knoxville, and in the Wilderness Campaign. After the wounding of General E. M. Law at Cold Harbor, Bowles was in temporary brigade command until the general's recovery. Bowles was no longer with his regiment when it surrendered with Lee at Appomattox. He served for a time as a judge after the war.

BOYCE, William Waters (1818-1890)

William W. Boyce can certainly be said to have enjoyed a "safe district" in the Confederate Congress, in more ways than one. He was unopposed in his three races for his seat and the district itself was not occupied by Union forces until the final months of the war. Boyce, a native South Carolinian—lawyer, planter, and former state legislator—was completing his fourth term in the U.S. House of Representatives when his state seceded on December 20, 1860. He resigned the next day. His committee assignments included those on: Executive Departments (Provisional Congress); Postal Affairs (Provisional Congress); Ways and Means (First Congress); and Naval Affairs (First and Second Congresses). He chaired the Committee on Naval

Affairs in the last congress. Having originally been a cooperationist before the war, Boyce favored the adoption of the U.S. Constitution with only a few changes. He favored incorporating the right of any state to secede and he succeeded in limiting the president to one six-year term. He wanted to remove the conduct of foreign policy from the hands of the executive and favored the creation of a general-in-chief to further limit Davis' authority on military matters. By 1864 Boyce was urging peace overtures be made. Wiped out by the war, he practiced law in the reunited nation's capital until his retirement.

BOYD, Belle (1843-1900)

One of the most famous of Confederate spies, Belle Boyd served the Confederate forces in the Shenandoah Valley. Born in Martinsburg—now part of West Virginia—she operated her spying operations from her father's hotel in Front Royal, providing valuable information to Generals Turner Ashby and "Stonewall" Jackson during the spring 1862 campaign in the Valley. The latter general then made her a captain and honorary aide-de-camp on his staff. As such she was able to witness troops reviews. Betrayed by her lover, she was arrested on July 29, 1862, and held for a month in the Old Capitol Prison in Washington. Exchanged a month later, she was in exile with relatives for a time but was again arrested in June 1863 while on a visit to Martinsburg. On December 1, 1863, she was released, suffering from typhoid, and was then sent to Europe to regain her health. The blockade runner she attempted to return on was

Belle Boyd, effective Confederate spy. (NA)

captured and she fell in love with the prize master, Samuel Hardinge, who later married her in England after being dropped from the navy's rolls for neglect of duty in allowing her to proceed to Canada and then England. Hardinge attempted to reach Richmond, was detained in Union hands, but died soon after his release. While in England Belle Boyd Hardinge had a stage career and published *Belle Boyd in Camp and Prison*. She died while touring the western United States. (Sigaud, Louis, A., *Belle Boyd, Confederate Spy*, and Scarborough, Ruth, *Belle Boyd: Siren of the South*)

BOYD, James William or Ward (ca. 1833-1865 or 1866)

A ruthless character, James W. Boyd has become in recent years a central point in Lincoln assassination theories. In 1977 a film and a book appeared, entitled *The Lincoln Conspiracy*, whose authors, David Balsiger and Charles E. Sellier, Jr., advanced the theory that several groups were involved in planning the kidnap or murder of Lincoln. All worked through John Wilkes Booth at one time or another. They included Confederate agents in Canada, Radical Republicans in Congress, northern cotton speculators, and New York financiers. At a time when Boyd was about to launch his own plan, having replaced Booth, the actor attacked at Ford's Theater. The most controversial part of this conspiracy theory is the claim that Boyd was killed at the Garrett farm in a case of mistaken identity while himself searching for Booth. The theory says that Booth in turn made good his own escape and there was a massive cover-up. There are major discrepancies in Boyd's career but he did serve in a Tennessee regiment, was cashiered, served as a Confederate secret agent, was captured, and offered to aid the U.S. War Department in western Tennessee. Enough evidence has now been found to show that Boyd actually was murdered on January 1, 1866, long after the shooting at the Garrett farm. Also the physical similarity of Boyd to Booth is not at all convincing. There was a 16-year difference in age, six inches in height, and eye and hair color differences.

BRAGG, Braxton (1817-1876)

Of the eight men who reached the rank of full general in the Confederate army Braxton Bragg was the most controversial. The North Carolinian West Pointer (1837) had earned a prewar reputation for strict discipline as well as a literal adherance to regulations. At one time, the story goes, he actually had a written dispute with himself while serving in the dual capacity of company commander and post quartermaster. His pre-Civil War career was highly distinguished. After seeing action against the Seminoles, he went on to win three brevets in the Mexican War, in which his battery of "flying artillery" revolutionized, in many respects, the battlefield use of that arm. In 1856 he resigned his captaincy—he was a lieutenant colonel by brevet—in the 3rd Artillery and became a Louisiana planter. His Confederate assignments included: colonel, Louisiana Militia (early 1861); major general, Louisiana Militia (early 1861); commanding Department of Louisiana (February

22-March 1861); brigadier general, CSA (March 7, 1861); commanding Pensacola, Florida (March 11-October 29, 1861); major general, CSA (September 12, 1861); commanding Department of Alabama and West Florida (October 14, 1861-February 28, 1862); also commanding Army of Pensacola (October 29-December 22, 1861); commanding Army of the Mississippi (March 6-17, May 7-July 5, August 15-September 28 and November 7-20, 1862); commanding 2nd Corps, Army of the Mississippi (March 29-June 30, 1862); general, CSA (April 12, 1862, to rank from the 6th); commanding Department #2 (June 17-October 24, 1862 and November 3, 1862-July 25, 1863); commanding Army of Tennessee (November 20, 1862-December 2, 1863); also commanding Department of Tennessee (August 6-December 2, 1863, except briefly in August); commanding Department of North Carolina (November 27, 1864-April 9, 1865, but under Joseph E. Johnston from March 6, 1865); and supervising Hoke's Division, Hardee's Corps, Army of Tennessee (April 9-26, 1865). Initially commanding in Louisiana, he was later in charge of the operations against Fort Pickens in Pensacola Harbor. Ordered to northern Mississippi in early 1862, he briefly commanded the forces gathering there for the attack on Grant at Shiloh. During the battle itself he directed a corps and was later rewarded with promotion to full general. As such he relieved Beauregard when he went on sick leave and was then given permanent command in the West. Having served during the Corinth siege, he led the army into Kentucky and commanded at Perryville, where he employed only a portion of his force. On the last day of 1862 he launched a vicious attack on the Union left at Murfreesboro but failed to carry through his success on the following days. Withdrawing from the area, he was driven into Georgia during Rosecrans' Tullahoma Campaign and subsequent operations. In September he won the one major Confederate victory in the West, at Chickamauga, but failed to follow up his success. Instead he laid seige to the Union army in Chattanooga and merely waited for Grant to break through his lines. In the meantime he had been engaged in a series of disputes with his subordinates—especially Leonides Polk, James Longstreet, and William J. Hardee—that severely injured the effectiveness of the Army of Tennessee. Several top officers left the army for other fields, and Longstreet and Simon B. Buckner were dispatched into East Tennessee. With the army thus weakened, Bragg was routed at Chattanooga and was shortly removed from command. Almost immediately he was appointed as an advisor to Jefferson Davis, his staunch supporter, and maintained an office in Richmond. Ineffective in the position of quasicommander in chief, he was dispatched to North Carolina in the waning day of the war. The forces under his command remained inactive during the second attack on Fort Fisher, allowing it to fall. When Joseph E. Johnston assumed command of all forces in North Carolina on March 6, 1865, Bragg was soon relegated to supervision of Hoke's division from his old department. In that capacity he surrendered near Durham Station. For a time after the war he served as Alabama's engineer and then settled in Texas where he died. He was the brother of Confederate Attorney General Thomas Bragg. (McWhiney, Grady C., *Braxton Bragg and Confederate Defeat*)

BRAGG, Thomas (1818-1872)

Resigning his U.S. Senate seat on March 8, 1861—and formally expelled from that body the following July 11—Thomas Bragg served the Confederacy as attorney general for four months and then was active in confronting the peace movement in his native North Carolina. A prominent lawyer, he had served in the state legislature and as a delegate to Democratic national conventions in the 1840s and 1850s before being elected governor in 1854. After serving two two-year terms he was named to the Senate, where he served until two-and-a-half months before the state's secession. Replacing Judah P. Benjamin in the cabinet on November 21, 1861, he was a close backer of Jefferson Davis and endorsed the establishment of a Confederate supreme court, which never came into existence. A strict legalist, he opposed the impressment of supplies for the army without full payment. Leaving the cabinet on March 18, 1862, he resumed his private practice but tried to thwart the calls for peace in North Carolina and tried to alleviate problems between Davis and Governor Zebulon Vance. Following the war he was active in efforts to bring the state back into the Union; a reluctant secessionist, he had never believed the South could establish its own country. (Patrick, Rembert W., *Jefferson Davis and His Cabinet*)

BRANCH, Lawrence O'Bryan (1820-1862)

Early in the war North Carolinian Lawrence O'B. Branch fought in an independent capacity, but at the time of his death he was in charge of a brigade under Lee. A veteran of the Seminole War, he embarked on such civil pursuits as law, journalism, and politics. Upon the secession of his state, he resigned from Congress and joined the South. His assignments included: quartermaster and paymaster general, North Carolina Troops (May 20, 1861); colonel, 33rd North Carolina (September 1861); brigadier general, CSA (November 16, 1861); commanding District of the Pamlico, Department of North Carolina (November 16, 1861-March 18, 1862); commanding 2nd Brigade, same district and department (March 17-22, 1862); commanding 2nd Brigade, same department (March 22-May 1862); commanding separate brigade, Department of Northern Virginia (May 1862); and commanding brigade, A.P. Hill's Division (in 1st Corps from June 29 and in 2nd Corps from July 27), Army of Northern Virginia (May 27-September 17, 1862). Preferring the field, he gave up his staff position to take command of a regiment but was soon promoted to brigadier and given a district on the state's coast. He was defeated by Burnside's expedition at New Bern on March 14 and a few days later was superseded by General French and later General Holmes. Sent to Virginia in May, his brigade acted as a link between Johnston's army on the Peninsula and J.R. Anderson's command facing McDowell near Fredericksburg. Merged into the newly created Light Division, he fought at Hanover Court House, the Seven Days, and under Jackson at Cedar Mountain, 2nd Bull Run, Chantilly, and Harpers Ferry. In Hill's charge to restore the Confederate right at Antietam, Branch played a leading role but was killed by a sharpshooter once the lines were stabilized. (Freeman, Douglas S., *Lee's Lieutenants*)

BRANDON, William Lindsay (1800 or 1802-1890)

The entire service of Mississippi planter William L. Brandon as a Confederate general was spent supervising the Bureau of Conscription in his native state. Along with some medical training and service in the state legislature, Brandon had been active in the militia when he joined the Confederacy. His assignments included: major general, Mississippi Militia (prewar); lieutenant colonel, 21st Mississippi (1861); colonel, 21st Mississippi (August 14, 1863); and brigadier general, CSA (June 18, 1864). Sent with his regiment to Virginia, he fought during the Seven Days and was severely wounded at Malvern Hill, where he lost a leg. Promoted to colonel in the summer of 1863, he returned to duty in time for the fighting at Chickamauga and Knoxville. Soon thereafter he was assigned to duty directing the draft and was promoted to brigadier general. He later retired to his plantation.

BRANTLEY, William Felix (1830-1870)

Having survived war wounds, Confederate General William F. Brantley died at the hands of an assassin five years after the close of hostilities. The Alabama-born Mississippi attorney sat in the state convention on secession before joining the army as captain of the Wigfall Rifles. His assignments included: captain, Company D, 15th Mississippi (1861); captain, Company D, 29th Mississippi (1862); colonel, 29th Mississippi (1862); commanding Walthall's-Benton's (old) Brigade, Hindman's-Anderson's-Johnson's-Hill's Division, Hood's-Lee's Corps, Army of Tennessee (July 22, 1864-April 26, 1865); and brigadier general, CSA (July 26, 1864). Wounded at Murfreesboro, he returned to command the regiment at Chickamauga and Chattanooga. During the Atlanta Campaign he commanded the consolidated 29th and 30th Mississippi until the Battle of Atlanta. In that action he succeeded the mortally wounded Samuel Benton in brigade command. Four days later he was named brigadier general. Accompanying Hood into middle Tennessee, he led his brigade at Franklin and Nashville and later in the Carolinas. After the surrender at Durham Station, he resumed his legal practice until killed by an unknown assailant near Winona, Mississippi.

BRATTON, John (1831-1898)

A South Carolina doctor, John Bratton rose through many grades to become a Confederate brigadier. His assignments included: private, 6th South Carolina (April 1861); second lieutenant, 6th South Carolina (July 1861); colonel, 6th South Carolina (April 1862); temporarily commanding Jenkins' Brigade, Pickett's Division, in the Department of Virginia and North Carolina (March-April 1, 1863); and in the Department of Southern Virginia (April 1-May 1863); commanding Jenkins' Brigade, Hood's Division, Longstreet's Corps, Army of Tennessee (September 19-November 5, 1863); commanding

Jenkins' Brigade, Hood's Division, Department of East Tennessee (November 5, 1863-February 1864); commanding Jenkins' (old) Brigade, Field's Division, 1st Corps, Army of Northern of Northern Virginia (May 6, 1864-April 9, 1865); and brigadier general, CSA (May 6, 1864). After service in Charleston Harbor, he went to Virginia and was named colonel upon the reorganization of the regiment. He led it at Yorktown, Williamsburg, and Seven Pines where he was wounded and captured. Exchanged he resumed command and led the regiment at Fredericksburg and in southeastern Virginia where he was in temporary brigade command. Sent to Georgia and Tennessee, he again led the brigade at Wauhatchie and Knoxville. He directed his regiment at the Wilderness until General Jenkins was killed. Promoted to brigadier, Bratton led the unit through Spotsylvania, North Anna, Cold Harbor, Petersburg, and surrendered at Appomattox. After the war he was a farmer and was prominent in South Carolina politics. (Freeman, Douglas S., *Lee's Lieutenants*)

BREATHED, James (1838-1870)

Marylander James Breathed is an example of the slowness of promotion faced by officers of artillery in the Confederate army and of their loyalty to their arm, refusing to seek advancement in the infantry or cavalry. Entering the army during the first summer of the war, he held the following assignments: private, Company B, 1st Virginia Cavalry (August 31, 1861); lieutenant, 1st Stuart Horse Artillery (March 23, 1862); captain, 1st Stuart Horse Artillery (to rank from August 9, 1862); major, artillery (February 27, 1864); commanding horse artillery battalion, in Cavalry Corps, Army of Northern Virginia and in Valley District, Department of Northern Virginia (March 1864-April 9, 1865). After service in the cavalry he joined with John Pelham to organize the first horse artillery battery to serve with Jeb Stuart. Serving as a subaltern, he took part in actions at Williamsburg, the Seven Days, 2nd Bull Run, and Antietam. Promoted to captain, he commanded the unit at Fredericksburg, Chancellorsville, and Gettysburg. In early 1864 he was promoted to field grade and was given command of a horse artillery battalion. In the Wilderness Campaign he distinguished himself by personally bringing off a gun with only two horses. Wounded at Yellow Tavern, he recovered to serve through the Shenandoah Valley Campaign of 1864 and returned to the Petersburg lines in time to take part in the retreat to Appomattox. At High Bridge he took part in hand to hand fighting. Following the surrender he resumed the practice of medicine in western Maryland. (Wise, Jennings C., *The Long Arm of Lee*)

BRECKINRIDGE, John Cabell (1821-1875)

The man who could have been president of the United States in 1861, John C. Breckinridge, fought for the neutrality of his native Kentucky but then joined the Confederacy, serving it as a general and cabinet member. He had served as a major in the 3rd Kentucky during the Mexican War but saw no action. Resuming his legal practice, he soon entered politics. He served in the state legislature and the U.S. Congress before being elected vice president on James Buchanan's ticket. The youngest man ever to hold that office, he was named to the U.S. Senate upon the completion of his term. However, in the meantime he had run as the 1860 candidate of the Southern faction of the split Democratic Party. In the four-way race he came in second in the electoral college with 72 votes but only third in the popular vote. Fighting to maintain Kentucky in the Union, he backed neutrality and retained his seat in the Senate. However, on October 2, 1861, he felt sufficiently threatened by the military government in his state that he fled. He soon joined the Confederate army and his assignments included: brigadier general, CSA (November 2, 1861); commanding Kentucky Brigade, 2nd (Buckner's) Division, Army of Central Kentucky, Department #2 (ca. November 1861-February 1862); commanding Kentucky Brigade, Reserve, Army of Central Kentucky, Department #2 (February-March 29, 1862); commanding Reserve Corps, Army of the Mississippi (ca. March 29-June 23, 1862 and August-October 1862); major general, CSA (April 14, 1862); commanding Breckinridge's Command, District of the Mississippi, Department #2 (June 23-August 19, 1862); commanding Army of Middle Tennessee, Department #2 (October 28-November 7, 1862); commanding division, Polk's Corps, Army of the Mississippi (November 7-20, 1862); commanding division, Polk's Corps, Army of Tennessee (November 20-December 12, 1862); commanding division, Hardee's Corps, Army of Tennessee (December 12, 1862-January 1863 and early 1863-May 24, 1863); commanding division, Department of the West (May 31-July 1863); commanding division, Department of Mississippi and East Louisiana (July-August 25, 1863); commanding division, Hill's Corps, Army of Tennessee (August 28-November 8, 1863); commanding the corps (November 8-December 15, 1863); commanding division, Hindman's Corps, Army of Tennessee (December 15, 1863-February 15, 1864); commanding Department of Western Virginia (March 5-May 25, 1864); commanding division, Army of Northern Virginia (May-June 1864); commanding division, Valley District, Department of Northern Virginia (June-September 1864); again commanding Department of Western Virginia (September 17, 1864-February 4, 1865); also commanding Department of East Tennessee (September 27, 1864-February 4, 1865); and Secretary of War (February 6-April 1865). For his action in joining the enemy, he was expelled by the Senate on December 4, 1861. In the meantime he had become a brigadier general and was given charge of a brigade of Kentuckians later to be known as the Orphan Brigade. Serving in central Kentucky, he took charge of that army's reserve when the rest of Buckner's division was sent to reinforce Fort Donelson. Joining the army forming at Corinth, Mississippi, under Albert Sidney Johnston, he led the Reserve Corps at Shiloh and during the Union drive on Corinth. He was then dispatched with his command to Vicksburg and later directed the Confederate attack on Baton Rouge, which proved unsuccessful. Ordered to rejoin Bragg's army, his division failed to arrive in time to take part in the campaign to liberate his native state. Instead he was given command in middle Tennessee and then finally was incorporated into the newly named Army of Tennessee. His division made

John C. Breckinridge, former vice president of the United States and Confederate general. (NA)

the disastrous attack, against Breckinridge's advice to Bragg, on the final day of fighting at Murfreesboro. Again sent to Mississippi the following spring, he served under Joseph E. Johnston in the attempt to relieve the pressure on Vicksburg and then took part in the unsuccessful defense of Jackson, Mississippi. Rejoining Bragg, he led his division at Chickamauga and a corps at Chattanooga. Transferred to Virginia, he was in departmental command when he won the Battle of New Market in the Shenandoah Valley. He joined Lee in time for Cold Harbor and then took part in the defense of Lynchburg. Under Jubal A. Early he fought at Monocacy and on the outskirts of Washington. Returning to his department in the late summer of 1864, his authority was extended over eastern Tennessee as well. Jefferson Davis then appointed him war secretary and he served in this post until the Confederacy's fall. He had been an advisor during the surrender negotiations of his former commander, Joe Johnston. He then fled in an adventurous escape to Cuba and eventually to England and Canada. Not returning to his home until 1869, he practiced law until his death. (Davis, William C., *Breckinridge: Statesman, Soldier, Symbol*)

BREVARD, Theodore Washington (1835-1882)

Serving almost the entire Civil War in Florida, Theodore W. Brevard became the last formally appointed general in the Confederate army. The North Carolina-born lawyer was serving as Florida's adjutant and inspector general when the Civil War broke out. His Civil War assignments included: major, 1st Florida Partisan Rangers Battalion (September 2, 1862); lieutenant colonel, 2nd Florida Battalion (change of designation June 24, 1863); colonel, 11th Florida (June 11, 1864); brigadier general, CSA (March 22, 1865); and possibly commanding Florida Brigade, Mahone's Division, 3rd Corps, Army of Northern Virginia (briefly March-April 1865). Throughout the early part of the war he led his troops in the sparsely manned areas of Florida. Although it is frequently reported that he was present with his command at the one major battle, Olustee, on the soil of his adopted state, there is no record of either he or his men being in the action. Joining the Army of Northern Virginia at Cold Harbor, he became colonel of a new regiment created from part of his own battalion and all of another. This he led through the Petersburg siege until promoted to brigadier general in late March 1865. There are some claims that he commanded the brigade during the early stages of the Appomattox Campaign but nothing appears in the *Official Records* to confirm this. Thereafter he engaged in the practice of law.

BRIDGFORD, David B. (?-?)

During the Civil War the equivalent of the modern day military police was the provost guard. It was in this line of work that David B. Bridgford spent most of the war. Of British descent, he was a merchant in New York City before the conflict, then migrated South. His assignments after going South included: captain, Company B, 1st Virginia Battalion Regulars (May 17, 1861); major, 1st Virginia Battalion Regulars (October 11, 1862); commanding Provost Guard, 2nd Corps, Army of Northern Virginia (fall 1862-June 4, 1863); and commanding Provost Guard, Army of Northern Virginia (June 4, 1863-April 9, 1865). He served at Cheat Mountain, Kernstown (commanding the battalion), McDowell, the Shenandoah Valley Campaign, the Seven Days, Cedar Mountain, and 2nd Bull Run. Promoted to battalion command he was soon detailed to provost duty for Jackson's Corps. As such he served at Fredericksburg. After Jackson's death he became provost marshal for the entire army, seeing action in the Petersburg and Appomattox campaigns. Following the surrender he returned to New York as a commission merchant and participated in a Cuban revolution.

BRIGHT, Daniel (?-1863)

One of the most sensitive questions raised in occupied areas during the Civil War was who was a guerrilla and who was a duly authorized soldier empowered to raise troops in areas near to or even behind enemy lines. For Daniel Bright the legal question was moot. He had been a member of Company L, 62nd Georgia (Cavalry), which was partly made up of North Carolinians. According to Edward A. Wild and the Union authorities he was a deserter from his unit engaged in guerrilla activities. Caught up in General Wild's December 1863 raid in northeastern North Carolina, he was captured at his home, given a drumhead court-martial and promptly hanged from a beam in his house on the 18th of the month. His body was left dangling for 40 hours with a placard on his back that read, "This guerrilla hanged by

order of Brigadier-General Wild." The Confederates were outraged and declared that Bright was on leave with an authorization from North Carolina's governor to raise a company in his home county. Confederate General George E. Pickett retaliated by hanging Private Samuel Jones, Company B, 5th United States Colored Troops, on January 12, 1864. A series of hostages were seized, including women, to guarantee treatment of captives as prisoners of war. The whole incident led to a lengthy series of communications between the two sides.

BROCK, Sallie Ann (1828-1911)

Mary Boykin Chesnut was not the only woman to write of her experiences in war-torn Richmond. Her close rival was Sallie Ann Brock, who in 1867 published *Richmond During the War: Four Years of Personal Observation* by "A Richmond Lady." Although she did not have Boykin's access to the Confederate centers of power, Brock provided a much more representative view of the capital, albeit from a somewhat darker side. Born in Madison County, Virginia, she had moved to the state capital a couple of years prior to the war and was involved in all the standard tasks of the women of the Confederacy: providing clothes for the troops and caring for them when wounded. She recorded the plight of the refugees, the shortages imposed by a war-torn economy, the endless inflation and the problems, real and imagined, that the war brought to race relations in the Old Dominion. Moving North after the war, she wrote four more books under the pen-name "Virginia Madison."

BROCKENBROUGH, John Mercer (1830-1892)

A farmer and Virginia Military Institute alumnus, John Brockenbrough was one of those temporary Confederate brigade commanders who was found wanting. He was appointed colonel, 40th Virginia on May 25, 1861. He commanded Field's Virginia Brigade, A.P. Hill's Division, Jackson's Corps, Army of Northern Virginia (August 29, 1862-March 5, 1863 and May 2-30, 1863) and same brigade, Heth's Division, A.P. Hill's Corps (May 30-July 1863) but was never promoted to the appropriate grade of brigadier general. During the Seven Days he led his regiment at Mechanicsville, Gaines' Mill, Frayser's Farm and later at 2nd Bull Run, where he assumed command of the brigade upon the wounding of General Field. He led the brigade at Chantilly, the capture of Harpers Ferry, Antietam, and Fredericksburg before being relieved by the assignment of General Heth to command the brigade. Brockenbrough commanded the regiment until Heth took command of the division and Brockenbrough the brigade during the fight at Chancellorsville. At Gettysburg he led his brigade on the first day and took part in driving the enemy back through the town. For some unexplained reason he was not with his brigade when it took part in Pickett's Charge on the third day. Later in July 1863, he was relieved of brigade command and resumed command of the 40th Virginia, which he led at Bristoe Station and Mine Run. On January 21, 1864, Brockenbrough resigned his commission, probably at least in part because his lieutenant colonel, Henry H. Walker, had been promoted to brigadier general and given command of the brigade over him. (Freeman, Douglas S., *Lee's Lieutenants*)

BROCKENBROUGH, John White (1806-1877)

A prominent federal judge before the Civil War, John W. Brockenbrough was sent by his native state of Virginia, along with other commissioners, to Washington to seek a peaceful separation of the country. This having failed and active military operations having begun, Brockenbrough was named, in June 1861, to the Provisional Confederate Congress where he was appropriately assigned to the Committee on the Judiciary. Representing a district in what was to become West Virginia, he supported the administration in its military efforts and in the search for means to finance them. However, most of his congressional time was spent in the organization of the new government and especially in getting the court system functioning. With institution of the permanent constitution, Brockenbrough left the legislature to accept appointment as Confederate States judge for the Western District of Virginia, the same jurisdiction he had held in the federal service and which was to become the new state of West Virginia in 1863. Here again he was an active supporter of the administration. After the war he ran the Lexington Law School, which soon became part of Washington College, of which he had been a trustee since 1852. He was instrumental in obtaining the school's presidency for Robert E. Lee, which eventually resulted in the institution becoming Washington and Lee University.

BROOKE, John Mercer (1826-1904)

The man who proposed the conversion of the scuttled USS *Merrimac* into an ironclad vessel, John M. Brooke, was also the Confederacy's chief gun designer. The Florida native had entered the U.S. Navy as an enlisted man in 1841 and, after four years' service, was appointed to the Naval Academy. Following his 1847 graduation from Annapolis he served on the coastal survey and at the naval observatory. He also plotted the route to China. Resigning his commission is April 1861, he joined the Confederacy; he was named a lieutenant in the navy and joined the staff, as an acting aide, of Robert E. Lee. It was he who suggested to the secretary of the navy, Stephen R. Mallory, a fellow Floridian, that the *Merrimac* be converted into the *Virginia*. Brooke's design of a submerged bow was used on this revolutionary craft. In recognition of his status as a scientist of the sea in 1863, he was named a commander for the duration of the war and in the latter stages of the war was chief of the Office of Ordnance and Hydrography. This may seem to have been a strange combination but Brooke had also been active in designing artillery pieces for the South. Many of his ideas appear to have come from Robert Parrott, and his best known work was a three-inch 10-pounder rifle.

BROOKE, Walker (1813-1869)

Although he had briefly served in the U.S. Senate, Walker

Brooke was unsuccessful in two attempts to gain a seat in the Confederate Senate. Born in Virginia, Brooke was admitted to the bar in that state before relocating to Mississippi where he eventually served in both houses of the state legislature. After completing Henry Foote's term in the Senate in 1852-53, he resumed his law practice. In the Mississippi secession convention he was basically a Unionist, but voted for secession in the end when he saw the futility of opposition. However, he urged that the secession ordinance be submitted to the people for a popular vote. This effort having failed, he was named to the Provisional Confederate Congress and assigned to the Committee on the Executive Departments and was chairman of the Committee on Patents. A firm supporter of a strong central government, he was an early Davis supporter. Following election defeats, he held several minor appointments including services in the military courts system. The war had broken him, and Brooke ran a failing law practice until his death.

BROOKS, John Hampden (?-?)

By the fall of 1864 the Confederacy was desperately looking for ways to fill its ever-thinning ranks. One source of manpower was the prisoner of war camps where many Union prisoners were willing to do almost anything to escape horrible conditions. John H. Brooks was assigned the task of organizing these men. His Confederate record included: captain, Company G, 7th South Carolina (April 16, 1861); captain, Company H, 7th South Carolina Battalion (July 14, 1862); and acting major, Brooks' Battalion Confederate Regular Infantry (November 16, 1864). After serving with his original regiment in Virginia, he resigned his commission in order to raise a company of partisan rangers. With this unit he served in the defense of Charleston until the spring of 1864 when the battalion was sent to Virginia to defend the Richmond-Petersburg area. That October he was ordered to proceed to Florence, South Carolina, to raise a battalion from those Union prisoners who were not U.S. citizens and were willing to take the oath of allegiance to join the Confederate army. His command of six companies, commanded by detailed officers, was mustered in on November 17. However, as soon as the unit took the field near Savannah mass desertions began. Then on the night of December 15 a mutiny led by the non-commissioned officers was crushed before it had fairly begun. The leaders were shot and, upon Brooks' recommendation, the battalion was broken up and the men returned to prison. Their commander returned to his former company.

BROOKS, Preston Smith (1819-1857)

Although he died almost four years before his home state of South Carolina seceded, Congressman Preston Brooks was an effective illustration of the violent feeling between the sections during the late ante-bellum period. A veteran of the Mexican War, Brooks was considered, even by some Republican friends, to be tolerant of interests other than his own—until May 19, 1856, when Massachusetts Senator Charles Sumner, an abolitionist Republican, began the two-day deliverance of his "Crime Against Kansas" speech. Part of the speech was a denunciation of South Carolina and one of her senators, Andrew P. Butler, a relative of Brooks. Brooks was outraged. On the 22nd he entered the chamber following an adjournment and, without offering Sumner time to make amends, he proceeded to mercilessly beat the senator with a gutta percha cane. Sumner, temporarily blinded, fell under his desk but rose, and the beating continued until the cane shattered. Others broke up the melee. While Brooks was being restrained, Lawrence Keitt, another South Carolina hothead, raced in with his cane raised, but Georgian Robert Toombs calmed Keitt and prevented a full-scale riot on the floor of the Senate. Brooks received praise from the South, and an expulsion resolution by the House failed to obtain the two-thirds required. He resigned anyway and was promptly reelected and presented with a cane with the motto "Hit him again." He was, however, fined $300 on an assault charge. He died a few months later from complications of a cold. (Donald, David, *Charles Sumner and the Coming of the Civil War*)

BROUN, William LeRoy (1827-1902)

There was great concern, whenever the Army of Northern Virginia got too far away from Richmond, that the capital would fall to a quick Union thrust. Therefore, emergency military units were formed, from the various government employees in the city, to be called upon when needed. William L. Broun, a native Virginian, was given command of one of these units. He was an ordnance officer and superintendent of the Richmond Arsenal. His employees were organized into a local defense unit on June 24, 1863, and he was made its lieutenant colonel. They were designated as the 5th Virginia Battalion, Local Defense Troops. After a year of this double duty he found that the military work was interfering with his work at the arsenal and on May 15, 1864, he submitted his resignation from the battalion. This was not accepted until August 11. He continued in his original post for the remainder of the war and served on a number of boards of review. He was subsequently a professor at several colleges and universities and a writer.

BROWN, Albert Gallatin (1813-1880)

His extreme views in the Confederate Senate and his post-war cooperationism have relegated Albert G. Brown to a less than popular place in Southern history. Emigrating from South Carolina to Mississippi as a child, Brown was admitted to the bar and became a militia general before launching his varied and lengthy political career. His service included the state legislature, where he was acting speaker for a time, two different periods of service in the U.S. House of Representatives, and governor of Mississippi. By the outbreak of the secession crisis, he had been serving in the U.S. Senate since 1853. With the secession of his state, he resigned his seat on January 12, 1861. Raising a company of infantry, Brown was commissioned captain, 18th Mississippi, early in 1861 and saw action at the Confederate victories at First Manassas and Ball's Bluff. Appointed to the Confederate Senate in November 1861, he left the army to take his seat at the convening of the First Confederate Congress in February 1862. His appointment being to

Senator Albert G. Brown, Davis opponent. (*Harper's*)

a four-year term, he served through the remainder of the war with assignment to the Committees on Naval Affairs and on Territories. Throughout his tenure he was chairman of the former. His primary concern for the new nation was the achievement of victory; he conceded that constitutional niceties might have to be sacrificed but could be corrected once independence had been secured. But he felt that these unlimited war powers rested with the legislative branch of the government and this led to an eventual break with Davis. He favored an expanded draft, the arming and emancipation of slaves, privateering, and increasing food production for the army at the expense of cotton planting. Feeling that a cooperationist attitude with the Northern authorities during Reconstruction would be more beneficial to the South than antagonism, he advised his fellow Southerners to in effect "shake hands." Labeled a submissionist, he retired to the life of a farmer for his remaining years. (Ranek, James B., *Albert Gallatin Brown, Radical Southern Nationalist*)

BROWN, Isaac N. (?-?)

A veteran of 27 years in the U.S. Navy, Kentucky-born Isaac Brown, a Mexican War veteran, returned from a cruise to find his country divided. He quickly switched his allegiance to the South. Having given up a lieutenant's commission in the old navy, he was, on June 6, 1861, appointed lieutenant, CSN, and assigned to the army's Department of the West with instructions to assist in the construction of batteries for the defense of the Mississippi River. He later worked on a similar project along the Cumberland. The advance of Union forces put an end to this work as it did to his next assignment—supervising the construction of four ironclads at New Orleans. On May 26, 1862, he was given command of the ironclad *Arkansas*, which was then nearing completion. He sailed his new vessel down the Mississippi through the entire Union fleet and safely anchored under the guns of Vicksburg. The entire naval outlook on the river had changed. Brown was absent sick the next month when the vessel moved down to Baton Rouge to aid in a land attack on the Union force there. He never saw his vessel again. It was blown up by its own crew when its cranky engines broke down. Brown gathered the remnants of his crew and performed shore duty at Port Hudson and later along the Yazoo River, where he helped blow up the Union vessels *DeKalb* and *Cairo* by torpedoes. He took part in the defense of Fort Pemberton. Already promoted to commander on August 25, 1862, Brown was, following Vicksburg's fall, ordered to command the ironclad *Charleston* in Charleston Harbor. Here he remained until the fall of the city. The war ended before he could assume his next command, that of naval defenses west of the Mississippi. (Scharf, J. Thomas, *History of the Confederate States Navy*)

BROWN, John (1800-1859)

Martyr for freedom, inciter of slave insurrections, murderer—all were titles given to John Brown, one of the most controversial characters to come out of the sectional conflict of the 1850s. Born in Connecticut, he had engaged in numerous businesses in various locations, usually unsuccessfully. While residing in Richmond, Ohio, he was a part of the Underground

Fanatical abolitionist John Brown. (NA)

Railroad. The dispute over Kansas attracted his attention and he moved there and helped establish a free state settlement at Osawatomie. Following the pro-slavery faction's sacking of Lawrence, Brown and six others—including four of his sons—raided along the Pottawatamie Creek in pro-slavery areas. In cold blood they murdered five men. Continuing his operations, he became the idol of some Eastern abolitionists, who then backed his plans to invade slave states and free the slaves. After arming them, he planned to set up a free state for blacks in the mountains of Virginia and Maryland. With a force of 21 men he took over the armory at Harpers Ferry, seizing hostages and killing six people. The next day Robert E. Lee and Jeb Stuart arrived with a detachment of marines. When the firehouse was stormed, ten of Brown's men and one marine were killed. Brown himself lost two sons and was taken prisoner after being knocked senseless. The October 1859 raid was finally over but its repercussions would further the movement toward secession and civil war. Following a trial in Charlestown, Virginia, Brown was hanged on December 2, 1859. To many in the North he became a martyr, even if many prominent abolitionists who had backed him secretly denied their involvement. (Oates, Stephen B., *To Purge This Land With Blood: A Biography of John Brown*)

BROWN, John Calvin (1827-1889)

Tennessee lawyer and minor politician John C. Brown rose to be one of the fighting division commanders of the Confederate Army of Tennessee. His assignments included: colonel, 3rd Tennessee (May 16, 1861); commanding 3rd Brigade, 2nd (Buckner's) Division, Central Army of Kentucky, Department #2 (October 28, 1861-February 11, 1862); commanding 3rd Brigade, Buckner's Division, Fort Donelson, Central Army of Kentucky, Department #2 (February 11-16, 1862); brigadier general, CSA (August 30, 1862); commanding brigade, 2nd (Anderson's Division, Left Wing, Army of the Mississippi (September-October 8, 1862); commanding Breckinridge's Division, Hardee's Corps, Army of Tennessee (December 1862, January 16-22, 1863, and February 2-June 6, 1863); commanding brigade, Stewart's Division, Hill's-Breckinridge's Corps, Army of Tennessee (June 6-August and October 1-November 12, 1863); commanding the division (August 1863); commanding brigade, Stewart's Division, Buckner's Corps, Army of Tennessee (September 1863); commanding brigade, Stevenson's Division, Hardee's Corps, Army of Tennessee (November 12-23, 1863 and November 24, 1863-February 20, 1864); commanding the division (November 23-24, 1863); commanding brigade, Stevenson's Division, Hood's-Lee's Corps, Army of Tennessee (February 20-July 1864); commanding Hindman's Division, Hood's Corps, Army of Tennessee (early July 1864); commanding Stewart's Division, Hood's Corps, Army of Tennessee (July 1864); commanding Bate's Division, Hardee's-Cheatham's Corps, Army of Tennessee (August-November 30, 1864); major general, CSA (August 4, 1864); commanding division, Cheatham's Corps, Army of Tennessee (April 2-9, 1865); and commanding division, Hardee's Corps, Army of Tennessee (April 9-26, 1865). After commanding a brigade in central Kentucky he was sent with it to reinforce the garrison of Fort Donelson where he was captured. Exchanged on August 27, 1862, he was named a brigadier general and commanded a brigade at Perryville where he was wounded. Returning to duty, he commanded a brigade during the Tullahoma Campaign and was again wounded at Chickamauga. At Chattanooga he briefly commanded the division. During the Atlanta Campaign he led his brigade and then a succession of divisions whose leaders were temporarily or permanently absent. Finally taking charge of Bate's division, he served through the rest of the siege and then accompanied Hood into middle Tennessee. There he was wounded at Franklin and did not return to his division until the very final weeks of the war in North Carolina, where he surrendered with Joseph E. Johnston. After the war he resumed his political and legal careers. He served two terms as governor and then went into railroading.

BROWN, John Thompson (1835-1864)

It was generally recognized that J. Thompson Brown's undistinguished showing as the new chief of artillery for the 2nd Corps at Gettysburg was really the fault of the corps commander, Richard S. Ewell. Nonetheless, he was superseded in his position two months later. Joining the artillery service four days after the secession of his native Virginia, lawyer Brown held the following appointments: lieutenant, Richmond Howitzers (April 21, 1861); captain, 2nd Company, Richmond Howitzers (May 1861); major, 1st Virginia Artillery (September 1861); lieutenant colonel, 1st Virginia Artillery (spring 1862); colonel, 1st Virginia Artillery (June 2, 1862); commanding battalion, Reserve Artillery, Army of Northern Virginia (early 1862-mid December 1862); commanding battalion, Artillery Reserve, 2nd Corps, Army of Northern Virginia (mid December 1862-May 2, 1863); chief of artillery, 2nd Corps, Army of Northern Virginia (May 2-September 23, 1863); commanding artillery battalion, 2nd Corps, Army of Northern Virginia (September 23, 1863-spring 1864); and commanding artillery division, 2nd Corps, Army of Northern Virginia (spring-May 6, 1864). After service at the battle of Big Bethel, he commanded a battalion in the Peninsula Campaign and at Antietam, Fredericksburg, and Chancellorsville. At the latter he took over direction of the corps' artillery upon the wounding of Colonel Crutchfield. Instead of being kept in permanent charge, he was replaced by General Long who had been promoted from a position on Lee's staff. As a consolation he was later given charge of three battalions in the Overland Campaign. At the Wilderness he was killed by a sharpshooter while placing his guns. (Wise, Jennings C., *The Long Arm of Lee*)

BROWN, Joseph Emerson (1821-1894)

A country born from the states' rights movement, the Confederacy nevertheless had to fashion a centralized government to fight the war. One who refused to accept this was Georgia's governor, Joseph Brown. Born in South Carolina, Brown was raised in northern Georgia and attended Yale Law School. Admitted to the bar, he practiced until 1849 when he took a

seat in the state legislature for one term. He served two years as a judge before being named as the surprise Democratic nominee for governor in 1857. Elected, he served for four two-year terms. Although pro-Union, he was known as an extreme states' rights man. On January 3, 1861, before the secession of the state, Georgia Militia, under Brown's direction, seized Fort Pulaski. Early in the conflict he was instrumental in raising troops in reply to calls by the Confederate administration. However, Davis' policy of appointing some field officers and later drafting men directly for the army, ignoring the state authorities, represented a violation of states' rights in Brown's eyes. In response to the Conscription Act he declared thousands of men to be necessary to his state's operations thus exempting them from the draft calls. He jealously guarded the Georgia Militia, withdrawing them from Confederate service whenever Georgia's borders were not threatened. He questioned taxation policies on literal readings of the Constitution. Throughout the war Davis and Brown exchanged long, angry letters arguing these points. Davis considered Brown to have been a major obstacle in the prosecution of the war. At the war's close he was arrested but shortly afterwards released. In June 1865 he resigned his office and turned to the Republicans, as the best way for the South to survive Reconstruction. Brown was despised by much of Georgia. In 1880, after returning to the Democrats, Brown was named to the U.S. Senate when former General John B. Gordon resigned. He was appointed by Governor Alfred Colquitt. The three men dominated Georgia politics for the next decade. Resigning in 1891, Brown died three years later. (Hill, Louise Biles, *Joseph E. Brown and the Confederacy*)

BROWN, Ridgely (1833-1864)

A farmer in his native Montgomery County, Maryland, Ridgely Brown had Southern sympathies, joined the Confederate army, and became a noted cavalryman before losing his life. Initially enlisting in a Virginia regiment, he later transferred to the Maryland Line. His assignments included: lieutenant, Company K, 1st Virginia Cavalry (1861); captain, Company A, Cavalry, Maryland Line (early 1862); major, 1st Maryland Cavalry Battalion (November 12, 1862); and lieutenant colonel, 1st Maryland Cavalry Battalion (August 20, 1863). Serving under Jeb Stuart, and later "Grumble" Jones, he was at 1st Bull Run. Transferred to the Maryland Line, he fought in the Shenandoah Valley Campaign and during the Seven Days on the Peninsula. He was wounded at Greenland Gap on April 25, 1863, but was able to serve in the advance of Richard S. Ewell's corps during the Gettysburg Campaign. When not with the main army he frequently participated in raids in West Virginia and western Maryland. While serving along the South Anna River he was shot in the head and killed on June 1, 1864.

BROWNE, Charles Farrar (1834-1867)

A professional humorist for the *Cleveland Plain Dealer*, Charles Browne took his pen-name, Artemus Ward, from the name of Revolutionary War General Artemas Ward, and became so popular during the Civil War that President Lincoln even recited his writings to cabinet meetings. Browne, an intimate friend of Samuel Clemens, styled his essays in the form of open letters signed "A. Ward, the showman." In his "Interview with President Lincoln," Ward condemned the horde of office-seekers who were descending upon the president-elect, declaring that he "hav no politics. Nary a one. I'm not in the bizniss." His advice on the division of the Union was that "if any State wants to secede, let 'em Sesesh!" When Abe asked about selecting the cabinet, A. Ward recommended, "Fill it up with Showmen, sir! Showmen is devoid of politics. They hain't gat any principles!" His career came to an end in England, where he was lecturing, when he died of tuberculosis at the age of 33. (Dudden, Arthur F., ed. *The Assault of Laughter* and Pullen, John J., *Comic Relief: The Life and Laughter of Artemus Ward, 1834-1867*)

BROWNE, William Montague (1823-1883)

In the waning days of the Confederacy, William M. Browne suffered the humiliation of having his appointment as a brigadier general rejected by an 18 to 2 vote in the Senate due to the animosity against Jefferson Davis, with whom he was so closely associated. The Dublin native had served in the Crimean War with the English army before settling in Washington where he was an editor with two political journals. Going over to the Confederacy, he obtained a staff position with the Confederate president and his assignments included: colonel, Cavalry (1861); and brigadier general, CSA (November 11, 1864). His request for field service turned down, he served most of the war in Richmond. When Robert M.T. Hunter left the post of secretary of state on February 17, 1862, Browne was appointed ad interim. This lasted until Judah P. Benjamin took over the portfolio on March 18, 1862. Browne then resumed his duties in the War Department's section dealing with organization until the fall of 1864. He was dispatched to Georgia to directly observe and report to Davis on Sherman's advance to the coast. At one point he commanded a brigade of local troops. Continuing in his reporting role during the Carolinas Campaign, he was included in Joseph E. Johnston's surrender. In the meantime he had been appointed and then rejected as a general officer. After the war he was a planter and educator. (Coulter, E. Merton, *William Montague Browne: Versatile Anglo-Irish American, 1823-1883*)

BROWNLOW, William Gannaway (1805-1877)

East Tennessee was a continuous thorn in the side of the Confederacy—its mountain people had little sympathy for the slave-holding class. One of the chief sources of this trouble was Parson William Brownlow. Converted to the Methodist faith, he served as a minister for a decade before, in 1839, founding the *Elizabethton Whig*, which eventually moved via Jonesboro to Knoxville. He kept all these communities in a virtually permanent state of political and religious uproar with his pro-Union, but pro-slavery, rhetoric. His extremist arguments, in support of the now defunct Whig Party, made him a victim of physical violence on at least one occasion. His anti-Confederate

tirades were tolerated during the first few months of the war, but reports linking him to railroad bridge-burning, and a final vicious attack in *Brownlow's Knoxville Whig*, proved too much for the rebels. He was imprisoned on December 6, 1861, and on March 15, 1862, he was physically expelled from the Confederacy. He promptly published *Sketches of the Rise, Progress, and Decline of Secession; with a Narrative of Personal Adventures among the Rebels*, which sold 100,000 copies in three months. Greeted with open arms by the North, he accompanied the Union army upon its return to East Tennessee and reestablished the *Knoxville Whig and Rebel Ventilator*. Favoring harsh treatment of rebels, he succeeded Andrew Johnson as governor in 1865 and held that post until appointed to the Senate. Retiring in 1875 he resumed his vitriolic journalism until his death. (Coulter, Ellis Merton, *William G. Brownlow, Fighting Parson of the Southern Highlands*)

BRUCE, Eli Metcalfe (1828-1866)

One of the few Confederate congressmen who did not come from a legal or planting background, businessman Eli M. Bruce closed his Northern-based chain of meat packing houses and reopened them in the South at the outbreak of the Civil War. Becoming a major supplier to the Confederate armies, Bruce also became known for his charity towards Kentucky troops and in early 1862 he was elected to represent Kentucky's 9th District in the First Congress. With his district soon overrun by enemy forces, Bruce favored carrying the war into the North and the use of privateers to raid Union commerce. During this congress he served on the Committee on Military Affairs. A great believer in Jefferson Davis' military abilities, Bruce urged him to take personal command of the field armies. Reelected to the Second Congress by the exile vote, Bruce was, in recognition of his business knowledge, assigned to the Committee on Ways and Means. His ethics were questioned in his withdrawal from the Erlanger Loan but he was later cleared. Moving to New York at the war's close, Bruce ran the Southern Hotel where ex-Confederates were always welcome with or without money.

BRUCE, Horatio Washington (1830-1903)

One of the Davis administration's most consistent supporters in Congress was the representative from Kentucky's 7th District, Horatio W. Bruce. The Kentucky-born Bruce, without college training, was admitted to the bar at 21 and served one term in the state legislature. In November 1861 he served in the convention that claimed to have taken the state out of the Union. With the state "admitted" to the Confederacy, Bruce was rewarded for his secessionist vote in the convention by being elected to the First Confederate Congress in January 1862. With his district soon occupied by Union troops, Bruce adopted a policy of supporting all measures, military and economic, necessary to win the war. He supported conscription and wanted the War Department to do with its forces as it pleased. He rarely criticized government leaders, military or civilian, and felt peace overtures to be fruitless. On the flight from Richmond, Bruce accompanied Davis as far as Augusta. After the war he practiced law in Louisville, served as a judge and taught law.

BRYAN, Goode (1811-1865)

West Pointer (1834) Goode Bryan served less than a year before resigning from the regular army but continued to be active in militia affairs in Alabama and then back in his native Georgia. During the Mexican War he was major, 1st Alabama. The remainder of his time before the Civil War was spent in engineering, on his plantations, or in politics. A member of the Georgia secession convention, he entered the Confederate army where his assignments included: captain, 16th Georgia (early 1861); lieutenant colonel, 16th Georgia (July 1861); colonel, 16th Georgia (February 15, 1862); commanding Semmes' (old) Brigade, McLaws'-Kershaw's Division, 1st Corps, Army of Northern Virginia (July 2-September 9, 1863 and April 12-June 2, 1864); brigadier general, CSA (August 29, 1863); commanding same brigade, McLaws' Division, Longstreet's Corps, Army of Tennessee (September 19-November 5, 1863); and commanding brigade, McLaws'-Kershaw's Division, Department of East Tennessee (November 5, 1863-April 12, 1864). Serving in Cobb's-Wofford's Brigade, he fought at Yorktown, the Seven Days, Fredericksburg, and Gettysburg, where he was assigned to command the brigade of the mortally wounded General Semmes. Promoted to brigadier shortly afterwards, his brigade did not arrive in time to take part in the Chickamauga fighting, when Longstreet went west. He did fight during the Knoxville Campaign and back in Virginia at the Wilderness, Spotsylvania, and Cold Harbor. On June 2, 1864, during the latter engagement, he relinquished command to Colonel James P. Simms and resigned, citing ill health, on September 20. He then retired to his Georgia home. (Freeman, Douglas S., *Lee's Lieutenants*)

BUCHANAN, Franklin (1800-1874)

Although the Confederacy's senior admiral constantly desired action, Maryland-born Franklin Buchanan had only two days of combat during the war—and was wounded both times. Entering the U.S. Navy in 1815 as a 14-year-old midshipman, Buchanan saw service in the Mediterranean, against pirates in the Caribbean, was co-founder and first superintendent of the Naval Academy at Annapolis, in the Mexican War, on Perry's expedition to Japan and as commander of the Washington Navy Yard. With the firing on the 6th Massachusetts in Baltimore, Buchanan assumed that Maryland would secede and join the Confederacy. Therefore, on April 22, 1861, he resigned his command and his commission as captain. But when the state did not secede, he tried to cancel his resignation. This being refused, he maintained a four-month-long neutrality before finally offering his services to the Confederacy. On September 5 he was appointed captain, CSN, and chief of the Bureau of Orders and Details, where he was faced with a lack of commands, for a surplus of officers, and a lack of trained crews. Highly effective in this administrative post, he was nonetheless desirous of an active command. His wish was fulfilled when, on February 24, 1862, he was given charge of the Chesapeake Bay

Squadron, with the just completed ironclad *Virginia* (or *Merrimack*) as his flagship. On March 8, 1862, he sailed his new command out of Norfolk, to attack the Union blockading fleet in Hampton Roads. His first target was the USS *Cumberland*, which he rammed and sank, losing in the process his ship's ram. Next turning his attention to the USS *Congress*, another wooden vessel, he gave her a series of broadsides that set her afire. The Union commander struck his flag, but when one of the *Virginia*'s escorts went to her relief, she was fired upon from shore by Union infantry. Enraged, Buchanan ordered the *Congress* destroyed and taking a rifle in hand himself opened fire on the stricken craft from an exposed position. He was struck in the thigh, taken below, and forced to relinquish command. He thus missed the next day's fight with the USS *Monitor*. Ironically, one of the Union officers aboard the *Congress* was his brother McKean Buchanan. Following a slow recovery from his wound and brief service on a court-martial, he was promoted to admiral, CSN, on August 21, 1862; in September he took over command of the Mobile defenses. After almost two years of work perfecting the defensive arrangements, he finally saw action again when Union Admiral Farragut entered the bay with his massive fleet. Aboard his flagship, the newly completed ironclad CSS *Tennessee*. Buchanan engaged the Union armada, repeatedly trying to ram Farragut's flagship, USS *Hartford*. With the rest of his fleet already gone and his flagship surrounded by the enemy, he suffered a broken leg from an iron splinter. Shortly after he turned over command, the *Tennessee* surrendered. Exchanged in March 1865, he was again captured in Mobile just after his resumption of command. After the war he served as a college president and in the insurance business until his retirement. (Lewis, Charles L., *Admiral Franklin Buchanan: Fearless Man of Action*)

BUCKNER, Simon Bolivar (1823-1914)

The organizer of the Kentucky State Guard, which largely joined the Confederacy, Simon B. Buckner rose to the rank of lieutenant general during the war. The Kentucky West Pointer (1844) served with the infantry in Mexico, winning two brevets and suffering a wound at Churubusco. He then returned to his teaching post at his alma mater. Feeling that the mandatory presence at Sunday chapel was a violation of his rights, he quit that post and returned to infantry service in 1849. In 1852 he transferred to the commissary branch but resigned three years later to engage in the real estate business. In the remaining years before the Civil War he was adjutant general of the Illinois militia and directed the reorganization of his native state's armed forces. His Civil War assignments included: major general and inspector general, Kentucky State Guard (spring 1860); brigadier general, CSA (September 14, 1861); commanding Central Geographical Division of Kentucky, Department #2 (September 18-October 28, 1861); commanding 2nd Division, Central Army of Kentucky, Department #2 (October 28, 1861-February 11, 1862); commanding division, Fort Donelson, Central Army of Kentucky, Department #2 (February 11-16, 1862); commanding the fort (February 16, 1862); major general, CSA (August 16, 1862); commanding division, Left Wing, Army of the Mississippi (ca. September-

November 20, 1862); commanding division, Hardee's Corps, Army of Tennessee (November 20-December 14, 1862); commanding District of the Gulf, Department #2 (December 14, 1862-April 27, 1863); commanding Department of East Tennessee (May 12-September 1863); commanding corps, Army of Tennessee (September 1863); commanding division, Cheatham's Corps, Army of Tennessee (October-November 1863); commanding division, Department of East Tennessee (November 26-December 1863); again commanding the department (April 12-May 2, 1864); second in command, Trans-Mississippi Department (June-August 4, 1864); commanding District of West Louisiana, Trans-Mississippi Department (August 4, 1864-April 19, 1865); also commanding 1st Corps, Trans-Mississippi Department (September 1864-May 26, 1865); lieutenant general, CSA (September 20, 1864); commanding the department (April 19-22, 1865); and commanding District of Arkansas and West Louisiana, Trans-Mississippi Department (April 22-May 26, 1865). As the head of the state's military forces he attempted to preserve its precarious neutrality but in July 1861 the Unionist-controlled military board of the state ordered the State Guard, which they considered pro-secessionist, to turn in its arms. Buckner resigned on July 20th and two months later was named a Confederate brigadier general, neutrality having come to an end. Initially in command in central Kentucky, he later led a division from there to reinforce Fort Donelson. He directed the attempted breakout from the encircled post on February 15, 1862, but was called back by his superiors, John B. Floyd and Gideon J. Pillow. Both of them fled across the Cumberland River rather than surrender and left the task to Buckner. He was outraged by Grant's demand for unconditional surrender, but he was somewhat mollified by later developments. He had paid Grant's New York hotel bill when the future Union general was on his way home, having resigned from the army. Grant returned the favor in kind, knowing that Buckner would have difficulty obtaining funds as a prisoner—and put his purse at the disposal of the vanquished. Exchanged on August 27, 1862, Buckner was promoted to major general and led his division at Perryville before being ordered to take command along the Gulf coast. The next spring he took over the Department of East Tennessee. On July 25, 1863, this command was merged into the Department of Tennessee under Braxton Bragg but was retained for administrative purposes. Thus Buckner was reporting to both Bragg and Richmond. This awkward situation led to ill-feelings later on. During the buildup prior to the battle of Chickamauga Buckner reinforced Bragg and his command became a corps for the battle. When Jefferson Davis visited the army shortly thereafter Buckner was one of the leading critics of Bragg's generalship. For this reason Bragg shunted Buckner back off to East Tennessee just before Chattanooga. There he served under Longstreet during the siege of Knoxville. He then held a number of special assignments until again being placed in charge of the Department of East Tennessee in the spring of 1864. During this period he spent much of his time in Richmond where he became known as "Simon the Poet" for his penchant for writing poetry. Later that spring he was ordered to the virtually cut-off Trans-Mississippi as E. Kirby Smith's

deputy. Not allowed to return to Kentucky for three years after the war, he resided for that period in New Orleans and then resurrected his fortune. After serving as a pallbearer at his old friend Grant's funeral he entered politics, serving a term as governor. In 1896 he ran for the vice presidency on John M. Palmer's Gold Democrats ticket. At the time of his death he was the only surviving Confederate officer over the rank of brigadier general. (Stickles, Arndt Mathias, *Simon Bolivar Buckner: Borderland Knight*)

BUFORD, Abraham (1820-1884)

At some 320 pounds, Abraham Buford was apparently the heaviest Confederate general. The native Kentuckian and West Pointer (1841) had won a brevet as a dragoon officer during the Mexican War and served on the frontier before resigning in 1854 as a captain in the 1st Dragoons. In the years before the Civil War he was a noted breeder of horses and cattle. When the sectional conflict broke into open warfare he maintained his own neutrality almost a year longer than his state. He became one of the few recruits gained during Bragg's invasion of the state in the summer and fall of 1862. Buford's assignments included: brigadier general, CSA (September 2, 1862); commanding brigade, Cavalry Division, Army of Tennessee (ca. December 1862-January 1863); commanding brigade, Loring's Division, Department of Mississippi and East Louisiana (ca. April-May 16, 1863); commanding brigade, Loring's Division, Department of the West (May 16-July 1863); commanding brigade, Loring's Division, Department of Mississippi and East Louisiana (July 1863-January 28, 1864); commanding brigade, Loring's Division, Department of Alabama, Mississippi and East Louisiana (January 28-March 2, 1864); commanding division, Forrest's Cavalry Corps, Department of Alabama, Mississippi and East Louisiana (February 18-May 4, 1865). Having finally made his decision, he covered the withdrawal from Kentucky and commanded a mounted brigade at Murfreesboro. Transferred to Mississippi, he was lightly engaged in actions against Grierson's raid and then took part in the early stages of the Vicksburg Campaign. Along with most of Loring's division, he was cut off from Pemberton's army after Champion Hill and joined the forces under Joseph E. Johnston. He took part in the defense of Jackson, Mississippi and in opposing Sherman's Meridian Campaign. Transferred to Forrest's cavalry, he fought in charge of a division at Brice's Crossroads, Tupelo, and during Andrew J. Smith's August 1864 invasion of Mississippi. Wounded at Lindville, Tennessee, on December 24, 1864, he was out of action for a time and was engaged in reorganizing the mounted forces under Richard Taylor when the end came. He then returned to horse raising but committed suicide after the deaths of his wife and son and financial losses.

BUFORD, Harry T.

See: *Velazquez, Loreta Janeta*

BULLOCH, James Dunwoody (1823-1901)

Never achieving his desire for a command of his own, James Bulloch fulfilled an even more important role for the Confederate navy—as purchasing agent in Europe providing many of the commerce raiders for a fledgling fleet. After 15 years in the U.S. Navy, rising to the rank of lieutenant, Bulloch resigned in 1854. Commanding the mail steamer *Bienville* at the outbreak of the Civil War, he refused to turn it over to the Confederate authorities when he offered his services, insisting on returning it to New York. Sent to Europe in May 1861 as a civilian purchasing agent for the rebel navy, he worked with the Fraser, Trenholm & Company financial office in Liverpool. Working in secrecy and through the loopholes in the British Neutrality Proclamation and the Foreign Enlistment Act, he contracted for numerous ships and naval stores. He ran the *Fingal*, laden with supplies, through the blockade at Savannah in late 1861. Returning to Europe with a commission as a commander, he looked forward to taking command of one of the commerce raiders under construction. But the "290," more famous as the *Alabama*, went to Raphael Semmes instead. Other vessels built in Britain included the *Florida* and *Shenandoah*. Working also in France Bulloch contracted for the ram *Stonewall*, which never reached the Confederacy. With the waning of Southern military fortunes, it became increasingly difficult to operate in Europe. Several vessels were seized in France and England when virtually completed. With the South's fall, Bulloch remained in England and became a naturalized citizen. He wrote *The Secret Service of the Confederate States in Europe* and was in the cotton trade.

BULLOCK, Robert (1828-1905)

A veteran of Seminole Indian fighting, North Carolina-born Floridian Robert Bullock rose to the rank of Confederate brigadier general before being wounded and put out of action during the Nashville Campaign. A teacher and court clerk before the war, his military assignments included: captain, Company H, 7th Florida (spring 1862); lieutenant colonel, 7th Florida (ca. April 26, 1862); colonel, 7th Florida (June 2, 1863); commanding Florida Brigade, Bate's Division, Hardee's-Cheatham's Corps, Army of Tennessee (ca. September 1-mid-December 1864); and brigadier general, CSA (November 29, 1864). His early war service came in East Tennessee in limited maneuvering and in fighting Unionist guerrillas in the area. Rising to command of the regiment, he led it to a junction with Braxton Bragg's main army and took part in the victory at Chickamauga. He missed Chattanooga but was advanced to brigade command during the Atlanta Campaign. He led the Floridian brigade at Franklin, and during the Nashville Campaign he fell severely wounded near Murfreesboro during a minor action. This ended his career in the field and the year after the close of hostilities he became an attorney. He was also active in politics and became a judge.

BURGWYN, Henry King, Jr. (1841-1863)

An 1861 graduate of the Virginia Military Institute, Henry Burgwyn had the dubious distinction of commanding the regiment that suffered the highest numerical loss of any regiment in a single engagement. Burgwyn entered the Confederate service as lieutenant colonel of the 26th North Carolina on August 27, 1861, and was promoted to full colonel on August 19, 1862. His regiment saw service at New Bern in North Carolina and in the Seven Days with the Army of Northern Virginia. Sent back to eastern North Carolina and southeastern Virginia the regiment rejoined the army in time for the Gettysburg Campaign. On the first day of the battle, Burgwyn led his regiment until he was wounded in both lungs. He died shortly thereafter. The remnants of the command took part in the famed Pickett's Charge on the third day. In the two days of heavy fighting the regiment suffered 588 killed and wounded plus 120 prisoners out of somewhat over 800 engaged.

BURKS, Jesse Spinner (1823-1885)

During Stonewall Jackson's campaigns in late 1861 and early 1862 his brigade commanders were falling so rapidly, either from enemy fire or his own displeasure with them, that few of them ever reached the appropriate grade of brigadier general. Native Virginian Jesse S. Burks is one example of this attrition. Although he had graduated from the Virginia Military Institute in 1844, he was living the life of a farmer by the time of the outbreak of the war. Entering the military his assignments included: colonel, 42nd Virginia (July 1861); commanding 6th Brigade, Army of the Northwest (summer and fall 1861); and commanding Gilham's (Old) Brigade, Army of the Northwest and later in the Valley District, Department of Northern Virginia (January 20-March 23, 1862). Commanding a brigade, he took part in Robert E. Lee's dismal Cheat Mountain Campaign and commanded another brigade during the winter at Romney, getting himself involved in the Loring-Jackson feud. At the battle of Kernstown, although in a supporting role, he fell wounded, after only two months in command. Never recovering sufficiently to take the field, he resigned on July 21, 1862. Returning to his farm, he served in the state legislature for a decade in the postwar years, he had also served one term 20 years earlier.

BURNETT, Henry Cornelius (1825-1866)

Kentucky's Henry C. Burnett was one of Jefferson Davis' friends in the Confederate Senate. Born in Virginia, Burnett had settled in Kentucky as a child and was eventually admitted to the bar. A Democrat, he served four terms in the U.S. Congress before being expelled on December 3, 1861, for his outspoken secessionist sentiments. This was only to be expected, since the preceding month he had presided over the convention that claimed to have taken Kentucky out of the Union. Initially sent to Richmond to gain the state's admittance into the Confederacy, Burnett was appointed as a representative to the Provisional Congress. He was also appointed colonel, 8th Kentucky, on November 11, 1861, resigning on February 10, 1862. With the adoption of the permanent constitution, he was appointed to the Senate where he served for the remainder of the war. A general supporter of the administration's war effort, he did, however, want to give the states more control over ex-

Enlightened diplomat Anson Burlingame. (NA)

emptions from the draft. With his state behind enemy lines, Burnett was a major proponent of the use of partisan rangers. His committee assignments in the Senate included those on: Buildings; Claims; Commerce; Engrossment and Enrollment; Judiciary; Military Affairs; Naval Affairs; and Pay and Mileage. He repeatedly used his influence with the president in an effort to get the Confederate army to invade Kentucky. He returned to the practice of law after the peace but died before he was 41.

BURNETT, Theodore Legrand (1829-1917)

One of the more troublesome members of Kentucky's generally Davis-friendly congressioinal delegation was the 6th District's Theodore L. Burnett. A native of the state, Burnett spent most of the antebellum period in his private law practice, with time out for service in the Mexican War and as a county attorney. With the recognition of the state's secession by the Richmond authorities, he was appointed to the Provisional Congress, but he only attended its sessions for one day. He was, however, elected to represent the 6th District in the First Congress. Here

he was assigned to the Committee on Claims and was named chairman of the Committee on Pay and Mileage. He demanded a hearing into the fall of Fort Donelson, which irritated the Davis administration. However, in the early years of the war he proved to be rather supportive of government policies. But by 1864 this had changed. No longer trusting Davis' military judgment, Burnett proposed that Congress name generals to high commands and frequently voted against giving the War Department additional powers. Ruined by the war, Burnett resumed his law practice and held minor elective office in Louisville.

BURT, Erasmus R. (?-1861)

In one of the relatively small actions early in the war Erasmus R. Burt is credited with killing the enemy commander before himself falling victim to enemy fire. Active in Mississippi politics and government and in helping the handicapped before the war, he became captain of the Burt Rifles. His assignments included: captain, Company K, 18th Mississippi (April 22, 1861) and colonel, 18th Mississippi (June 7, 1861). After leading his men in some of the fringe operations at 1st Bull Run, he took an active part in the Battle of Ball's Bluff. Here, some accounts have him firing the pistol shot that killed the Union commander, Edward D. Baker. A short while later he was mortally wounded, dying after five days, on October 26, 1861.

BURTON, James H. (?-?)

After running into trouble with the Confederate Congress in his role as an official in the ordnance department, Virginian James H. Burton went on to run an armory. Originally working for the Virginia state government, he transferred to the Confederate ordnance department under Josiah Gorgas. When push came to shove, he set up the Macon, Georgia, armory. He not only produced arms there, but also traveled to Europe to purchase ordnance machinery. In the final year of the war he was charged with inspecting the armories of the Confederacy.

BUTLER, Andrew P. (1796-1857)

South Carolina Senator Andrew Butler may not have been alive when the Civil War really got started but he was, in some respects, a participant in one of the first physical actions of that war. Butler was respected by his legislative colleagues, and many Northern senators, including Stephen Douglas, were uneasy with the vehemence of attacks heaped upon him during Senator Charles Sumner's two-day, 1856 speech, "Crime Against Kansas." Butler had been highly critical of Sumner, an abolitionist Republican, in recent months but this attack on the defender of slavery was too much for some to take. A relative of Butler, Congressman Preston Brooks, decided to take punitive action. On May 23, 1856, Brooks assaulted Sumner on the Senate floor with a cane. A full-fledged fight between the sections nearly erupted in the halls of Congress. On June 12 Butler supported Brooks' attack during a debate, and a move to expel Brooks failed to gain approval. Butler died almost exactly a year after the incident.

BUTLER, Matthew Calbraith (1836-1909)

South Carolina lawyer and state legislator M.C. Butler followed Wade Hampton throughout the war. His assignments included: captain, Hampton (S.C.) Legion (early 1861); major, Hampton Legion (July 21, 1861); colonel, 2nd South Carolina Cavalry (August 1862); brigadier general, CSA (September 1, 1863); commanding brigade, Hampton's Division, Cavalry Corps, Army of Northern Virginia (early spring-summer 1864); commanding the division (summer 1864-January 19, 1865); major general, CSA (September 19, 1864); commanding cavalry division, Department of South Carolina, Georgia and Florida (January-February 1865); commanding division, Hampton's Cavalry Command (March-April 9, 1865); and commanding division, Hampton's Cavalry Command, Army of Tennessee (April 9-26, 1865). He fought with the legion at 1st Bull Run and on the Peninsula before being given command of a new cavalry regiment. He saw further action at Antietam and Fredericksburg and was severely wounded in the foot by a shell. While recovering from the amputation of the limb he was promoted to brigadier and assigned to a brigade. However, when it become apparent that he would be out of action for some time, Colonel P.M.B. Young was given charge in his stead. When in the spring of 1864 he did report for duty, he was given a brigade of three regiments just arrived from South Carolina and led them through the Overland Campaign and took over the division at Petersburg. At the beginning of 1865 he was sent with his division to South Carolina to reinforce the opposition to Sherman's drive. Failing in this he fought at Bentonville and surrendered with Johnston. After the war he was active in Democratic politics and sat as a senator in Washington for three terms. He was a major general of volunteers, in blue, during the war with Spain. He was also an officer of the Southern Historical Association. (Freeman, Douglas S., *Lee's Lieutenants*, and Brooks, U.R., *Butler and His Cavalry*)

C

CABELL, Henry Coalter (1820-1889)

It is a comment on the slowness of promotions in the Confederate artillery that Henry C. Cabell, although a colonel and battalion commander for most of the war, never made it to the rank of general. A Richmond lawyer, he raised an artillery company early in the conflict and his assignments included: captain, Richmond Fayette Artillery (April 25, 1861); lieutenant colonel, 1st Virginia Artillery (September 12, 1861); colonel, Artillery (July 4, 1862); chief of artillery, Magruder's Command, Department of Northern Virginia (April 12-June 1862); commanding Artillery Battalion, McLaws' Division, 1st Corps, Army of Northern Virginia (summer 1862-July 1863); commanding artillery battalion, 1st Corps, Army of Northern Virginia (July-September 1863 and May 1864-April 9, 1865); and commanding battalion, Artillery Reserve, Army of Northern Virginia (September 1863-May 1864). Initially serving on the Peninsula, he saw action on the Yorktown lines. He subsequently led his battalion at Antietam, Fredericksburg, Chancellorsville, and Gettysburg. When the corps went west with Longstreet, Cabell's Battalion was assigned to the army's reserve. With the return of Longstreet in the spring of 1864, Cabell served through the Wilderness and Petersburg campaigns, sometimes as acting corps chief of artillery. On the retreat to Appomattox, his battalion was assigned to General Walker's column bound for Lynchburg and thus was not present at the surrender. He resumed his private practice after the war. (Wise, Jennings, C., *The Long Arm of Lee*)

CABELL, William Lewis (1827-1911)

Having resigned from the old army at the outbreak of hostilities, Virginian West Pointer (1850) William L. Cabell has been credited with helping Beauregard and Joseph E. Johnston design the Confederate battleflag. Upon his graduation he was posted to the infantry for eight years before being transferred to the quartermaster's department. He resigned as a captain on April 20, 1861, and was almost immediately com-missioned in the Southern army. His assignments included: major and assistant quartermaster (April 1861); chief quartermaster, Army of the Potomac (1861); chief quartermaster, Department of Northern Virginia (1862); commanding 1st Brigade, McCown's Division, Army of the West, Department #2 (spring-summer 1862); commanding cavalry brigade, Steele's Division, District of Arkansas, Trans-Mississippi Department (ca. February-late 1863); brigadier general, CSA (April 23, 1863 to rank from January 20); commanding brigade, Fagan's Cavalry Division, District of Arkansas, Trans-Mississippi Department (early 1864-September 18, 1864); commanding brigade, Fagan's Cavalry Division, Army of Missouri, Trans-Mississippi Department (September 18-October 25, 1864); and also commanding 1st (Arkansas) Cavalry Brigade, 1st (Arkansas) Cavalry Division, Cavalry Corps, Trans-Mississippi Department (September-October 25, 1864). After staff duty in northern Virginia he was transferred to the Trans-Mississippi and as an acting brigadier general was given charge of a mounted brigade, which he led across the Mississippi. He was wounded at Corinth and the Hatchie River. He returned to duty early in 1863 and continued to command a cavalry brigade in Arkansas until captured at Marais des Cygnes during Sterling Price's invasion of Missouri. Not exchanged until August 1865, he took up the practice of law, moved to Texas, entered railroading, was a U.S. marshal, and was connected with the Louisiana Lottery. He also served four terms as mayor of Dallas and was active in veterans' affairs. (Harvey, Paul, Jr., *Old Tige: General William L. Cabell, CSA*)

CALHOUN, John Caldwell (1782-1850)

Although he died more than a decade before secession became a reality, the ideas on states' rights of John C. Calhoun make him the leading contender for the titles of father of secession and father of the Confederacy. A South Carolina lawyer, he was secretary of war under Monroe from 1817 to 1825 and vice president under John Quincy Adams and Andrew Jackson. In the latter administration he broke with the president over a protective tariff and developed his theory of nullification, which claimed that a state had the right to void any federal law that in its opinion violated the agreement made at the time of entry into the Union. If a compromise had not been achieved the Civil War might have been fought decades earlier, since Jackson was threatening the use of force. Calhoun later went to the U.S. Senate where he continued to focus on states' rights. "The Great Nullifier," as he was then known, earned another sobriquet for his outspoken defense of slavery: "The Napoleon of Slavery." After a brief return to his plantation he was Tyler's secretary of state in 1844-1845. Then returning to the Senate, he died in office. (Thomas, John L., *John C. Calhoun, A Profile*)

CALLAHAN, Samuel Benton (1833-1911)

Despite the fact that he was only one-eighth Creek, Samuel B. Callahan managed to serve in the Second Confederate Congress as a nonvoting representative for the Creek and Seminole nations. After working as a journalist in Texas, the Alabama-born Callahan moved to the Indian Territory and, based upon his mother's being one-quarter Creek, obtained Creek citizenship in 1858. He had been a commissioner to Washington but, being a slaveholder, felt that the Creeks should align themselves with the Confederacy. He served as captain, 1st Creek Cavalry. When the Creek and Seminole nations were given the right to alternately elect a nonvoting delegate to the Confederate Congress, Callahan was named to the position, taking his seat on May 30, 1864. Unable to vote, he took very little part in the activities of the legislature, but only considered matters relating to the Indians. After the war he resumed his ranching and farming operations and held various positions, often representing the Creeks, in the Indian Territory and later in Oklahoma, the state formed from the Indian Territory.

CAMPBELL, Alexander William (1828-1893)

It was not until the final months of the war that Tennessee native Alexander W. Campbell received the wreath of a brigadier general around his three stars. The lawyer's Confederate assignments included: major and assistant inspector general, Provisional Army of Tennessee (ca. May 9, 1861); colonel, 33rd Tennessee (October 18, 1861); acting assistant inspector general, Forrest's Cavalry Corps, Department of Alabama, Mississippi and East Louisiana (February 18-ca. March 1865); brigadier general, CSA (March 1, 1865); and commanding brigade, Jackson's Division, Cavalry Corps, Department of Alabama, Mississippi and East Louisiana (ca. March-May 2, 1865). Following initial service in a staff position he was given charge of a regiment, which due to the lack of arms could not take the field until early 1862. At Shiloh he suffered a severe wound and following a lengthy recovery he found that he had not been reelected when his unit was reorganized on May 8, 1862. He served on Leonidas Polk's staff and then engaged in conscript and recruiting duties. While on the latter in July 1863 he was taken prisoner at Lexington, Tennessee. Apparent-

ly held for a year and a half before being exchanged, he served briefly as Nathan Bedford Forrest's inspector before taking charge of a mounted brigade until the Confederacy's demise. Returning to the legal profession, he lost a bid for the Democratic gubernatorial nomination in the postwar years.

CAMPBELL, John Archibald (1811-1889)

Although he had opposed secession, U.S. Supreme Court Justice John A. Campbell resigned to follow Alabama out of the Union and became the Confederacy's assistant secretary of war. The native of Georgia attended West Point for three years until the death of his father prompted his resignation. Taking up the practice of law, he spent two sessions in the Alabama legislature. A national reputation as a lawyer made him the choice of the other judges on the Supreme Court, and he was accordingly appointed to join them by Franklin Pierce on March 22, 1853, and then confirmed by a Senate voice vote three days later. In the *Dred Scott* case he ruled that since Scott was still a slave he was not a citizen and did not have the right to sue before a state or national court. Wishing to avoid war, he finally resigned on April 26, 1861, less than two weeks after Fort Sumter. Setting up a practice in New Orleans, he was appointed assistant secretary of war by Jefferson Davis on October 21, 1862. For the balance of the war his primary duties were related to the draft. In early 1865 he was one of three Confederate peace commissioners to meet with Lincoln and Secretary of State Seward in the Hampton Roads Peace Conference. At the close of the war he was confined for six months at Fort Pulaski. He then returned to the Crescent City and built a substantial practice. During the Tilden-Hayes presidential election dispute, he was one of Tilden's legal advisors. (Connor, Henry Groves, *John Archibald Campbell, Associate Justice of the United States Supreme Court*)

CAMPBELL, John Arthur (1823-1886)

The dreadful attrition rate in Stonewall Jackson's command during the campaigns of 1862 is exemplified by the case of John A. Campbell. He was the third commander of one of his brigades in a little over two months and he was destined to last two months himself. Having attended both the Virginia Military Institute and the state's secession convention put him in good stead to become an officer in the Confederate army. His assignments there included: colonel, 48th Virginia (September 1861); commanding 2nd Brigade, Valley District, Department of Northern Virginia (March 23-May 17, 1862); and commanding 2nd Brigade, Jackson's Division, Valley District, Department of Northern Virginia (May 17-25, 1862). Having commanded his regiment in the Cheat Mountain and Romney campaigns, he missed the battle of Kernstown but succeeded to the command of the brigade upon the wounding of Colonel Jesse S. Burks. Having led his new command at Front Royal, he moved on to Winchester where he was wounded at the side of Stonewall Jackson. Out of action until the fall, he resigned on October 16, 1862, out of resentment over the promotion of John R. Jones to brigadier general and Jones' assignment to command what Campbell felt was rightfully his brigade.

CANTEY, James (1818-1874)

Plagued by illness, Confederate General James Cantey was frequently absent from his various commands. The South Carolina native had practiced law and sat in the state legislature before serving as a second lieutenant of South Carolina infantry during the Mexican War. Unlike many volunteer officers in that conflict he saw action and was wounded. The veteran of the Palmetto Regiment then settled in Alabama where he lived as a planter until the outbreak of the Civil War. His assignments included: colonel, 15th Alabama (July 27, 1861); brigadier general, CSA (January 8, 1863); commanding Eastern Division, Department of the Gulf (early 1863-summer 1863); commanding 1st Brigade, Western Division, Department of the Gulf (summer-August 1863); commanding Mobile, Department of the Gulf (August-September 1863); commanding 1st Brigade, Department of the Gulf (September 1863-April 6, 1864); commanding 1st Brigade, District of the Gulf, Department of Alabama, Mississippi and East Louisiana (April 6-April 1864); commanding brigade, Army of Mississippi, Department of Alabama, Mississippi and East Louisiana (April-May 19, 1864); commanding brigade, French's Division, Polk's Corps (or Army of Mississippi), Army of Tennessee (May 19-May 1864); and commanding division, Polk's-Stewart's Corps, Army of Tennessee (May-June 1864). He led his regiment in the Shenandoah Valley and during the Seven Days under Stonewall Jackson but was absent during the fights at Cedar Mountain, 2nd Bull Run, Antietam, and Fredericksburg. Promoted to brigadier general, he was ordered to Mobile where he served for somewhat over a year before joining the Army of Tennessee for the Atlanta Campaign in the early stages of which he was in charge of a brigade and then a division. However, after June 1864 he does not appear to have commanded his division in any major action although it was engaged at Franklin, Nashville, and in the Carolinas. Following the surrender he returned to his plantation.

CAPERS, Ellison (1837-1908)

South Carolina Military Academy graduate Ellison Capers rose to the rank of brigadier general in the Confederate service and subsequently wrote the South Carolina volume of *Confederate Military History*. The native South Carolinian and 1857 graduate became a professor at his alma mater, with the rank of second lieutenant, two years later. He was engaged in these educational pursuits during the lengthy secession crisis, then offered his services. His assignments included: major, 1st South Carolina Rifles (fall 1860); lieutenant colonel, 24th South Carolina (April 1, 1862); colonel, 24th South Carolina (January 1864); commanding Gist's Brigade, Cheatham's Division, Hardee's Corps, Army of Tennessee (August-September 1864); brigadier general, CSA (March 1, 1865); and commanding Gist's (old) Brigade, Bate's Division, Cheatham's Corps, Army of Tennessee (ca. March 1865). As a field officer he witnessed the bombardment of Fort Sumter and for a time served in northern Virginia before becoming second in command of a regiment enlisted for the war. With this unit he served mostly on the South Carolina coast—seeing action at Secessionville—

until ordered to join Joseph E. Johnston in Mississippi in an attempt to relieve the pressure on Vicksburg. During these operations he was wounded at Jackson while commanding the regiment. Joining Bragg's army he succeeded to command again at Chickamauga and was again wounded. His regiment fought at Chattanooga and he was made its permanent commander early in 1864. During the Atlanta Campaign he commanded Gist's brigade for a time and later was wounded again at Franklin. Promoted to brigadier general, he led the brigade briefly in the Carolinas and apparently was captured at Bentonville. Following the war he rose to a high position in the Episcopal Church and also engaged in educational and veterans' affairs.

CAPERTON, Allen Taylor (1810-1876)

Originally a Unionist, Allen T. Caperton used his seat in the Confederate Senate to fight against those government policies that he felt were making the Confederacy's fight for independence a rich man's war and a poor man's fight. A lawyer and planter in west Virginia, Caperton had served for a decade in both houses of the state legislature before attending the Virginia secession convention where he opposed immediate secession—until Lincoln made a call for troops on Virginia to fight the rest of the South. With the death of Senator William B. Preston in November 1862, Caperton became one of five candidates for the vacant seat. After 20 ballots he took his seat on January 26, 1863. A personal animosity toward President Davis colored his voting record. From his position as chairman of the Committee on Accounts he fought for the maintenance of a strong internal economy, not willing to let it be sacrificed to the military effort. He fought Davis' policies on the land tax, the draft, the suspension of the writ of habeas corpus, foreign policy, and, albeit too late, the arming of slaves. He was a constant critic of Davis' cabinet appointees. After the war he was instrumental in developing the resources of the new state of West Virginia, serving as its senator in the 1870s. He was also an official of the James River and Kanawha Canal.

CARRINGTON, Isaac Howell (1827-1887)

When shortly after the close of the Civil War Major Isaac H. Carrington was arrested by the Federal authorities, he was able to prove, through a complete records file, that he was innocent of any wrongdoing in the disposition of monies belonging to prisoners of war. A native of Richmond, he was a lawyer when he accepted a commission as major, 38th Virginia, in June 1861. After service on the Manassas lines during the winter and later on the Peninsula, he failed to gain reelection in the spring reorganization. He was, however, kept in grade and in July 1863 was assigned to duty as a commissioner dealing with matters pertaining to prisoners of war. He later served as a provost marshal for the city of Richmond from February 1864 through the city's fall. During this time some funds taken from Union prisoners were deposited with him. He kept a complete file of the orders under which he made any disbursements from these monies. Thus any shortfall was due to his superiors. He was promptly released from arrest when this became clear. During the final stages of the war he attempted to find a route out of Richmond for the treasury funds of the dying nation. After the war he resided in Richmond and presumably practiced law.

CARROLL, William Henry (ca. 1810-1868)

On the day before his division commander, George B. Crittenden, was arrested on charges of drunkenness, Confederate General William H. Carroll was himself arrested on that same charge plus those of incompetence and neglect of duty. A planter and postmaster before the war, the Tennessee native was also active in the state militia. His Confederate assignments included: brigadier general, Tennessee Militia (prewar); inspector general, Provisional Army of Tennessee (May 9, 1861); colonel, 1st East Tennessee Rifles (October 1861); brigadier general, CSA (October 26, 1861); commanding 2nd Brigade, District of East Tennessee, Department #2 (January-February 23, 1862); and commanding 1st Brigade, 2nd (Crittenden's) Division, Army of Central Kentucky, Department #2 (February 23-March 31, 1862). Following service in organizing the state forces he took command of a regiment from East Tennessee, which was later designated the 7th Tennessee, Provisional Army, and the 37th Tennessee. Within days he was named a Confederate brigadier general and eventually was given a brigade in East Tennessee. This he led at Mill Springs where he came in for his share of the criticism for the defeat there. While commanding his brigade under William J. Hardee he was relieved and placed under arrest on the above-mentioned charges. Following a court of inquiry he resigned on February 1, 1863, and joined his exile family in Canada. In the remaining five years of his life he never returned to the United States.

CARSWELL, Reuben W. (1828-1886)

Worn out by campaigning in Virginia, Reuben W. Carswell returned to his native Georgia and fought in its defense as a militia general. His assignments included: lieutenant, Company C, 20th Georgia (June 14, 1861); captain, Company E, 48th Georgia (March 1862); lieutenant colonel, 48th Georgia (March 22, 1862); brigadier general, Georgia Militia (May 1864); and commanding 1st Brigade, 1st Division, Georgia Militia (May 1864-early 1865). After service on the Manassas line with his first company, Carswell became a field officer in a new regiment with which he saw action during the Seven Days. Next the unit fought at 2nd Bull Run and Antietam. At Chancellorsville he distinguished himself while in command of the regiment. Some time after this he left the unit and while in Georgia was made a general of militia. He commanded a brigade in the Atlanta Campaign. While opposing Sherman's March to the Sea, he resigned his commission in the 48th Georgia on November 12, 1864. He was also involved in the defense of Savannah.

CARTER, John Carpenter (1837-1864)

Serving through most of the battles of what was to become the Army of Tennessee, John C. Carter became one of six Confederate generals to be fatally struck during the suicidal attack at Franklin. The native of Georgia was a Memphis attorney when the war broke out; he soon enlisted in the Southern army where his assignments included: captain, Company B, 38th Tennessee (September 23, 1861); colonel, 38th Tennessee (May 1862); commanding Wright's (old) Brigade, Cheatham's Division, Hardee's Corps, Army of Tennessee (spring-September 1864); brigadier general, CSA (July 7, 1864); and commanding Maney's (old) Brigade, Brown's Division, Cheatham's Corps, Army of Tennessee (September-November 30, 1864). Leading his company at Shiloh, he seized the regimental colors and was later wounded. He returned in time to fight at Perryville and Murfreesboro and take part in the Tullahoma Campaign. At Chickamauga he led a field consolidation of the 38th Tennessee and Murray's 22nd Tennessee Battalion. Carter's regiment was detached at Charleston, Tennessee, during the fight at Chattanooga and was cut off from the army when Bragg's forces werre compelled to retire. Moving into East Tennessee they eventually rejoined the Army of Tennessee in time for the Atlanta Campaign during which Carter was named a brigadier general, having led a brigade throughout. After the fall of the city he was given charge of another brigade, which he led into middle Tennessee with Hood. In the assaults of November 30, 1864, at Franklin he fell mortally wounded. He died on December 10th, not far from the battlefield.

CARTER, Thomas Hill (1831-1908)

Educated at the Virginia Military Institute, Virginian Thomas H. Carter put his skills to good use as one of the senior artillerists in Lee's army. His assignments included: captain, King William Artillery (June 1, 1861); major, Artillery (to rank from December 12, 1862); commanding Artillery Brigade, D.H. Hill's-Rodes' Division, 2nd Corps, Army of Northern Virginia (early 1863-July 1863); lieutenant colonel, Artillery (March 2, 1863); commanding artillery battalion, 2nd Corps, Army of Northern Virginia (July 1863-spring 1864); commanding artillery division, 2nd Corps, Army of Northern Virginia (spring 1864-September 2, 1864 and March-April 9, 1865); colonel, Artillery (February 27, 1864); chief of artillery, Valley District, Department of Northern Virginia (ca. September 2-late October 1864 and November 1864-January 1865); and commanding artillery battalion, Valley District, Department of Northern Virginia (late October-November 1864). Commanding his battery, he distinguished himself at Seven Pines and fought at the Seven Days, Antietam, and Fredericksburg. After being promoted, he commanded a battalion at Chancellorsville and Gettysburg. He directed a pair of artillery battalions through the Overland Campaign. After service on the Petersburg front, he was sent to join Early in the Valley and soon was serving as his artillery chief in the absence of General Long. He saw action at Cedar Creek, following which many of his guns were captured by Union cavalry. Returning east in the early part of 1865, he commanded a group of battalions on the Richmond front and finally surrendered at Appomattox. He was a doctor and farmer after the war. (Wise, Jennings. C., *The Long Arm of Lee*)

CARUTHERS, Robert Looney (1800-1882)

Due to the federal occupation of the state of Tennessee, Robert L. Caruthers was never able to take up his gubernatorial duties. A native Tennesseean, Caruthers had a distinguished antebellum career as lawyer, legislative clerk, judicial clerk, journalist, state's attorney, state legislator, educator, and congressman. At the outbreak of the Civil War, he had been serving on the Tennessee supreme court for nine years. Although a long-time secessionist, he attended the Washington peace convention. This having failed, he was appointed to represent Tennessee's 5th District in the Provisional Confederate Congress. Serving on the Committee on the Judiciary, he proved to be, when present, a supporter of the administration's program. He lost the race for the Senate of the First Regular Congress on the 32nd ballot in October 1861. For some reason he did not attend the sessions of the Provisional Congress in the first two months of 1862. In 1863 Caruthers was elected governor to succeed the also-exiled Isham G. Harris, who, however, continued to exercise the limited powers of an exiled governor when it was found impossible to inaugurate the new governor. Meanwhile, Andrew Johnson was serving as Union military governor in Nashville. Following the war, Caruthers became a law professor at Cumberland University.

CARY, Hetty (1836-1892)

To much of the Confederacy, Hetty Cary was the epitome of Southern womanhood, and it is perhaps appropriate that she suffered the fate of so many Southern women—widowhood. Born near Baltimore she belonged to an old Virginia family related to the Jeffersons and Randolphs. A firm supporter of secession she was eventually forced either to leave Baltimore or face imprisonment. After visiting the troops at Manassas Junction and a short stay in Charlottesville, she settled in Richmond with her sister, Jennie, and her cousin Constance. The trio immediately became part of the capital's social life, and Hetty was considered by many to be the most beautiful belle in the country. For the next three years she was involved in patriotic work and attracted the attention of many military figures. Finally, one of Lee's division commanders, General John Pegram, won her hand, and they were married on January 19, 1865, in a ceremony that was one of the highlights of a dismal winter. Joining her new husband's headquarters on the lines around Petersburg, she became very popular with his men. Three days after a triumphant review of the division, Pegram was killed in the battle of Hatcher's Run on February 5, 1865. No one had the heart to tell the widow, so his body was brought back to his quarters and she was brought down to see it. Exactly three weeks after the wedding the Pegrams were back at St. Paul's Church for the funeral. Returning to Baltimore after the war, Hetty Pegram was arrested, but General Grant ordered her release with an apology. She later taught and toured Europe and remarried in 1879.

CARY, Richard Milton (ca. 1824-1886)

When in the spring of 1862 the Confederate one-year regiments were reorganized, they were given the opportunity of electing new officers. This was very disruptive to the command structure and many commanders opposed it, including Richard M. Cary. A Richmond lawyer, he had been active in military affairs before the war and promptly entered the service when the war began. His assignments included: captain, 1st Virginia (early 1861); colonel, 30th Virginia (June 13, 1861); lieutenant, Artillery (June 4, 1862); captain, Artillery (March 26, 1863); and major, Artillery (September 10, 1863). After commanding his regiment in the Aquia District and the Department of North Carolina, he refused to stand for reelection on principle. He was elected over his protests but declined to serve. Thus a qualified regimental commander, who had penned an infantry drill manual, was lost to the service. Two months later, in June 1862, he accepted assignment as a lieutenant and was detailed to ordnance duty. Receiving two promotions, he continued in this duty for the remainder of the conflict. Settling in England after the war, he was in the tobacco and cotton business.

CAWTHORN, James (?-1861)

The battle of Wilson's Creek, although relatively small when compared to later engagements, was nonetheless devastating to the officer corps of the Missouri State Guard. Having joined up at the beginning of the conflict, Colonel James Cawthorn was commanding the 2nd (Cavalry) Brigade, 2nd Division during the early part of August 1861. At Wilson's Creek on the 10th he dismounted his troopers and held his position throughout the fight, mostly unsupported by infantry. His unit paid a price for this action—87 casualties, including their mortally wounded commander.

CEVER, Charles (?-?)

A veteran balloonist before the Civil War, Captain Charles Cever donated his skills to the Confederate cause. Working in Charleston, he accumulated silk frocks from the patriotic ladies of the city. Piecing them together, he constructed the second Confederate balloon. It was shipped, already inflated, to the Richmond area and placed on board the *Teaser*. Moving downriver on its first mission in the aerial service, the vessel ran aground and Cever's balloon was captured by the USS *Monitor* and USS *Maratanza*.

CHALMERS, James Ronald (1831-1898)

Following up his membership in the Mississippi secession convention, Virginia-born lawyer James R. Chalmers served as a brigadier general in both the Confederate infantry and cavalry. His assignments included: captain, Infantry (March 1861); colonel, 9th Mississippi (April 1861); brigadier general, CSA (February 13, 1862); commanding 2nd Brigade, 1st Corps, 2nd Grand Division, Army of the Mississippi (March 29-late June 1862); commanding 2nd Brigade, Reserve Corps, Army of the Mississippi (late June-July 2, 1862); commanding 2nd Brigade, Reserve Division, Army of the Mississippi (July 2-August 15, 1862); commanding 2nd Brigade, Withers' Division, Right Wing, Army of the Mississippi (August 15-

November 20, 1862); commanding 2nd Brigade, Withers' Division, Polk's Corps, Army of Tennessee (November 20-December 31, 1862); commanding 5th Military District, Department of Mississippi and East Louisiana (April-summer 1863); commanding cavalry brigade, Department of Mississippi and East Louisiana (summer-October 18, 1863); commanding cavalry division, Department of Mississippi and East Louisiana (October 18-November 1863); commanding division, Lee's Cavalry Corps, Department of Mississippi and East Louisiana (November 1863-January 11, 1864); commanding division, Forrest's Cavalry Corps, Department of Mississippi and East Louisiana (January 11-28, 1864); and commanding division, Forrest's Cavalry Corps, Department of Alabama, Mississippi and East Louisiana (January 28, 1864-May 4, 1865). Initially stationed at Pensacola, he was promoted to brigadier general and was part of the Confederate buildup at Corinth, Mississippi, just before Shiloh. He led his brigade at that battle and during the Union drive on the Confederate base at Corinth. He was engaged against Philip H. Sheridan's cavalry at Booneville and then took part in Bragg's Kentucky Campaign. On the last day of the year he was severely wounded in the head at Murfreesboro in the fighting for the Round Forest. Upon his recovery he was assigned to district command in Mississippi. He led a cavalry brigade and then a division in the northern part of the state. Early in 1864 he joined Nathan Bedford Forrest's command and fought at Tupelo and faced Andrew J. Smith's August 1864 invasion of the state. He was also engaged on some of Forrest's raids. Cooperating with Hood's forces in middle Tennessee, he was present at Nashville, and he ended his Civil War career facing Wilson's raid through Alabama and Georgia. In the postwar years he served three terms in Congress and then resumed his legal practice.

CHAMBERS, Henry Cousins (1823-1871)

Coming from the Southern plantation society and its acceptance of violence, Henry C. Chambers used a novel method to get himself elected to the First Regular Congress—he killed his opponent. The Alabama-born Chambers, after graduating from Princeton College, settled in Mississippi, enjoying the life of a substantial planter. At the outbreak of the war he was serving in the state legislature. In October 1861 he ran for the Confederate House from Mississippi's 4th District, along the Mississippi River. The race became heated, and Chambers provoked a duel with his opponent, William A. Lake. With rifles at 50 paces, Lake died. Chambers was unopposed in 1863. Taking his seat in February 1862, Chambers served on the Committees on Commerce; Enrolled Bills; Flag and Seal; and Military Affairs. He favored impressment as a means of supplying the army and opposed the idea of local defense, preferring stronger armies in the field. Thus he exhibited a strong centralist tendency. He did, however, oppose the arming of the slaves. He returned to farming after the war.

CHAMBLISS, John Randolph, Sr. (1809-1875)

Although a late convert to secession, in April 1861, John R.

Chambliss proved to be an active supporter of the war for independence in his one term in the Confederate Congress. A Virginia native, Chambliss held numerous nonelective public offices and as a delegate to the Virginia constitutional conventions was at first a Unionist. Elected in November 1861 from southeastern Virginia's 2nd District, he took his seat in the First Confederate Congress in February 1862. Here he served on the Committee on Naval Affairs. Initially opposed to the draft, he later worked to tighten up the list of exemptions. He favored giving the War Department a freer hand in determining army organization and was willing to allow the central government extensive control over the country's economy. He did, however, resist the extension of the suspension of the writ of habeas corpus. In 1863 he dropped out of the race for reelection. Impoverished after the war, he worked to improve the county's police and economic base. His son was Brigadier General John R. Chambliss, Jr.

CHAMBLISS, John Randolph, Jr. (1833-1864)

The son of Confederate congressman John R. Chambliss, Sr., West Pointer (1853) John R. Chambliss, Jr., remained in the mounted rifles for less than a year before resigning. Later, he left his Virginia plantation to join the Confederacy. He had long been active in the militia and as such was an aide to the governor. When he transferred to Confederate service his assignments included: colonel, 41st Virginia (July 1861); colonel, 13th Virginia Cavalry (July 1862); commanding W.H.F. Lee's Brigade, Cavalry Division, Army of Northern Virginia (June 9-September 9, 1863); commanding W.H.F. Lee's Brigade, F. Lee's Division, Cavalry Corps, same army (September 9, 1863-ca. April 23, 1864); brigadier general, CSA (December 19, 1863); and commanding brigade, W.H.F. Lee's Division, Cavalry Corps, same army (ca. April 23-August 16, 1864). After service in the infantry, near Norfolk and on the Peninsula, Chambliss was transferred to the head of a newly formed cavalry regiment. Initially this unit served along the Rappahannock River with other troops, all under his command. Becoming a part of the Army of Northern Virginia, it fought at Fredericksburg and opposed Stoneman's raid during the Chancellorsville Campaign. He succeeded the wounded "Rooney" Lee in brigade command at Brandy Station and led the unit at Aldie, Middleburg, Gettysburg, and in the Bristoe Campaign. Promoted to brigadier on a permanent basis and with the brigade shifted to "Rooney" Lee's newly created division, he fought through the Overland Campaign and was killed in fighting at Deep Bottom near Richmond on August 16, 1864. (Freeman, Douglas S., *Lee's Lieutenants*)

CHAPMAN, Conrad Wise (1842-1910)

Although Conrad Chapman had left the Old Dominion when only six years old, he returned from his family's home in Rome to join the Virginia forces and become the Confederate artist of the Charleston defenses. Unable to get to Virginia from New York, Chapman ended up as a private in Company D, 3rd Kentucky, enlisting on September 30, 1861. He soon resumed his painting and his comrades began calling the accented eccentric "Old Rome." On the second day at Shiloh, Chapman was severely wounded in the head and upon his recovery joined Company A, 46th Virginia, by the request of General Henry A. Wise and the urging of Wise's close friend, Conrad's father, John G. Chapman. Conrad Chapman served in Virginia from September 1862 until the next year when Wise's Brigade was transferred to the Charleston defenses. Wise suggested that Chapman, who had become a professional artist, under his artist father's tutorship, be detailed to depict Charleston fortifications. Chapman began a comprehensive study, often under enemy fire, until March 1864, when he returned to Italy on furlough to visit his ill mother. Failing to rejoin his command before the collapse of the Confederacy, and having landed in Texas, Chapman joined those ex-Confederates who went to Mexico to join Maximilian. After the war he completed his sketches and continued to work, often in poverty, in Rome, Paris, London, New York, and Mexico before settling in Virginia, where he continued to work until his death.

CHAPMAN, William Henry (1840-1929)

As second-in-command to Confederate partisan leader John S. Mosby, William Henry Chapman was the man who arranged the meeting of that leader with Union General Hancock, which led to the disbandment—but not the surrender—of the partisans at the war's close. A native of Virginia, he lived in Fauquier County, which would become part of "Mosby's Confederacy." His Confederate assignments included: lieutenant, Monroe "Dixie" (Va.) Artillery (June 21, 1861); captain, Monroe "Dixie" (Va.) Artillery (December 8, 1861); captain, Company C, 43rd Virginia Cavalry Battalion (December 7, 1863); and lieutenant colonel, Mosby's (Va.) Cavalry Regiment (December 7, 1864). As an artillery battery commander, he fought at the Seven Days, 2nd Bull Run, and Antietam before his command was consolidated with other units in October 1862. Made a supernumerary by this action, he served as a recruiting officer until given charge of a company in Mosby's command. Operating behind Union lines, it was highly disruptive of Union communications. When the battalion was increased to a regiment, Chapman became its lieutenant colonel. He met with Hancock after Lee's surrender to arrange the Mosby meeting; Chapman himself was paroled at Winchester on April 22, 1865. After the war he worked for the revenue service in various cities. (Jones, Virgil Carrington, *Gray Ghosts and Rebel Raiders*)

CHEATHAM, Benjamin Franklin (1820-1886)

Serving throughout the Civil War in what would become the Confederate Army of Tennessee, Tennesseean Benjamin F. Cheatham proved himself to be a highly capable commander at brigade through corps level. A farmer, he had served as a captain in the 1st Tennessee and as the colonel of the 3rd Tennessee during the Mexican War. Active in the state militia during the interwar years, he was one of the state's senior officers during the

period before it merged its forces into the Confederate army. His Civil War assignments included: major general, Tennessee Militia (prewar); brigadier general, Provisional Army of Tennessee (May 9, 1861); brigadier general, CSA (July 9, 1861); commanding 1st Brigade, 1st Geographical Division, Department #2 (September 7-October 24, 1861); commanding 2nd Division, 1st Geographical Division, Department #2 (October 24, 1861-March 9, 1862); major general, CSA (March 10, 1862); commanding 2nd Division, 1st Corps, Army of the Mississippi (March 29-July 2, 1862); commanding 1st Division, Army of the Mississippi (July 2-August 15, 1862); commanding division, Right Wing, Army of the Mississippi (August 15-November 20, 1862); commanding division, Polk's-Hardee's Corps, Army of Tennessee (November 20, 1862-October 23, 1863, January-July, and September-October 1864); commanding the corps (October 23-November 1863 and October 1864-April 9, 1865); and commanding division, Hardee's (new) Corps, Army of Tennessee (April 9-26, 1865). He led a division at Belmont and Shiloh, where he was wounded, and during the defense of Corinth, Mississippi. Having been promoted to major general before Shiloh, he fought as a division commander temporarily in charge of the wing at Perryville and later at Murfreesboro. After participating in the Tullahoma Campaign he fought in the Confederate victory at Chickamauga. Absent at Chattanooga—the one major action of the army that he missed—he returned for the Atlanta Campaign. When William J. Hardee left the army due to conflicts with Braxton Bragg, Cheatham took over the corps for the invasion of middle Tennessee. Just before the fight at Franklin the Confederates lost an opportunity to destroy a large portion of John M. Schofield's Union forces at Spring Hill. Instead of attacking, the enemy was allowed to slip by unmolested. Recriminations followed as Hood focused on Cheatham, who retaliated in kind. Most historians believe that the facts are on Cheatham's side. In any event Cheatham went on to fight at Nashville and shortly thereafter Hood asked to be relieved. Cheatham then went on to the Carolinas where in the April 9, 1865 reorganization and consolidation he was reduced to command of a division. This he led until the surrender near Durham Station, North Carolina. He then returned to his farm and briefly entered politics as an unsuccessful congressional candidate. He was later a prison official and postmaster.

CHESNUT, James, Jr. (1815-1885)

Although less well-known than his wife and her diary, James Chesnut, Jr., held several important posts in the Confederacy. A lawyer and former state legislator, he resigned a seat in the U.S. Congress on November 10, 1860, more than a month before the secession of his native South Carolina, to help move the state in that direction. At the secession convention he was one of the authors of the ordinance itself. Named to the Provisional Confederate Congress, he sat on the Committees on Naval Affairs and Territories. A product of the plantation society to which his father belonged, he advocated the legalization of the internationally prohibited African slave trade. During the recess between the first and second sessions he served, as an aide-de-camp to Beauregard, at the bombardment of Fort Sumter and later at 1st Bull Run. As a colonel, he served on the president's staff. The next year, as a member of his state's executive council, he was charged with the organization of the militia, but resigned this post to rejoin the chief executive. His later military assignments included: brigadier general, CSA (April 23, 1864); commanding brigade of reserves and militia, Department of South Carolina, Georgia and Florida (December 1864-January 1865); and commanding same brigade, McLaws' Division, same department (early January 1865). Sent to organize the reserve forces in his native state, he took a brigade to Georgia to participate in the Savannah Campaign but soon returned to his administrative duties. Following the South's collapse he was active in ending carpetbag rule.

CHESNUT, Mary Boykin (1823-1886)

Deservedly so, Mary Boykin Chesnut is the best known of Civil War diarists. Born into the South Carolina plantation aristocracy, as Mary Boykin Miller, she was married at 17 to a prominent lawyer and plantation owner, James Chesnut, Jr. Her husband's position in the Confederate government, as congressman, general and aide to Jefferson Davis, brought Mary into the inner social circles of the Confederacy, and she was active in politics. On February 15, 1861, she began her famous diary and continued it throughout the war. Her high connections in both the civilian and military sectors and her gossipy nature make for informative and interesting reading. She never got over the defeat of the South, and the couple lost much of their fortune in the war. She lived on for another two decades, trying to rebuild a part of their lives in the style of the antebellum period and revising her war diary. (Woodward, C. Van, *Mary Chesnut's Civil War*)

CHEVES, Langdon (1814-1863)

An engineering officer, Captain Langdon Cheves overcame the shortages of virtually everything in the Confederacy and constructed the first Southern balloon. Born and raised in Philadelphia, he went to college in South Carolina and for a time at the U.S. Military Academy. A lawyer, he married into the Southern plantation society. Becoming active in politics as a Democrat, he attended the secession convention of his adopted state. As an aide to General Thomas F. Drayton at Port Royal he took part in the defense of Forts Walker and Beauregard. For the next year and a half he worked on the fortifications on the coast, principally at Charleston and Savannah. While in the latter city he built a patchwork silk balloon that was sent to Virginia to observe the enemy's movements. On July 10, 1863, he was killed by a shell fragment from one of the monitors firing on Morris Island in Charleston Harbor.

CHEW, Robert Stanard (1828-1886)

A Fredericksburg physician turned field officer in Pickett's Division, Robert S. Chew may have survived the Civil War only because he was lucky enough to have served in the one brigade of the division that was not present at Gettysburg. His assignments included: captain, Company B, 30th Virginia (April 22, 1861); lieutenant colonel, 30th Virginia (April 19, 1862); colonel, 30th Virginia (November 5, 1864); and commanding Corse's Brigade, Pickett's Division, 1st Corps, Army of Northern Virginia (briefly in 1864). He served with his regiment in the Aquia District and the Department of North Carolina and during the Seven Days Battles. At Antietam he was in command of the regiment and was wounded. After service at Fredericksburg, the unit served in southeastern Virginia and was guarding Hanover Junction during the Gettysburg Campaign. Thus Chew missed the disastrous charge in which most of the division's field grade officers were cut down. He next served in western Virginia and back in the Department of North Carolina while most of the corps was off in Georgia and Tennessee with Longstreet. He took part in the initial defense of Petersburg before joining Lee at the North Anna and fighting at Cold Harbor. Returning to Petersburg, he took part in the siege of the town and part of the time was in command of the brigade. He surrendered with his regiment at Appomattox.

CHEW, Roger Preston (1843-1921)

Virginian Roger P. Chew raised and commanded the first Confederate horse artillery battery. After receiving some military education at the Virginia Military Institute just prior to the outbreak of the war, he held the following positions: captain, Ashby (Va.) Horse Artillery (September 1861); major, Artillery (February 27, 1864); executive officer, Horse Artillery Battalion, Cavalry Corps, Army of Northern Virginia (March 19-April 29, 1864); commanding Horse Artillery, Cavalry Corps, Army of Northern Virginia (April 29, 1864-April 9, 1865); and lieutenant colonel, Artillery (February 18, 1865). His unit was raised with the intention that it should serve with Turner Ashby's cavalry in the Shenandoah Valley. Thus Chew saw action at Kernstown and in the Shenandoah Valley Campaign before the death of his commander. Joining Lee's army in 1862, he took part in the actions at 2nd Bull Run, Antietam, Fredericksburg, Chancellorsville, Gettysburg, and in the Bristoe and Mine Run campaigns. Promoted to chief of the cavalry's guns, he served through the Wilderness, Petersburg, and Appomattox campaigns before the surrender of the latter. In time Jeb Stuart, shortly before his death, came to the conclusion that Chew was a fitting successor to "The Gallant Pelham." After the war Chew returned to the Valley and served three terms in the state legislature. (Wise, Jennings C., *The Long Arm of Lee*)

CHILTON, Robert Hall (1815-1879)

Frustrated in his ambitions for promotion, Virginia native Robert H. Chilton left Lee's staff and took a desk post in Richmond. The West Pointer (1837) had been posted to the dragoons with a brief stint in the quartermaster's branch. He saw frontier service and won a brevet in the Mexican War. In 1854 he transferred to the pay department and resigned his commission as a major on April 29, 1861. His Confederate assignments included: lieutenant colonel and assistant adjutant general, CSA (spring 1861); chief of staff, Army of Northern Virginia (June 4, 1862-April 1, 1864); and brigadier general, CSA (October 20, 1862). Joining Lee's staff days after Lee took over command of the Army of Northern Virginia, Chilton soon became its head. As such he served during the Seven Days and at 2nd Bull Run, Antietam, Fredericksburg, Chancellorsville, Gettysburg, and during the Bristoe and Mine Run campaigns. Named a brigadier general in the fall of 1862, he suffered a loss of rank when the Senate refused to confirm the appointment on April 11, 1863. Reverting to the rank of lieutenant colonel, he continued to serve for another year, but on April 1, 1864, his request for relief from field duty was granted and he spent the balance of the war in Richmond as an inspector. Settling in Georgia after Appomattox, he ran a manufacturing firm.

CHILTON, William Paris (1810-1871)

Serving through all three of the Confederate congresses, Alabama's 6th District representative, William P. Chilton, held an unusually high number of committee chairmanships and was considered one of the more hard working members of the legislative branch. Born in Kentucky, Chilton studied law in Tennessee and subsequently settled in Alabama. Active in Whig politics, he served in the state legislature and was unsuccessful in a bid for a seat in the U.S. House of Representatives. Appointed to the state's supreme court in 1847, he was its chief justice for the last four years of his tenure. He retired to private practice in 1856. At the beginning of the Civil War he was again in public office, having been elected to the state legislature's upper house in 1859. A convert to secessionism, he was named to the Provisional Congress and he remained in the legislature until the end of the Confederacy. Throughout the war he was chairman of the Committee on Post Offices and Post Roads. In the First Regular Congress he also chaired the Committee on the Quartermaster's and Commissary Departments and in the Second Congress the Committee on the Flag and Seal. Being very industrious, he was rewarded with additional committee appointments including the committees on: Buildings (Provisional Congress); Printing (Provisional Congress); Patents (Provisional Congress); the Judiciary (Second Congress); and Rules and Officers (Second Congress). His oratory attracted visitors to the galleries. A strong supporter of the war effort, he was accused of wanting to raise the black flag—fighting to the bitter end, with no prisoners. After the war he rebuilt his law practice and recouped much of his wartime losses.

CHISOLM, John Julian (1830-1903)

At the outbreak of the war Charleston physician and surgeon, John J. Chisolm wrote the guide for untrained field surgeons, *Manual of Military Surgery*. A native of South Carolina, he received his medical education there as well as in London and Paris. At the outbreak of the war he was a professor at the South Carolina Medical College. As a military surgeon he was present at Fort Sumter and then went into the production of the necessary medicines for the war effort. After the war he returned

to the field of medical education. (Cunningham, Horace Herndon, *Doctors in Gray*)

CHURCHILL, Thomas James (1824-1905)

Kentucky-born lawyer Thomas J. Churchill, serving most of the war west of the Mississippi River, rose to the rank of Confederate major general in its final months. After practicing in his native state he served as a first lieutenant of Kentucky cavalry during the Mexican War. Thereafter he was an Arkansas planter and was Little Rock's postmaster when secession came. His assignments included: colonel, 1st Arkansas Mounted Rifles (June 9, 1861); brigadier general, CSA (March 4, 1862); commanding cavalry brigade, Trans-Mississippi Division, Department #2 (ca. March-April 15, 1862); commanding 2nd Brigade, McCown's Division, Army of the West, Department #2 (April 15-June 27, 1862); commanding 2nd Brigade, McCown's Division, Department of East Tennessee (June 27-ca. September 1862); commanding division, Division of Arkansas, Trans-Mississippi Department (January-January 11, 1863); commanding brigade, Price's Division, District of Arkansas, Trans-Mississippi Department (ca. January-March 24, 1864); commanding 1st (Arkansas) Division, District of Arkansas, Trans-Mississippi Department (March 24-April 1, mid-April-early August, and August 4-late August 1864); commanding Detachment, District of Arkansas, District of West Louisiana, Trans-Mississippi (April 1-mid-April 1864); commanding District of Arkansas, Trans-Mississippi Department (August-August 4, 1864); commanding 1st (Arkansas) Division, 2nd Corps (or District of Arkansas), Trans-Mississippi Department (September 1864-May 26, 1865); and major general, CSA (March 18, 1865). He led his regiment at Wilson's Creek and Pea Ridge and was then promoted to brigadier general and assigned to command a cavalry brigade, which he led across the Mississippi to Corinth. There he took charge of an infantry brigade and took part in the siege of Corinth. Early that summer he was transferred with the rest of the division to East Tennessee and went on the invasion of Kentucky, fighting at Richmond. Shortly thereafter he was relieved and was commanding at Fort Hindman or Arkansas Post when he was forced to surrender to John. A. McClernand early in 1863. Following his release he led two divisions in the Red River Campaign and then one division at Jenkins' Ferry against Steele's drive against Camden, Arkansas. He finished out the war in division command in Arkansas.

CLANTON, James Holt (1827-1871)

Although he was killed six years after the end of the Civil War, Confederate General James H. Clanton was just as much a casualty of that conflict as those who fell on the field of battle. Born in Georgia, he entered upon the practice of law in Alabama. A state legislator, he was a Unionist until the last moment. In 1860 he backed the presidential bid of John Bell on the Constitutional Union ticket. Joining the Confederacy, his assignments included: captain, Company K, 1st Alabama Cavalry (1861); colonel, 1st Alabama Cavalry (March 18, 1862 to rank from December 3, 1861) brigadier general, CSA

(November 16, 1863); commanding 2nd Brigade, Department of the Gulf (ca. November 1863-early 1864); aide-de-camp, Polk's Corps (Army of Mississippi), Army of Tennessee (spring 1864); commanding cavalry brigade, District of Central and Northern Alabama, Department of Alabama, Mississippi and East Louisiana (summer-September 24, 1864); commanding brigade, District of Central Alabama, Department of Alabama, Mississippi and East Louisiana (September 24-late November 1864); and commanding brigade, District of the Gulf, Department of Alabama, Mississippi and East Louisiana (early 1865-March 25, 1865). He led his regiment at Shiloh but the terrain gave the cavalry little opportunity for action. Later he took part in the defense of Corinth, Mississippi, and fought at Farmington and Booneville. Promoted to brigadier general, he led a brigade in various parts of Alabama. During the early stages of the Atlanta Campaign he was Leonidas Polk's aide and, after the corps commander's death, returned to his brigade. While serving in the District of the Gulf he was wounded at Bluff Spring, Florida, on March 25, 1865, and shortly thereafter he was taken prisoner. Released at the end of the war, he resumed his legal and political career until assassinated by an ex-Union officer "under the influence."

CLARK, Charles (1811-1877)

Invalided out of the army, Charles Clark became the last Confederate governor of Mississippi. A planter and politician on the state level, he had served during the Mexican War as colonel, 2nd Mississippi, but had not seen any action. Upon the secession of his adopted state—he was Ohio-born and Kentucky-educated—he entered its service and later that of the Confederacy. His assignments included: brigadier general, Army of Mississippi (early 1861); major general, Army of Mississippi (April 15, 1862); brigadier general, CSA (May 22, 1861); commanding Longstreet's (old) Brigade, Longstreet's Division in the 1st Corps, Army of the Potomac (October 14-22, 1861) and in the Potomac District, Department of Northern Virginia (October 22-November 2, 1861); commanding independent brigade, Central Army of Kentucky, Department #2, (November 1861-February 1862); commanding 1st Division, 1st Corps, Army of the Mississippi (March 12-April 6 and April 8-July 1862); and commanding 1st Division, Breckinridge's Command, District of the Mississippi, Department #2 (July-August 5, 1862). After initial service in Tennessee, Virginia, and Kentucky, he was wounded on the first day at Shiloh but returned to duty in a matter of days. Transferred farther south, he was wounded and captured in the unsuccessful attack on Baton Rouge. Exchanged in February 1863, he was so crippled that he had to use crutches for the rest of his years and resigned his commission on October 31. Earlier that month he had been elected governor and served through the Confederacy's collapse when he was removed by the Union authorities despite his urging compliance with the laws of the occupation. After his release from prison he resumed his law practice.

CLARK, Henry Toole (1808-1874)

A non-elected governor of North Carolina, Henry T. Clark had a great deal of difficulty in gaining support in the face of the Confederate defeats along the coast in early 1862. A native of the state, he had been admitted to the bar but was never active in the profession. Instead he entered politics in 1840, winning the position of court clerk. Ten years later he was a state senator and was that body's speaker from 1858. With the death of Governor John W. Ellis on July 7, 1861, Clark succeeded to the gubernatorial post. An effective organizer, he established military districts within his domain and arranged for the overseas purchase of arms and equipment. Since his senate term had expired an attempt was made by William W. Holden to oust him from the state house. Declining reelection, he left office on September 8, 1862, at the expiration of Ellis' term and returned to his plantation. Not having been pardoned by the Union occupation, he was refused his seat in the state senate in 1865 when elected to that post. He then retired from politics. (Wheeler, John, *Reminiscences and Memoirs of North Carolina and North Carolinians*)

CLARK, John Bullock, Sr. (1802-1885)

Because of his personality, John B. Clark had frequent difficulties with other politicians but was able to keep coming back after elections. Born in Kentucky, Clark moved to Missouri and was admitted to the bar. He served as a judicial clerk, colonel in the Black Hawk War, militia officer and state legislator. At the outbreak of the Civil War he had been serving, since 1857, in the U.S. Congress. Having joined the Missouri State Guard as a brigadier general, he was expelled on July 13, 1861. He commanded the 3rd Division at Carthage and Wilson's Creek. In October 1861 he was named to the Provisional Confederate Congress and was assigned to the Committees on Foreign Affairs and Indian Affairs. When appointed to the Senate in the First Congress he drew a two-year term. Here he served on the equivalent committees plus those on: Post Offices and Post Roads; Printing; Public Lands; and Territories. He supported local defense units, partisan rangers, and the war effort in general. He was, however, sensitive to discrimination against Missouri and fought to end the draft in areas threatened by invasion or guerrillas. He antagonized Davis by trying to limit his powers of appointment in the army, preferring the seniority system. By the end of his term, Clark was in hot water with Missouri Governor Thomas Reynolds who believed that Clark was a drunkard, a liar, and immoral. Reynolds dropped his previous support for Clark and he failed to gain reelection to the Senate. He was, however, elected to the House by the exile vote of Missouri's occupied 3rd Division. Here he served on the Committees on Elections and Military Affairs. After the war he resumed his law practice. His son, John Bullock, Jr., was a Confederate brigadier.

CLARK, John Bullock, Jr. (1831-1885)

The son of Confederate Congressman John B. Clark, Sr., John B. Clark, Jr., rose to be a brigadier general. The Missouri native and graduate of Harvard Law School was practicing his profession upon the outbreak of the Civil War. His assignments included: lieutenant, Missouri State Guard (1861); captain,

Missouri State Guard (1861); major, 1st Infantry, 3rd Division, Missouri State Guard (1861); colonel, 1st Infantry, 3rd Division, Missouri State Guard (1861); commanding 3rd Division, Missouri State Guard (March 1862); colonel, 9th Missouri (spring 1862); commanding brigade, Price's-Frost's Division, District of Arkansas, Trans-Mississippi Department (April-fall 1863); commanding Drayton's Brigade, Price's Division, District of Arkansas, Trans-Mississippi Department (January-February 1864); commanding brigade, Price's Division, District of Arkansas, Trans-Mississippi Department (March-March 24, 1864); brigadier general, CSA (March 6, 1864); and commanding in Trans-Mississippi Department: 1st Brigade, 1st (Missouri) Division, District of Arkansas (March 24-March and April-ca. September 18, 1864); 1st Brigade, 1st (Missouri) Division, Detachment, District of Arkansas, District of West Louisiana (March-April 1864); brigade, Marmaduke's Cavalry Division, Army of Missouri (September 18-December 18, 1864); also 2nd (Missouri) Cavalry Brigade, 1st (Missouri) Cavalry Division, Cavalry Corps (September 1864-early 1865); and Army of Missouri (temporarily December 1864). With the Missouri State Guard he fought at Carthage, and Wilson's Creek and at Pea Ridge led one of its divisions. Joining the Confederate volunteers, he continued to serve west of the Mississippi. He took part in the defense of Little Rock. The next year he fought in the Red River Campaign and at Jenkins' Ferry in the repulse of Steele's drive on Camden, Arkansas. That fall he led a cavalry brigade in Sterling Price's invasion of Missouri. A postwar lawyer, he also sat for five terms in the U.S. Congress.

CLARK, Meriwether Lewis (1809-1881)

The son of famed explorer William Clark, Meriwether Lewis Clark is sometimes mistakenly identified as a Confederate general. In fact he was never higher than a colonel in that service but was a brigadier in the Missouri State Guard early in the war. A native of Missouri and a West Pointer (1830), he had served three years in the regular army and commanded a volunteer artillery battalion in the Mexican War. Made a brigadier general in the Missouri State Guard, he commanded its 9th Military District in the latter part of 1861. Early the following year he served successively as chief of artillery for the Guard, Price's Division, and the Army of the West. On July 17, 1861, he was named the chief artillerist in Department #2. Having transferred to Confederate service, he rose in this period from major to colonel of artillery. In charge of Bragg's guns, he took part in the battle of Murfreesboro. In the summer of 1864 he was assigned to ordnance duty as an inspector. He held this post until the end of the war and was subsequently a faculty member at the Kentucky Military Institute.

CLARK, Willis Gaylord (1827-1898)

As the co-editor of a Confederate newspaper, Willis G. Clark went to the front to cover the fighting for his readership. Born in New York, he studied in Illinois before becoming a lawyer in Mobile. His first journalism endeavor was editing the Democratic *Southern Magazine*. By the outbreak of the Civil

War he was editing the *Mobile Daily Advertiser,* which soon merged with the *Mobile Register* of which he became co-editor. After his work as a war correspondent he was active in manufacturing and railroading. He also wrote *History of Education in Alabama.*

CLARKE, Kate

See: *King, Kate*

CLARKE, Marcellus Jerome (ca. 1843-1865)

Newspaper publicity brought a minor Confederate guerrilla, Marcellus J. Clark, to the gallows near the end of the Civil War. The son of a prominent Kentucky family, he had entered the Confederate army in the first year of the conflict and had served under John Hunt Morgan. In September 1864 he began a career leading small independent bands against military targets. But like most guerrillas he was also something of a bandit. *Louisville Courier* editor George D. Prentice was, unfortunately for Clarke, engaged in a political feud with the Union commander in the area, Stephen G. Burbridge, and launched a journalistic campaign to embarrass the general. Since Clark was of slight stature, Prentice labelled him a mere woman that the Union forces could not deal with. Borrowing the name of a notorious black woman in the city, Prentice dubbed Clarke "Sue Mundy." His efforts against Burbridge may have had some effect since the general was removed and replaced by John M. Palmer. Meanwhile Clarke/Mundy continued his operations and in February 1865 worked with the notorious bushwhacker William C. Quantrill in a number of minor operations. On March 12, 1865, Clarke was captured by some of Palmer's men while tending a wounded associate. Following a perfunctory court-martial, Clarke was hanged three days later.

CLAY, Clement Claiborne, Jr. (1816-1882)

Certainly one of the shining lights in the generally less-than-distinguished Confederate Congress was Alabama's Senator Clement C. Clay, Jr. Clay was a graduate of both the University of Alabama and the University of Virginia's law school. In his early years he worked as editor of the *Huntsville Democrat*, acquired a large plantation, and served as state legislator and as a county judge. In the meantime he practiced law. He was serving his second term in the U.S. Senate at the time of the secession crisis. On January 21, 1861, he was one of the five Southern senators, whose states had seceded, who made farewell speeches and then dramatically withdrew from the Senate chamber. Long a supporter of states' rights, Clay was offered the position of secretary of war by Jefferson Davis but declined in favor of Leroy P. Walker. Elected to the Senate of the First Regular Congress in November 1861, on the tenth ballot, he took his seat in February 1862 and drew a two-year term. He chaired the Committee on Commerce and also served on the committees on Indian Affairs and Military Affairs. A friend of Secretary of the Navy Stephen R. Mallory, who had left the U.S. Senate at the same time as Clay, he used his chairmanship of a special joint

Confederate Senator Clement C. Clay, Jr. (*Harper's*)

committee investigating the Navy Department for a whitewash protecting Mallory. A supporter of Davis' war effort, Clay did show much independence. He was well respected by both the pro- and anti-Davis forces for his non-dogmatic openness. Failing at reelection in November 1863, he left Congress in February 1864. Two months later he was sent to Canada to assist Jacob Thompson on a secret peace mission. Acknowledging failure, Clay returned South just in time for the final collapse of the Confederacy. Upon hearing that he was a suspect in the Lincoln murder, he surrendered to Union authorities and was confined at Fort Monroe for virtually a year without trial. Restrictions upon his activities limited him to his law practice after the war. (Nuremberger, Ruth K., *The Clays of Alabama: A Planter-Lawyer-Politician Family*)

CLAYTON, Alexander Mosby (1801-1889)

Although he only served a few months in the Confederate Congress, Alexander M. Clayton played a major role in shaping the new nation. Born in Virginia, he had moved via Tennessee to Mississippi where he was a lawyer, judge, and planter. He was

briefly, in 1853, U.S. consul to Havana. Lincoln's election converted Clayton into an immediate secessionist, and at the Mississippi convention he was instrumental in drawing up the ordinance that took the state out of the Union. Appointed to the Provisional Confederate Congress, he chaired the Committee on the Judiciary where he played a key role in securing the rights of the states within the new federal system. He was also instrumental in the creation of the new court system. Having supported Jefferson Davis for the presidency, he was rewarded by being named judge for the District of Mississippi, a post that he held until removed at the war's close. After the war Clayton served as a judge until removed in 1869 under Reconstruction by the U.S. Congress. Then he was a lawyer, planter, educator, banker, and was active in the railroad business.

CLAYTON, Henry DeLamar (1827-1889)

Georgia-born Alabama lawyer and state legislator Henry D. Clayton rose to division command in the Confederate Army of Tennessee but in the final reorganization appears to have become a supernumerary officer. His assignments included: colonel, 1st Alabama (March 27, 1861); colonel, 39th Alabama (May 15, 1862); commanding brigade, Stewart's Division, Hill's-Breckinridge's-Hindman's-Hood's Corps, Army of Tennessee (ca. April-September 1, 1863 and early 1864-July 7, 1864); brigadier general, CSA (April 22, 1863); commanding brigade, Stewart's Division, Buckner's Corps, Army of Tennessee (September 1-October 1, 1863); major general, CSA (July 7, 1864); and commanding Stewart's (old) Division, Hood's-Lee's Corps, Army of Tennessee (July 7, 1864-April 9, 1865). Initially stationed at Pensacola, he was relieved of command of his first regiment on January 18, 1862, upon the expiration of its original one-year term of enlistment. He then took command of a new regiment and led it in the Kentucky Campaign, although it was not present at Perryville, and at Murfreesboro where he was wounded. Returning to duty, he was promoted to brigadier general and commanded a brigade in the Tullahoma Campaign. Again wounded at Chickamauga, he returned in time to command the brigade in the Atlanta Campaign. During the campaign he was promoted to major general and took charge of Alexander P. Stewart's division when that officer took over Polk's Army of Mississippi. This division he led through the balance of the campaign and then went with Hood to middle Tennessee. The division was left south of the Duck River and thus missed the disastrous fight at Franklin but was present at Nashville where Clayton was praised for his role in covering the first part of the retreat. Moving on to the Carolinas, he led the division until the April 9, 1865, reorganization and consolidation of the Army of Tennessee. He appears to have been left without a command but remained with the army in some capacity since he was included in Joseph E. Johnston's surrender. After the war he returned to his plantation and resumed his legal practice, eventually becoming a judge.

CLAYTON, Philip (1815-1877)

A former U.S. treasury auditor, Philip Clayton quit his post as the Confederacy's assistant secretary of the treasury in a dispute with the secretary. A native Georgian lawyer and Democrat, he had also been a planter and journalist before taking the auditor's post. He then served as Buchanan's assistant treasury secretary and following secession took the same post in the Confederacy. Resenting the excessive demands of his boss, Christopher G. Memminger, he resigned in 1863. Washing his hands of the Confederacy, he became a Republican after the war and was a bank teller before becoming Grant's representative in Peru. He died there in 1877.

CLEBURNE, Patrick Ronayne (1828-1864)

The most popular Confederate division commander was the "Stonewall of the West"—Patrick R. Cleburne. Appropriately, the native of County Cork was born on St. Patrick's Day and became the only product of the Emerald Isle to become a Confederate major general. Failing the language requirements for a druggist's degree, he served with the British 41st Regiment of Foot as an officer for a number of years before purchasing his way out. Emigrating to America, he became a druggist and then a highly successful property attorney. He joined the Confederacy, and his military assignments included: captain, Company F, 1st Arkansas State Troops (early 1861); colonel, 1st Arkansas State Troops (early 1861); colonel, 15th Arkansas (designation change July 23, 1861); commanding 2nd Brigade, 1st (Hardee's) Division, Army of Central Kentucky, Department #2 (fall 1861-March 29, 1862); commanding 2nd Brigade, Hardee's Division, Army of the Mississippi (July 2-August 15, 1862); commanding 2nd Brigade, Buckner's Division, Left Wing, Army of the Mississippi (August 15-30, October-October 8, and October-November 20, 1862); commanding 2nd Brigade, Buckner's Division, Hardee's-Breckinridge's Corps, Army of Tennessee (November 20-December 1862); major general, CSA (December 20, 1862 to rank from the 13th); commanding the division (December 1862-November 30, 1863); commanding division, Hardee's (Polk's old)-Cheatham's Corps, Army of Tennessee (November 30, 1863-January 1864, January-August 31, and September 2-November 30, 1864); and commanding the corps (August 31-September 2, 1864). At the head of the Yell Rifles, he served in Arkansas before being named as commander of the state unit. Transferred with William J. Hardee to central Kentucky, he was promoted to brigadier general and fought at Shiloh and during the siege of Corinth. Taking part in the Kentucky Campaign, he was wounded at both Richmond and Perryville. Promoted to major general, he commanded a division at Murfreesboro, during the Tullahoma Campaign, and at Chickamauga. A favorite of Jefferson Davis, he is credited with covering the retreat from Chattanooga after his splendid defense of Tunnel Hill. That winter he and William H.T. Walker proposed that in order to reinforce the Confederate armies slavery would have to be abolished in a "reasonable time" and blacks be recruited for military service on the promise of their freedom. The proposal was rejected by the Richmond authorities and would not be passed by the Confederate Congress until a couple of months after Cleburne's death. Cleburne went on to command his division, and briefly the corps, through the Atlanta Campaign and then with Hood into middle Tennessee. At the battle of Franklin he became the senior of six Confederate generals to die in this fight, which did little more than commit mass suicide against the Union works. (Purdue, Howell and Elizabeth, *Pat Cleburne, Confederate General*)

CLEMENS, Samuel Langhorne (1835-1910)

Writing under the pen-name, Mark Twain, which he adapted from his days as a Mississippi River steamboat pilot, Sam Clemens is most remembered for his stories of boyhood in Hannibal, Missouri: *Tom Sawyer* (1876) and *Huckleberry Finn* (1884). He vented his bitterness toward the base condition of human civilization in many of his works—clearly in his account of his experiences as a citizen-soldier during the early days of the Civil War in Missouri, when he served for less than a month in a Confederate company, the Marion Rangers. His short story entitled "The Private History of a Campaign that Failed" uses laughter to soften the horror of young men and boys going off to fight a war, the reasons for which were unclear in their minds. This tragicomic approach was a constant theme in his post war writings, especially in condemning American actions in the Philippines.

"Mark Twain," or Samuel Clemens, at center with George Alfred Townsend (left) and David Gray. (NA)

CLINGMAN, Thomas Lanier (1812-1897)

North Carolina lawyer and politician Thomas L. Clingman spent most of his Confederate military service in the Carolinas

Coastal defender Thomas L. Clingman. (NA)

and served only briefly under Lee in Virginia. He resigned his seat in the U.S. Senate on March 28, 1861 (he had previously sat in the lower house), to offer his services to his state. His assignments included: colonel, 25th North Carolina (August 15, 1861); brigadier general, CSA (May 17, 1862); commanding brigade, District of the Cape Fear, Department of North Carolina (November 20, 1862-February 1863); commanding brigade, 1st Military District of South Carolina, Department of South Carolina, Georgia and Florida (February-April 30, 1863); commanding brigade, Department of North Carolina (May-July 1863); commanding 2nd Subdivision, 1st Military District of South Carolina, Department of South Carolina, Georgia and Florida (July-August and September-October 1863); commanding brigade, same subdivision, district and department (August-September 1863); commanding brigade, same district and deparment (October-November 1863); commanding brigade, Department of North Carolina (December 1863-May 1864); commanding brigade, Hoke's Division, Department of North Carolina and Southern Virginia (May-June and June-August 19, 1864); and commanding brigade, Hoke's Division, Hardee's Corps, Army of Tennessee (ca. April 9-26, 1865). After initial service with his regiment in the Carolinas and southern Virginia he was promoted and eventually given a brigade at Wilmington, North Carolina. Traveling between Charleston and Petersburg, he and his brigade saw action at Goldsboro Bridge, Charleston, and New Bern. After fighting at Drewry's Bluff in May 1864, the division was sent to reinforce

Lee at Cold Harbor, where Clingman was wounded. Soon returning to duty, he served in the early stages of the siege of Petersburg until wounded at the Weldon Railroad on August 19. Incapacitated for field duty, he did not return to his brigade until the final month of the war when it was serving under Joe Johnston in North Carolina. Surrendered at Greensboro, he returned to the law and took up surveying in the Alleghenies. (Freeman, Douglas S., *Lee's Lieutenants*)

COBB, Howell (1815-1868)

A prominent Georgia Unionist, Howell Cobb served before the war as a lawyer, state legislator, solicitor general, U.S. congressman (including as Speaker of the House), governor, and secretary of the treasury. In February 1861 he was named the presiding officer of what became the Provisional Confederate Congress. He had advocated secession after Lincoln's election. A rival candidate for president at the Montgomery convention, he soon became known as an opponent of Davis. He left the congress to join the army, where his assignments included: colonel, 16th Georgia (July 15, 1861); brigadier general, CSA (February 12, 1862); commanding brigade, McLaws' Division, Department of the Peninsula (ca. February 12-April 12, 1862); commanding brigade, McLaws' Division, Magruder's Command, Department of Northern Virginia (April 12-June 1862); commanding brigade, Magruder's Division, Magruder's Command, Army of Northern Virginia (June-July 1862); commanding brigade, McLaws' Division, 1st Corps, same army (July-October 1862); commanding District of Middle Florida, Department of South Carolina, Georgia and Florida (November 11, 1862-ca. October 6, 1863); major general, CSA (September 9, 1863); commanding District of Northwest Georgia, Department of Tennessee (November 1863); commanding reserve forces in Georgia (December 1863-September 28, 1864); and commanding District of Georgia, Department of Tennessee and Georgia (September 28, 1864-March 27, 1865). After fighting at Yorktown, the Seven Days, and South Mountain, he was assigned to Florida and in the summer of 1863 served on a court investigating the disasters at Vicksburg, Port Hudson, and Jackson. He held various commands in Georgia and had to pacify the troublesome Governor Brown. He was involved in the operations to halt Wilson's raid through Alabama in the spring of 1865. Returning to the law after the war, he was active in opposition to the harsher aspects of Reconstruction until his death on a business trip to New York. (Montgomery, Horace, *Howell Cobb's Confederate Career*)

COBB, Silas T. (?-?)

The role of Sergeant Silas T. Cobb in the escape of John Wilkes Booth after the assassination of Lincoln, and Cobb's escape from punishment, have led to many suspicions and conspiracy theories. That April night the soldier was on guard duty at the western end of the Navy Yard Bridge across the Anacostia River. His orders were that no one was to cross without the password. However, Booth appeared at 10:30 or 11:00, as Cobb later testified, and explained that he lived in Maryland and had been unavoidably detained past the 9:00 P.M. deadline. He was allowed to cross. It must be remembered that the war was all but over and security was somewhat lax. But many claim that Secretary of War Edwin M. Stanton deliberately left this route open.

COBB, Thomas Reade Rootes (1823-1862)

The younger brother of Howell Cobb, Thomas R.R. Cobb, was a prominent Georgia lawyer before the Civil War who became an immediate secessionist upon the election of Lincoln. Named to the Provisional Confederate Congress, he served as chair of the Committee on Printing and was active in the establishment of the judicial system for the new nation. He left the Congress to raise a mixed force of infantry and cavalry. His military assignments included: colonel, Cobb's (Ga.) Legion (August 28, 1861); brigadier general, CSA (November 1, 1862); and commanding Howell Cobb's (old) Brigade, McLaws' Division, 1st Corps, Army of Northern Virginia (November 6-December 13, 1862). After service on the Peninsula, including action in the Yorktown operations and the Maryland Campaign, he was promoted and given charge of his brother's former command. In defense of the famed stone wall at Fredericksburg he was wounded in the thigh and bled to death in a short time. (McCash, William B., *Thomas R.R. Cobb: The Making of a Southern Nationalist*)

COCKE, Philip St. George (1809-1861)

Philip Cocke resigned from the regular army two years after graduating from West Point in 1832 to pursue the life of a planter and philanthropist—until he was called upon and appointed brigadier general of Virginia State Troops on April 21, 1861. Three days later he was assigned to command the Alexandria Line opposite Washington. He was transferred to Confederate service as colonel, 19th Virginia, on May 10 but retained command of the Alexandria Line until superseded by General Bonham on the 21st. On June 20, 1861, he was given command of a brigade in the Army of the Potomac, the newly organized successor to the Alexandria command. During the 1st Battle of Bull Run, Cooke had command of his own brigade plus Colonel Nathan Evans' demi-brigade. His knowledge of the battlefield was put to good use as he directed reinforcements to Evans' aid and finally, at the close of the battle, abandoned his sector of the line, which was then not seriously threatened, and took his own brigade to the main battle area. Promoted to brigadier general, CSA, on October 21, 1861, he shortly afterwards returned home, a man broken by the rigors of field service, and on the day after Christmas took his own life. (Freeman, Douglas S., *Lee's Lieutenants*)

COCKRELL, Francis Marion (1834-1915)

Starting the Civil War as a company commander in the Missouri State Guard, native Missourian lawyer Francis M. Cockrell rose to a brigadier generalship in the regular Confederate service and was in charge of a division when the end came. His assignments included: captain, 3rd Infantry, 1st Brigade, 2nd Division, Missouri State Guard (early 1861); captain, Company H, 2nd Missouri (January 15, 1862); lieutenant colonel, 2nd Missouri

(May 1862); colonel, 2nd Missouri (June 29, 1862); commanding 1st (Missouri) Brigade, Bowen's Division, Department of Mississippi and East Louisiana (April 17-July 4, 1863); commanding brigade, French's Division, Polk's (Army of Mississippi)-Stewart's Corps, Army of Tennessee (May-July and August-November 30, 1864); and commanding French's Division, District of the Gulf, Department of Alabama, Mississippi and East Louisiana (March-April 12, 1865). With the Missouri State Guard, he fought at Carthage and Wilson's Creek. Early in 1862 he transferred to the Confederate service and fought at Pea Ridge. Crossing the Mississippi, he took part in the defense of Corinth and was then engaged in thwarting Grant's lengthy operations against Vicksburg. Finally captured, in command of the Missouri Brigade, upon the fall of the city, he was exchanged on September 12, 1863. In the meantime he had been promoted to brigadier general. A hand wound suffered in the siege did not prevent him from leading the brigade through most of the Atlanta Campaign. Accompanying Hood on his drive into middle Tennessee, Cockrell suffered three wounds at Franklin. During the final months of the war he commanded the division at Mobile. Following the surrender of the city on April 12, 1865, he was paroled and resumed his practice. Later he spent six terms in the U.S. Senate and sat on the Interstate Commerce Commission. (Anderson, Ephraim McD., Edwin C. Bearss, ed., *Memoirs: Historical and Personal; Including the Campaigns of the First Missouri Confederate Brigade*)

COLBERT, Wallace Bruce (1834-1865)

As the colonel of the 40th Mississippi, W. Bruce Colbert was in command of a brigade for a month early in the war but he never graduated to the position permanently. He became colonel upon the unit's organization in mid-1862 and fought at the battle of Iuka. Due to the death of division commander Little and the ascension of General Hébert to division level, Colbert commanded Hébert's (2nd) Brigade, Little's (1st) Division, Price's Corps, Army of West Tennessee, Department No. 2 (September 19-mid October 1862). At this higher level he fought at Corinth. He next took part in the Vicksburg Campaign and was captured with his command upon the river city's fall. Exchanged, he led his regiment in the Department of Alabama, Mississippi and East Louisiana until it accompanied General Polk to northern Georgia to help oppose Sherman's drive on Atlanta. He took part in the campaign until mid-June 1864. He rejoined the army of Tennessee for Hood's disastrous Tennessee Campaign, including fighting at Franklin and Nashville. This was his last service. He died in 1865.

COLEMAN, Henry Eaton (1837-1890)

During the Civil War Virginia-born Henry E. Coleman was forced to leave his regiment on two occasions, first when he failed to gain reelection and second when he was wounded at Spotsylvania. In fact he was not even with his regiment when he achieved his greatest glory. Leaving his native North Carolina to serve the Confederacy, he held the following assignments: captain, Company B, 12th North Carolina (April 26, 1861); lieutenant colonel and volunteer aide-de-camp (early 1863); and colonel, 12th North Carolina (August 11, 1863 to rank from May 4, 1863). As with so many other qualified officers, he had attended the Virginia Military Institute, but he failed to gain reelection to his captaincy during the May 1862 reorganization of the regiment. Less than a year later he was serving on the staff of General Iverson, the 12th's brigade commander, and after distinguishing himself at Gettysburg he was commissioned colonel and assigned to his old regiment. He led this unit through the Bristoe and Mine Run campaigns and at the Wilderness. At Spotsylvania Court House, on May 12, 1864, he was wounded so severely that he was never able to rejoin his unit. While recovering from his injury, he took part in the defense of the Staunton River Bridge on June 25. He was cited for his gallant conduct in this action against Wilson's Union cavalry.

COLQUITT, Alfred Holt (1824-1894)

One of Lee's brigade commanders who failed the grade, Alfred H. Colquitt was traded, with his brigade, for another then serving in North Carolina but was back under Lee again a year later. His legal practice had been interrupted by the Mexican War in which he served as a paymaster of volunteers. Entering politics, he served his native Georgia in Congress and later in the state legislature. In the Civil War his assignments included: captain, Infantry (1861); colonel, 6th Georgia (May 27, 1861); commanding brigade, Department of the Peninsula (October 1861); commanding Rains' (old) Brigade, D.H. Hill's Division (in 1st Corps from June 29 and 2nd Corps from July 27), Army of Northern Virginia (June 18, 1862-May 20, 1863); brigadier general, CSA (September 1, 1862); commanding brigade (in the District of the Cape Fear in July), Department of North Carolina (May-July 1863); commanding 3rd Subdivision (Morris Island), 1st Military District of South Carolina, Department of South Carolina, Georgia and Florida (August 1863); commanding Western Division (or 2nd Sub-District), 7th Military District of South Carolina, same department (October 22, 1863-January 1864); commanding brigade, same district and department (January-February 1864); commanding brigade, District of (until February 23: East) Florida, same department (February-May 1864); commanding division, Department of North Carolina and Southern Virginia (mid-May 1864); commanding brigade, Hoke's Division, same Department (May-October 19, 1864); commanding brigade, Hoke's Division, Anderson's Corps, Army of Northern Virginia (October 19-December 20, 1864); commanding brigade, Hoke's Division, Department of North Carolina (December 1864-March 1865); commanding brigade, Hoke's Division, Hardee's Corps (March-April 9, 1865); and commanding brigade, same division and corps, Army of Tennessee (April 9-26, 1865). Sent to the Peninsula of Virginia in the first year of the war, Colquitt and his regiment fought at Yorktown, Williamsburg, and Seven Pines. He succeeded General Rains in brigade command for the Seven Days and later led it at Antietam. Promoted to the position permanently, he led the unit at Fredericksburg and Chancellorsville. At the latter he put in a poor performance during Jackson's attack on May 2. He halted his brigade because of the fear of enemy cavalry on his right. Although he redeemed himself somewhat the next day, his brigade was swapped for Junius Daniel's from the Department of North Carolina. After serving in the Carolinas, he led his brigade to Florida and took part in the victory at Olustee. Three months later he was back in Virginia, under Beauregard, and fought at Drewry's Bluff, temporarily in charge of a small division. Attached to Hoke's division, he soon joined Lee for Cold Harbor and took part in the first months of the siege of Petersburg. Sent in December 1864 to the Wilmington area, he later fought at Bentonville and surrendered with Johnston. After the war he spent a stormy term, full of charges of dishonesty, as governor and later sat in the U.S. Senate. (Freeman, Douglas S., *Lee's Lieutenants*)

COLQUITT, Peyton H. (1832-1863)

The brother of Confederate General Alfred H. Colquitt, Peyton H. Colquitt did not live long enough to reach that rank. The Georgian's assignments included: colonel, 46th Georgia (March 17, 1862); commanding 4th and 5th Military District of South Carolina, Department of South Carolina, Georgia and Florida (April-May 6, 1862); commanding Gist's Brigade, Department of the West (May-June 1863); and commanding Gist's Brigade, Walker's Division, Reserve Corps, Army of Tennessee (September-September 20, 1863). Assigned with his regiment to the Atlantic seaboard, he was for a time in command of two districts in South Carolina before being ordered to Mississippi in the spring of 1863. Serving under Joseph E. Johnston in the attempts to relieve Vicksburg, he led a brigade at the battle of Jackson and after the river city's fall in the defense of Jackson against Sherman. Part of the Confederate buildup in northern Georgia prior to Chickamauga, he led his brigade toward that bloody field. He became very impatient with the railroad engineers for delays, fearing that he would miss the battle. However, on the second day of the fight, September 20, he was killed in action.

COLSTON, Raleigh Edward (1825-1896)

Paris-born Raleigh E. Colston was found wanting by General Lee and was relegated to the less active areas of the war. Granted U.S. citizenship, he was educated at the Virginia Military Institute and served there for a decade and a half as a French professor. His Civil War assignments included: colonel, 16th Virginia (May 1861); brigadier general, CSA (December 24, 1861); commanding 1st Brigade, Department of Norfolk (late 1861-early April 1862); commanding same brigade, McLaws' Division, Department of the Peninsula (early April-April 12, 1862); commanding brigade, McLaws' Division, Magruder's Command, Department of Northern Virginia (April 1862); commanding brigade, Longstreet's Division, same department (April-June 1862); commanding brigade, in Elzey's Command (December 20-late December 1862) and in French's Command (late December 1862-March 24, 1863), Department of Virginia and North Carolina; commanding Taliaferro's (old) Brigade, Jackson's (old) Division, 2nd Corps, Army of Northern Virginia (April and May 1863); commanding division (April-May 1863); commanding brigade, District of

Georgia, Department of South Carolina, Georgia and Florida (October 20, 1863-April 16, 1864); commanding 1st Military District, Department of North Carolina and Southern Virginia (May 14, 1864-June 1, 1864); and commanding Post at Lynchburg, Virginia (June 4, 1864-April 1865). After serving around Norfolk, he moved to the Peninsula where he saw action at Williamsburg and Seven Pines. Sick for six months, he returned to command in the Richmond and Petersburg area before joining Lee's army. After a poor performance as a division leader at Chancellorsville he was shunted aside to less vital fields and after serving in Georgia finished the war at Lynchburg. A military educator after the war, he was paralyzed from the waist down in a camel accident while serving as a colonel in the Egyptian army. (Freeman, Douglas S., *Lee's Lieutenants*)

COLTART, John Gordon (?-?)

In the final stages of the life of the Confederate Army of Tennessee the attrition among general officers was so great that John G. Coltart was commanding a division at Bentonville with the rank of colonel. His war assignments included: captain, Company E, 3rd (Coltart's) Battalion (April 2, 1861); lieutenant colonel, 3rd (Coltart's) Battalion (April 2, 1861); lieutenant colonel, 7th Alabama (May 18, 1861); colonel, 7th Alabama (January 1862); colonel, 26th (Coltart's) Alabama (April 3, 1862); commanding Deas' Brigade, Withers' Division, 1st Corps, Army of Tennessee (December 31, 1862-early 1863 and July-August 1863); colonel, 50th Alabama (June 6, 1863); commanding Deas' Brigade, Hindman's Division, 2nd Corps, Army of Tennessee (May-July 26 and July 28-August 1864); and commanding D.H. Hill's Division, 2nd Corps, Army of Tennessee (March 1865). His original unit was enlarged into a 12-months regiment, the 7th Alabama, with which he served at Pensacola and in Tennessee. Upon its expiration of service he was given a new regiment, the 26th, later designated the 50th. A few days after taking command he was wounded on the first day at Shiloh. He recovered in time to fight at Murfreesboro where he took command of the brigade on the first day. He was at Chickamauga and Chattanooga as a regimental commander. In the Atlanta Campaign he was at times directing the brigade and was wounded. He went to Tennessee with Hood, seeing action at Franklin and Nashville. After those disasters, the remains of the army went to North Carolina trying to stop Sherman. His last service was as a division commander at Bentonville. This was two command levels above his appropriate rank due to heavy losses among generals. He does not appear to have been at the surrender in April.

CONNALLY, John Kerr (1839-1904)

After attending the U.S. Naval Academy at Annapolis, John Connally entered the Confederate land forces and became an example of the problems caused by "honor" in the Southern military. A resident of Yadkin County, he was appointed captain, Company B, 21st North Carolina, on May 12, 1861. After seeing service at the battle of 1st Bull Run, Connally became colonel, 55th North Carolina, on May 19, 1862. During Longstreet's siege of Suffolk in April 1863, Connally's regiment was assigned the task of protecting the Confederate guns in Fort

Huger. On the evening of the 19th a Union force attacked and captured five guns and 137 soldiers. There was negligence on the part of both Connally and General Law, both of whom tried to blame the other. Captains Terrell and Cussons of Law's staff reported that the 55th had acted in a cowardly manner. Connally demanded satisfaction and was joined by Major Belo in challenging the two staff officers to a duel. While Belo and Cussons fired two rounds at each other, Connally and Terrell settled the quarrel without violence, and all parties resumed the business of killing Yankees instead of each other. Joining the Army of Northern Virginia, Colonel Connally was wounded and captured at Gettysburg. He was not exchanged until March 1864. He fought in the Wilderness and at Spotsylvania, handicapped by the loss of one arm, and was again wounded at Cold Harbor and at Petersburg. He resigned on March 7, 1865, and became a lawyer. After nearly being killed in a collapse of part of the Virginia state capitol, he became a minister. (Freeman, Douglas S., *Lee's Lieutenants*)

CONNER, James (1829-1883)

It took two wounds in the same leg to permanently place James Conner out of commission for further field service. As a district attorney in his native South Carolina he had prosecuted both slave traders and a member of William Walker's Central American filibustering expedition. Nonetheless, he was an active secessionist and had pushed for the secession convention of which he was a member but did not vote on the ordinance itself. He declined appointment as a district attorney for the Confederacy preferring to enter the military. His assignments included: captain, Infantry Company A, Hampton's (S.C.) Legion (May 1861); major, Hampton's Legion (July 21, 1861); colonel, 22nd North Carolina (June 13, 1862); brigadier general, CSA (June 1, 1864); commanding McGowan's Brigade, Wilcox's Division, 3rd Corps, Army of Northern Virginia (June 4-summer 1864); and commanding Kershaw's (old) Brigade, Kershaw's Division, 1st Corps, Army of Northern Virginia (summer-October 13, 1864). At the head of the Washington Light Infantry, part of Hampton's Legion, he fought at 1st Bull Run and succeeded to its command upon the wounding of Colonel Wade Hampton. Promoted to major, he fought at Yorktown, West Point, and Seven Pines before being appointed colonel of a North Carolina regiment. At Mechanicsville, at the start of the Seven Days, he was wounded in the leg. Apparently not rejoining his regiment, he resigned on August 13, 1863, and became a member of the military court of the 2nd Corps in the fall of 1863. Appointed brigadier the following spring, he was given temporary charge of the wounded McGowan's Brigade. Upon the latter's return, Conner took command of Kershaw's old Brigade and led it to the Shenandoah Valley. In a small action near Fisher's Hill on October 13, 1864, he was again wounded in the same leg necessitating its amputation. This ended his field service. He was active in law and politics after Appomattox. (Moffett, Mary C., ed. *Letters of General James Conner, C.S.A.*)

CONNER, Zephaniah Turner (1811-1866)

Stonewall Jackson was known for his tendency to condemn

subordinate officers, often on questionable grounds, but Zephaniah T. Conner was certainly deserving of the general's wrath. He had entered the Confederate army at the beginning of the war and his assignments included: private, Company A, 1st Georgia that 15, 1861); lieutenant colonel, 12th Georgia (July 2, 1861); colonel, 12th Georgia (December 13, 1862); and commanding 1st Brigade, Army of the Northwest (ca. April-May 1862). After seeing action at Cheat Mountain, Romney, and McDowell he took part in the beginning stages of Jackson's Shenandoah Valley Campaign. When the Confederates scored a complete victory at Front Royal, capturing a large amount of supplies and some prisoners, it was the 12th Georgia which was detailed to guard the area while the rest of the army went on towards Winchester. But on May 30 Conner was faced with the advance of a Union column from the east. Losing his head, he took off for Winchester to report to Jackson. His regiment set fire to the captured supplies and withdrew after him. When Conner reported to Jackson that he had suffered no men killed or wounded, the general immediately placed him under arrest. The court-martial kept being delayed by the lack of officers for the court during a season of active campaigning. Finally, on about January 22, 1863, Conner resigned. He died a year after the war ended. (Freeman, Douglas, S., *Lee's Lieutenants*)

CONRAD, Charles Magill (1804-1878)

One of the members of the Confederate Congress whose experiences typified those of Southern politicians in general, was Charles M. Conrad. Born in Virginia, Conrad moved to Louisiana with his family. He was in due course admitted to the bar in New Orleans and engaged in politics as a Jacksonian Democrat and later as a Whig. He developed a large plantation and was a successful duelist. He served in the state legislature and in both houses of the U.S. Congress, before becoming secretary of war under President Fillmore. In the mid and late 1850s he was highly successful in private practice but maintained an interest in politics, supporting the Constitutional Union ticket in 1860. He started his Confederate career as one of Louisiana's delegates to the Provisional Congress. He remained in the legislative branch for the entire war. During his three terms representing the New Orleans district in Congress he served on the following committees: Executive Departments; Naval Affairs; Ordnance and Ordnance Stores; Public Buildings; and Ways and Means. While chairing the Committee on Naval Affairs, Conrad suggested the Navy Department's merger with the War Department in an effort to get rid of Secretary of the Navy Stephen R. Mallory. It is perhaps for this reason that Conrad was given a different committee assignment in the Second Congress. He felt that the conduct of the war should be left to the executive branch and the military, and he basically supported all war measures that Davis proposed. With his plantation confiscated, Conrad resumed the practice of law after Appomattox.

CONROW, Aaron H. (1824-1865)

Although he died after the end of hostilities, Missouri Congressman Aaron H. Conrow certainly was a casualty of the Civil

War, dying in Mexico while trying to flee to England in order to avoid the uncertainties of defeat. Born north of the Ohio River, in Cincinnati, his family moved by way of Illinois to Missouri where he eventually became a lawyer and judge. His sympathies ultimately were with the South, so he became a secessionist and raised a company for the Missouri State Guard in which he was commissioned a colonel. With the alleged "secession" of Missouri Conrow was named to the Provisional Confederate Congress and remained in that body and the regular congresses throughout the war. A slow convert to the idea of total war, he soon became a supporter of the Davis administration. Representing the 4th District in the northwestern corner of Missouri, which was in enemy hands for most of the war, Conrow was reelected by the exile vote. His committee assignments included those on: Finance; Post Offices and Post Roads; Public Buildings; and Quartermaster's and Commissary Departments. With the collapse of the Confederacy, Conrow accompanied General Mosby M. Parsons and two staff officers through Mexico in an effort to reach California and take ship for England. Attacked by Juarista troops on August 15, 1865, Conrow and the officers all perished.

COOK, George Smith (1819-1902)

Although overshadowed by Brady and other Northern photographers, George Cook was an outstanding artist who covered the war in Charleston Harbor. Moving to the South at the age of 14, the Connecticut-born Cook entered the field of photography and traveled throughout the South establishing daguerreotype studios. He settled in Charleston in 1849 and two years later, when Brady went overseas, Cook took over his gallery in New York and opened one of his own. He later set up shop in Chicago and Philadelphia. But with the coming of war, he concentrated his enterprises in Charleston. With an eye for history, he took the famous shot of Major Robert Anderson and his staff at Fort Sumter. Following the fort's fall, Cook continued to cover the war, in addition to his portrait business, photographing the fort after its fall and during the subsequent siege by the Union forces. He frequently exposed himself to enemy fire to acquire images. He scored a photographic first by capturing three monitors in action. On September 8, 1863, while exposing a view of Fort Sumter's interior, a Union shell exploded and he captured it on film—a rare occurrence. He remained financially solvent during the inflationary life of the Confederacy by requiring payment in gold. Cook remained active in photography, in New York, Richmond, and Charleston, until his death. (Kocher, A. Lawrence and Dearstyne, Howard, *Shadows in Silver*)

COOK, Philip (1817-1894)

A Georgia attorney, Philip Cook rose from the ranks to the command of a brigade in Lee's army. His assignments included: private, Company I, 4th Georgia (May 1861); first lieutenant and adjutant, 4th Georgia (1861); lieutenant colonel, 4th Georgia (ca. August 15, 1862); colonel, 4th Georgia (November 1, 1862); commanding Doles' (old) Brigade, Rodes' Division, 2nd Corps, Army of Northern Virginia (June 2-13,

1864); commanding same brigade, Rodes'-Grimes' Division, Valley District, Department of Northern Virginia (June 13-December 1864); brigadier general, CSA (August 5, 1864); and commanding brigade, Grimes' Division, 2nd Corps, Army of Northern Virginia (December 1864-March 25, 1865). Having seen some action against the Seminoles, he was soon rewarded with the position of adjutant. After serving in the Norfolk area, the regiment moved to the Peninsula and fought at Seven Pines and in the Seven Days. As a field officer he served at Antietam and succeeded George Doles in command when that officer took charge of the brigade. He was wounded at Chancellorsville and did not return for several months. In the Overland Campaign he succeeded Doles in brigade command and was promoted to brigadier in August. He joined Early in the Valley and saw action at 3rd Winchester, Fisher's Hill, and Cedar Creek. Moving into the trenches at Petersburg in December, he was severely wounded in the assault on Fort Stedman on March 25. He was captured in a hospital upon the fall of the city and was not released until July. He was a lawyer, congressman, and member of the governor's cabinet after the war. (Thomas, Henry W., *A History of the Doles-Cook Brigade, Army of Northern Virginia*)

COOKE, James Wallace (?-1869)

Resigning from the old navy as a lieutenant on May 1, 1861, James W. Cooke rose through the ranks to become a captain in the Confederate navy. On May 4, 1861, he was appointed a lieutenant in the Virginia navy. Transferred with the same rank to the Confederate service, he was assigned to the batteries at Aquia Creek blockading the Potomac River. Sent to North Carolina shortly after the battle of 1st Manassas, Cooke was given command of a small one-gun steamer, the *Ellis*. During this period he placed obstructions in Albemarle Sound to delay the enemy. At the battle of Roanoke Island on February 8, 1862, Cooke kept his vessel fighting until he had fired off the last round of his ammunition and that of a disabled Confederate gunboat. Two days later, at Elizabeth City, Cooke was forced to order his ship abandoned. It was already surrounded and being boarded by men from two Union gunboats, but his orders to destroy the ship were not carried out. With a bullet wound in the arm and a bayonet cut in the leg, Cooke himself was taken prisoner. Paroled, he returned home until exchanged in September. On the 17th he was promoted to commander, CSN. Sent to the Roanoke River, he received instructions to construct the ironclad *Albemarle*. His efforts to obtain supplies earned him the nickname of the "Iron Captain." With his vessel completed, he joined in the successful April 1864 attack on Plymouth, North Carolina. For this battle and an action in the Roanoke River on May 5, Cooke was promoted to captain, CSN, and given command of all naval forces in the Plymouth area. He held this position until the area was abandoned at the close of the war. He then retired to his home in Portsmouth, Virginia. (Scharf, J. Thomas, *History of the Confederate States Navy*)

COOKE, John Esten (1830-1886)

An established writer before the Civil War, John Esten Cooke used his experiences as the milieu for his postwar works. In the antebellum period he had written to further the secessionist cause, often appearing in the *Southern Literary Messenger*. As a member of the elite Richmond Howitzers artillery company he was present at the capture of John Brown at Harpers Ferry. Early in the Civil War he joined the staff of his cousin's husband, Jeb Stuart, and served through most of the illustrious cavalryman's campaigns. Meanwhile his uncle, Philip St. George Cooke, had become a Union general and his cousin, John R. Cooke, a Confederate one. After Stuart's death in 1864, he served as an inspector of horse artillery. Following his surrender at Appomattox, he resumed his writing career with both novels and histories. His biographies include *The Life of Stonewall Jackson* and *The Life of R.E. Lee*. His historical novels include *Surry of Eagle's Nest* and *Wearing of the Gray*. When not writing he was involved in agricultural pursuits. (Beatty, John O., *John Esten Cooke, Virginian*)

COOKE, John Rogers (1833-1891)

Confederate Brigadier General John R. Cooke's own case is an example of a family divided by the Civil War. His father was Union General Philip St. George Cooke, his brother-in-law Confederate Major General Jeb Stuart, and his cousin John Esten Cooke was on Stuart's staff. He had held an infantry lieutenant's commission in the Old Army for almost six years when he resigned on May 30, 1861, to go with the South. His assignments included: first lieutenant, Infantry (1861); major, Artillery (February 1862); colonel, 27th North Carolina (April 24, 1862); brigadier general, CSA (November 1, 1862); commanding Walker's (old) Brigade, Ransom's Division, 1st Corps, Army of Northern Virginia (November 6-December 13, 1862); commanding brigade, 3rd Military District of South Carolina, Department of South Carolina, Georgia and Florida (ca. January-April 23, 1863); commanding brigade, District of the Cape Fear, Department of North Carolina (April 26-May 1, 1863); commanding brigade, same department (May-July 1863); commanding brigade (in Ransom's Division from late July), Department of Richmond (July-August 1863); and commanding a brigade (assigned to Heth's Division ca. October 3), 3rd Corps, Army of Northern Virginia (September-October 14, 1863 and early 1864-April 9, 1865). After serving with General Holmes in Virginia and North Carolina he was elected colonel of a regiment that led in the Seven Days and at the capture of Harpers Ferry. At Antietam he made a charge with one other regiment, which was commended, and was promoted to command the brigade six weeks later. Wounded at Fredericksburg, he went with his command to South Carolina, North Carolina, and finally to the Richmond vicinity during the Gettysburg Campaign. He rejoined Lee's army and was again wounded in the assault at Bristoe Station. He recovered in time for the Wilderness and led his men through Spotsylvania, Cold Harbor, Petersburg, and to the surrender at Appomattox. A Richmond merchant, he helped found the Confederate Soldiers' Home. (Freeman, Douglas S., *Lee's Lieutenants*)

COOPER, Douglas Hancock (1815-1879)

A native Mississippian, Douglas H. Cooper was a veteran of the Mexican War, having served as a captain in the 1st Mississippi Rifles, and in 1853 was appointed as U.S. commissioner to the Choctaws, one of the Five Civilized Tribes, of the southeastern United States. Because of this connection with the Indians, he was appointed by the Confederacy as a representative to deal with the Five Tribes. Working with Albert Pike, he succeeded in getting portions of all five tribes to join with the South. On May 25, 1861, he was adopted into the Chickasaw tribe. Raising an Indian unit, he held the following assignments: colonel, 1st Choctaw and Chickasaw Mounted Rifles (1861); brigadier general, CSA (May 2, 1863); commanding District of Indian Territory, Trans-Mississippi Department (July 21, 1864-February 14 and February 21-May 1865); and also commanding Indian Division, Cavalry Corps, Trans-Mississippi Department (fall 1864-May 1865). Leading his mixed regiment, he took part in the pursuit of the Unionist Upper Creeks fleeing under Opothleyohola. He subsequently fought at Newtonia, having missed the action at Pea Ridge because the Indians refused to serve outside Indian Territory until they were paid. During Price's Missouri operations in 1864, Cooper commanded the Indian forces. By the end of the war he was in command of all the Indians serving in the Trans-Mississippi. After the peace he continued action against the U.S. government by pressing, and winning, claims for losses during the war for the Indians.

COOPER, Samuel (1798-1876)

By the time of the Civil War, New Jersey-born West Pointer (1815) Samuel Cooper, having served mostly on staff assignments in the Seminole and Mexican wars, had become the adjutant general of the U.S. Army. Having married a Virginian, he resigned his position on March 7, 1861, and offered his services to the Confederacy. On March 16, 1861, the day after he arrived in Richmond, Jefferson Davis appointed him a brigadier general in the regular army of the Confederacy with the joint position of adjutant and inspector general. In this position, for which he was most qualified by his experience in the "Old Army," he was responsible for the organization of an army from scratch. On August 31, 1861, he was promoted to full general with rank from May 16. This made him the senior officer in the rebel military command. Although he is little remembered, he was largely responsible for having kept the Confederate forces in the field. He retained his position until the collapse of the rebel nation when he turned over the records of his department to the Washington authorities. Without this treasure, the *Official Records* would be much less reliable and valuable. After the war, Cooper took up farming near Alexandria, Virginia. However, by 1870 he was in such poor financial straits that General Lee raised $300 from ex-Confederates and added $100 himself for Cooper's relief.

CORBIN, William F. (?-1863)

A prominent Kentuckian, William F. Corbin had the misfortune to become the focal point in a dispute between the warring authorities over the status of recruiting officers found behind enemy lines. Under orders, he had entered Kentucky in search of Confederate recruits. On April 9, 1863, he and another officer, T.B. McGraw, were arrested while in civilian clothes and escorting enlistees to the Southern lines. The two were tried by court-martial and shot on May 15 at Johnson's Island. In retaliation, Richmond selected two captive captains, Henry W. Sawyer and John M. Flinn, for the gallows. General Burnside's position was that the two Confederates were considered to be spies since they were out of uniform and thus subject to the death penalty.

CORLEY, James Lawrence (1828-1883)

Although he served on the staff of Robert E. Lee throughout his tenure as commander of the Army of Northern Virginia, Chief Quartermaster James L. Corley was not really a member of Lee's headquarters family. The South Carolina-born officer had graduated from West Point (1850) and served in the infantry before the war, part of the time as a regimental quartermaster. With the war already begun, he resigned his commission in the old army on May 4, 1861, and went South. His appointments included: captain and quartermaster (July 1861); lieutenant colonel, 60th Virginia (October 13, 1861); and chief quartermaster, Army of Northern Virginia (June 1862-April 9, 1865). After serving on the staff of General Garnett in western Virginia during the first summer of the war, he became second in command of the 60th Virginia. He served with this unit until his resignation on March 10, 1862. He took a position as judge advocate in the Department of South Carolina, Georgia, and Florida but, just prior to the Seven Days Battles, he returned to Virginia and was assigned to direct the Quartermaster's Department for Lee's army. Serving as head of a staff department, he was not strictly speaking a member of Lee's personal staff. After serving through all the army's campaigns he was given the task of reducing the amount of mules, horses, wagons, etc., for the transportation of the army on the dismal retreat to Appomattox. Settling in Norfolk after the war he was involved in the insurance business. He also served as an escort for his former chief during much of his Southern tour. (Freeman, Douglas S., *R.E. Lee*)

CORSE, Montgomery Dent (1816-1895)

A Virginia banker and veteran of the Mexican War, as a captain in the 1st Virginia, Montgomery D. Corse was skillfully prepared for the Civil War. In 1860 he organized the Old Dominion Rifles and became its captain. Following the secession of the state his assignments included: major, 6th Virginia Battalion (early 1861); colonel, 17th Virginia (spring 1861); commanding Kemper's Brigade, Kemper's Division, 1st Corps, Army of Northern Virginia (early August-August 30, 1862); brigadier general, CSA (November 1, 1862); temporarily commanding Garnett's brigade, Pickett's Division, same corps and army (November 6-26, 1862); commanding new brigade, same division, corps and army (November 26, 1862-February 25, 1863; May-September 23, 1863; and May 1864-April 6, 1865); commanding brigade, Pickett's Division, in the

Department of Virginia and North Carolina (February 25-April 1, 1863) and in the Department of Southern Virginia (April 1-May 1863); commanding brigade Ransom's Division, Department of Western Virginia (September 1863-January 1864); and commanding brigade (in Hoke's Division in May), Department of North Carolina (January-May 1864). Corse commanded his regiment at Blackburn's Ford, 1st Bull Run, Yorktown, Williamsburg, Seven Pines, and in the Seven Days. At 2nd Bull Run he was in brigade command until wounded. The next month he was again wounded at both South Mountain and Antietam at the head of the regiment. A new brigade was created for him in November. After being lightly engaged at Fredericksburg he accompanied Longstreet to southeastern Virginia. During the Gettysburg Campaign he was detached from the division to guard vital Hanover Junction north of Richmond. The division was detached from the corps when Longstreet went to Georgia, with Corse's Brigade assigned to western Virginia. In January 1864 Corse and the brigade joined Pickett for the attack on New Bern, North Carolina. After seeing action at Drewry's Bluff the entire division rejoined Lee and fought at Cold Harbor and through the siege of Petersburg. After the disaster at Five Forks the retreat to Appomattox began and Corse was captured at Sayler's Creek on April 6, 1865. Following his July release he returned to banking in his native Alexandria. (Freeman, Douglas S., *Lee's Lieutenants*)

COSBY, George Blake (1830-1909)

Transferring from the staff to the line in the middle of the Civil War, native Kentuckian George B. Cosby served throughout the western theater as commander of mounted troops. The West Pointer (1852) had been posted to the Regiment of Mounted Riflemen and with them was wounded fighting Indians at Lake Trinidad, Texas on May 9, 1854. The next year he was transferred to the cavalry, and he resigned as first lieutenant, 2nd Cavalry, on May 10, 1861. His Confederate assignments included: captain, Cavalry (ca. May 1861); major and assistant adjutant general (September 1861); colonel, Cavalry (1862); commanding brigade, Jackson's Division, Cavalry Corps, Department of Mississippi and East Louisiana (January 1863); commanding brigade, Martin's Division, Cavalry Corps, Department of Mississippi and East Louisiana (February-March 1863); brigadier general, CSA (April 23, 1863 to rank from January 20); commanding brigade, Jackson's Cavalry Division, Department of the West (June 9-July 1863); commanding brigade, Jackson's Cavalry Division, Department of Mississippi and East Louisiana (July-August 1863); commanding brigade, Jackson's Division, Lee's Cavalry Corps, Department of Mississippi and East Louisiana (August-December 24, 1863 and January-January 28, 1864); commanding brigade, Jackson's Division, Lee's Cavalry Corps, Department of Alabama, Mississippi and East Louisiana (January 28-February 1864); and commanding Hodge's (old) Brigade, Department of Western Virginia and East Tennessee (September 5, 1864-ca. April 1865). As a staff officer with Simon B. Buckner, he served in central Kentucky and was part of the force sent to reinforce Fort Donelson. As Buckner's staff chief he carried the first com-

munications with Grant concerning a possible surrender. Not exchanged until August 27, 1862, he was promoted to a colonelcy. Early the next year he took command of a cavalry brigade and fought at Thompson's Station before being promoted to brigadier general. He took part in the unsuccessful defense of Jackson. Late in 1864 he was given command of another brigade in southwestern Virginia and eastern Tennessee, which he led until the end of the war. A postwar California farmer, he also was a public office holder. He committed suicide, allegedly due to his old wound (probably from Indian fighting).

COURTNEY, Alfred Ranson (1833-1914)

For his failure to accompany two of his batteries to the field at Antietam, Alfred Ranson Courtney faced a court-martial for dereliction of duty and so requested a transfer out of the Army of Northern Virginia. He had entered the Confederate service early in 1861 and his assignments included: captain, Richmond "Courtney" Artillery (July 8, 1861); major, Artillery (July 14, 1862); commanding Artillery Battalion, Ewell's Division, Jackson's Command, Army of Northern Virginia (July 14-fall 1862); commanding Artillery Battalion, Hindman's Division, 2nd Corps, Army of Tennessee (November 1863-February 1864); and commanding artillery battalion, 2nd Corps, Army of Tennessee (February-May 14, 1864 and summer-fall 1864). He led his battery in the Shenandoah and Peninsula campaigns before being promoted to command Ewell's artillery. In this capacity, he served through Cedar Mountain, 2nd Bull Run, and the capture of Harpers Ferry. Of the six batteries of his battalion only two were ordered into Maryland to join in the battle of Antietam. He chose to remain in Harpers Ferry with the majority of his command. For this action charges were preferred against him. Upon his own request he was assigned to staff duty in Richmond on April 20, 1863. Three months later he was directed to report to East Tennessee. Joining the Army of Tennessee, he fought at Chattanooga and in the early stages of the Atlanta Campaign. He was wounded at Resaca but returned to duty in time for the final unsuccessful battles for the city. He subsequently served at gathering up the fragments of the artillery after Hood's disastrous foray into Tennessee. A postwar lawyer, he served in the Virginia legislature and as an official of the masonic order.

COX, Samuel, Jr. (?-?)

A strong Southern sympathizer during the Civil War, Samuel Cox, Jr., provided aid to the fleeing John Wilkes Booth and David Herold. At about midnight on April 15, 1865, the pair of fugitives appeared at the home of the wealthy Maryland planter. Following a conversation, which was whispered so that the fugitive's black guide, Oswald Swann, could not hear it, Cox ordered them from his house in a loud and clear manner. However, Swann later noticed the assassins returning to the house where they were given food and allowed to stay in the nearby woods. Cox then sent for his foster brother Thomas Jones to arrange for their further flight into Virginia. Strangely enough, Cox was never prosecuted for his role in the affair.

COX, William Ruffin (1832-1919)

Suffering some 11 Civil War wounds, five at Chancellorsville, William R. Cox lived to be one of the last surviving general officers. A North Carolina lawyer and militia officer, he entered the service of the state even before its secession. His assignments included: major, 2nd North Carolina (May 8, 1861); lieutenant colonel, 2nd North Carolina (April 2, 1863, to rank from September 17, 1862); colonel, 2nd North Carolina (March 21, 1863); brigadier general, CSA (May 31, 1864); commanding Ramseur's (old) Brigade, Rodes'-Grimes' Division, 2nd Corps, Army of Northern Virginia (June 4-13 and December 1864-April 9, 1865); and commanding brigade, Rodes'-Grimes' Division, Valley District, Department of Northern Virginia (June 13-December 1864). After service near Fredericksburg, Virginia, and Wilmington, North Carolina, his regiment served at the Seven Days, South Mountain, Antietam, and Fredericksburg. In command of the unit at Chancellorsville he suffered multiple wounds on May 3 but was able to rejoin the regiment on August 1. He fought in the Bristoe Campaign and received two more wounds at Kelly's Ford. After Spotsylvania he was promoted to the temporary rank of brigadier and command of Ramseur's former command. He led this brigade for the remainder of the conflict including service with Early at Monocacy, on the outskirts of Washington, at 3rd Winchester, Fisher's Hill, and Cedar Creek. Directing his men in the trenches around Petersburg until its fall, he surrendered at Appomattox. A postwar politician he sat in congress for three terms. (Freeman, Douglas S., *Lee's Lieutenants*)

CRAWFORD, Martin Jenkins (1820-1883)

A moderate secessionist and a strong proponent of States' rights, Congressman Martin Crawford resigned his seat upon the secession of his native Georgia. In February he was appointed by Jefferson Davis as one of the three commissioners to the United States during the crisis over Forts Sumter and Pickens. When his commission failed, he returned to the South and entered the Provisional Congress where he served on the Accounts and the Commercial Affairs committees and was a supporter of Howell Cobb for the chief executive's position. Following the adjournment of the provisional body in February 1862, Crawford was appointed colonel, 3rd Georgia Cavalry, a newly organized regiment, on May 28. His military career was not a success. Near New Haven, Kentucky, Colonel Crawford and a large portion of his command was surprised while on outpost duty, and was New Haven, Kentucky, on September 29, 1862, Colonel Crawford and a large portion of his command was surprised while on outpost duty, and was captured without the Union cavalry having to fire a shot. After being paroled, Crawford was found guilty by a general court-martial and sentenced to "three months' suspension from rank and pay and to be reprimanded in orders by the general commanding." Before his suspension was over, Crawford resigned on March 13, 1863. He subsequently served as an unofficial aide to General Howell Cobb. After the war, he resumed his career as a lawyer and went on to become a judge on the state supreme court.

CRENSHAW, William Graves (?-?)

A prominent Richmond businessman in the import-export field, William G. Crenshaw raised and equipped a Confederate artillery battery, but his talents were soon determined to be more useful in his own field. A native of the city, he was engaged in the running of his firm in 1861 when he raised the Richmond "Crenshaw" Artillery and became its captain. He led the unit during the Seven Days, at 2nd Bull Run, and Antietam. Missing Fredericksburg, he resigned in 1863 to accept an assignment to purchase supplies and naval vessels in England. Successful in this, he was however unable to achieve a second part of his assignment—to gain recognition and outright support from the London government. After the war he was highly successful in the mining field.

CREWS, Charles Constantine (?-?)

It is sometimes claimed that Colonel Charles C. Crews was promoted to brigadier general during the final days of the Confederate Army of Tennessee. However, despite his being in charge of a brigade for extended periods, there is no record of a formal appointment. His assignments included: captain, Company A, 2nd Georgia Cavalry (May 7, 1862); colonel, 2nd Georgia Cavalry (November 1, 1862); commanding brigade, Wharton's Division, Wheeler's Cavalry Corps, Army of

Martin J. Crawford, legislator turned cavalryman. (*Harper's*)

Tennessee (summer-fall 1863); commanding brigade, Martin's Division, Wheeler's Cavalry Corps, Army of Tennessee (December 1863-February 29, 1864); and commanding brigade, Allen's Division, Wheeler's Cavalry Corps, Department of South Carolina, Georgia and Florida (September 1864-early 1865). During a raid in central Kentucky in the fall of 1862, he was captured but released in time to receive promotion to regimental command. After service in middle Tennessee he fought at Chickamauga, Knoxville, and in the Atlanta, Savannah, and Carolinas campaigns. He was wounded in the last-named campaign. By this time Wheeler's cavalry was serving with Johnston's army and he was mentioned as a colonel on April 15, 1865. The army surrendered on April 26. It is during this eleven-day period that it is claimed that he received promotion.

CRITTENDEN, George Bibb (1812-1880)

The son of the great compromiser of 1860, John J. Crittenden, George B. Crittenden's military career was greatly damaged by charges of drunkenness in the face of the enemy. The native Kentuckian and West Pointer (1832) had served in the Black Hawk War before resigning in 1833 while still a brevet second lieutenant of infantry. Relocating to Texas, he joined the army there and in 1843 was captured during the Mier invasion of Mexico. He escaped the fate of his compatriots when he drew the white bean and his life was spared. During the Mexican War, he was recommissioned as a captain in the Regiment of Mounted Riflemen and won a brevet. In 1848 he was cashiered from the Army but was reinstated the next year. By the time of his June 10, 1861, resignation he was the lieutenant colonel of the regiment. He offered his services to the Confederacy, and his assignments included: brigadier general, CSA (August 15, 1861); assigned command 4th Brigade, 2nd Division, Potomac District, Department of Northern Virginia (October 22, 1861); major general, CSA (November 9, 1861); commanding District of East Tennessee, Department #2 (December 8, 1861-February 23, 1862); commanding 2nd Division, Army of Central Kentucky, Department #2 (February 23-April 1, 1862); and commanding Departments of East Tennessee and Western Virginia (May 31-June 22, 1864). Appointed a brigadier general, he was assigned to a brigade in northern Virginia but the record is unclear whether or not he actually commanded one there. Promoted to major general, he was given command in East Tennessee. He lost the battle of Mill Springs in Kentucky early in 1862. Despite the fact that he was apparently drunk at the time much of the blame belongs to his subordinate, Felix K. Zollicoffer, who was killed in the action brought on by his own rashness. Nonetheless Crittenden came in for the bulk of the censure—much of it deserved—and was arrested for drunkenness on April 1, 1862. He resigned the following October 23rd. For much of the rest of the war he served on the staff of John S. Williams with the apparently unofficial rank of colonel. In the spring of 1864 he was briefly in departmental command in his old bailiwick. His brother Thomas L. Crittenden remained loyal to the Union and became a general officer. After the war George B. Crittenden served as Kentucky's state librarian.

CROSSLAND, Edward (1827-1881)

A Kentucky farmer, lawyer, and politician, Edward Crossland served throughout the war in various theaters but did not earn his greatest distinction until his command was mounted and assigned to Forrest's Cavalry. His assignments included: captain, Company E. 1st Kentucky (April 23, 1861); major, 1st Kentucky (1861), lieutenant colonel, 1st Kentucky (1862); colonel, 7th Kentucky (May 20, 1862); commanding 3rd Brigade, Buford's Division, Forrest's Cavalry Corps, Department of Alabama, Mississippi and East Louisiana (May-July 14, 1864); and commanding independent brigade, Forrest's Cavalry Corps, Department of Alabama, Mississippi and East Louisiana (spring 1865). After seeing action at Dranesville, his original 12-months unit was mustered out in May 1862 and he was elected colonel of the veteran 7th. He led it at Baton Rouge, Corinth, Champion Hill, and Jackson. Having been cut off at Champion Hill with the rest of Loring's Division, he was not included in the capture of Vicksburg. On March 1, 1864, the regiment was mounted and joined the cavalry. Within a few days he was in command of the brigade and led it at Brice's Crossroads and Tupelo, where he was wounded, under Forrest. Returning to duty in August, he found that the brigade had been assigned to General H.B. Lyon. He resumed regimental command until early 1865 when he directed a separate brigade in opposing Wilson's Raid through Alabama. Crossland's command surrendered May 6, 1865, at Columbus, Mississippi.

CRUIKSHANK, Marcus Henderson (1826-1881)

One of the most obstructionist of congressmen during the Second Confederate Congress was Alabama's 4th District representative, Marcus H. Cruikshank. A native Alabamian, Cruikshank practiced law and owned a small farming operation. On the political side, he was a half-owner of the *Alabama Reporter* and served for many years as the mayor of Talladega. A lifelong Whig he supported the Union and was an outspoken opponent of secession. Nonetheless, after running a saltworks during the early part of the war, he defeated Jabez L.M. Curry, the 4th District's incumbent, in the fall of 1863. Taking his seat in February 1864 he was named chairman of the Committee on Enrolled Bills and promptly became a thorn in the side of the Davis administration. He immediately moved to cancel the authorization to suspend the writ of habeas corpus and opposed virtually all war measures. Peace proposals always found favorable consideration with Cruikshank. He also served on the committees on Ordnance and Ordnance Stores and on Printing. He followed the legal and journalistic professions after the war as well as helping the poor until his death in a riding accident.

CRUMP, William Wood (1819-1897)

An ardent secessionist and prominent attorney, William W. Crump served as the assistant secretary of the treasury in the Confederate government. A native Virginian he had been admitted to the bar in 1840 and after serving a year as a judge returned to private practice, preferring to work before a jury. During the war he worked to protect younger bureaucrats from military service. He was sitting in the state legislature when military rule was established after the war's close. Returning to his law practice, he worked on Jefferson Davis' defense and held no further public office excepting one term in the legislature. For the remaining years of his life he was a prominent defense attorney.

CRUTCHFIELD, Stapleton (1835-1865)

The battle of Chancellorsville deprived the Confederacy not only of Stonewall Jackson but also of Stapleton Crutchfield, one of the South's most able artillerists, who lost his leg in the battle, and a probable promotion to brigadier and further active service. Six years after graduating number one in his Virginia Military Institute class of 1855 he entered Confederate service. His assignments included: major, 9th Virginia (July 1861); major, 58th Virginia (October 1861); lieutenant colonel, 58th Virginia (early 1862); colonel, 16th Virginia (May 1862, declined); colonel, Artillery (May 5, 1862); chief of artillery, Valley District, Department of Northern Virginia (May 5-June 25, 1862); chief of artillery, 2nd Corps, Army of Northern Virginia (June 25, 1862-May 2, 1863); commanding Artillery Brigade, Department of Richmond (January 7-April 2, 1865); and commanding brigade, G.W.C. Lee's Division, attached to Army of Northern Virginia (April 2-6, 1865). After early service in the infantry on Crany Island and in western Virginia, he transferred to the artillery and served with Stonewall Jackson in the Shenandoah and at the Seven Days, Cedar Mountain, 2nd Bull Run, Antietam, Fredericksburg, and Chancellorsville. He was under active consideration for promotion to brigadier general but after losing his leg on the second day at Chancellorsville, he was incapacitated for further service in the field. Upon his recovery in March 1864, he was assigned to duty as an artillery inspector. In the following January he was given command of the stationary artillery defenses of Richmond. With the fall of the city, his gun crews formed a brigade of infantry. Joining Lee's army in the retreat, he was decapitated by a cannonball at Sayler's Creek on April 6, three days before the surrender at Appomattox. (Wise, Jennings C., *The Long Arm of Lee*)

CULP, John Wesley (ca. 1838-1863)

Although born in Gettysburg, John Culp, better known by his middle name of Wesley, served in the Confederate army. Having worked for a number of years in Virginia, young Culp had politically become a Southerner. On April 20, 1861, he was enlisted in the Hamtranck Guards, officially Company B, 2nd Virginia, at Harpers Ferry. After initial service in the Shenandoah Valley, the company, from Shepherdstown, fought at the battle of 1st Bull Run. Early in 1862, Culp received a furlough but was captured by Union troops during his leave. He thus missed the Valley and Peninsula campaigns. Exchanged on August 5, 1862, he soon rejoined his regiment. The regiment, in the famed "Stonewall" Brigade, fought at Cedar Mountain, 2nd Bull Run, Antietam, Fredericksburg, and Chancellorsville. The next campaign, Lee's second invasion of the North, would take Culp to his hometown and to his death. Culp took part in the 2nd battle of Winchester on the way to Pennsylvania. Late on the second day of the battle of Gettysburg, Culp's division moved onto Culp's Hill, which was named for his family. In the fighting the next morning, as the Union forces retook the hill, Culp fell dead. His body was never identified and he lies with the unknown dead.

CUMMING, Alfred (1829-1910)

Promotion to brigadier general in the Confederate service brought Georgia West Pointer (1849) Alfred Cumming a transfer to the western theater. Upon his graduation he was posted to the infantry and served on the frontier. He took part in the Utah operations against the Mormons and served on the staff of David E. Twiggs for a time. Resigning as a captain in the 7th Infantry on January 19, 1861—the very day his native state seceded—he joined the Confederacy. His assignments included: major, Infantry (March 16, 1861); lieutenant colonel, Augusta Volunteer Battalion (spring 1861); lieutenant colonel, 10th Georgia (June 1861); colonel, 10th Georgia (September 25, 1861); commanding Wilcox's (Ala.) Brigade, Anderson's Division, Longstreet's Corps, Army of Northern Virginia (September 14-17, 1862); brigadier general, CSA (October 29, 1862); commanding 3rd Brigade, Stevenson's Division, Department of Mississippi and East Louisiana (April 15-July 4, 1863); commanding brigade, Stevenson's Division, Hill's-Breckinridge's Corps, Army of Tennessee (October 17-November 23, 1863); commanding brigade, Stevenson's Division, Hardee's Corps, Army of Tennessee (November 23, 1863-February 20, 1864); and commanding brigade, Stevenson's Division, Hood's-Lee's Corps, Army of Tennessee (February 20-August 31, 1864). Moving with his regiment to Virginia, he was stationed on the Peninsula and took part in the siege of Yorktown. During the Seven Days he was wounded at Malvern Hill but recovered in time to take part in the invasion of Maryland. He fought at Crampton's Pass on South Mountain and was again wounded at Antietam. During both actions he was detailed to command another brigade. The next month he was promoted to brigadier general and upon his recovery was sent to John C. Pemberton's army near Vicksburg. He commanded a brigade in the defense of that city until its fall and was exchanged in September 1863 in time to take part in the defeat at Chattanooga. He served throughout the Atlanta Campaign, at the head of his brigade, until severely wounded at Jonesboro. This ended his field career and after the war he became a farmer. In the late 1880s he was a U.S. military representative to Korea.

CUMMING, Kate (ca. 1833-?)

A nurse with the Army of Tennessee, Kate Cumming served from the battle of Shiloh through the final surrender. Born in Scotland, her family settled in Mobile, where her brother enlisted in the Confederate army. She then volunteered for hospital duty and treated the wounded following the battle of Shiloh. She was present through the campaigns in Mississippi, Tennessee, Kentucky, and Georgia. After serving in the Atlanta Campaign she completed the war in a hospital. In 1866 she published *A Journal of Hospital Life in the Confederate Army of Tennessee from the Battle of Shiloh to the End of the War.*

CUNNINGHAM, Richard H., Jr. (1834-1862)

The rate of attrition in the officers' ranks of Stonewall Jackson's command during the campaigns of 1862 was so great that Richard H. Cunningham, Jr., was commanding his regiment as a captain and his brigade as a lieutenant colonel. A merchant in Virginia's capital he had served in a local volunteer company long before the war. His unit volunteered for service a few days after the state's secession and his assignments included: first lieutenant, Company F, 21st Virginia (April 21, 1861); captain, Company F, 21st Virginia (May 1861); lieutenant colonel, 21st Virginia (April 21, 1862); and commanding 2nd Brigade, Jackson's Division, Jackson's Command, Army of Northern Virginia (June 26 and July 1-mid July 1862). After participating in the Cheat Mountain Campaign, he succeeded to command of the regiment, as a captain, during the Romney Campaign and became involved in the Loring-Jackson feud during the winter encampment there. Continuing in regimental command, he fought at Kernstown, McDowell, and in the Shenandoah Valley Campaign, where he was entrusted with escorting the prisoners captured at Front Royal and Winchester up the Valley. Moving to the defense of Richmond he commanded the brigade at Gaines' Mill while two grades short of the appropriate rank of brigadier. Relieved by Brigadier General John R. Jones, he resumed command of the 21st and led it through the rest of the Seven Days Battles before again taking over the brigade upon the wounding of Jones at Malvern Hill. Leaving an ambulance, where he had been for several days, to command his regiment at Cedar Mountain, he was killed while trying to rally his broken unit.

CURRY, Jabez Lamar Monroe (1825-1903)

Although he played an active role in the events of 1861-65, Jabez L.M. Curry's greatest service to the South was performed in the postwar period. Born in Georgia, Curry moved to Alabama and began the practice of law. After several terms in the state legislature, he was elected to the U.S. House of Representatives in 1856 where he remained until the secession of his state. An early secessionist, he was named to the Provisional Confederate Congress and served on the committees on: Comercial Affairs; Flag and Seal; and Postal Affairs. Running unopposed, he took his seat in the First Regular Congress. He chaired the Committee on Commerce and sat on the Committee on Elections. A consistent supporter of the war effort, he urged President Davis to take the field personally. As a lame duck, having been defeated for reelection in the 1863 elections, Curry was a driving force behind the call for additional sacrifices made by the First Congress as it adjourned. Having also lost a bid for a senatorship, Curry was appointed lieutenant colonel, 5th Alabama Cavalry, and commanded the regiment in central Alabama during the final stages of the war. His only previous military experience had been a brief stint in the Mexican War. Becoming a Baptist preacher, he became involved in education, establishing a public school system throughout most of the former Confederacy. His work was occasionally interrupted by

Confederate Congressman Jabez L.M. Curry. (*Harper's*)

diplomatic appointments, but he was active in education until his death. (Alderman, Edwin and Gordon, Armistead, *J.L.M. Curry: A Biography*)

CUSSONS, John (1837-?)

An English-born Alabama journalist in the Southern army, John Cussons' most notable moment in the Civil War came when he suffered a wounded hat in an affair of honor with a fellow officer. Entering the Confederate army as a lieutenant in the 4th Alabama, the newspaper publisher served on the staffs of Generals Lee and Whiting and Colonel E.M. Law. With the latter officer he served at Thoroughfare Gap, 2nd Bull Run, and Antietam. Having been promoted to captain, Cussons was present at the action at Fort Huger—during Longstreet's half-hearted siege of Suffolk—on April 19 when some five guns and 137 men were captured by the enemy in a surprise attack. There was much recrimination among the various units involved, especially between officers of the 55th North Carolina and Law's Brigade. Cussons and fellow staff officer Captain Terrell filed a report that questioned the North Carolinians' bravery and Colonel Connally and Major Belo, of that regiment, challenged them to a duel. Thus Cussons and Belo found themselves facing one another over the sights of Mississippi rifles. In the first discharge Cussons' hat was hit. In the second round of fire, Belo suffered a nicked neck. Before a third round could be fired, word came that Terrell and Connally had resolved the dispute without violence and the matter was closed. Cussons was later captured at Gettysburg and confined at Forts McHenry and Delaware, Johnson's Island, and Point Lookout. After eight months he was exchanged and rejoined his division. He later served with Forrest's cavalry. He went into the hotel and printing businesses following the war. (Cussons, John, *A Glance at Current History*)

CUTSHAW, Wilfred Emory (1828-1907)

It was natural for Wilfred E. Cutshaw to have so much of his Civil War career connected with the Shenandoah Valley, since he had been born at Harpers Ferry. A graduate of the Virginia Military Institute, he was an instructor at another military academy when he joined the Confederacy, where his assignments included: lieutenant, Infantry (October 31, 1861); captain, Winchester (Va.) Artillery (March 1862); major, Artillery (February 27, 1864); commanding artillery battalion, 2nd Corps, Army of Northern Virginia (March 19-August 1864 and February-April 6, 1865); and commanding artillery battalion, Valley District, Department of Northern Virginia (August 1864-February 1865). During the first winter of the war, he commanded an improvised section of artillery, which was captured in an affair at Hanging Rock on January 7, 1862. Soon taking command of a new battery, he led it through the early stages of Jackson's Shenandoah Valley Campaign. Heavily engaged at 1st Winchester on May 25, the command lost all of its officers, including Cutshaw who was wounded and captured. Upon his exchange in April 1863, it was found that he was unfit for field service and he was assigned as acting commandant of cadets at VMI. Desiring a more active role, he obtained an assignment as inspector of artillery with the 2nd Corps in September. As such he served through the Bristoe and Mine Run campaigns. He led his newly assigned battalion at the Wilderness and Spotsylvania where he was wounded. He was

detached from the Petersburg lines and sent with Kershaw to reinforce Early in the Valley in August 1864. There he took part in the action at Cedar Creek. His battalion having suffered heavily, especially in horses, it was returned to Richmond the following February and assigned to stationary guns. With the fall of the city, he joined in the retreat to Appomattox and was severely wounded, losing a leg, at Sayler's Creek. He later was a civil engineer in Richmond and a VMI professor.

CUTTS, Allen Sherrod (1827-ca. 1895)

A veteran of the Mexican War, as an enlisted artilleryman, Allen Cutts became one of the earliest artillery battalion commanders in the Army of Northern Virginia. Between the wars, Cutts was a planter in Americus, Georgia. At the outbreak of the Civil War he began organizing an artillery battery for Confederate service. His assignments included: captain, Sumter (Ga.) Flying Artillery (July 6, 1861); major, Artillery (May 22, 1862); commanding an artillery battalion, Reserve Artillery, Army of Northern Virginia (May 22, 1862-June 2, 1863); lieutenant colonel, Artillery (May 26, 1862); and commanding artillery battalion, 3rd Corps, Army of Northern Virginia (June 2, 1863-early 1865). Taking part in the battle of Dranesville, in command of his battery, Cutts was noticed by Jeb Stuart for bravery; he was seen to actually load the guns himself. Promoted the next spring, he was given command of a battalion that was known as the Sumter Battalion. He led his men in the Peninsula Campaign and at Antietam and Chancellorsville. In 1864 he fought from the Wilderness to Petersburg, where he had his greatest moment in the repulse of the Union attack on June 20. During much of the last campaign he was in charge of his own and Richardson's Battalions. He was often referred to as a full colonel, but there is no official record of his promotion. After the war, Cutts was a state legislator, mayor, and law officer. (Wise, Jennings Cropper, *The Long Arm of Lee*)

D

DABNEY, Robert Lewis (1820-1898)

A Presbyterian minister, professor, and editor, Robert L. Dabney served on Stonewall Jackson's staff for only three months but nonetheless wrote a biography, *Life and Campaigns of Lieut.-Gen. Thomas J. Jackson*. The native Virginian became chaplain of the 18th Virginia upon the outbreak of the Civil War and in April 1862 reluctantly accepted the post of chief of staff for Jackson's Valley District. He was commissioned as a major and assistant adjutant general. Henry Kyd Douglas declares that while Dabney was a good staff officer in camp he was not up to the job in the field. After serving in the Shenandoah Valley Campaign and the Seven Days, he resigned in July 1862. Known for carrying an umbrella instead of a sword, he was once ridiculed by Jackson's "foot cavalry" when he was seen on the march with it opened against the weather. Resuming his religious pursuits, he never reconciled himself to the South's fall and proposed the emigration of the white populace. His Jackson biography had to be corrected on a number of points by a tactful General Lee. (Johnson, Thomas Cary, *Life and Letters of Robert Lewis Dabney*)

DANIEL, John Moncure (1825-1865)

As editor of the *Richmond Examiner*, John M. Daniel became increasingly critical of the Davis administration. Lacking an interest in the study of law, he gave it up to become a librarian and by 1847 was the editor of this new newspaper. In the 1850s he held a diplomatic post in Italy but was not very capable at the art of diplomacy. Returning home at the outbreak of the war, he served two stints in the army in staff positions and was slightly wounded in the summer of 1862. Returning to his paper, he developed intense dislikes for many of the figures in the Confederacy and even fought a duel with the Confederate treasurer in 1864 in which he was again wounded. Struck down by illness, he died a few days before his plant was destroyed in the fire upon the capture of Richmond. (Bagby, G.W., *John M. Daniel's Latch-key*)

DANIEL, Junius (1828-1864)

A West Pointer (1851), Junius Daniel spent most of his Confederate career in brigade command. The North Carolinian had resigned an infantry commission in 1858 to run a Louisiana plantation but returned to his native state upon the outbreak of the war. His assignments included: colonel, 14th North Carolina (June 3, 1861); colonel, 45th North Carolina (ca. April 14, 1862); commanding brigade, Holmes' Division (from the Department of North Carolina), Army of Northern Virginia (June-July 1862); commanding brigade, Department of North Carolina (July-August 1862); commanding brigade (in Elzey's Command from December 12 and in French's-D.H. Hill's Command from late December), Department of Virginia and North Carolina (August 1862-April 1, 1863); brigadier general, CSA (September 1, 1862); commanding brigade, Department of North Carolina (April 1-May 1863); and commanding brigade, Rodes' Division, 2nd Corps, Army of Northern Virginia (June 1863-May 12, 1864). Commanding his original regiment at Yorktown, he transferred to a new regiment upon the reorganization. He commanded a brigade in the Seven Days, seeing action at Malvern Hill. After service near Drewry's Bluff and in North Carolina, he was sent with his men to Lee's army, with which they suffered heavily on the first day at Gettysburg. He served through the autumn campaigns and in the Wilderness. At Spotsylvania on May 12, 1864, he was mortally wounded while trying to recapture the trenches at the Bloody Angle. He died the next day. (Freeman, Douglas, S., *Lee's Lieutenants*)

DARGAN, Edmund Strother (1805-1879)

Being primarily self-educated, Edmund S. Dargan was a successful lawyer and former chief justice of the Alabama supreme court by the time of the secession crisis, during which he urged immediate disunion without the nicety of referring the ordinance to the people. Representing Alabama's 9th District, including Mobile, Dargan utilized his seat on the Committee on the Judiciary to busy himself with the judicial organization of the new nation. He also chaired the investigation of the Erlanger Loan. In order to win the war he was willing to bend and even violate the constitution until the emergency was past. In what can be cited as an example of the legislative behavior of the times, Dargan drew a knife on fellow representative Henry S. Foote. With his term in the First Congress coming to an end, Dargan declined to stand for reelection. He resumed his law practice.

DAVIDSON, Henry Brevard (1831-1899)

Transferring from the staff to the line, Tennessee West Pointer (1853) Henry B. Davidson became a brigadier general of Confederate cavalry. He had served in the Mexican War as a private and sergeant in Company K, 1st Tennessee, and his performance earned him his appointment to the academy. Upon his graduation he served on the frontier with the dragoons. On July 30, 1861, he was dropped from the rolls as captain, 1st Dragoons, when he did not report after his leave expired. In the meantime he had joined the Confederacy where his assignments included: major and assistant adjutant general (early 1861); colonel and assistant adjutant general (late 1862); commanding Post of Staunton, Virginia (late 1862); brigadier general, CSA (August 18, 1863); commanding brigade, Pegram's Division, Forrest's Cavalry Corps, Army of Tennessee (September-October 1863); commanding brigade, Wharton's Division, Wheelers' Cavalry Corps, Army of Tennessee (October 1863-early 1864); commanding Jackson's (old) Brigade, Lomax's Cavalry Division, Valley District, Army of Northern Virginia (fall 1864-January 1865); and commanding Cavalry Brigade, Valley District, Army of Northern Virginia (January-March 1865). His early service came in the West as a staff officer with John B. Floyd, Simon B. Buckner, Albert Sidney Johnston, and William W. Mackall. Captured at Island #10, he was not exchanged until August 27, 1862. Promoted to colonel, he was assigned to post duty for a time and then was advanced to brigadier general. Commanding a mounted brigade, he fought at Chickamauga and then was transferred back to Virginia. Commanding a cavalry brigade in the Shenandoah Valley, he fought at Cedar Creek and at Waynesboro. Then he apparently joined Joseph E. Johnston in North Carolina and was included in Johnston's surrender. A civil engineer in California after the war, he was also engaged in railroading and held minor state office.

DAVIDSON, Thomas J. (?-1862)

During the defense of Fort Donelson Confederate brigade commander Thomas J. Davidson had to be relieved due to illness but this did not save him from capture, imprisonment, and death as a prisoner. In 1861 he became a colonel of a regiment that was variously designated as the 2nd and 3rd Mississippi. While serving in Kentucky, on November 19, 1861 the designation was officially changed to the 23rd. Sent to the aid of the beleaguered fort, he commanded a brigade, Johnson's Division, Fort Donelson, Department #2 (February 9-15, 1862). On the morning of the planned breakout attempt Davidson was

so ill that he had neglected to give the order for his troops to move to the jumpoff point. General Bushrod Johnson saw the problem and relieved him of duty. But the timing of the attack was ruined and the move failed. With the fall of the fort, Davidson became a prisoner and was sent to Fort Warren in Boston Harbor. The Union authorities were anxious to exchange him quickly, perhaps because they knew his situation was serious and he might die before they could get one of their colonels back for him. On April 29, 1862, he died.

DAVIS, George (1820-1896)

Although he had long been an opponent of secession, George Davis wound up serving in both the legislative and executive branches of the Confederate government. Active in Whig politics, lawyer Davis did not, however, run for public office. He did attend the Washington Peace Conference whose recommendations he criticized as dishonorable for the South. With the secession of his native North Carolina, he was named to an at-large seat in the Provisional Confederate Congress. After 25 ballots in September 1861 he was appointed to the Senate of the First Regular Congress, but it turned out to be only a two-year term. In the First Congress he chaired the Committee on Claims and also served on those on Buildings, Finance, and Naval Affairs. Becoming a strong nationalist, even favoring appellate jurisdiction over state courts for the proposed supreme court, Davis became unpopular with much of the North Carolina delegation. The same feeling permeated the state legislature and he failed to be reelected in the summer of 1863. While serving as a lame duck, he was tapped by Jefferson Davis to serve as attorney general. He was confirmed by the Senate on January 2, 1864, and, with only six weeks to go in his term, he resigned his seat to take up his new duties. Here his nationalist tendencies became even more pronounced as he sided with the central government opinions against the individual states. Fleeing Richmond at the war's close and heading for Europe, Davis was captured at Key West and imprisoned until New Year's Day 1866. He resumed his law practice and was successful enough at it to decline an 1878 offer of the chief justice's seat on the state supreme court, for financial considerations.

DAVIS, James Lucius (1813-1871)

A graduate of West Point (1833) and a veteran of three years in the 4th Artillery, Virginian J. Lucius Davis was well qualified to write a cavalry manual for the Confederate army. With the outbreak of war, he returned to the military where his assignments include: colonel, 46th Virginia (June 24, 1861); lieutenant colonel, 8th Virginia Cavalry Battalion (early 1862); colonel, 10th Virginia Cavalry (officially September 24, 1862, although he appears to have acted as such since the spring); and commanding Chambliss' Brigade, W.H.F. Lee's Division, Cavalry Corps, Army of Northern Virginia (August 16-October 1864). After initial service with the infantry in western Virginia, he transferred to the cavalry, seeing action at Williamsburg, the Seven Days, Fredericksburg, and Gettysburg. During the retreat from the latter he was wounded and captured at Hagerstown, on July 6, 1863. Declared exchanged on March 10, 1864, he commanded the regiment during the siege of Petersburg. He commanded Chambliss' Brigade for about two months after that officer was killed. He appears to have been absent from October 1864 until his resignation on February 2, 1865. He retired to Buckingham County, Virginia, after the war.

DAVIS, Jefferson (1808-1889)

The only president of the Confederacy, Jefferson Davis proved to be something less than the revolutionary leader necessary to lead a fledgling nation to independence; he himself would have preferred to serve as a military leader. Born in Kentucky, he was graduated from West Point in 1828 and was posted to the Pacific Northwest. There he served with the infantry until 1833 when he transferred to the dragoons. Two years later he resigned as a first lieutenant when he eloped with the daughter of his commander, Zachary Taylor. Thereafter a Mississippi planter, he lost his wife shortly after the wedding and then married Varina Howell. Elected as a Democrat to Congress he served in the House of Representatives from 1845 to 1847. During the Mexican War he compiled an enviable record as colonel of the 1st Mississippi Rifles. Wounded at Buena Vista, he turned down a commission as a brigadier general. He then won a seat in the U.S. Senate, which he held until named Franklin Pierce's war secretary in 1853. He held this post for the full tenure of the Pierce presidency and then won reelection to the Senate. A staunch supporter of states' rights, he backed his state's secession and made a powerful speech on the floor of the Senate when he and four other senators withdrew from that body on January 21, 1861. Almost immediately named commander of the state military forces with the rank of major general—in recognition of his Mexican War service—he became a compromise candidate for the provisional presidency of the Confederacy and was so elected on February 9, 1861. Inaugurated nine days later in Montgomery, Alabama, he was elected as regular president for a six-year term on November 6, 1861, and was reinaugurated on Washington's Birthday in Richmond. His interest in the military defense of his country soon became apparent; his early war secretaries served as little more than clerks as he himself supervised the affairs of the department. He made frequent forays into the field, arriving at 1st Bull Run just as the fight was ending, and was later under fire at Seven Pines where he placed Robert E. Lee in command of what became the Army of Northern Virginia. Later he toured the western theater where he supported his old friend Braxton Bragg against the criticisms of his subordinates. His handling of the high command was extremely controversial. There were long-standing feuds with Beauregard and Joseph E. Johnston. His defense of certain non-performing generals, such as Bragg and Pemberton, irritated many in the South. On the political front his autocratic ways fostered a large and well-organized anti-Davis faction in the Confederate Congress, especially in the Senate. His attempts to manage the war effectively by placing more power in the hands of the central government were often thwarted by the states' rights philosophy that had led to its very founding. It is quite apparent that he is more popular in the

President Jefferson Davis. (Leslie's)

South today than he was during his tenure. Upon the fall of Richmond he fled south with the remnants of his government and was finally captured near Irwinville, Georgia, on May 10, 1865. He was sent off to prison at Fort Monroe, faced with charges of treason. Never brought to trial, he was finally released on bail after two years of confinement. Always contentious, he wrote his autobiography entitled *The Rise and Fall of the Confederate Government*. In this 1881 work he refought the war, including his views of those feuds with officers like Beauregard and Johnston who received much of the blame for the Confederacy's demise. He lived out his remaining years in Mississippi, never seeking to have his citizenship restored. In spite of this, it was restored during the presidency of Jimmy Carter. (Eaton, Clement, *Jefferson Davis*)

DAVIS, Joseph (ca. 1858-1864)

Both Presidents Lincoln and Davis lost a son during their tenures in their respective White Houses. At mid-day on April 30, 1864, little Joe Davis was playing with the other children of the White House, when his mother went to take lunch to the president. While in the presence of the family nurse, the five-year old fell off the gallery railing and struck his head on the brick floor of the garden. The parents raced to his side but he was dead within a few minutes. The bereaved father soon had to deal with the double crisis of the advances of Grant into the Wilderness and Sherman towards Atlanta—while the executive mansion was in a state of mourning.

DAVIS, Joseph Robert (1825-1896)

When the Confederate Senate received the nomination of Joseph R. Davis to be a brigadier general it was rejected and the president was charged with nepotism. A few days later, after some bargaining, the nephew of Jefferson Davis was finally confirmed. The former Mississippi state senator and lawyer had entered the army at the head of a local company and his assignments included: captain, 10th Mississippi (spring 1861); lieutenant colonel, 10th Mississippi (April 1861); colonel and aide-de-camp to President Davis (August 31, 1861); brigadier general, CSA (September 15, 1862); commanding brigade (in French's Command from early 1863), Department of Virginia and North Carolina (fall 1862-April 1, 1863); commanding brigade, Department of Southern Virginia (April 1-May 1863); commanding brigade, Heth's Division, 3rd Corps, Army of Northern Virginia (May 30-July and August 1863-April 9, 1865). After brief service in the Pensacola area, he joined the staff of his uncle and was assigned to several fact-finding missions. Following the delay in his confirmation he was given a brigade, which he led in the Richmond area and in southeastern Virginia. Sent to reinforce Lee's army, he fought at Gettysburg where he allowed two of his regiments to be decimated in the railroad cut on the first day. He also led the brigade in Pickett's Charge two days later. Later the same month he was taken ill and Lee considered breaking up the brigade but felt that he could not because it was the president's nephew. Davis fought through the rest of the campaigns of the army including the Wilderness, Spotsylvania, Cold Harbor, Petersburg and the surrender at Appomattox. He practiced law for the next three decades. (Freeman, Douglas S., *Lee's Lieutenants*)

DAVIS, Reuben (1813-1890)

Although he shared the same family name and the same home state as the Confederate president, Mississippi's Senator Reuben Davis was one of that body's most vehemently anti-administration members. Davis was born in Tennessee and raised in Alabama before moving to Mississippi to study and practice medicine. He later switched to the law. He served as a district attorney and a judge before serving as colonel, 2nd Mississippi, in the Mexican War. After serving in the state legislature, Davis took a seat in the U.S. Congress and was there when his state seceded. Believing disunion to be a disaster but inevitable, he was considered by many to be a fire-eater. With the outbreak of the war, he saw some limited service in Kentucky as a brigadier general of state troops. In the fall elections he was named as the representative of the 2nd District to the First Regular Congress. Opposed to the war effort, Davis fought against the draft, and attempted to abolish the House's Committee on Military Affairs, but when this failed he resigned from the committee. Defeated as an anti-war candidate for governor in 1863, he resigned from Congress before the final session of the First Congress and rendered the Confederacy no further service. After the war Davis was a highly successful defense attorney and was a supporter of harsh treatment of freed blacks. (Davis, Reuben, *Recollections of Mississippi and Mississippians*)

DAVIS, Samuel (1842-1863)

Convicted Confederate spy Samuel Davis went to the gallows rather than provide the information demanded by the Union authorities. The 21-year-old had been caught by some of Grenville M. Dodge's command with maps and papers describing the Federal dispositions and likely plans. The capture had taken place near Pulaski, Tennessee, and he was taken into the town for court-martial. Convicted and sentenced to hang, he was offered a commutation of his sentence if he would reveal information about enemy spying activities. What the Union was most interested in was the identity of a Captain E. Coleman, Braxton Bragg's fictitious chief of scouts. Coleman was actually Captain Henry Shaw, but Davis refused to reveal this. In fact, Shaw witnessed the November 27, 1863, hanging from his cell in the same jail that had held Davis. (Whitley, Edythe Johns Rucker, *Sam Davis: Confederate Hero*)

DAVIS, Varina Howell (1826-1906)

The second wife of Jefferson Davis, Varina Howell became the butt of much of Richmond's gossip during the Civil War years. Born in Mississippi she had met the future Confederate president in 1844 and married him the next year. During his years in the U.S. Senate she managed the family plantation. When he was inaugurated in Montgomery, she was not present, but she soon arrived and moved with the Confederate capital to Richmond. As the country's first lady, she was roundly criticized for the almost royal manner in which the new nation's

Ruben Davis, one of Jefferson Davis' harshest critics. (*Harper's*)

White House was run. She clashed with the wives of many prominent Southern leaders but was informed on Richmond matters. After the war she lived for a time in England when her husband was released from custody. She then helped with his memoirs and wrote her own *Memoir of Jefferson Davis*. After his death she retired in New York. (Ross, Ishbel, *First Lady of the South* and Randall, Ruth P., *I Varina: A Biography of the Girl Who Married Jefferson Davis and Became the First Lady of the South*)

DAVIS, William George Mackey (1812-1898)

After donating $50,000 to the Confederate cause, William G.M. Davis resigned his brigadier general's commission to become something of a profiteer. The Virginia native had sailed the high seas before settling in Florida where he engaged in the cotton brokerage business and practiced law. He was engaged in these pursuits when the Civil War broke out and he offered his services. His assignments included: colonel, 1st Florida Cavalry (January 1, 1862); commanding 2nd Brigade, 2nd (Heth's) Division, Department of East Tennessee (ca. July 3-ca. October 31, 1862); commanding 1st Brigade, 3rd (Heth's) Division, Department of East Tennessee (ca. October 31-December 1862); brigadier general, CSA (November 4, 1862); commanding 1st Brigade, District, Department of East Tennessee (December 1862-early 1863); and commanding the department (spring-April 25, 1863). In command of a mounted regiment, he spent the first couple of months of his service in eastern Florida before being sent to East Tennessee in March 1862. There the regiment served dismounted and Davis soon found himself in brigade command. His remaining service being in that department, he was promoted to brigadier general and for a time commanded it. Resigning on May 6, 1863, he engaged in directing blockade-running operations. Once restrictions were lifted after the close of the conflict he resumed his legal career.

DAWKINS, James Baird (1820-1883)

By the time he was elected to the U.S. House of Representatives in 1860, James B. Dawkins was a devout secessionist and never took his seat because of the rapid development of the crisis. Instead, the South Carolina-born and-educated lawyer and planter served on the committee of the Florida convention, which drew up the document that took the state out of the Union. In November 1861 he was elected to represent the eastern half of Florida in the First Regular Confederate Congress, where he served on the committees on: Elections; Naval Affairs; and Quartermaster's & Commissary departments. Dawkins concerned himself primarily with matters relating directly to his home state, including the urging of construction of a military railroad for Florida. Elected to a judgeship in the Suwanee district, he resigned his congressional seat on December 8, 1862. His judicial appointment lasted until the Confederacy's fall. Following Reconstruction, during which he was banned from politics, he again served as a judge until his death.

DEARING, James (1840-1865)

Finding the promotion potential of the artillery too limited, Virginian James Dearing transferred to the cavalry—and was destined to be the last general officer of the Army of Northern Virginia to be fatally shot. He was three-quarters of the way through his studies at West Point when they were interrupted by the outbreak of war; he resigned, on April 22, 1861, to go with his state. First commissioned in the state forces as a lieutenant of artillery, he served at 1st Bull Run attached to the Washington Artillery of New Orleans. His later assignments included: captain, Lynchburg (Va.) Artillery (1861); major, Artillery (early 1863); commanding Artillery Battalion, Pickett's Divison, Department of Southern Virginia (April 16-May 1863); commanding Artillery Battalion, Pickett's Division, 1st Corps, Army of Northern Virginia (May-July 1863); lieutenant colonel, Artillery (ca. July 1863); commanding artillery battalion, same corps and army (July-September 1863); commanding artillery battalion, Department of North Carolina (fall 1863-January 1864); colonel, 8th Confederate Cavalry (January 13, 1864); brigadier general, CSA (April 29, 1864); commanding Cavalry Brigade, Whiting's Division, Department of North Carolina and Southern Virginia (mid-May 1864); commanding Cavalry Brigade, same department (May-September 1864); commanding independent brigade, Cavalry Corps, Army of Northern Virginia (September-November 1864); commanding brigade, W.H.F. Lee's Division, same corps and army (November 1864-March 1865); and commanding brigade, Rosser's Division, same corps and army (March-April 6, 1865). Commanding his guns he fought with Pickett's Brigade and later his division at Yorktown, Williamsburg, Seven Pines, and Fredericksburg. He was given command of a battalion under Pickett and served in southeastern Virginia and at Gettysburg. Again serving south of Richmond, he was assigned to command the army's horse artillery but apparently never joined, having previously been named colonel of a cavalry regiment. He was promoted to brigadier and given a brigade when his regiment was disbanded in April 1864. He then served through the Petersburg Campaign, eventually being incorporated into the cavalry with Lee's army. In the fighting at High Bridge during the retreat to Appomattox, he engaged in a close-range pistol duel with Union General Theodore Read. Read was killed and Dearing was wounded. On April 23, the wound proved fatal. By that time Lee's army was no more. (Freeman, Douglas S., *Lee's Lieutenants* and Wise, Jennings C., *The Long Arm of Lee*)

DEARING, St. Clair (1833-?)

It was not until less than a month before Appomattox that the Confederate government finally decided to recruit black soldiers. One of the officers detailed to this service was a native Georgian, St. Clair Dearing. Commissioned directly into the regular army in 1855, he had served in the infantry and artillery. He resigned as second lieutenant, 2nd Artillery, on February 7, 1861. His Confederate assignments included: lieutenant colonel, 25th North Carolina (August 15, 1861) and second lieutenant, Cavalry, CSA (December 6, 1864 to rank from November 16, 1864). After serving with his regiment in North Carolina he claims that he declined reelection out of "petulance," but other records indicate he was under charges for excessive drinking. After this April 1862 departure he served on the staffs of General Ripley, during the April 1863 bombardment of Fort Sumter, and General Gist, supervising slaves detailed to work on fortifications. These services were as a volunteer. After petitioning Jefferson Davis for any commission, he was appointed a lieutenant and when final congressional approval was given he was sent to Georgia to recruit slaves into the army. The war ended before they could take the field.

DEAS, Zachariah Cantey (1819-1882)

A wealthy Alabama cotton broker, Zachariah C. Deas raised his regiment at his own expense and rose to the rank of Confederate brigadier general. Although born in South Carolina he had made his fortune in Alabama. A veteran, as an enlisted man, of the Mexican War, he immediately threw himself into the Confederate cause and raised a regiment of which he became colonel. His assignments included: colonel, 22nd Alabama (October 25, 1861); commanding Gladden's Brigade, 2nd (Withers') Division, 2nd Corps, Army of the Mississippi (April 6, 1862); brigadier general CSA (December 13, 1862); and commanding in the Army of Tennessee: Gardner's (old) Alabama Brigade, Withers'-Hindman's Division, Polk's Corps (December 14, 1862-November 1863); brigade, Hindman's-Anderson's-Johnson's-Hill's Division, Breckinridge's-Hindman's-Hood's-Lee's Corps (November 1863-January 1864, January-May 1864, and August 1864-ca. March 1865); and the division (January 1864). On the first day at Shiloh his brigade commander Adley H. Gladden was mortally wounded and his successor, Daniel W. Adams, also fell wounded. At this point Deas took charge but also was hit. Upon his recovery he took part in the Kentucky Campaign but was not present at Perryville. Appointed brigadier general, he also appears to have been absent at the time of Murfreesboro. However, he served in the Tullahoma Campaign and fought at Chickamauga and Chattanooga. He led his brigade during parts of the Atlanta Campaign and then went on Hood's invasion of middle Tennessee. After fighting at Franklin and Nashville he moved on to the Carolinas where he served until illness forced him to relinquish command in the final months of the war. After the war he joined the New York Stock Exchange.

DeBOW, James Dunwoody Brownson (1820-1867)

As the editor of *DeBow's Review* James D.B. DeBow played a very important restraining role in the sectional crisis but eventually did embrace secession. Failing as a lawyer—as an orphan he had struggled through his education—he found his niche writing for the *Southern Quarterly Review* on philosophical and political topics. The first of his reviews, which appeared under varying titles, appeared in 1846 but was soon forced to close down for financial reasons. But he eventual-

ly got the publication on its feet. Being primarily an economic journal, it tried to remain above the politics that were tearing the country apart. This was difficult because the native Charlestonian was an admirer of John C. Calhoun. DeBow did, however, maintain a more national perspective. In the 1850s he was head of the Census Bureau and in 1854 he published *Statistical View of the United States*. A Breckinridge backer in 1860, he supported the secession movement after the election of Lincoln and during the war itself was an adherent of Jefferson Davis. Continuing to publish the *Review*, he was enthusiastic about the prospects for the new nation and also served in the Treasury Department, working on foreign loans to be backed by cotton. He died shortly after the fall of the South, having continued in journalism and railroading. (Skipper, Otis Clark, *J.D.B. DeBow, Magazinist of the South*)

DeBRAY, Xavier Blanchard (1819-1895)

Cut off from Richmond by the fall of Vicksburg, Trans-Mississippi Department commander E. Kirby Smith was forced to promote deserving officers like Xavier B. DeBray without the formalities of presidential appointment and senate confirmation. A native of France, DeBray had been educated at the French military school, St. Cyr, and had served as a diplomat. Settling in Texas in 1852, he became the governor's aide-de-camp upon the outbreak of war. His later assignments in the Trans-Mississippi Department included: major, 2nd Texas (August 1861); lieutenant colonel, DeBray's (Tex.) Cavalry Battalion (1861); colonel, 26th Texas Cavalry (December 5, 1861); commanding 2nd Brigade, 2nd Division, District of Texas, New Mexico and Arizona (June 25-November 11, 1863); commanding brigade, District of Texas, New Mexico and Arizona (November 11-December 15, 1863); commanding cavalry brigade, 2nd Division, District of Texas, New Mexico and Arizona (December 1863); brigadier general, CSA, by Smith (April 13, 1864); commanding 6th Texas Cavalry Brigade, 2nd Texas Cavalry Division, 1st Corps (ca. April 13, 1864-early 1865); and commanding brigade, Bee's Division, Cavalry Corps (early 1865-May 1865). With his regiment he took part in the fight at Galveston during his stationing in Texas. In the spring of 1864 he was sent as part of the reinforcements to the District of West Louisiana to face Banks during the Red River Campaign. It was during this operation that he was promoted to brigadier by Smith. He finished out the war in Louisiana and served as a translator back in Texas.

De FONTAINE, Felix Gregory (1834-1896)

A prewar reporter, Felix G. De Fontaine moved to Columbia, South Carolina, shortly before the war and as founder and editor of the *Daily South Carolinian* became an ardent Southern apologist, although he had been born in Boston. Maintaining his connections with the *New York Herald*, in February 1861 he wrote a defense of the actions of the South, which was later published in book form as *A History of American Abolitionism Together with a History of the Southern Confederacy*. His friendship with Beauregard enabled him to write the first report of the bombardment of Fort Sumter to appear in the Northern papers. He later went to the Virginia front, apparently with the honorary rank of major, with the 1st South Carolina as a military correspondent. Signing most of his writings as "Personne," he produced much Southern propaganda until his press was destroyed in the fire following the Union occupation of Columbia. After the war he wrote to keep Southerners active in the defense of their values, but soon moved to New York where he was editor for the *Telegram* and then the *Herald*. He held the latter post for the remainder of his life.

DEGATAGA

See: *Watie, Stand*

de LAGNEL, Julius Adolph (1827-1912)

For somes unexplained reason Julius A. de Lagnel turned down a commission as a Confederate brigadier general early in the war and completed his service in the ordnance branch. The New Jersey native received a direct commission into the regular army from Virginia in 1847. He served as a subaltern in the 2nd Artillery until he resigned as a first lieutenant on May 17, 1861, in order to join the South. His Confederate assignments included: captain, artillery (March 16, 1861); chief of artillery, Army of the Northwest (June-July 11, 1861); brigadier general, CSA (July 31, 1862 to rank from April 18, 1862); and lieutenant colonel, Ordnance (1862). With Robert S. Garnett he was sent to western Virginia during the first spring of the war. When the forces of George B. McClellan advanced into the area de Lagnel was stationed at Rich Mountain with a small force—numbering a few companies and only one gun—with which to face the column under William S. Rosecrans. In the subsequent battle the Confederates made a heroic stand but were eventually forced from their positions by the force of numbers. Falling severely wounded, their chief secreted himself until he could make his getaway. By the time that he had recovered in a mountain cabin the enemy was between him and the Confederate lines. Captured in an attempt to join them, he was not exchanged until December 20, 1861. The next summer he was promoted to brigadier general but declined on July 31, 1861. As an ordnance officer, he served frequently on inspection duty. Engaged in shipping after the war, he eventually settled in the reunited nation's capital.

De LEON, Edwin (1818-1891)

One of the few high ranking Confederate officials of the Jewish faith, Edwin De Leon resigned his U.S. consular post in Egypt to join his native South. Born in South Carolina, he studied law and had a journalistic career that included the editorship of the *Savannah Republican*, the *Columbia Telegraph*, and *The Southern Press* in Washington, before becoming a diplomat in 1854. Returning to North America, he was appointed as a Confederate agent in Europe and was primarily concerned with propaganda. He was based in Paris and came into conflict with John Slidell. By February 1864 he had become so disillusioned with the idea of French aid or recognition that he publicly denounced that government, effectively ending his usefulness. He did not return to the United States until 14 years after Appomattox, having lived in both Europe and Egypt. He had spent most of his own wealth in the service of the Confederacy. In his later years he introduced the telephone to Egypt and wrote *The Kedive's Egypt, Under the Stars and Crescent*, and *Thirty Years of Life in Three Continents*.

DESHLER, James (1833-1863)

Within two months of receiving his promotion to brigadier general in the Confederate service, Alabamian West Pointer (1854) James Deshler was dead. Initially posted to the artillery, he transferred to the infantry in 1855. Before being dropped on July 15, 1861, as a first lieutenant in the 10th Infantry—for failing to return following a leave—he had seen action against the Sioux and on the expedition against the Mormons in Utah. His Confederate assignments included: captain, Artillery (1861); colonel, Artillery (early 1862); chief of artillery, Department of North Carolina (spring 1862); commanding Artillery, Holmes' Division, Army of Northern Virginia (June-July 1862); commanding brigade, Churchill's Division, District of Arkansas, Trans-Mississippi Department (January-January 11, 1863); brigadier general, CSA (July 28, 1863); commanding Artillery Reserve, Army of Tennessee (ca. July-August 13, 1863); and commanding brigade, Cleburne's Division, Hill's Corps, Army of Tennessee (August 13-September 20, 1863). Sent to western Virginia, he served as Henry R. Jackson's adjutant during the campaigning there late in 1861 and was severely wounded on December 13 at Allegheny Summit. Promoted to colonel, he was dispatched to North Carolina where he became Theophilus H. Holmes' chief gunner. As such he served through the Seven Days and was later sent to the West. Commanding a brigade at Arkansas Post he was taken prisoner and upon his exchange was named a brigadier general. After leading the Army of Tennessee's reserve guns for a time he took charge of an infantry brigade and on the second day at Chickamauga he was killed by the explosion of a shell.

DEVINE, Thomas Jefferson (1820-1890)

A Texas judge and secessionist, Thomas J. Devine was a special trade negotiator with the Mexican authorities. Born in Halifax, Nova Scotia, he reached maturity in Florida and studied law in Mississippi and Kentucky before emigrating to the Lone Star state in 1843. Practicing law in San Antonio, he served a year as attorney for the city and in 1851 became a district judge. Still a judge, he attended the secessionist convention and worked hard to gain possession of federal property and to assure the removal of national forces from the state. That same year he was appointed to the state supreme court. He went to Mexico City in 1863 and upon his return, at the war's close, he was arrested and indicted for treason but not tried. After practicing law he was again named to the supreme bench in 1873. Resigning in 1875, he ran unsuccessfully for the governor's chair three years later. (Johnson, Sidney Smith, *Texans Who Wore the Gray*)

DIBRELL, George Gibbs (1822-1888)

Although not promoted to Confederate brigadier until the war was virtually over, Tennessee farmer and merchant George G. Dibrell was frequently in command of a brigade in the early years of the war. A Unionist at the secessionist convention, he nonetheless joined the Confederate army. His assignments included: lieutenant colonel, 25th Tennessee (August 10, 1861); colonel, 13th (unofficially 8th) Tennessee Cavalry (September 1862); commanding brigade, Forrest's Cavalry Division, Army of Tennessee (August-September 1863); commanding brigade, Armstrong's Division, Forrest's Cavalry Corps, Army of Tennessee (September-October 1863); commanding brigade, Armstrong's Division, Wheeler's Cavalry Corps, Army of Tennessee (October-November 1863); commanding brigade, Armstrong's Division, Martin's Detachment of Wheeler's Cavalry Corps, Department of East Tennessee (November-December 1863); commanding division, Cavalry, Department of East Tennessee (February-March 1864); commanding brigade, Kelly's-Humes' Division, Wheeler's Cavalry Corps, Army of Tennessee (April-late 1864); commanding brigade, Humes' Division, Wheeler's Cavalry Corps, Department of South Carolina, Georgia and Florida (late 1864-March 1865); brigadier general, CSA (January 28, 1865 to rank from July 26, 1864); and commanding brigade, Humes' Division, Wheeler's Cavalry Corps, Army of Tennessee (March-April 26, 1865). With his initial regiment he fought at Mill Springs but failed to gain reelection on May 10, 1862. He then became commander of a mounted regiment, which was originally organized as partisan rangers but quickly converted to normal cavalry. This he led on Nathan Bedford Forrest's first raid in western Tennessee during the winter of 1862-63. The following summer he took charge of a brigade and fought at Chickamauga and Knoxville. He served through the Atlanta Campaign in brigade command but during its latter stages was cut off from the main army while on a raid in east Tennessee. Before he could rejoin it he commanded his few troops in the fight at Saltville, Virginia. Rejoining Wheeler he participated in the opposition to Sherman's March to the Sea and fought in the Carolinas campaign, seeing action at Averysboro and Bentonville. Surrendered with Joseph E. Johnston, his final years were spent in a series of enterprises that included finance, mercantile, rail, and mining ventures. He also sat for five terms in the U.S. House of Representatives.

DICKISON, John J. (?-?)

With most of the Florida troops ordered out of the state for service with the Armies of Northern Virginia and Tennessee, there was ample opportunity for small-unit commanders like John J. Dickison, still in the state, to gain more distinction than equally-ranked Floridians elsewhere. His Confederate assignments included: first lieutenant, Marion (Fla.) Light Artillery (December 12, 1861); captain, Lee (Fla.) Dragoons (August 21, 1862); and captain, Company H, 2nd Florida Cavalry (December 4, 1862). Upon the reorganization of the artillery unit in the spring of 1862, he decided that he preferred the cavalry service and was granted authority to raise a company.

At first independent, the company was assigned to the 2nd Florida Cavalry but rarely served with more than a few of its sister companies. Operating independently in Palatka and the St. Johns River region, he proved the bane of Union detachments and supply trains. One typical foray occurred in February 1865 when he attacked a portion of the 17th Connecticut, which was guarding 10 wagons. Although outnumbered two to one he captured the train and killed or captured the entire escort. Dickison himself mortally wounded the 17th's commander. Events elsewhere ended the war for Dickison. (Dickison, John J., "Florida," *Confederate Military History*, Vol. XI)

DILL, Benjamin Franklin (?-ca. 1866)

Along with co-editor John R. McClanahan, Benjamin Dill led the *Memphis Appeal* in one of the most outstanding odysseys of journalism. Having directed the paper for a decade, supporting the candidacy of Stephen A. Douglas and the preservation of the Union, Dill finally threw his wholehearted support behind the Confederacy. His editorial line never wavered during a three-year series of relocations due to military defeats. The refugee paper published in Grenada, Jackson, and Meridian, Mississippi, Atlanta, and lastly in Montgomery, Dill was the last editor to close up shop in Atlanta before Sherman took the city. Finally, in April 1865, Dill's, and his paper's luck ran out. They were captured with most of the equipment and staff, at Columbus, Georgia. Although McClanahan managed to smuggle the press to Macon, the commander of the Union cavalry was still ecstatic at the capture of their long-sought quarry. The fight against equipment and supply shortages was over. On November 5, 1865, with the press brought back from Macon, Dill published the first edition of the *Appeal* in its old home. He died shortly after. The paper later become the *Memphis Commercial Appeal*. (Baker, Thomas Harrison, *The Memphis Commercial Appeal*)

DILLARD, R.K. (?-?)

Thoroughly acquainted with the area along the James River in Virginia, a civilian, R.K. Dillard, took part in the most devastating Confederate sabotage attacks. In late July 1864 Dillard was hired by John Maxwell, a secret agent belonging to "Captain Z. McDaniel's Company, Secret Service," as a guide and accomplice in the detonation of an invention of Maxwell's, a "horological" device or time bomb. On the 26th the pair left Richmond and soon decided on the immense Union supply center at City Point as their target. On August 9, 1864, Dillard remained about half a mile outside the base while Maxwell managed to get the explosives planted on a Union ordnance boat. The resulting explosion caused two million dollars in damage and 169 casualties. Rejoining Maxwell, Dillard slipped back out of the Union lines. For several days the two continued their spying operations on the river. The records are silent on Dillard's further activities. (Stern, Philip Van Doren, *Secret Missions of the Civil War*)

DIXON, George E. (?-1864)

An army officer, Lieutenant George E. Dixon, gave his life in command of the first successful sinking of a vessel by a submarine. While serving with the 21st Alabama in the defenses of Mobile, Dixon was witness to some of the early trials of the *H.L. Hunley*, a submersible craft. In command of one trial, his crew of nine remained submerged for two hours and 35 minutes. Dixon maintained interest in the vessel despite its sinking in Mobile and at least three times in Charleston, with heavy loss of life including that of its inventor, Horace L. Hunley. With the loss of at least 33 lives, General Beauregard stopped further trials until Dixon requested permission to try again. But there was a condition imposed that required the vessel to remain only partially submerged. On February 17, 1864, Dixon, with eight men operating the crank propulsion system, made for the blockading fleet. The submarine's spar torpedo was detonated under the USS *Housatonic*, which quickly went to the bottom with the loss of five lives. But the *Hunley* was missing. The Confederate authorities long hoped that the crew had been captured or drifted out to sea and would yet return. It was not until after the war that the wreck was located next to the first victim of a submarine.

DOCKERY, Oliver Hart (1830-1906)

As the Civil War progressed, there was a growing Unionist sentiment in North Carolina, and it even affected some of the early volunteers like Oliver H. Dockery. A Wake Forest plantation owner, he entered the Confederate army in the first fall of the war and his assignments included: captain, Company E, 38th North Carolina (October 30, 1861) and lieutenant colonel, 38th North Carolina (January 17, 1862). After serving in North Carolina during the first winter of the war, he was defeated during the April 1862 reorganization elections. Gradually he became a Unionist and even claimed that he had really removed himself from the race because of a desire to support the federal government. After the war he became a scalawag serving in the Reconstruction state legislature and failed in a bid to become governor. He also represented his district in the U.S. Congress.

DOCKERY, Thomas Pleasant (1833-1898)

All of Thomas P. Dockery's service as a Confederate general was spent in the western theater. Born in North Carolina, he had been raised in Tennessee and Arkansas. His Civil War assignments included: colonel, 5th Arkansas State Troops (summer 1861); colonel, 19th Arkansas (May 12, 1862); commanding Middle Sub-District of Arkansas, District of Arkansas, Trans-Mississippi Department (late 1862); commanding Green's (old) Brigade, Bowen's Division, Department of Mississippi and East Louisiana (June 27-July 4, 1863); brigadier general, CSA (August 10, 1863); and commanding brigade, Fagan's Cavalry Division, District of Arkansas, Trans-Mississippi Department (April 1864). In command of a regiment of state troops he fought at Wilson's Creek and the next spring became colonel of a regiment of Arkansas troops in Con-

federate service. Crossing the Mississippi he took part in the defense of Corinth and that fall fought in the battle there. During the siege of Vicksburg he succeeded Martin E. Green, who had been killed, in brigade command. Captured upon the fall of the city, he was paroled the same day and later exchanged. In the spring of 1864 he commanded a cavalry brigade at Jenkins' Ferry, an action in the effort to drive back Steele's campaign in support of Nathaniel P. Banks in Louisiana. In the postwar years he was a civil engineer in Texas.

DODD, David Owen (1846-1864)

Given a last-minute reprieve from his scheduled execution as a Confederate spy, if he would reveal the names of his accomplices, Arkansan David O. Dodd refused to betray a trust and instead went to the gallows. Born in Texas, he was only 17 at the time of his hanging. With the capture of Little Rock, the family home, Dodd's father returned secretly to smuggle the family to Mississippi. However, the elder Dodd left behind some unfinished business and sent his son back to tie up the loose ends. It is not known how he also came to be given a spying assignment, but on his return journey to the Confederate lines young Dodd was taken in for questioning by Union pickets. In his possession they found a small pocket notebook that included a page in Morse Code (young Dodd had previously worked as a telegraph operator). Deciphered, the message proved to be a report on the strength of Union forces in the Little Rock area. Tried on the last day of 1863, he was found guilty and sentenced to hang. At the last moment Union General Frederick Steele offered Dodd his life in return for the names of those who had aided him in gathering the intelligence. The reply, "I can die, but I cannot betray the trust of a friend," were his last words. The bungled hanging took eight minutes. There is speculation that the "friend" was his girlfriend, Mary Dodge, who was quickly sent to her former Vermont home by special government transport.

DOLES, George Pierce (1830-1864)

A Georgia businessman, George P. Doles had been active in the militia before the war and was captain of the Baldwin Blues, which enlisted shortly after the fall of Fort Sumter. Doles led them and his later assignments included: captain, Company H, 4th Georgia (April 1861); colonel, 4th Georgia (April 26, 1861); commanding brigade D.H. Hill's-Rodes' Division, 2nd Corps, Army of Northern Virginia (September 17, 1862-June 2, 1864); and brigadier general, CSA (November 1, 1862). After serving in the Norfolk area, Doles led his regiment to the Peninsula where they saw action at Seven Pines and in the Seven Days. Having distinguished himself in the defense along South Mountain, he succeeded to command of the brigade when General R.S. Ripley was wounded at Antietam. Promoted to brigadier six weeks later and given permanent charge of the brigade, he led it at Fredericksburg, Chancellorsville, Gettysburg, and the Wilderness. At Spotsylvania, despite his vigilance, a large number of his men and a battery were captured when Union troops under Emory Upton made a sudden assault on his lines on May 10. Doles fought through the rest of the battle and the actions at the North Anna. Countering Grant's next side step toward Richmond, Doles was killed by a sniper at Bethesda Church while checking his lines on June 2, 1864. (Thomas, Henry W., *A History of the Doles-Cook Brigade, Army of Northern Virginia*)

DONELSON, Daniel Smith (1801-1863)

Five days after his death the man who had given his name to the Cumberland River fort, Daniel S. Donelson, was promoted to major general, apparently when the authorities in Richmond were not yet aware of his demise. The Tennessee native and West Pointer (1825) had served less than a year when he resigned as a second lieutenant in the 3rd Artillery. A planter and politician, he was the speaker of the lower house of the state legislature at the outbreak of the Civil War. In the meantime he had been active in the militia and his assignments included: brigadier general, Tennessee Militia (prewar); adjutant general, Provisional Army of Tennessee (May 9, 1861); brigadier general CSA (July 9, 1861); commanding 3rd Brigade, Army of Northwestern Virginia (summer-December 16, 1861); commanding brigade, Department of South Carolina and Georgia (December 1861-spring 1862); commanding 1st Brigade, 2nd (Cheatham's) Division, 1st Corps, Army of the Mississippi (spring-July 2, 1862); commanding 1st Brigade, Cheatham's Division, Army of the Mississippi (July 2-August 15, 1862); commanding 1st Brigade, Cheatham's Division, Right Wing, Army of the Mississippi (August 15-November 20, 1862); temporarily commanding the division (October 8, 1862); commanding 1st Brigade, Cheatham's Division, Polk's Corps, Army of Tennessee (November 20, 1862-January 17, 1863); commanding Department of East Tennessee (January 17-April 17, 1863); and major general, CSA (April 22, 1863 to rank from January 17). While serving in the state forces he determined the location for Fort Donelson and, following his commission in the Confederate service, he led a brigade under Lee in the Rich Mountain Campaign in western Virginia. Late in the year his brigade was transferred to the South Carolina coast and in the spring joined Bragg's army in Mississippi. For the balance of his life Donelson was to serve under Bragg and to earn his respect. Taking part in the Kentucky Campaign in the fall of 1862, he was in temporary command of a division at Perryville. He resumed command of his brigade and led it at Murfreesboro. Shortly after that action he was assigned to command in East Tennessee with a recommendation for promotion to major general. However, on April 17, 1863, he died of disease at Montvale Springs, Tennessee. Five days later he was confirmed at the higher grade by the Confederate Senate, backdated to his assumption of departmental command.

DORTCH, William Theophilus (1824-1889)

A wealthy North Carolina lawyer and planter, William T. Dortch was serving as the speaker of the state legislature's lower houses during the secession crisis. Although professing an attachment to the Union, Dortch actually worked with the immediate secessionists during the crisis winter. He did not, however, attend the state's secession convention. In late 1861, a deadlocked state legislature named Dortch as a compromise appointee to the Senate of the First Regular Confederate Congress. He was assigned to the committees on: Accounts; Commerce; Naval Affairs; and Engrossment and Enrollment, being chairman of the latter. He often served as a liaison between the central government and North Carolina's touchy governor Zebulon Vance. While working to strengthen the war effort, Dortch did try to protect local rights from excessive measures being used indiscriminately. His was one of the few North Carolina legislative voices to oppose peace negotiations. After the war Dortch rebuilt his law practice and his plantation, served in the state legislature, was a railroad director, and supervised the revision of the state's laws.

DOUGLAS, Henry Kyd (1838-1903)

A veteran of the campaigns in the Shenandoah Valley and with the Army of Northern Virginia, Henry Kyd Douglas had served on the staffs of Generals Jackson, Edward Johnson, Gordon, and Early before being assigned to the command of a brigade at the close of the war. Time ran out before he could be commissioned a brigadier general. He had studied law before returning to his hometown of Shepherdstown, Virginia, to enlist in the Confederate army. His assignments included: private, Company B, 2nd Virginia (April 1861); corporal, Company B, 2nd Virginia (1861); sergeant, Company B, 2nd Virginia (1861); second lieutenant, Company B, 2nd Virginia (August 1861); assistant inspector general, Valley District, Department of Northern Virginia (spring-June 1862); assistant inspector general, Jackson's Command, Army of Northern Virginia (June-November 11, 1862); captain, Company B, 2nd Virginia (ca. November 11, 1862); major and assistant adjutant general (May 1863); assistant adjutant general, Johnson's Division, 2nd Corps, Army of Northern Virginia (May-July 1863 and May 1864); assistant adjutant general, Gordon's Division, 2nd Corps, Army of Northern Virginia (May 1864); assistant adjutant general, Early's Division, 2nd Corps, Army of Northern Virginia (May 1864); assistant adjutant general, 2nd Corps, Army of Northern Virginia (May-June 1864); assistant adjutant general, Valley District, Department of Northern Virginia (June-December 1864); assistant adjutant general, 2nd Corps, Army of Northern Virginia (December 1864-March 1865); and commanding Walker's (old) Brigade, Ramseur's (old) Division, 2nd Corps, Army of Northern Virginia (March-April 1865). As an enlisted man he served at Harpers Ferry and fought at 1st Bull Run. Promoted to a lieutenancy, he joined Stonewall Jackson's staff in the spring of 1862 and served at Kernstown and during the Shenandoah Valley Campaign of 1862. He then fought at Cedar Mountain, 2nd Bull Run, Harpers Ferry, and Antietam before being given the captaincy of his old company. As such he fought at Fredericksburg and Chancellorsville. He then joined Johnson's staff as adjutant until his wounding and capture at Gettysburg. Not released until March 1864 he served successively on the staffs of Johnson, Gordon, and Early. He took part in the Overland, Shenandoah Valley, and Petersburg campaigns. Shortly before the Appomattox Campaign he was assigned to command of a Virginia brigade with the unfulfilled intention that he be made a brigadier general. During this campaign he suffered the last two of his six wartime wounds. Arrested after the surrender, he was a witness at the trial of the Lincoln conspirators through his acquaintance with some suspects. Long after the war he wrote a lively account of his war experiences, *I Rode With Stonewall.*

DOUGLASS, Marcellus (1830-1862)

Although his military service was relatively brief, Marcellus Douglass did manage to serve in three theaters of operation. Following attendance at the Georgia secession convention he entered the Confederate army. His assignments included: captain, Company E, 13th Georgia (June 19, 1861); lieutenant colonel, 13th Georgia (July 8, 1861); colonel, 13th Georgia (February 1, 1862); and commanding Lawton's Brigade, Ewell's Division, Jackson's Corps, Army of Northern Virginia (August 28-September 17, 1862). He served in the Kanawha Valley, in what is now West Virginia, in the latter part of 1861 before his unit was recalled to protect the Georgia coast. Then in June 1862 when Robert E. Lee was trying to scratch together enough men for the defense of Richmond, the 13th, as part of Lawton's brigade, returned to Virginia. As a part of Jackson's Division they fought through the Seven Days with Douglass at their head. Serving in Ewell's Division, Douglass fought at 2nd Bull Run and assumed command of the brigade when Lawton took over the division from the wounded Ewell. He held this position through the rest of the battle and during the Maryland invasion, including participation in the capture of Harpers Ferry. At Antietam he was struck down by enemy fire, dying before he could earn a permanent promotion.

DOWLING, Richard W. (ca. 1848-1867)

A native of County Galway, Ireland, Dick Dowling commanded the only Confederate soldiers to receive a medal for valor. Entering the Confederate service, he was appointed a first lieutenant in the Davis Guards on August 13, 1861. His first service was along the Rio Grande. In October 1862, the company became Company F, 1st Texas Heavy Artillery. On January 1, 1863, Dowling saw his first action in the attack on Galveston Island. Sent to Sabine Pass, Dowling and his men were placed upon two steamers, the *Uncle Ben* and the *Josiah H. Bell*, and sent out to attack the Union blockaders, two of which, the *Morning Light* and *Velocity*, were captured on January 21. Returning to shore he continued to serve in the defenses of the pass until September 8, 1863, when a Union expedition up the Sabine River was stopped by Dowling and 42 others—with only six guns—from their mud earthwork, Fort Griffin. The first wave of the Union fleet was composed of four gunboats and seven transports carrying the first of some 4,000 troops. After an artillery duel, the *Clifton* and *Sachem* surrendered, with about 200 prisoners, and the other two Union gunboats withdrew. The garrison received the thanks of the Confederate Congress for stopping the invasion of southeastern Texas. Dowling continued with his company until July 28, 1864, when he was reported sick, but was paroled at Houston as a major on June 21, 1865. He died of yellow fever two years later in Houston where he was involved in the local gaslight company, real estate, and oil speculation. (Tolbert, Frank X., *Dick Dowling at Sabine Pass*)

DOWNER, William S. (?-?)

As the Civil War progressed, the Confederate capital became subject to Union cavalry raids, often without many regular line troops to defend it. As a result the Local Defense Troops were established utilizing the manpower employed by the various government agencies. Among those placed in these units were the workmen under William S. Downer at the Richmond Armory. He had been the superintendent of the armory since 1861 and when the 1st Virginia Local Defense Troops Battalion, or the "Armory Battalion," was organized in mid-1863 he was made its major and first commander. However, he was relieved on August 6, 1863, so that he could devote his full energies to the armory. He held this post for most of the war.

DRAKE, Joseph (?-1878)

Capture of Fort Donelson ended the Confederate military career of Colonel Joseph Drake of the 4th Mississippi. Named to head the regiment in 1861, he commanded it at Fort Henry, and, after the initial bombardment by the Union fleet, he was ordered to move it over to Fort Donelson. There he was given command of a brigade in Johnson's Division (February 9-16, 1862). With the surrender of the fort, he was confined at Fort Warren in Boston Harbor. Exchanged on August 27, 1862, he was not reelected upon the reorganization of the regiment.

DRAYTON, Thomas Fenwick (1808-1891)

In order to dispose of a failed brigadier, Thomas F. Drayton, General Lee used the expedient of breaking up his brigade and leaving him without a command. He had graduated from West Point (1828) in the same class as Jefferson Davis and served eight years in the infantry before retiring to his South Carolina plantation. Although active in railroading and politics, as a state legislator, Drayton kept up his military interests through the local militia. Offering his services to the South, they included: brigadier general, CSA (September 25, 1861); commanding 3rd Military District, Department of South Carolina (September-November 1861); commanding 5th Military District of South Carolina, Department of South Carolina and Georgia (December 1861-early 1862); commanding 6th (known as 4th after May 28) Military District of South Carolina, Department of South Carolina, Georgia and Florida (early 1862-July 1862); commanding brigade, D.R. Jones' Division, 1st Corps, Army of Northern Virginia (August-September 1862); commanding brigade, McLaws' Division, same corps and army (September-November 26, 1862); commanding brigade, Price's Division, District of Arkansas, Trans-Mississippi Department (ca. August 26, 1863-January 11, 1864 and March 1864); commanding the division (January 11-March 1864 and March 16-April 1864); commanding Western Sub-District of Texas, District of Texas, New Mexico and Arizona, Trans-Mississippi Department (June 26-fall 1864); commanding Central Sub-District of Texas, same district and department (fall 1864-March 8, 1865); and also commanding 3rd Texas Cavalry Division, 3rd Corps, Trans-Mississippi Department (September 1864-March 8, 1865). Assigned to duty in South Carolina, he led the unsuccessful defense of Port Royal in November 1861. He joined Lee's army in August 1862 and promptly displayed an incapacity for command by failing to launch his brigade into the attack at 2nd Bull Run on time. After further poor showings at South Mountain and Antietam, his regiments were divided among three other brigadiers. Assigned to court duty, he returned to the field in Arkansas and later in Texas. The war ended while he was sitting on the court investigating the 1864 Missouri expedition of General Price. He was in insurance and farming after the war. (Freeman, Douglas S., *Lee's Lieutenants*)

DRED SCOTT

See: *Scott, Dred*

DREW, John (?-?)

Cherokee chief John Drew organized a regiment, the 1st Cherokee Mounted Rifles, when his nation seceded from the United Staes and allied itself with the Confederacy at the behest of Albert Pike. He was commissioned colonel on October 4, 1861. Serving initially in the Indian Territory, today Oklahoma, his command proved of dubious value. In pursuit of loyal Creeks, who were fleeing to Union-controlled areas under their chief Opothleyohola, Drew's braves refused to attack when it was discovered that there were some Cherokees among them. Drew and his command formed part of Pike's Brigade at Pea Ridge but, having become dissatisfied with Confederate service and coming under Union artillery fire, they tried to defect to the enemy. Fighting broke out between them and Stand Watie's regiment of Cherokee Confederates. During the night following the first day's battle the regiment dispersed and headed home. Then in June 1862 a Union force of whites and Indians entered the Cherokee country and many of Drew's men joined the Union army, becoming part of the 3rd Indian Home Guard. Drew was humiliated by this defection and the following year was reported as negotiating his surrender with only some 40 followers. (Monaghan, Jay, *Civil War on the Western Border, 1854-1865*)

DROUYN De L'HUYS, Édouard (?-?)

When French Emperor Napoleon III found that his desire for intervention in the sectional conflict in America was not being furthered by his foreign minister, Édouard Thouvenel, he replaced the man on October 15, 1862, with Édouard Drouyn de L'Huys. Thought to be more conservative, and thus more amenable to an interventionist policy, the latter was entering the third of his four stints in ministerial posts. However, when he examined the situation he realized that the abstentionist policy of his predecessor was the prudent one for France. With the empire already involved in adventures in Italy and Mexico, he feared that further commitments across the Atlantic would be unwise, especially in the face of Bismarck's German threat.

Thus he rode out the war across the ocean, keeping the country from becoming embroiled in the American conflict. (D'Harcourt, Bernard, *Diplomatie et diplomates, les quatre ministères de M. Drouyn de L'Huys*)

DUBOSE, Dudley McIver (1834-1883)

A Georgia lawyer, Dudley M. DuBose rose rapidly in rank in the Confederate army. His assignments included: lieutenant, 15th Georgia (1861); captain, 15th Georgia (1862); colonel, 15th Georgia (1862); colonel, 15th Georgia (January 1863); brigadier general, CSA (November 16, 1864); and commanding Wofford's (old) Brigade, Kershaw's Division, 1st Corps, Army of Northern Virginia (December 5, 1864-April 6, 1865). As a junior officer he served in the Peninsular and 2nd Manassas campaigns. He fought at Antietam on the staff of his father-in-law, Brigadier General Robert Toombs. Promoted to the colonelcy of his regiment, he took part in the campaign under Longstreet in southeastern Virginia in early 1863. He rejoined the Army of Northern Virginia in time for Gettysburg where he was especially distinguished in extricating his command from virtual encirclement. Going west with Longstreet, he was wounded at Chickamauga but returned to duty for the Knoxville Campaign. Back in Virginia, his command fought through the Overland Campaign, at Richmond and Petersburg and in the Shenandoah. In the retreat from the trenches around Richmond, DuBose was captured at Sayler's Creek three days before Appomattox. He was not released until July after which he resumed the practice of law and served one term in the U.S. Congress.

DUKE, Basil C. (1815-?)

A border state physician, Basil C. Duke had sought to preserve the Union by supporting John Bell for the presidency in 1860, but once the Lower South had seceded he joined the Confederacy, despite the fact that Kentucky remained in the Union. He had received his medical training in Baltimore. His military assignments included: private, 5th Kentucky (1861); surgeon, 5th Kentucky (late 1861); and medical director, District of Abingdon, Department of Southwestern Virginia (ca. May 1862-May 1863). Serving in the mountain area of southwestern Virginia, eastern Kentucky, and east Tennessee, he was under the command of General Humphrey Marshall. Apparently he was recommended for a brigadier generalship. Following the war and settlement in Memphis, the former Whig became a democrat and resumed his private practice. (Cunningham, Horace Herndon, *Doctors in Gray*)

DUKE, Basil Wilson (1838-1916)

Kentuckian Basil W. Duke, brother-in-law of John H. Morgan, succeeded the fallen raider in command of the brigade, was promoted to Confederate brigadier general, and remained in the service until well after the flight of the government from Richmond had begun. Practicing law in St. Louis at the outbreak of the Civil War, he was a staunch secessionist and eventually returned to his native state and sought to raise a company. However, he ended up enlisting as a private in Morgan's Lexington Rifles. His assignments included: private, Morgan's Cavalry Company (1861); first lieutenant, Company A, Morgan's Kentucky Cavalry Squadron (October 1861); first lieutenant and acting adjutant, Morgan's Kentucky Cavalry Squadron (October 1861); lieutenant colonel, 2nd Kentucky Cavalry (June 1862); colonel, 2nd Kentucky Cavalry (December 7, 1862); commanding Morgan's Brigade, Department of Western Virginia and East Tennessee (September 4, 1864-April 10, 1865); brigadier general, CSA (September 15, 1864); and commanding brigade, Jefferson Davis' Escort (April-May 8, 1865). Wounded on the first day at Shiloh, he returned to take part in the Kentucky Campaign and join in on some of Morgan's famous raids. In the summer of 1863 he took part in the raid north of the Ohio river and was captured at Buffington Island, Ohio. Not exchanged until August 3, 1864, he rejoined Morgan just before he was killed, then took over the remnants of Morgan's command for the balance of the war. Promoted to brigadier general, he took most of the brigade to join Jefferson Davis when Lee surrendered and Richmond fell. For a time he escorted the remaining treasury of the Confederacy and then set off as a decoy to lure Union cavalry away from Davis' trail. In the postwar years he resumed his practice, sat in the legislature, and entered journalism. In matters relating to the war he served as as commissioner for the park at Shiloh and engaged in historical writing. (Duke, Basil Wilson, *Reminiscences of General Basil W. Duke, C.S.A.* and *Morgan's Cavalry*)

DUNCAN, Johnson Kelly (1827-1862)

Residence in the South overrode Johnson K. Duncan's northern birth and led him into the Confederate army and up to the rank of brigadier general before his death. The native Pennsylvanian and West Pointer (1949) served on the frontier and in Florida before resigning in 1855 to engage in civil engineering in Louisiana. His Confederate assignments included: major, Artillery (ca. March 1861); colonel, Artillery (1861); commanding Coast Defenses, Department #1 (1861-April 28, 1862); brigadier general, CSA (January 7, 1862); commanding 4th Brigade, Reserve (Withers') Division, Right Wing, Army of the Mississippi (August-October 12, 1862); commanding the division (October 12-November 10, 1862); and chief of staff, Department #2 (November-December 18, 1862). In the early stages of the war he was placed in charge of the fortifications along the lower Mississippi (Forts Jackson and St. Philip). Taking overall charge of the defenses of the coasts of Alabama, Mississippi, and Louisiana, he was promoted to brigadier general early in 1862. With the majority of his organized units ordered north to Corinth, Mississippi, in the pre-Shiloh Confederate buildup there, he was left with inadequate means for defending the approaches to New Orleans. Obliged to surrender on April 28, 1862, he was declared exchanged on August 27, 1862, and was then given charge of an infantry brigade during the operations in Kentucky. After briefly commanding a division he became Bragg's staff chief but died of typhoid fever in Knoxville on December 18, 1862.

DUNGAN, Robert H. (1834-1903)

By the time that Robert H. Dungan took over the command of the old 2nd Brigade of Jackson's original division it had been reduced to the size of a single regiment, and it was soon consolidated into one. An educator before the war, Dungan entered the Confederate army and his assigments included: lieutenant, Company A, 48th Virginia (May 18, 1861); captain, Company A, 48th Virginia (April 21, 1862); lieutenant colonel, 48th Virginia (October 16, 1862); colonel, 48th Virginia (late 1863 to date from May 3, 1863); commanding Jones' 2nd Brigade, Johnson's Division, 2nd Corps, Army of Northern Virginia (July 2-3, 1863 and May 5-14, 1864); and commanding 21st, 25th, 42nd, 44th, 48th and 50th Virginia consolidated (May 14-late October 1864). As a company officer, he took part in the Cheat Mountain and Romney campaigns and fought at Kernstown and Cedar Mountain. In each of the latter two he was wounded. He returned to duty in time to be promoted and then suffer a third wound at Chancellorsville. On the second day at Gettysburg he succeeded to brigade command but was relieved the next day. He then served in the Bristoe and Mine Run campaigns and at the Wilderness he took over the brigade again when General J.M. Jones was killed. After suffering heavily at Spotsylvania on May 12, the brigade was consolidated into a single regiment. Dungan commanded this field organization through Early's Shenandoah Valley Campaign seeing action at Monocacy, 3rd Winchester, Fisher's Hill, and Cedar Creek. He later commanded the remnants of the 48th at Petersburg and surrendered the command at Appomattox.

DUNLOP, George

See: *Peter, Walter*

DUNN, Ambrose C. (1835 or 1840-post 1907)

Twice thrown out of the Confederate army, Georgian Ambrose C. Dunn managed to get reinstated each time. His assignments included: captain, Company A, 60th Georgia (August 21, 1861); and lieutenant colonel, 37th Virginia Cavalry Battalion (August 2, 1862). His command of a Georgia infantry company lasted less than three months before he was ousted by order of a court-martial on November 20, 1861. Going to western Virginia he raised a battalion of partisan rangers and became their commander. This time he lasted 15 months before he was dismissed on charges of disobedience of orders brought by then-Colonel William L. Jackson. Eight months later he was back in command, having been reinstated, and led his command at Monocacy, the burning of Chambersburg, 3rd Winchester, Fisher's Hill, and Cedar Creek. With the war coming to a close, Dunn resigned on March 31, 1865. After the war he moved to New York City.

DUNOVANT, John (1825-1864)

Appointed to the temporary rank of brigadier in the Confederate cavalry, John Dunovant held the post for a little over a month before he was felled by enemy fire. He had served as an enlisted man in the Palmetto regiment during the war with Mexico and gained a regular army captaincy upon the 1855 expansion of the military. Resigning that commission nine days after the secession of his native South Carolina, he was present at the firing on Fort Sumter as a major in his state's forces. His later assignments included: colonel, 1st South Carolina Regulars (July 22, 1861); colonel, 5th South Carolina Cavalry (ca. Janaury 18, 1863); brigadier general, CSA (August 22, 1864); and commanding Butler's (old) Brigade, Hampton's-Butler's Division, Cavalry Corps, Army of Northern Virginia (August 22-October 1, 1864). He was charged with drunkenness while serving in the Charleston area in June 1862 and was dismissed on November 7. However, two months later he was appointed to the colonelcy of a new cavalry regiment with which he served for over a year in his native state before being sent to Virginia. After serving through the Overland Campaign and the early portion of the Petersburg siege, he was advanced to the temporary grade of brigadier and given charge of Butler's brigade while that officer led the division. On October 1 he was killed in action along the Vaughan Road near Petersburg.

DUPRÉ, Lucius Jacques (1822-1869)

A native Louisiana lawyer and judge, Lucius J. Dupré, began his Confederate career by enlisting in the 18th Louisiana, but in November 1861 he won an uncontested election to represent the state's 4th District in the First Congress. He served on the committees on: Indian Affairs; Judiciary; and Printing, chairing the latter in the Second Congress. A believer in a strong military effort, he repeatedly called for the reconquest of New Orleans. But his financially conservative views led him to demand economy from the commanders in the field. He felt that the Davis administration should be given a free hand by Congress to direct the purely military aspects of the war. With the South's fall he resumed his legal pursuits.

DURBEC, F.E. (fl. 1861-1866)

The Union navy's blockade of Charleston was probably responsible for the breakup of the photographic partnership of F.E. Durbec and James M. Osborn. The pair had been running a "Photographic Mart" at 223 King Street before the war. Shortly after the surrender of Fort Sumter the two artists took their stereo camera to the fort and the surrounding batteries to capture the historic scene. The resulting extensive record of the sites was impressive considering the relative novelty of war photography. Unfortunately their inability to obtain quantities of chemicals and other supplies prevented the wide distribution of their work and discouraged them from other endeavors in the field. By the end of the war they had dissolved their partnership.

E

EARLY, Jubal Anderson (1816-1894)

Always an irascible officer, Jubal A. Early suffered overwhelming defeats in the Shenandoah Valley and went on after the conflict to wage a literary war with a fellow Confederate corps commander. A West Pointer (1837) from Virginia, Early had served one year in the artillery, and later in the Mexican War as a major of volunteers, before taking up law. Also involved in politics, he served in the legislature. Although he voted against secession at the convention, he entered the military where his assignments included: colonel, 24th Virginia (early 1861); commanding 6th Brigade (in 1st Corps from July 20), Army of the Potomac (June 20-October 22, 1861); brigadier general, CSA (July 21, 1861); commanding brigade, Van Dorn's-D.H. Hill's Division (in Potomac District until March), Department of Northern Virginia (October 22, 1861-May 5, 1862); commanding Elzey's Brigade, Ewell's Division, 2nd Corps, Army of Northern Virginia (July 1-September 17, 1862); commanding the division (September 17, 1862-November 1863; ca. December 4-15, 1863; February-May 7; and May 21-27, 1864); major general, CSA (April 23 to rank from January 17, 1863); commanding the corps (November-ca. December 4, 1863 and May 27-June 13, 1864); commanding Valley District, Department of Northern Virginia (December 15, 1863-February 1864 and June 13, 1864-March 29, 1865); commanding 3rd Corps, Army of Northern Virginia (May 7-21, 1864); and lieutenant general, CSA (May 31, 1864). Leading a brigade at 1st Bull Run and Williamsburg, he was wounded at the latter. Returning to duty, he was given another command on the day of Malvern Hill. At Cedar Mountain and 2nd Bull Run he directed this unit and continued until he succeeded to division level at Antietam. He went on to Fredericksburg, Chancellorsville, and Gettysburg and commanded the corps in the Mine Run operations. Detached, he commanded in the Shenandoah during the winter of 1863-64. After the battle of the Wilderness he took over temporary control of Hill's Corps during the operations at Spotsylvania. He directed his division at the North Anna and took over Ewell's Corps before Cold

Harbor. A couple of weeks later this command was sent back to the Valley and Early invaded Maryland, fighting at Monocacy and on the outskirts of Washington. Falling back to Virginia, he dispatched part off his cavalry to burn Chambersburg, Pennsylvania, in retaliation for Union devastation. In September and October he was defeated in a series of disasters at the hands of Sheridan. The reverses at 3rd Winchester, Fisher's Hill, and Cedar Creek ended his power in the Valley and the old 2nd Corps and was recalled to Lee in December. However, Early remained with a small force that was destroyed at Waynesborough the following March. Lee then removed him, explaining that he was forced to by public reaction and the fact that he could not defend his subordinate without revealing how weak the Confederacy was. Early fled to Mexico but soon returned to practice law. He was connected with the Louisiana Lottery and was president of the Southern Historical Society. Becoming a defender of Lee, he feuded with Republican convert James Longstreet until his death. (Bushong, Millard K., *Old Jube*)

ECHOLS, John (1823-1896)

Virginia lawyer and state legislator John Echols served as a Confederate general officer mostly in western Virginia and the Shenandoah Valley. His assignments included: lieutenant colonel, 27th Virginia (May 30, 1861); colonel, 27th Virginia (October 14, 1861); brigadier general, CSA (April 16, 1862); commanding Department of Southwestern Virginia (October 16-November 19, 1862); commanding brigade, Department of Western Virginia (November 19, 1862-May 1864); commanding brigade, Breckinridge's Division, Army of Northern Virginia (May-June 1864); commanding brigade, Breckinridge's Division, Valley District, Army of Northern Virginia (June-July 9, 1964); commanding the division (July 9, 1864); and commanding Department of Western Tennessee (January-February and March 29-April 12, 1865). He commanded his regiment, in what became the Stonewall Brigade, at 1st Bull Run and was later wounded at Kernstown in the Valley.

Promoted to brigadier general, he was assigned to western Virginia where he remained until the spring of 1864. At that time he took part in the victory at New Market over Franz Sigel and then went to Lee's army, seeing action at Cold Harbor. Heading west he took part in the defense of Lynchburg and served for a time in the Valley again before taking command in southwestern Virginia. Engaged in business after the war he was a leading force in the rebuilding of the commonwealth's railroads.

ECTOR, Matthew Duncan (1822-1879)

The loss of a leg in the Atlanta Campaign put an end to the active military career of Georgia-born Confederate General Matthew D. Ector. The lawyer and Texas legislator enlisted first as a private and then became a staff officer with Joseph L. Hogg. As such he was present for part of the Corinth siege and was then named to a colonelcy. His later assignments included: colonel, 14th Texas Cavalry (May 1862); brigadier general, CSA (August 23, 1862); commanding brigade, McCown's Division, Department of East Tennessee (fall-December 1862); commanding brigade, McCown's Division attached to Hardee's Corps, Army of Tennessee (December 1862-January 1863); commanding brigade, McCown's Division, Smith's Corps, Army of Tennessee (January-March 1863); commanding brigade, McCown's Division, Polk's Corps, Army of Tennessee (March-ca. May 1863); commanding brigade, Walker's Division, Department of the West (May 19-July 1863); commanding brigade, Walker's Division, Department of Mississippi and East Louisiana (July-August 25, 1863); commanding brigade, Walker's Division, Hill's Corps, Army of Tennessee (August 28-September 1863); commanding brigade, Walker's Division, Reserve Corps, Army of Tennessee (September 1863); commanding brigade, Walker's Division, Polk's Corps, Army of Tennessee (September-September 22, 1863); commanding brigade, French's Division, Department of Mississippi and East Louisiana (September 22, 1863-January 28, 1864); commanding brigade, French's Division, Department of Alabama, Mississippi and East Louisiana (January 28-May 4, 1864); commanding brigade, French's Division, Polk's (Army of Mississippi)-Stewart's Corps, Army of Tennessee (May 4-July 22, 1864); and commanding brigade, French's Division, District of the Gulf, Department of Alabama, Mississippi and East Louisiana (spring 1865). Transferred from the Corinth area to East Tennessee, Ector led a brigade there and at Richmond, Kentucky. Attached to Bragg's army, he fought at Murfreesboro and in the attempt under Joseph E. Johnston to relieve Vicksburg. Returning to Bragg, he fought at Chickamauga and a few days later was ordered back to Mississippi. In the spring of 1864 he accompanied Leonidas Polk to northern Georgia and served through the Atlanta Campaign until wounded outside the city. The loss of a leg kept him out of action for some time. In the meantime his brigade had fought in middle Tennessee with Hood before being dispatched to Mobile where he apparently rejoined it in the war's final days. Postwar he was a lawyer and judge.

EDWARDS, J.D. (ca. 1831-?)

New Hampshire-born J.D. Edwards has been called the "Photographer of the Confederacy" for his early war work. Little is known of him before or after the war but he had apparently opened his New Orleans business by 1860 or shortly before. With the outbreak of war he packed his equipment and headed for the front at Pensacola. There he took an amazing series of images of the camps, guns, men, and fortifications under the command of Braxton Bragg. In a May 14, 1861, newspaper advertisement he offered some 39 views for sale. However, it is now apparent that he probably exposed about twice as many images. Some of his views were pirated as woodcuts in *Harper's Weekly*. He also took images around Mobile and, it is suspected, also in New Orleans. However, after early 1862 he disappears from the field—possibly due to the lack of photographic supplies—although there are statements that he was later in the Confederate secret service.

ELLIOTT, John Milton (1820-1879)

Born in Virginia and raised in Kentucky, John Milton Elliott had practiced law and served in both the state legislature and the U.S. House of Representatives before launching his career in the Confederate Congress—a career that would be as long as the life of that body itself. While serving again in the state legislature, Elliott was tapped by the provisional pro-Southern government of Kentucky to serve in the Provisional Confederate Congress. Taking his seat, he soon became identified as an ardent supporter of both the Davis administration and the war effort. Reelected to both of the regular congresses he was appointed to the committees on: Indian Affairs; Post Offices and Post Roads; and Enrolled Bills, of which he was chairman in the First Congress. Once the issue of local defense troops was moot in relation to Kentucky, Elliott was willing to grant almost anything to the army. Ater the war he served as a lawyer and judge. While serving on the state's highest court, on March 26, 1879, Elliott was struck down by a shotgun blast fired by an irate litigant in a land case.

ELLIOTT, Stephen, Jr. (1830-1866)

South Carolina plantation owner and state legislator Stephen Elliott, Jr., served most of the war in his native state. His assignments included: captain, Company A, 11th South Carolina (early 1861); major and lieutenant colonel, Artillery (1863); colonel, Holcombe (S.C.) Legion (early 1864); brigadier general, CSA (May 24, 1864); commanding brigade, Johnson's Division Department of North Carolina and Southern Virginia (May-July 30, 1864); commanding brigade, Taliaferro's Division, Department of South Carolina, Georgia and Florida and Hardee's Corps (January 2-April 9, 1865); and commanding brigade, Anderson's division, Stewart's Corps, Army of Tennessee (April 1865). At the head of the Beaufort Artillery, he reported to the state authorities and the company soon became part of an infantry regiment. Elliott attached himself to another unit to take part in the bombardment of Fort Sumter. During the next three years he served as the chief of artillery for various districts in the state and for a time commanded in the rubble known as Fort Sumter. During the early part of the war he had fought at Port Royal and had earned a reputation as a daring raider. Transferred to Virginia in the spring of 1864, heading a legion, he was soon promoted brigadier and assigned a brigade on the Petersburg lines. Part of his brigade was blown up at the Crater on July 30, and he himself was wounded while organizing a counterattack. After a lengthy recovery he directed a brigade of former Charleston defenders in North Carolina, suffering another wound and eventually surrendering with Johnston. He died of his wounds and debilitation from the war a few months later. (Freeman, Douglas S., *Lee's Lieutenants*)

ELLIS, John Willis (1820-1861)

The death of North Carolina Governor John W. Ellis on July 7, 1861, from overwork deprived the Confederacy of a loyal supporter at the head of that state. A North Carolina native, he practiced law before entering politics as a Democrat. He served in the legislature in the 1840s and was also a militia officer. During the late 1840s and 1850s he served as a judge. A moderate on secession, he was elected governor in 1858 and was reelected two years later. Following John Brown's raid on Harpers Ferry he became a believer in military preparedness and reorganized the militia. He favored the calling of a convention of the Southern states but his proposal was defeated by a popular vote. Trying to avoid hostilities, he returned two forts to federal authorities after they had been seized by the citizenry during the secession crisis. The firing on Fort Sumter galvanized him into action and he called for 30,000 troops. He called the legislature back into session, and they in turn established the secession convention that took the state out of the Union. On a trip to Red Sulpher Springs, now in West Virginia, he died from the complications arising from stress. (Boykin, James, *North Carolina in 1861*)

ELLSWORTH, George A. (1834-1899)

Canadian-born telegrapher George A. Ellsworth became a major asset to Confederate raider John Hunt Morgan's command. Working in Texas at the outbreak of hostilities, he enlisted in a local regiment but was not allowed to go to the front, his services being considered too valuable at home. But he eventually made his way to Mobile where he joined up with Morgan. On the cavalryman's July 1862 raid into Kentucky, Ellsworth's value became apparent when he began to tap enemy communications, gathering valuable information. When the Confederates found an intact, abandoned telegraph station, he was able to provide the frantic Union forces with faulty information as to Morgan's whereabouts. Subsequently he served with Morgan until the latter's capture, then on Simon Buckner's staff, and was wounded at Chickamauga. Briefly he was an agent in Kentucky but fled to Canada, his native country, in April 1864. After the war he was in and out of trouble with the law but continued to find jobs in the United States in his old trade.

ELZEY, Arnold (1816-1871)

A career soldier, Arnold Elzey had dropped the family name of Jones about the time he graduated from West Pont in 1837. Having served in the artillery for nearly a quarter century, earning a brevet in Mexico, Captain Elzey resigned on April 25, 1861, to offer his services to the South—despite the fact that his native Maryland never joined the Confederacy. His assignments included: major, Artillery (spring 1861); colonel, 1st Maryland (1861); commanding brigade, 2nd Corps, Army of the Potomac (July 21-October 22, 1861); brigadier general, CSA (July 21, 1861); commanding brigade, E.K. Smith's-Ewell's Division, Potomac District (Valley District after April), Department of Northern Virginia (October 22, 1861-June 8, 1862); commanding brigade, Ewell's Division, Jackson's Command, Army of Northern Virginia (June 26-27, 1862); major general, CSA (December 4, 1862); commanding Elzey's Command, Department of Virginia and North Carolina (December 12, 1862-April 1, 1863); commanding Department of Richmond (April 1, 1863-April 25, 1864); and chief of artillery, Army of Tennessee (September 8, 1864-February 17, 1865). He succeeded to brigade command at 1st Bull Run and continued in charge until wounded at Port Republic at the end of the Shenandoah Valley Campaign. His wound being slight, he soon returned to duty but was severely wounded in the head at Gaines' Mill, his first action in the Seven Days. Unfit for active field duty he was given charge of the captal's defenses. In April 1864 he was sent to Staunton, Virginia to work on the long-delayed organization of the Maryland Line. That fall and winter he was artillery chief under Hood but was apparently not in the Franklin-Nashville Campaign. After his parole he retired to a Maryland farm.

EMMETT, Daniel Decatur (1815-1904)

If he had known in advance that his song "Dixie" would become an unofficial national anthem of the Confederacy, Ohio Unionist Daniel Emmett would probably have never written it. Although he had no formal musical education, Emmett early developed a talent for music. During the Black Hawk War he served as a fifer and drummer in the 6th Infantry until his father had him discharged as a minor. However, he had mastered the drum sufficiently to write the army's first manual for drummers, *Emmett's Standard Drummer*. He then joined a series of small circuses until he formed possibly the first blackface minstrel show. He did all the writing and costume designing for the show himself. While working for another minstrel show (his own had gone broke on a English tour) as a songwriter and performer, Emmett wrote "I Wish I was in Dixie's Land," which was copyrighted in 1860. The next year it was played at the inauguration of Jefferson Davis, and was enthusiastically adopted by the troops. Throughout the war he continued to write for the New York minstrel company. But none of his works achieved the fame of "Dixie." A fan of General McClellan, Emmett wrote, "Mac Will Win the Union Back." Maybe if he had been right it would have become famous. After the war and until his retirement in 1888 he worked as a theater manager and conductor. Eventually his song, which Lincoln had declared to be captured property at the war's close, became a force for reuniting the country. (Galbreath, Charles Burleigh, *Daniel Decatur Emmet*)

ESHLEMAN, Benjamin Franklin (1830-1909)

A member of the famed Washington Artillery of New Orleans, Benjamin F. Eshleman rose to command the unit in the latter stages of the Civil War. He was a student at West Point when the war began but resigned to offer his services to the South despite the fact that he had been born in Pennsylvania. His assignments included: captain, 4th Company, Washington Artillery Battalion (May 26, 1861); major, Washington Artillery Battalion (March 26, 1862); commanding Washington Artillery Battalion, Reserve Artillery, 1st Corps, Army of Northern Virginia (June 4-July 1863); commanding Washington Artillery Battalion, 1st Corps, Army of Northern Virginia (July-September 1863); commanding Washington Artillery Battalion, Department of North Carolina (September 1863-May 1864); lieutenant colonel, Washington Artillery Battalion (February 22, 1864); commanding another artillery battalion, Department of North Carolina and Southern Virginia (May 1864); and commanding Washington Artillery Battalion, 3rd Corps, Army of Northern Virginia (June 1864-April 9, 1865). Severely wounded at Blackburn's Ford, he missed the battle of 1st Bull Run three days later. He returned to command his battery at 2nd Bull Run, Antietam, Fredericksburg, and Chancellorsville, sometimes commanding the battalion. Following the last action he was promoted to major, to date from the previous spring. After leading the battalion in action at Gettysburg, he was left with his command in the Department of North Carolina while the corps went to Georgia and East Tennessee. The new lieutenant colonel was given command of a new artillery battalion, which he led in the defense of Petersburg, before resuming direction of the Louisiana unit in order to join Lee in time for Cold Harbor. He served through the Petersburg Campaign and during the retreat he was assigned to the column under General Walker bound for Lynchburg and thus was not present at the surrender. He returned to New Orleans and was active in business affairs as a merchant. (Owen, William M., *In Camp and Battle With the Washington Artillery of New Orleans*)

EVANS, Augusta Jane (1835-1900)

A novelist of some note who had received recognition for her second novel *Beulah* shortly before the Civil War, Augusta Jane Evans threw herself wholeheartedly into the Confederate cause. During the conflict itself she was a nurse in a hospital in Mobile, where she had been raised, and an advisor to Confederate Congressman J.L.M. Curry. The Georgia-born author wrote another novel, *Macaria*, in 1863, predicting dire consequences in the emancipation of the slaves. It was popular in both the South and North, and some Union commanders such as George H. Thomas banned the book because of its adverse affect on morale. Highly critical of the Davis regime, she wrote

numerous articles favoring Beauregard over Bragg for command in the West. She continued her career until her sudden death. (Fidler, William Percy, *Augusta Jane Evans Wilson, 1835-1900*)

EVANS, Clement Anselm (1833-1911)

A Georgia lawyer and politician, Clement A. Evans became a division commander in the last months of the war. His assignments included: major, 31st Georgia (November 19, 1861); colonel, 31st Georgia (May 13, 1862); commanding Lawton's-Gordon's Brigade, Ewell's-Early's Division, 2nd Corps, Army of Northern Virginia (September-October and December 13, 1862-ca. April 11, 1863 and May 8-21, 1864); commanding brigade, Gordon's Division, Valley District, Department of Northern Virginia (June 13-July 9 and late summer-December 1864); and commanding Gordon's Division, 2nd Corps, Army of Northern Virginia (December 1864-April 9, 1865). Wounded in the Seven Days Battles, he was back on duty in time to succeed to command of the brigade at Fredericksburg. Replaced by General Gordon, he commanded the 31st at Gettysburg and the Wilderness. When Gordon was raised to division command, Evans took over the brigade and a few days later was transferred with Gordon to the remnants of Johnson's Division after Spotsylvania. Evans fought at Cold Harbor and then accompanied the corps to the Valley. In the invasion of Maryland he was wounded at Monocacy but returned in time to fight at 3rd Winchester, Fisher's Hill, and Cedar Creek. Returning to Lee's army, he directed the division in the Petersburg trenches and surrendered at Appomattox. Becoming a minister after the war, he wrote *Military History of Georgia* and edited *Confederate Military History*, a 13-volume work.

EVANS, Nathan George (1824-1868)

Of all the Confederacy's early heroes, one of the most troublesome was South Carolinian Nathan G. Evans. A West Pointer (1848), he was a veteran of 13 years in the mounted service when he resigned his captaincy on February 27, 1861. Not receiving immediate appointment in the Confederate service, he entered that of his state and his assignments included: major, S.C. Army (ca. March 1861); captain, Cavalry (May 21, 1861); major and colonel, Cavalry (July 1861); commanding 7th Brigade, 1st Corps, Army of the Potomac (ca. July 21-25, 1861); commanding a new 7th Brigade, 1st Corps, Army of the Potomac (July 25-October 22, 1861); brigadier general, CSA (October 21, 1861); commanding 4th Brigade, 4th Division, Potomac District, Department of Northern Virginia (October 22-November 24, 1861); commanding 3rd (called 2nd after June) Military District of South Carolina, Department of South Carolina, Georgia and Florida (December 18, 1861-July 1862); commanding independent brigade (in McLaws' Division from late September), 1st Corps, Army of Northern Virginia (August-November 6, 1862); commanding brigade, Department of Virginia and North Carolina (November 6, 1862-April 1, 1863); commanding brigade, Department of North Carolina (April 1-11, 1863); commanding subdivision, 1st Military District of South Carolina,

Department of South Carolina, Georgia and Florida (April 11-May 15, 1863); commanding brigade, Loring's Division (May-June 1863), Breckinridge's Division (June 1863), and French's Division (June 21-August 4, 1863), Department of the West; commanding 2nd Subdivision, 1st Military District of South Carolina, Department of South Carolina, Georgia and Florida (August-October 5, 1863); and commanding the district (March 21-April 1864). As a staff officer, he witnessed the attack on Fort Sumter before going to Virginia where he became a hero of 1st Bull Run, slowing a surprise Union flank attack. He was in general command at the Ball's Bluff victory and later at Secessionville in South Carolina. With a new brigade in Virginia, he fought at 2nd Bull Run. Also in control of Hood's Division, he placed that officer under arrest in a dispute over some captured ambulances. Hood was later freed by Lee at Antietam. After that battle Evans was transferred to North Carolina where he got into a dispute with his regimental commanders. He placed one of them under arrest and, in retaliation, another brought him up on charges of drunkenness. Eventually they were both acquitted. Evans' brigade served in South Carolina and Mississippi during the Vicksburg Campaign where he got in a scrape over disobediance and, although acquitted, was kept off duty by Beauregard until March 1864. The next month he was injured in a fall from his horse and never returned to command his "Tramp Brigade," so named because of its travels. Evans recovered but he was passed over for assignment to duty. After the war he claimed to have undergone a moral reformation. (Freeman, Douglas S., *Lee's Lieutenants*)

EWELL, Richard Stoddert (1817-1872)

As Stonewall Jackson's successor, the gallant Richard S. Ewell proved to be a disappointment and the argument as to why is still around today. Some claim it was the loss of a leg, others that it was the influence of the "Widow Brown" who he married during his recovery. But the fact of the matter is that he was ill-prepared by Jackson for the loose style of command practiced by Lee. A West Pointer (1840) and veteran of two decades as a company officer, he never quite made the adjustment to commanding large-scale units. He once went out foraging for his division and returned—with a single steer—as if he was still commanding a company of dragoons. Resigning his captaincy on May 7, 1861, to serve the South, he held the following assignments: colonel, Cavalry (1861); brigadier general, CSA (June 17, 1861); commanding brigade (in 1st Corps after July 20), Army of the Potomac (June 20-October 22, 1861); commanding brigade, Longstreet's Division, Potomac District, Department of Northern Virginia (October 22, 1861-February 21, 1862); major general, CSA (January 23, 1862); commanding E.K. Smith's (old) Division, same district and department (February 21-May 17, 1862); commanding same division, Valley District, same department (May 17-June 26, 1862);

"Old Baldy" Richard S. Ewell. (*Leslie's*)

commanding division, 2nd Corps, Army of Northern Virginia (June 26-August 28, 1862); commanding the corps (May 30, 1863-May 27, 1864); lieutenant general, CSA (May 23, 1863); and commanding Department of Richmond (June 13, 1864-April 6, 1865). After serving at 1st Bull Run he commanded a division under Jackson in the Shenandoah Valley Campaign where he complained bitterly about being left in the dark about plans. Jackson's style of leadership was to prove the undoing of Ewell once Jackson was gone. Ewell fought through the Seven Days and at Cedar Mountain before being severely wounded and losing a leg at Groveton, in the beginning of the battle of 2nd Bull Run. After a long recovery, he returned to duty in May 1863 and was promoted to command part of Jackson's old corps. At 2nd Winchester he won a stunning victory and for a moment it looked like a second Stonewall had come. But at Gettysburg he failed to take advantage of the situation on the evening of the first day when given discretionary orders by Lee. He required exact instructions, unlike his predecessor. After serving through the fall campaigns he fought at the Wilderness where the same problem developed. At Spotsylvania one of his divisions was all but destroyed. After the actions along the North Anna he was forced to temporarily relinquish command due to illness but Lee made it permanent. He was given command in Richmond and was captured at Sayler's Creek on April 6, 1865, during the retreat to Appomattox. After his release from Fort Warren in July "Old Baldy" retired to a farm in Tennessee. (Hamlin, Percy Gatling, *"Old Bald Head"*)

F

FAGAN, James Fleming (1828-1893)

An early Arkansas Confederate, Kentucky-born lawyer and Mexican War veteran—as a second lieutenant in Yell's Arkansas Regiment—James F. Fagan rose to a major generalcy in charge of a mounted division. His assignments included: colonel, 1st Arkansas (May 8, 1861); brigadier general CSA (September 12, 1862); commanding brigade, Frost's Division, 1st Corps, Trans-Mississippi Department (December 1862-January 1863); commanding brigade, Hindman's-Price's Division, District of Arkansas, Trans-Mississippi Department (January-July 23 and August 17-late 1863); commanding Price's Division, District of Arkansas, Trans-Mississippi Department (July 23-August 17, 1863); commanding cavalry division, District of Arkansas, Trans-Mississippi Department (late 1863-September 18, 1864); major general, CSA (April 25, 1864); and commanding in Trans-Mississippi Department: cavalry division, Army of Missouri (September 18-late 1864); also 1st (Arkansas) Cavalry Division, Cavalry Corps (September 1864-early 1865); and Cavalry, District of Arkansas (February 1-spring 1865). He led his regiment at Shiloh and during the defense of Corinth, Mississippi. Promoted to brigadier general and transferred west of the Mississippi, he fought at the head of a brigade at Prairie Grove, Helena, and Little Rock. During the repulse of Steel's Arkansas expedition in April 1864 Fagan led a mounted division at Jenkins' Ferry and that fall went on Sterling Price's invasion of Missouri. Surrendering on June 14, 1865, he was a postwar farmer, U.S. marshal, and minor goverment official.

FAULKNER, W.W. (?-?)

The Union forces in the West seemed to have a great deal of difficulty in controlling one partisan leader, W.W. Faulkner. Commanding as a captain an irregular band of Confederate cavalry in northern Mississippi and western Tennessee, he had led a raid on Island #10 in the Mississippi River on October 17, 1862. In this attack he and a number of his command were taken prisoner. At first the Union authorities refused to consider them as regular Confederate soldiers subject to the normal procedures for exchange. Confederate General Pemberton eventually got them to agree to an exchange but it was already too late. On November 15, 1862, less than a month after his capture, Faulkner escaped while being transferred from Alton, Illinois, to Johnson's Island, Ohio. What made it even worse for the Union authorities was that he had publicly boasted of his planned break ahead of time and subsequently sent a letter to one of his fellow prisoners while on the run. He later became colonel, 12th Kentucky Cavalry, and served under Nathan Bedford Forrest. At the battle of Tupelo in July 1864 he led a charge and kept going after being wounded. He was finally stopped by a second wound. During Forrest's operations against A.J. Smith's second Mississippi invasion in August 1864, he commanded the 3rd Brigade, Buford's Division, Forrest's Cavalry Corps, Department of Alabama, Mississippi, and East Louisiana. His final action of the Civil War was in opposing Wilson's Raid through Alabama.

FAUNTLEROY, Thomas Turner (1795-1883)

A veteran of two and a half decades in the regular army, Thomas T. Fauntleroy was not pleased with the treatment he received at the hands of the Virginia and Confederate authorities and resigned his commission as a brigadier general in the state forces. A native of Virginia, he had served as a lieutenant in the War of 1812 and entered the regular service in 1836 as a major of dragoons. On May 13, 1861, he resigned his commission as colonel, 1st Dragoons, and was soon thereafter appointed a brigadier in the provisional army of Virginia. On May 19 he was given command of the forces in and around Richmond. Tendered a brigadier generalship in the Confederate army with assignment to command of the militia serving with General J.E. Johnston near Harpers Ferry on July 9, 1861, he declined. After much of his command was taken from his jurisdiction he requested to be relieved of duty on August 17. The formal order was issued on the 30th. (Freeman, Douglas S., *Lee's Lieutenants*)

FEATHERSTON, Winfield Scott (1820-1891)

A Tennessee-born youth, Winfield Scott Featherston had fought in the Creek War before becoming a Mississippi lawyer. He took time out from his practice to sit for two terms in Congress in the late 40s and early 50s. Once the Civil War began, his services included: colonel, 17th Mississippi (spring 1861); brigadier general CSA (from March 4, 1862); commanding brigade, D.H. Hill's Division, Department of Northern Virginia (April 6-May 1862); commanding a different brigade, Longstreet's Division, Army of Northern Virginia (June 1862); commanding brigade, Wilcox's Division, 1st Corps, same army (August-September 1862); commanding brigade, Anderson's Division, same corps and army (November 1862-January 19, 1863); commanding brigade, Loring's Division (in 2nd Military District until April), Department of Mississippi and East Louisiana (ca. February-June 1863 and August 1863-January 28, 1864); commanding brigade, Loring's Division, Department of Alabama, Mississippi and East Louisiana (January 28-May 4, 1864); commanding brigade, Loring's Division, Army of Mississippi (May 4-June 14 and July 7-26, 1864); commanding the division (June 14-July 7, 1864); commanding brigade, Loring's Division, Stewart's Corps, Army of Tennessee (July 26-28 and September-December 1864 and early April-April 26, 1865); and commanding the division (July 28-September 1864). Sent to Virginia, he took part in the victories at 1st Bull Run and Ball's Bluff and the following spring was given a brigade composed of the old Manassas garrison. He fought at Yorktown and Williamsburg and was wounded at Glendale on June 30, 1862, during the Seven Days. He fought at 2nd Bull Run commanding several brigades on the field. Sick at the time of Antietam, he was slated to be replaced by Carnot Posey but returned to duty, upsetting Lee's plan. After the victory at Fredericksburg Featherston requested—there may have been some hints—transfer to his threatened state. Assigned to a brigade under Loring, he fought at Champion Hill; he and the division were cut off from Vicksburg, joining the forces under J.E. Johnston. He later was engaged in the Atlanta Campaign, at times in charge of the division, and in Hood's invasion of Tennessee. He appears to have been off duty for a time following Franklin and Nashville but assumed command of a brigade in Johnston's reorganized army in the final weeks of the war in North Carolina; he surrendered at Greensboro. As a lawyer and politician he campaigned against the carpetbaggers and served in the legislature. (Freeman, Douglas S., *Lee's Lieutenants*)

FERGUSON, Champ (?-1865)

On October 25, 1865, Confederate guerrilla Champ Ferguson was hanged in front of a detachment of United States Colored Troops for his role in the massacre of black prisoners after the fight at Saltville, Virginia the previous year. From the mountainous region of East Tennessee, he had raised a company of irregulars, which at times served with conventional troops, most notably under Joseph Wheeler. When Union forces tried to seize the vital salt works at Saltville, he took part in the October 2, 1864, battle there. The next day he proved to be one of the leaders in the massacre of wounded and captured blacks and their white officers. Confederate General John Breckinridge had him arrested and reported the incident to the authorities. Ferguson had already developed an unsavory reputation and was seized surreptitiously by federal forces. Tried for the murders of 53 persons, including 14 at Saltville, he was sentenced to the gallows. There is some evidence that a Confederate general was also involved in the massacre, and it is speculated that it was Felix H. Robertson who ironically lived to be the last living ex-general of the Confederacy. (Sensing, Thurman, *Champ Ferguson, Confederate Guerilla*)

FERGUSON, Samuel Wragg (1834-1917)

When, in August 1864, there was talk of promoting Samuel W. Ferguson to major general, Confederate cavalryman Joseph Wheeler protested so forcefully that not only was the promotion not made but Ferguson appears not to have held a significant command thereafter. The South Carolinian West Pointer (1857) had taken part in the expedition against the Mormons before resigning on March 1, 1861, as a second lieutenant with the 1st Dragoons. His Confederate assignments included: brigadier general, CSA (July 23, 1863); commanding cavalry brigade, Department of Mississippi and East Louisiana (late August 1863-January 1864); commanding brigade, Jackson's Division, Lee's Cavalry Corps, Department of Mississippi and East Louisiana (January-January 28, 1864); commanding brigade, Jackson's Division, Lee's Cavalry Corps, Department of Alabama, Mississippi and East Louisiana (January 28-May 4, 1864); commanding brigade, Jackson's Cavalry Division, Polk's-Stewart's (Army of Mississippi) Corps, Army of Tennessee (May 4-July 26, 1864); and commanding brigade, Jackson's Cavalry Division, Army of Tennessee (July 26-late August 1864). Initially he performed staff duty, mostly with Beauregard, before transferring to the line midway through the conflict. He commanded at first an independent brigade in Mississippi and as part of William H. Jackson's division took part in the Atlanta Campaign. It was during the siege of that city that dispute over discipline within the brigade and Ferguson's often insubordinate attitude came to the fore. Relegated to minor duties for the balance of the war, he later took up the practice of law and was a minor officeholder in Mississippi.

FIELD, Charles William (1828-1892)

A devastating wound at 2nd Bull Run kept Kentucky-born career soldier Charles W. Field out of active service for a year and a half but he returned to command a division for the final battles. A West Pointer (1849), he had spent a dozen years in the mounted service when he resigned his captaincy on May 30, 1861. His assignments for the Confederacy included: captain, Cavalry (spring 1861); colonel, 6th Virginia Cavalry (summer 1861); brigadier general, CSA (March 9, 1862); commanding brigade, Aquia District, Department of Northern Virginia

(March 27-May 27, 1862); commanding brigade, A.P. Hill's Division (in 1st Corps from June 29 and 2nd Corps from July 27), Army of Northern Virginia (May 27-August 29, 1862); and commanding Hood's (old) Division, 1st Corps, same army (April 1864-January 1865 and March-April 9, 1865). Initially serving in Jeb Stuart's cavalry, he was promoted and transferred to command a brigade of Virginia troops near Fredericksburg. He served with the forces facing McDowell's overland advance in connection with the Peninsula Campaign. Assigned to Hill's Light Division, he fought at the Seven Days and later with Jackson at Cedar Mountain and 2nd Bull Run. Wounded at the latter, he was incapacitated for months. After serving for a time in Richmond on conscript duty, he was assigned to take charge of Hood's former command, then in East Tennessee with Longstreet, in February 1864 but does not appear to have joined it until about the time that it reached Virginia in April. He fought through the Overland and Petersburg campaigns and surrendered with Lee. He was in private business after the war and was a colonel of engineers in Egypt. Returning to the United States, he worked as a government engineer. (Freeman, Douglas S., *Lee's Lieutenants*)

FINEGAN, Joseph (1814-1885)

An Irish-born Florida planter and mill operator, Joseph Finegan spent most of the war commanding the small and widely scattered forces in that state. A member of the secession convention, he supervised the state's military affairs under Governor Milton until he entered the Confederate service. His assignments included: brigadier general, CSA (April 5, 1862); commanding Department of East and Middle Florida (April 18-October 7, 1862); commanding District of Middle and Eastern Florida, Department of South Carolina, Georgia and Florida (October 7-November 4, 1862); commanding District of East Florida, same department (November 4, 1862-February 23, 1864); also temporarily commanding District of Middle Florida, same department (August 7-November 11, 1863); and commanding Florida Brigade, Anderson's-Mahone's Division, 3rd Corps, Army of Northern Virginia (May 28, 1864-March 20, 1865). The high point of his Florida service came in February 1864, when he defeated a Union expedition at Olustee. Sent with some Florida reenforcements to the Army of Northern Virginia in May 1864, he was given charge of the enlarged Florida Brigade under Lee. He fought at Cold Harbor and in the trenches at Petersburg. In the late winter of 1864-65 he was ordered back to Florida but there is no record of his arriving before the close of hostilities. A state legislator immediately after the war, he was for a while in the cotton trade in Savannah before returning to Florida.

FINLEY, Jesse Johnson (1812-1904)

Giving up a Confederate judgeship, Tennessee native Jesse J. Finley enlisted as a private and rose to the rank of brigadier general. A lawyer, he had also been active in politics in Tennessee, Arkansas, and Florida. A judge at the outbreak of the Civil War, he continued in the same position under the Confederate government until early 1862. At that time—having

been a company commander in Seminole fighting—he decided to rejoin the military. His assignments included: private, Company D, 6th Florida (March 1862); captain, Company D, 6th Florida (March 1862); colonel, 6th Florida (April 14, 1862); brigadier general, CSA (November 16, 1863); commanding Florida Brigade, Breckinridge's-Bate's Division, Breckinridge's Corps, Army of Tennessee (November 1863-January 1864); and commanding Florida Brigade, Bate's Division, Hardee's Corps, Army of Tennessee (February-September 1, 1864). His unit served in Florida until June 1862 when it was ordered to East Tennessee. After taking part in the Kentucky Campaign that fall, Finley returned to East Tennessee until ordered to join Bragg's army shortly before Chickamauga. He led his regiment on that field and was rewarded with the rank of brigadier general and assigned to command the newly constituted Florida Brigade. This he led at Chattanooga and during the Atlanta Campaign. During the latter he was severely wounded at Resaca and Jonesboro. The second wound incapacitated him for field service and he finished the war in administrative assignments. He was a U.S. congressman after the war.

FISER, John Calvin (1838-1876)

A highly popular officer with his command, John C. Fiser proved to be one of the heroes of the battle of Fredericksburg. A native of Tennessee, he had been raised in Mississippi. He entered the Confederate service at the war's commencement and his assignments included: lieutenant, Company H, 17th Mississippi (May 27, 1861); first lieutenant and adjutant, 17th Mississippi (June 7, 1861); lieutenant colonel, 17th Mississippi (April 26, 1862); colonel, 17th Mississippi (February 26, 1864); colonel, Provisional Army (mid-1864); and commanding brigade, McLaw's Division, Department of South Carolina, Georgia and Florida (December 24, 1864-ca. April 9, 1865). As regimental adjutant, he fought at 1st Bull Run and Ball's Bluff before being promoted to field officer. During the Seven Days Battles, he succeeded to command of the regiment when the colonel was wounded at Malvern Hill. He continued in command at Antietam and at Fredericksburg he directed a detachment of Barksdale's Brigade in the town itself. This command held up the Union crossing of the river for several hours by delaying the placement of pontoon bridges. Although hit by a falling wall when Union gunners opened up, he retained command. He subsequently was wounded at Gettysburg after again assuming regimental command, fought at Chickamauga, and took part in the siege of Knoxville. Here he led the 17th at the head of one of the assaulting columns at Fort Sanders. It cost him his right arm. Promoted to colonel that winter, he was unable to perform his duties and resigned on June 12, 1864. Soon thereafter he was appointed a colonel in the Provisional Army and joined his old division commander, McLaws, on the coast. He was later given a brigade, composed mostly of Georgia Reserves, and opposed Sherman during the Carolinas Campaign. After the war he settled in Memphis as a merchant.

FLAGG, Benjamin (?-?)

Together with William Glaze of South Carolina, Massachusetts musket manufacturer Benjamin Flagg was awarded on April 15, 1851, a contract with the state of South Carolina—which a decade later would fire on Fort Sumter—to provide 9,000 firearms and 2,000 swords and sabers. Flagg's Milbury, Massachusetts plant provided the equipment to make 1842 model muskets and pistols. The work itself was done at Glaze's Palmetto Iron Works in Columbia, South Carolina.

FLANAGIN, Harris (1817-1874)

New Jersey-born Arkansas lawyer Harris Flanagin left the field as a Confederate colonel to become governor of his adopted state following a special election. He had taught school in Pennsylvania before relocating to Arkansas where he was admitted to the bar. A former state Legislator, he gave up his practice to enter the Confederate army. His assignments included: captain, Company E, 2nd Arkansas Mounted Rifles (July 29, 1861); and colonel, 2nd Arkansas Mounted Rifles (May 8, 1862). He fought at Wilson's Creek, and Pea Ridge before being transferred to the east side of the Mississippi. While still in the field he was elected to the governorship in a special election and resigned on November 8, to take up his duties on November 15, 1862. During his term much of the state fell under Union control and he was effectively removed from office on April 18, 1864. He resumed the practice of law and attended the 1874 state constitutional convention.

FLETCHER, Thomas (1819-1900)

A native of Arkansas, Thomas Fletcher held the governorship of that state for only 11 days. A teacher and farmer, he was serving as sheriff of Pulaski county upon the outbreak of the Civil War. In 1862 he became the president of the new state senate organization under the pro-Confederate constitution. When Governor Henry M. Rector was in effect forced from office by the new document on November 4, 1862—for his uncooperative attitude toward the Richmond authorities—Fletcher automatically assumed the governorship temporarily. He promptly called new elections and served until November 15 when Harris Flanagin was able to take office. After the war he farmed, practiced law, and served again as sheriff and later as a U.S. marshal.

FLOURNOY, Thomas Stanhope (1811-1883)

By the time of the Civil War the cavalry charge had pretty much become a thing of the past and those that were made were frequently made out of desperation and were disastrous. An exception on both counts was the charge of Thomas S. Flournoy and his 6th Virginia Cavalry at Front Royal, Virginia. With no apparent previous military experience the native Virginian had entered the Confederate army as a captain, on August 19, 1861. On November 20, 1861, his unit was assigned to the 6th Virginia Cavalry as Company G. Rising to colonel by the time of the Shenandoah Valley Campaign of 1862, he commanded all the cavalry of Ewell's Division at the battle of Front Royal. After first cutting the railroad into the town, to prevent reenforcements, he led part of his regiment across the Shenandoah River and charged upon the Union 1st Maryland which had been driven from its positions by the Confederate infantry. Although outnumbered by about four to one, the pursuing cavalry managed to gather in most of the Union force as prisoners. Flournoy continued the pursuit into the night. Jackson praised the cavalry's actions. Remaining in the Valley when Jackson moved to Richmond, the 6th became part of the Laurel Brigade and joined the army for the battle of 2nd Bull Run. It was detailed to gather up abandoned weapons on the field and did not rejoin the Army of Northern Virginia until after the battle of Antietam. Less than a month later, on October 15, 1862, Flournoy resigned. After the war he resided in Halifax County, Virginia.

FLOYD, John Buchanan (1806-1863)

One of the greatest rogues ever to serve in high position in both the U.S. and Confederate governments must have been John B. Floyd. A native Virginian lawyer and politician, he became James Buchanan's war secretary in 1857. During his tenure he became embroiled in a controversy over the misuse—possibly for personal purpose—of funds earmarked for the Indians. He survived this and other disputes. But when Buchanan refused to order Robert Anderson's garrison back from Fort Sumter to Fort Moultrie, Floyd resigned on December 29, 1860. Raising a brigade for the Confederacy, his assignments included: brigadier general, CSA (May 23, 1861); commanding Army of the Kanawha (August 12, 1861-January 1862); commanding division, Army of Central Kentucky, Department #2 (January-February 13. 1862); commanding Fort Donelson, Army of Central Kentucky, Department #2 (February 13-15, 1862); and major general, Virginia State Line (May 17, 1862). Commanding an independent force in western Virginia, he displayed a singular inability to cooperate with his fellow commanders in the region. Sent west with his command, he took command of Fort Donelson from Gideon J. Pillow. With the post besieged, he launched a breakout attempt but lost his nerve and recalled the troops at the moment an escape could have been made. That night he relinquished command and turned it over to Pillow who did the same, passing it on to Simon B. Buckner. Floyd then commandeered some river steamers and ferried his own division across the Cumberland River, abandoning the rest of the troops. Jefferson Davis relieved Floyd of his commission on March 11, 1862, without any formal hearing. The displaced general was then appointed to a state military post two months later but his health failed and he died on August 26, 1863.

FOOTE, Henry Stuart (1804-1880)

A violent-tempered man, Henry Foote was a perpetual opponent of Jefferson Davis in both the U.S. and Confederate Congresses. Born in Virginia, Foote had practiced law in Richmond before moving to Alabama and then Mississippi. Having served in the state legislature, he was, in 1847, named to the Senate where, in an effort to reconcile the two sections of the country, he supported the Compromise of 1850, the only member of the Mississippi congressional delegation to do so. This conciliatory nature brought him into confrontation with his fellow Mississippi senator, Davis; it had already resulted in a fistfight between the two on Christmas Day 1847. The two faced each other in the 1851 gubernatorial election and Foote won the seat for a two-year term. His Unionist policies being unpopular, he spent the following four years in California. Returning, he soon moved to Nashville. Following the secession of Tennessee, he was elected to the Confederate 1st and 2nd congresses, from the 5th District. He continued to serve, although his district was soon behind Union lines. He served on the Quartermaster's and Commissary Department Committee and was chairman of the Foreign Affairs Committee in the 1st Congress. From his first entry into the House, in February 1862, he was a vocal opponent of the rebel president. Long in favor of negotiating a return to the Union, he resigned from the Foreign Affairs Committee on December 20, 1864, and headed for Washington to try to open negotiations. He was captured but, soon released, he tried again. Getting to the Union lines, he was met coolly as Lincoln was about to attend the Hampton Roads Conference. Foote was held in custody until he sailed for Europe. Returning six weeks later, in violation of State Department orders, he was promptly arrested. Again directed to leave the country, he went to Canada until things calmed down following Lincoln's assassination. After the war he served as superintendent of the mint in New Orleans before returning home to Nashville. (Foote, Henry S., *Casket of Reminiscences*)

FORD, Antonia (ca. 1838-1871)

From her home within the Union lines surrounding Washington, Antonia Ford was able to provide the Confederates with much valuable information about the Union forces in and around Fairfax, Virginia, and she spent many months in the Old Capitol Prison for her efforts. Early in the war she rode to warn the Southerners of a ruse that the federals were planning for an upcoming battle. As a reward Jeb Stuart granted her a whimsical commission as a major and aide-de-camp. She carefully studied troop positions around Fairfax and pumped the officers quartered in her father's home for more information. This she provided to Mosby who used it to plan his raids. Following the raid in which General Edwin H. Stoughton was captured, she was investigated and four days later arrested. Confined for many months, she became the object of a campaign to gain her freedom. In poor health she was finally released and before the end of the war married the Union officer who had been instrumental in obtaining her release. Her early death was, by many Southerners, blamed upon her poor diet in the prison. (Jones, Virgil Carrington, *Gray Ghosts and Rebel Raiders*)

FORNEY, John Horace (1829-1902)

Resigning from the old army 12 days after the secession of his adopted state, Alabama, North Carolina-born West Pointer (1852) John H. Forney rose to the rank of major general in the Confederate service while performing duty in most of the major theaters of the war. After frontier duty and participation in the

campaign against the Mormons in Utah he resigned as a first lieutenant in the 10th Infantry on January 23, 1861. His Confederate assignments included: colonel, Alabama Artillery (early 1861); captain, Infantry (March 16, 1861); colonel, 10th Alabama (June 4, 1861); commanding 5th Brigade, Army of the Shenandoah (July 21-October 1861); also commanding detachment (still in Shenandoah Valley), Army of the Shenandoah (July 21-July 1861); brigadier general, CSA (March 10, 1862); commanding Department of Alabama and West Florida (April 28-June 27, 1862); commanding District of the Gulf, Department #2 (July 2-December 8, 1862); major general, CSA (October 27, 1862); commanding division, 2nd Military District, Department of Mississippi and East Louisiana (early 1863-April 17, 1863); commanding Maury's (old) Division, 2nd Military District, Department of Mississippi and East Louisiana (April 17-April 1863); commanding division, Department of Mississippi and East Louisiana (April-July 4, 1863 and fall 1863-February 1864); and commanding 1st (Texas) Division, 1st Corps (or District of West Louisiana), Trans-Mississippi Department (September 1864-ca. May 26, 1865). Although it is frequently stated that he fought at 1st Bull Run, in fact on that very day he took command of the Army of the Shenandoah's 5th Brigade and other forces from that army that were still in the Shenandoah Valley. However, fighting at Dranesville that December he was wounded. Promoted to brigadier general that winter, he was assigned to command along the Gulf coast for most of 1862. As a major general he was transferred to Mississippi where he commanded a division at Vicksburg. Following his exchange he again took charge of the division until early 1864. Transferred to the Trans-Mississippi West he led a division in western Louisiana for the balance of the war. Returning to Alabama, he became a planter and civil engineer.

FORNEY, William Henry (1823-1894)

North Carolina-born lawyer William Forney was a Mexican War veteran when he became captain of a company in the 10th Alabama in June 1861. He accompanied his regiment to Virginia where it served in the 5th Brigade, Army of the Shenandoah. Colonel John Forney, the regimental commander and William Forney's brother, took command of this brigade on July 21, 1861. In August William Forney was promoted to major. Joining Johnston's army, later known as the Army of Northern Virginia, the regiment was engaged at Dranesville on December 20, 1861, where Forney was wounded. On March 17, 1862, he was promoted to lieutenant colonel. At Williamsburg he was wounded and later captured in the hospital. After four months in prison he rejoined his regiment, having been made its colonel as of June 27. He led his men at Fredericksburg, Chancellorsville, and at Gettysburg where on the second day he was again wounded and captured. Imprisoned for over a year, he did not rejoin his command until November 1864 when he, as senior colonel, took command of the brigade in Mahone's Division, A.P. Hill's Corps, Army of Northern Virginia. The previous commander, General Sanders, had been killed some three months earlier, and the brigade had been without a regular commander ever since. Forney commanded the brigade through the rest of the Petersburg siege, finally achieving the rank of brigadier general on February 15, 1865. On April 9 he surrendered the remnant of his brigade at Appomattox. After the war he resumed his law practice and served as member of congress for 18 years. (Freeman, Douglas S., *Lee's Lieutenants*)

FORNO, Henry (1797-1866)

Although he survived a war wound that many considered to be fatal, Henry Forno did not long outlast the war, dying in a railroad accident less than a year later. He was born in Louisiana when it belonged to the Spanish and was a veteran of the Mexican War, having served in the infantry and the artillery. In the decade before the Civil War he was chief of police in New Orleans. Reentering military service, this time for the Confederacy, his assignments included: lieutenant colonel, 5th Louisiana (May 10, 1861); colonel 5th Louisiana (July 31, 1862); and commanding Taylor's (old) Brigade, Ewell's Division, Jackson's Corps, Army of Northern Virginia (ca. August 8-29, 1862). He served through the battles at Yorktown, the Seven Days, Cedar Mountain, and 2nd Bull Run. Severely wounded at the latter, he was feared by some to be mortally hurt. He eventually recovered and served as commander of the post garrison at Andersonville in late 1864. He was subsequently on recruiting duty. (Freeman, Douglas S., *Lee's Lieutenants*)

FORREST, French (1796-1866)

Already 65 by the outbreak of the Civil War, French Forrest failed to measure up as the commander of the Confederacy's James River Squadron. The Maryland native was a veteran of five decades in the navy including the War of 1812 battle of Lake Erie and service at Alvarado and Vera Cruz during the Mexican War. He joined the Southern war effort in 1861, and his assignments included: captain, Virginia Navy (1861); commanding Norfolk Navy Yard (ca. April 25, 1861-ca. May 9, 1862); captain, CSN (1861); chief, Office of Orders and Detail (1862-63); and commanding James River Squadron (1863-ca. May 1864). When the Union fleet abandoned Norfolk, Forrest was dispatched by the Virginia authorities to take charge of the naval equipment and stores there. During the famous fights of the *Virginia* and *Monitor* in Hampton Roads he was aboard the tugboat *Harmony*. After the fall of Norfolk he was made a bureau chief in the Navy Deaprtment and then took charge of the small flotilla on the James. During 1863 the squadron's poor behavior was blamed on Forrest who was relieved by John K. Mitchell in early 1864. While Forrest's name had appeared on the naval register of January 1, 1864, it was missing from that of June 1, and it must be assumed that he had been dropped from the rolls. In any event he barely outlived the war.

FORREST, Nathan Bedford (1821-1877)

With no formal military training, Nathan Bedford Forrest became one of the leading cavalry figures of the Civil War. The native Tennesseean had amassed a fortune, which he estimated at $1,500,000, as a slave trader and plantation owner before enlisting in the Confederate army as a private in Josiah H. White's cavalry company on June 14, 1861. Tapped by the governor, he then raised a mounted battalion at his own expense. His assignments included: lieutenant colonel, Forrest's Tennessee Cavalry Battalion (October 1861); colonel, 3rd Tennessee Cavalry (March 1862); brigadier general, CSA (July 21, 1862); commanding cavalry brigade, Army of the Mississippi (summer-November 20, 1862); commanding cavalry brigade, Army of Tennessee (November 20, 1862-summer 1863); commanding cavalry division, Army of Tennessee (summer 1863); commanding cavalry corps, Army of Tennessee (ca. August-September 29, 1863); commanding West Tennessee, (probably in) Department of Mississippi and East Louisiana (November 14, 1863-January 11, 1864); major general, CSA (December 4, 1863); commanding cavalry corps, Department of Mississippi and East Louisiana (January 11-28, 1864); commanding District of Mississippi and East Louisiana, Department of Alabama, Mississippi and East Louisiana (January 27-May 4, 1865); also commanding cavalry corps, Department of Alabama, Mississippi and East Louisiana (January 28-May 4, 1865); and lieutenant general, CSA (February 28, 1865). When the mass Confederate breakout attempt at Fort Donelson failed, Forrest led most of his own men, and some other troops, through the besieging lines and then directed the rear guard during the retreat from Nashville. At Shiloh there was little opportunity for the effective use of the mounted troops and his command again formed the rear guard on the retreat. The day after the close of the battle Forrest was wounded. After serving during the Corinth siege he was promoted to brigadier general, and he raised a brigade with which he captured Murfreesboro, its garrison and supplies. In December 1862 and January 1863 he led another raid, this time in west Tennessee, which contributed to the abandonment of Grant's campaign in central Mississippi; the other determining factor was Van Dorn's Holly Springs raid. Joining up with Joseph Wheeler, Forrest took part in the unsuccessful attack on Fort Donelson which resulted in Forrest swearing he would never serve under Wheeler again. His next success came with the capture of the Union raiding column under Abel D. Streight in the spring of 1863. On June 14, 1863, he was shot by a disgruntled subordinate, Andrew W. Gould, whom Forrest then mortally wounded with his penknife. Recovering, he commanded a division that summer and then a corps at Chickamauga. Having had a number of disputes with army commander Braxton Bragg, Forrest was humiliated by being placed under Wheeler again. His request for transfer to west Tennessee was granted and he was dispatched there with a pitifully small force. Recruiting in that area, he soon had a force large enough to give Union commanders headaches. Sherman kept ordering his Memphis commanders to catch him. When Forrest captured Fort Pillow a controversy developed over reports of a massacre of the largely black garrison. Apparently a massacre did occur as there are numerous Confederate firsthand accounts of it. He defeated Samuel D. Sturgis at Brice's Crossroads and under Stephen D. Lee fought Andrew J. Smith at Tupelo. He again faced Smith during August 1864 and then provided the cavalry force for Hood's invasion of middle

Tennessee that fall. Finally the force of numbers began to tell when he proved incapable of stopping Wilson's Raid through Alabama and Georgia in the final months of the war. His diminished command was included in Richard Taylor's surrender. Wiped out financially by the war, he resumed planting and became engaged in railroading. Joining the Ku Klux Klan shortly after the war, he was apparently one of its early leaders. Forrest once summed up his military theory as "Get there first with the most men." (Wyeth, John, *Life of Nathan Bedford Forrest* and Henry, Robert Selph, *"First with the Most" Forrest*)

FORSYTH, Alexander John (fl. 1805)

It took some three decades for the percussion cap invented by Reverend Alexander J. Forsyth to be adopted for use on military weapons. The Scottish cleric had developed his improvement over the flintlock firing system in 1805 but it took a long time for the small metal caps to gain acceptance and supersede the flint. Even at the outbreak of the Civil War the conversion was not complete. Many regiments, especially Confederate, still went into the field with flintlocks or with flintlocks poorly altered and adapted to the percussion system.

FORSYTH, John (1812-1879)

The mayor of Mobile, John Forsyth was chosen by Jefferson Davis to be one of the peace commissioners sent to Washington to negotiate the turning over of Forts Sumter and Pickens to the new Confederacy. Convinced of the hopelessness of his endeavors, Forsyth, a Douglas supporter in 1860, threw his full efforts into the secessionist movement. As editor of the Mobile *Register*, Forsyth was able to provide propaganda for the rebel nation. Forsyth was instrumental in the planning of the defense of the city from the Union fleet, carrying on an extensive correspondence with the Richmond authorities. Having served as mayor throughout the war, he used his paper as a critical voice against the postwar policies of Andrew Johnson's administration. (Swanberg, W.A., *First Blood*)

FRAZER, John Wesley (1827-1906)

The fall of Cumberland Gap into the hands of the Union Army under Burnside in late 1863 unfairly cost John W. Frazer his reputation as a Confederate general. This unfairness was recognized by Jefferson Davis but not until 1883. The Tennessee-born West Pointer (1849) was posted to the infantry with which he performed frontier and routine garrison duties until his March 15, 1861, resignation as a captain in the 9th Infantry. His Confederate assignments included: captain, Infantry (March 1861); lieutenant colonel, 8th Alabama (June 11, 1861); colonel, 28th Alabama (March 1862); brigadier general, CSA (May 19, 1863); and commanding brigade, Department of East Tennessee (May-September 9, 1863). With his first regiment—the first to enlist for the war—he served in Virginia until he accepted the colonelcy of a new unit. This he led in the defense of Corinth, Mississippi, at Munfordville and Murfreesboro. Promoted to brigadier general, he was ordered to

East Tennessee and was eventually stationed at Cumberland Gap. With a small force, and his supports called into northern Georgia in the buildup for Chickamauga, he was faced with an impossible dilemma when Burnside's forces approached the gap. Most of his troops were untried and untrusted; rather than sacrifice his command he surrendered on September 9, 1863. There was a public outcry throughout the South against this "cowardly" action and the Confederate Senate rejected his nomination as brigadier general on February 16, 1864. Frazer himself was not released from Fort Warren, Boston Harbor, until the summer of 1865. Afterwards he was an Arkansas planter and New York City businessman. It was 20 years before Davis' mollifying comments were printed in his memoirs.

FRENCH, Samuel Gibbs (1818-1910)

Despite his Northern birth Samuel G. French joined the Confederate army and rose to the rank of major general. The New Jersey native and West Pointer (1843) won two brevets and was wounded at Buena Vista while serving as an artillery officer in Mexico. Transferring to the quartermaster department in 1848, he resigned as a captain eight years later. He spent the next five years managing his Mississippi plantation—he had married into a prominent family there—and answered his new country's call. His assignments included: chief of ordnance, Mississippi forces (early 1861); major, Artillery (April 1861); brigadier general CSA (October 23, 1861); commanding Evansport, Department of Fredericksburg (November 14-22, 1861); commanding 1st Brigade, Aquia District, Department of Northern Virginia (November 22, 1861-February 1862); commanding Department of North Carolina and Southern Virginia (February 17-26, 1862); commanding District of the Pamlico, Department of North Carolina (March 18-20, 1862); commanding District of the Cape Fear, Department of North Carolina (ca. March 20-ca. September 1862); commanding French's Command (North Carolina), Department of North Carolina and Southern Virginia (ca. September 1862-April 1, 1863); major general, CSA (October 22, 1862, to rank from August 31); commanding division, Department of the West (June-July 1863); commanding division, Department of Mississippi and East Louisiana (July 1863-January 28, 1864); commanding division, Department of Alabama, Mississippi and East Louisiana (January 28-May 4, 1864); commanding division, Polk's Louisiana (January 28-May 4, 1864); commanding division, Polk's (Army of Mississippi)-Stewart's Corps, Army of Tennessee (May 4-mid-December 1864); and commanding division, District of the Gulf, Department of Alabama, Mississippi and East Louisiana (spring 1865). In the early part of the war he served in various fringe commands in Virginia and North Carolina before being dispatched to command a division under Joseph E. Johnston in Mississippi. As such he took part in the unsuccessful attempt to free the garrison of Vicksburg. He later faced Sherman's movements against Jackson and Meridian before accompanying Leonidas Polk to northern Georgia for the Atlanta Campaign. Following the fall of that city he was ordered northward by Hood to cut Sherman's communication lines. He commanded the unsuccessful attack on Allatoona, which was defended by troops under John M. Corse. Later he went with

Hood into middle Tennessee and commanded his division at Franklin. Just before the battle of Nashville he was forced to relinquish command due to a severe eye infection. Returning to duty, his unit was soon transferred to the Mobile area and he finished the war there. He then returned to his plantation. (French, Samuel G., *Two Wars: An Autobiography*)

FROST, Daniel Marsh (1823-1900)

The only Confederate general to be dropped from the army's rolls was New York native Daniel M. Frost for, in effect, desertion. The West Pointer (1844) had been posted initially to the artillery but transferred to the Regiment of Mounted Riflemen in 1846. During the Mexican War he won one brevet and then served on the frontier and a tour of duty in Europe before resigning as a first lieutenant in 1853. He then went into business in St. Louis and sat in the state legislature. Having been in the militia for a number of years, he joined the Southern faction in 1861. His Southern assignments included: brigadier general, Missouri Militia (prewar); brigadier general, Missouri State Guard (early 1861); commanding 7th and 9th Divisions, Missouri State Guard, Trans-Mississippi District, Department #2 (March 1862); commanding Artillery Brigade, Price's Division, Trans-Mississippi District, Department #2 (March 17-April 15, 1862); commanding Artillery Brigade, Army of the West, Department #2 (April 15-April 1862); inspector general, Army of the West, Department #2 (May 8-26, 1862); commanding division, 1st Corps, Trans-Mississippi Department (late 1862-January 1863); brigadier general, CSA (October 10, 1862, to rank from March 3); commanding brigade, Hindman's Division, District of Arkansas, Trans-Mississippi Department (January-March 2 and March 30-May 1863); commanding the division (March 2-30, 1863); and commanding division, District of Arkansas, Trans-Mississippi Department (May-fall 1863). It was his command at Camp Jackson that Nathaniel Lyon seized in order to protect the arsenal in St. Louis. At Pea Ridge he commanded two tiny divisions of the State Guard and then took command of an artillery brigade, which he took across the Mississippi. During the siege of Corinth he served as an inspector and then recrossed the river. At Prairie Grove he led a division, having been named a brigadier general in the Confederate service. He continued in Arkansas until he joined his wife and family in Canada where they had gone to flee the Union occupation of St. Louis. Not having tendered his resignation, he was simply dropped on December 9, 1863. After the war he returned to the St. Louis area and engaged in farming.

FRY, Birkett Davenport (1822-1891)

Wounded four times during the Civil War, Virginian Birkett D. Fry rose to the rank of Confederate brigadier general but is largely forgotten because he spent so little time in command. A graduate of the Virginia Military Institute, he flunked out of the 1866 class at West Point for a deficiency in mathematics. The Mexican War, however gave him another chance as he was commissioned directly into the Regiment of Voltigeurs—which was raised especially for that conflict—as a

first lieutenant. During a part of the war he served as the unit's adjutant. Mustered out in 1848, he settled in California. In the late 1850s he accompanied William Walker's filibustering expedition to Nicaragua. Managing a cotton mill in Alabama at the outbreak of the Civil War, he joined the Confederacy. His assignments included: colonel, 13th Alabama (July 19, 1861); commanding Archer's Brigade, A.P. Hill's Division, 2nd Corps, Army of Northern Virginia (May 3, 1863); commanding Archer's brigade, Heth's Division, 3rd Corps, Army of Northern Virginia (July 1-3, 1863); commanding Barton's Brigade, Ransom's Division, Department of North Carolina and Southern Virginia (May 1864); and brigadier general, CSA (May 24, 1864). With his regiment he fought on the Peninsula, seeing action at Yorktown, Williamsburg, Seven Pines (wounded), and the Seven Days. He fought at Antietam and was wounded a second time. At Chancellorsville he took over the brigade when James J. Archer took over the division but soon fell wounded again. When Archer was captured on the first day at Gettysburg, Fry again took over. During Pickett's Charge on the third day Fry was wounded a fourth time and captured. Not exchanged until April 1864, he fought under Beauregard at Drewry's Bluff and was rewarded with promotion to brigadier general. In the fall of 1864 he was dispatched to Augusta, Georgia, to command in that area in the face of Sherman's March to the Sea. After three years in Cuban exile he returned to the cotton business in Alabama. (Freeman, Douglas S., *Lee's Lieutenants*)

FULKERSON, Samuel Vance (1822-1862)

Although a favorite of Stonewall Jackson, Samuel V. Fulkerson did not live long enough to receive his rightful promotion to a brigadier generalship. A native of Virginia, he served in a Tennessee regiment as adjutant during the Mexican War. A lawyer and judge at the outbreak of the Civil War, he reentered military service where his assignments included: colonel, 37th Virginia (May 28, 1861); commanding 3rd Brigade, Jackson's Division, Valley District, Department of Northern Virginia (ca. February-April 13, 1862 and May 1862); and commanding the same brigade, Jackson's Division, Jackson's Corps, Army of Northern Virginia (June 27, 1862). He commanded the regiment in the Cheat Mountain and Romney campaigns and got involved in the Loring-Jackson feud near the latter place. He then took part in the Shenandoah Valley Campaign, sometimes commanding the brigade. Again in brigade command he was killed at the battle of Gaines' Mill during the Seven Days.

FULLER, William A. (ca. 1836-1905)

The conductor of the train pulled by *The General*, which was hijacked by Union raiders under James J. Andrews, became the Confederate hero of the raid. With the Western and Atlantic train making a scheduled breakfast stop at Big Shanty, Georgia, William A. Fuller was astonished to see the engine and three box cars leaving the station without him and the rest of his crew. Thinking deserters from a nearby Confederate camp were responsible for the theft, Fuller and a handful of other railroad employees gave chase—on foot! Soon picking up a pushcart, they continued the pursuit at a faster pace. Derailed by a track torn up by the raiders, Fuller continued on foot until he picked up the first of three pursuit engines. Changing trains several times and sometimes running backwards, the pursuers easily pushed aside any obstructions laid by the fugitives. Finally, after about 87 miles, the raiders were forced by a lack of fuel to abandon *The General* and were soon captured by the alerted authorities. Fuller's pursuit prevented the raiders from inflicting any serious damage to the line. With the excitement of April 12, 1862, over, Fuller resumed his duties with the road and in 1864 was made a captain of Georgia Local Defense Troops assigned to protecting the railroad. With the impending fall of Atlanta, it was Fuller who was responsible for the removal of most of the railroads engines to safer areas. (O'Neill, Charles, *Wild Train: The Story of the Andrews Raiders*)

FULTON, John S. (1828-1864)

In a little over two years of active service John S. Fulton took part in military operations in several major theaters of the Civil War. His Confederate assignments included: private, Company G or K, 44th Tennessee (March 27, 1862); captain, Company F, 44th Consolidated Tennessee (April 18, 1862); major, 44th Consolidated Tennessee (April 19, 1862); colonel, 44th Consolidated Tennessee (May 15, 1862); temporarily commanding Johnson's Brigade, Johnson's Provisional Division, Army of Tennessee (September 19-20, 1863); colonel, 25th and 44th Tennessee Consolidated (October 1863); commanding Johnson's Brigade, Buckner's-Johnson's Division, Department of East Tennessee (November 26, 1863-April 1864); commanding same brigade, Hoke's Division, Department of North Carolina and Southern Virginia (May 1864); and commanding same brigade, Johnson's Division, Department of North Carolina and Southern Virginia (ca. May 21-June 30, 1864). Following the heavy losses suffered at Shiloh, he became captain of his company, but a few days later the 44th was merged with the 55th (McKoin's) Tennessee. He became, in quick succession, captain of a consolidated company, major and colonel. Commanding the new regiment, he fought at Perryville and Murfreesboro. At Chickamauga he commanded the brigade. Having again suffered severe casualties, the regiment was "temporarily" united the 25th Tennessee. Still in command of the brigade, Fulton fought at Knoxville and, after moving to Virginia, at Port Walthall Junction, Swift Creek, and Drewry's Bluff. Taking position in the Petersburg trenches, he was struck by a shell fragment on the last day of June 1864. He died four days later.

FUNSTEN, David (1819-1866)

Having provided his initial service to the Confederacy in the army, David Funsten became an innovative legislator in the field of military affairs. A native Virginian, he had served one term in the state legislature before the war. His army assignments included: captain, 11th Virginia (early 1861); lieutenant colonel, 11th Virginia (May 16, 1861); and colonel, 11th Virginia May 23, 1862). He saw action at 1st Manassas and Seven Pines, where he was severely wounded. His wound eventually forced his resignation on September 24, 1863. Running for the 9th Congressional District's seat, which had been vacated by William Smith, Funsten won election to both the unexpired portion of the term in the First Congress and for the Second. Taking his seat at the commencement of the next session on December 7, 1863, Funsten was assigned to the Committees on Naval Affairs and on Flag and Seal, as well as numerous special bodies. An extreme proponent of all-out warfare, he favored the drafting of whites and even blacks, heavy taxes, impressments, military control of railroads and minerals, and the suspension of the writ of habeas corpus on the slightest of pretexts. Drawing on his military experiences, he initiated legislation that consolidated decimated field units and provided for limited service by invalided soldiers. Returning to his home near Alexandria, Virginia, he died of pneumonia, a complication from his war wound, less than a year after Lee's surrender.

G

GANO, Richard Montgomery (1830-1913)

A veteran of Texas Indian fighting, Richard M. Gano got his early Civil War cavalry training under John Hunt Morgan. The Kentucky-born doctor had sat in the Texas legislature before the Civil War. His Confederate assignments included: captain, Texas Cavalry Squadron (1861); captain, Company A, 7th Kentucky Cavalry (May 6, 1862); colonel, 7th Kentucky Cavalry (September 2, 1862); commanding brigade, Maxey's Cavalry Division, District of Arkansas, Trans-Mississippi Department (April 1864); commanding 5th (Texas) Cavalry Brigade, 2nd (Texas-Maxey's) Cavalry Division, 1st Corps (or District of West Louisiana), Trans-Mississippi Department (September 1864-ca. March 1865); and brigadier general, CSA (March 17, 1865). He took part in a number of Morgan's raids and was given command of a regiment during the Kentucky Campaign. Transferred to the far side of the Mississippi, he commanded a mounted brigade during the repulse of Steele's drive on Camden, Arkansas, in the spring of 1864. During these operations he was wounded but returned to duty to command the brigade again and receive promotion to brigadier general in the final months of the war. He then became a minister in the Christian Church for the remainder of his life. He was also active in veterans' affairs.

GARDNER, Franklin (1823-1873)

During the Civil War Jefferson Davis came in for much criticism for his predilection of appointing Northern-born officers to important commands—where they were frequently unsuccessful. Such is the case of New York City-born Franklin Gardner who surrendered the last major Confederate post on the Mississippi River. The West Pointer (1843) had received his appointment from Iowa and was then posted to the infantry. He won two brevets in Mexico, fought the Seminoles, was stationed on the frontier, and campaigned against the Mormons. With the secession crisis reaching its peak, he abandoned his post and was dropped as a captain in the 10th Infantry on May 7, 1861.

Joining the Confederacy, his assignments included: lieutenant colonel, Infantry (March 16, 1861); commanding Cavalry Brigade, 2nd Grand Division, Army of the Mississippi (March 25-29, 1862); brigadier general, CSA (April 11, 1862); commanding Cavalry, 2nd Division, 2nd Corps, Army of the Mississippi (ca. May-late June 1862); commanding 1st Brigade, Reserve Corps, Army of the Mississippi (late June-July 2, 1862); commanding 1st Brigade, Reserve (Withers') Division (Right Wing from August 15), Army of the Mississippi (July 2-November 20, 1862); commanding 1st Brigade, Withers' Division, Polk's Corps, Army of Tennessee (November 20-December 1862); major general, CSA (December 13, 1862); commanding 3rd Military District (or District of Eastern Louisiana), Department of Mississippi and East Louisiana (December 28, 1862-May 6, 1863 and May 6-July 8, 1863); also temporarily commanding District of the Gulf, Department of Mississippi and East Louisiana (April 27, 1863); commanding District of the Gulf, Department of Alabama, Mississippi and East Louisana (early September 1864); commanding the department (September 1864); and commanding District of Mississippi and East Louisiana, Department of Alabama, Mississippi and East Louisiana (October 4, 1864-May 4, 1865). Early in the war he served in Tennessee and Mississippi. During the battle of Shiloh he was in charge of the cavalry in the rear, but due to the terrain his command played little part in the fight. He commanded a brigade—which was not present at Perryville—during the Kentucky Campaign in the fall of 1862. Promoted to major general, he was ordered to the Mississippi Valley with principal responsibility for Port Hudson, which next to Vicksburg was the most important Confederate stronghold on the river. The fall of Vicksburg on July 4, 1863, virtually made Port Hudson untenable and Gardner surrendered the post on the 8th, having repulsed several determined Union assaults during the seven weeks of siege. Not exchanged until August 1864, his promotion to major general was not confirmed by the Senate until two months earlier due to the anti-Davis sentiment in that body. He spent the balance of the war in district command and took part in no further major battles. Surrendered under the terms of Richard Taylor's capitulation, he lived out his years as a planter in Louisiana.

GARDNER, William Montgomery (1824-1901)

Resigning his regular army commission on the date of his native Georgia's secession, William M. Gardner rose to the rank of brigadier general in the Confederate service. The West Pointer (1846) had been posted to the infantry with which he was wounded on two consecutive days in Mexico. For this he was brevetted. The interwar years were spent mostly on the frontier and by the time of his resignation on January 19, 1861, he was a captain in the 2nd Infantry. His Confederate assignments included: major, Infantry (March 16, 1861); lieutenant colonel, 8th Georgia (ca. June 1861); colonel, 8th Georgia (August 21, 1861 to rank from July 21); brigadier general, CSA (November 14, 1861); commanding District of Middle Florida, Department of South Carolina, Georgia and Florida (November 11, 1863-February 23, 1864); and commanding Post of Richmond, Department of Richmond (January-April 2, 1865). Badly wounded at 1st Bull Run, he was promoted to colonel and brigadier general during his lengthy recovery. Late in 1863 he finally returned to duty as a district commander in Florida. Although most sources state that he fought at Olustee there is no evidence of this in the *Official Records*. Shortly thereafter he was placed in charge of all prisoner of war camps east of the Mississippi River except in Alabama and Georgia. During the final months of the conflict he commanded the post at Richmond. After Appomattox he returned quietly to his home.

GARLAND, Augustus Hill (1832-1899)

The youngest member of the Confederate Congress, Augustus H. Garland was a late convert to the secessionist cause, not committing himself to the idea until the call for troops made by Lincoln following the fall of Fort Sumter. The Tennessee-born and Arkansas-raised Garland was a successful lawyer by this time and took an active role in the Arkansas secession convention. He was promptly sent to Montgomery as an at-large delegate to the Provisional Congress. In a disputed election in November 1861, Garland won reelection as representative for the 3rd District in the southeastern corner of the state. Defeated in an attempt to gain election to the senate in 1862, he continued to serve in the House, into the Second Congress, before taking a seat in the Senate on November 8, 1864, upon the death of the incumbent. Although a staunch supporter of the Davis administration's war policies and favoring an extended draft, Garland became known as one of the most articulate opponents of the suspension of the writ of habeas corpus and of martial law. After the war, he played a key role in the overturning of the "iron-clad oath," required by Congress before a lawyer could argue a case before the U.S. Supreme Court. He later served as governor, senator, and as Cleveland's attorney general. He died, fittingly, while presenting arguments before the Supreme Court. (Newberry, Farrar, *A Life of Mr. Garland of Arkansas*)

GARLAND, Samuel, Jr. (1830-1862)

A graduate of the Virginia Military Institute, Samuel Garland, Jr., was a practicing attorney but active in military affairs at the outbreak of the Civil War. He promptly joined the Virginia forces and his assignments included: captain, Company G, 11th Virginia (April 24, 1861); colonel, 11th Virginia (April 1861); brigadier general, CSA (May 23, 1862); and commanding Early's (old) Brigade, D.H. Hill's Division, Army of Northern Virginia (May 24-September 14, 1862). He fought at 1st Bull Run, Dranesville, and was wounded at Williamsburg but remained on duty. Later that month he was promoted and transferred to command the wounded General J.A. Early's Brigade. He led this unit at Seven Pines, in the Seven Days, and on the fringes of the 2nd Bull Run Campaign. In the invasion of Maryland, he was assigned to hold Fox's Gap in South Mountain on September 14, 1862. In its defense he fell mortally wounded, dying later that day. (Freeman, Douglas S., *Lee's Lieutenants*)

GARNETT, John Jameson (1839-1902)

One of the artillery battalion commanders of the Army of Northern Virginia who failed to make the grade was John J. Garnett. He was scheduled to graduate from West Point in the spring of 1861 when the outbreak of hostilities interrupted his studies. Joining the Confederacy immediately, he received the following assignments: lieutenant, Artillery (March 16, 1861); lieutenant, 3rd Company, Washington (La.) Artillery Battalion (June 20, 1861); major, Artillery (June 16, 1862); chief of artillery, D.R. Jones' Division, Magruder's Command, Army of Northern Virginia (June 16-July 1862); inspector of ordnance and artillery, 1st Corps, Army of Northern Virginia (November 14, 1862-early 1863); commanding Artillery Battalion, Anderson's Division, 1st Corps, Army of Northern Virginia (early 1863-June 2, 1863); commanding Artillery Battalion, Heth's Division, 3rd Corps, Army of Northern Virginia (June 2-July 1863); commanding artillery battalion, 3rd Corps, Army of Northern Virginia (July 1863-February 18, 1864); and commanding Post at Hicksford, 1st Military District, Department of North Carolina and Southern Virginia (summer-November 30, 1864). He was initially assigned to duty with the Washington Artillery of New Orleans with which he served at 1st Bull Run. He was a divisional artillery chief during the Seven Days, 2nd Bull Run, and Antietam. He was an inspector during the battle of Fredericksburg but was again in charge of a battalion at Chancellorsville and Gettysburg. His performance not being up to the standards required, he was suspended from duty on February 18, 1864, and relieved of duty with the army six weeks later. The army's chief artillerist, General Pendleton, had felt him better qualified for conscript duty than field command. He was assigned to post duty and finished the war as artillery inspector with the Army of Tennessee. (Wise, Jennings C., *The Long Arm of Lee*)

GARNETT, Richard Brooke (1817-1863)

Like his cousin, Robert S. Garnett, Richard B. Garnett rose to be a Confederate brigadier and lost his life in the war. Graduating from West Point in 1841, he spent two decades in the old army before resigning as captain, 6th Infantry on May 17, 1861. The veteran of the Seminole and Utah campaigns received the following assignments: major, Artillery (May 1861); brigadier general, CSA (November 14, 1861); commanding Stonewall Brigade, Valley District, Department of Northern Virginia (November 1861-April 1, 1862); commanding Pickett's Brigade, Jones' Division, 1st Corps, Army of Northern Virginia (September 5-late September 1862); commanding brigade, Pickett's Division, same corps and army (September 1862-February 25, 1863 and May-July 3, 1863); and commanding brigade, Pickett's Division, in the Department of Virginia and North Carolina (February 25-April 1, 1863) and in the Department of Southern Virginia (April 1-May 1863). Given command of the famed Stonewall Brigade, he commanded it in the Romney Campaign and at Kernstown where he withdrew it when his ammunition was exhausted, much to the displeasure of Jackson. He was placed under arrest on April 1, but the requirements of active campaigning prevented completion of the court-martial. Ordered back to duty on September 5, 1862, he led Pickett's old command at Antietam, Fredericksburg, in southeastern Virginia, and at Gettysburg. In Pickett's Charge on the third day he was killed and buried in a mass grave. Less than two months earlier he had served as pallbearer for his accuser, Stonewall Jackson. (Robertson, James I., Jr., *The Stonewall Brigade*)

GARNETT, Robert Selden (1819-1861)

The first general officer to die in action during the Civil War was Confederate Robert S. Garnett. The Virginian and West Pointer (1841) was a veteran of the infantry, artillery, and cavalry, and had received two brevets for the Mexican War. He resigned as major, 9th Infantry, on April 30, 1861, and entered the service of his state as adjutant general of Virginia troops. Working on the staff of Robert E. Lee, he became more of a chief of staff than any other officer was to become during the conflict. Transferred to Confederate service his assignments included: brigadier general, CSA (June 6, 1861) and commanding Army of the Northwest (June 8-July 13, 1861). Departing Richmond, he took command in what is now West Virginia. Covering a withdrawal in the face of Union forces under General Rosecrans, he was killed at Carrick's Ford on July 13. His cousin, General Richard Brooke Garnett was destined to die two years later in Pickett's Charge. (Freeman, Douglas S., *R.E. Lee*)

GARNETT, Thomas Stuart (1825-1863)

On both occasions when Virginian Thomas S. Garnett took over command of his brigade he soon fell victim to enemy fire. A former student at the Virginia Military Institute, he had served as a first lieutenant in the 1st Virginia during the Mexican War. When the Civil War began he gave up his medical practice and entered the Confederate army where his assignments included: captain, Company C, 9th Virginia Cavalry (May 1861); lieutenant colonel, 48th Virginia (mid 1861); commanding

J.R. Jones' (2nd) Brigade, Jackson's (old) Division, Jackson's Corps, Army of Northern Virginia (summer 1862-August 9, 1862 and May 2-3, 1863); and colonel 48th Virginia (October 16, 1862). After initial service with his company, Lee's Light Horse, he was promoted to field officer with the 48th Virginia. With this command he served through the Cheat Mountain and Romney campaigns and fought at Kernstown and part of the 1862 Shenandoah Valley Campaign. At Cedar Mountain he commanded the brigade and was wounded but did not relinquish command until the fight was concluded. He returned, with the rank of colonel, and led his regiment at Chancellorsville. When on the night of May 2, General Jones left the field he took over the brigade. The next day he was mortally wounded, living until the following morning. (Freeman, Douglas S., *Lee's Lieutenants*)

GARRETT, Richard H. (?-?)

The Virginia farm of Richard H. Garrett was the scene of one of the last episodes of the Civil War—the death of John Wilkes Booth. On the 24th of April 1865 John Wilkes Booth was left at the farm, between Port Conway and Bowling Green, by Willie Jett. The next day he was rejoined by David Herold who had been guiding him on his escape. They came to believe that federal cavalry were pursuing them and asked Mr. Garrett for horses to take them to the next railroad station. When he became suspicious and refused, the two conspirators asked to sleep in the tobacco shed. When the cavalry arrived in the early hours of April 26 Garrett refused to reveal that the pair were on the farm and in hiding. The shed was surrounded and Herold came out to surrender. The barn was then set ablaze and Booth was shot either by Boston Corbett, one of the soldiers, or by himself. Dragged from the flaming structure fatally wounded, Booth died on Garrett's porch.

GARROTT, Isham Warren (1816-1863)

Although appointed a brigadier general in the Confederate army, Isham Garrott never knew it. At the time of the secession movement, Garrott had been a lawyer and local politician in Mobile. He was sent by Alabama's governor to the state of his birth, North Carolina, to induce it to join the Confederate cause. His military assignments included: lieutenant colonel, 20th Alabama (September 9, 1861); colonel, 20th Alabama (October 8, 1861); temporarily commanding Tracy's old Brigade, Stevenson's Division, Department of Mississippi and East Louisiana (May 1-mid May 1863); and brigadier general (May 28, 1863). After his initial service in the Army of Mobile, Colonel Garrott and the 20th were sent to the Department of East Tennessee early in 1862. Here he saw action at Cumberland Gap in June; in December, the 20th along with the rest of Stevenson's Division, was ordered to Mississippi and took part in the defense at Chickasaw Bluff over the New Year holiday. Garrott then led his men in the battle of Port Gibson, the first fight in Grant's victorious drive on Vicksburg. When General E.D. Tracy was killed, Garrott took over temporary command of the brigade until he was superseded by General S.D. Lee. He again led his regiment at Champion's Hill and in the siege of

Vicksburg. On June 17, 1863, while on the skirmish line, Garrott was killed by a sharpshooter's bullet. Word had not yet been received that he had been named brigadier general to rank from May 28, 1863.

GARTRELL, Lucius Jeremiah (1821-1891)

An early and extreme states' righter and secessionist, Lucius J. Gartrell carried his convictions into the field and into the halls of the Confederate Congress. A native Georgian, Gartrell had been a lawyer, former judge, former state legislator, and former Whig by 1861, when he was serving as a Democratic member of the U.S. House of Representatives. With the secession of Georgia, he resigned his seat and in May 1861 was commissioned colonel, 7th Georgia. With this command he fought at 1st Manassas where his son was killed and where Colonel and Congressman Francis S. Bartow died in his arms. Elected in November 1861 to be Georgia's 8th District representative in the First Regular Confederate Congress, he resigned his commission on February 13, 1862, in order to take his seat. During his term in Congress, Gartrell chaired the Committee on the Judiciary. Supporting the Davis administration he favored abolishing exemptions from conscription, nationalizing some vital industries, suspending the writ of habeas corpus, and government price regulation. He even went so far as to support the Davis administration before the less than friendly Georgia legislature. It may have been his unpopular views that prompted his decision not to seek reelection. Instead he was commissioned brigadier general, CSA, on August 22, 1864 and assigned to duty in Georgia, where his assignments included: the organization of the Georgia Reserves, a portion of which he commanded in the Savannah Campaign until wounded on December 9 near Coosawhatchie. He was a lawyer and unsuccessful politician after the war.

GARY, Martin Witherspoon (1831-1881)

A South Carolina defense attorney and state legislator, Martin W. Gary served from 1st Bull Run to Appomattox. His mother's home was the scene of one of the last Confederate cabinet meetings. His assignments included: captain, Company B, Infantry Battalion, Hampton (S.C.) Legion (June 12, 1861); lieutenant colonel, Hampton Legion (ca. April 1862); colonel, Hampton Legion (late 1862); brigadier general, CSA (May 19, 1964); commanding Cavalry Brigade, Department of Richmond (ca. May 19-December 1864 and January 1865); and commanding brigade, F. Lee's Cavalry Division, Cavalry Corps, Army of Northern Virginia (January-April 9, 1865). With the legion's infantry he fought at 1st Bull Run, at the head of his company, the Watson Guards. As a field officer he fought at Seven Pines, the Seven Days, 2nd Bull Run, Antietam, and Fredericksburg. The unit served with Longstreet, in southeastern Virginia in early 1863 and during the Gettysburg Campaign was in the vicinity of Richmond. Rejoining Longstreet, the command was too late for Chickamauga but served in East Tennessee before being sent to South Carolina to secure horses in early 1864. As mounted infantry the legion went to the Richmond front in May 1864. Promoted to brigadier, Gary led the mounted defenders of the capital until his command was absorbed into the cavalry of Lee's army early in 1865. He continued to serve near the city until its fall when he was the last general officer to leave. At Appomattox he cut his way out and joined President Davis in North Carolina and escorted him in part of his flight, with the stop at his mother's residence. After the war he was part of the powerful Hampton-Butler faction but eventually broke with them, leading to his defeat in two bids for a senatorship. He had previously served in the state legislature. (Freeman, Douglas S., *Lee's Lieutenants*)

GATES, Elijah (ca. 1829-?)

A Missouri farmer, Elijah Gates served with the Missouri Brigade of the western armies up until the battle of Franklin and was often in command. His Confederate assignments included: lieutenant colonel, 1st Cavalry, 5th Division, Missouri State Guard (early 1861); colonel, 1st Missouri Cavalry (December 31, 1861); commanding 1st Brigade, 1st Division, Army of the West, Department #2 (June-July 1862); commanding 1st Brigade, 1st Division, Price's Corps (Army of the West), Army of West Tennessee, Department #2 (July-October 1, 1862); commanding 1st Brigade, 1st Division, Price's Corps, Department of Mississippi and East Louisiana (October 1862); and commanding Cockrell's Brigade, French's Division, Stewart's Corps, Army of Tennessee (July-August 1864). After leading

Confederate legislator Lucius J. Gartrell. (*Harper's*)

his regiment at Pea Ridge, he went with the rest of the Army of the West to the east bank of the Mississippi to join in the attack at Shiloh but arrived too late. At this time the regiment was dismounted and served for the remainder of the war as infantry. After serving in the siege of Corinth in the spring of 1862, he commanded the brigade at Iuka and Corinth. During the Vicksburg Campaign he was captured at Big Black River Bridge but escaped two days later and rejoined his command for the siege. Captured and exchanged, he joined Johnston's army in the Atlanta Campaign and was wounded on June 20, 1864, at Lattimer's Mills. During the latter part of the campaign and the beginning of the siege he commanded the brigade. On August 23, 1864, he suffered another wound during the siege. Following Atlanta's fall he accompanied Hood northward seeing action at Allatoona. In the invasion of Tennessee he took part in the futile charge at Franklin. He returned from the repulse with his horse's reins in his teeth, having been wounded in both arms. His left arm had to be amputated, ending his military service. (Anderson, Ephraim McD., *Memoirs: Historical and Personal: Including the Campaigns of the First Missouri Confederate Brigade* 2nd ed.—Notes and Foreword by Edwin C. Bearss)

GATLIN, Richard Caswell (1809-1896)

Veteran infantryman and West Pointer (1832), Richard Gatlin became the Confederate scapegoat for the fall of New Bern in early 1862. A veteran of the Black Hawk, Seminole and Mexican wars and the Mormon Expedition, Gatlin was a major in the 5th Infantry when hostilities began. Captured and paroled by Arkansas forces, he soon resigned his commission and returned to his native state North Carolina and became adjutant general of the state militia. His Confederate assignments included: colonel (ca. June 22, 1861); commanding Southern Department, Coast Defenses (June 22-August 20, 1861); brigadier general, CSA (July 8, 1861); and commanding Department of North Carolina (August 20, 1861-March 19, 1862). Commanding in North Carolina he was responsible for the defense of that state in the face of general Burnside's expedition against the coast. After a string of defeats, General J.R. Anderson relieved him, the day after the Union capture of New Bern. After relinquishing command on March 29, 1862, Gatlin served for the rest of the war as adjutant and inspector general of North Carolina and resigned his Confederate commission on September 8, 1862. The explanation for his removal from command was officially listed as "ill health." Moving to Arkansas after the war, Gatlin was a farmer until his death.

GATLING, Richard Jordan (1818-1903)

This North Carolina doctor—he had studied medicine only to treat himself following a bout with smallpox—living in the North is credited with manufacturing the first practical machine gun. An inventor of some note, Richard J. Gatling had primarily engaged in the design and manufacture of farming implements before the Civil War. His rapid-fire gun, capable of firing 250 rounds a minute, was not accepted by the War Department until 1865, too late to see official active service. However, some had previously been placed upon gunboats and two saw some action with Butler at Petersburg. In addition, General Hancock ordered a dozen for his prestigious First Veteran Volunteer Corps but his unit never saw action. Subsequently Gatling perfected his gun and sold the rights to the Colt Fire Arms Company. President of the American Association of Inventors and Manufacturers for six years, he was working on a motorized plow when he died.

GAUL, Gilbert (1855-1919)

Although of Northern birth and too young to have participated in the Civil War, Gilbert Gaul became one of the outstanding artists in the depiction of the "Lost Cause." Receiving his artistic training at the National Academy of Design in New York, he developed an early interest in things military and subsequently spent most of his creative time in depicting the Civil War, and frequently the Confederate side of it. He traveled widely, researching army life, an experience that greatly enhanced the realism of his work. Many of his works, including "With Fate Against Them" and "Waiting for the Dawn," show a strong sympathy for the Confederate soldier and his tribulations. Some of his other famous works include: "Sergeant Hart Nailing the Colors to the Flagstaff of Fort Sumter," "General Thomas' Bivouac," and "Between the Lines During a Truce." Many of Gaul's works were reproduced in the Century Magazine's publication, *Battles and Leaders*.

GEE, John Henry (1819-1876)

Unlike his fellow prison camp commander, Henry Wirz, John H. Gee was acquitted in his war crimes trial. A physician before the war, he entered the Confederate army. His assignments included: captain, Company G, 1st Florida (April 5, 1861); major, 4th Florida Battalion (May 2, 1863); major, 11th Florida (June 11, 1864); and commanding post at Salisbury, North Carolina (August 24, 1864-April 1865). After initial service in Florida, he was sent to reinforce the Army of Northern Virginia in the spring of 1864. His battalion was merged into a new regiment, and he was soon thereafter assigned to command the prison camp at Salisbury. The prison had a good reputation for being spacious for a mixed population of prisoners of war, deserters, and convicts, but later it became overcrowded. On November 25 a mass escape attempt was made and had to be contained in part by the use of artillery. There were casualties on both sides. Gee was arrested in November 1865 and charged with ordering these and other "murders." There were also the usual charges of cruel conditions. After a trial that lasted over five months, he was acquitted and released in August 1866. He died fighting a fire in Florida where he had returned to practice medicine.

GENTRY, Meredith Poindexter (1809-1866)

After a distinguished career in the U.S. Congress, Meredith P. Gentry sank into virtual obscurity during his term in the Confederate Congress. To a large extent the North Carolina-born Gentry was a self-educated man, and although he had been

"With Fate Against Them" by Gilbert Gaul. (*B&L*)

admitted to the bar in Tennessee, he rarely practiced. Instead he built-up his plantation and devoted his interest to politics. After three years in the state legislature, he was sent to the U.S. Congress where he remained, on and off, for 12 years. Here he was noted for his opposition to the Mexican War, his moderation on the issue of slavery, and his oppositon to secession. Having retired to his plantation in 1855, he was finally convinced of the propriety of secession with the firing in Charleston Harbor. Elected to the First Regular Confederate Congress in November 1861 from Tennessee's 6th District, he failed in a bid to become the House's speaker. He is said to have made only one speech in Richmond and became known as one disenchanted with the idea of secession itself and with the war effort. He stopped attending the congressional meetings on October 13, 1862, but had been frequently absent from the deliberations previously. Taken into Federal custody at home in 1864, he died on his impoverished farm two years later.

GHOLSON, Samuel Jameson (1808-1883)

Having spent most of the Civil War as a Mississippi state officer, Kentucky-born Samuel J. Gholson served only briefly as a Confederate brigadier general. A lawyer in both Alabama and Mississippi, he sat in the latter's state legislature and represented it in Congress. He was a district judge upon the

outbreak of hostilities when he entered the army as captain of the Monroe Volunteers. His assignments included: captain, Company I, 14th Mississippi (1861); major general, Mississippi State Troops (April 1863); brigadier general, CSA (May 6, 1864); commanding brigade, Forrest's Cavalry Corps, Department of Alabama, Mississippi and East Louisiana (May-June 1864); and commanding brigade, Adams' Cavalry Division, Department of Alabama, Mississippi and East Louisiana (June-August 1864). As a company commander, he was wounded and captured at Fort Donelson. He then appears to have carried messages and seen service in East Tennessee until appointed to a major generalcy in the state forces when Vicksburg was being threatened. He had a brush with a portion of Grierson's raiders. Gholson also came into conflict with the regular Confederate officers in his area. The next spring he became a Confederate brigadier general and led a brigade of cavalry in Mississippi and Alabama. A wound at Egypt, Mississippi, on December 27, 1864—which cost him an arm—appears to have put him out of the war. Following the peace he was again a state legislator.

GHOLSON, Thomas Saunders (1808-1868)

Having no prior legislative experience, Virginia Congressman Thomas S. Gholson did not become a leader in the Second Confederate Congress but nonetheless became known as a proponent of a vigorous war effort. A native of Virginia, Gholson was a lawyer who had been prominent in civic improvements in his adopted home of Petersburg. By the time of the outbreak of the Civil War he was serving as a circuit judge, a position he continued to hold under the Confederate regime. Then in 1863 he defeated the incumbent in a race for the 4th District's seat in the Second Congress. Here he naturally served on the committee on the Judiciary. Considering any infringements to the new constitution to be only temporary emergency measures, he threw his entire effort behind the military effort. About the only thing he would not grant the Davis administration was the recruiting of slaves. He favored wartime nationalization of many industries and wanted to grant the War Department full powers over all state forces. He also felt that the writ of habeas corpus was dispensable. Following the fall of Richmond, Gholson fled to England and went into the cotton and tobacco business.

GIBBS, George Cooper (1822-1873)

Although the colonel of an infantry regiment, Floridian George C. Gibbs spent most of the Civil War guarding prisoners of war. His Confederate assignments included: captain, Infantry (May 20, 1861); major, Infantry (1861); and colonel, 42nd North Carolina (April 22, 1862). By the first summer of the war he was commanding the prison guard forces in Richmond. Then on January 11, 1862, he was ordered to Salisbury, North Carolina, to take command of the prison at that place. He was also given authority to raise three or four companies to serve as guards. Shortly thereafter he was authorized to raise a regiment for service in the field. He recruited the guard companies into this regiment. Moving his unit to Virginia, he was soon in command of the prison at Lynchburg. On January 7, 1864, he resigned his regimental commission but continued in prison work. On June 2, 1864, he wsa transferred to command the post at Andersonville, with the infamous prison a part of his jurisdiction. He was respected by the prisoners at Salisbury and Macon as a fair jailer. He was later a witness at the trial of Major Henry Wirz.

GIBSON, Randall Lee (1832-1892)

Kentucky-born Yale graduate Randall L. Gibson had had a distinguished prewar career as a lawyer and diplomat in Madrid before entering the Confederate army and rising to brigadier general. He had been raised in his family's home state, Louisiana, and upon the secession crisis coming to a peak he became an aide to the governor, Thomas O. Moore. His later military assignments included: captain, 1st Louisiana Artillery (March 1861); colonel, 13th Louisiana (September 16, 1861); commanding 1st Brigade, 1st (Ruggles') Division, 2nd Corps, Army of the Mississippi (ca. March 29-April 1862); commanding Adams' Brigade, 1st (Breckinridge's) Division, Hardee's Corps, Army of Tennessee (December 31, 1862-early 1863); commanding Adams' Brigade, Breckinridge's Division, Hill's-Breckinridge's Corps, Army of Tennessee (September 20-November 12, 1863); commanding Adams' Brigade, Stewart's-Clayton's Division, Breckinridge's-Hindman's-Hood's-Lee's

Corps, Army of Tennessee (November 12, 1863-early 1865); brigadier general, CSA (January 11, 1864); and commanding Louisiana Brigade, District of the Gulf, Department of Alabama, Mississippi and East Louisiana (early 1865-April 8, 1865). He led a brigade at Shiloh and then the regiment during the Corinth siege and at Perryville. At Murfreesboro he was in charge of the consolidated 13th and 20th Louisiana and succeeded the wounded Daniel W. Adams in brigade command. At Chickamauga he was again at the head of the paired regiments when called upon, the second day, to take over brigade leadership from the wounded and captured Adams. He retained command, thereafter fighting at Chattanooga and then being promoted to brigadier general. As such he served throughout the Atlanta Campaign. During the battle of Franklin his division was still south of the Duck River so it did not take part in the action. He did however fight at Nashville and early the next year was sent with his brigade to the Gulf coast. There he directed the unsuccessful defense of Spanish Fort near Mobile. After the war he returned to his law practice and served in both houses of the national legislature.

GIFT, George W. (1833-1879)

Lieutenant George W. Gift of Tennessee was one of the Confederacy's more unorthodox naval officers. A graduate of Annapolis in 1848, he had resigned from the navy in 1852 to enter the banking business in California. Returning East at the outbreak of the war, he entered the Confederate army but on March 18, 1862, was transferred to the navy as a lieutenant. Assigned to the CSS *Arkansas*, then under construction, he commanded two of the ironclad's guns during its run through the Union fleet on the Mississippi, from the Yazoo to Vicksburg. After the *Arkansas'* destruction at Baton Rouge in August 1862, Gift performed shore duty for a time. In February 1864 he was in command of one portion of John Taylor Wood's expedition, which destroyed the *Underwriter*. Having served as executive officer with the *Chattahoochee* on the Appalachicola River, until that vessel accidentally blew up there on May 27, 1863, Gift was placed in command of it when it was reraised. Returning from the *Underwriter* raid in North Carolina, Gift and his officers devised a plan to attempt with small boats, the seizure of the two Union blockaders guarding the mouth of the river. The expedition was a disaster, with all but one of the seven craft lost. Gift's boat was driven 15 miles across the sound to St. George's Island. He was forced to turn over command due to illness on the way to the island. After two days of near starvation, eating alligators, the crew returned to the mainland. With the abandonment of the river, the *Chattahoochee* was destroyed. After the war Gift returned to California and edited the *Napa City Reporter*. (Scharf, J. Thomas, *History of the Confederate Navy*)

GILHAM, William (1818-1872)

The fact that William Gilham was ordered away from the field to resume his duties on the faculty of the Virginia Miliary Institute, seems to indicate that he was more in demand to train future officers—than to fight a war himself. But it may in fact be more truthful to conclude that the order resulted from a dispute with his superior, Stonewall Jackson. An Indianan, Gilham had graduated fifth in his 1840 class at West Point. The Civil War found him serving as an instructor and commandant of cadets at VMI. Having authored a drill manual, his first service to the Confederacy was as drill master at Camp Lee at Richmond. His later assignments included: colonel, 21st Virginia (July 1861); and commanding brigade, Army of the Northwest (July 1861-January 20, 1862). He led his brigade in Robert E. Lee's failure at Cheat Mountain and continued campaigning in western Virginia into the winter. He got involved in the Loring-Jackson feud over the stationing of the former's command at Romney under dismal conditions. The latter pressed charges against Gilham for neglect of duty. It was at about this time on January 20, 1862, that he was relieved of brigade command and ordered back to the school. Here he devoted his full time to his courses and dropped the position of commandant. The postwar economic crunch at the academy forced him to become a chemist for a private firm. (Wise, Jennings C., *The Military History of the Virginia Military Institute from 1839 to 1865*)

GILMER, Jeremy Francis (1818-1883)

A North Carolinian by birth, Jermey Gilmer was the premier engineer in the service of the Confederacy. Graduating fourth at West Point in 1839, Gilmer's entire antebellum service was in the engineers; he was serving as a captain when he resigned on June 29, 1861. His Confederate assignments included: lieutenant colonel, Engineers (September 1861); chief engineer, Department #2 (September 1861-April 7, 1862); chief engineer, Department of Northern Virginia (August 4-September 25, 1862); chief of Engineer Bureau (September 25, 1862-August 17, 1863); colonel, Engineers (October 4, 1862); chief engineer, Department of South Carolina, Georgia and Florida (August 17-31, 1863); major general, CSA (August 25, 1863); second in command of the department (August 31, 1863-May 25, 1864); and chief of Engineer Bureau (June 1864-April 1865). Serving under General A.S. Johnston in Kentucky and Tennessee, Gilmer saw action at Forts Henry and Donelson, escaping capture at the latter, and at Shiloh where Johnston was killed on the first day and Gilmer was wounded on the second. Returning to duty, Gilmer was assigned to Lee's command but spent most of his time working on the defenses near Richmond. He then headed the bureau at the War Department until sent to South Carolina. Much of the time he was in charge of the Savannah defenses and also worked on the Atlanta fortifications. He again served, for the last year of the war, as head of the Engineer Bureau in Richmond. For 16 years before his death, Gilmer was the head of the Savannah Gaslight Company.

GILMER, John Adams (1805-1868)

A congressman from the Piedmont region of North Carolina, John Gilmer often voted against some of his more radical colleagues from the rest of the South. In 1858, he opposed the admission of Kansas as a slave state under the Lecompton Con-

stitution. Following the election of Lincoln, Gilmer still maintained hopes for peace, despite the secessionist movement. During the winter of 1860-61, Gilmer personally paid for and franked an estimated 100,000 pieces of Unionist mail to North Carolina, with more going to the rest of the Upper South. Lincoln offered the position of Secretary of the Interior to Gilmer in a move to prevent the states of the Upper South from joining those of the Lower South. While waiting for the Inaugural Address, he urged Lincoln to be conciliatory and grant the South its meaningless and "foolish abstraction of Congressional protection to slavery in the Territories." The failure to get a truly conciliatory message from the incoming president and the makeup of the rest of the blatantly pro-Union cabinet led Gilmer to refuse the appointment. After Fort Sumter, he declared, "All hope is now extinguished." Serving in local posts for the first years of the Confederacy, Gilmer was elected to the Second Confederate Congress, which convened on May 2, 1864. He chaired the House Elections Committee and served on the Ways and Means Committee. Gilmer was a vocal opponent of Jefferson Davis and supported higher taxes and less impressment of supplies (some of his own whiskey had been impressed). After the war he returned to his law practice. He died on May 14, 1868. (Croft, Daniel W., "A Reluctant Unionist: John A. Gilmer and Lincoln's Cabinet," *CWH*, September 1978)

GILMER, John Alexander, Jr. (1838-1892)

The son of prominent North Carolina Unionist John Adams Gilmer, John Alexander Gilmer adopted "Jr." to distinguish them. Not in tune with his father's sentiments, he joined the Confederacy at the outbreak of the Civil War. His assignments included: second lieutenant, Company B, 27th North Carolina (April 20, 1861); first lieutenant and adjutant, 27th North Carolina (November 18, 1861); major, 27th North Carolina (January 6, 1862); lieutenant colonel, 27th North Carolina (November 1, 1862); and colonel, 27th North Carolina (December 5, 1862). He commanded the regiment in the disaster at New Bern and then fought at the Seven Days, Harpers Ferry, Antietam, and Fredericksburg. Wounded at the latter, he rejoined the regiment and led it in South Carolina, North Carolina, and in the Department of Richmond. With the brigade ordered to rejoin the Army of Northern Virginia it took part in the charge at Bristoe Station. For a second time Gilmer was struck in the leg. Upon his recovery, he was assigned, on June 8, 1864, to command the post and prisoner of war camp at Salisbury, North Carolina. Relieved on August 24, 1864, he was directed to rejoin his regiment. Apparently he was still unfit for field service since he never reported to his command. Finally, on January 11, 1865, he was retired to the Invalid Corps. After the war he served in the North Carolina legislature and on its supreme court.

GILMOR, Harry W. (1838-1883)

With a turf between those of other partisan leaders—John S. Mosby to the east and John H. McNeill to the west—Harry Gilmor was an effective scout and raider in the Shenandoah Valley and western Maryland. A native Baltimorean, (he dropped his middle initial), he had lived in Wisconsin and the Nebraska Territory before the war. His Civil War assignments included: private, Company G, 7th Virginia Cavalry (August 31, 1861); captain, Company F, 12th Virginia Cavalry (March 27, 1862); and major, 2nd Maryland Cavalry Battalion (May 27, 1863). Beginning his service under Turner Ashby, he became one of Ashby's company commanders in time for the Shenandoah Valley Campaign. In the aftermath of the Maryland Campaign, he was captured while on a raiding mission in western Maryland during September 1862. Exchanged five months later, he was soon commanding a battalion of Marylanders who, despite being labeled as regular cavalry, were frequently engaged in irregular warfare. In the Gettysburg Campaign he led his battalion in advance of Ewell's Corps in Pennsylvania. He continued to be a bane to federal commanders during the 1864 Shenandoah Valley Campaign. Finally on February 4, 1865, he was captured in bed in Moorefield, West Virginia by Major Harry Young of Sheridan's staff with a command dressed in Confederate uniforms. Confined in Boston Harbor, he was not released until July 24, 1865, but had meanwhile compiled a series of historical sketches of his career, which were later developed into a book, ghostwritten by Francis H. Smith, and published as *Four Years in the Saddle*. In 1874-79 Gilmor served as Baltimore's police commissioner. (Jones, Virgil Carrington, *Gray Ghosts and Rebel Raiders*)

Partisan Harry Gilmor. (NA)

GILTNER, Harry Liter (?-?)

While the two principal armies of the Confederacy were usually kept relatively close to the authorized level of general officers, many of the fringe commands were not so fortunate, with colonels like Henry L. Giltner commanding brigades for a year or more. His assignments included: captain, Kentucky cavalry company (September 10, 1862); colonel, 4th Kentucky Cavalry (October 5, 1862); commanding Williams' Cavalry Brigade, Department of Southwestern Virginia (November-December 1863); commanding cavalry brigade, Department of East Tennessee (February-May 23, 1864); and commanding cavalry brigade, Department of Western Virginia and East Tennessee (May 23, 1864-April 12, 1865). Serving in western Virginia and eastern Tennessee, Giltner led his regiment in frequent operations against Union raiders and in protecting railroads and salt works. Joining Longstreet, he commanded the brigade during the siege of Knoxville. In December 1864 he directed the initial defense of Saltville against the Union cavalry. Although his role in protecting the supplies and supply lines for the major armies was vital, it was not considered crucial enough for his promotion to brigadier. He commanded his brigade in the region until after Lee's surrender.

GIRARDEY, Victor Jean Baptiste (1837-1864)

Thirteen days was the length of time that Victor J.B. Girardey held his appointment as a brigadier after being promoted four grades from staff captain to general officer. Born in France and raised as an orphan in Georgia and Louisiana, he entered the Confederate military early in the war. His assignments included: first lieutenant and aide-de-camp (October 12, 1861); captain and assistant adjutant general (January 1862); brigadier general, CSA (August 3 to date from July 30, 1864); and commanding Wright's Brigade, Mahone's Division, 3rd Corps, Army of Northern Virginia (August 3-16, 1864). On the staff of General A.R. Wright he fought through the Seven Days, Chancellorsville, and Gettysburg. At Manassas Gap that summer he directed the operations of half the brigade. He was at the Wilderness and Spotsylvania before being transferred to the staff of General Mahone on May 21, 1864. He so impressed General Lee during the battle of the Crater in bringing up two brigades to plug the gap, that he was shortly after promoted four grades and given command of Wright's Brigade. He died on August 16 while repulsing a Union assault at Fussell's Mill near Richmond. (Freeman, Douglas S., *Lee's Lieutenants*)

GIST, States Rights (1831-1864)

With a given name such as his there could be little doubt of which side his parents wanted States Rights Gist to fight on, and so he ended up giving his life as a Confederate brigadier general. The South Carolina native graduated from Harvard Law School and was practicing his profession in his native state when the secession movement reached crisis proportions. Realizing this, he entered the militia and his Civil War-era assignments included: brigadier general, South Carolina Militia

(1859); adjutant and inspector general, South Carolina Army (1861); colonel and volunteer aide-de-camp (July 1861); brigadier general, CSA (March 20, 1862); commanding James Island, Department of South Carolina, Georgia and Florida (May-June, July-September 25, 1862, and October 17, 1862-May 1863); commanding James Island, 1st Military District of South Carolina, Department of South Carolina, Georgia and Florida (June-July 1862); commanding the district (September 25-October 17, 1862); commanding brigade, Department of the West (May-June 1863); commanding brigade, Walker's Division, Department of the West (June-July 1863); commanding brigade, Walker's Division, Department of Mississippi and East Louisiana (July-August 25, 1863); commanding brigade, Walker's Division, Hill's Corps, Army of Tennessee (August 28-September 1863); commanding Walker's Division, Reserve Corps, Army of Tennessee (mid-September 1863); commanding brigade, Walker's Division, Polk's Corps, Army of Tennessee (September-September 26, 1863); commanding brigade, Walker's Division, Longstreet's Corps, Army of Tennessee (September 26-November 12, 1863); commanding brigade, Walker's Division, Hardee's Corps, Army of Tennessee (November 12-November 1863 and November 1863-July 24, 1864); commanding the division (late November 1863); and commanding brigade Cheatham's-Brown's Division, Hardee's-Cheatham's Corps, Army of Tennessee (July 24-November 30, 1864). As a state officer, he was present at the reduction of Fort Sumter and then went to Virginia as a volunteer aide to Barnard E. Bee. There Bee was killed at 1st Bull Run, all the field officers of the 4th Alabama being put hors de combat Gist took command of it. After the battle he returned to his state post until appointed a brigadier general in the Confederate service. For over a year he served on the South Carolina coast until ordered to Mississippi with a brigade in May 1863. There he joined Joseph E. Johnston in his attempt to relieve the garrison of Vicksburg and after the fall of the river city defended Jackson, Mississippi, for a time. As part of William H.T. Walker's division, he joined Bragg's army and led the division at Chickamauga while Walker exercised temporary corps command. At Chattanooga Gist was again in charge of the division. He served throughout the Atlanta Campaign—being transferred to Cheatham's division when Walker's was broken up following his death—and then accompanied Hood into middle Tennessee. In the suicidal assault at Franklin on November 30, 1864, Gist became one of six generals to be fatally struck. He died instantly.

GLADDEN, Adley Hogan (1810-1862)

Adley Gladden was destined to die in his first major battle as a Southern officer. His Confederate services included: colonel, 1st Louisiana Regulars (early 1861); brigadier general, CSA (September 30, 1861); commanding 1st Brigade, Army of Pensacola (late September 1861-January 27, 1862); temporarily commanding the army (from October 22, 1861); commanding brigade, Army of Mobile (January 27-March 1862); commanding 2nd Corps, 2nd Grand Division, Army of the Mississippi (March 9-29, 1862); and commanding 1st Brigade, 2nd Division, 2nd Corps, Army of the Mississippi (March 29-

April 6, 1862). After serving on the Florida coast, and under the Union bombardment in late November 1861, and at Mobile, Adley Gladden was ordered the following March to Corinth in northern Mississippi to oppose forces under General Grant gathering along the Tennessee River. After briefly commanding a "corps," in reality only a division, he was given command of a brigade of troops brought up from the Gulf coast and led it in the surprise attack on the Union army at Shiloh on April 6, 1862. At about 8:00 A.M., while overrunning the federal camps, Gladden was hit by a cannon projectile and mortally wounded. He lingered, back in Corinth, until April 12.

GLASSEL, William T. (? -1879)

If any man can be said to have been enlisted for Confederate service by the U.S. government it was Lieutenant William T. Glassel, USN. The North Carolinian had returned aboard the USS *Hartford* from a lengthy voyage to China in mid-1862 and was promptly confronted with a demand that he take a new oath of allegiance or be imprisoned. He felt the oath conflicted with the original one he took upon entering the service and he refused. On August 5, 1862, he was sent into imprisonment at Fort Warren in Boston Harbor. Exchanged later that month as a prisoner of war and delivered into the Confederate lines, he was promptly appointed lieutenant, CSN, to date from his original confinement and he was assigned to duty with the *Chinora* in Charleston Harbor. He took part in the attempt to raise the blockade on January 31, 1863, and was involved in the employment of spar torpedoes. Following the collapse of the Confederacy he settled in California. (Scharf, J. Thomas, *History of the Confederate States Navy*)

GLAZE, William (?-?)

Almost a decade before secession, and foreshadowing its role as the first state to secede from the Union, South Carolina had become the only Southern state to begin in-state manufacture of weapons to prepare for war. On April 15, 1851, it issued a contract to William Glaze of South Carolina and Benjamin Flagg of Massachusetts, calling for the production of 9,000 firearms—rifles, muskets and pistols—and 2,000 swords and sabers. Glaze was the proprietor of the Palmetto Iron Works of Columbia and he converted it to the manufacture of what became known as Palmetto Arms. Continuing in its new military role during the Civil War, Glaze's plant switched to the production of munitions and was severely damaged when Sherman took the city in 1865.

GODWIN, Archibald Campbell (1831-1864)

A rancher and miner in California, Archibald C. Godwin returned to his native Virginia in 1861 and became a captain, later major and provost marshal of Richmond. Transferred to Salisbury, North Carolina, he continued in charge of prisoners. He then raised a regiment and transferred to the line where his assignments included: colonel, 57th North Carolina (July 17, 1862); commanding Hoke's Brigade, Early's Division, 2nd Corps, Army of Northern Virginia (July 2-November 7, 1863); brigadier general, CSA (August 5, 1864); and commanding

Hoke's (old) Brigade, Ramseur's Division, Valley District, Department of Northern Virginia (August 5-September 18, 1864). His first action came at Fredericksburg, and he went on to fight in the Fredericksburg portion of the battle of Chancellorsville. At Gettysburg he succeeded to brigade command and led a brigade until captured at Rappahannock Bridge on November 7, 1863. Exchanged in 1864, he was promoted to brigadier and relieved temporary Brigadier William G. Lewis in command of Hoke's Brigade. The next month he was killed at 3rd Winchester. At both Libby and Salisbury he was remembered for his cruelty toward the captives, and there was some discussion of trying him after the war (until it was discovered that he was already dead).

GOGGIN, James Monroe (1820-1889)

For some unexplained reason James M. Goggin's appointment as brigadier was canceled shortly after its issuance and he reverted to his position as a staff oficer. The Virginia-born former West Point student had not graduated from the military academy but had served briefly in the army of the Republic of Texas and served the postal department in California before he settled in Memphis, where he was a businessman when the war began. He returned to his native state to enlist and his assignments included: major, 32nd Virginia (July 1, 1861); major and assistant adjutant general (spring 1862); and brigadier general, CSA (December 4, 1864). Serving on the Peninsula, he soon held a position on Lafayette McLaws' staff. He was distinguished at Yorktown and Williamsburg but lost his commission when all the field officers of the regiment failed to gain reappointment at the May 21, 1862, reorganization. McLaws, however, had him appointed to a formal staff position. Sometimes as inspector but mostly as adjutant, Goggin was with his chief at the Seven Days, Harpers Ferry, South Mountain, Antietam, Fredericksburg, Chancellorsville, and Knoxville. At the latter he advised Longstreet on the futility of continuing the attack on Fort Sanders. He fought through the Overland Campaign on Kershaw's staff and went to the Shenandoah Valley where he commanded Conner's, formerly Kershaw's own, Brigade at Cedar Creek. In December 1864 he was appointed brigadier, probably intended for the same brigade. However this was revoked, possibly because he was a Virginian designated to direct South Carolinians. Back on Kershaw's staff he served through part of the Petersburg operations and was captured at Sayler's Creek on the retreat. He resided in Texas after his release.

GOODE, John, Jr. (1829-1909)

One of the closest friends of the Davis administration in the Virginia congressional delegation was John Goode, Jr., of the 6th District. A native Virginian, Goode was a practicing attorney and active in politics before the Civil War. Favoring secession in the event of Lincoln's election, he attended the convention that eventually took Virginia out of the Union. Serving in the 2nd Virginia Cavalry and on the staff of Colonel Jubal A. Early, he saw action at 1st Manassas. Without campaigning he was elected to represent his district in the First Regular Congress in November 1861. Taking his seat the following

February, he served on the committees on: Enrolled Bills; Indian Affairs; and the Medical Department. Following his reelection, again without any campaigning, he served on the committees on Printing and Commerce. A convert to the need for conscription, he favored its rigid enforcement and the supplying of the army through impressments. A Davis confidant, he broke with the president on the issue of freeing the slaves, although he would accept their being armed for the nation's defense. Resuming the practice of law after the war, he continued to be active in politics into the 20th century, serving in the U.S. Congress and as U.S. solicitor general. (Goode, John, *Recollections of a Lifetime*)

GOODE, John Thomas (1835-1916)

Despite the fact that his command was designated as a heavy artillery regiment, John Thomas Goode was usually leading infantry. A native Virginian, he had attended the Virginia Military Institute before being commissioned directly into the regular army in 1855. He saw service against the Seminoles, in the Kansas troubles, and during the Mormon expedition. After tendering his services to the state of Virginia he was dismissed from the old army on July 3, 1861. His Confederate assignments included: captain, Artillery (March 16, 1861); major, Artillery (October 1861); lieutenant colonel, Artillery (April 1862); colonel, 4th Virginia Heavy Artillery (May 12, 1862); colonel, 34th Virginia (early 1864); commanding Wise's Brigade, Johnson's Division, Department of North Carolina and Southern Virginia (ca. June 1-ca. October 17, 1864); and commanding Wise's Brigade, Johnson's Division, 4th Corps, Army of Northern Virginia (ca. October 17-December 1864). After serving as chief of artillery during the siege of Yorktown, he was given command of an artillery regiment. Lacking a sufficient number of artillery pieces in the defenses of Richmond, he had his men equipped with rifles. It was not until 1864 that this change was officially recognized and the unit was given an infantry designation. His unit was sent to Charleston in September 1863 and did not return to Virginia until the following spring. Assigned to the Petersburg-Richmond lines Goode led his regiment and then the brigade at Stony Creek, Port Walthall Junction, the Petersburg assaults, and the battle of the Crater. The next spring he was in command of the regiment at Hatcher's Run, Boydton Plank Road, Sayler's Creek, and at the Appomattox surrender. After the war he served a term in the state legislature.

GORDON, B. Frank (?-?)

By the time that B. Frank Gordon was appointed a brigadier general by General E. Kirby Smith, the president of the dying Confederacy was already a prisoner. Gordon's assignments included: adjutant, 1st Brigade, 2nd Division, Missouri State Guard (1861); major, 5th Missouri Cavalry (1862); lieutenant colonel, 5th Missouri Cavalry (1862); commanding Shelby's Brigade, Marmaduke's Division, District of Arkansas, Trans-Mississippi Department (August 1863); colonel, 5th Missouri Cavalry (ca. December 15, 1863); commanding 1st Missouri Cavalry Brigade, 1st Missouri Cavalry Division, Cavalry Corps,

Trans-Mississippi Department (October 25, 1864-May 1865); and brigadier general, CSA, by Smith (May 16, 1865). With the Missouri State Guard he served in the battle of Wilson's Creek before becoming an officer in Shelby's cavalry regiment. While Shelby commanded a brigade, Gordon led the regiment at Newtonia, Helena, and Little Rock. During a part of the latter action he was in temporary command of the brigade. He joined Price's expedition to reclaim Missouri for the South and took command of the brigade after the division commander, J.S. Marmaduke, was captured. With the war virtually over, Smith promoted Gordon to the wreathed stars of a general in recognition of his months in charge of a brigade. Ten days later the department was surrendered.

GORDON, George Washington (1836-1911)

In the battle that cost the Army of Tennessee six general officers killed or mortally wounded, the Confederacy also lost the services of Brigadier General George W. Gordon, who was wounded and captured. The native Tennessean and graduate of Nashville's Western Military Institute was working as a surveyor when the Civil War began. His Confederate assignments included: drillmaster, 11th Tennessee (June 1861); captain, Company I, 11th Tennessee (1861); lieutenant colonel, 11th Tennessee (1862); colonel, 11th Tennessee (December 1862); brigadier general, CSA (August 15, 1864); and commanding Vaughan's Brigade, Cheatham's-Brown's Division, Hardee's-Cheatham's Corps, Army of Tennessee (September-November 30, 1864). Initially serving in East Tennessee he gradually rose to command of the regiment, which had been James E. Rains', and was wounded at its head at Murfreesboro. He later fought at Chickamauga but missed Chattanooga. Serving in the Atlanta Campaign, he was promoted to brigadier general and shortly after the city's fall took command of a Tennessee brigade. This he led at Franklin in the futile assaults and was wounded and captured. Confined in Boston Harbor's Fort Warren, he was not released until July 1865. After the war he was active in veterans' affairs and took up the practice of law. After holding a series of minor public offices he was elected to Congress. During much of the postwar period he was also a planter.

GORDON, James Byron (1822-1864)

It was the death of Confederate General James Byron Gordon that led Union General Francis C. Barlow to believe that his benefactor at Gettysburg, in reality John Brown Gordon, had been killed in the war. Like Barlow's Gordon, James Gordon had no prior military experience but served throughout his career as a cavalry officer. A farmer, businessman, and state legislator, he had served briefly as an enlisted man and officer in an infantry company. His later assignments included: major, 1st North Carolina Cavalry (May 16, 1861); colonel, 1st North Carolina Cavalry (July 23, 1863); commanding Baker's (intended) Brigade, Hampton's Division, Cavalry Corps, Army of Northern Virginia (September 9, 1863-ca. April 23, 1864); brigadier general, CSA (September 28, 1863); and commanding brigade, W.H.F. Lee's Division, same corps and army (ca.

April 23-May 12, 1864). As a regimental officer, he served through the major campaigns of the army including the Seven Days, Antietam, Fredericksburg, and Gettysburg. With the September 1863 reorganization of the cavalry, an all-North Carolina brigade was created for General L.S. Baker who had been wounded the month before. For a time Gordon commanded the unit as a colonel but was promoted to brigadier when it became apparent that Baker would not be fit for field duty for a long period. Gordon led his fellow North Carolinians through the Bristoe, Mine Run, and Overland campaigns. He fought at Yellow Tavern, where Stuart was mortally wounded, and himself fell with a mortal hurt the next day, May 12, fighting Sheridan's raid at Meadow Bridge. He died six days later. (Cowles, William H., *The Life and Services of James B. Gordon* and Freeman, Douglas S., *Lee's Lieutenants*)

GORDON, John Brown (1832-1904)

A civilian turned soldier, John B. Gordon became a trusted corps commander under Lee in the final days of the Confederacy. Involved in the coal industry in his native Georgia, Gordon raised the Racoon Roughs for the Southern cause. His assignments included: captain, Company I, 6th Alabama (May 1861); major, 6th Alabama (ca. May 14, 1861); colonel, 6th Alabama (April 28, 1862); commanding Rodes' brigade, D.H. Hill's Division, Department of the Virginia (May 31-June and July 1862); brigadier general, CSA (November 1, 1862; not confirmed and reappointed May 7, 1863); commanding Lawton's (old) Brigade, Early's Division, 2nd Corps, Army of Northern Virginia (April 11, 1863-May 8, 1864); command-

Civilian General John B. Gordon. (NA)

ing the division (May 8-21, 1864); major general, CSA (May 14, 1864); commanding Johnson's (old) Division, same corps and army (May 21-June 13, 1864); commanding same division, Valley District, Department of Northern Virginia (June 13-December 1864); and commanding 2nd Corps, Army of Northern Virginia (December 1864-April 9, 1865). Having fought at 1st Bull Run, he was elected colonel upon the regiment's reorganization and led it at Williamsburg. At Seven Pines he distinguished himself when he assumed command of the brigade. He fought through the Seven Days, part of the time in brigade command. He led the regiment at Antietam where he was wounded in the head and lived to relate how a hole in his cap from a bullet earlier in the day saved him from drowning in his own blood, which had accumulated in it. Recovering, he was given command of a Georgia brigade with which he fought at Chancellorsville and Gettysburg. At the latter he aided a wounded Union general, Francis C. Barlow, whom he met, decades later, each thinking the other had died in the war. They were friends until Barlow's death. Gordon received Lee's praise for planning a successful attack on the Union right at the Wilderness, and two days later Lee juggled a number of commands so that Gordon could lead Early's Division. At Spotsylvania, Gordon earned permanent promotion to major general and was soon given the remnants of Johnson's former division plus his own Georgia brigade. This unit he led at Cold Harbor and in the Shenandoah Valley Campaign during which he was sometimes in charge of an informal corps. He saw action at Monocacy, on the outskirts of Washington, at 3rd Winchester, Fisher's Hill, and Cedar Creek. Rejoining Lee in the trenches at Petersburg, he directed the corps and planned the attack on Fort Stedman. At Appomattox his men made the last charge of the Army of Northern Virginia. It is often claimed that he was a lieutenant general, but Gordon himself is silent on the matter in his *Reminiscences of the Civil War* in which he recounts each of his other promotions. He went on to a distinguished career in politics, serving as governor and senator and was active in veterans' affairs. (Tankersley, Allen P., *John B. Gordon: A Study in Gallantry*)

GORGAS, Josiah (1818-1883)

Taking advantage of the fact that his entire service in the U.S. Army was in the ordnance branch, the Confederacy utilized Josiah Gorgas as its chief ordnance officer throughout the war. The Pennsylvanian West Pointer (1841) had risen to the rank of captain before he resigned on April 3, 1861. Five days later he was commissisoned in the Confederate service and his assignments included: major, Ordnance (April 8, 1861); chief, Bureau of Ordnance (April 8, 1861-April 1865); lieutenant colonel, Ordnance (from March 16, 1861); colonel, Ordnance (1863); and brigadier general, CSA (November 10, 1864). His task was an extremely difficult one; given the Union blockade of Confederate ports and the lack of materials for weapons and ammunition at home. He was amazingly successful in keeping the armies in the field relatively well supplied. Recognizing that his best source of munitions was abroad, he organized a small fleet of blockade runners on his own authority. Jospeh E. Johnston was a great admirer of Gorgas. After Appomattox

Gorgas was engaged in the iron business and then in education. (Gorgas, Josiah, *Civil War Diary*)

GOULD, Andrew Wills (1840-1863)

The officer corps of the Confederate army was very sensitive about what they considered slights to their honor and hindrances to their careers. The June 13, 1863, affair at Columbia, Tennessee, between General Nathan Bedford Forrest and a young artillery lieutenant, Andrew Wills Gould, is a typical example. At the outbreak of the war Gould, a graduate of Cumberland University, was attending the military school of the University of Nashville. Leaving school he joined his cousin Colonel Alonzo Napier's Tennessee Cavalry Battalion. The command captured two artillery pieces from a Union transport and Gould was placed in charge. After serving with Forrest in west Tennessee, Gould's section was assigned on December 23, 1862, to Morton's Tennessee Battery. Gould became a first lieutenant in the new unit. The commander of Forrest's other battery had been killed on April 10, 1863, and it was widely rumored that Gould would get the command, but first came operations against Streight's Raid. On April 30, in the fight at Sand Mountain, Gould was forced to abandon his guns, which had been serving on the skirmish line. Word of his gallant action in spiking the pieces unaided in the face of enemy did not reach Forrest, only the loss of the section. Forrest was outraged and questioned Gould's courage. The vacant battery command was given to another lieutenant in May. Back in Columbia Gould went to confront Forrest and, not being satisfied with an order transferring Gould to Bragg's army, started to draw his pistol, which went off before he had fully raised it. The ball hit Forrest in the hip. Forrest opened a penknife with his teeth and stabbed the subordinate in the ribs. Gould fled across the street to a tailor shop where a doctor began to treat him. Forrest burst in with two borrowed pistols, intent upon killing the man who had, according to preliminary diagnosis, mortally wounded him. Forrest fired but hit a staff officer instead and Gould again fled. Forrest's rage subsided when informed that his wound was not serious, and he directed that Gould be well treated. On the other hand, Gould was fatally injured and he died a few days later. It has been alleged that the general forgave his dying lieutenant in a bedside visit. But this meeting has been denied by many then present in Columbia.

GOVAN, Daniel Chevilette (1829-1911)

As a Confederate officer, North Carolina-born Daniel C. Govan rose from command of a company to that of a brigade and received the three stars and the wreath of a general officer. A veteran of the 1849 gold rush, he was an Arkansas planter when the war came. His assignments included: captain, Company F, 2nd Arkansas (June 5, 1861); lieutenant colonel, 2nd Arkansas (June 1861); colonel, 2nd Arkansas (January 6, 1862); commanding Liddell's Brigade, Liddell's Division, Reserve Corps, Army of Tennessee (September 1863); commanding Liddell's-Govan's Brigade, Cleburne's Division, Hardee's-Cheatham's Corps, Army of Tennessee (November 1863-September 1, 1864 and ca. October-December 16, 1864); brigadier general, CSA

(December 29, 1863); and commanding brigade, Brown's Division, Hardee's Corps, Army of Tennessee (April 9-26, 1865). He led his regiment at Shiloh and it fought at Perryville. After fighting at Murfreesboro he commanded a brigade at Chickamauga and Chattanooga. Rewarded with the rank of brigadier general, he led Liddell's old brigade through the Atlanta Campaign until he was captured at Jonesboro. Exchanged on September 20, 1863, he resumed command and led his men at Franklin and Nashville. For a time thereafter he appears not to have been on duty but reappears as a brigade commander in the final stages of the Carolinas Campaign. Surrendered at Durham Station, he returned to planting and served for a time as an Indian agent.

GRAHAM, William Alexander (1804-1875)

If any Confederate congressional election race can be considered a rebuke to a perceived movement toward military rule in the new nation, it was the North Carolina victory of William A. Graham over the incumbent Senator George Davis. Graham had had a distinguished career in politics before the Civil War, serving as: state legislator (including the speakership); governor; secretary of the navy; and unsuccessful vice-presidential candidate in 1852. During the secession crisis he opposed taking the drastic step, was prominent in the Constitutional Union movement, and attended the Washington Peace Conference. While he was attending the North Carolina convention as a unionist, Lincoln's call for troops moved Graham into the secessionists' camp. In the election campaign for the Senate seat of George Davis for the Second Congress, Graham prevailed. Serving on the committees on Finance and Naval Affairs, he quickly became known for his opposition to the administration. He condemned an effective draft without exemption, arming the slaves, suspension of the writ of habeas corpus, and most presidential vetoes and legislative requests. By the end of the war he was calling for each Confederate state to make a separate peace with the enemy. After the war he held a respected position in the eyes of his fellow North Carolinians.

GRANBURY, Hiram Bronson (1831-1864)

Starting the war as a captain, Hiram Granbury rose to comand the Texas brigade of Cleburne's Division and died in the assault at Franklin, Tennessee. The local politician from Texas raised the Waco Guards and became its first captain. His later assignments included: major, 7th Texas (November 1861); colonel, 7th Texas (August 29, 1862); commanding Smith's old Brigade, Cleburne's Division, Hardee's-Cheatham's Corps, Army of Tennessee (November 25, 1863-November 30, 1864); and brigadier general, CSA (February 29, 1864). Sent to Kentucky, Granbury's regiment later moved into Fort Donelson, where he was captured on February 16, 1862. Imprisoned at Fort Warren in Boston Harbor, he was allowed to visit Baltimore on parole to attend his wife while she was undergoing an operation. He was exchanged on August 27, 1862, for two lieutenants and almost immediately promoted to colonel. But the 7th Texas was not exchanged until November and was then consolidated with the 49th and 55th Tennessee regiments

under Colonel J.E. Bailey. This left Granbury without a command until January 1863 when the unit was again independent. He led the regiment at Raymond and Jackson in the Vicksburg Campaign as part of Johnston's command and went to the Army of Tennessee in time for Chickamauga where he was wounded. At Chattanooga, Granbury assumed command of the brigade upon the wounding of General J.A. Smith and led it until Smith resumed command after the Atlanta Campaign had started. Granbury, having been promoted to brigadier, was again in command by the end of the campaign. He led his men in Hood's invasion of Tennessee, where, in the desparate Confederate attacks on the Union positions at Franklin, he was one of six rebel generals killed. He died almost within the Union positions.

GRAY, Henry (1816-1892)

By the time that South Carolina native Henry Gray was officially named a brigadier general he was representing western Louisiana in the Confederate Congress. Before the Civil War he was a lawyer and politician in Mississippi and Louisiana. Upon the outbreak of the conflict he enlisted in a regiment from the former state. His later assignments included: colonel, 28th Louisiana (ca. May 17, 1862); brigadier general, CSA (per E.K. Smith, April 15, 1864); commanding brigade, Mouton's-Polignac's Division, District of West Louisiana, Trans-Mississippi Department (ca. April-October 1864); and brigadier general, CSA (March 18, 1865, to rank from the 17th). In 1862 his regiment was stationed at Vicksburg and defended it from the early Union attempts to take it. He was then dispatched to western Louisiana and took part in the Teche Campaign of 1863, being wounded in the battle there. During the Red River Campaign he led a brigade at Mansfield and Pleasant Hill. On October 17, 1864, he was elected, without his knowledge, to represent Louisiana's 5th District in the Second Confederate Congress. Taking his seat on December 28, 1864, he was assigned to the Judiciary Committee. He was a noted opponent of peace overtures. During the final session he was confirmed as a brigadier general, a position he had held informally under E.K. Smith for almost a year. Following a term in the state senate he retired from politics.

GRAYSON, John Breckinridge (1806-1861)

Although a brigadier general in the Confederate army, John Grayson did not get a chance to serve his country in combat. Graduated from West Point (1826), Grayson served in the artillery and as commissary during the Seminole and Mexican wars. At the outbreak of the Civil War he resigned his major's commission and on May 25, 1861, was named brigader general of state forces by the governor of North Carolina. On August 15, 1861, he was transferred to Confederate service with the same rank and six days later was assigned to command of the Department of Middle and Eastern Florida. Suffering from a lung ailment, he was relieved by the War Department on October 10, 1861, and succumbed to the disease 11 days later.

GREEN, Martin Edwin (1815-1863)

Two days after being slightly wounded, Confederate General Martin E. Green was fatally struck at Vicksburg. The Virginia native had settled in Missouri in the 1830s and was running a sawmill at the outbreak of the Civil War. Siding with the South, his assignments included: colonel, Green's Cavalry Regiment, Missouri State Guard (1861); brigadier general, Missouri State Guard (ca. September 1861); commanding 2nd Division, Missouri State Guard (ca. September 1861-ca. March 17, 1862); commanding 4th Brigade, Trans-Mississippi District, Department #2 (ca. March 17-April 15, 1862); commanding 3rd Brigade, Price's Division, Army of the West, Department #2 (April-May 1862); commanding 3rd Brigade, 1st (Little's) Division, Army of the West, Department #2 (June-October 4, 1862); brigadier general, CSA (July 21, 1862); commanding the division (October 4-20, 1862); commanding 2nd Brigade, Bowen's Division, Price's Corps (or Army of the West), Army of West Tennessee, Department of Mississippi and East Louisiana (October 20-22, 1862); commanding 1st Brigade, Bowen's Division, Price's Corps (or Army of the West), Department of Mississippi and East Louisiana (October 22, 1862-early 1863); and commanding brigade, Forney's-Bowne's Division (in 2nd Military District during April), Department of Mississippi and East Louisiana (April-June 27, 1863). Raising a cavalry regiment he took part in the capture of Lexington, Missouri, and was soon thereafter promoted to brigadier general in the Missouri State Guard. As such he commanded a division at Pea Ridge and that summer was named to the same rank in the Confederate service. He fought at Iuka and succeeded to command of Little's Division at Corinth when Louis Hébert reported himself as too ill to command. He led a brigade in opposing Grant's campaign in central Mississippi and then commanded it during the beginning of the Vicksburg Campaign fighting at Port Gibson. Falling back with the rest of Pemberton's command into the city's defenses, he was wounded during the siege on June 25, 1863. Two days later he was killed when he exposed himself to a sharpshooter.

GREEN, Thomas (1814-1864)

Virginia native and a veteran of the Texas independence movement and the Mexican War, Thomas Green gave his life for the Confederacy. After studying law in Tennessee, he moved in 1835 to what would later become the Lone Star Republic and served in its army. He commanded a company of the 1st Texas Rifles in Mexico and was a court clerk at the time of the state's secession from the Union. Joining the Confederate army, his assignments included: colonel, 5th Texas Cavalry (August 1861); brigadier general, CSA (May 20, 1863); commanding cavalry brigade, District of Western Louisiana, Trans-Mississippi Department (late 1863); commanding Cavalry Division, District of Western Louisiana, Trans-Mississippi Department (November 1863 and March 16-April 12, 1864); and commanding cavalry brigade, District of Texas, New Mexico and Arizona, Trans-Mississippi Department (early 1864). Early in 1862 he took part in Henry H. Sibley's campaign in the New Mexico Territory and fought at Valverde.

Returning to Texas after the unsuccessful conclusion of the operation, he played a leading role in the fight at Galveston on the first day of 1863. Promoted to brigadier general he served under Richard Taylor in western Lousiana and during the Red River Campaign fought at Mansfield and Pleasant Hill. In an attack on the Union gunboats at Blair's Landing he was killed by a shell on April 12, 1864. (Nunn, W. Curtis, Ed., *Ten More Texans in Gray*)

GREENHOW, Rose O'Neal (1817-1864)

One of the most effective female Confederate spies, Rose O'Neal Greenhow continued her activities even during her imprisonment. Born in Port Tobacco, Maryland, she had become a Washington belle and friend of politicians as diverse as James Buchanan and John C. Calhoun. A staunch Southerner, she backed Calhoun's call for a separation of the states. By the time of the Civil War she was a widow and one of the most traveled women in the capital. Working for the Confederate espionage system, she was able to supply much information gleaned from her admirers. She is credited with providing Richmond with the intelligence of McDowell's advance in time to provide for the uniting of Johnston and Beauregard for the victory at 1st Bull Run. Imprisoned in her own home in August 1861, she continued to send messages south. The following January she was transferred to the Old Capitol Prison and for five months—despite tightening security—managed to continue some clandestine activities. Finally in May she was sent into the Confederate lines along with her young daughter, Rose, who had also been confined. In August 1863 she was sent to England and France to plead the Confederacy's cause. From abroad she published *My Imprisonment and the First Year of Abolition Rule at Washington*. Returning aboard the *Condor*—her mission a failure—she was at her own request placed in a small craft in order to land when they arrived off Wilmington, North Carolina, on October 1, 1864, in the midst of a raging storm. Her vessel swamped and the weight of the gold she was carrying for the cause forced her under. She was given a military funeral and her grave is decorated on Confederate Memorial Day. (Ross, Ishbel, *Rebel Rose: Life of Rose O'Neal Greenhow, Confederate Spy*)

GREGG, John (1828-1864)

A native of Alabama, lawyer John Gregg had emigrated to Texas a decade before the Civil War and served as a judge and as a member of the secession convention. Named to the Provisional Confederate Congress, he was admitted on February 15, 1861, and served on the committees on Accounts; Claims; and Military Affairs. He left the capital to raise a regiment for the war effort. His military assignments included: colonel, 7th Texas (September 1861); brigadier general, CSA (August 29, 1862); commanding brigade, 3rd Military District, Department of Mississippi and East Louisiana (late 1862-May 1863); commanding brigade (in Walker's Division from June), Department of the West (May-July 1863); commanding brigade, Walker's Division, in Department of Mississippi and East Louisiana (July-September 1863) and in Reserve Corps, Army of Tennessee (September 1863); and commanding Texas Brigade, Field's Division, in Department of East Tennessee (January 11-April 12, 1864) and in 1st Corps, Army of Northern Viriginia (April 12-October 7, 1864). Captured at Fort Donelson he was exchanged and promoted. Assigned to command a brigade in eastern Louisiana, he was detached to fight at Chickasaw Bayou in December 1862. He returned to Louisiana until May 1863 when he again went to Mississippi and joined Johnston in his attempt to save Pemberton at Vicksburg; he was wounded on the first day at Chickamauga. Upon recovering he was assigned to the Texas Brigade and led it at the Wilderness, Spotsylvania, Cold Harbor, and around Richmond and Petersburg. He was killed on the Darbytown Road on October 7, 1864. (Freeman, Douglas S., *Lee's Lieutenants*)

GREGG, Maxcy (1814-1862)

Although a regular army major in the Mexican War, South Carolina lawyer and amateur scientist Maxcy Gregg did not see any action there. A longtime proponent of states' rights, he was a member of the state secession convention. His military assignments included: colonel, 1st South Carolina, Provisional Army (January 1861); brigadier general, CSA (December 18, 1861); commanding brigade, Department of South Carolina, Georgia, and Florida (early 1862); commanding same brigade, J.R. Anderson's Command (April-May 27, 1862) and A.P. Hill's Division (May 27-July 1862), Department and Army of Northern Virginia; and commanding brigade, A.P. Hill's Division, Jackson's Corps, Army of Northern Virginia (July-December 13, 1862). After observing the capitulation of Fort Sumter, Gregg took his regiment to Virginia where on June 17 it attacked a train full of Ohio troops at Vienna. After reorganizing his regiment in the summer Gregg returned to Virginia during the fall until promoted and ordered back to South Carolina in December. Given a brigade he led it at Beaver Dam Creek, Gaines' Mill, at Frayser's Farm during the Seven Days Battles, and at Cedar Mountain. Known for carrying a scimitar, instead of a sword, Gregg led the brigade at 2nd Bull Run where it held the extreme left of Jackson's line and Gregg was wounded. Taking part in the capture of Harpers Ferry, the brigade arrived just in time to drive back the final Union advance at Antietam. At Fredericksburg his men were placed behind a supposedly impenetrable gap in the line. Surprised by the breakthrough of Meade's Union Division, Gregg was trying to rally his men when he was killed. (Caldwell, J.F.J., *The History of a Brigade of South Carolinians*)

GREGG, William (1800-1867)

A leading advocate of Southern industry, Virginia-born William Gregg was recognized before the Civil War as the leader in cotton manufacturing. Having completed his apprenticeship in Kentucky, he eventually established the Graniteville Manufacturing Company in South Carolina. Arguing for more internal manufacturing of cotton, he also urged the South to prepare financially for secession. In 1845 he wrote *Essays on Domestic Industry*. Before the war he served two years in the state legislature but was unsuccessful in an attempt to gain election to the upper house in 1858. Having bought new equipment before the outbreak of hostilities, the manufacturer was able to keep his enterprise running throughout the war. Through his articles in *DeBow's Review* and his signing of South Carolina's secession document, he played an important role in bringing about the war for which he had prepared. He rebuilt his plant after the war but died soon thereafter from exposure while repairing a mill dam. (Mitchell, Broadus, *William Gregg, Factory Master of the Old South*)

GREER, Elkanah Brackin (1825-1877)

Having served under Jefferson Davis in the 1st Mississippi Rifles during the Mexican War, Tennessee native Elkanah B. Greer received a commission of brigadier general from the Confederate president. A Texas farmer and businessman, he had been a leader in the pro-expansion of slavery Knights of the Golden Circle. This group would later become a band of Southern sympathizers in the North during the Civil War. Joining the Confederate army, his assignments included: colonel, 3rd Texas Cavalry (July 1, 1861); brigadier general, CSA (October 8, 1862); chief, Bureau of Conscription, Trans-Mississippi Department (October 8, 1862-May 26, 1865); also commanding Texas Reserve Forces (1864); and also commanding Reserve Corps, Trans-Mississippi Department (March 27-May 26, 1865). At the head of his regiment—then known as the South Kansas-Texas Mounted Regiment—he fought at Wilson's Creek. Slightly wounded at Pea Ridge, he was promoted to brigadier general the next fall and assigned to conscript duty. In the final stages of the war he was also in charge of the reserve forces in Texas. After the war he resettled in Texas and later moved to Arkansas.

GRENFELL, George St. Leger (1807-1868?)

Not, strictly speaking, a soldier of fortune, since he had recently inherited funds adequate enough to enable him to serve the Confederacy without pay, George St. Leger Grenfell was certainly a military adventurer. Born in England, he was denied his father's permission to join the French army. He subsequently served as a French Foreign Legion officer, with various Arab chieftains, against Mediterranean pirates, as a British officer, with the Turks in the Crimean War, against the Sepoy Mutiny, and with Garibaldi in both South America and Italy before heading to America in early 1862 to join the Confederacy. Although lacking a commission, he served as Morgan's adjutant for half a year before a dispute with the general led to his departure. From November 1862 until the following spring he was a cavalry inspector with the Army of Tennessee. In May 1863 he was appointed a lieutenant colonel of cavalry, legitimatizing his position on General Wheeler's staff. But Grenfell got himself arrested in June for aiding a slave to escape. Bailed out by General Bragg, he went east and, in September 1863, joined Jeb Stuart's cavalry in Virginia. This lasted until January when he rejoined Morgan for two months before leaving the South. Taking the amnesty oath in Washington he went "hunting" in Illinois. Here he got caught up in the conspiracy to free the prisoners at Camp Douglas and stage an uprising in the Northwest. The depth of his involvement is a matter of dispute. He was arrested on November 6, 1864, and convicted, early the next year, primarily on the testimony of ex-Confederate captain John Shanks with whom Grenfell had had a dispute in 1862. Of all the conspirators, Grenfell received the harshest sentence—death. His sentence was commuted to life imprisonment on Dry Tortugas. Being the last conspirator in confinement and despairing of being released, Grenfell on March 7, 1868, fled the island prison, with three other prisoners and a bribed guard. None of the five was ever seen again, apparently drowning in the rough seas. (Starr, Stephen Z., *Colonel Grenfell's Wars: The Life Of A Soldier Of Fortune*)

GRIFFITH, Richard (1814-1862)

Jefferson Davis' adjutant during the Mexican War, Richard Griffith, became a Confederate brigadier and, in late 1861, a focal point in the feud between Davis and General Joseph E. Johnston. After serving in the 1st Mississippi Rifles in Mexico, Griffith, a former Vicksburg teacher, became a banker in Jackson and was the state's treasurer at the time of its secession. As the first colonel of the 12th Mississippi, he went to Virginia and arrived at Manassas a few days after 1st Bull Run. His later assignments included: brigadier general (November 2, 1861); commanding Clark's old Brigade, First Corps, Army of the Potomac (November 2-9, 1861); commanding a Mississippi Brigade, Forces at Leesburg, Potomac District, Department of Northern Virginia (November 9, 1861-early 1862); commanding same brigade, D.H. Hill's Divison, Department of Northern Virginia (early 1862-April 18, 1862); and commanding same brigade, Magruder's Division, Department of Northern Virginia (April 18-June 29, 1862). While serving around Leesburg, it was decided in Richmond that Mississippi regiments should be assigned to the brigades of Griffith and General W.H.C. Whiting. Johnston, however, felt that it was not advisable to reorganize in the face of the enemy. This dispute continued for months. In the end, Griffith led his brigade to the Peninsula, and in the battle of Savage Station on June 29, 1862, during McClellan's retreat from in front of Richmond, Griffith was mortally wounded. He died in Richmond that evening. (Freeman, Douglas S., *Lee's Lieutenants*)

GRIGSBY, Andrew Jackson (1819-1895)

Profanity may have been the root cause of Virginian Andrew Jackson Grigsby's leaving the Confederate army. A Shenandoah Valley farmer, he had seen service in a Missouri unit during the Mexican War. Based upon this experience he was quickly commissioned in the Southern army. His assignments included: major, 27th Virginia (June 12, 1861); lieutenant colonel, 27th Virginia (October 14, 1861); colonel, 27th Virginia (May 28, 1862); commanding Stonewall Brigade, Jackson's (old) Division, Jackson's Corps, Army of Northern Virginia (August 30-September 17, 1862); and commanding the division (from September 17, 1862). After serving at 1st Bull Run, Kernstown, and in the early part of Shenandoah Valley Campaign of 1862, he was promoted to command of the regi-

ment. Following the close of the campaign, the 27th moved to the Richmond area and took part in the Seven Days Battles where Grigsby was wounded at Malvern Hill. Missing the fighting at Cedar Mountain, he rejoined the army in time for 2nd Bull Run where he was slightly wounded at Groveton on August 28, 1862. Two days later he assumed command of the Stonewall Brigade upon the death of Colonel W.S.H. Baylor. He suffered a third wound later that day but remained in command for the rest of the battles. After serving at the capture of Harpers Ferry, Grigsby commanded the brigade at Antietam and succeeded to the direction of the division. Knowing that Stonewall Jackson was going to appoint a staff officer to the permanent command of the brigade, Grigsby resigned on November 19, 1862. Legend has it that the pious Jackson refused to promote a man who swore so much. But Jackson had other concerns. The 27th had an extremely high casualty rate and he feared that this was due to its commanders. He was also worried about a lack of discipline in the regiment and Grigsby's failure to deal promptly with a mutiny. Grigsby was also a leader in the conspiracy of silence against a previous brigade commander. (Robertson, James, I., Jr., *The Stonewall Brigade*)

GRIMES, Bryan (1828-1880)

North Carolina planter Bryan Grimes survived Civil War injuries only to be assassinated a decade and a half after the war's close. His Confederate assignments included: major, 4th North Carolina (May 16, 1861); lieutenant colonel, 4th North Carolina (May 1, 1862); colonel, 4th North Carolina (June 19, 1862); commanding Ramseur's Brigade, D.H. Hill's Division, 2nd Corps, Army of Northern Virginia (December 1862); brigadier general, CSA (May 19, 1864); commanding Daniel's (old) Brigade, Rodes' Division, same corps and army (June 4-13, 1864); commanding brigade, Rodes' Division, Valley District, Department of Northern Virginia (June 13-September 19 and September 20-October 19, 1864); commanding the division (September 19-20 and October 19-December 1864); commanding division, 2nd Corps, Army of Northern Virginia (December 1864-April 9, 1865); major general, CSA (February 15, 1865). He served with his regiment at Yorktown and Williamsburg and commanded it at Seven Pines and South Mountain. Kicked by a horse in the latter, he was out of action for several months but returned to lead the brigade at Fredericksburg. He led the 4th at Chancellorsville, suffering another wound, Gettysburg, the Wilderness, and Spotsylvania. He was promoted and transferred to command the brigade of deceased General J. Daniel, which he led from Cold Harbor to the outskirts of Washington. At 3rd Winchester he succeeded to the command of Rodes' Division when Rodes was killed. Replaced by General Ramseur the next day, he led his brigade at Fisher's Hill. When Ramseur was killed at Cedar Creek, Grimes took over the division and led it from Petersburg to Appomattox. He was the last major general assigned to Lee's army. He ran his plantation until his assassination in a deportation case. (Freeman, Douglas S., *Lee's Lieutenants*)

GUILD, Lafayette (?-?)

From the Seven Days to the trenches of Petersburg the medical needs of the Army of Northern Virginia were met by Surgeon Lafayette Guild, the army's medical director. He joined Lee's departmental staff in the spring of 1862. Throughout the war he fought against supply and transportation problems in an effort to provide the best treatment possible to wounded and ill Confederates. He is truly one of the unsung heroes of the Civil War.

GURLEY, Frank B. (?-1920)

The legitimate killing of Union General Robert L. McCook on August 5, 1862, brought Frank B. Gurley seemingly endless trouble. A member of Forrest's cavalry, he had been detailed to organize a company for the yet to be organized 4th Alabama Cavalry. At the time of the incident Gurley had succeeded in raising most of his company, and it was with this force together with another company that he attacked an ambulance and its escort. In riding past the ambulance, in pursuit of the escort, he fired at the man whipping the horses to higher speed. He wounded McCook in the abdomen. Returning later he heard of who he had shot and talked with the mortally wounded officer. Despite the rag-tag appearance of his attackers, McCook apparently believed them to be legitimate soldiers and never said anything to the contrary before he died the next day. But the North did not look at it that way. Although Gurley had a commission to raise troops from Forrest it was not legal since only Jefferson Davis, under Confederate law, could issue such authority. This meant Gurley was a guerrilla. Furthermore, Union accounts claimed that McCook had been shot—murdered—while lying in the vehicle. Gurley was officially mustered in as captain, Company C, 4th (Russell's) Alabama Cavalry, on November 23, 1862, and rejoined Forrest. After fighting at Chickamauga illness forced him to take a leave at home. He was captured there in October 1863 and almost immediately placed on trial. On January 11, 1864, he was found guilty and sentenced to the gallows. He was fortunate to have his case repeatedly delayed, and in January 1865, apparently by mistake, he was exchanged. After the close of the war Gurley thought his troubles were over, but he was wrong. Late in 1865 a nationwide search for the "murderer" of McCook was launched. He was arrested at his Madison County, Alabama, home on November 28, 1865, and was again scheduled for the hangman, but proceedings were suspended by Andrew Johnson two days later. He was finally released in April 1866. After that he hosted annual reunions for his regiment.

H

HAGOOD, Johnson (1829-1898)

Despite becoming a lawyer during the antebellum period, Johnson Hagood never forgot his military education at the South Carolina Military Academy, the Citadel, and served in the state militia. By the outbreak of the war he was a brigadier but soon transferred to the volunteers. His assignments included: colonel, 1st South Carolina Volunteers (January 8, 1861); brigadier general, CSA (July 12, 1862); commanding 2nd Military District of South Carolina, Department of South Carolina, Georgia and Florida (July 19, 1862-June 1863); commanding brigade, 1st Subdivision, 1st Military District of South Carolina, same department (September-October 22, 1863); commanding Eastern Division (or 1st Sub-District), 7th Military District of South Carolina, same department (October 22, 1863-January 1864); commanding brigade, same district and department (January-April 1864); commanding brigade, Hoke's Division, Department of North Carolina and Southern Virginia (May-October 19, 1864); commanding brigade, Hoke's Division, Anderson's Corps, Army of Northern Virginia (October 19-December 20, 1864); commanding brigade, Hoke's Division, Department of North Carolina (December 1864-March 1965); commanding brigade, Hoke's Division, Hardee's Corps (March-April 9, 1865); and commanding brigade, same division and corps, Army of Tennessee (April 1865). After service in Charleston Harbor during the firing on Fort Sumter, Hagood took his regiment to Manassas, but it returned to South Carolina to reorganize prior to going into Confederate service. Hagood remained behind and as a volunteer private in Kershaw's 2nd South Carolina fought at 1st Bull Run. He led the reorganized unit at Secessionville and soon thereafter received a commission as brigadier. For almost two years he was stationed in his native state but in the spring of 1864 he was sent to the Petersburg area and fought at Port Walthall Junction, Drewry's Bluff, joined Lee at Cold Harbor, and then served through the first months of the Petersburg siege. In December 1864 the division was sent to North Carolina and after fighting at Bentonville was surrendered as a part of J.E. Johnston's army. Hagood had been sent a short time before to South Carolina to recruit for his unit. He played an active role in the wresting of power from the Reconstruction forces and eventually was elected governor. (Hagood, Johnson, *Memoirs of the War of Secession*)

HAMPTON, Wade (1818-1902)

One of the largest plantation and slave owners in the South, Wade Hampton, with no military training, rose to the second highest rank in the Confederate army. Organizing and equipping a legion of infantry, cavalry, and artillery in his home state of South Carolina, he offered it to the government. His assignments included: colonel, Hampton's (S.C.) Legion (July 1861); commanding brigade, Whiting's-Smith's Division (known as Forces Near Dumfries in Potomac District until March), Department of Northern Virginia (fall 1861-May 31, 1862); brigadier general, CSA (May 23, 1862); commanding 3rd Brigade, Jackson's (old) Division, Jackson's Command, Army of Northern Virginia (June 28-July 1862); commanding brigade, Cavalry Division, same army (July 28, 1862-July 3, 1863); major general, CSA (September 3, 1863); commanding division, Cavalry Corps, same army (December 1863-August 11, 1864); commanding Cavalry Corps, same army (August 11, 1864-January 19, 1865); commanding Cavalry, Johnston's Command (February-April 9, 1865); lieutenant general, CSA (February 15, 1865); and commanding Cavalry, Army of Tennessee (April 9-26, 1865). He distinguished himself and was slightly wounded leading his infantry at 1st Bull Run. Commanding a brigade he was wounded at Seven Pines but returned in time to command a different brigade in the latter part of Seven Days. Transferring to the cavalry, with which he was to become famous, he fought at Antietam and took part in Stuart's ride around McClellan's army in Maryland. He was at Fredericksburg and made a series of raids that winter. He was wounded in the cavalry fight at Gettysburg and, when he returned to duty late that year, he had already been given a division and a major generalcy. He fought at the Wilderness, but after Stuart's death he was not given charge of the cavalry, despite the fact that he was the senior division commander. Instead, Lee had the three cavalry divisions report directly to him. Hampton fought at Trevilian Station and on the flanks of the siege lines at Petersburg. In August he was finally given overall command of the mounted troops. In September 1864 he staged a brilliant raid, bringing in 2,500 head of cattle for the hungry Confederates. On one occasion he is reported to have released a bathing federal soldier he came across but he kept his clothes. True to the soldier's word to name a son for the Confederate, Hampton met a Northern youngster years later, while he was serving in the Senate, who identified himself as the naked soldier's son and said that he had been named in honor of the Confederate cavalryman. Early in 1865, Hampton was detached from Lee's army to recruit his old division and was then promoted and assigned to command Wheeler's Cavalry Corps and his own former division under M.C. Butler. Thus in charge of all Johnston's cavalry, he fought at Bentonville and surrendered with Johnston. He reentered politics and after Reconstruction dominated South Carolina for many years, serving as governor and senator. (Wellman, Manly Wade, *Giant in Gray: A Biography of Wade Hampton of South Carolina*)

HANGER, James E. (1843-1919)

A college sophomore, Jim Hager left school to join Captain Franklin Sterrett's Virginia company, the Churchville Cavalry, in the spring of 1861. On June 3 his company was present when the battle of Philippi, or more aptly the "Philippi Races," occurred. Among the few Confederate casualties was Private Hanger who had been struck in the leg by a cannonball and captured. His leg amputated, he was exchanged and returned home to work secretly for several months designing and constructing a homemade artificial limb out of barrel staves. His whittling became popularly known and he started to make these "Hanger Limbs" for other unfortunate Confederates. He eventually received a commission from the state government to manufacture even more. His enterprise became J.E. Hanger Comapny, still in business today.

HANNON, Moses Wright (1827-?)

General Joseph Wheeler claims that one of his brigade commanders, Moses W. Hannon, received a promotion to brigadier general in the final stages of the war, but there is no official record of this. Hannon's assignments included: lieutenant colonel, 1st Alabama Cavalry (ca. December 3, 1861); colonel, 53rd Alabama Partisan Rangers (November 5, 1862); commanding brigade, Hume's Division, Cavalry Corps, Army of Tennessee (April-May 1864); commanding brigade, Kelly's Division, Cavalry Corps, Army of Tennessee (May-fall 1864 and April 9-26, 1865); commanding brigade, Kelly's Division, Wheeler's Cavalry Corps, Department of South Carolina, Georgia and Florida (fall 1864-April 9, 1865). The Georgia-born merchant entered the Confederate army upon the outbreak of the war and, after his initial regiment served at Shiloh, he raised a regiment of partisans, which at first served under General Roddey in northern Alabama. Joining Wheeler, he

fought at Chickamauga and commanded a small brigade in the Atlanta Campaign, after he was detached from Roddey's command. This may have had something to do with his resignation the previous December, which had been revoked in January. He served in the delaying actions against Sherman in the Savannah and Carolinas campaigns. His command was ordered disbanded on January 2, 1865, but the order appears never to have been carried out. He was praised by Wheeler for his service in the final campaigns and after the war he was a merchant in Alabama and Louisiana and a planter in Texas.

HANSON, Roger Weightman (1827-1863)

When Roger W. Hanson received the order to make a suicidal attack in his first, and last, battle as a Confederate brigadier general, he reportedly wanted to go to army headquarters and kill Braxton Bragg. Following service as the first lieutenant of an independent company of volunteers from his native Kentucky during the Mexican War, he was admitted to the bar. In the late 1850s he lost a bid for the U.S. Congress and, as a conservative on secession, backed John Bell for president in 1860; he then favored the neutrality of his state during the early stages of the war. Finally won over to secession, his assignments included: colonel, Kentucky State Guard (August 19, 1861); colonel, 2nd Kentucky (September 3, 1861); commanding 1st (Kentucky) Brigade, Army of Middle Tennessee, Department #2 (ca. September-November 20, 1862); commanding 4th (Kentucky) Brigade, 1st (Breckinridge's) Division, Hardee's Corps, Army of Tennessee (November 20, 1862-January 2, 1863); and brigadier general, CSA (December 13, 1862). Following initial service in central Kentucky, he was detached with his regiment to join the garrison at Fort Donelson where he was captured. Exchanged for Michael Corcoran on August 27, 1862, he took command of the Kentucky Brigade. Known for his strict discipline he was "Old Flintlock" to his men. In the antebellum period he had been wounded in the leg during a duel. Never recovering full use of the leg, he was also nicknamed "Bench Leg." Promoted to brigadier general he led the Orphan Brigade at Murfreesboro. There on January 2, 1863, Breckinridge's division was ordered to assault the Union left. Breckinridge and his brigade commanders realized it was futile but obeyed orders. Hanson was mortally wounded and died on the 4th. (Davis, William C., *The Orphan Brigade*)

HARBIN, Thomas (?-?)

Like his brother-in-law Thomas Jones on the Maryland side of the Potomac River, Thomas Harbin ran a Confederate signal station on the Virginia shore, reporting on Union naval movements. He was called upon to aid in the escape of John Wilkes Booth and David Herold. When the fugitive pair finally managed to cross the river on April 22, 1865, Harbin met them and turned them over to a guide who took them to the home of Dr. Richard H. Stewart. There is also some evidence that Harbin had been part of the original plan to kidnap Lincoln and smuggle him South to Richmond for a prisoner exchange.

HARDEE, William Joseph (1815-1873)

Problems with Braxton Bragg affected only slightly the outstanding record of the premier lieutenant general to serve in the Confederate Army of Tennessee. By the time that this Georgian West Pointer (1838) resigned as lieutenant colonel, 1st Cavalry, on January 31, 1861, he was one of the most distinguished and well-known officers in the old army. Serving in the Seminole and Mexican conflicts, he won two brevets in the latter and was wounded at La Rosia, Mexico. He returned to his alma mater as a tactics instructor and served as commandant of cadets. His textbook *Rifle and Light Infantry Tactics*, or more familiarly *Hardee's Tactics*, became the standard textbook and was widely used by both sides during the Civil War. Joining the Confederacy, his assignments included: colonel, Cavalry (March 16, 1861); brigadier general, CSA (June 16, 1861); commanding Upper District of Arkansas, Department #2 (July 22-October 1861); major general, CSA (October 7, 1861); commanding 1st Division, Central Army of Kentucky, Department #2 (October 28-December 5, December 18-December 1861, and February 23-March 29, 1862); commanding the army (December 5-18, 1861 and December 1861-February 23, 1862); commanding 3rd Corps, Army of the Mississippi (March 29-July 5, 1862); commanding the army (July 5-August 15, 1862); commanding Left Wing, Army of the Mississippi (August 15-November 20, 1862); lieutenant general, CSA (October 10, 1862); commanding 2nd Corps, Army of Tennessee (November 20, 1862-July 14, 1863); commanding Army of the Department of Mississippi and East Louisiana (July 14-November 1863); commanding 1st (Polk's old) Corps, Army of Tennessee (November-December 2, 1863, December 22-January 1864, early 1864-August 31, and September 2-October 5, 1864); commanding the army (December 2-22, 1863); commanding his own and Lee's corps, Army of Tennessee (August 31-September 2, 1864); commanding Department of South Carolina, Georgia and Florida (October 5, 1864-February 16, 1865); commanding Hardee's Corps, cooperating with Joseph E. Johnston's forces (February 16-April 9, 1865); and commanding corps, Army of Tennessee (April 9-26, 1865). As a brigadier general, he served in Arkansas and was then promoted to major general and assigned to central Kentucky. He commanded one of the corps in the Confederate attacks at Shiloh where he was wounded. He led his corps during the defense of Corinth, Mississippi, and after leading the Army of Mississippi into Kentucky under Bragg, he commanded the left at Perryville. One of the original lieutenant generals allowed under Confederate law, he led an official corps at Murfreesboro and during the Tullahoma Campaign. In order to get away from the despised army commander, Bragg, he took an assignment in Mississippi under Joseph E. Johnston but after taking part in the minor operations there was recalled to the Army of Tennessee to take over Leonidas Polk's corps at Chattanooga and during the Atlanta Campaign. During the final stages of the latter, i.e., at Jonesboro, he was in charge of two corps in the Confederate attacks. Disenchanted with Hood's leadership, he accepted transfer to command of the Atlantic coast and served there for the balance of the war. He was unable to stop Sherman's March to the Sea but successfully evacuated Savannah at the last minute. Forced to abandon Charleston as Sherman's command bypassed it, he continued to withdraw into North Carolina with his "corps" drawn from the coastal defenders. Joining Johnston's forces, his last fight was at Bentonville. It was also the last for his only son who was killed there. In the final reorganization and consolidation of the Army of Tennessee he retained corps command. His new corps comprised two divisions of Army of Tennessee men who had previously served under him and one from the Department of North Carolina. This force he surrendered along with Johnston's command on April 26, 1865. "Old Reliable" refused command of the army just after the disaster at Chattanooga but seems to have found his appropriate position as a top corps leader. After the war he settled on an Alabama plantation. (Hughes, Nathaniel C., *General William J. Hardee: Old Reliable*)

HARDEMAN, William Polk (1816-1898)

This veteran of the War for Texan Independence and the Mexican War saw his entire Confederate service west of the Mississippi, and eventually rose to the rank of brigadier general. William P. Hardeman's assignments included: captain, 4th Texas Cavalry (1861); lieutenant colonel, 4th Texas Cavalry (1862); colonel, 4th Texas Cavalry (late 1862); commanding 3rd (Texas) Cavalry Brigade, 1st (Texas) Cavalry Division, 2nd Corps (or District of Arkansas), Trans-Mississippi Department (September 1864-March 1865); brigadier general, CSA (March 18, 1865); and commanding brigade, Bee's Division, Cavalry Corps, Trans-Mississippi Department (March-May 26, 1865). Taking part in the operations in New Mexico, he fought at Valverde. He then held various assignments in Texas while rising to command of his regiment by late 1862. He led it in the Red River Campaign and in the last eight months of the war was in command of a mounted brigade in Arkansas and Texas. Having been promoted to brigadier general two months before the surrender, he was a planter and minor office holder. During the war he had been known to his troops as "Gotch."

HARDING, Abner Clark (1807-1874)

In his only significant military action of the war, Abner C. Harding managed to administer a bloody repulse to Confederate cavalrymen Joe Wheeler and Nathan Bedford Forrest and was rewarded with the star of a brigadier general. The Connecticut native became an Illinois lawyer and politician, moving through a series of party affiliations to become a Republican. His Civil War services included: colonel, 83rd Illinois (August 21, 1862); and brigadier general, USV (March 13, 1863). His regiment was initially assigned to routine guard duty before being assigned as part of the garrison of Fort Donelson, which had been captured in February 1862. Taking command of the post early in 1863, he was called upon to surrender by the enemy cavalry. Refusing, he invited the Confederates to attack and on February 3, 1863, they did. The results was disastrous for the troopers and they were forced to withdraw. Harding was promoted and Forrest swore he would never serve under Wheeler again. Failing eyesight forced Harding to resign on June 3, 1863. However, the next year he was elected as a Republican congressman and served two terms from March 4,

1865, to 1869. Not seeking reelection in 1868, he went into railroading and banking.

HARDINGE, Belle Boyd

See: *Boyd, Belle*

HARRIS, David Bullock (1814-1864)

Engineering officer David B. Harris is another example of the South's penchant for postwar grade inflation. A West Pointer (1833), Harris served two years in the regular artillery before resigning to become a civil engineer in his native Virginia. A planter by the outbreak of the Civil War, he offered his services to the state and held the following appointments: captain, Virginia Engineers; major, Engineers; lieutenant colonel, Engineers; and colonel, Engineers. He played a distinguished role at the battle of 1st Bull Run. On the staff of General Beauregard he worked on the fortifications at Columbus, Kentucky, Island #10, Fort Pillow, Vicksburg, Charleston, Drewry's Bluff, and Petersburg. He was Beauregard's chief engineer when the latter commanded the Department of South Carolina, Georgia, and Florida and later of North Carolina and Southern Virginia. Returning to Charleston in the fall of 1864, he succumbed to yellow fever on October 10. There is no record of his holding any rank above that of colonel, although several postwar accounts credit him with being a brigadier general, but they cite no date of appointment.

HARRIS, Isham Green (1818-1897)

Following the election of Abraham Lincoln, Tennessee's Isham G. Harris, governor since 1857, was the foremost voice calling for secession. As a native Democratic lawyer he served two terms in Congress before rejecting renomination in order to return to his private Memphis practice. Called back into politics, he was elected governor in 1857 and reelected two and four years later. When called upon by Washington for troops he replied, "Tennessee will not furnish a single man for the purpose of coercion, but 50,000 if necessary for the defense of our rights and those of our Southern brothers." With the secession of the state, he turned over twice that number to the Confederacy. With the capture of Forts Henry and Donelson and the imminent fall of Nashville, he tried to move the state government to Memphis, but he was soon driven from the state and Andrew Johnson was installed as military governor. He then served on the staffs of Generals Albert S. Johnston, Pierre G.T. Beauregard, Braxton Bragg, Joseph E. Johnston, and John B. Hood. All of this service was as a volunteer. With a price of $5,000 on his head for treason he fled to Mexico and England. Following over two years of exile he returned to his Memphis practice and served in the U.S. Senate from 1878 until his death. (Connelly, Thomas Lawrence, *Army of the Heartland*)

HARRIS, John V. (?-?)

With the federal drive on Vicksburg, it became necessary for some Mississippi state forces to join in the campaign. These forces were officially known as Mississippi State Troops (the governor called them "Minute Men") and were under command of state Brigadier General John V. Harris. They were called into service in the fall of 1862 and the brigade of one regiment and one battalion was assigned to the 1st Military District, Department of Mississippi and East Louisiana. In the final campaign for the river fortress, Harris and his men were attached to Vaughn's Brigade, Smith's Division, Department of Mississippi and East Louisiana. Harris was included among the prisoners after the siege but was declared exchanged on July 16, 1863. On August 26, 1863, he was ordered to pay off and muster out the paroled men in his command. This ended his active service. Harris is sometimes erroneously listed as a Confederate general officer when in fact he was only in the state service.

HARRIS, Nathaniel Harrison (1834-1900)

A Vicksburg lawyer, Nathaniel H. Harris entered the Southern military at the head of the Warren Rifles on May 8, 1861. His later assignments included: captain, Company C, 19th Mississippi (June 1, 1861); major, 19th Mississippi (May 5, 1862); lieutenant colonel, 19th Mississippi (November 24, 1862); colonel, 19th Mississippi (April 2, 1863); commanding Posey's (old) Brigade, Anderson's-Mahone's Division, 3rd Corps, Army of Northern Virginia (October 14, 1863-April 9, 1865). He served in the Shenandoah, northern Virginia, and then on the Peninsula where he saw action at Williamsburg. The regiment went on to fight at Seven Pines, the Seven Days, 2nd Bull Run, Antietam, and Fredericksburg. Attrition among the field officers resulted in his promotion through grades to the colonelcy. He directed the 19th at Chancellorsville and Gettysburg. At Bristoe Station he succeeded the wounded Carnot Posey in command of the brigade, and when Posey's wound proved fatal Harris was promoted to brigadier general. He served through the Overland Campaign and in the siege lines at Petersburg. His troops held Forts Gregg and Whitworth during the final collapse of the defenses of the city. His surrender came at Appomattox a week later. A lawyer and businessman postwar, he eventually made his home in California and died on a business trip to England. (Harris, W.M., *From the Diary of General Nat. H. Harris*)

HARRISON

See: *Harrison, Henry Thomas*

HARRISON, George Paul, Jr. (1841-1922)

It may have been that, since he commanded in a relative backwater of the war, George P. Harrison, Jr., never received the rank of brigadier general proper for the various brigade-size units he led in the last half of the Civil War. Born in Georgia, he was a student at the Georgia Military Institute when he took part in the seizure of Fort Pulaski even before the state seceded. He then enlisted and his assignments included: second lieutenant, 1st Georgia Regulars (January 1861); first lieutenant and adjutant, 1st Georgia Regulars (ca. May 1861); colonel, 5th Georgia State Troops (April 1862); colonel, 32nd

Georgia (late 1862); commanding 2nd Brigade, District of East Florida, Department of South Carolina, Georgia and Florida (February 1864); commanding brigade, McLaws' Division, Department of South Carolina, Georgia and Florida or Hardee's Corps (December 28, 1864-April 9, 1865); and commanding brigade, Walthall's Division, Stewart's Corps, Army of Tennessee (April 9-26, 1865). Following his enlistment he was detailed back to the military school to complete his studies and serve as commandant of cadets. Graduating at the top of his class, he rejoined his regiment and served with it in western Virginia. Returning to Georgia, he commanded a regiment of state troops for six months before recruiting the 32nd Georgia. With this regiment he fought at Pocotaligo, Coosawhatchie, and at Charleston, including the defense of Battery Wagner. He was twice wounded in the defense of the city where secession had been born. Sent to the defense of Florida he commanded one of the two brigades in the Confederate victory at Olustee and was again wounded. Shortly thereafter he was assigned to command the prison camp at Florence, South Carolina. Serving there for most of 1864, he became known for his fair treatment of his charges. As a reward his family was guarded and fed by Union troops when they occupied Savannah. Returning to field duty before the end of the year, he commanded a brigade in the composite forces facing Sherman's march through the Carolinas. After seeing action at Bentonville, he was surrendered with the rest of Joe Johnston's command. He subsequently became a lawyer in Alabama, served in the state legislature and the U.S. Congress.

HARRISON, Henry Thomas (ca. 1832-post 1900)

Long a mystery who was known to history simply as "Harrison," Henry T. Harrison was an effective spy for the South. His most famous coup came after spying in Washington, when he reported back to his chief, James Longstreet, near Chambersburg, Pennsylvania, on June 28, 1863. He brought the first news that the Confederates received of George G. Meade's relief of Joseph Hooker in command of the Army of the Potomac. He also reported that that army had crossed its namesake river. With this information passed along to Lee the stage was set for the battle of Gettysburg. In 1970 historian James Bakeless claimed to have identified the mysterious Harrison as a Richmond actor, James Harrison. However, in the mid-1980s James O. Hall, working through the National Archives and other sources, positively identified the spy as one Henry Thomas Harrison. This Harrison had been one of the original Mississippi Scouts serving with the Confederate army in northern Virginia during the first year of the war. In 1862 he became a special agent with Secretary of War James A. Seddon. The following spring he served with Longstreet in southeastern Virginia and then went on his Washington information hunt. In the fall of 1863 he appears to have been paid off for his services due to the security risks of his heavy drinking. But within a couple of months, while Longstreet was serving in East Tennessee, he was sought out by his old chief for further work. He could not be located. After the war he allegedly went to

Mexico to aid Maximilian and later disappeared in the Montana Territory until 1900, when he again vanished into oblivion. (Hall, James O., "The Spy Harrison," *Civil War Times Illustrated*, February 1986)

HARRISON, James Edward (1815-1875)

Serving throughout the war in the Trans-Mississippi West, James E. Harrison rose to the rank of brigadier general in the Confederate army. The native South Carolinian had served in the Alabama state senate before moving on to Texas where he was charged with negotiating with the Indians in the pre-Civil War years. His Confederate assignments included: lieutenant colonel, 15th Texas (ca. May 20, 1862); commanding cavalry brigade, District of West Louisiana, Trans-Mississippi Department (fall 1863); colonel, 15th Texas (1864); brigadier general, CSA (November 22, 1864); commanding brigade, District of Texas, New Mexico and Arizona, Trans-Mississippi Department (March-April 7, 1865); and commanding 1st Brigade, Maxey's Division, District of Texas, New Mexico and Arizona, Trans-Mississippi Department (April 7-May 26, 1865). Before being named a brigadier general he served in the Teche and Red River campaigns, his principal field service. Returning home to Texas after the surrender of E. Kirby Smith's department, he was active in education.

HARRISON, Thomas (1823-1891)

Having served as an enlisted man in Jefferson Davis' 1st Mississippi Rifles in Mexico, Thomas Harrison received a commission as brigadier general from the Confederate president. Born in Alabama, he was raised in Mississippi. Taking up the practice of law in Texas before the Mexican War, he returned to it after his first round of military service. Sitting in the state legislature, he was also active in the militia. His Confederate assignments included: captain, 8th Texas Cavalry (1861); major, 8th Texas Cavalry (early 1862); colonel, 8th Texas Cavalry (November 18, 1862); commanding brigade, Wharton's Division, Wheeler's Cavalry Corps, Army of Tennessee (July-November 1863); commanding brigade, Wharton's Division, Martin's detachment of Wheeler's Cavalry Corps, Department of East Tennessee (November-December 1863); commanding brigade, Armstrong's Division, Martin's detachment of Wheeler's Cavalry Corps, Department of East Tennessee (December 1863-February 1864); commanding brigade, Humes' Division, Wheeler's Cavalry Corps, Army of Tennessee (February-fall 1864 and February-April 26, 1865); commanding brigade, Humes' Division, Wheeler's Cavalry Corps, Department of South Carolina, Georgia and Florida (fall 1864-February 16, 1865); and brigadier general, CSA (January 14, 1865). He was a field officer in the Texas Rangers by the time of Shiloh and went on to the Corinth and Perryville operations. He commanded the regiment at Murfreesboro and during the Tullahoma Campaign. Leading a brigade at Chickamauga, Knoxville, and during the Atlanta and Savannah campaigns, he was not, however, named a brigadier general until the beginning of the Carolinas Campaign. Following the surrender in North Carolina he was a judge and politician. His older brother was a general in the Trans-Mississippi region.

HART, Charley

See: *Quantrill, William Clarke*

HARTRIDGE, Julian (1829-1879)

One of the best orators in the Confederate Congress, Julian Hartridge generally used his skills to the benefit of the Davis administration. Born in South Carolina, Hartridge received his education in Georgia and later took up the practice of law in Savannah. He subsequently served a term in the state legislature and attended the Democratic convention in 1860. With Lincoln's election, he embraced secession. With war at hand, he was commissioned lieutenant, Chatham (Ga.) Artillery, and saw service in coastal defense. He won an easy election to the First Regular Congress during the first year of the war and took his seat in February 1862 where he served on the committees on: Commerce; Ordnance and Ordnance Stores; and Ways and Means. His reelection to the Second Congress was a closer contest but he was made chairman of the Committee on Commerce, dropping his other two committee assignments. Although highly critical of some administration appointees, especially Secretaries Mallory and Memminger and General Bragg, Hartridge generally backed the Davis regime. He usually supported the national interest over those of the states. However, he broke with the administration on the issues of the suspension of the writ of *habeas corpus* and arming the slaves. Rebuilding his financial status through his legal practice, he reentered politics after Reconstruction, eventually serving in the U.S. Congress, a position he held at the time of his death.

HASKELL, John Cheves (1841-1906)

Although he did not join the artillery of the Army of Northern Virginia until the second half of the war, John Cheves Haskell soon became one of the more distinguished of its battalion commanders. He entered the Confederate army at the outbreak of the conflict and his assignments included: lieutenant, Company A, 1st South Carolina Artillery (May 18, 1861); major and commissary (December 21, 1861); major, Artillery (April 13, 1863); executive officer, Henry's Artillery Battalion, Hood's Division, 1st Corps, Army of Northern Virginia (June-July 1863); executive officer, Henry's Artillery Battalion, 1st Corps, Army of Northern Virginia (July-September 1863); commanding artillery battalion, 1st Corps, Army of Northern Virginia (September 1863-April 9, 1865); and lieutenant colonel, Artillery (February 18, 1865). After serving on the South Carolina coast, he joined G.W. Smith's, and later D.R. Jones', staff in Virginia. He was wounded, losing his right arm, at Gaines' Mill during the Seven Days Battles. Recovering, he served in the artillery in the Department of North Carolina in the spring of 1863 before joining Lee. He was second in command of Hood's artillery at Gettysburg. When Major Henry was transferred, Haskell took over the battalion. During the absence of the 1st Corps in Georgia and Tennessee the battalion served in the army reserve and temporarily with the 3rd Corps. When the corps returned in the spring of 1864, Haskell and his guns rejoined it. Haskell served through the Overland

Confederate artillerist John C. Haskell. (NA)

Campaign and in the defense of Petersburg where he was especially distinguished. He surrendered at Appomattox. After the war he was a lawyer and legislator in South Carolina and a plantation owner in Mississippi. (Wise, Jennings C., *The Long Arm of Lee* and Haskell, John, *The Haskell Memoirs*)

HATTON, Robert Hopkins (1826-1862)

A lawyer and Know-Nothing congressman from Tennessee, Robert Hatton was made colonel of the 7th Tennessee on May 26, 1861. After a brief stint in East Tennessee, the regiment was mustered into Confederate service in July, then sent to western Virginia where it served in General S.R. Anderson's Brigade under Loring and Lee at Cheat Mountain and under Jackson in the unsuccessful Romney Campaign that winter. On February 24, 1862, the 7th and 14th Tennessee regiments were sent to Johnston's army at Manassas and organized with another regiment into a new brigade for General Anderson. On May 10, 1862, General Anderson resigned due to ill health and Colonel Hatton was commissioned a brigadier general on May 23, 1862, and given comand of the Tennessee Brigade. By this time the brigade was serving on the Peninsula and was a part of General G.W. Smith's Division, Department of Northern Virginia. On May 31, during the battle of Seven Pines, Hatton was shot in the head and killed north of Fair Oaks Station. (Drake, James Vaulx, *Life of General Robert Hatton*)

Confederate General Robert H. Hatton, killed at Seven Pines. (NA)

HAWES, James Morrison (1824-1889)

Considering the amount of military training and experience that James M. Hawes had acquired prior to the Civil War, it is surprising that he saw only limited action as a Confederate brigadier general. The native Kentuckian and West Pointer (1845) had furthered his education in France at the Saumur cavalry school for two years. He also taught at his alma mater. In the field he won a brevet in the Mexican War and served on the frontier and in troubled Kansas. Resigning on May 9, 1861, as a captain in the 2nd Dragoons, he joined the Confederacy. His assignments included: captain, Cavalry (May 1861); major, Cavalry (June 16, 1861); colonel, 2nd Kentucky Cavalry (June 26, 1861); brigadier general, CSA (March 14, 1862, to rank from the 5th); commanding brigade, Reserve Corps, Army of the Mississippi (April 26-late June 1862); and commanding in the Trans-Mississippi Department: brigade, District of Arkansas (October 1862-63); brigade, Walker's Division, District of West Louisiana (November 1863); cavalry brigade, Green's Division, District of West Louisiana (March 16-March 1864); 1st Sub-District, District of Texas, New Mexico and Arizona (April-December 1864); also 5th (Texas) Brigade, 2nd (Texas) Division, 3rd Corps (or District of Texas, New Mexico and Arizona) (September 1864-spring 1865); and Defenses of Galveston, District of Texas, New Mexico and Arizona (December 1864-April 1865). After commanding the cavalry

under Albert S. Johnston until Shiloh, he asked to be relieved and was placed in charge of an infantry brigade. Transferring west of the Mississippi, his principal action came at Milliken's Bend. He finished the war in the Galveston area and then went into the hardware business in Kentucky.

HAWES, Richard (1797-1877)

With the state of Kentucky divided in its loyalties, Richard Hawes became the unrecognized governor of the pro-Southern faction. A native of Virginia and veteran of the Black Hawk War, he was a lawyer and Whig member of the Kentucky legislature and the U.S. Congress. Joining the Democratic Party in 1856, he backed John C. Breckinridge in the 1860 presidential race and then supported the state's neutrality during the secession crisis and the early part of the Civil War. Believing that this stance had to be upheld by force, he became major, 5th Kentucky, and eventually became part of the Confederate army and served at Shiloh. In May 1862, following the death of George W. Johnson at Shiloh, he became the provisional governor of the state in exile. It was not until Bragg's invasion of Kentucky that he could be sworn in at the capitol in Frankfort on October 4, 1862. After the battle of Perryville, he was forced to flee with the Confederate army. He continued in his role in exile and returned again to the state before being forced finally to leave in 1864. Returning after the war, he resumed his private practice and became a judge. (Clift, G. Glenn, *Governors of Kentucky*)

HAWTHORN, Alexander Travis (1825-1899)

After having been twice defeated for reelection to the colonelcy of two different regiments, Alexander T. Hawthorn was named a Confederate brigadier general. The Alabama native was practicing law in Arkansas in 1861. Joining the army, his assignments included: lieutenant colonel, 6th Arkansas (June 7, 1861); colonel, 6th Arkansas (October 15, 1861); colonel, Hawthorn's Arkansas Regiment (November 4, 1862); brigadier general, CSA (February 18, 1864); commanding brigade, Arkansas (Churchill's) Division, District of Arkansas, Trans-Mississippi Department (ca. February-September 1864); and commanding 4th (Arkansas) Brigade, 1st (Arkansas) Division, 2nd Corps (or District of Arkansas), Trans-Mississippi Department (September 1864-May 26, 1865). After leading his regiment at Shiloh he was defeated for reelection at the reorganization on May 14, 1862, but that fall he took command of a new regiment. This he led at Helena and Little Rock but on January 5, 1864, he was again defeated for continuance as colonel. The next month he was named a brigadier general, and he led a brigade in Arkansas for the balance of the war, seeing action at Jenkins' Ferry facing Steele's expedition against Camden. After nearly a decade in Brazil he became an Atlanta businessman and then a Baptist minister in Texas.

HAYNES, Landon Carter (1816-1875)

In the prewar years, Landon C. Haynes was one of the staunchest secessionists in East Tennessee, an area heavily pro-Union in sentiment. A native of his region, Haynes was a preacher, lawyer, and farmer before becoming active in politics. He later served in both houses of the state legislature (including the speakership of the lower chamber) and as a presidential elector before being named to a six-year term in the Confederate Congress. Taking his seat in February 1862 he was appointed to the committees on: the Judiciary; Patents; Post Offices and Post Roads; Printing; and (in the Second Congress) Commerce. His fiscal and economic conservatism proved to be a thorn in the side of the war effort. However, he did support the Davis administration on the purely military aspects. His excessive states' rights views, which views had really launched the secession movement and the Confederacy, were to prove the Confederacy's demise by denying it the means to achieve its independence. Uncomfortable with the Unionist dominance in East Tennessee, Haynes moved to Memphis shortly after the war's end and resumed the practice of law.

HAYS, Harry Thompson (1820-1876)

A New Orleans lawyer and politician, Harry T. Hays had been born in Tennessee and raised in Mississippi and had some military experience from the Mexican War, where he served as a first lieutenant and regimental quartermaster in the 5th Louisiana. With the outbreak of the Civil War he reentered the military and his assignments included: colonel, 7th Louisiana (1861); brigadier general, CSA (July 25, 1862); commanding 1st Louisiana Brigade, Ewell's-Early's Division, 2nd Corps, Army of Northern Virginia (September 17, 1862-December 15, 1863 and February-May 18, 1864); commanding the division (December 15, 1863-February 1864); commanding his and Stafford's brigades, Johnson's Division, same corps and army (May 8-10, 1864); and major general, CSA, by E.K. Smith (May 10, 1865). After fighting at 1st Bull Run he was in the Shenandoah Valley Campaign until wounded at Port Republic. Promoted to brigadier while recovering, he returned to duty on the day of the battle of Antietam. He went on to Fredericksburg, Chancellorsville, and Gettysburg. At times he was in command of the division during the absence of General Early but directed only his brigade at the Wilderness and both Louisiana brigades at Spotsylvania, being severely wounded on May 10, 1864. On July 9 he was ordered to the Trans-Mississippi Department to round up absentees from western units serving east of the Mississippi. He was engaged in this work until the fall of the Confederacy and was promoted extra-legally by General E.K. Smith to the rank of major general only weeks before his surrender. Subsequently he resumed his law practice and was briefly sheriff in New Orleans. (Freeman, Douglas S., *Lee's Lieutenants*)

HÉBERT, Louis (1820-1901)

Twice a prisoner, West Pointer (1845) Louis Hébert rose to the rank of brigadier general in the Confederate army. Posted to the engineers, the native Louisianan resigned as a brevet second lieutenant the year after his graduation. While engaged in the sugar business he also kept up his interest in military affairs through the state militia. In the antebellum period he was a civil engineer and served in the state legislature. Offering his services to the Confederacy, his assignments included: colonel, 3rd Louisiana (May 11, 1861); commanding 2nd Brigade, McCulloch's Division, Department #2 (late 1861-March 8, 1862); commanding 2nd Brigade, 1st Division, District of Trans-Mississippi, Department #2 (March-April 1862); commanding 2nd Brigade, Price's Division, Army of the West, Department #2 (April-September 1862); brigadier general, CSA (May 26, 1862); commanding 2nd Brigade, 1st Division, Price's Corps (or Army of the West), Army of West Tennessee, Department #2 (September-October 4, 1862); commanding 1st Brigade, Bowen's Division, Price's Corps (or Army of the West), Army of West Tennessee, Department of Mississippi and East Louisiana (October 20-22, 1862); commanding brigade, Maury's Division, Price's Corps (or Army of the West), Army of West Tennessee, Department of Mississippi and East Louisiana (October 22-late 1862); commanding brigade, Maury's-Forney's Division, 2nd Military District, Department of Mississippi and East Louisiana (April-July 4, 1863); commanding Heavy Artillery, District of the Cape Fear (ca. February-April 18, 1864); commanding Heavy Artillery, District of the Cape Fear, Department of North Carolina (April 18-May 19, 1864); and commanding Defenses Mouth of the Cape Fear, 3rd Military District, Department of North Carolina and Southern Virginia (May 19, 1864-January 15, 1865). His regiment fought well at Wilson's Creek but the next spring much of it including Hébert was captured at Pea Ridge. Exchanged on March 20, 1862, he resumed command of a brigade and led it at Iuka and Corinth until illness forced him to relinquish command. Transferred to the Vicksburg area, he was again captured. Paroled on July 4, 1863, he was exchanged on the 13th. Thereafter he was concerned with artillery and engineering matters near Fort Fisher. After the war he was engaged in education and journalism. (Tunnard, W.H., *A Southern Record: The History of the Third Regiment Louisiana Infantry*)

HÉBERT, Paul Octave (1818-1880)

Serving throughout the war in the trans-Mississippi region, Paul O. Hébert took part in only one major action, Milliken's Bend, during the Civil War. The Louisiana West Pointer (1840) had served five years before resigning as a second lieutenant of engineers. Donning the uniform again for the Mexican War, he served as lieutenant colonel of the 3rd and 14th Infantry, winning a brevet before being mustered out in 1848. In the early 1850s he served as his state's governor. His Confederate assignments included: colonel, 1st Louisiana Artillery (early 1861); commanding Department of Louisiana (April 16-17, 1861); brigadier general, CSA (August 17, 1861); temporarily commanding Trans-Mississippi Department (spring 1862); commanding District of West Louisiana and Texas, Trans-Mississippi Department (fall-December 1862); commanding 6th (Texas) Brigade, 2nd (Texas) Division, 3rd Corps, Trans-Mississippi Department (fall 1864-May 26, 1865); also commanding Eastern Sub-District of Texas, District of Texas, New Mexico and Arizona, Trans-Mississippi Department (January 1865); and temporarily commanding 2nd (Texas) Division, 3rd Corps, Trans-Mississippi Department (February 1865). During the Vicksburg Campaign he attempted to relieve the pressure on Vicksburg from the Louisiana side of the Mississippi River but this failed. Much of his service was performed even farther west in Texas. Included in the surrender of E. Kirby Smith, he returned to his native state and again engaged in politics.

HEIMAN, Adolphus (?-1862)

Native Prussian Adolphus Heiman spent most of his Confederate career at Fort Henry on the Tennessee River, but led most of its garrison over to Fort Donelson before the attack on the latter work. Coming to America, he had served as adjutant of the 1st Tennessee during the Mexican War. Upon the outbreak of the Civil War he was named colonel of the 10th Tennessee in May 1861. This unit was organized in the state army at Fort Henry and was active in the fort's construction. A subsidiary work was constructed on the opposite bank, in Kentucky, and named after him. For much of 1861 he was in command of the two fortifications. On February 5, 1862, Heiman was ordered to lead the garrison, except the heavy artillery, to Fort Donelson since Fort Henry was flooded and indefensible. His superior, General Tilghman, remained behind with the heavy guns. At Donelson, Heiman commanded a brigade in Johnson's Division (February 9-16, 1862). After a defense of several days that post also fell to the enemy. Heiman was imprisoned until paroled with the regiment the following September. The unit was reorganized in October but Heiman died from the effects of his incarceration the next month, at about the time that his command was declared exchanged. (Hamilton, James, *The Battle of Fort Donelson*)

HEISKELL, Joseph Brown (1823-1913)

A veteran of the state legislature in his native Tennessee, Joseph B. Heiskell became a secessionist only upon the call for troops by Lincoln following the firing on Fort Sumter. Although he was elected to the Provisional Confederate Congress, he voluntarily never took his seat because the candidate for his East Tennessee district running for the U.S. House of Representatives had drawn twice as many votes on the same day. While he did not serve, his opponent was imprisoned by the Confederates! Reelected in the November 1861 elections, Heiskell finally took his place in the Confederate Congress the next February. He was assigned to the Committee on the Judiciary. Reelected to the Second Congress in 1863 he served on the committees on: Claims; Elections; and Patents. His primary concern during his tenure was with those citizens living in enemy-occupied territories. He favored a vigorous war effort, especially when it held out the prospect of recovery of lost areas. While visiting his home in 1864 he was captured by Union forces and not released until after the close of the war. After the war he moved to Memphis, where pro-Confederate sympathies provided a more friendly home than East Tennessee. He resumed the practice of law, served as state attorney general, and as state reporter, compiled *Heiskell's Reports* for eight years.

HELM, Benjamin Hardin (1831-1863)

In an example of how the Civil War tore families apart, the U.S. White House went into mourning when Confederate General Benjamin H. Helm was mortally wounded at Chickamauga. The Kentucky native and West Pointer (1851) resigned the next year as a second lieutenant in the 2nd Dragoons in order to practice law. Marrying the half-sister of Mary Todd Lincoln in 1856, he formed a close friendship with the future Civil War president. When the secession crisis came to a head Lincoln offered Helm the position of paymaster with the rank of major. This was refused after a few days' deliberation. Joining the Confederacy, Helm's assignments included: colonel, 1st Kentucky Cavalry (October 19, 1861); brigadier general, CSA (March 14, 1862); commanding 3rd Brigade, Reserve Corps, Army of the Mississippi (spring-June 1862); commanding 2nd Brigade, 1st Division, Breckinridge's Command, District of the Mississippi, Department #2 (July-August 5, 1862); commanding Kentucky Brigade, Breckinridge's Division, Hardee's Corps, Army of Tennessee (January 31-May 1863); commanding Kentucky Brigade, Breckinridge's Division, Department of the West (May-August 1863); and commanding Kentucky Brigade, Breckinridge's Division, D.H. Hill's Corps, Army of Tennessee (August-September 20, 1863). Raising a regiment of mounted troops, Helm served in Mississippi before being promoted to brigadier general. He was then given charge of a brigade under John C. Breckinridge, which he led in the Confederate attack on Baton Rouge. In the operations against that city he was injured by the fall of his horse. Not returning to duty immediately, he spent some time serving along the Gulf coast. He then took command of the Kentucky Brigade, again under Breckinridge, and led it in the expedition to relieve the pressure on Vicksburg. With Rosecrans' advance through middle Tennessee, the brigade and its division rejoined Bragg just before Chickamauga. In the Confederate attacks on the second day of that battle Helm fell mortally wounded. He died on the next day, September 21, 1863. (Davis, William C., *The Orphan Brigade* and McMurtry, R. Gerald, *Ben Hardin Helm: "Rebel Brother-In-Law of Abraham Lincoln"*)

HELPER, Hinton Rowan (1829-1909)

Not even *Uncle Tom's Cabin* garnered more Southern wrath than the 1857 publication, *The Impending Crisis of the South: How To Meet It*, and its author, Hinton Helper—all the more so because Helper was one of their own. Orphaned at an early age, Helper was an indentured servant in antebellum North Carolina before absconding with money from his employer, going to New York, and then joining the California Gold Rush. Returning to New York broke, he observed that the North was far advanced over the South in culture, trade, and society in general. Blaming this situation on the relatively small slaveholding class, he became a practical abolitionist, not from any compassion for the blacks but rather as a means to rectify the regional imbalance. His book, which had been rejected by several major publishing houses in fear of losing the Southern market, projected this thesis in a highly incendiary and somewhat less than purely factual manner. Reaction was immediate and harsh. It became illegal through most of the South to read or even possess a copy; the speaker of the House of Representatives, John Sherman, lost his post for his endorsement; and men were hanged in Arkansas for supporting Helper's thesis. In the 1860 elections the Republicans used excerpts as campaign literature. Although the book had a wide distribution, it brought Helper little financial reward, and he was penniless when appointed consul in Argentina where he served throughout the Civil War. In the postwar period he had little success, went insane, and finally committed suicide. (Bailey, Hugh C., *Hinton Rowan Helper, Abolitionist Racist*)

HENAGAN, John Williford (1822-1865)

A dependable Confederate officer, John W. Henagan fell victim to the advanced technology of the Union forces. A native South Carolinian, he had served in that state's legislature and as a sheriff. Capitalizing on his experience in the militia, where he had risen to the rank of brigadier general, he offered his services to the South. His assignments included: lieutenant colonel, 8th South Carolina (April 13, 1861); colonel, 8th South Carolina (May 14, 1862); and commanding Kershaw's Brigade, Kershaw's Division, 1st Corps, Army of Northern Virginia (April-May 1864). He saw early action at 1st Bull Run, Williamsburg, and the Seven Days before being wounded at South Mountain. Returning, he commanded the regiment at Chancellorsville, Gettysburg, Chickamauga, and Knoxville. At the Wilderness and Spotsylvania he led the brigade and in both instances spearheaded the corps' advance. He subsequently fought at Cold Harbor and Petersburg before being sent to the Shenandoah Valley to reenforce General Early. In a small action near Winchester on September 13, 1864, Union General John B. McIntosh led his cavalry brigade, armed with repeating rifles, across the Opequon on a reconnaissance. The prize was nearly the entire 8th South Carolina, including Colonel Henagan. Confined at Johnson's Island, Henagan died on April 26, 1865, the same day the remnant of the 8th laid down their arms. (Dickert, D. Augustus, *History of Kershaw's Brigade*)

HENNINGSEN, Charles Frederick (1815-1877)

A military adventurer of some note, Charles F. Henningsen had only a brief career in the Confederate army. The native of Brussels, Belgium, had served the Carlists in Spain and fought with Kossuth in Hungary before immigrating to the United States in the early 1850s. He became a noted author, recounting his adventures, and was involved in the expansionist plots of William Walker in Central America. Offering his services to the South, he was commissioned colonel, 59th Virginia, on August 1, 1861. Serving under General Wise, he took part in the campaigns in western Virginia, North Carolina, and on the Peninsula. Much of the time he directed the artillery of Wise's Legion. When the regiment was reorganized under the Conscript Act in November 1862 he was relieved of his command. He subsequently lived in Washington, D.C.

HERBERT, Arthur (1829-1919)

By the time Arthur Herbert got to command a brigade there were only three days left in its life. A native of Alexandria, Virginia, he was a barber at the outbreak of the war when he helped raise a local company. His Confederate assignments included: lieutenant, Company G, 6th Virginia Battalion (early 1861); captain, Company H, 17th Virginia (April 17, 1861); major, 17th Virginia (April 27, 1862); lieutenant colonel, 17th Virginia (November 1, 1862); colonel, 17th Virginia (July 8, 1864); and commanding Corse's Brigade, Pickett's Division, 1st Corps, Army of Northern Virginia (April 6-9, 1865). He saw action at Blackburn's Ford, 1st Bull Run, Yorktown, Williamsburg, Seven Pines, the Seven Days, and 2nd Bull Run. In the latter battle he succeeded to command of the regiment upon the wounding of the lieutenant colonel. Again, at Antietam, he moved up to regimental command, this time when Colonel M.D. Corse was injured. After being only lightly engaged at Fredericksburg, the division took part in Longstreet's campaign, in southeastern Virginia, missing the battle of Chancellorsville. During the Gettysburg Campaign, the brigade, now under Corse, was left in Virginia to guard Hanover Junction. In the fall and winter of 1863-64 the brigade was again detached from the army, with Herbert and the 17th serving in southern Virginia. Rejoining the army in May 1864, he fought at North Anna, Cold Harbor, Petersburg, Five Forks, and Sayler's Creek. In the last action, he took over the brigade after General Corse was captured. Three days later he surrendered the command at Appomattox. Returning to Alexandria, he was active in banking.

HERBERT, Caleb Claiborne (ca. 1814-1867)

Confederate congressmen from the Trans-Mississippi area were generally advocates of states' rights within the new nation, demanding that their region not be stripped of troops. One of the most vehement of these radicals was Caleb C. Herbert of Texas' 2nd District. Born in Virginia, Herbert had moved to Texas where he became a wealthy farmer. In the immediate prewar years he served in the state legislature's upper house where he furthered the movement toward secession. Winning election to the First Regular Congress in November 1861, he served on the committees on Ordnance and Ordnance Stores; and Post Offices and Post Roads. As chairman of a special committee investigating the treatment of Union prisoners, Herbert wrote a minority report condemning the management of Castle Thunder. Considering the draft to be class discrimination and a drain upon the defenses of the Texas frontier, he even threatened the secession of the state from the Confederacy. He rejected all administration proposals, especially those threatening his constituents' cotton crop. Winning by a narrow margin in his 1863 reelection campaign, he served on the committees on Claims and Commerce. With the impending doom of the Confederacy, Herbert supported the Davis administration's foreign policy and opposed peace negotiations. After the war he was twice refused admittance to the U.S. Congress and two years after the war was shot and killed, apparently a case of the "wrong man."

HEROLD, David E. (1842-1865)

On the flight from Ford's Theater, it was an unemployed druggist's clerk, David E. Herold, who was the almost constant companion of John Wilkes Booth. He went to the gallows for it. Meeting Booth through his acquaintance with John Surratt, he had become involved in the plan to capture Lincoln and spirit him off to Richmond where he would be exchanged for Confederate prisoners of war. Apparently at least one attempt was made. When the plan was changed to assassination following Appomattox, Herold was assigned to aid Lewis Paine to make his escape through Maryland after killing Secretary of State William H. Seward. Herold had grown up in the area and was thoroughly familiar with the roads and terrain. In advance of the planned murders he placed guns in the Maryland countryside to facilitate the plotters' getaway. In the actual event Herold hooked up with Booth on the far side of the Anacostia River, having passed Silas T. Cobb, the sentry on the Navy Yard Bridge. From there their route took them to Dr. Samuel A. Mudd, then across the Potomac and eventually to the tobacco shed on the Richard H. Garrett farm near Port Royal, Virginia. When surrounded by Union cavalrymen, Herold begged to be allowed to come out and surrender and did so, being cursed by Booth. With Booth in a maimed condition, Herold had already shown extreme loyalty in staying with him this far; he had always been going off to get aid for his friend. Following Booth's death Herold was taken to Washington and tried by a military court. He went to the hangman on July 7, 1865.

HETH, Henry (1825-1899)

Graduating at the very bottom of his 1847 class at West Point, Henry Heth served 14 years on frontier duty before resigning his infantry captaincy on April 25, 1861, to serve his native Virginia. His assignments included: captain, Infantry (spring 1861); colonel, 45th Virginia (1861); brigadier general, CSA (January 6, 1862); commanding District of Lewisburg (February 6-May 8, 1862); commanding division, Department of East Tennessee (July 3-December 1862); commanding the District, same department (December 1862); commanding the department (January 1863); commanding Field's (old) Brigade, A.P. Hill's Division, 2nd Corps, Army of Northern Virginia (March 5-May 2, and late May 1863); major general, CSA (May 24, 1863); commanding the division (May 2-3, 1863) commanding division, 3rd Corps, same army (May 30-July 1 and July 1863-February 1865 and March-April 9, 1865); and commanding the corps (February-March 1865). His initial service came in the Kanawha Valley and the Lewisburg area of western

David Herold on wanted poster. (AC)

Henry Heth, whose division opened the battle of Gettysburg. (NA)

Virginia. He joined Kirby Smith in East Tennessee in the summer of 1862 and commanded a division and briefly the department. At the request of Robert E. Lee, who called the brigadier by his first name, allegedly the only case of Lee doing this with his generals, Heth was transferred to the Army of Northern Virginia. Commanding a Virginia brigade he fought at Chancellorsville and was in command of the division until wounded. Returning to duty he was soon promoted (an October 1862 appointment as major general had not been confirmed), and given a division in the new 3rd Corps. On the first day at Gettysburg he was wounded but recovered to fight at Falling Waters, Bristoe Station, and Mine Run before the end of the year. The next spring and summer he guided his men through the Overland Campaign and supervised them in the trenches around Petersburg, often sallying forth to defeat Union attempts to cut the railroads and highways into the beleaguered city. Briefly in corps command during the final winter of the conflict, he surrendered with his chief at Appomattox. He was involved in insurance after the peace. (Morrison, James L., ed., *The Memoirs of Henry Heth*)

HEYWARD, William Cruger (1808-1863)

West Pointer (1830) and ex-brevet second lieutenant in the 3rd Infantry, William C. Heyward was living on his plantation in South Carolina when the Civil War prompted him to reenter the military, which he had left in 1832. In July 1861 he was named colonel, 11th South Carolina. This unit was sometimes referred to as the 9th. On the morning of November 7, 1861, he was placed in command of Fort Walker at Port Royal. The Union fleet attacked within a few hours and when he was about out of ammunition, he ordered the fort's evacuation. The following spring he was not reelected to the colonelcy and he was accordingly dropped in May. He retired to his plantation where he died on September 1, 1863, a couple of months after most of his slaves were lost to Union raiders.

HIGGINS, Edward (1821-1875)

Being twice captured while commanding river defenses, Confederate artillerist Edward Higgins rose to the rank of brigadier general. Born in Virginia, he had spent nearly two decades in the navy before resigning as a lieutenant in 1854 and entering the mail steamer business on his own hook. Residing in New Orleans at the outbreak of the war, he offered his services and his assignments included: captain, 1st Louisiana Artillery (April 1861); lieutenant colonel, 21st Louisiana (February 1862); colonel, Artillery (post April 1862); commanding River Batteries, Vicksburg, Department of Mississippi and East Louisiana (winter-July 4, 1863); brigadier general, CSA (October 29, 1863); commanding 3rd Brigade, Department of the Gulf (fall 1863-early 1864); and commanding brigade, District of the Gulf, Department of Alabama, Mississippi and East Louisiana (spring-fall 1864). His initial service came as an aide to David E. Twiggs on the Louisiana coast and then in command of Forts Jackson and St. Philip. When the Union fleet passed his outposts on the way to New Orleans and captured the city he faced mutinies by the garrisons and was forced to surrender.

Eventually exchanged, he was promoted to colonel and commanded the batteries commanding the river at Vicksburg. When that city fell he again became a prisoner of war and was not exchanged until October 27, 1863. Two days later he was named a brigadier general and he spent most of the balance of the war on the Gulf coast. However, he disappears from the records in the fall of 1864. In the postwar years he engaged in various business enterprises on both the East and West coasts.

HILL, Ambrose Powell (1825-1865)

Known for his red battle shirt and his hard-hitting attacks at the head of the famed Light Division, Ambrose P. Hill proved to be an example of the Peter principle. A West Pointer (1847) and veteran artilleryman, he resigned as a first lieutenant on March 1, 1861, and joined the South, where his services included: colonel, 13th Virginia (spring 1861); brigadier general, CSA (February 26, 1862); commanding brigade, Longstreet's Division, Department of Northern Virginia (ca. February 26-May 27, 1862); major general, CSA (May 26, 1862); commanding Light Division (in 1st Corps from June 29 and 2nd Corps from July 27, 1862), Army of Northern Virginia (May 27, 1862-May 2, 1863); commanding 2nd Corps, Army of Northern Virginia (May 2 and 6-30, 1863); lieutenant general, CSA (May 24, 1863); and commanding 3rd Corps, Army of Northern Virginia (May 30, 1863-May 7, 1864 and May 21, 1864-April 2, 1865). In reserve at 1st Bull Run, he fought at Yorktown and Williamsburg before being given command of a division. On the day he assumed command he directed the fight at Hanover Court House. He then took part in the Seven Days, distinguish-

A.P. Hill, Confederate corps commander killed in the final days of the war. (NA)

ing himself. After fighting at Cedar Mountain, 2nd Bull Run, and the capture of Harpers Ferry, he launched powerful counterattacks at the right moment at both Antietam and Fredericksburg. At Chancellorsville he was on Jackson's famed march around the Union left flank. When Jackson was wounded, Hill took command of the corps but was wounded carrying his chief to the rear. At the end of the month he was given command of the new 3rd Corps, which he led to Gettysburg where, suffering from a now unidentifiable illness, he put in a lackluster performance. He was responsible for the disaster at Bristoe Station that fall and, again ill, was virtually circumvented at the Wilderness when Lee in effect took over command of the corps. He relinquished command temporarily after the battle and missed Spotsylvania but returned for the North Anna and Cold Harbor. Taking part in the siege of Petersburg, he was again ill during part of the winter of 1864-65. With the lines around the city collapsing on April 2, 1865, he was shot and killed in an encounter with a stray group of federal soldiers. Interestingly enough, both Stonewall Jackson and Lee called for Hill and his division in their dying delirium. It must have been the old Hill they were recalling. (Hassler, William W., *A.P. Hill: Lee's Forgotten General* and Schenck, Martin, *Up Came Hill: The Story of the Light Division and of its Leaders*)

HILL, Benjamin Harvey (1823-1882)

One of the politicians most adept at flowing with the times was Georgia's Benjamin H. Hill, who at one time or another served under just about every political banner of the mid- and late-19th century. Initially an opponent of secession, the plantation owner and lawyer had been active in Whig politics before becoming a Know-Nothing upon the breakup of the Whigs. In the 1860 election he backed the Constitutional Union ticket, but with the election of Lincoln he determined that secession was inevitable and signed the document taking Georgia out of the Union, rather than cause division in his state. Having served in both houses of the state legislature, he was named to the Provisional Confederate Congress where he was active in the organization of the new government. With the adoption of the regular constitution he was named to the Senate for both of the regular congresses. His congressional service included appointments to the following committees: Claims; the Judiciary; Naval Affairs; Patents; Postal Affairs; and Printing. From his position chairing the Committee on the Judiciary, he tried to establish a Confederate supreme court but this was never accomplished. A general supporter of the president, he opposed the creation of the position of general in chief (for Robert E. Lee), fearing that it would weaken Davis' authority. Although he would sometimes oppose administration requests, once they were enacted he would act as liaison to Georgia in support of the administration's policy. Confined for three months after the war, Hill soon reentered politics, eventually accepting the harsh Reconstruction policies of the Radical Republicans. Five years later, the resulting furor in Georgia over his acceptance of the political realities having died down, he was elected to the U.S. House of Representatives and later the Senate, where he fought for southern rights. He died in office. (Pearce, Haywood

Jefferson, *Benjamin H. Hill, Secession and Reconstruction* and Hill, Benjamin Harvey, Jr., *Senator Benjamin H. Hill of Georgia*)

HILL, Benjamin Jefferson (1825-1880)

Native Tennessee merchant Benjamin J. Hill spent most of the war serving with the infantry, but once he was promoted to be a Confederate brigadier general he was transferred to the mounted arm. His assignments included: colonel, 5th Tennessee, Provisional Army (September 11, 1861); colonel, 35th Tennessee (designation change November 1861); commanding Cleburne's Brigade, Buckner's Division, Left Wing, Army of the Mississippi (August 30 and October 1862); provost marshal general, Army of Tennessee (late 1863-August 24, 1864); and brigadier general, CSA (November 30, 1864). He led his regiment at Shiloh and during the Corinth siege. During the Kentucky Campaign he commanded the brigade at Richmond and succeeded to the command again when Patrick R. Cleburne was wounded at Perryville. He led his regiment at Murfreesboro and Chickamauga and at Chattanooga he directed the consolidated 35th and 48th Tennessee. During most of the Atlanta Campaign he served as provost marshal and then resumed command of his regiment. This he led at Franklin and he was then promoted to brigadier general. Transferred to the cavalry, he eventually surrendered to Henry M. Judah on May 16, 1865. He was a lawyer postwar.

HILL, Daniel Harvey (1821-1889)

Criticism of his army commander, Braxton Bragg, to Jefferson Davis cost South Carolinian West Pointer (1842) Daniel H. Hill his corps command and his promotion to lieutenant general in the Confederate army. Posted to the artillery, he had won two brevets in the Mexican War before resigning as a first lieutenant in the 4th Artillery in 1849. Active in education until the outbreak of the Civil War, he was superintendent of the North Carolina Military Institute in 1861. His Southern assignments included: colonel, 1st North Carolina Volunteers (May 11, 1861); commanding Department of the Peninsula (May 31-June 1861); brigadier general, CSA (July 10, 1861); commanding Department of Fredericksburg (July 17-July 1861); commanding District of the Pamlico, Department of North Carolina (ca. October 4-November 16, 1861); commanding 1st Brigade, 3rd (Longstreet's) Division, Potomac District, Department of Northern Virginia (November 16, 1861-January 1862); commanding Forces at Leesburg, Potomac District, Department of Northern Virginia (January-March 1862); major general, CSA (March 26, 1862); commanding 4th (Van Dorn's old) Division, Department of Northern Virginia (March-July 17, 1862); commanding Department of North Carolina (July 17-August 1862 and April 1-July 1, 1863); commanding division, Jackson's Corps, Army of Northern Virginia (August 1862-April 1, 1863); temporarily commanding Valley District, Army of Northern Virginia (September 6, 1862); lieutenant general, CSA (July 11, 1863); commanding 2nd (Hardee's old) Corps, Army of Tennessee (July 24-November 8, 1863); volunteer aide-de-camp, Department of North Carolina and Southern Virginia (May 5-18 and May 21-ca. June 1864); commanding division, Department of North Carolina and Southern Virginia (May 18-21, 1864); commanding District of Georgia, Department of South Carolina, Georgia and Florida (January 21-ca. March 1865); commanding division, Lee's Corps, Army of Tennessee (ca. March and late March-April 26, 1865); and commanding the corps (late March 1865). Commanding a regiment of six-months volunteers, he played a leading role in the Confederate victory at Big Bethel. Promoted to brigadier general, he served for a time in northern Virginia and then returned to the Peninsula as a division leader with the rank of major general. He saw action at Yorktown, Williamsburg, Seven Pines, and during the Seven Days. Left in southeastern Virginia during the 2nd Bull Run Campaign, he rejoined Lee's army for the Maryland Campaign, performing well at both South Mountain and Antietam. His last battle with the Army of Northern Virginia came at Fredericksburg. He then returned to command the Department of North Carolina until named a lieutenant general and ordered to Bragg's army. He took over Hardee's old corps, leading it at Chickamauga. Disgusted with Bragg's failure to reap the benefits of the victory he made his view known to the president, who still supported his friend. Hill was relieved of corps command and Davis refused to submit his nomination as lieutenant general to the Senate. Thus he reverted to a major generalcy on October 15, 1863. His next action came as a volunteer on Beauregard's staff at Drewry's Bluff and Petersburg. He was in command of a provisional division for a couple of days. Ordered to the Atlantic coast he finished out the war with Joseph E. Johnston's army in the Carolinas as a division commander. After the surrender he returned to education and engaged in literary and historical writing. (Bridges, Leonard Hal, *Lee's Maverick General, Daniel Harvey Hill*)

HILLIARD, Henry Washington (1808-1892)

Although he only commanded it for about half a year, Henry W. Hilliard raised one of the larger commands of the Civil War. Born in North Carolina, he moved to Alabama and was a lawyer, state and national legislator, and diplomat before the war. An opponent of secession, he nonetheless went along with his adopted state. On April 24, 1862, he was commissioned a colonel and authorized to raise a legion for Confederate service. When it was complete in June its 3,000 men were divided into a cavalry battalion, three battalions of infantry, and one of artillery, which served mostly as infantry. His principal service was in East Tennessee during the latter part of 1862. However, on December 1, 1862, he resigned. After Reconstruction he served as U.S. minister to Brazil. (Hilliard, Henry Washington, *Politics and Pen Pictures at Home and Abroad*)

HILTON, Robert Benjamin (1821-1894)

Born Robert B. Smith in Virginia, Hilton changed his name and moved to Florida where he worked his way up in the journalism profession to the editorship of the *Tallahassee Floridian*. He later moved to Georgia, where he had previously worked, and became editor and owner of the *Savannah Georgian*. He divided his time between his journalism pursuits and the practice of law. Having supported secession as far back as 1850, it is not surprising that Hilton never took his seat in the U.S. Congress, following his election in the fall of 1860. Instead, he received a commission as captain, 1st Florida, with which he served at Pensacola. In November 1861 he won election to be the western 2nd District's representative to the First Regular Confederate Congress, and he was reelected in 1863. Within a month of taking his seat he proposed limiting the planting of cotton in favor of foodstuffs for the military. He generally supported the war effort, although he tried to prevent the War Department from draining away Florida's military defenders for other fronts. During his two terms in Congress Hilton served on the committees on: Elections; Military Affairs; Patents; Post Offices and Post Roads; and Territories and Public Lands. Wiped out by the war, Hilton resumed his legal and journalistic pursuits, eventually becoming a judge.

HINDMAN, Thomas Carmichael (1828-1868)

Surviving a Civil War wound, which put him out of action for the balance of the war, Thomas C. Hindman died at the hands of an unknown assassin four years later. Born in Tennessee, he had seen heavy action as a second lieutenant in the 2nd Mississippi during the Mexican War and then took up the practice of law in Arkansas. For a time a state legislator, he was about to begin his second term in Congress when his state seceded. Instead, he rejoined the military—this time the Southern—and his assignments included: colonel, 2nd Arkansas (spring 1861); brigadier general, CSA (September 28, 1861); commanding 1st Brigade, 1st Hardee's Division, Central Army of Kentucky, Department #2 (October 28, 1861-March 29, 1862); commanding 1st Brigade, 3rd Corps, Army of the Mississippi (March 29-April 1862); also commanding 3rd Brigade, 3rd Corps, Army of the Mississippi (April 6-7, 1862); major general, CSA (April 18, 1862); commanding Trans-Mississippi District, Department #2 (May 31-July 30, 1862); commanding District of Arkansas, Trans-Mississippi Department (August 20-September 26, 1862); commanding 1st Corps, Trans-Mississippi Department (fall 1862-early 1863); commanding Wither's (old) Division, Polk's Corps, Army of Tennessee (August 13-September 20, 1863); commanding division, Breckinridge's-Hindman's-Hood's Corps, Army of Tennessee (December 1863 and February 25-June 27, 1864); and commanding the corps (December 15, 1863-February 25, 1864). Following service in central Kentucky he commanded two brigades at Shiloh and was rewarded with promotion to major general. Transferred west of the Mississippi, he was in command in the Confederate defeat at Prairie Grove. In 1863 he asked to be relieved of duty in Arkansas and in the summer was posted back to what had become the Army of Tennessee. He was wounded at Chickamauga while leading a division but recovered and after briefly commanding the corps led his division in the Atlanta Campaign until severely wounded in the face, and partially blinded at Kennesaw Mountain on June 27, 1864. Incapable of performing further field duty, he went to

Mexico for three years after the surrender and then resumed his practice in Arkansas. His killing was probably related to the throes of Reconstruction.

HOBART-HAMPDEN, Augustus Charles (1822-1886)

Resigning a Royal Navy commission, Augustus C. Hobart-Hampden sought the immense profits possible in the trade with the Confederate States by successfully running the Union blockade. Before the war he had operated against the African slave trade. Aboard the *Don* in 1863 he began his dangerous career as a blockade runner. Using a series of aliases, he always made it through safely. After the war he published his account, *Never Caught*. After rejoining the Queen's fleet, he again quit to serve in the Turkish navy and earned the title of "Hobart Pasha."

HODGE, George Baird (1828-1892)

Although he had been a member of the Confederate House of Representatives, George B. Hodge had the disappointment of twice seeing his nomination as a brigadier general rejected by the Senate. The native Kentuckian and lawyer had graduated from Annapolis in 1845 and served five years before resigning as a passed midshipman. Taking up the practice of law, he also entered politics and lost an 1852 bid for a congressional seat. Having sat in the state legislature in the late 1850s, he backed his fellow Kentuckian, John C. Breckinridge, for the presidency in 1860. Briefly serving as a Confederate private, he was appointed to the Provisional Confederate Congress where he held no committee assignments. In the elections for the First Regular Confederate Congress he was elected from Kentucky's 8th District, located just across the Ohio River from Cincinnati. In that Congress he sat on the committees on Naval Affairs and Ordnance and Ordnance Stores. However, he was frequently absent in the field as a staff officer to Breckinridge. As such he fought at Shiloh. His military assignments included: captain (1861); major (May 6, 1862); colonel and assistant adjutant general (May 6, 1863); commanding brigade, Armstrong's Division (detached in Department of East Tennessee), Wheeler's Cavalry Corps, Army of Tennessee (November 1863-early 1864); reappointed brigadier general, CSA (August 4, 1864); commanding District of Southwest Mississippi and East Louisiana, Department of Alabama, Mississippi and East Louisiana (ca. August 25, 1864-February 3, 1865); and commanding District of South Mississippi and East Louisiana, District of Mississippi and East Louisiana, Department of Alabama, Mississippi and East Louisiana (March 14-May 4, 1865). Having been promoted from captain through colonel on staff duty, he transferred to the line as a brigadier general of cavalry. Leading a brigade of Wheeler's cavalry he fought in East Tennessee during the Knoxville Campaign, before having his appointment rejected on February 17, 1864. Reappointed six months later, he held district command in Mississippi and Louisiana, and his appointment was again turned down on February 8, 1865. Nonetheless he was paroled as a brigadier general when Richard Taylor's department

surrendered. Thereafter he practiced law and sat in the state legislature.

HOGG, Joseph Lewis (1806-1862)

Lawyer, planter, politician, and Mexican War veteran Joseph Hogg voted for the secession of his adopted state of Texas at its convention on February 1, 1861. Appointed colonel of Texas troops shortly thereafter, Hogg was active in raising troops for the field. Appointed brigadier general in Confederate service, February 14, 1862, Hogg was sent to Arkansas and assigned to command a brigade of Arkansas and Texas troops. This brigade subsequently became part of McCown's Division, Army of the West. On March 22, 1862, the Army of the West was ordered to Corinth, Mississippi, to join the army of General A.S. Johnston. However, the command failed to join before the battle of Shiloh and Hogg's Brigade was in Memphis on April 23. It did reach Corinth by the end of April. However, on May 16, before he could lead his men into battle, Joseph Hogg died of dysentery, which was ravaging the army then under Beauregard.

HOKE, Robert Frederick (1837-1912)

When serving in a semi-independent fashion Robert F. Hoke proved to be a capable division leader but it later turned out that he lacked the ability to coordinate with others. Having been educated at the Kentucky Military Institute, the North Carolinian left the family cotton and iron businesses to join the Confederate military. His assignments included: second lieutenant, 1st North Carolina (spring 1861); major, 33rd North Carolina (ca. September 20, 1861); major, 33rd North Carolina (ca. September 20, 1861); lieutenant colonel, 33rd North Carolina (ca. September 20, 1861); lieutenant colonel, 33rd North Carolina (ca. January 17, 1862); colonel, 21st North Carolina (fall 1862, to rank from August 5); commanding Trimble's (old) Brigade, Ewell's-Early's Division, 2nd Corps, Army of Northern Virginia (fall 1862-May 4, 1863); brigadier general, CSA (April 23, to rank from January 17, 1863); commanding brigade, Department of North Carolina (January-April 1864); major general, CSA (April 20, 1864); commanding division, Department of North Carolina and Southern Virginia (May-October 19, 1864); commanding division, 4th Corps, Army of Northern Virginia (October 19-December 20, 1864); commanding division, Department of North Carolina (December 20, 1864-ca. March 25, 1865); commanding division, Hardee's Corps from Department of South Carolina, Georgia and Florida (ca. March 25-April 9, 1865); and commanding division, Hardee's Corps, Army of Tennesseee (April 9-26, 1865). As a company officer he fought at Big Bethel and became a field officer in the 33rd after the 1st was mustered out. After the colonel was captured at New Bern, he led the regiment at Hanover Court House, the Seven Days, Cedar Mountain, 2nd Bull Run, and Antietam. Transferred to the 21st as colonel, he directed a brigade at Fredericksburg and until wounded at Chancellorsville. Upon his recovery he was detached to deal with deserters in western North Carolina. He joined Pickett for the action against New Bern and played a leading role in the capture of Plymouth. By now a major general and division commander, he took part in the fighting at Bermuda Hundred and Cold Harbor where he displayed a lack of cooperation in joint operations. After serving several months in the Petersburg trenches, his division ws transferred to the defenses of Wilmington, North Carolina, in December 1864. Following the fall of that port, the division joined the composite forces trying to halt Sherman in the Carolinas. After seeing action at Bentonville, Hoke surrendered as part of Johnston's army. After the war he returned to the iron business. (Freeman, Douglas S., *Lee's Lieutenants*)

HOLCOMBE, James Philemon (1820-1873)

Although he had never previously had any desire to become really active in politics, James P. Holcombe became prominent in Virginia politics during the crisis winter of 1860-61 because of his strong secessionist views. Lacking real interest in the actual practice of law, Holcombe had become a legal authority, authoring several law texts and teaching at the University of Virginia's law school. In the decade before the Civil War he penned several defenses of slavery and justifications for secession. In November 1861 he was elected to the First Regular Confederate Congress from the 7th District. Naturally he was assigned to the Committee on the Judiciary. He proved to be one of Virginia's more flexible representatives in his willingness to accept questionable constitutional measures during the emergency of the war. He supported heavy, but equalized, taxation, punishment of speculators and military control over the means of production whenever necessary. Originally an opponent of conscription, he eventually accepted it as a necessary evil. Declining reelection, Holcombe was sent in February 1864 to Nova Scotia where he defended some unauthorized Confederate privateers. Afterwards he worked with the Confederate agents in Canada and upon his return to Richmond urged active operations to foster war weariness in the North and to attempt to provoke the northwestern states to secede into their own confederacy. After the war Holcombe was active in literary and educational pursuits.

HOLDEN, William Woods (1818-1892)

A North Carolina journalist and would-be politician, William W. Holden traversed the spectrum of beliefs on Civil War issues. Admitted to the bar in 1841, he became a Democrat in order to become the editor of the *North Carolina Standard* in Raleigh. He became an ardent supporter of secession and served a term in the legislature. However, his efforts to gain the governorship and a senatorship met with defeat. In 1860 he attended the Democratic conventions in Charleston and Baltimore and switched his allegiance from Douglas to Breckinridge. Inexplicably he was a Union delegate to the secession convention but then backed the disruption of the Union. Continuing his editorship, he came into opposition with the war party and the Davis administration and favored peace. His presses were wrecked for his sentiments. He ran as a peace candidate for governor in 1864 but lost to Zebulon Vance. He was the fonder of the "Heroes of America," also known as the

"Red Strings," as a secret society working for an end to the war. Andrew Johnson appointed him provisional governor on May 29, 1865, and instructed him to call a state convention to abolish slavery and void secession. In the election later that year he was defeated for a regular term, and a diplomatic assignment to San Salvador was not confirmed by the Senate. His editorials took up a decidedly Radical Republican slant and he became an organizer of the party in the state. As a party member, he was elected governor in 1868 and served until 1870, overseeing a corrupt regime. The state legislature impeached and removed him from office in 1870. He moved to Washington and edited the *Daily Chronicle* and held a diplomatic post in Peru before splitting with the party over black voting rights, which he had formerly backed, and other issues. (Folk, Edgar, *W.W. Holden, Political Journalist*)

HOLLIDAY, Frederick William Mackey (1828-1899)

Utilizing his record as an early secessionist and as a regimental commander in the famed Stonewall Brigade, Frederick W.M. Holliday managed to defeat incumbent Virginia 10th District Representative Alexander R. Boteler in the race for the Second Confederate Congress. A native Virginian, Holliday was a commonwealth attorney at the outbreak of the Civil War when he entered the military service. His grades included: captain, 33rd Virginia (May 10, 1861); major, 33rd Virginia (April 22, 1861); and colonel, 33rd Virginia (February 1, 1863). During this period of service the regiment saw action at 1st Manassas, during the Shenandoah Valley Campaign of 1862, and in the Seven Days Battles around Richmond. At Cedar Mountain on August 9, 1862, a preliminary action in the Manassas Campaign, Holliday was severely wounded, losing an arm. His wound forced him resign on March 21, 1864. The previous year he had defeated Boteler and taken his seat in February 1864. In Congress he served on the committees on: Claims; and Quartermaster's and Commissary Departments. His primary interest in legislative matters was in relation to military affairs. Working to improve organization, supplies, and pay, he also tried to find useful employment for disabled soldiers in the war effort. Returning to the law and his farm after the war, he served a term as governor during which he halted the movement to cancel the debt incurred during the war.

HOLLINS, George Nichols (1799-1878)

Dressed as a woman, Captain George N. Hollins, CSN, scored his first victory for the Confederacy. The veteran of action against the Barbary pirates, the War of 1812, and in Nicaragua had resigned his captain's commission in order to join the Confederacy. In the early hours of June 29, 1861, disguised as a women, Hollins seized the Chesapeake Bay steamer *St. Nicholas*. From July 10-31, 1861, he was in command of the naval defense along the James River. He then took over the naval station at New Orleans trying to keep the port open despite the Union blockade. With pressure growing on the upper Mississippi, Hollins moved his small fleet north. Returning to threatened New Orleans in April 1862, he was assigned to the court of inquiry investigating the scuttling of the *Virginia* before the fall of the city. For the remainder of the war Hollins served on numerous boards and courts. Paroled, he became a court officer in Baltimore after the war. (Scharf, J. Thomas, *History of the Confederate States Navy*)

HOLMES, Theophilus Hunter (1804-1880)

A case of partial deafness did not help Theophilus H. Holmes repeat his distinguished Mexican War career for the South. The North Carolinian West Pointer (1829) had won a brevet south of the border and fought the Seminoles and Navajos before resigning on April 22, 1861, as major, 8th Infantry. Joining the Confederacy, his assignments included: brigadier general, CSA (June 5, 1861); commanding Department of Fredericksburg (June 5-October 22, 1861); major general, CSA (October 7, 1861); commanding Aquia District, Department of Northern Virginia (October 22, 1861-March 23, 1862); commanding Department of North Carolina (March 25-July 17, 1862); commanding Trans-Mississippi Department (July 30, 1862-March 18, 1863); lieutenant general, CSA (October 10, 1862); com-

manding District of Arkansas, Trans-Mississippi Department (May 18-July 24, 1863 and September 25, 1863-March 16, 1864); and commanding Reserve Forces of North Carolina (April 18, 1864-Arpil 1865). Placed in command along the Rappahannock in Virginia, he took a small brigade of two regiments to join Beauregard at 1st Bull Run but did not get into the action. He continued to command in that area as a major general until ordered to command in North Carolina. He led a division to join Robert E. Lee in June 1862 for the Seven Days but performed poorly. Due to his deafness, at times he did not even know if there was a fight in progress. In Lee's general housecleaning the next month Holmes was displaced but his friend Jefferson Davis found him a place west of the Mississippi. There he was in overall charge, as a lieutenant general, during the defeat at Prairie Grove. Even Holmes deemed himself too old to command the vast department and was pleased when E. Kirby Smith arrived to succeed him. Retaining command in Arkansas, he directed the unsuccessful attack on Helena. This was designed to relieve the pressure on Vicksburg, which coincidentally fell on the same day. Smith soon felt that Holmes was too old and slow for even his more limited district command and so informed the Richmond authorities. An incensed Holmes resigned. Davis then put him in charge of organizing the reserves in North Carolina, a duty he performed for the remaining year of the war. After the war he was a small-scale farmer in his native state. (Freeman, Douglas S., *Lee's Lieutenants*)

HOLTZCLAW, James Thadeus (1833-1893)

His brother's death caused James T. Holtzclaw to skip the West Point education he had been selected for, but the Civil War still brought him the three stars and wreath of a Confederate general. Born when his parents were on a visit to Georgia, he was raised in Alabama and practicing law there in 1861. His Confederate assignments included: lieutenant, Montgomery True Blues (1861); major, 18th Alabama (September 1861); colonel, 18th Alabama (May 10, 1862); commanding Clayton's Brigade, Stewart's Division, Breckinridge's Corps, Army of Tennessee (November 1863); brigadier general, CSA (July 7, 1864); commanding Clayton's (old) Brigade, Clayton's Division, Hood's-Lee's Corps, Army of Tennessee (July 7-September 1864 and ca. October 1864-January 26, 1865); and commanding brigade, District of the Gulf, Department of Alabama, Mississippi and East Louisiana (ca. January-May 4, 1865). As a field officer he was wounded at Shiloh and was elected colonel during the regiment's reorganization the following month. Wounded again at Chickamauga, he was in charge of the brigade at Chattanooga two months later. During the Atlanta Campaign he led the regiment until promoted and given permanent command of Henry D. Clayton's brigade when that officer took over Alexander P. Stewart's division. During the fight at Franklin the division was still south of the Duck River and thus missed the action. However Holtzclaw did fight at Nashville and played a leading role in covering the retreat. Early the next year he and his brigade were transferred to the Gulf and he was surrendered with the rest of Richard Taylor's forces on May 4,

Oliver Wendell Holmes, future Supreme Court justice. (NA)

1865. Resuming his practice he was active in Democratic circles.

HOMER, Winslow (1836-1910)

Although he had been apprenticed to a lithographer in Boston, the Civil War and country artist Winslow Homer was primarily self-taught in his trade. As a free-lance artist he had already developed a reputation by the outbreak of the Civil War when he joined *Harper's Weekly* as a special correspondent. Covering the routine of army life his works frequently appeared in the weekly editions of the paper and depicted the boredom and frustations of life in the field. Working from his field sketches he finished his paintings in a New York studio and in 1864, he was elected an associate of the National Academy. The next year he was advanced to be an academician. Some of his most famous works include: "Defiance: Inviting a Shot Before Petersburg, Va., 1864," "Prisoners From the Front," "A Rainy Day in Camp," and "Pitching Horseshoes." Leaving the field of journalism at the close of the war, Homer concentrated on the depiction of country life.

HOOD, John Bell (1831-1879)

A premier example of the Peter principle is the case of John B. Hood who excelled as a brigade and division leader, was uncooperative as a corps commander, and was an unqualified disaster at the head of an army, which he all but destroyed. A Kentucky-born West Pointer (1853), he became associated with Texas while with the 2nd Cavalry. Resigning the first lieutenant's commission on April 16, 1861, he joined the South. His assignments included: first lieutenant, Cavalry (spring 1861); colonel, 4th Texas (October 1, 1861); commanding Texas Brigade, Whiting's Division (known as Forces Near Dumfries and in the Potomac District until March and the Valley District in June), Department of Northern Virginia (February 20-June 1862); brigadier general, CSA (March 3, 1862); commanding Texas Brigade, Whiting's Division, 2nd Corps, Army of Northern Virginia (June 26-July 1862); commanding the division, 1st Corps, same army (July-August 30, 1862; September 14, 1862-February 25, 1863; and May-July 2, 1863); major general, CSA (October 10, 1862); commanding division in the Department of Virginia and North Carolina (February 25-April 1, 1863); in the Department of Southern Virginia (April 1-May 1863); temporarily commanding the corps (September 20, 1863); lieutenant general, CSA (February 1, 1864); commanding 2nd Corps, Army of Tennessee (February 28-July 18, 1864); temporary rank of general, CSA, and commanding the army (July 18, 1864-January 23, 1865); and also commanding Department of Tennessee and Georgia (August 15, 1864-January 25, 1865). He organized cavalry on the Peninsula and was distinguished at the small action at West Point and saw later action at Seven Pines and Seven Days. He delivered a powerful attack at 2nd Bull Run but was arrested by General Nathan G. Evans after a dispute over some captured ambulances. Allowed to accompany his division, in arrest, he was released by Lee on the morning of South Mountain. After distinguishing himself at Antietam he was promoted to major

general and fought at Fredericksburg. After service in southeastern Virginia he led his division at Gettysburg where he suffered a crippling wound in his arm. He resumed command as Longstreet was headed for Georgia and while commanding the corps at Chickamauga—Longstreet was directing a wing—was wounded in the leg. Recovering in Richmond from the amputation, he received a promotion and was permanently assigned to the Army of Tennessee. It was at this time that Hood underwent a change. He had a great deal of difficulty in coordinating with the other corps commanders during the Atlanta Campaign, especially General Hardee. With the army having fallen back to the outskirts of Atlanta, Hood was appointed a temporary general and replaced Joe Johnston. In a series of disastrous attacks over the next several days he failed to drive Sherman from the city. After a siege he was forced to evacuate and that fall resorted to attacking Union supply lines to force Sherman north. This failing, he launched a move into middle Tennessee, hoping that a threat to the Ohio Valley might dislodge the enemy from Georgia. After a missed opportunity at Spring Hill, he threw his infantry into a bloody frontal attack at Franklin that decimated them. Besieging the Union forces in Nashville, he attacked in mid-December 1864 and his army was annihilated. Retreating into the deep South with the fragments of the army he relinquished his command and his temporary commission in January 1865. After the war he settled in New Orleans and was a prosperous merchant until an 1878 financial crisis. He died the next year in a yellow fever epidemic. His memoirs are entitled *Advance and Retreat*. (McMurry, Richard M., *John Bell Hood and the War for Southern Independence*)

John Bell Hood, a success as a division commander, proved a dismal failure as head of the Army of Tennessee. (NA)

HOTCHKISS, Jedediah (1828-1899)

A transplanted New Yorker, Jedediah Hotchkiss became the most famous of Confederate topographers. After a tour of Virginia in the late 1840s he settled there and founded an academy. In 1861 he gave up teaching and offered his services as a map maker to General Garnett in western Virginia. After serving at Rich Mountain and mapping out General Lee's planned campaign in the mountains, he fell ill with typhoid fever. In March 1862 he joined Stonewall Jackson in the Shenandoah Valley as a captain and chief topographical engineer of the Valley District. Often personally directing troop movements he took part in the actions of the Valley Campaign and at Cedar Mountain, Chantilly, Harpers Ferry, Antietam, and Fredericksburg. At Chancellorsville he found the route by which Jackson was able to launch his surprise flank attack on the Union 11th Corps. After the death of his chief he served the next two commanders of the corps, Generals Ewell and Early, but was frequently assigned to work for Lee's headquarters. In this dual role he served at Gettysburg and in the Mine Run and Wilderness campaigns. Accompanying Early to the Shenandoah, he served through the campaigns there until after the disaster at Waynesborough. He gave himself up upon notification of Lee's surrender. By now a major, he was arrested but General Grant had him released and returned his maps. Grant even paid for the right to copy some of them for his own reports. Most of the Confederate maps in the atlas of the *Official Records* were drawn by Hotchkiss. After the war he was energetic in trying to develop the economy of his adopted state. Also involved in veterans' affairs, he authored the Virginia volume of *Confederate Military History*. (Hotchkiss, Jedediah, *Make Me A Map of the Valley*)

HOTZE, Henry (1833-1887)

A prewar journalist and diplomat, Henry Hotze was sent to Europe and became one of the Confederacy's leading propagandists. A native of Zürich, Switzerland, he had emigrated to the United States and settled in Mobile. He soon became an editor for the *Mobile Register* and served at a Belgian diplomatic post in 1858-59. At the outbreak of the Civil War he enlisted in the Mobile Cadets, which served in the harbor defenses. Sent to Europe in August 1861 on a purchasing mission, within three months he had become a commercial agent posted to London. He edited the Confederate propaganda organ the *Index* in London for over three years and worked hard to gain European recognition and support. He was also active on the propaganda front in France working with Edwin De Leon. In a move to gain diplomatic capital he favored the arming of the slaves in return for their freedom. After the Confederacy's collapse he remained as a journalist in Europe, dying in Zug, Switzerland. (Cullop, Charles P., *Confederate Propaganda in Europe*)

HOUGHTON G.H. (?-?)

A Vermont landscape photographer, G.H. Houghton recognized the Civil War as a fertile ground for the relatively new art of photography and proved to be one of the art's more daring practitioners in his coverage of troops from his native state. He visited the Vermont Brigade in the Army of the Potomac on two or more occasions in 1862 and 1863. Not limiting his views to soldiers in the safety of the camps, he took his equipment daringly close to the actual front lines. Back home there was a tremendous market for his unusually-large-format prints. Returning to Brattleboro, he resumed his more orthodox photographic pursuits. (Davis, William C., ed., *The Image of War 1861-1865*)

HUBBARD, David (1792-1874)

A wounded veteran of the battle of New Orleans, David Hubbard served the Confederacy as its commissioner of Indian affairs in the latter part of the Civil War. A lawyer and Democrat, he was in the manufacturing and railroad businesses and employed slave labor. He served two nonconsecutive terms in the U.S. Congress from Alabama, supported John C. Breckinridge in 1860, and favored secession. In 1863 he took over the troubling job of dealing with the Indians and preventing their defection to the Union. He met with mixed success. Impoverished by the war, he ran a tannery in Tennessee.

HUGER, Benjamin (1805-1877)

Having spent most of his tour in the old army in staff positions, South Carolinian West Pointer (1825) Benjamin Huger proved to be another early failure as a Confederate general. Initially posted to the artillery upon his graduation, he transferred to the ordnance branch in 1832 and won three brevets in Mexico on Winfield Scott's staff. Resigning as a captain on April 22, 1861, he joined the Confederacy and his assignments included: commanding Department of Norfolk (May 26, 1861-April 12, 1862); brigadier general, CSA (June 17, 1861); major general, CSA (October 7, 1861); commanding Department of Norfolk under the Department of Northern Virginia (April 12-May 1862); and commanding division, Department of Northern Virginia (May-July 12, 1862). Assigned to command at Norfolk, he came in for his share of the blame for the loss of Roanoke Island, North Carolina, which was part of his department. His command was placed under that of Joseph E. Johnston on April 12, 1862, and the next month the Confederate withdrawal from the Yorktown lines compelled him to abandon the port city and also resulted in the scuttling of the *Virginia*. Joining Johnston's forces with what was now styled a division he fought at Seven Pines and later, under Lee, in the Seven Days. He performed poorly in the latter campaign and fell victim to Lee's weeding out process the next month. For the balance of the war the major general performed routine inspection duty for ordnance and artillery mostly west of the Mississippi. His postwar years were spent as a farmer. (Rhoades, Jeffrey, *Scapegoat General: The Story of Major General Benjamin Huger, C.S.A.*)

HUGER, Frank (1837-1897)

Virginian Frank Huger was one of those relatively recent graduates of West Point (1860) who resigned their commissions to serve the South and whose military skills brought them rapid advancement. Resigning from the 10th Infantry on May 21, 1861, he launched his Confederate career, which included the following assignments: captain, Norfolk (Va.) Artillery (June 1861); major, Artillery (March 2, 1863); executive officer, Alexander's Battalion, Reserve Artillery, 1st Corps, Army of Northern Virginia (April 16-July 1863); executive officer, Alexander's Artillery Battalion, 1st Corps, Army of Northern Virginia (July-September 1863); executive officer, Alexander's Artillery Battalion, Longstreet's Corps, Army of Tennessee (September-November 1863); commanding Alexander's-Huger's Artillery Battalion, Department of East Tennessee (November 1863-April 1864); lieutenant colonel, Artillery (February 27, 1864); commanding artillery battalion, 1st Corps, Army of Northern Virginia (April 1864-April 6, 1865); and colonel, Artillery (February 18, 1865). After initial service in the Norfolk area, including duty as an aide-de-camp to his father, General Benjamin Huger, he led his battery in the Seven Days and at Fredericksburg. He served under E. Porter Alexander at Chancellorsville and Gettysburg but arrived too late at Chickamauga when the battalion accompanied Longstreet to Georgia. He led the battalion in the Knoxville Campaign and was named to its permanent command in early 1864. Back with Lee's army, he fought at the Wilderness, Spotsylvania, Cold Harbor, and in the siege of Petersburg. During the retreat to Appomattox he was captured in the rear guard action at Sayler's Creek on April 6, 1865. He was active in railroading after the war. (Wise, Jennings C., *The Long Arm of Lee*)

HUGER, Thomas B. (?-1862)

In the rather dismal performance of the Southern naval forces on the Mississippi at New Orleans, the skipper of the gunboat *McRae*, Lieutenant Thomas B. Huger, was one of the shining stars. But he also lost his life. A veteran of a quarter-century in the U.S. Navy, Huger resigned his commission as first lieutenant of the USS *Iroquois* upon the secession of South Carolina, his native state. After early service in the ordnance department and commanding shore batteries at Charleston, Huger was given command of the 7-gun *McRae* at New Orleans. When on April 24, 1862, Farragut's Union fleet passed Forts Jackson and St. Philip below the city they were met by a ragtag Confederate fleet. It was past Confederate Navy vessels, part Louisiana State vessels and part the southern division of the River Defense Fleet, former riverboats commanded by steamboatmen under the loose direction of the War Department. The net result was a confused action in which many vessels declined to take part, especially parts of the River Defense Fleet. Huger's *McRae* was an exception however. Engaging his vessel in the unequal contest, he fell mortally wounded and was succeeded in command by Lieutenant Charles W. Read. Huger died the next day. (Scharf, J. Thomas, *History of the Confederate States Navy*)

HUGHS, John M. (ca. 1832-?)

Rising from company officer to acting brigade commander,

John M. Hughs was finally found wanting. A native of Tennessee he entered the Confederate service from Overton County. His assignments included: lieutenant, Company D, 25th Tennessee (August 1, 1862); major, 25th Tennessee (summer 1862); colonel, 25th Tennessee (July 21, 1862); and commanding Johnson's Brigade, Department of Richmond (August 1864-January 1865). He saw action at Mill Springs, Perryville, and Murfreesboro, commanding the regiment at the latter two engagements. Having suffered a wound at Murfreesboro, he rejoined his command but was detached in August 1863 to conscript duty. Cut off for a time, he rejoined the Army of Tennessee in Georgia but found that his regiment had been transferred to Virginia. After the battle of Chickamauga, where it had suffered heavily, it had been consolidated with another unit and he was now a supernumerary. Therefore he was given various forces over the next few months with which he raided Union garrisons in Kentucky and Tennessee. With the death of Colonel John S. Fulton of the consolidated regiment, Hughs was sent to Virginia where he took over command of the brigade in the defenses of Richmond. He was relieved in January 1865 when the brigade was consolidated with Archer's old Brigade and was found to be incompetent by an examining board. He resigned on March 17, 1865, citing the reduced state of his old regiment.

HUMES, William Young Conn (1830-1882)

Although he did not transfer from the staff to the line until late in 1863, William Y.C. Humes rose to the rank of brigadier general in the Confederate cavalry and the command of a mounted division. The Virginia native had graduated one place from the top of the 1851 class at the Virginia Military Institute before becoming a Tennessee lawyer. His military assignments included: lieutenant, Artillery (April 1861); lieutenant, Bankhead's Tennessee Battery (May 13, 1861); captain, Artillery (June 1861); captain, Keiter's (Tenn.) Battery (November 8, 1861); chief of artillery, Wheeler's Cavalry Corps, Army of Tennessee (March-November 1863); major, Artillery (May 15, 1863); brigadier general, CSA (November 16, 1863); commanding brigade, Armstrong's Division, Martin's Detachment, Wheeler's Cavalry Corps, Department of East Tennessee (November 1863); commanding brigade, Kelly's Division, Wheeler's Cavalry Corps, Army of Tennessee (January-ca. March 5, 1864); commanding division, Wheeler's Cavalry Corps, Army of Tennessee (ca. March 5-late 1864); commanding division, Wheeler's Cavalry Corps, Department of South Carolina, Georgia and Florida (late 1864-February 16, 1865); and commanding division, Wheeler's Cavalry Corps, Army of Tennessee (spring-April 26, 1865). Serving as a staff artillerist he was captured at Island #10 and subsequently exchanged. As chief of artillery to Wheeler, he attracted the general's attention and won the rank of brigadier general commanding brigades at Chickamauga and Knoxville. He had quickly risen to division command in time for the Atlanta Campaign and went on to serve opposing the March to the Sea of William T. Sherman and Sherman's drive through the Carolinas. Included in Joseph E. Johnston's surrender, he returned to his practice.

manding brigade, Kelly's Division, Wheeler's Cavalry Corps, Army of Tennessee (January-ca. March 5, 1864); commanding division, Wheeler's Cavalry Corps, Army of Tennessee (ca. March 5-late 1864); commanding division, Wheeler's Cavalry Corps, Department of South Carolina, Georgia and Florida (late 1864-February 16, 1865); and commanding division, Wheeler's Cavalry Corps, Army of Tennessee (spring-April 26, 1865). Serving as a staff artillerist he was captured at Island #10 and subsequently exchanged. As chief of artillery to Wheeler, he attracted the general's attention and won the rank of brigadier general commanding brigades at Chickamauga and Knoxville. He had quickly risen to division command in time for the Atlanta Campaign and went on to serve opposing the March to the Sea of William T. Sherman and Sherman's drive through the Carolinas. Included in Joseph E. Johnston's surrender, he returned to his practice.

HUMPHREY, William T.

See: *Smith, Hiram*

HUMPHREYS, Benjamin Grubb (1808-1882)

Despite having been expelled from West Point in 1827 over a Christmas Eve riot the previous year, Benjamin G. Humphreys rose to the rank of brigadier during the Civil War. A planter and state legislator before the war, he promptly entered the military in 1861. His assignments included: captain, 21st Mississippi (May 18, 1861); colonel, 21st Mississippi (September 11, 1861); commanding Barksdale's (old) Brigade, McLaws'-Kershaw's Division, 1st Corps, Army of Northern Virginia (July 2-September 9, 1863 and April 12-September 13, 1864); brigadier general, CSA (August 14, 1863); commanding same brigade, McLaws' Division, Longstreet's Corps, Army of Tennessee (September 19-November 5, 1863); commanding brigade, McLaws'-Kershaw's Division, Department of East Tennessee (November 5, 1863-April 12, 1864); and commanding District South of Homochitto, Department of Alabama, Mississippi and East Louisiana (spring 1865). He led his regiment at Yorktown, the Seven Days, Antietam, Fredericksburg, Chancellorsville, and Gettysburg. In the latter he succeeded to brigade command upon the mortal wounding of General William Barksdale on the second day. Promoted to brigadier, he led the unit west to Chickamauga and Knoxville. Returning to Virginia, he led the brigade at the Wilderness, Spotsylvania, Cold Harbor, and in the defense of Richmond and Petersburg. Sent to reinforce Early in the Shenandoah in the late summer of 1864, he was wounded at Berryville on September 13. Upon his recovery he was assigned to command in southern Missisipi and eastern Louisiana. He was governor of his native Mississippi during much of Reconstruction and later retired to his plantation. (Freeman, Douglas S., *Lee's Lieutenants*)

HUNLEY, Horace L. (?-1863)

Although he would not live to see the day, Horace L. Hunley was the inventor of the first submarine to sink an enemy vessel. Hunley had made two previous attempts to create a submersible fighting craft during the Civil War before his third effort, although it cannot be called completely successful, scored its victory. The first attempt, the *Pioneer*, had to be destroyed when Union forces occupied its home port of New Orleans. Hunley moved on to Mobile, where his second effort failed with the swamping of his invention in rough weather during an attempt to attack the blockaders. Hunley financed the third venture himself and the craft was dubbed the *H.L. Hunley* in his honor. Manned by a crew of nine, the vessel was operated by hand cranks and could be propelled under water. However, when submerged the vessel lacked light and fresh air. Nonetheless, it could remain below the surface for as along as two hours and 35 minutes. The vessel also had an unfortunate tendency to sink quickly to the bottom. The first disaster in Mobile drowned the entire crew. After moving to Charleston, two more accidents occurred, killing 15 more crew members. Hunley then took charge of a volunteer crew and made several successful dives. Then on October 15, 1863, the *Hunley* failed to resurface. Hunley and his second in command had suffocated and the remainder of the crew drowned. In February 1864 Hunley's dream came true when his invention, under the command of Lieutenant George E. Dixon, sank the USS *Housatonic*—but was itself lost with all hands.

HUNTER, Robert Mercer Taliaferro (1809-1887)

In a forlorn attempt to salvage the Confederacy Confederate Senator Robert M.T. Hunter—and two other commissioners, Alexander Stephens and John A. Campbell—met with Lincoln and Seward in the Hampton Roads Peace Conference in February 1865. A Calhoun states' righter and Democratic lawyer, Hunter came from one of the first families of Virginia. He began his political career as an independent in the state legislature in 1834 and three years later he entered the U.S. House of Representatives as a Whig. In his second term he served as its speaker and continued to be reelected, but not as a speaker, until defeated in 1842. He returned to Congress in 1845 as a Calhoun Democrat. His U.S. Senate career began in 1847. From then until the Civil War he proved to be a moderate secessionist willing to compromise to preserve the Union. Having backed Breckinridge in 1860, he nonetheless remained in the Senate well after Lincoln's inauguration, hoping for a settlement. He finally withdrew on March 28, 1861, and was expelled on July 11, 1861. On May 10 he was admitted as a member of the Virginia delegation to the Provisional Confederate Congress where he served on the Committee on Finance. With the resignation of Secretary of State Robert Toombs, Hunter was given the portfolio on July 25, 1861. Resigning on February 17, 1862, he took his seat as one of Virginia's representatives in the Confederate Senate where he served on his old committee for the remainder of the war. During the First Confederate Congress he also sat on the Committee on Foreign Affairs. His policy positions were a mix of support for the war effort and restrictions on the power of the central government and the president. After the failure of the February 3, 1865, conference and the fall of the Confederacy he spent several months confined in Fort Pulaski. With his estate looted during the war and its aftermath, he served as Virginia's treasurer and as a port collector. (Simms, Henry Harrison, *Life of Robert M.T. Hunter*)

HUNTER, William Wallace (1803-?)

With nearly four decades of service in the old navy, including capture by and escape from pirates in the West Indies, it was natural that when Commander William W. Hunter resigned his commission he was appointed captain, CSN, immediately. Assigned to duty in New Orleans, he was given responsibility for the protection of the Louisiana and Texas coasts. Highly successful here, he was transferred to Virginia where he supervised the batteries at the mouth of the Rappahannock River for four months. After service in Richmond, he became the last commander of the Savannah River Squadron. With his fleet of nine craft, he cooperated with Lieutenant General William Hardee in the defense of Savannah against Sherman's armies. At the fall of the city, Hunter was able to save two of his gunboats by running them up the river to August. He and the remnants of his command were included in the surrender of General Joe Johnston. (Scharf, J. Thomas, *History of the Confederate States Navy*)

HUNTON, Eppa (1822 or 1823-1908)

Fighting bouts of illness, Eppa Hunton, who had distinguished himself early in the war, rose to brigadier general in the Confederate army. An attorney and militia brigadier, he was a member of the secession convention of his native Virginia and soon thereafter entered the army. His assignments included: colonel, 8th Virginia (spring 1861); commanding Pickett's Brigade, Longstreet's Division, Army of Northern Virginia (June 27-30, 1862); commanding Pickett's Brigade, Kemper's Division, 1st Corps, same army (August-September 5, 1862); brigadier general, CSA (August 9, 1863); commanding Garnett's (old) Brigade, Pickett's Division same corps and army (August 15-September 23, 1863; May 1864-January 1865; and March-April 6, 1865); and commanding brigade, Department of Richmond (September 23, 1863-May 19, 1864). He distinguished himself at 1st Bull Run and, despite being ill, at Ball's Bluff. Again fighting illness, he took over brigade command at Gaines' Mill but was forced to leave the field by exhaustion three days later at Glendale. He led the brigade at 2nd Bull Run and the regiment at South Mountain and Antietam. Wounded in Pickett's Charge at Gettysburg, he recovered to be promoted and given command of the brigade, replacing deceased General Richard B. Garnett. After services in the defenses of Richmond, he rejoined the reconstituted Pickett's Division and fought with Lee at Cold Harbor and along the Richmond and Petersburg siege lines. After the debacle at Five Forks, he took part in the retreat toward Appomattox until he was captured at Sayler's Creek on April 6, 1865. He returned to the law after his release and sat in both houses of congress. (Hunton, Eppa, *Autobiography of Eppa Hunton*)

HUSE, Caleb (1831-1905)

Although he had been born in Massachusetts, Caleb Huse became the chief, and for much of the war, the only purchaser abroad of supplies for the Confederate army. After graduating from West Point in 1851 and serving there as a professor for a number of years, Huse was a first lieutenant of the 1st Artillery by late 1859 when he was granted a six-months leave of absence for a tour of Europe. On this trip he obtained the knowledge of European armament industries that would serve him so well in the Civil War. Returning to the United States in May 1860, he accepted an appointment, with the rank of colonel in the state forces, as commandant of cadets at the University of Alabama under a special arrangement whereby he was given an additional year's leave from the army after which he was to resign if he liked his new post. In February 1861, with conflict looming, his leave was revoked and he resigned on the 25th. In April he was appointed a captain, and soon promoted to major, in the Confederate army and assigned to the duty of purchasing ordnance supplies in Europe. After much difficulty traveling through the North with almost no funds, he made his way to England on May 10. Here he entered upon his work at which he was very successful. He managed to wrest the full production of the London Armory Company away from U.S. agents for the length of the war. He astounded many by his purchase from the Austrian government of 10 fully equipped artillery batteries and 100,000 rifles. A critic of the contract system for running the blockade, whereby contractors made huge profits, Huse was often in conflict with Confederate diplomats. Charges of corruption were leveled at him but disproved and Jefferson Davis gave him complete independence from political officers in Europe. Working through the Liverpool financial firm of Fraser, Trenholm & Company, in reality a branch of the Charleston firm John Fraser & Company, he continued his purchasing until the close of the war. Returning to the United States in 1868, he launched a number of unsuccessful business enterprises before establishing a successful prep school for West Point. (Huse, Caleb, *The Supplies for the Confederate Army*)

HYAMS, Godfrey Joseph (?-?)

The Civil War was full of shady characters operating in Canada for both sides. One of the more untrustworthy was Godfrey Hymans. Living in Arkansas early in the war he was evicted by the Union occupation forces who also appropriated his property. He moved to St. Louis but soon went to Canada to offer his services to the Confederacy. Meeting Dr. Luke Blackburn at the end of 1863, he was offered $60,000, and more fame than General Lee, if he would hold himself ready for a special assignment from Blackburn. He agreed, according to his own account, but denied interest in acquiring wealth from his service. This seems strange since earlier in the war he had sold lists of Confederate sympathizers to Union authorities. Later, he provided damaging testimony against Confederate agents and the famed St. Albans raiders. In May 1864 he was directed by a letter from Blackburn to proceed to Halifax for a meeting. In the July 18 meeting Hyams was directed take some trunks, filled with infected clothing from yellow fever victims in Havana, and distribute them throughout the North in places likely to reach the forces in the field. They were sent to Washington, New York, Philadelphia and Norfolk and Hyams was convinced that one trunk reached New Bern, North Carolina, because an epidemic broke out there shortly afterwards. In fact he was not responsible for the 2,000-plus deaths because yellow fever, it is now known, can only be transmitted by a mosquito. With the plot revealed in April 1865, Hyams testified to his own involvement. Not enough proof ever existed to convict either Hyams or Blackburn in the germ warfare plot.

I

IMBODEN, John Daniel (1823-1895)

The commander of a group of partisan rangers, John D. Imboden was relieved of duty when it was found that his men, while capable as raiders, were not effective as regular cavalry. A former state legislator, he had failed in a bid to attend the secession convention but raised a battery upon the withdrawal of his native Virginia from the Union. His assignments included: captain, Staunton Artillery (April 1861); colonel, 1st Virginia

John D. Imboden, escort of the ambulances from Gettysburg. (NA)

Partisan Rangers later known as 62nd Virginia Mounted Infantry (ca. July 1862); brigadier general, CSA (January 28, 1863); commanding Northwestern Brigade, Department of Northern Virginia (ca. January 28-July 28, 1863); commanding Valley District, same department (July 28-December 15, 1863 and early 1864-June 1864); commanding Northwestern Brigade, same district and department (December 15, 1863-early 1864); and commanding brigade, Ransom's-Lomax's Cavalry Division, same district and department (June-December 6, 1864). After participating in the occupation of Harpers Ferry he directed his guns at 1st Bull Run. The next summer he organized a regiment of partisans to serve in the Valley and the western part of the state. Promoted to the command of a brigade reporting directly to Lee he was active in raiding operations. He covered the advance in Pennsylvania in June 1863 but angered Lee when the brigade went off to rest at Hancock, Maryland, without informing him. Following the defeat at Gettysburg Imboden was charged with escorting the wagon train including the ambulances to the Potomac. Placed in command in the Valley, he served under Breckinridge in the New Market victory the next spring. In June Early took over the district and Imboden led his brigade in the advance via Monocacy to the outskirts of Washington. Back in the Shenandoah proper, he fought at 3rd Winchester, Fisher's Hill, and Cedar Creek. Following a bout with typhoid, he was relieved of his command. Ransom had recommended his replacement as early as August 1864 for inefficiency. Imboden finished out the war guarding prisoners at Aiken, South Carolina. A businessman and lawyer after the surrender, he wrote several articles for the *Century Magazine's Battles and Leaders* series. (Freeman, Douglas S., *Lee's Lieutenants*)

INGRAHAM, Duncan N. (1802-1891)

Having entered the U.S. Navy at the age of ten, South Carolinian Duncan N. Ingraham was, by the outbreak of the Civil War, a veteran of almost half a century of naval service including the War of 1812, the Mexican War, command of the

Philadelphia Navy Yard, a diplomatic incident with Austrian warships over a naturalized U.S. citizen, and duty as chief of the Bureau of Ordnance and Hydrography. When his state seceded, Ingraham was commanding the USS *Richmond* in the Mediterranean. He promptly returned home and resigned his commission. On March 26, 1861, he was appointed captain, CSN, and following some duty on a board studying the problems of building a navy from scratch was assigned to duty at Pensacola. Then on November 16, 1861, he was ordered to Charleston Harbor and given command of the naval defenses of South Carolina. One of his first accomplishments in his new command was the supervision of the construction of the *Palmetto State*, an armored ram. On the night of January 30, 1863, Ingraham sailed out of the harbor aboard the *Palmetto State*, accompanied by another ironclad, the *Chicora*. The next day they "lifted" the Union blockade of Charleston. In the attack, the blockading vessels, *Mercedita* and *Keystone State* were severely damaged and the former barely avoided sinking. Other blockaders were less severely damaged and the rest of the fleet was driven off. Later that day the Confederate authorities declared the blockade lifted and even had foreign consuls verify the fact. However, it was not recognized by other nations. The blockade resumed. In March 1863, Ingraham was relieved of sea duty, being thought to be too old, but retained command of the shore station. (Scharf, J. Thomas, *History of the Confederate States Navy*)

IVERSON, Alfred, Jr. (1829-1911)

Although he had originally urged the promotion of Alfred Iverson, Jr., General Lee found it necessary to get rid of him quietly. A second lieutenant of Georgia volunteers in the Mexican War, Iverson had received a commission as a first lieutenant directly into the 1st Cavalry in 1855. He resigned on March 21, 1861, to go with the South and his assignments included: captain, PACS (spring 1861); colonel, 20th North Carolina (August 20, 1861); brigadier general, CSA (November 1, 1862); commanding Garland's (old) Brigade, D.H. Hill's-Rodes' Division, 2nd Corps, Army of Northern Virginia (November 6, 1862-July 1, 1863); commanding 2nd Louisiana Brigade, Johnson's Division, same corps and army (July 21-October 6, 1863); commanding brigade, Martin's Division, Wheeler's Cavalry Corps, Army of Tennessee (February 29-fall 1864); commanding division, Wheeler's Cavalry Corps, Department of South Carolina, Georgia and Florida (fall 1864-February 1865); and commanding Cavalry Division, District of Georgia and South Carolina, same department (February-March 25, 1865). Wounded at Gaines' Mill during the Seven Days Battles, he returned to fight at South Mountain and Antietam. Promoted and given command of the brigade, he fought at Fredericksburg and Chancellorsville. In the latter his performance was less than shining. In the heavy fighting on the first day at Gettysburg he suffered a breakdown when he saw what looked like his whole brigade surrendering. He had to be relieved by his assistant adjutant general and later in the day General S.D. Ramseur took command of the brigade as well as his own. Three weeks later Iverson was placed in charge of a brigade of Louisiana troops but in October Lee got his way and sent the Georgian to his native state to work with the reserve forces. In early 1864, Iverson took command of a cavalry brigade under Wheeler and fought throughout the Atlanta Campaign including the capture of raider Stoneman. He directed a division during the Savannah Campaign and part of the Carolinas Campaign. In late March he was ordered to leave his division and report to Wade Hampton in North Carolina, but it apprears that he never made it as he was paroled at his home in Georgia in May. He became a Florida citrus farmer after the Confederacy's collapse. (Freeman, Douglas S., *Lee's Lieutenants*)

J

JACKMAN, Sidney D. (?-?)

Missourian Sidney D. Jackman was one of the final batch of general officers appointed extralegally by General E. Kirby Smith in his Trans-Mississippi Department. Early in the war Jackman had proved a nuisance to the Union occupation forces in Missouri at the head of small groups of irregulars. In 1863 he raised a regiment which was designated the 7th Missouri Infantry, but sometimes designated as the 14th or 16th, and became its colonel. He subsequently commanded a cavalry regiment in the District of Arkansas and the District of Indian Territory. During Price's invasion of Missouri he commanded a brigade in Shelby's Division, Army of Missouri. In recognition of his service at brigade level, Smith promoted him in orders to brigadier general on May 16, 1865. However this could not be made official since President Davis was a prisoner and the senate was no longer in session.

JACKSON, Alfred Eugene (1807-1889)

Age may have been a major factor in bringing to an end the active field career of Confederate General Alfred E. Jackson. A farmer, manufacturer and merchant from Tennessee, he entered the Confederate service in the quartermaster's branch. His assignments included: major and assistant quartermaster (1861); major and paymaster (1862); brigadier general, CSA (October 29, 1862); commanding brigade, Department of East Tennessee (March-fall 1863); reappointed brigadier general, CSA (April 22, 1863, to rank from February 9); commanding brigade, Department of Southwestern Virginia and East Tennessee (January 1864); commanding brigade, Ransom's Division, Department of East Tennessee (January-February 1864); commanding brigade, Department of East Tennessee (February-March 1864); and commanding brigade, Buckner's Division, Department of East Tennessee (spring 1864). As a quartermaster he served on the staff of Felix K. Zollicoffer until his death at Mill Springs. Transferring to the pay branch he served until he received his first appointment as a brigadier general, which was canceled. Reappointed the next spring, he

led a brigade in East Tennessee and southwestern Virginia until 1864. At times his command was composed principally of William H. Thomas' Legion of North Carolinian mountaineers and Cherokee Indians. On November 23, 1864, he was reported as unfit for field duty and appears to have finished the war in staff assignments. After the war he was engaged in farming for a time.

JACKSON, Claiborne Fox (1806-1862)

After leading a rump session of the Missouri state legislature into exile, Governor Claiborne F. Jackson was effectively removed from office by federal authorities. A former cashier in the state bank, he had served several terms in the state legislature, including holding the speakership. After several candidacies he was finally elected governor by the proslavery faction of the state in 1860. The Kentucky-born politician entered upon his new duties on January 3, 1861, and was promptly embroiled in the secession crisis. Advocating separation from the Union, he was active in preparing the state for war. Mobilizing the Missouri State Guard, he also called for 50,000 volunteers to resist federal coercion. In May 1861 he authorized General Sterling Price to negotiate a settlement with Union General William S. Harney, but his purpose was by this time merely to gain time for further war preparations. Forced by military operations from the state capital, he was effectively replaced by Hamilton R. Gamble on July 31, 1861. That November he headed a portion of the legislature in a meeting in Neosho that resulted in the issuance of a secession ordinance. He was active in pressing for Confederate aid in support of the exiled Rebel government of his state. He died on December 6, 1862. (Snead, Thomas L., *The Fight for Missouri*)

JACKSON, Henry Rootes (1820-1898)

It is ironic that a leading Savannah lawyer who had prosecuted the owners and crew of the slaver *Wanderer* in 1859, Henry R. Jackson, became a Confederate brigadier general, while one of the principal defendants in the case, John E. Farnum, became a brevet brigadier general in the Union army. A Democrat, the native Georgian attended both of the divided party's conventions in 1860, backed Breckinridge, and attended his native state's secession convention. His Confederate military assignments included: brigadier general, CSA (June 4, 1861); commanding Army of the Northwest (July 14-20, 1861); commanding brigade, Army of the Northwest (July 20-November 22, 1861); commanding 1st Division, Army of the Northwest (November 22-December 2, 1861); major general, Georgia State Troops (December 1861); reappointed brigadier general, CSA (September 23, 1863); and commanding Stevens' (old) Brigade, Bate's-Brown's-Bate's Division, Hardee's Cheatham's Corps, Army of Tennessee (July 29-September and October-December 16, 1864). During the first year of the war he served in western Virginia, taking part in Robert E. Lee's dismal Cheat Mountain operations. Resigning on December 2, 1861, he took a position with the state forces until they were absorbed into the confedereate army. Recommissioned in that service, he held a number of positions before taking charge of the deceased Clement H. Stevens' brigade during the battles around Atlanta.

He led the brigade through the rest of that camapign and at Franklin and Nashville. At the latter he was captured and not released until July 1865. Following his confinement in Boston Harbor's Fort Warren he resumed his distinguished practice and served as a diplomat in Mexico.

JACKSON, James T. (?-1861)

An Alexandria, Virginia, hotel owner, James T. Jackson became the South's first martyr to the cause of secession. Despite the dangerous proximity of the town to the Union buildup of volunteers in the capital, Jackson insisted upon flying a banner proclaiming his support for the new Confederacy. Then, on May 24, 1861, it happened. Union forces occupied the town. One unit of the invading force was the 11th New York or "Ellsworth's Fire Zouaves." Late that day, Colonel Ellsworth spied the secession flag floating over Jackson's establishment, the Marshall House. Awakened by the commotion of the federals in his hotel, Jackson denied any knowledge of the flag, claiming to be a boarder. He then went for his shotgun and confronted the Union colonel as he descended with his trophy.

Confederate martyr James Jackson. (*Leslie's*)

Firing at close range, he killed Ellsworth. Union private Francis E. Brownell then shot the rebel in the head and ran him through with his bayonet. From this wasteful incident each side could claim a martyr.

JACKSON, James W. (ca. 1832-?)

The case of Colonel James W. Jackson shows that not all of the officers of the Army of Northern Virginia were heroes. He entered Confederate service in the second year of the war and his assignments included: captain, Company I, 47th Alabama (May 20, 1862); lieutenant colonel, 47th Alabama (May 22, 1862): colonel, 47th Alabama (August 11, 1862); and commanding Taliaferro's Brigade, Jackson's (old) Division, Jackson's Corps, Army of Northern Virginia (September 17, 1862). After seeing action at 2nd Bull Run he took part in the Maryland Campaign, briefly commanding the brigade at Antietam until he was wounded. He rejoined the regiment in time for Gettysburg, but, as Major James M. Campbell put it in his battle report, was "left behind." After praising the 21 officers taking part in the attack on Little Round Top, the major made it clear that "The colonel and adjutant are not included in this number." A week later, on July 10, 1863, Jackson resigned.

JACKSON, John King (1828-1866)

Confederate Brigadier General John K. Jackson barely survived the Civil War. A practicing attorney in Augusta, Georgia, he was active in military matters well before the sectional conflict burst into war. His assignments in the Confederate service included: captain, Oglethorpe Infantry (prewar); lieutenant colonel, Augusta City Battalion (1861); colonel, 5th Georgia (May 1861); brigadier general, CSA (January 14, 1862); commanding 3rd Brigade, 2nd (Withers') Division, 2nd Corps, Army of the Mississippi (March 29-July 2, 1862); commanding 3rd Brigade, Reserve (Withers') Division, Army of the Mississippi (July 2-August 15, 1862); commanding 3rd Brigade, Withers' Division, Right Wing, Army of the Mississippi (August 15-November 20, 1862); commanding brigade, Withers' Division, Polk's Corps, Army of Tennessee (November 20-December 1862); commanding independent brigade, Hardee's-Hill's Corps, Army of Tennessee (December 1862-August 23, 1863); commanding brigade, Cheatham's Division, Polk's-Hardee's Corps, Army of Tennessee (August 23, 1863-February 20, 1864); commanding brigade, Walker's Division, Hardee's Corps, Army of Tennessee (February 20-July 3, 1864); and commanding District of Florida, Department of South Carolina, Georgia and Florida (July-September 29, 1864). Following initial service at Pensacola he was promoted to brigadier general and commanded a brigade at Shiloh and in the delaying action back towards Corinth. He led his brigade into Kentucky with Bragg but did not fight at Perryville. His command was made independent from any division late in the year but fought at Murfreesboro attached to Breckinridge's division. He continued in an independent status in the Tullahoma Campaign and a month before Chickamauga was assigned to Benjamin F. Cheatham's division. Missing Chattanooga, he

fought through the Atlanta Campaign until ordered to the Georgia coast in July 1864. He served through parts of the Savannah Campaign and then held administrative and supply positions in the Carolinas Campaign. Before dying of pneumonia in February 1866 he briefly resumed his legal career.

JACKSON, Mary Jane (1836-?)

Known as "Bricktop," one of New Orleans' most notorious and vicious street criminals, Mary Jane Jackson was freed from prison as a result of the Civil War. A prostitute by the age of 13, she had been thrown out of several whorehouses because of her violent streak which kept the other girls in a state of fear. By 1861 she had killed at least three men and then got into a fight with her lover, John Miller, who also ended up dead. Sent to prison for 10 years, she was confined in the Parish Prison when the Union forces captured the city. A Union general, George F. Shepley, was appointed military governor and one of his early acts was the issuance of a blanket pardon virtually emptying the jails, enraging the citizenry, especially in Jackson's case. Following her release, she apparently left the city.

JACKSON, Thomas Jonathan (1824-1863)

Next to Robert E. Lee himself, Thomas J. Jackson is the most revered of all Confederate commanders. A graduate of West Point (1846), he had served in the artillery in the Mexican War, earning two brevets, before resigning to accept a professorship at the Virginia Military Institute. Thought strange by the cadets, he earned "Tom Fool Jackson" and "Old Blue Light" as nicknames. Upon the outbreak of the Civil War he was commissioned a colonel in the Virginia forces and dispatched to Harpers Ferry where he was active in organizing the raw recruits until relieved by Joe Johnston. His later assignments included: commanding 1st Brigade, Army of the Shenandoah (May-July 20, 1861); brigadier general, CSA (June 17, 1861); commanding 1st Brigade, 2nd Corps, Army of the Potomac (July 20-October 1861); major general, CSA (October 7, 1861); commanding Valley District, Department of Northern Virginia (November 4, 1861-June 26, 1862); commanding 2nd Corps, Army of Northern Virginia (June 26, 1862-May 2, 1863); and lieutenant general, CSA (October 10, 1862). Leaving Harpers Ferry, his brigade moved with Johnston to join Beauregard at Manassas. In the fight at 1st Bull Run they were so distinguished that both the brigade and its commander were dubbed "Stonewall" by General Barnard Bee. (However, Bee may have been complaining that Jackson was not coming to his support). The 1st Brigade was the only Confederate brigade to have its nickname become its official designation. That fall Jackson was given command of the Valley with a promotion to major general. That winter he launched a dismal campaign into the western part of the state that resulted in a long feud with General William Loring and caused Jackson to submit his resignation, which he was talked out of. In March he launched an attack on what he thought was a Union rear guard at Kernstown. Faulty intelligence from his cavalry chief, Turner Ashby, led to a defeat. A religious man, Jackson always regretted having fought on a Sunday. But the defeat had the

"Stonewall" Jackson. (NA)

desired result, halting reinforcements being sent to McClellan's army from the Valley. In May Jackson defeated Frémont's advance at McDowell and later that month launched a brilliant campaign that kept several Union commanders in the area off balance. He won victories at Front Royal, 1st Winchester, Cross Keys, and Port Republic. He then joined Lee in the defense of Richmond but displayed a lack of vigor during the Seven Days. Detached from Lee, he swung off to the north to face John Pope's army and after a slipshod battle at Cedar Mountain, slipped behind Pope and captured his Manassas Junction supply base. He then hid along an incomplete branch railroad and awaited Lee and Longstreet. Attacked before they arrived, he held on until Longstreet could launch a devastating attack which brought a second Bull Run victory. In the invasion of Maryland, Jackson was detached to capture Harpers Ferry and was afterwards distinguished at Antietam with Lee. He was promoted after this and given command of the now-official 2nd Corps. It had been known as a wing or command before this. He was disappointed with the victory at Fredericksburg because it could not be followed up. In his greatest day he led his corps around the Union right flank at Chancellorsville and routed the 11th Corps. Reconnoitering that night, he was returning to his own lines when he was mortally wounded by some of his own men. Following the amputation of his arm, he died eight days later. A superb commander, he had several faults. Personnel problems haunted him, as in the feuds with Loring and with Garnett after Kernstown. His choices for promotion were often not first rate. He did not give his subordinates enough latitude,

which denied them the training for higher positions under Lee's loose command style. This was especially devastating in the case of his immediate successor, Richard Ewell. Although he was sometimes balky when in a subordinate position, Jackson was supreme on his own hook. (Henderson, G.F.R., *Stonewall Jackson and the American Civil War*; Vandiver, Frank E., *Mighty Stonewall*; and Chambers, Lenoir, *Stonewall Jackson*)

JACKSON, William Hicks (1835-1903)

Known to his troopers as "Red," Tennessean William H. Jackson became one of the hard-hitting Confederate cavalry division commanders in the West. The West Pointer (1856) had been posted to the Regiment of Mounted Riflemen with which he served until his resignation as a second lieutenant on May 16, 1861. His Confederate assignments included: captain, Artillery (1861); captain, Jackson's Tennessee Heavy Artillery Company (July 1861); captain, Company D, 1st Tennessee Light Artillery (August 12, 1861); colonel, 7th (AKA 1st) Tennessee Cavalry (April 1, 1862); brigadier general, CSA (December 29, 1862); commanding 1st Division, Cavalry Corps, Department of Mississippi and East Louisiana (late 1862-early 1863); commanding Cavalry Division, Department of the West (June 9-July 1863); commanding Cavalry Division, Department of Mississippi and East Louisiana (July-August 1863); commanding division, Lee's Cavalry Corps, Department of Mississippi and East Louisiana (August 1863-January 28, 1864); commanding division, Lee's Cavalry Corps, Department of Alabama, Mississippi and East Louisiana (January 28-May 4, 1864); commanding Cavalry Division, Polk's (Army of Mississippi)-Stewart's Corps, Army of Tennessee (May 4-July 26, 1864); commanding cavalry division, Army of Tennessee (July 26, 1864-ca. February 1865); and commanding division, Forrest's Cavalry Corps, Department of Alabama, Mississippi and East Louisiana (ca. February-May 4, 1865). When his battery could not make it across the Mississippi in time to take part in the fight at Belmont Jackson joined Gideon J. Pillow's staff as a volunteer and was wounded. Upon his recovery he became colonel of a Tennessee mounted regiment. With this unit he took part in Earl Van Dorn's raid on Holly Springs. He was rewarded with promotion to brigadier general and later led a division under Joseph E. Johnston on the fringes of the Vicksburg Campaign. He fought at Jackson and during the Meridian Campaign. Accompanying Leonidas Polk to northern Georgia, he took part in the Atlanta Campaign and then went with Hood on the campaign into middle Tennessee. Joining Forrest's forces, he tried to defend against Wilson's raid through the deep South and was included in Richard Taylor's surrender. Thereafter he engaged in horse breeding and agricultural pursuits.

JACKSON, William Lowther (1825-1890)

In order to prevent confusion with his more famous second cousin, William L. Jackson became known as "Mudwall" Jackson. A lawyer, judge, and former lieutenant governor in his native Virginia, he entered the Confederate army as a private but was soon commissioned as an officer. His assignments included: lieutenant colonel, 31st Virginia (June 1861); colonel, 19th Virginia Cavalry (April 11, 1863); commanding cavalry brigade, Department of Western Virginia and East Tennessee (December 1863-January 1864); commanding cavalry brigade, Department of Western Virginia (January-June 1864); commanding brigade, Ransom's Cavalry Division, Valley District, Department of Northern Virginia (summer 1864); commanding brigade, Lomax's Cavalry Division, Valley District, Department of Northern Virginia (September-October and November-December 1864) and brigadier general, CSA (December 19, 1864). Following service in western Virginia, he joined his cousin's staff as a volunteer aide, seeing action in the Shenandoah Valley, during the Seven Days, and at 2nd Bull Run and Antietam. Raising a mounted regiment he became its colonel and served in Virginia and Tennessee. He participated in the defense of Lynchburg and then went on Jubal A. Early's drive on Washington, fighting at Monocacy. Back in the Valley he fought at 3rd Winchester, Fisher's Hill, and Cedar Creek. Disbanding his command on April 15, 1865, rather than surrender, he ended his military career as a brigadier general and fled to Mexico. Eventually settling in Kentucky, he resumed his practice and was again named to the judicial bench.

JAMES, Frank (1843-1915)

The elder brother of the more famous Western outlaw Jesse James, Frank James received his training in brigandage under the noted Confederate guerrilla William Quantrill. Frank took part in the bloody massacre at Lawrence, Kansas; after the breakup of the gang due to dissension among the leaders he remained loyal to Quantrill and went with him to Kentucky, from James' native Missouri, where Quantrill was killed at the very end of the war. By this time brother Jesse had joined the irregulars, and in 1866 the two Jameses linked up with the four criminal Younger Brothers and continued their violent ways. Robbing banks, fairs, and the hated railroads, they were seen by many as the stuff of legend since they were, in many Southern eyes, still fighting Northern (business) oppression. The Jameses were forced into three years of semi-retirement following the disastrous 1876 Northfield, Minnesota, bank raid. After his brother's murder in 1882—the gang had been reconstituted three years earlier—Frank James turned in his guns at the governor's office and stood trial in both Missouri and Alabama. However, the legend made it impossible to constitute a jury that would convict him. Following his release he was a farmer and held a number of odd jobs, but to many he was always a hero, his ruthlessness ignored.

JAMES, Jesse (1847-1882)

With his older brother, Frank, already a longtime member of the bloody gang of Confederate guerrillas under William C. Quantrill, Jesse James joined the irregulars in 1864, when he was only 17. By this time Quantrill's band had dissolved, and Jesse joined that remnant now under Quantrill's former lieutenant, "Bloody Bill" Anderson. That year they attacked the railroad station at Centralia, Missouri, and killed several unarmed Union soldiers on furlough. They also killed some

Noted outlaw Jesse James, with his brother Frank and two of the Youngers. (LC)

passengers who hid their valuables. When Union troops followed, they were ambushed and slaughtered, with Jesse noted for his brutality. With the death of Anderson, Jesse joined brother Frank in Quantrill's reconstituted gang and resumed pillaging, this time in Kentucky. In 1866, with the war over and Quantrill dead, the Jameses joined the Youngers to continue their depredations. Their robberies of banks and the despised railroads made them heroes to many, who saw them as fighting Northern business aggression. An unfounded legend developed that Jesse was America's Robin Hood. The fact is that he never helped the poor and was nothing more than a brutal bandit. The James-Younger gang operated until the disaster of the 1876 Northfield, Minnesota, bank robbery. With the band decimated the Jameses went into three years of semi-retirement. In 1879 Jesse formed a new gang but three years later he was betrayed and assassinated by one of his new recruits, Bob Ford, on April 3, 1882.

JEMISON, Robert, Jr. (1802-1871)

A long-standing political opponent of William L. Yancey, Robert Jemison, Jr., nonetheless succeeded him in the Confederate Congress and became part of the faction which sought peace. Born in Georgia, he was an Alabama planter and Whig politician before the war. From 1837 to 1863 he served in both houses of the state legislature, with only a few interruptions. Much of the time he was chairman of the Committee on Ways and Means and became an expert in financial and banking matters. He attended the secession convention as the leader of the Unionists and roundly condemned Yancey's call for immediate separation from the Washington government. He replaced the deceased Yancey in the Confederate Senate on December 28, 1863, and served on the Committee on Finance in both the First and Second Congresses. His other assignments included the committees on Claims (First Congress); Naval Affairs (First Congress); and Post Offices & Post Roads (Second Congress). His loyalty came into question with his departing speech in the state senate as he expressed his desire for a just peace settlement. In Richmond he failed to vote for the sacrifices that were necessary for a military victory and favored local defense rather than moves to increase the main field armies. After June 1864 he ceased to attend any sessions and looked after his personal business interests. Retired from politics after the war, he was involved in railroading.

JENKINS, Albert Gallatin (1830-1864)

Accomplished as raiders in their own region, the western Virginia cavalry brigade of Albert G. Jenkins was found to be less than effective when serving as regular cavalry under Lee. A lawyer, Jenkins had been representing his district in the western part of Virginia in the U.S. Congress when the secession crisis came. Resigning his seat he organized a cavalry company with which he gained a reputation as an independent raider. Although made a lieutenant colonel in the 8th Virginia Cavalry

Albert G. Jenkins, loser at Cloyd's Mountain, also lost his life. (NA)

in about January 1862, he had also been elected to the First Confederate Congress and left to take his seat in February. He served only briefly in the legislative body but did serve on the committees on Printing and Territories and Public Lands. Resigning on August 5, he accepted another field appointment. His assignments included: brigadier general, CSA (August 5, 1862); commanding cavalry brigade, Department of Western Virginia (August 1862-spring 1863); commanding brigade, Cavalry Division, Army of Northern Virginia (spring-July 2, 1863); and commanding cavalry brigade, Department of Western Virginia (fall 1863-May 9, 1864). His early activities as a general were in raids in western Virginia and one into Ohio. He was attached to Lee's army during the Gettysburg Campaign and was wounded during the main battle, when many of his men deserted rather than serve away from home. He apparently resumed command in the fall when the brigade was back in its proper department. This is not certain, since the brigade was operating in widely scattered detachments over much of the following months. However, on May 9, 1864, he was the senior officer on the field at Cloyd's Mountain where he was severely wounded in the arm and captured. Following amputation of his arm he died on May 21. (Freeman, Douglas S., *Lee's Lieutenants*)

JENKINS, Micah (1835-1864)

A graduate of the South Carolina Military Academy, Micah Jenkins spent the prewar years affiliated with the King's Mountain Military School. Offering his services to the South, they included: colonel, 5th South Carolina (April 13, 1861); colonel, Palmetto (S.C.) Sharpshooters (April 1862); temporarily commanding R.H. Anderson's Brigade, Longstreet's Division, Department of Northern Virginia (May 5; May 31-June 1; and June 29-July 1, 1862); commanding Anderson's (old) Brigade, Longstreet's Division, 1st Corps, Army of Northern Virginia (July 14-August 1862); brigadier general, CSA (July 22, 1862); commanding brigade, Kemper's Division, same corps and army (August 1862); commanding brigade, Pickett's Division, same corps and army (ca. November 1862-February 25, 1863); commanding brigade, Pickett's Division, in the Department of Virginia and North Carolina (February 25-April 1, 1863) and in the Department of Southern Virginia (April 1-May 1863); commanding brigade, in the Department of North Carolina (May-July 1863) and in Ransom's Division, Department of Richmond (July-September 1863); commanding brigade, Hood's Division, Longstreet's Corps, Army of Tennessee (September 1863); commanding the division (September-November 1863); commanding division, Department of East Tennessee (November 1863-February 1864); commanding brigade, Hood's (old) Division, same department (February-April 12, 1864); and commanding brigade, Field's Division, 1st Corps, Army of Northern Virginia (April 12-May 6, 1864). After leading his regiment at 1st Bull Run he commanded a brigade on a temporary basis at Williamsburg, Seven Pines, and in the latter stages of the Seven Days. Given permanent command of the brigade, he led it and was wounded at 2nd Bull Run. He returned in time for Fredericksburg but was only lightly engaged. After serving with Longstreet in southeastern Virginia, his brigade was detached from its division and remained in the area until it was attached to Hood's Division during the movement to Georgia. Arriving too late for Chickamauga, he directed the division at Wauhatchie and Knoxville, where the division's effectiveness was lessened by the dispute between Jenkins and General Law. Returning to Virginia, he led the brigade in the second day's fighting at the Wilderness until he was mortally wounded, at the same time that Longstreet was hit, by Confederate troops. He died after babbling in his delirium for the troops to move forward. His wound being in the brain he never knew he was hit. (Freeman, Douglas S., *Lee's Lieutenants*)

JETT, Willie (?-?)

When Confederate Captain Willie Jett was on his way home from the war, he and two other ex-Confederate officers met John Wilkes Booth and David Herold at the Port Conway ferry across the Rappahannock River. Told of their identities, he agreed to help them and left Booth at the farm of Richard H. Garrett without informing Garrett that Booth was Lincoln's assassin. Jett then rode on to visit his girl in Bowling Green. Meanwhile, the Union cavalry detachment under Lieutenant Edward P. Doherty found out at the ferry that Booth had crossed with Jett and that Jett would probably head to his girl's house. The cavalry caught Jett in Bowling Green and demanded to know where Booth was. Jett was then taken back to Garrett's and witnessed the scene there as a prisoner. Detective L.B. Baker took charge of him, and Booth's corpse, and rode ahead of the main body. Apparently Jett made good his escape. Unpopular in his home area over his role in the affair, he eventually died in a Maryland mental facility.

JOHNSON, Adam Rankin (1834-1922)

For his ingenious capture of Newburgh, Indiana, on July 18, 1862, Kentuckian Adam R. Johnson won the nickname "Stovepipe." Having settled in Texas in the prewar years, he worked as a surveyor and mail contractor and also engaged in various Indian fights. He started his Civil War career as a scout under Nathan Bedford Forrest, escaping with him from Fort Donelson. He then fought as an irregular in his native state. Capturing the Union town of Newburgh in the summer of 1862 with only 12 men and parts of stovepipes on the running gear of a wagon to resemble a cannon, he was promoted to the colonelcy of a partisan rangers unit. His later assignments included: colonel, 10th Kentucky Partisan Rangers (August 1862); brigadier general, CSA (September 6, 1864, to rank from June 1); and commanding Department of Western Kentucky (September 6-26, 1864). On August 21, 1864, in a fight at Grubbs Crossroads in Kentucky, he was severely wounded. Both of this eyes were totally blinded. He spent the rest of his life in Texas, remaining active in civic affairs despite his disability. He was also at work in historical writing. (Johnson, Adam Rankin, *The Partisan Rangers*)

JOHNSON, Bradley Tyler (1829-1903)

Despite his state remaining in the Union, Maryland lawyer Bradley T. Johnson rose to the rank of Confederate brigadier general and took part in the burning of Chambersburg, Pennsylvania, late in the war. He had backed John C. Breckinridge at both Democratic conventions in 1860 and in the general election. His military assignments included: major, 1st Maryland Battalion (1861); colonel, 1st Maryland (early 1862); commanding J.R. Jones' Brigade, Jackson's Division, Jackson's Corps, Army of Northern Virginia (late August-September 17, 1862); brigadier general, CSA (June 28, 1864); and commanding brigade, Ransom's-Lomax's Cavalry Division, Valley District, Department of Northern Virginia (summer-November 1864). He fought at 1st Bull Run and commanded his regiment in the Shenandoah Valley and during the Seven Days. He led a brigade, as colonel, at 2nd Bull Run and until wounded at Antietam. Promoted to brigadier general in the early summer of 1864, he led a mounted brigade at Monocacy and to the very gates of Washington. He then took part in the ransoming attempt at Chambersburg, in retaliation for the destruction in the Shenandoah Valley, and subsequent burning. Returning to Virginia, he fought against Sheridan at 3rd Winchester, Fisher's Hill, and Cedar Creek. The heavy losses in the Valley cavalry necessitated a consolidation and Johnson became supernumerary in November 1864. Ordered to North Carolina, he commanded the prison at Salisbury for the balance of the conflict. In his later years he resumed his legal practice and sat in the Virginia legislature. He also wrote biographies of George Washington and Joseph E. Johnston. (Freeman, Douglas S., *Lee's Lieutenants*)

JOHNSON, Bushrod Rust (1817-1880)

After spending a lifetime in the military, Ohio-born Bushrod R. Johnson found himself without a command when Lee's army surrendered. A West Pointer (1840) and veteran of the Seminole and Mexican wars, he resigned in 1847 to teach at military schools in Kentucky and Tennessee. Active in the militia, he sided with the South in the secession crisis. His assignments included: colonel and chief engineer, Provisional Army of Tennessee (June 28, 1861); brigadier general, CSA (January 24, 1862); commanding, Fort Donelson, Department #2 (February 7-9, 1862); commanding division, Fort Donelson, Department #2 (February 9-16, 1862); commanding brigade, 2nd Division, 1st Corps, Army of the Mississippi (March-April 6, 1862); commanding 3rd Brigade, Buckner's Division, Left Wing, Army of the Mississippi (ca. September 1862-November 20, 1862); commanding 3rd Brigade, Buckner's Cleburne's Division, Hardee's Corps, Army of Tennessee (November 20, 1862-May 20, 1863); commanding brigade, Stewart's Division, Hardee's-Hill's-Breckenridge's Corps, Army of Tennessee (May 20-November 1863); commanding provisional division (temporarily in September 1863); commanding Buckner's Division, Department of East Tennessee (November 26, 1863-April 1864); commanding brigade (part of the time in Hoke's Division), Department of North Carolina and Southern Virginia (May 1864); major general, CSA (May

21, 1864); commanding division, same department (May-October 19, 1864); and commanding division, Anderson's Corps, Army of Northern Virginia (October 19, 1864-April 8, 1865). He escaped the debacle at Fort Donelson by slipping through enemy lines after the capitulation and was assigned to command a brigade which he led at Shiloh until wounded. He rejoined the army for the Kentucky Campaign, leading his brigade at Pettyville and later at Murfreesboro. At Chickamauga he directed a provisional division and later led Buckner's Division to aid Longstreet in the Knoxville Campaign. Transferred to Virginia in the spring of 1864, he fought at Drewry's Bluff and in the early defense of Petersburg. His new division held a portion of the trenches once Lee's army arrived and it was part of his command that was blown up when Grant set off the mine explosion on July 30. In the retreat to Appomattox his division was badly cut up at Sayler's Creek and two days later he was relieved of duty by Lee. He was still with the army the next day when the surrender came. Johnson returned to the field of education. (Cummings, Charles M., *Yankee Quaker, Confederate General: The Curious Career of Bushrod Rust Johnson*)

JOHNSON, Edward (1816-1873)

Twice captured during 1864, Confederate Major General Edward Johnson finished the Civil War as a prisoner of war. The Virginia-born and Kentucky-raised West Pointer (1838) had been posted to the infantry with which he saw action in the Seminole War, on the frontier, and during the Mexican War. In the latter conflict he won two brevets. Resigning as a captain in the 6th Infantry on June 10, 1861, he joined the Southern forces. His assignments included: colonel, 12th Georgia (June 15, 1861); commanding brigade, 1st Division, Army of the Northwest (November 22-December 1861); brigadier general, CSA (December 13, 1861); commanding Army of the Northwest (spring 1862); major general, CSA (February 28, 1863); commanding division, 2nd Corps, Army of Northern Virginia (May 8, 1863-May 12, 1864); and commanding Hindman's-Anderson's (old) Division, Lee's Corps, Army of Tennessee (September 1-December 16, 1864). Sent into western Virginia, he commanded his regiment under Lee during the Cheat Mountain Campaign, and then a brigade. Taking his army to join Stonewall Jackson, he was severely wounded, as a brigadier general, at McDowell on May 8, 1862. By the time he returned to field duty he was a major general and was placed in command of a division. This he led on Culp's Hill at Gettysburg and during the Bristoe and Mine Run operations. During Grant's Overland Campaign he fought in the Wilderness and then held the angle of the Confederate lines at Spotsylvania. When the line was broken he was taken prisoner along with much of his division. Exchanged in the summer of 1864, he was ordered to the Army of Tennessee and given charge of a division. This he led in the final stages of the defense of Atlanta and then took it into middle Tennessee under Hood. After fighting at Franklin he was captured in the Confederate rout at Nashville. Due to a new exchange policy, whereby release was determined by the date of capture, the requests of

Robert E. Lee to have him exchanged were rejected by the Confederate War Department. Not released until July 1865, "Old Allegheny" became a farmer (Freeman, Douglas S., *Lee's Lieutenants*)

JOHNSON, George W. (1811-1862)

Having been forced to flee Kentucky with the Confederate forces in early 1862, George W. Johnson became the only Civil War governor to die of wounds received in action. A native of the state, he was a lawyer and large-scale planter. A Democrat and former state legislator, he strongly supported John C. Breckinridge for the presidency in 1860 and backed the secession of the state, which never came about. He became the first governor of the provisional Confederate government of the state in 1861 and joined the military forces of Albert Sidney Johnston at Bowling Green where he served as an advisor. After the fall of Forts Henry and Donelson, the Confederates at Bowling Green were forced to withdraw from the state and Johnson went with them. On the first day at Shiloh he was a volunteer aide to General Breckinridge and had his horse shot out from under him. That night he enlisted as private, 1st Kentucky. He fell mortally wounded on the second day and died on April 9. (Clift, G. Glenn, *Governors of Kentucky*)

JOHNSON, Herschel Vespasian (1812-1880)

A Southern Democrat seeking a compromise between the sections, Herschel V. Johnson was the running mate of Stephen A. Douglas in 1860. Reluctantly going with his state, he represented Georgia in the Confederate Senate where he took typical states' rights positions. A native Georgian lawyer, he served his state as a U.S. senator, judge, and governor. His quest for moderation brought him to support the Compromise of 1850 and the Kansas-Nebraska Act. He was deeply troubled by the excessive violence on both sides in the fighting in Kansas. After his defeat for the vice presidency he attended the state secession convention where he tried to achieve unified action on the part of the Southern states rather than individual secession. When Robert A. Toombs refused a senate seat, Johnson was named in his place and was admitted to the First Confederate Congress on January 19, 1863. He won reelection to the Second Congress and served during both congresses on the Committee on Naval Affairs. During the First Congress he also sat on the committees on: Finance; Foreign Affairs; and Post Offices and Post Roads. He favored a heavy income tax but opposed other tax increases and generally failed to make the hard decisions necessary to win the war. He was active in seeking a peaceful settlement and eventually favored reunion if slavery could be guaranteed. After the Confederacy's fall he presided over the state constitutional convention and was elected to the U.S. Senate but was denied admission. He then returned to his practice and was named a judge in 1873. (Flippen, Percy Scott, *Herschel V. Johnson of Georgia*)

JOHNSON, Jonathan Eastman (1824-1906)

An established genre painter, Eastman Johnson traveled widely to observe at first hand the inspiration for his scenes. Born in Maine, he early showed an aptitude for drawing with crayons and soon took an apprenticeship in Boston. A portrait painter early on, he worked in New England and Washington, where he did black and white drawings of famous men in the Capitol itself. He studied for many years in Germany, Italy, France, and the Netherlands. Returning to the United States, he opened a studio in New York in 1858, having in the meantime become a genre painter. He traveled through the South to gain close knowledge of Negro life for his work He also executed several works upon the Civil War. The most famous of these is "The Wounded Drummer Boy" which it is believed that he did from personal observation at Antietam. He was still painting into the next century.

JOHNSON, Robert Ward (1814-1879)

As Arkansas' congressional representative for most of the Civil War, Robert W. Johnson proved to be a strong supporter of the Davis administration except for the fact that he wanted Western troops kept in the Trans-Mississippi Department. Born in Kentucky, he moved to Arkansas where he practiced law and served as a prosecutor. He went to Congress and then became a senator. He did not seek reelection in 1860 and left office at the peak of the secession crisis. Despite his connections with the slave powers he favored compromise and supported the Kansas-Nebraska Act. The election of Lincoln, however, converted him into an immediate secessionist. The state secession convention named him to the Provisional Confederate Congress, and he subsequently won a seat in the Confederate Senate. He took his seat in Montgomery on May 18, 1861, only two days before the decision to move the capital to Richmond. He was given a seat on the Committee on Indian Affairs and in both regular congresses he chaired it. Throughout his service he also sat on the Committee on Military Affairs. His other assignments included the committees on: Accounts (First Congress); Naval Affairs (First Congress); Public Lands (Second Congress); and Rules (Second Congress). He pursued a liberal policy toward the Indians and favored an independent status for the western Confederate states. He proposed that cabinet officers be reconfirmed every two years—a distinct limitation on the executive power. Missing the final session, he wanted to flee to Mexico but instead sought a pardon in Washington, which was granted. He ran a marginal law practice with Albert Pike in Washington after the war and failed in a bid for a U.S. Senate seat. (Thomas, Davis Yancey, *Arkansas in War and Reconstruction, 1861-1874*)

JOHNSON, Waldo Porter (1817-1885)

A friend of Jefferson Davis, Waldo P. Johnson nonetheless became highly critical of two of his cabinet members and a number of Western generals. Born in what is now West Virginia, he established a law practice in Missouri and served as a private in the Mexican War before taking a seat in the state legislature. He later served as a judge and continued his private practice. With the coming of the secession crisis he attended the Washington Peace Conference and was elected as a Democrat to the U.S. Senate. Taking his seat on March 17, 1861, he was expelled from that body on January 10, 1862, for having joined the Confederate army. His military assignments included: major, 1st Missouri Battalion (1861); and lieutenant colonel, 4th Missouri (1861 or early 1862). Twice wounded at the battle of Pea Ridge, he worked to transfer the Missouri troops into Confederate service. With the death of Missouri Senator Robert L.Y. Peyton, the governor named Johnson to fill the unexpired term. He was admitted on December 24, 1863, and was seated on the Committee on Claims in the First Confederate Congress. In the next he also sat on the committees on: Engrossment and Enrollment; Foreign Relations; and Indian Affairs. He favored heavy taxation to fund the war effort but was highly critical of Davis appointments, especially those of cabinet secretaries Benjamin and Memminger and of General Braxton Bragg. He wanted the war switched from Davis' hands to those of Generals Lee, Beauregard, and Joseph E. Johnston. After the Confederacy's collapse he spent a year in Canadian exile before returning to his Missouri practice.

JOHNSON, William A. (?-?)

Since the brigade which William A. Johnson commanded during the spring and summer campaigns of 1864 was not officially sanctioned by the War Department, he was not considered for promotion to brigadier general. His Confederate assignments included: major, 4th (Roddey's) Alabama Cavalry (October 21, 1862); lieutenant colonel, 4th (Roddey's) Alabama Cavalry (April 23, 1863); colonel, 4th (Roddey's) Alabama Cavalry (August 3, 1863); and commanding brigade, Roddey's Cavalry Division, Department of Alabama, Mississippi and East Louisiana (April-September 24, 1864). He served at first in Mississippi and northern Alabama but joined Wheeler's cavalry for the victory at Chickamauga shortly after his promotion to regimental command. Returning to northern Alabama, he was given command of an unofficial brigade in the spring of 1864 when General Roddey decided to divide his brigade into two brigades. Johnson led one to reinforce Forrest's cavalry in Mississippi, seeing action at Brice's Crossroads and Tupelo. Rejoining Roddey, his brigade was merged with the other brigade and Roddey became commander of the District of Northern Alabama on September 24, 1864. Three days later Johnson was wounded at Pulaski, Tennessee, and it is unclear whether he ever rejoined the regiment.

JOHNSTON, Albert Sidney (1803-1862)

At the beginning of the Civil War it was almost universally agreed that the finest soldier, North or South, was Albert Sidney Johnston. But his Civil War career was a definite disappointment to the Confederacy. The Kentucky-born Johnston was appointed to West Point from Louisiana and graduated eighth in the class of 1826. After eight years of service he resigned to care for his terminally ill wife. A failure at farming, he went to Texas and joined the revolutionary forces as a private.

He rose to the forces' chief command as senior brigadier the next year. He served as secretary of war in the Republic of Texas and commanded the 1st Texas Rifles in the Mexican War. Reentering the regular army in 1849 as a major and paymaster, he became colonel, 2nd (old) Cavalry, in 1855. For his services in the 1857 campaign against the Mormons in Utah he was brevetted brigadier general. He resigned his commission on April 10, 1861, but did not quit his post on the West Coast until his successor arrived. Relieved, he began the long trek to Richmond overland. Meeting with Jefferson Davis, he entered Confederate service where his assignments included: general, CSA (August 30, 1861, to date from May 30, 1861); commanding Department #2 (September 15, 1861-April 6, 1862); and in immediate command of the Central Army of Kentucky, Department #2 (October 28-December 5, 1861 and February 23- March 29, 1862). As the second ranking general in the Southern army he was given command of the western theater of operations. Establishing a line of defense in Kentucky from the Mississippi River to the Appalachians, he held it until it was broken at Mill Springs in January and at Forts Henry and Donelson in February 1862. Abandoning Kentucky and most of Tennessee, he fell back into northern Mississippi where he concentrated his previously scattered forces. In early April he moved against Grant's army at Shiloh. In what was basically a surprise attack, he drove the enemy back. While directing frontline operations he was wounded in the leg. Not considering his wound serious, he bled to death. Grant, writing in his memoirs, considered Johnston as having failed to live up to earlier expectations. (Roland, Charles P., *Albert Sidney Johnston: Soldier of Three Republics*)

JOHNSTON, George Doherty (1832-1910)

Alabama lawyer and politician George D. Johnston entered the Confederate army and rose to the rank of brigadier general, serving mostly in the western theater. The North Carolina-born officer's assignments included: second lieutenant, Company G, 4th Alabama (May 7, 1861); major, 25th Alabama (January 1862); lieutenant colonel, 25th Alabama (April 6, 1862); colonel, 25th Alabama (September 14, 1863); brigadier general, CSA (July 26, 1864); commanding Deas' Brigade, Hindman's Division, Lee's Corps, Army of Tennessee (July 26-28, 1864); commanding Quarles' Brigade, Walthall's Division, Stewart's Corps, Army of Tennessee (fall 1864-late March 1865); and commanding the division (late March-ca. April 9, 1865). Commissioned in the Marion Light Infantry, he fought at 1st Bull Run before being promoted to field officer in a new regiment in the West. He succeeded to command of the unit at Shiloh and then served in the Corinth, Murfreesboro, and Tullahoma campaigns. Made colonel a few days before Chickamauga, he led the regiment there and at Chattanooga. During the Atlanta Campaign he received the three wreathed stars of a brigadier general and two days after being given charge of a brigade was wounded at Ezra Church. Returning to duty that fall, he took command of another brigade but did not command it at Franklin. In charge at Nashville, he later fought at Bentonville during the Carolinas Campaign and soon thereafter rose to command the division. When the army was reorganized about April 9, 1865, he became supernumerary and was en route to the Department of Alabama, Mississippi and East Louisiana when the Confederacy collapsed. Resuming his practice, he was also involved in military education and held national appointive office.

JOHNSTON, Joseph Eggleston (1807-1891)

Petty considerations over rank and military etiquette and wounds cost the Confederacy, for lengthy periods, the services of one of its most effective, top commanders, Joseph E. Johnston. The Virginia native and West Pointer (1829), rated by many as more capable than Lee, was the highest-ranking regular army officer to resign and join the Confederacy. With the staff rank of brigadier general, he had been the national army's quartermaster general for almost a year when he quit on April 22, 1861. His earlier career had included eight years in the artillery before he was transferred to the topographical engineers in 1838, when he rejoined the army a year after his resignation. During the Mexican War he won two brevets and was wounded at both Cerro Gordo and Chapultepec. He had also been brevetted for earlier service against the Seminoles in Florida. Having been appointed quartermaster general on June 28, 1860, he remained in the service until after the secession of his native state. His Virginia and Confederate assignments included: major general, Virginia Volunteers (April 1861); brigadier general, CSA (May 14, 1861); commanding Army of the Shenandoah (June 30-July 20, 1861); commanding Army of the Potomac (July 20-October 22, 1861); general, CSA (August 31, 1861, to rank from July 21); commanding Department of Northern Virginia (October 22, 1861-May 31, 1862); commanding Department of the West (December 4, 1862-December 1863); commanding Army of Tennessee (December 27, 1863-July 18, 1864); commanding Army of Tennessee and Department of Tennessee and Georgia (February 25-April 26, 1865); also commanding Department of South Carolina, Georgia and Florida (February 25-April 26, 1865); and also commanding Department of North Carolina (March 16-April 26, 1865). Initially commissioned in the Virginia forces, he relieved Thomas J.—later "Stonewall"—Jackson in command at Harpers Ferry and continued the organization of the Army of the Shenandoah. When the Virginia forces were absorbed into the Confederate army he was reduced to a brigadier generalship. When the Union army under Irvin McDowell moved out of Washington and Alexandria to attack Pierre G.T. Beauregard at Manassas, Johnston managed to totally fool Pennsylvania General Robert Patterson with a small force in the Shenandoah Valley and move the bulk of his forces to Beauregard's support. During the battle of 1st Bull Run, Johnston, although senior to Beauregard, left the general direction of the battle to the junior officer due to a lack of familiarity with the terrain. Johnston was basically engaged in forwarding freshly arrived Valley troops to the threatened sectors. The two generals shared the glory and were critical of supply problems which they felt prevented a march on Washington. The next month Johnston became one of five men advanced to the grade of full general—all Confederate

Joseph E. Johnston, a capable Confederate army commander, was handicapped by his feud with President Davis. (NA)

generals wore the same insignia of rank, three stars in a wreath—but was not pleased with the relative ranking of the five. He felt that since he was the senior officer to leave the "Old" service and join the Confederacy he sould not be ranked behind Samuel Cooper, Albert Sidney Johnston, and Robert E. Lee. Only Beauregard was placed behind Johnston on the list. This led to much bad blood between Johnston and Jefferson Davis. There would be more. With his increased rank, Johnston was given command of the Department of Northern Virginia and became engaged in what was virtually a phony war with the Washington-based army of George B. McClellan. Throughout the winter of 1861-62 he maintained his position at Manassas Junction and then withdrew just as McClellan's superior force advanced. In the meantime he had engaged in a dispute with his president over a policy of brigading troops from the same state together. Johnston argued that a reorganization could not with propriety be carried out in the face of an active enemy. When he withdrew his army from the line of Bull Run he reinforced John B. Magruder on the Peninsula east of Richmond and took command there. With McClellan again facing him, he held Yorktown for a month before pulling back just before his opponent again advanced. His forces fought a rearguard action at Williamsburg and were then encamped on the very outskirts of the new nation's capital. In an effort to drive McClellan off, Johnston launched an attack south of the Chickahominy River at the end of May 1862. The battle of Seven Pines, or Fair Oaks, turned out to be a confusion of errors in the confusing terrain.

For years afterwards there was acrimonious debate among various Confederate generals over who was to blame for the limited success. On the first day of the battle Johnston reexhibited his tendency to attract enemy bullets and was succeeded the next day by Robert E. Lee who was to lead the Army of Northern Virginia for the balance of the war. Upon his recovery he was given charge of a largely supervisory command entitled the Department of the West. He was in charge of Braxton Bragg's Army of Tennessee and John C. Pemberton's Department of Mississippi and East Louisiana. With few troops under his immediate command he proved powerless in attempting to relieve the besieged garrison of Vicksburg under Pemberton. Following the river city's fall, he made a feeble attempt to hold Jackson, Mississippi, against the advance of William T. Sherman. Following Bragg's disastrous defeat at Chattanooga, Johnston was given immediate command of his army and the next spring and summer directed a masterful delaying campaign against Sherman during his advance on Atlanta. However, his continued withdrawals raised the ire of Jefferson Davis, and he was relieved in front of the city. His successor, John B. Hood, then began his destruction of the Army of Tennessee with reckless tactics. With Sherman having marched clear through Georgia and begun his drive through the Carolinas, a clamor arose in the Confederate Congress for Johnston's resumption of command. Davis finally relented in early 1865 and the general took eventual command of three departments. Unfortunately for the Confederacy his forces were heavy on generals but weak on men. He could do little but hope for a linkup with Lee's army so that they could turn on either Grant or Sherman and then on the other. It never came off and he surrendered his forces following some difficulties over terms, bordering on the political, on April 26, 1865, at the Bennett House near Durham Station, North Carolina. He had been one of the most effective Confederate commanders when he was not hampered by directives from the president. Following the war he sat in Congress and was a federal railroad commissioner. Engaged in much debate over the causes of the Confederate defeat, he wrote his *Narrative of Military Operations* which was highly critical of Davis and many of his fellow generals. In an example of the civil relationships between former wartime opponents, Johnston died of a cold caught while attending the funeral of his arch-opponent, Sherman. (Govan, Gilbert E. and Livingood, James W., *A Different Valor: The Story of General Joseph E. Johnston*)

JOHNSTON, Robert Daniel (1837-1919)

A North Carolina lawyer with some militia experience, Robert D. Johnston entered Confederate service early in the war and rose to be a brigadier. His assignments included: captain, Company K, 23rd North Carolina (July 15, 1861); lieutenant colonel, 23rd North Carolina (April 16, 1862); brigadier general, CSA (September 1, 1863); commanding Iverson's (old) Brigade, Rodes' Division, 2nd Corps, Army of Northern Virginia (September 8, 1863-May 8, 1864); commanding same brigade, Early's Division, same corps and army (May 8-12, 1864); commanding brigade, Ramseur's-Pegram's Division,

Valley District, Department of Northern Virginia (August-December 1864); commanding brigade, Pegram's Division, 2nd Corps, Army of Northern Virginia (December 1864-February 1865); and commanding the division (February-March 1865). He saw action at Williamsburg and succeeded to command of the regiment at Seven Pines where he was wounded. He returned to duty in time to fight at South Mountain and Antietam and at Chancellorsville he was placed in command of the 12th North Carolina when that unit had lost all of its field officers. Back with his own regiment he was again wounded at Gettysburg but recovered to accept promotion and charge of the brigade. He fought at the Wilderness and, in a different division, at Spotsylvania, suffering a third wound. Returning to duty in August he served through Early's Valley Campaign, fighting at 3rd Winchester, Fisher's Hill, and Cedar Creek before moving to the Petersburg trenches. After briefly leading the division, he was detached to round up deserters. With the war ending while he was on this duty, he resumed his law practice in his native state and later became a banker in Alabama. (Freeman, Douglas S., *Lee's Lieutenants*)

JOHNSTON, William Preston (1831-1899)

The son of General Albert Sidney Johnston, William Preston Johnston became one of the leading participants in the controversy over the battle of Shiloh. A Louisville lawyer, he had some military training at the Western Military Institute. His Confederate assignments included: major, 2nd Kentucky (early 1861); lieutenant colonel, 1st Kentucky (ca. July 3, 1861); and colonel and aide-de-camp to Jefferson Davis (May 1862). He saw action at Dranesville with the second unit and upon its muster-out in the spring of 1862, he joined the president's staff. After being present at Seven Pines, he was sent to Mississippi to report upon the situation in the western theater where his father had lost Kentucky and most of Tennessee and, at Shiloh, his life. The younger Johnston reported that the Confederates had been on the verge of victory when his father had been mortally wounded and his successor, General Beauregard, had muffed the opportunity. This lost opportunity thesis was further stated in his *The Life of Albert Sidney Johnston*, published in 1878, and in an article for the *Century Magazine*. Continuing on Davis' staff, Johnston saw action in the vicinity of Richmond whenever it was threatened. Fleeing with his chief, he was captured in Georgia and jailed. He resided in Canada briefly after regaining his liberty and then became a professor and university president. (Shaw, Arthur Marvin, *William Preston Johnston: A Transitional Figure of the Confederacy*)

JOMINI, Baron Antoine Henri (1779-1869)

On both sides of the Atlantic in the mid-1800s the works on the theory of war by Baron Antoine H. Jomini were considered the leading authorities in the field. His principal work was published in French and translated as *Summary of the Art of War*. The historian and theorist of the Napoleonic Wars was challenged in his preeminence in Europe by the German General Karl von Clausewitz and his *Vom Kriege* (*On War*). But on the other side of the ocean there was no English-language version available before the Civil War and Clausewitz had little impact on the combatants. Jomini however was read by many of the cadets at West Point. It is interesting to note that Grant claimed never to have read anything by him.

JONES, Arnold Elzey

See: *Elzey, Arnold*

JONES, Catesby ap Roger (1821-1877)

Having supervised the armament of the CSS *Virginia*—the armored version of the USS *Merrimac*—former U.S. naval officer Catesby ap R. Jones commanded her in the historic encounter with the USS *Monitor*. The Virginia native had entered the U.S. Navy in 1836 as a midshipman and was a passed midshipman during the Mexican War, during which he was assigned to the Pacific Squadron but did not see any action. Promoted to lieutenant in 1849, he served with John A. Dahlgren on ordnance projects during the 1850s. Resigning in 1861, his Confederate assignments included: captain, Virginia Navy (1861); lieutenant, CSN (1861); executive officer, CSS *Virginia* (March 1862); commanding CSS *Virginia* (March 8-9, 1862); commanding CSS *Chattahoochie* (1862); and commander, CSN (1863). After aiding in the construction of the revolutionary vessel, he was its second in command when it sailed out into Hampton Roads to engage the wooden Union fleet. On March 8, 1862, it put two Union warships out of action and was threatening a third. Meanwhile the ship's skipper, Franklin Buchanan, was wounded and Jones took over. The next day the *Monitor* appeared and the first battle between iron-clad vessels was under way. Although a draw, Jones withdrew and the *Virginia* rarely ventured out of its port again. Jones later commanded another vessel and then directed the naval foundry and ordnance works at Selma, Alabama. Promoted to commander in 1863, he appears to have left the service in the first six months of 1864. Engaged in business in the postwar years, he died in a quarrel with one J.S. Harral who shot him dead.

JONES, David Rumph (1825-1863)

It was heart disease and not enemy action that deprived the Confederacy of a capable, but not brilliant, division leader, David R. Jones. The South Carolinian was a West Pointer (1846) and Mexican War veteran when he resigned as a brevet staff captain on February 15, 1861, to serve the South. His assignments included: major, CSA (early 1861); brigadier general, CSA (June 17, 1861); commanding 3rd Brigade (in 1st Corps after July 20), Army of the Potomac (June 20-October 22, 1861); commanding a different brigade, Longstreet's Division, Potomac District, Department of Northern Virginia (October 22, 1861-February 17, 1862); commanding S. Jones' (old) Brigade, G.W. Smith's Division, in Potomac District until March), Department of Northern Virginia (February 17-April 1862); major general, CSA (April 5, to rank from March 10, 1862); commanding division, Magruder's Command, same department (April-July 3, 1862); and commanding division, 1st Corps, Army of Northern Virginia (July 3-October 1862).

After serving as Beauregard's chief of staff during the bombardment of Fort Sumter he was given command of a Virginia brigade which he led at 1st Bull Run. He then commanded a South Carolina and later a Georgia brigade before leading a division on the Peninsula. There he fought in the Seven Days. In the 2nd Bull Run campaign he distinguished himself when Longstreet forced his way through Thoroughfare Gap in order to join Jackson. He saw further action at 2nd Bull Run and played a key role guarding a gap in South Mountain. He resisted Burnside's attack on the Confederate right at Antietam and joined A.P. Hill in driving the enemy back. Shortly afterwards heart trouble forced him to give up his command. He died the following January 15. (Freeman, Douglas S., *Lee's Lieutenants*)

JONES, George Washington (1806-1884)

As the chairman of the Committee on Rules and Officers of the House in the First Regular Confederate Congress, George W. Jones was one of Tennessee's top states' righters in the congressional delegation. A native of Virginia he had worked as a saddler, justice of the peace, state legislator, and court clerk before the Civil War. Named to the Washington Peace Conference in 1861, he failed to attend and worked instead for the secession of his adopted Tennessee. In November 1861 he was elected to represent the 7th District in the Confederate Congress, where he also served on the Committee on Ways and Means. He worked to keep the control of the army in the hands of the states, granting the president only the right to select his own cabinet officers and direct foreign policy. He did not seek reelecton to his seat and in 1870 attended the state constitutional convention.

JONES, Hilary Pollard (1833-1913)

Opinion upon the military merits of artillerist Hilary P. Jones was divided when he received a promotion over the strenuous objections of Stonewall Jackson and his artillery chief, Stapleton Crutchfield. A teacher at the outbreak of the war, he entered the Confederate army, where his assignments included: lieutenant, Morris (Va.) Artillery (August 1861); captain, Morris (Va.) Artillery (February 1862); major, Artillery (May 28, 1862); commanding battalion, Reserve Artillery, Army of Northern Virginia (June 1862-fall 1862); commanding Artillery Battalion, D.H. Hill's Division, 2nd Corps, Army of Northern Virginia (fall 1862-January 1863); commanding Artillery Battalion, Jackson's (old) Division, 2nd Corps, Army of Northern Virginia (January-June 2, 1863); lieutenant colonel, Artillery (March 2, 1863); commanding Artillery Battalion, Early's Division, 2nd Corps, Army of Northern Virginia (June 2-July 1863); commanding artillery battalion, 2nd Corps, Army of Northern Virginia (July 1863-March 19, 1864); colonel, Artillery (February 27, 1864); commanding artillery battalion, 1st Corps, Army of Northern Virginia (March 19-early May 1864); commanding Artillery, Department of North Carolina and Southern Virginia (early May-October 1864); and commanding Artillery, Anderson's Corps, Army of Northern Virginia (October 1864-April 9, 1865). As a battalion com-

mander, he saw service at the Seven Days, Antietam, and Fredericksburg. Before Chancellorsville he was promoted upon the recommendation of the army's chief artillerist, General William Pendleton, despite the objections of the corps commander and chief of artillery. He then fought at Chancellorsville, 2nd Winchester, where he distinguished himself, and Gettysburg before being transferred to the Petersburg area. As Beauregard's chief of artillery he directed operations at Drewry's Bluff and the initial attacks on Petersburg. When Beauregard's command was absorbed into the Army of Northern Virginia, he directed the guns of the new corps. In this capacity he served throughout the rest of the siege and in the retreat to Appomattox where he was surrendered. He resumed his role as an educator after the war. (Wise, Jennings C., *The Long Arm of Lee*)

JONES, John Beauchamp (1810-1866)

Athough he served for a time in the Local Defense Troops, units composed of government and other vital workers in Richmond who were only called out when the city was seriously threatened, Baltimore-born John Jones is better known for his diary chronicling the homefront and military affairs as he viewed them from the Confederate capital. Having previously worked as an editor for the *Southern Monitor*, a proslavery Philadelphia weekly, Jones offered his services to the new government early in 1861 and was given a clerkship in the rebel War Department. Serving under all six Secretaries of War, Jones was well placed, in his passport office, to gain intimate knowledge of the military and civil affairs of the Confederacy. His diary is full of the ups and downs of the Southern Peoples' hopes, the spiraling inflation and profiteering that wreaked havoc on the homefront. Jones recounts the bread riots of 1863 and the repeated scares of enemy raids, and provides evaluations of military and civil leaders. While his diary was going to press in early 1866, Jones died. (Jones, John B., *A Rebel War Clerk's Diary*)

JONES, John Marshall (1820-1864)

On May 21, 1863, there occurred in the Army of Northern Virginia one of the most confusing command changes in Confederate history. John M. Jones was assigned to the command of a brigade which up until a couple of weeks earlier had been directed by General John Robert Jones. John M. was a graduate of West Point (1841) and had resigned his commission as captain, 7th Infantry, on May 27, 1861, in order to offer his services to his native Virginia. His assignments included: captain, CSA (spring 1861); lieutenant colonel, CSA (ca. September 1861); brigadier general, CSA (from May 15, 1863); and commanding brigade, Trimble's-Johnson's Division, 2nd Corps, Army of Northern Virginia (May 21-July 2, 1863 and August 1863-May 5, 1864). From September 1861 he served as adjutant general, and sometimes also as inspector general, for Generals Ewell and Early. In this capacity he saw action at Front Royal, Winchester, Cross Keys, Port Republic, the Seven Days, Cedar Mountain, 2nd Bull Run, Fredericksburg, and Chancellorsville. Promoted to brigadier, he took over the brigade formerly belonging to John R. Jones whose courage had become a matter of question. In the assault on Culp's Hill on the evening of the second day at Gettysburg, he was severely wounded. He returned to command for the Bristoe and Mine Run campaigns. He was wounded in the head in a skirmish in the latter campaign but returned to duty within a few days. Then, on the first day of battle at the Wilderness, he was killed while trying to rally his brigade in the face of a Union onslaught. (Freeman, Douglas S., *Lee's Lieutenants*)

JONES, John Robert (1827-1901)

Stonewall Jackson had a tendency to name new generals for brigades from outside the units which they were to direct. This policy led to much friction in the officer corps; often, as in the case of John R. Jones, Jackson's choices were not top-notch. A native Virginian and graduate of the Virginia Military Institute, Jones had been active in military affairs in Florida and Maryland before returning to the Shenandoah Valley where he raised the Rockingham Confederates at the outbreak of the Civil War. His unit was assigned to what became the Stonewall Brigade and his assignments included: captain, Company I, 33rd Virginia (July 1861); lieutenant colonel, 33rd Virginia (early 1862); brigadier general, CSA (June 23, 1863); commanding 2nd Brigade, Jackson's (old) Division, Jackson's Corps, Army of Northern Virginia (ca. June 27-July 1, 1862 and December 12, 1862-May 2, 1863); and commanding the division (September 7-17 and September 18-December 12, 1862). He served at 1st Bull Run and in the Shenandoah Valley before being tapped to command the 2nd Brigade. His appointment led to the resignation of a former brigade commander, Colonel John A. Campbell. Joining the command during the Seven Days, he led it at White Oak Swamp and Malvern Hill, where he was wounded. Rejoining the army in Maryland he took command of Jackson's (old) Division for the operations against Harpers Ferry. At Antietam he was stunned, although not hit by, a bursting shell and forced to relinquish command. Sent to the Valley to gather stragglers, he resumed command of the division until the day before Fredericksburg. He was praised by his superiors for the manner in which he handled his brigade there, but charges of cowardice were also leveled at him by subordinates. He apparently sheltered himself behind a tree. In his next action, Chancellorsville, he left the field complaining of an ulcerated leg. Never allowed to resume command, he also had the humiliation of not receiving confirmation of his appointment. Seized by Union troops in Tennessee on July 4, 1863, he was imprisoned for the duration with no desire on the part of the Richmond authorities to effect his exchange. After his release he was a businessman and minor office holder in Harrisonburg, Virginia. (Freeman, Douglas S., *Lee's Lieutenants*)

JONES, Joseph (1833-1896)

A medical professor before the Civil War, Joseph Jones served in the latter part of the war as a surgeon at the Andersonville prisoner of war compound in his native Georgia. He received his training in South Carolina, New Jersey, and Pennsylvania. He was a professor of medicine at several Georgia colleges when in 1861 he joined the Confederate army as a surgeon. In 1864 he was assigned to Andersonville and out of necessity became a specialist in the treatment of gangrene. Despite his training and efforts the high mortality rate continued at the camp. Moving to New Orleans after the war, he was again involved in education and was active in historical circles, writing his three-volume *Medical and Surgical Memoirs*.

JONES, Robert McDonald (1808-1872)

A Choctaw Indian and large plantation owner—with an estimated 500 slaves—Robert M. Jones was for economic reasons very inclined to the Confederacy. He was the principal negotiator for his tribe in its dealings with Albert Pike, the Confederate Indian commissioner. He signed the treaty of alliance and was named as the non-voting representative of both his own tribe and the Chickasaws in the Confederate Congress. He was admitted on January 17, 1863, but held no committee assignments. When his term expired he was supposed to have made way for a representative from the Chickasaws, but they had already returned to their allegiance with the Union. So Jones continued in office for a second term. Before his admission to Congress he had raised a battalion of Choctaws for Confederate service at his own expense. He represented the tribe in negotiations in Washington after the Confederacy's collapse. He then returned to his devastated plantation.

JONES, Samuel (1819-1887)

West Pointer (1841) and veteran of two decades in the artillery, Samuel Jones served the Confederacy in most of the major theaters. He resigned his commission as captain on April 27, 1861, to change his allegiance. His assignments included: colonel, Artillery (early 1861); brigadier general, CSA (July 21, 1861); commanding brigade, 2nd Corps, Army of the Potomac (summer-fall 1861); commanding brigade, G.W. Smith's Division, Potomac District, Department of Northern Virginia (October 22, 1861-January 10, 1862); commanding Army of Pensacola, Department of Alabama and West Florida (January 27-March 3, 1862); commanding the department (March 3-24 and April 2-28, 1862); major general, CSA (March 10, 1862); commanding 1st Division, Army of the West, Department #2 (May-June 1862); commanding Hindman's (old) Division, 2nd Corps, Army of the Mississippi, Department #2 (June 1862); commanding the corps (June-July 1862); commanding District of Middle Tennessee, Department #2 (September 27-November 4, 1862); commanding Department of Western Virginia (December 10, 1862-March 5, 1864); commanding Department of South Carolina, Georgia and Florida (April 20-October 5, 1864); commanding District of South Carolina (also called a division), same department (October 17-December 1864); and commanding District of Florida, same department (February 2-May 1865). After serving as Beauregard's chief artillerist at 1st Bull Run and commanding a brigade in northern Virginia he was assigned to the Gulf coast. He next served in northern Mississippi and middle Tennessee before being assigned to command in western Virginia. Here he guarded supply sources and lines and quibbled with Lee over certain regiments and to whom they belonged. Sent to the southern coast, he apparently initiated the keeping of prisoners within the range of the guns bombarding Charleston. This led to a series of retaliations to no purpose. He finished the war in Florida. After the war he was a farmer and government clerk. (Jones, Samuel, *The Siege of Charleston*)

JONES, Thomas (ca. 1821-1895)

At the behest of his foster brother, Samuel Cox, Jr., Thomas Jones provided the boat that ferried John Wilkes Booth and David Herold across the Potomac River in their flight from Washington. During the Civil War, being of Southern leanings, he had been in charge of a signal station along the river which reported the movements of federal shipping. He was introduced to Booth in a thicket near his foster brother's home and agreed to help. His first assignments were in gathering information on the public reaction to the assassination. In addition to bringing back newspapers he gathered local opinion. He himself believed the assassination to have been a great act, but later felt that it had badly hurt the South. Never prosecuted for his role in the escape, he did however lose his subsequent job in the Washington Navy Yard for political reasons.

JONES, William Edmondson (1824-1864)

Former regular army officer William E. "Grumble" Jones lived up to his nickname in his feud with his superior, Jeb Stuart, and the latter had the subordinate court-martialed for disrespect. A West Pointer (1848), Jones had served almost a decade in the mounted riflemen until he resigned to manage his estate in southwestern Virginia. His Confederate assignments included: captain, Washington Mounted Rifles (spring 1861); major, Virginia Volunteers (May 1861); colonel, 1st Virginia Cavalry (September 24, 1861); colonel, 7th Virginia Cavalry (ca. June 1862); brigadier general, CSA (September 19, 1862); commanding Laurel Brigade, Cavalry Division, Army of Northern Virginia (November 8, 1862-September 9, 1863 but detached in the Valley District fall 1862-spring 1863); also commanding Valley District, Department of Northern Virginia (December 29, 1862-May 1863); commanding brigade, Hampton's Division, Cavalry Corps, Army of Northern Virginia (September 9-October 9, 1863); commanding cavalry brigade, Ransom's Division, Department of Western Virginia (October 1863-February 1864 but detached with Longstreet in East Tennessee in November and December); commanding brigade, Cavalry, Department of East Tennessee (February-March and April-May 1864); commanding division, Cavalry Corps, same department (March-April 1864); commanding cavalry brigade, Department of Western Virginia (May 1864 and June 1-5, 1864); and temporarily commanding the department (May 25-31, 1864). After serving in western Virginia, he succeeded Jeb Stuart in command of the 1st Virginia Cavalry, but his strict old army discipline cost him his chance of reelection at the spring 1862 reorganization. However, he was soon given charge of a portion of Ashby's cavalry and fought at Cedar Mountain and 2nd Bull

Run. Promoted to brigadier, he led the Laurel Brigade in the Valley and on a raid to Beverly in western Virginia. He joined Lee's army for the Gettysburg Campaign but did not shine. His feud with Stuart coming to the fore, he was deprived of his command and sent to southwestern Virginia to organize cavalry. He directed a brigade there and in the Knoxville Campaign. After a brief stint in departmental command he was in overall command in the fighting at Piedmont on June 5, 1864, and was killed. (Freeman, Douglas S., *Lee's Lieutenants* and McDonald, William N., *A History of the Laurel Brigade*)

JORDAN, Thomas (1819-1895)

Although a Confederate brigadier, Thomas Jordan rarely commanded troops in the field. An 1840 graduate of West Point, where he had roomed with William Sherman, he served in the infantry and as a quartermaster until he resigned his captaincy on May 21, 1861. His assignments for the Confederacy included: colonel and assistant adjutant general (early 1861); brigadier general, CSA (April 14, 1862); and commanding 3rd Military District of South Carolina, Department of South Carolina, Georgia and Florida (May 1864). On the staff of Beauregard, the Virginian served at 1st Bull Run, Shiloh, and in the Corinth siege. In the summer of 1862 he was on Bragg's staff but soon rejoined his old chief on the Southern coast. Here he participated in the defense of Charleston. He briefly commanded a district in May 1864 but mostly performed vital staff work. However, his connection with Beauregard did not make him a favorite of the president and his circle. When Richmond was threatened late in September 1864, he tendered his services as he was temporarily in the city, but the offer went unanswered. For a time he edited the *Memphis Appeal* after the war and in 1869 joined the revolutionaries in Cuba. With the revolt's collapse he returned to the United States and resumed writing. Several of his articles appear in *Battles and Leaders*.

JUAREZ, Benito (1806-1872)

In 1861, at the outbreak of the American Civil War, the president of Mexico, Benito Juarez, announced a two-year moratorium on the payment of Mexico's national debt. This prompted a joint military operation by the British, Spanish, and French. After her allies had departed, France maintained a presence and eventually forced Juarez out and placed Archduke Maximilian of Austria on an imperial throne. Juarez, the former president, became the leader of the republican revolutionary forces and received aid from the United States, which feared possible French intervention on behalf of the Confederacy. Juarez in return prohibited trade with the South. After the Civil War in the United States, the French withdrew their troops and Maximilian soon fell, being executed in 1867. Juarez again became president and held office until his death.

JUMPER, John (?-?)

A pure-blood Seminole, John Jumper was a chief of the old treaty faction of the tribe, part of the Five Civilized Tribes, dating back to the removal west of the Mississippi River. Having adopted many of the white Southerner's ways, he urged many of his fellow tribesmen to agree to the treaty with the Confederacy being negotiated by Albert Pike. When a sizeable portion of the nation agreed, Jumper organized the 1st Seminole Battalion on September 21, 1861, and became first its major and later its lieutenant colonel. In 1864 the battalion was increased to a regiment with Jumper as colonel. In November and December 1861, Jumper and his men took part in the pursuit of Opothleyohola of the Upper Creeks who was leading his people and some non-Confederate Cherokees and Seminoles to Kansas and Union protection. The remainder of his Civil War service was in the Indian Territory and along the borders of Kansas, Missouri, and Arkansas. (Monoghan, Jay, *Civil War on the Western Border, 1854-1865*)

K

KEAN, Robert Garlick Hill (1828-1898)

For the final three years of the Confederacy's life Virginia lawyer Robert G.H. Kean served as the head of the War Department's Bureau of War. A longtime backer of states' rights, he became an early believer in secession and, when the Civil War came, promptly enlisted. When his father-in-law George W. Randolph was promoted to brigadier general, Kean joined his staff as assistant adjutant general. He then followed his relative into the War Department and succeeded Albert T. Bledsoe in the Bureau of War. Holding the post until the fall of the would-be nation, he served under several secretaries of war and then returned to his practice. (Younger, Edward, ed., *Inside the Confederate Government: The Diary of Robert Garlick Hill Kean*)

KEENE, John (?-1865)

A resident of Memphis at the outbreak of the Civil War, John Keene was a criminal wanted by both sides, but it was a miners' court which finally got him. Enlisting in the Confederate navy, he fled after striking his captain on the head with a marlinespike. On his way back to Memphis, he killed one or two men. Back in Union-controlled Memphis, he was safe from Confederate authorities, but he soon got on the wrong side of the occupation forces by killing another man. Under the name Bob Black, he headed a band of cutthroats who pillaged the countryside and kept troops busy hunting them. Caught and confined, he made good his escape and became a fence in St. Paul, Minnesota. When the heat got too much for him he headed to Utah but soon had to flee to Montana where his association with the Innocents bandit gang earned him a notice to leave or face lynching. Instead, he shot a sleeping enemy. Within an hour of his sentencing by the miners he was swinging from a nearby tree.

KEENE, Laura (1826-1873)

Under the stage-name of Laura Keene an English actress really had only one connection with the Civil War: She starred in the show which lured Abraham Lincoln to the scene of his murder. She had made her American debut in 1852 and was a pioneer as a woman manager until 1863. It was one of her more popular performances as the female lead in *Our American Cousin* which had drawn the president to Ford's Theater in April 1865. Her career was already in decline but she continued to work as a playwright, editor, actor, and lecturer until her sudden death, said to have been from overwork. (Creahan, John, *The Life of Laura Keene*)

KEITT, Lawrence Massillon (1824-1864)

A longtime supporter of states' rights, even to the extent of South Carolina seceding alone, Lawrence Keitt had served in the U.S. House of Representatives until the South Carolina Secession convention, of which he was a member, voted the state out of the Union. During the first year of the new nation he was a member of the Confederate Provisional Congress, serving on the Foreign Affairs, Indian Affairs and Rules committees. In this body he was a frequent critic of Jefferson Davis and is said to have despised him; he supported Howell Cobb for the presidency. He was also instrumental in the drafting of the Confederate Constitution. He favored an early attack on Fort Sumter. With the Provisional Congress coming to an end, Keitt was elected colonel, 20th South Carolina, on January 11, 1862. With this unit he served on the South Carolina coast, mostly in Charleston Harbor, until ordered to Virginia in mid-May 1864. Arriving on the South Anna River, the 20th was assigned to Kershaw's (old) Brigade, Kershaw's Division, First Corps, Army of Northern Virginia, about May 28. With Kershaw commanding the division, Keitt was the senior officer present in the brigade, the other regiments having suffered heavily in three years of arduous service. Four days later the inexperienced combat officer led the brigade in the battle of Cold Harbor. Kershaw's (old) Brigade, Kershaw's Division, 1st Corps, Army of Northern Virginia, about May 28. With Kershaw commanding the division, Keitt was the senior officer present in the brigade, the other regiments having suffered heavily in three years of arduous service. Four days later the inexperienced combat officer led the brigade in the battle of Cold Harbor. Kershaw's and Hoke's divisions were to make a major attack but Keitt, needlessly mounted, failed to keep his command in order and the entire effort collapsed. In trying to rally his regiment before the confusion spread to other units, Keitt fell mortally wounded. (Dickert, D. Augustus, *History of Kershaw's Brigade*)

KELL, John McIntosh (1823-1900)

A veteran of 17 years in the old navy, John M. Kell joined the Southern navy and served mostly under Raphael Semmes on commerce raiders. The Georgia-born graduate of Annapolis had served in the Mexican War and sailed to Paraguay and Japan. He resigned his lieutenant's commission at the outbreak of the war, and his Confederate assignments included: lieutenant, CSN (early 1861); executive officer, CSS *Sumter* (April 18, 1861-early 1862); executive officer, CSS *Alabama* (August 24, 1862-1864); commanding CSS *Richmond* (early 1864); and commander, CSN (1864). He took part in the famous cruises of the *Sumter* and *Alabama* as a first lieutenant and then was placed in charge of the ironclad *Richmond* in the James River. In this latter capacity he took part in the operations near Drewry's Bluff. After the fall of the Confederacy he took up farming in his native state. In the year of his death he published his memoirs, *Recollections of a Naval Life*, one of the prime sources of information on Confederate commerce raiders. (Delaney, Norman C., *John McIntosh Kell of the Raider* Alabama)

KEMPER, James Lawson (1823-1895)

A Virginia lawyer with a meager experience in military matters, gained as a regimental quartermaster and an assistant quartermaster of volunteers in the Mexican War, James L. Kemper had served as chairman of the military affairs committee in the Virginia legislature before the Civil War. When he entered the Confederate army his assignments included: colonel, 7th Virginia (May 2, 1861); commanding A.P. Hill's (old) Brigade, Longstreet's Division (in the 1st Corps from June 29), Army of Northern Virginia (May 27-July 1862); brigadier general, CSA (June 3, 1862); commanding division, 1st Corps, same army (August-September 1862); commanding brigade, Jones' Division, same corps and army (September-October 1862); commanding brigade, Pickett's Division, in 1st Corps, Army of Northern Virginia (October 1862-February 25 and May-July 3, 1863), in the Department of Virginia and North Carolina (February 25-April 1, 1863), and in the Department of Southern Virginia (April 1-May 1863); and major general, CSA (September 19, 1864). After fighting at 1st Bull Run, Yorktown, and Williamsburg, he took over Hill's former command. He fought through the Seven Days Battles and then commanded a temporary division, formed from half of Longstreet's old command, at 2nd Bull Run. This force was merged into Jones' Division before Antietam and later became part of Pickett's Divison. Lightly engaged at Fredericksburg, he participated in the southeastern Virginia campaign under

James L. Kemper, a survivor of Pickett's Charge. (NA)

Longstreet. At Gettysburg he was severely wounded and captured in Pickett's Charge. Exchanged in September 1863, he returned to duty in May 1864 and was assigned to organize the reserve forces of Virginia. He finished the war in this post and resumed his legal and political careers, becoming governor in 1874. (Freeman, Douglas S., *Lee's Lieutenants*)

KENEALY, Jim (?-?)

At the head of his band of counterfeiters, Big Jim Kenealy devised a plan in 1876 to steal the body of the martyred president, Abraham Lincoln. Once the casket was in their possession, they would contact the authorities with a ransom demand. When they got their money they would unearth the coffin from its hiding place and return it. They never got that far. Their group had been infiltrated by a Secret Service informer working on counterfeiting matters, and the Secret Service was notified. Agents arrived just as the plotters were about to remove the casket. Fleeing, they were all caught within 10 days. Big Jim then informed the authorities that there was no law against stealing a corpse, no matter whose it was. The prosecutors knew he was right but countered by charging them with the attempted theft of the casket. Each got the maximum sentence of one year for their plot. This event and several other similar attempts resulted in the casket being moved from one hiding place to another 17 times from 1865-1901.

KENNEDY, John Doby (1840-1896)

Despite being wounded six times and struck by 15 spent balls,

John D. Kennedy managed to survive the Civil War. A young lawyer at the outbreak of hostilities, the South Carolina native entered the Confederate army where his assignments included: captain, Company E, 2nd South Carolina (January 8, 1861); colonel, 2nd South Carolina (May 13, 1862); commanding Kershaw's (old) Brigade, Kershaw's Division, 1st Corps, Army of Northern Virginia (October 1864-January 3, 1865); commanding same brigade, McLaws' Division, Department of South Carolina, Georgia and Florida (January-April 9, 1865); and commanding same brigade, Walthall's Division, Stewart's Corps, Army of Tennessee (April 9-26, 1865). After witnessing the bombardment of Fort Sumter from Morris Island, he went with his company, the Camden Volunteers, to Virginia. There he took part in the fights at 1st Bull Run, Yorktown, Seven Pines, and the Seven Days. After the battle of Savage Station in the latter he was incapacitated. Returning to duty, he was wounded at Antietam but recovered to fight at Fredericksburg and Chancellorsville. He was also wounded at Gettysburg, on the second day, and at Knoxville. Returning to Virginia, he fought at Petersburg and was present during a portion of the Shenandoah Valley Campaign under Early. In early January 1865 the brigade, which he had been commanding since October, for which he received promotion to brigadier in December, was ordered to the Carolinas to help stop Sherman. He fought at Bentonville and was surrendered with Johnston's army. A lawyer and state legislator after the war, he also served as consul general in Shanghai. (Dickert, D. Augustus, *History of Kershaw's Brigade*)

KENNEDY, Robert Cobb (1835-1865)

For his role in the attempt to burn New York City on November 25, 1864, Robert C. Kennedy paid with his life. Born in Georgia, he was raised in Alabama and Louisiana. A member of the West Point class of 1858, he was expelled in 1856 for poor grades and conduct. Running his father's plantation at the outbreak of the Civil War, he joined Company G, 1st Louisiana, on April 30, 1861, and soon became its captain. Wounded at Shiloh, he later served on the staff of General Jospeh Wheeler and while on an errand was captured near Trenton, Georgia, on October 16, 1863. After nearly a year's captivity at Johnson's Island, Ohio, he made good his escape on the night of October 4, 1864, and made his way to Canada. His escape went unnoticed for some two weeks due to a ruse by his fellow prisoners. Sent by Jacob Thompson, Captain Kennedy and seven others set off for New York with the intention of setting the city aflame on election day. However, Union precautions prompted a delay until the 25th. The fires set in several hotels and P.T. Barnum's Museum proved highly ineffective, and the conspirators returned to Canada. Kennedy later took part in the failed raid to free captured Confederate generals being transferred by train near Buffalo, New York. It was in this misadventure that John Yates Beall was captured. Kennedy himself determined to return to the Confederacy and, with a companion, set off on December 28, 1864. He was captured near Detroit—his companion made good his escape—and was sent to New York for trial, by a military commission headed by General Fitz-Henry Warren, as a spy. Convicted, he was hanged at Fort Lafayette on

the following May 25th. (Brandt, Nat, *The Man Who Tried to Burn New York*)

KENNER, Duncan Farrar (1813-1887)

One of the great ironies of the Civil War was the plan of Confederate Congressman Duncan F. Kenner to abolish slavery in order to gain European recognition for the Confederacy—which to a large degree had been established because of slavery. Having studied law, but not practiced, the native Louisianan had become a successful plantation owner and horse breeder. He served in both houses of the state legislature and upon the formation of the Confederacy was named to the Provisional Congress where he served on the committees on Finance and Patents. During both regular congresses he served as chairman of the Committee on Ways and Means, where he favored higher taxes. Realizing that foreign recognition was vital to the survival of his country, he reasoned that the abolition of slavery would achieve that end. Approaching Jefferson Davis, he was, with misgivings, dispatched to Europe to discuss the subject. However, by that time interest in the Confederacy had waned in the face of military failures. His trip via New York in disguise had been for naught. After the war he returned to his devastated plantation, served in the legislature, and was active in supplanting the Radical Republican government in the state. His agricultural operations became even more profitable without slavery and he was active in horse racing. Defeated for the U.S. Senate in 1878, he was on President Arthur's tariff commission four years later.

KERSHAW, Joseph Brevard (1822-1894)

A solid brigade and division commander in Lee's army, Joseph B. Kershaw is a fine example of the citizen turned soldier who proves capable despite a tendency to sound off about his abilities. He had served as a first lieutenant of South Carolina troops in the Mexican War, much of the time wracked with fever, before returning to his law career and entering politics. A member of the secession convention in his native South Carolina, he raised a militia regiment which went into state and then Confederate service. His assignments included: colonel, 2nd South Carolina (February 2, 1861); commanding Bonham's (old) Brigade, Van Dorn's (old) Division, Potomac District, Department of Northern Virginia (January 29-April 12, 1862); brigadier general, CSA (February 13, 1862); commanding brigade, McLaw's Divison, Magruder's Command, Army of Northern Virginia (April 12-July 1862); commanding brigade, McLaws' Division, 1st Corps, Army of Northern Virginia (July 1862-September 9, 1863); commanding brigade, McLaws' Division, Longstreet's Corps, Army of Tennessee (September 19-November 5, 1863); commanding the division (September 20, 1863); commanding brigade, McLaws' Division, Department of East Tennessee (November 5-December 17, 1863); commanding the division (December 17, 1863-January and February-April 12, 1864); commanding Division, 1st Corps, Army of Northern Virginia (April 12, 1864-April 6, 1865); and major general, CSA (June 2, to date from May 18, 1864). He was present with the regiment on Morris Island during the bombardment of Fort Sumter. Moving to Virginia, he played a key role at 1st Bull Run but annoyed General Beauregard by not filing a report with him and instead writing an article for a South Carolina newspaper in which it appeared that he won the battle himself. Beauregard later referred to him as "that militia idiot." Despite Beauregard's views, Kershaw went on to command a brigade at Williamsburg, Savage Station in the Seven Days, Antietam, Fredericksburg, Chancellorsville, and Gettysburg. He was especially distinguished at Fredericksburg. Going west with Longstreet, he commanded that portion of the division which arrived in time to fight at Chickamauga. He took part in the Knoxville Campaign and succeeded to division command when McLaws was relieved. Returning to Virginia he was still a brigadier but in charge of the division at the Wilderness where he led a crucial assault on the second day. He also helped save the life of General Longstreet by yelling "Friends!" when he had been wounded by fellow Confederates. He went on to fight at Spotsylvania, Cold Harbor, and around Richmond and Petersburg. Promoted, he led the division to the Shenandoah in late summer and fought at Cedar Creek. Returning to the lines at Richmond, he was captured at Sayler's Creek during the retreat to Appomattox. He was released in July, and later served as a lawyer, state senator, judge, and postmaster in South Carolina. (Dickert, D. Augustus, *History of Kershaw's Brigade*)

KEWEN, Edward J.C. (?-?)

The 1862 arrest of secessionist Edward J.C. Kewen in California is a ludicrous example of suppression in that state far off from Civil War combat. A native of Mississippi he had settled in the Los Angeles area and on September 3, 1862, was elected as a pro-Southern Democrat to the California assembly. However, the defeated Union candidate contested the results on October 6, charging the victor had spoken out in favor of the rebellion. The very next day Kewen found himself under arrest and on his way to Alcatraz. The incident was one of many which occurred in the fall of 1862. At that time the war was going badly for the North and the War Department had issued a series of orders which authorized the suppression of newspapers and the military confinement of dangerous secessionists. On the West Coast this was taken to the extreme. While the secessionists had been a power in California in the 1850s, by this time most of them had gone east to join the Confederates and many of the others were swept out of office. The remaining secessionist activity was actually confined mostly to the drunken firing of guns accompanied by cheers for Jeff Davis and various Confederate generals. Finally, on October 24, 1862, department commander Wright ordered Kewen's release upon payment of a $5,000 bond and the taking of the oath of allegiance. If anything, Kewen's political standing was enhanced by the unnecessary incarceration.

KEYES, Wade, Jr. (1821-?)

A noted Alabama attorney, Wade Keyes, Jr., served throughout the life of the Confederacy as its assistant attorney general and at one point briefly headed the Justice Department. He had practiced his profession in Kentucky, Florida, and Alabama and had written a couple of legal treatises. Appointed to the number two legal position in the new government, he quickly became its guiding force, citing many U.S. precedents in support of government positions in the unprecedented war. When Thomas H. Watts left the cabinet late in 1863 to take up his duties as governor of Alabama, Keyes became acting attorney general until George Davis was appointed to the post. After the war Keyes returned to Alabama and resumed his practice.

KICKING BIRD (?-1875)

The principal voice for peace within his tribe, Kiowa chief Kicking Bird may have paid for his beliefs with his life. During the Civil War he was already known as peaceful but nonetheless the Indian agent Jesse H. Leavenworth reported him as leading some of the depradations occurring in 1865 following the Sand Creek massacre. Kicking Bird was a signer of the 1867 Treaty of Medicine Lodge and thereafter was staunchly for peace. In the Red River War of 1874-75 he managed to get his people back to the agency, where they were then imprisoned. The military decided that 26 Kiowas must be sent to confinement in Florida. They insisted that Kicking Bird make the selections of those to be so punished. Reluctantly, he did. Upon their departure one of the chained Indians accused Kicking Bird of being a big man with the whites and threatened to make sure that he did not live long. Two days later, on May 5, 1875, Kicking Bird died suddenly after drinking a cup of coffee—probably poisoned. (Brown, Dee, *Bury My Heart At Wounded Knee*)

KING, Kate (1842-?)

The mistress of Missouri bushwhacker William C. Quantrill, Kate King (sometimes rendered Clarke) used the money gained from his will to open a posh St. Louis brothel. She had been kidnapped by the Confederate guerrillas—in actuality nothing more than bandits—early in the war. She was frequently with Quantrill and upon his death came into half of his loot from the war. A chance reference to Quantrill as a mere butcher led to the demise of one of her clients by the outraged madam. She recruited many of her clients from the ranks of the former guerrillas. Following her marriage she disappeared from history.

KING, Wilburn Hill (1839-1910)

Although his appointment as a brigadier general was never recognized by the Richmond authorities, Wilburn H. King served in that grade for the final year of the war in the Trans-Mississippi. His assignments in the Trans-Mississippi Department included: major and quartermaster, CSA (October 15, 1861) major, lieutenant colonel and colonel, 18th Texas; brigadier general, CSA by Smith (April 16, to rank from April 8, 1864); commanding brigade, Walker's Division, District of West Louisiana (spring-July 17, 1864); commanding Walker's Division, District of West Louisiana (July 17-September 2, 1864); commanding 4th Texas Brigade, Polignac's Division, 1st Corps (September 1864-February 27, 1865); and commanding brigade, Forney's Division, 1st Corps (February 27-May

1865). Most of his service was in western Louisiana, including action at Bayou Bourbeau in November 1863 and in the Red River Campaign. He was appointed a brigadier in orders by General E. Kirby Smith in the spring of 1864 and held brigade and higher commands for the rest of the war but was never legally promoted.

KIRBY-SMITH, Edmund

See: *Smith, Edmund Kirby*

KIRKLAND, Richard R. (1841-1863)

Following the disastrous charges of the Union forces against the stone wall at Fredericksburg, the victorious Confederates were forced to remain under cover and to listen to the piteous cries of their fallen foes. This proved to be too much for Richard Kirkland, a sergeant in the 2nd South Carolina. A veteran of all the regiment's battles since 1st Bull Run, he pleaded with his brigade commander for permission to leave the safety of the Sunken Road and carry water to the suffering Federals. His request granted, he asked, as an after-thought, to be allowed to wave a white handkerchief. This was refused. Still, he jumped over the wall and into the face of almost certain death, but no shots were fired for the hour and half during which he succored the enemy's wounded. Ten months later, "The Hero-Sergeant of Fredericksburg" fell at Chickamauga. (Kershaw, C.D., comp., *Richard Kirkland, CSA*)

KIRKLAND, William Whedbee (1833-1915)

It happened twice: When William W. Kirkland returned to duty after being wounded he found that he had been supplanted in his command and had to be assigned to other duties. He had attended West Point for a while but instead entered the Marine Corps, resigning his commission the year before the war. His Confederate assignments included: colonel, 11th North Carolina Volunteers (July 3, 1861); colonel, 21st North Carolina (designation change on November 14, 1861); reappointed colonel, 21st North Carolina (April 21, 1863); brigadier general, CSA (August 29, 1863); commanding Pettigrew's (old) Brigade, Heth's Division, 3rd Corps, Army of Northern Virginia (September 7-October 14, 1863 and early 1864-June 2, 1864); commanding Martin's (old) brigade, Hoke's Division, Department of North Carolina and Southern Virginia (August 19-October 19, 1864); commanding brigade, Hoke's Division, Anderson's Corps, Army of Northern Virginia (October 19-December 1864); commanding brigade, Hoke's Division, Department of North Carolina (December 1864-March 1865); commanding brigade, Hoke's Division, Hardee's Corps (in Army of Tennessee from April 9) (March-April 26, 1865). He fought at 1st Bull Run but failed to gain reelection at the spring 1862 reorganization. However, when the victor declined appointment, Kirkland was appointed acting colonel. Wounded in Jackson's Valley Campaign at 1st Winchester, he

recovered to serve as chief of staff to Patrick Cleburne, seeing action at Murfreesboro. During his convalescence a permanent colonel for the 21st had been named and that is what forced him to look for other duty. When the new man was promoted, Kirkland was reappointed to his old regiment. After fighting at Gettysburg he was promoted and transferred to the command of another brigade. Wounded in a futile attack at Bristoe Station, he returned to fight at the Wilderness and Spotsylvania. Again wounded at Cold Harbor, he returned to find his brigade had gone to William MacRae. In August 1864 he was assigned to another North Carolina brigade and served at Petersburg and Richmond before being sent to North Carolina. He served near Fort Fisher and then fought at Bentonville, finally surrendering with Johnston at Greensboro. (Freeman, Douglas S., *Lee's Lieutenants*)

KNOBELOCH, Margaret Anna Parker (1833-1916)

Born in the North and raised in the South, Margaret A.P. Knobeloch was driven by compassion to approach the U.S. War Department with an unusual request. She wanted to distribute aid to Confederate prisoners of war from funds provided by Southerners living in Europe. The Philadelphia native had married a German immigrant, John Knobeloch, in Charleston, South Carolina, and the couple had moved to Philadelphia upon the outbreak of the Civil War. John returned to Germany in order to avoid the draft but Margaret remained. In the summer of 1862 she approached Secretary of War Edwin M. Stanton with her proposal, utilizing her connections in the South and in Europe. Informal permission was granted and she began her work in the hospitals of her native city and in nearby Fort Delaware. She kept her work up until the end of the war. In subsequent years she wrote of her experiences in relief work.

KOSSUTH, Louis (1802-1894)

For a number of years just after the Mexican War Louis Kossuth and his failed 1848-49 Hungarian uprising attracted the interest of the public. Upon the collapse of his revolution, Kossuth had fled to Turkey, and in 1851 he received a hero's welcome upon a visit to the United States. Seeking to gain support for his cause, he was also courted by the abolitionists for their cause. When he announced his neutrality upon the slavery question, interest quickly faded. While he gained sympathy from Secretary of State Daniel Webster, Webster was quick to state—for Austrian consumption—that it was his personal opinion not official policy. In the summer of 1851 Kossuth sailed away, his mission a failure. He lived out his years in exile in Italy but had a lasting impact on America, with at least one Confederate unit being called the "Kossuth Hunters." (Spencer, Donald S., *Louis Kossuth and Young America: A Study of Sectionalism and Foreign Policy, 1848-1852*)

L

LAIRD, John (1805-1874)

One of the first to construct ships of iron and the first to build one with guns was Englishman John Laird. He had been constructing vessels for several decades, and selling throughout the British Empire and to the United States, when the American Civil War came. That same year he retired from his firm and became a member of Parliament. The company continued under his sons and constructed the *Alabama* for the Confederacy. Later in the war two rams were contracted for by the South under the cover of being intended for the Egyptian government. After prolonged pressure from Washington, the Laird rams were seized by the British authorities on September 5, 1863. While in Parliament and until his death, John Laird continued to play a role in maritime affairs.

LAMAR, Gazaway Bugg (1798-1874)

A Georgia-born banker in New York, Gazaway B. Lamar provided his first service to the Confederacy in November 1860 by purchasing and shipping 10,000 muskets to Georgia. In 1834 he had introduced iron steamships to America, only to see his first wife and six of his seven children drowned in the sinking of one of his vessels, the *Pulaski*. In the early months of the Civil War he remained in New York as a Confederate intelligence and postal agent. Moving to Savannah to head the Bank of Commerce, he was chairman of the 1861 banking convention in Atlanta. Seeking ways to weaken the blockade, he negotiated with former New York mayor Fernando Wood to bribe the appropriate persons to allow his blockade runners through. Lamar was sharply criticized in the South when this became public knowledge. He took the Union loyalty oath upon the seizure of Savannah to try to save his property. Soon thereafter he was arrested for a bribery plot. Following his release in late 1865 he returned to New York.

LAMAR, Lucius Quintus Cincinnatus (1825-1893)

For L.Q.C. Lamar the Civil War was just one episode in a varied career. A lawyer and educator he had developed an interest in Democratic politics, become a defender of states' rights, and served in the Georgia legislature. Moving to Mississippi, he was elected to the U.S. House of Representatives. Originally opposed to individual state action, he assisted in the drafting of Mississippi's secession ordinance. Entering the military, he held the following appointments: lieutenant colonel, 19th Mississippi (June 11, 1861); and colonel, 19th Mississippi (May 5, 1862). Seeing action at Williamsburg, he succeeded to regimental command when the colonel was killed, but suffering from vertigo, he resigned on November 24, 1862. He then served as a special commissioner to England, France, and Russia. Never confirmed by the Senate, he returned home in late 1863 and became a vocal supporter of the president. On December 3, 1864, he reentered the military service as a judge on the court of the 3rd Corps, Army of Northern Viriginia. As such he received a parole at Appomattox. He later served as representative, senator, secretary of the interior, and as a justice on the Supreme Court. (Cate, Wirt Armistead, *Lucius Q.C. Lamar*)

LAMB, William (1835-1909)

It was not until the final few weeks of his Confederate career that William Lamb saw heavy action. A Norfolk publisher, he entered the army the day after Virginia's secession. His assignments included: captain, Company C, 6th Virginia (April 18, 1861); major and quartermaster, CSA (September 24, 1861); colonel, 2nd North Carolina Artillery (May 14, 1862); and commanding Fort Fisher, North Carolina (July 4, 1862-January 15, 1865). After only brief service in the Norfolk area he resigned his company command on August 6, 1861. Given a staff appointment the next month he was ordered to Wilmington, North Carolina. He resigned this position to

Confederate diplomat L.Q.C. Lamar. (*Harper's*)

accept a new appointment following his election as colonel of an artillery unit. His unit was for a long time a fluid paper organization for the various batteries serving in the District of the Cape Fear. Lamb was given command of Fort Fisher below Wilmington and had little to do with the regiment until its organization was stabilized and most of its companies were assigned to the fort late in the war. On December 24-25, 1864, the garrision beat off the first Union assault on the fort. On January 15, 1865, a joint army-navy expedition against the fort was more successful. With Union troops, sailors, and marines already over the wall, Lamb fell wounded. The fort soon surrendered and Lamb was held as a prisoner until after the war's close.

LANE, James Henry (1833-1907)

A graduate and former professor at the Virginia Military Institute, James Henry Lane was teaching at the North Carolina Military Institute when the war began. Leading the cadet corps to war, he held the following assignments: major, 1st North Carolina Volunteers (May 11, 1861); lieutenant colonel, 1st North Carolina Volunteers (September 3, 1861); colonel, 28th North Carolina (September 21, 1861); commanding Branch's

(old) Brigade, A.P. Hill's Division, 2nd Corps, Army of Northern Virginia (September 17, 1862-May 30, 1863); brigadier general, CSA (November 1, 1862); commanding brigade, Pender's-Wilcox's Division, 3rd Corps, same army (May 30-July 2; July 3; mid-July 1863-February 1865; and March-April 9, 1865); and commanding the division (July 2-3; July 3-mid July 1863; and February-March 1865). He fought from Big Bethel to Appomattox in Virginia. After the small actions at the former and Hanover Court House, he was twice wounded during the Seven Days, at Frayser's Farm and the next day at Malvern Hill. Still on duty, he moved north with Jackson and participated in operations at Cedar Mountain, 2nd Bull Run, Harpers Ferry, and Antietam where he succeeded the slain General L. O'B. Branch. Lane led his brigade at Fredericksburg and Chancellorsville and was in temporary command of the division on the second day at Gettysburg. Relieved the next day, before Pickett's Charge, he returned from the famed assault again in charge of the division since his replacement had fallen. The Virginian led his North Carolinians through the Overland and Petersburg operations and surrendered with Lee at Appomattox. (Freeman, Douglas S., *Lee's Lieutenants*)

LANE, Joseph (1801-1881)

Running for the vice presidency on the ticket of John C. Breckinridge effectively ended the political career of Joseph Lane. The North Carolina native had engaged in trade in Indiana and sat in the state legislature. During the Mexican War he entered the military as colonel of the 2nd Indiana but within a month was named a brigadier general of volunteers. During the course of the war he won the brevet of major general and was mustered out in the summer of 1848. From 1848-1850 he was territorial governor of Oregon and then became its House of Representatives delegate. In 1859 he became one of the new state's two senators. Noted for his proslavery and secession views he was chosen by the Southern faction of the Democratic party as its vice presidential nominee. After the defeat he remained a Southern partisan but lost most of his political clout.

LANE, Walter Paye (1817-1892)

Definitely an adventurer, Walter P. Lane rose to the rank of brigadier general in the final days of the Confederacy. The native of County Cork had been brought to the United States by his parents in 1821. They settled in Ohio but Lane eventually went off to Texas and, joining the forces of Sam Houston, fought at San Jacinto. He then served on a Texas privateer in the Gulf of Mexico and fought Indians until the Mexican War. During that conflict he served as a first lieutenant in the Texas Rifles and then as major of a battalion of Texas mounted volunteers. Some of his quieter activities included teaching and mining, with mixed success, in the United States and Peru. Joining the Confederacy, his assignments included: lieutenant colonel, 3rd Texas Cavalry (early 1861); colonel, 1st Texas Partisan Rangers (ca. 1864); brigadier general, CSA (March 17, 1865); and commanding brigade, Steele's Division, Cavalry Corps, Trans-Mississippi Department (March-May 26, 1865). He fought at Wilson's Creek and on December 26, 1861, against the Creeks at Chustenahlah. He also participated in the defense of Corinth, Mississippi. Given command of a regiment of partisan rangers, he served in Louisiana until wounded at Mansfield during the Red River Campaign. Returning to duty in western Louisiana, he was eventually promoted to brigadier general and in the final months of the war led a mounted brigade. Returning to Texas, he engaged in mercantile pursuits and was active in veterans' affairs. (Lane, Walter Paye, *The Adventures and Recollections of Walter P. Lane*.)

LANG, David (1838-1917)

Rising from the enlisted ranks, David Lang became the temporary commander of the Florida Brigade shortly before Appomattox. A native Georgian, he graduated from Georgia Military Institute before moving to Florida and becoming a surveyor. Entering the Confederate army his assignments included: private, Company H, 1st Florida (early 1861); sergeant, Company H, 1st Florida (April 1862); captain, Company C, 8th Florida (May 10, 1862); colonel, 8th Florida (October 2, 1862); commanding Perry's Brigade, Anderson's Division, 3rd Corps, Army of Northern Virginia (spring 1863-fall 1863); and commanding Finegan's Brigade, Mahone's Division, 3rd Corps, Army of Northern Virginia (early 1865-April 9, 1865). After serving his 12-month enlistment, he raised his own company and was soon sent with it to Virginia. He saw action at 2nd Bull Run, Antietam, and Fredericksburg where he was severely wounded in the head while commanding the regiment. He recovered in time to command the brigade at Gettysburg. He then led his regiment at the Wilderness, Spotsylvania Court House, Cold Harbor, and Petersburg. Again in command of the brigade, he led it through the final stages of the Petersburg siege and the Appomattox Campaign. After the surrender, he served in civil and military appointive positions in the state of Florida. (Freeman, Douglas S., *Lee's Lieutenants*)

LANIER, Sidney (1842-1881)

A firm believer in the myth of the "Old South" as fostered by the novels of Sir Walter Scott, poet Sidney Lanier supported the secession of his home state of Georgia. He enlisted in June 1861 in the Macon County Volunteers, which became Company I, 4th Georgia, and reported to Virginia. On March 9, 1862, he witnessed the battle between the *Monitor* and the *Merrimac*. His next action was defending Drewy's Bluff, Virginia, against the *Monitor* and other Union vessels on May 15, 1862. Transferring to the Signal Corps, Lanier served on the staff of Major General S.G. French. In May 1863, he visited the battlefield of Chancellorsville, thus inspiring the 1865 poem, "The Dying Words of Jackson." He was subsequently captured while serving on a blockade-runner and confined principally at Point Lookout, Maryland. Although he rarely wrote about the war, his novel *Tiger-Lilies* dealt with prison life. Released four months later, his health was permanently impaired and he died of tuberculosis at the age of 39. His unhappiness with Northern reconstruction policies led to his condemnatory, and sometimes racist poems: "Laughter in the Senate," "The Raven Days," "Civil Rights," "Betrayal," and "The Ship of the Earth."

(Parks, Ed Winfield, *Sidney Lanier: The Man, The Poet, The Critic*)

LATIMER, Joseph White (1843-1863)

Interrupting his studies at the Virginia Military Institute, young Joseph W. Latimer became one of the most promising artillery field officers in the Army of Northern Virginia. His assignments included: first lieutenant, Richmond Courtney Artillery (September 15, 1861); captain, Richmond Courtney Artillery (ca. July 14, 1862); commanding Courtney's Artillery Battalion, Ewell's Division, 2nd Corps, Army of Northern Virginia (fall 1862-ca. March 2, 1863); major, Artillery (March 2, 1863); commanding Andrew's Artillery Battalion, Ewell's-Early's Division, 2nd Corps, Army of Northern Virginia (ca. March 2-ca. April 4, 1863); and commanding Andrew's Artillery Battalion, Johnson's Division, 2nd Corps, Army of Northern Virginia (June 15-July 2, 1863). After having served as a cadet drillmaster for the Richmond Hampden Artillery in the spring and summer of 1861, he received a commission in a new battery with which he saw action in the Shenandoah Valley Campaign, the Seven Days, Cedar Mountain, 2nd Bull Run, and Harpers Ferry. He especially distinguished himself at 1st Winchester, in the Valley, and at Cedar Mountain. Remaining at Harpers Ferry, his battery did not see action at Antietam, but Latimer took over battalion command soon thereafter when his superior, Major A.R. Courtney, was brought up on charges for his behavior there. He commanded the battalion at Fredericksburg and the next winter received promotion to major and assignment as executive officer in Andrews' Battalion. He commanded part of the unit at 2nd Winchester and took over the battalion when Andrews was wounded at Stephenson's Depot the next day. On the second day at Gettysburg, he was fatally wounded while withdrawing his battalion from an unequal artillery duel supporting the attack on Culp's and Cemetery Hills. He died on August 1. (Wise, Jennings C., *The Long Arm of Lee*)

LAW, Evander McIvor (1836-1920)

A distinguished brigade commander, E. McIvor Law became embroiled in a dispute with another brigadier which virtually destroyed the efficiency of Hood's former division. A graduate of the South Carolina Military Academy, he became involved with a number of such academies in his native South Carolina and in Alabama. With the outbreak of hostilities he raised a company and joined the Confederacy where his assignments included: captain, Company B, 4th Alabama (spring 1861); lieutenant colonel, 4th Alabama (May 1861); colonel, 4th Alabama (October 28, 1861); commanding Whiting's Brigade, Smith's-Whiting's Division (in the Valley District in June), Department of Northern Virginia (May-June 1862); commanding same brigade, Whiting's Division, 2nd Corps, Army of Northern Virginia (June 26-July 1862); commanding brigade, Whiting's-Hood's-Field's Division, 1st Corps, Army of Northern Virginia (July 1862-February 25, 1863; May-July 2, 1863; and April-June 3, 1864); brigadier general, CSA (October 3, 1862); commanding brigade, Hood's Division, in the Department of Virginia and North Carolina (February 25-April 1, 1863) and in the Department of Southern Virginia (April 1-May 1863); commanding Hood's Division, 1st Corps, Army of Northern Virginia (July 2-September 1863); commanding brigade, Hood's Division, Longstreet's Corps, Army of Tennessee (September-November 5, 1863); temporarily commanding the division (September 20, 1863); commanding brigade, Hood's-Field's Division, Department of East Tennessee (November 5-December 19, 1863); and commanding brigade, Butler's Division, Hampton's Cavalry Command with Johnston's army (March-April 1865). After being severely wounded at 1st Bull Run, he was promoted to regimental command. Leading the brigade he fought at Seven Pines, the Seven Days, 2nd Bull Run, and Antietam before being promoted to brigadier general. After fighting at Fredericksburg he served in southeastern Virginia with Longstreet and then returned to Lee's army. At Gettysburg he succeeded to divisional command upon the wounding of General Hood. Going west, he led the division temporarily at Chickamauga while Hood led the corps. Hood was wounded again but Law was relieved by Micah Jenkins who was senior brigadier in the division but had long been detached with his brigade. During the battle of Wauhatchie and in the East Tennessee Campaign there were charges of a lack of cooperation. Eventually Law took his resignation to Richmond, having taken it back from Longstreet. He was talked out of it, but Longstreet filed charges against Law for stealing the document. He was reinstated by the War Department in time for the Wilderness, and he fought later at Spotsylvania and North Anna before being badly wounded at Cold Harbor. Returning to duty in the final months of the war, he commanded a cavalry brigade in North Carolina and fought at Bentonville. After the war he was active in education, journalism, and veterans' affairs. (Freeman, Douglas S., *Lee's Lieutenants*)

LAWTON, Alexander Robert (1818-1896)

South Carolina-born Alexander R. Lawton's service with the Army of Northern Virginia was brief, and he finished out the war in a thankless military job—quartermaster general. A West Pointer (1839), he served only a year in the artillery before resigning to attend Harvard Law School. Settling in Savannah to practice, he entered politics, serving in both state houses. Also involved in railroads and the militia, he seized Fort Pulaski, as colonel of the 1st Georgia, even before the state seceded. His later assignments included: brigadier general, CSA (April 13, 1861); commanding District of Savannah (April 17-October 26, 1861); commanding Department of Georgia (October 26-November 5, 1861); commanding District of Georgia, Department of South Carolina, Georgia and Florida (May 28-June 1862); commanding brigade, Jackson's Division, in the Valley District, Department of Northern Virginia (June 1862) and in Jackson's Command, Army of Northern Virginia (June 26-mid-August 1862); commanding brigade, Ewell's Division, Jackson's Command, Army of Northern Virginia (mid-August-August 28, 1862); commanding the division (August 28-September 17, 1862); and quartermaster general, CSA (August 10, 1863-April 1865). After serving on the coast

he was sent to Virginia where he arrived too late to participate in the Valley Campaign but fought in the Seven Days. His brigade was left guarding the trains during the fighting at Cedar Mountain so that a junior officer, General Winder, could lead the division. Transferred to Ewell's Division, he fought at 2nd Bull Run, taking over the division until he was wounded at Antietam. After a long recovery he was assigned to the staff department. Active in law and politics after the war, he served as U.S. minister to Austria. (Freeman, Douglas S., *Lee's Lieutenants*)

LEADBETTER, Danville (1811-1866)

A career engineer, Danville Leadbetter was highly respected by some of the top Confederate commanders but came in for much criticism from a fellow engineer, E. Porter Alexander. The Maine native and West Pointer (1836) had shifted back and forth a couple of times between the artillery and engineers in his first two years after graduation. From then until his resignation as a captain in 1857 he served in the latter. Having for a time been stationed in Mobile, he spent the remaining antebellum years as Alabama's chief engineer. Adopting Southern political beliefs, he entered the Confederate service and his assignments included: lieutenant colonel, Alabama Troops (1861); major, Engineers, CSA (summer 1861); acting chief, Engineer Bureau (August 3-November 11, 1861); brigadier general, CSA (March 6, 1862, to rank from February 27); commanding Leadbetter's Command, District of East Tennessee, Department #2 (early 1862); and chief engineer, Army of Tennessee (1863-64). His earliest service came in constructing the defenses at Mobile. Throughout the war he kept returning to this post for further engineering work. During the first summer of the war he was in temporary charge of the War Department's engineering branch. Promoted to brigadier general, he held brief command of line troops at Chattanooga and Knoxville. When Bragg besieged the former city, Leadbetter designed the lines on Missionary Ridge and Lookout Mountain. It was at Knoxville that he came into conflict with Alexander over the advice given to the operation's commander, James Longstreet. Apparently his work was not of the best—there were especially grievous faults in the works at Chattanooga. After the war Leadbetter went via Mexico to Canada where he died.

LEE, Charles Cochrane (1834-1862)

Although he was well qualified, having graduated fourth in his 1856 class at West Point, and having served as an instuctor at the Charlotte Military Academy after his resignation from the regular army in 1859, Charles Lee was deprived of his general's wreath by an early death. The former ordnance second lieutenant was appointed lieutenant colonel, 1st North Carolina Volunteers, on May 11, 1861. Lee participated in the small, early Confederate victory in the battle of Big Bethel on June 10. On September 1, 1861, he was promoted to colonel of the regiment, then dubbed the "Bethel Regiment," and served until it was discharged at the end of its term of service. On November 20 he was made colonel of a new unit, the 37th North Carolina. After participating in the battle of New Bern on March 15,

1862, the regiment moved to Virginia as part of General Branch's Brigade which was made part of General A.P. Hill's Division. Lee took part in the battle of Hanover Court House on May 27. In the Seven Days Battles Branch's Brigade was held in reserve at Beaver Dam Creek but was engaged at Gaines' Mill and Frayser's Farm. In the latter battle, Colonel Lee was killed leading a charge.

LEE, Edwin Gray (1836-1870)

The least-known of the Confederate Generals Lee, Edwin G. Lee finished out the war as a Southern agent in Canada. A second cousin of *the* General Lee, Edwin was a lawyer in what is now West Virginia and was a son-in-law of General William N. Pendleton. Lee gave up his practice to join the Confederacy as an officer in the Hamtranck Guards, a company he had been associated with since John Brown's raid. His assignments included: second lieutenant, Company B, 2nd Virginia (1861); first lieutenant and adjutant, 2nd Virginia (1861); lieutenant colonel, 33rd Virginia (ca. April 22, 1862); colonel, 33rd Virginia (to date from August 28, 1862); and brigadier general, CSA (September 23, 1864). As part of the Stonewall Brigade he served at Harpers Ferry and 1st Bull Run on Jackson's staff. He then served through the Shenandoah Valley Campaign and the Seven Days. After Cedar Mountain and 2nd Bull Run he was promoted to colonel. Shortly after Antietam, he was captured while visiting his ill father but was freed in time to fight at Fredericksburg. Upon his doctor's advice he resigned that winter. Later in 1863 he was reappointed but assigned to less arduous duty, although he did see action at Drewry's Bluff and Bermuda Hundred in May 1864. The next month he was ordered to Staunton to organize the reserve forces in the Valley District and a few months later was promoted to brigadier. The appointment was rejected by the Senate in February but by then he was already on a mission to Canada. By the time he had set up shop as successor to Jacob Thompson and Clement Clay the war was ending. He remained in Canada until early 1866, dispensing funds to needy Confederates in exile. Returning, he was a witness at the trial of John Surratt whom he had known in Montreal. He had also looked after the interests of the St. Albans raiders while they were in a Canadian prison. The next few years were spent in an unsuccessful attempt to improve his long-failing health.

LEE, Fitzhugh (1835-1905)

The nephew of two of the Confederacy's top generals, R.E. Lee and Samuel Cooper, Fitzhugh Lee himself held the rank of major general in both a gray and blue uniform. A West Pointer (1856) and a wounded veteran of Texas Indian fighting, Lee resigned a first lieutenancy in the 2nd Cavalry on May 21, 1861, to go with his native Virginia. His assignments included: first lieutenant, Cavalry (1861); lieutenant colonel, 1st Virginia Cavalry (August 1861); colonel, 1st Virginia Cavalry (April 1862); brigadier general, CSA (July 24, 1862); commanding brigade, Cavalry Division, Army of Northern Virginia (July 28, 1862-September 9, 1863); major general, CSA (August 3, 1863); commanding division, Cavalry Corps, same army

(September 9, 1863-August 1864 and January-March 1865); commanding cavalry division, Valley District, Department of Northern Virginia (August-September 19, 1864); and commanding Cavalry Corps, Army of Northern Virginia (March-April 11, 1865). He served at 1st Bull Run as a staff officer and the next month was named a field officer in the 1st Virginia Cavalry. Promoted to colonel in the spring 1862 reorganization, he led the regiment in Stuart's first ride around McClellan's army and served through the Seven Days. Promoted and given a brigade, he fought at 2nd Bull Run, South Mountain, Antietam, in the December 1862 raids, at Kelly's Ford, and with the main army at Chancellorsville. After participating in Stuart's wide swing around the Union army in the Pennsylvania Campaign, he fought in the cavalry action on the third day at Gettysburg. Back in Virginia he was given charge of a newly organized division. At Spotsylvania he held off the Union forces until Lee's infantry arrived on the field. After serving on the Petersburg-Richmond lines, he was sent to the aid of Early in the Valley but was soon wounded out of action at 3rd Winchester. Not returning to duty until the beginning of the next year he found his division by that time back from the Shenandoah, and led the cavalry on the Richmond front. In the final month of the war he headed the mounted corps and cut his way out of the Appomattox encirclement with a portion of his command but surrendered two days after Lee. A farmer after the war, he became governor of the state and was a diplomat in Cuba just before the war with Spain. Donning the blue, he was a major general of volunteers and soon thereafter was placed on the retired list of the regular army at the same grade. (Freeman, Douglas S., *Lee's Lieutenants*)

LEE, George Washington Custis (1832-1913)

Robert E. Lee's eldest son, George W.C. Lee, chaffed in his position as an aide-de-camp to Jefferson Davis, desiring instead a field position. Having been graduated at the head of his 1854 class at West Point, he had accordingly been assigned to the engineers. He had resigned his first lieutenant's commission on May 2, 1861, to follow his father into the service of their native Virginia. His assignments included: captain, Engineers (July 1, 1861); colonel, Cavalry, and aide-de-camp (August 31, 1861); brigadier general, CSA (June 25, 1863); commanding Local Defense Troops Brigade, Department of Richmond (October 1864-January 1865); major general, CSA (to rank from October 20, 1864); commanding division, Department of Richmond (March-April 2, 1865); and commanding separate division, Army of Northern Virginia (April 2-6, 1865). Initially assigned to the designing of the capital's defenses, Lee was tapped by the president as an aide. In addition he finally got a troop assignment with the organization of the government workers into the Local Defense Troops. Whenever these units were called into active duty he would command. The remainder of his time would be spent serving the chief executive. During the Richmond-Petersburg operations he was regularly at the head of his brigade. In the final month, he directed a division of Local Defense units, reserves, regular line troops, and landlocked sailors and marines. In the retreat to Appomattox he was with his father's army and was captured at Sayler's Creek. Quickly paroled to tend to his ill mother, he eventually succeeded his father as president of Washington College. (Freeman, Douglas S., *R. E. Lee*)

LEE, Robert Edward (1807-1870)

The idol of the South to this day, Virginian Robert E. Lee had some difficulty in adjusting to the new form of warfare that unfolded with the Civil War, but this did not prevent him from keeping the Union armies in Virginia at bay for almost three years. The son of Revolutionary War hero "Light Horse" Harry Lee—who fell into disrepute in his later years—attended West Point and graduated second in his class. During his four years at the military academy he did not earn a single demerit and served as the cadet corps' adjutant. Upon his 1829 graduation he was posted to the engineers. Before the Mexican War he served on engineering projects in Georgia, Virginia, and New York. During the war he served on the staffs of John Wool and Winfield Scott. Particularly distinguishing himself scouting for and guiding troops, he won three brevets and was slightly wounded at Chapultepec. Following a stint in Baltimore Harbor he became superintendent of the military academy in 1852. When the mounted arm was expanded in 1855, Lee accepted the lieutenant colonelcy of the 2nd Cavalry in order to escape from the painfully slow promotion in the engineers. Ordered to western Texas, he served with his regiment until the 1857 death of his father-in-law forced him to ask for a series of leaves to settle the estate. In 1859 he was called upon to lead a force of marines, to join with the militia on the scene, to put an end to John Brown's Harpers Ferry Raid. Thereafter he served again in Texas until summoned to Washington in 1861 by Winfield Scott who tried to retain Lee in the U.S. service. But the Virginian rejected the command of the Union's field forces on the day after Virginia seceded. He then accepted an invitation to visit Governor John Letcher in Virginia. His resignation as colonel, 1st Cavalry—to which he had recently been promoted—was accepted on April 25, 1861. His Southern assignments included: major general, Virginia's land and naval forces (April 23, 1861); commanding Virginia forces (April 23-July 1861); brigadier general, CSA (May 14, 1861); general, CSA (from June 14, 1861); commanding Department of Northwestern Virginia (late July-October 1861); commanding Department of South Carolina, Georgia and Florida (November 8, 1861-March 3, 1862); and commanding Army of Northern Virginia (June 1, 1862-April 9, 1865). In charge of Virginia's fledgling military might, he was mainly involved in organizational matters. As a Confederate brigadier general, and later full general, he was in charge of supervising all Southern forces in Virginia. In the first summer of the war he was given his first field command in western Virginia. His Cheat Mountain Campaign was a disappointing fizzle largely due to the failings of his superiors. His entire tenure in the region was unpleasant, dealing with the bickering of his subordinates—William W. Loring, John B. Floyd, and Henry A. Wise. After this he became known throughout the South as "Granny Lee." His debut

in field command had not been promising, but Jefferson Davis appointed him to command along the Southern Coast. Early in 1862 he was recalled to Richmond and made an advisor to the president. From this position he had some influence over military operations, especially those of Stonewall Jackson in the Shenandoah Valley. When Joseph E. Johnston launched his attack at Seven Pines, Davis and Lee were taken by surprise and rode out to the field. In the confusion of the fight Johnston was badly wounded, and that night Davis instructed Lee to take command of what he renamed the Army of Northern Virginia. He fought the second day of the battle but the initiative had already been lost the previous day. Later in the month, in a daring move, he left a small force in front of Richmond and crossed the Chickahominy to strike the one Union corps north of the river. In what was to be called the Seven Days Battles the individual fights—Beaver Dam Creek, Gaines' Mill, Savage Station, Glendale, White Oak Swamp, and Malvern Hill—were all tactical defeats for the Confederates. But Lee had achieved the strategic goal of removing McClellan's army from the very gates of Richmond. This created a new opinion of Lee in the South. He gradually became "Uncle Robert" and "Marse Robert." With McClellan neutralized, a new threat developed under John Pope in northern Virginia. At first Lee detached Jackson and then followed with Longstreet's command. Winning at 2nd Bull Run, he moved on into Maryland but suffered the misfortune of having a copy of his orders detailing the disposition of his divided forces fall into the hands of the enemy. McClellan moved with unusual speed and Lee was forced to fight a delaying action along South Mountain while waiting for Jackson to complete the capture of Harpers Ferry and rejoin him. He masterfully fought McClellan to a standstill at Antietam and two days later recrossed the Potomac. Near the end of the year he won an easy victory over Burnside at Fredericksburg and then trounced Hooker in his most creditable victory at Chancellorsville, where he had detached Jackson with most of the army on a lengthy flank march while he remained with only two divisions in the immediate front of the Union army. Launching his second invasion of the North, he lost at Gettysburg. On the third day of the battle he displayed one of his major faults when—as at Malvern Hill and on other fields—he ordered a massed infantry assault across a wide plain, not recognizing that the rifle, which had come into use since the Mexican War, put the charging troops under fire for too long a period. Another problem was his issuance of general orders to be executed by his subordinates. Returning to Virginia he commanded in the inconclusive Bristoe and Mine Run campaigns. From the Wilderness to Petersburg he fought a retiring campaign against Grant in which he made full use of entrenchments, becoming known as "Ace of Spades" Lee. Finally forced into a siege, he held on to Richmond and Petersburg for nearly 10 months before beginning his retreat to Appomattox, where he was forced to surrender. On January 23, 1865, he had been named as commander in chief of the Confederate armies but he found himself too burdened in Virginia to give more than general directives to the other theaters. Later in 1865 he became president of Washington College (now Washington and Lee University) in Lexington, Virginia, and

Robert E. Lee, Confederate commander-in-chief at war's end. (NA)

his reputation revitalized the school after the war. He died of heart disease which had plagued him since the spring of 1863. Somehow, his application for restoration of citizenship was mislaid, and it was not until the 1970's that it was found and granted. (Freeman, Douglas S., *R.E. Lee* and Connelly, Thomas L., *The Marble Man: Robert E. Lee and His Image in American Society*)

LEE, Stephen Dill (1833-1908)

One of the Confederacy's most capable lieutenant generals, Stephen D. Lee has been overshadowed by the likes of Stonewall Jackson and James Longstreet. The native South Carolinian and West Pointer (1854) had seen service with the artillery against the Seminoles and on the frontier before resigning as a first lieutenant with the 4th Artillery on February 20, 1861. His Confederate assignments included: captain and aide-de-camp, South Carolina Army (spring 1861); captain, Artillery, Hampton (S.C.) Legion (1861); major, Artillery (November 1861); lieutenant colonel, Artillery (June 1862); chief of Artillery, Magruder's Command, Army of Northern Virginia (June 17-July 1862); temporarily commanding 4th Virginia Cavalry (July 1862); colonel, Artillery (ca. July 1862); commanding battalion, Artillery, Longstreet's Corps, Army of Northern Virginia (ca. July-November 1862); brigadier general, CSA (November 6, 1862); commanding Provisional Division, 2nd Military District, Department of Mississippi and

East Louisiana (December 1862-January 1863); commanding brigade, Smith's Division, 2nd Military District, Department of Mississippi and East Louisiana (January-April 1863); chief of Artillery, Department of Mississippi and East Louisiana (May-July 4, 1863) major general, CSA (August 3, 1863); commanding cavalry corps, Department of Mississippi and East Louisiana (August 1863-January 28, 1864); commanding cavalry corps, Department of Alabama, Mississippi and East Louisiana (January 28-May 9, 1864); commanding the department (May 9-July 26, 1864); lieutenant general, CSA (June 23, 1864); and commanding Hood's (old) Corps, Army of Tennessee (July 26-December 1864 and late March-April 26, 1865). Highly commended by Beauregard for his staff services at Fort Sumter, he went to Virginia with the Hampton Legion and was engaged in closing the Potomac to Union shipping. Transferred to the Peninsula, he fought at Seven Pines and became Magruder's artillery chief for the Seven Days. Briefly in command of a cavalry regiment in the summer of 1862, he led an artillery battalion under Longstreet at 2nd Bull Run and played a vital role in repulsing the Union assaults and paving the way for Longstreet's steamroller attack. After fighting at Antietam, he was named a brigadier general and ordered to Mississippi where he played a leading role in the repulse of Sherman's attacks at Chickasaw Bayou at the end of 1862. For a time he commanded an infantry brigade at and near Vicksburg, and during the siege of the city itself he was Pemberton's chief artillerist. Paroled and exchanged by July 13, 1863, he was promoted to major general and assigned to command the cavalry in Mississippi and eastern Louisiana. As such he greatly hampered Sherman's Meridian expedition the next year. For a time in charge of the department, he was named a lieutenant general—the youngest in the Confederacy—and was soon engaged against Andrew J. Smith at Tupelo. Ordered to Georgia, he took over Hood's former corps and led it through the balance of the Atlanta Campaign. He continued under Hood into middle Tennessee. He fought at Franklin and at Nashville where his corps was forced to retreat when the others did. Covering the retrograde movement, Lee was wounded. He rejoined the army in the Carolinas in the final days of the war and was surrendered with Joseph E. Johnston. Besides being active in veterans' affairs after the war he was a farmer, legislator, and college president. (Hattaway, Herman, *General Stephen D. Lee*)

LEE, Sydney Smith (1805-1869)

Brother of General Robert E. Lee, father of Major General Fitzhugh Lee, and uncle of Major General W.H.F. Lee, Captain Sydney Smith Lee, CSN, is little remembered in Civil War history. Born in New Jersey, while his Virginia congressman father was attending a session of Congress in Philadelphia, Lee was raised in Virginia. At the age of 14 Lee entered the navy and saw action during the Mexican War. His later services included: command of the Philadelphia Navy Yard, commandant at Annapolis, commanding the USS *Mississippi* on Perry's Japan mission, and chief of the Bureau of Coast Survey. With the secession of Virginia, he resigned his captain's commission and received one of like grade from the Confederacy. He was assigned initially to duty at the Norfolk Navy Yard until its evacuation. Next assigned to command at Drewry's Bluff, he arrived during the Union naval attack. Declining to relieve his predecessor during the action, Lee gave him all the assistance possible in the Confederate victory. Subsequently, he served on several courts-martial, as an examiner in the Confederate States Naval Academy, and as chief of the Bureau of Orders and Detail. Following the war he retired to live out his final four years in Virginia. (Scharf, J. Thomas, *History of the Confederate States Navy*)

LEE, William Henry Fitzhugh (1837-1891)

The eldest and most famous of Robert E. Lee's sons, "Rooney" Lee was a Harvard graduate and regular army veteran when he entered the cavalry service of the South in which he was to rise to division leadership. In the period from 1857 to 1859 he had served as a second lieutenant of infantry but resigned to run a family plantation. His Civil War assignments included: captain and major, Cavalry (May 1861); lieutenant colonel, 9th Virginia Cavalry (January 1862); colonel, 9th Virginia Cavalry (ca. April 28, 1862); brigadier general, CSA (to rank from September 15, 1862); commanding brigade, Cavalry Division, Army of Northern Virginia (November 10, 1862-June 9, 1863); major general, CSA (April 23, 1864); and commanding division, Cavalry Corps, same army (ca. April 23, 1864-April 9, 1865). After service as Loring's cavalry chief in western Virginia, Lee was sent to the Aquia District to organize the cavalry along the Rappahannock River. He was upped from lieutenant colonel to colonel upon the reorganization of the 9th Virginia Cavalry for the war and led it in Stuart's ride around McClellan on the Peninsula and during the Seven Days, 2nd Bull Run, and Antietam. Promoted and given charge of a newly formed brigade, he fought at Fredericksburg and in opposing Stoneman's raid during the Chancellorsville Campaign. The next month he was wounded in the great cavalry battle at Brandy Station. While recuperating at home he was captured and got caught up in the retaliation for the Confederate threat to hang two Union captains. Kept in close confinement under threat of death, he was finally exchanged in March 1864 only to find that his wife had died during his incarceration. A new division of cavalry was formed for him and he was promoted to a major generalcy. He led his division through the Overland and Petersburg campaigns. After Appomattox, he was a farmer, he sat in the state senate and in the U.S. Congress, and he served as president of the state agricultural society. (Freeman, Douglas, S., *R. E. Lee* and *Lee's Lieutenants*)

LE MAT, J.A.F. (?-?)

Popular with many of the top Confederate generals were the revolvers designed by J.A.F. Le Mat. Born in France, the New Orleans doctor sometimes referred to himself as "Colonel." His weapon was of an eight-shot design with an extra lower barrel which was capable of firing a charge of buckshot. A few hundred were manufactured in the Crescent City immediately prior to the Civil War, but with the outbreak of the conflict Le Mat found it too difficult to continue manufacturing and sailed for France. Later he produced his sidearms in Britain and Belgium. In all some 3,000 made it through to the Confederacy, where they were carried by the likes of Jeb Stuart and Beauregard.

LEOPOLD I, King of Belgium (1790-1865)

Like Queen Victoria of Britain and Emperor Napoleon III of France, King Leopold I of Belgium was lobbied by Confederate agents for his recognition of the fledgling nation. By the outbreak of the Civil War Leopold had been on his throne for three decades. While toying with the Southern agents, he, like his fellow monarchs, never acceded to the pleas of such Confederate diplomats as, principally, Ambrose D. Mann. He died the same year the American war ended.

LESLIE, Frank (1821-1880)

A pioneer in the field, Frank Leslie published an illustrated weekly newspaper that was, for the first time, able to present pictures of events as soon as they were reported. Born in England, he had declined to enter his father's glove-making business, preferring to pursue his wood-carving and engraving interests. After working for the *Illustrated London News* under the name Frank Leslie (he had been named Henry at birth), he immigrated to the United States. There he worked for a number of publications and became the head of the engraving department of the *Illustrated News*. Here he scored a major coup by producing a two-page illustration, that would normally have taken four months, in only three days. His method was to divide the drawing into 34 parts and assign an engraver to each. After starting several papers of his own, he launched *Frank Leslie's Illustrated Newspaper* on December 15, 1855. During the Civil War his paper was one of the two national pictorial weeklies dispatching swarms of artist-correspondents to the armies. There was also a German edition, *Illustrierte Zeitung*. He ran several papers in the post war years but died in bankruptcy.

LETCHER, John (1813-1884)

To the Confederacy John Letcher was the opposite of Joseph Brown of Georgia—a cooperative governor. Born in the Shenandoah Valley, he became a lawyer and editor of the *Lexington Valley Star*, a Democratic organ. A champion of his section of the state against the historic domination of the Tidewater, he was propelled to a seat in Congress in 1851. Although a states' righter he opposed the extreme doctrines of John C. Calhoun. He kept his seat in Congress until 1859 when he ran for and was elected to a four-year term as Virginia's governor. Taking office at the start of 1860, he supported Douglas for president and urged a convention of the states to attempt to iron out the nation's difficulties. At the same time, as a precaution, he strengthened Virginia's military position. His planned convention was not called by the state legislature until a year after he took office; by this time it was too late, Lincoln having been elected and several states having seceded. He delayed calling a state convention, which might take the state out of the Union, until January 1861. Thanks in large part to his efforts, the convention had a large cooperationist element and refused to secede in February and March. With the firing on Fort Sumter and Lincoln's call for troops from Virginia, Letcher promptly refused and in a matter of days Virginia was out of the Union. Letcher supervised the organization of the Virginia land and naval forces and their eventual incorporation into the Confederate service. One of his chief accomplishments was the appointment of such officers as Lee and Jackson. During the war he opposed many of Jefferson Davis' war measures, especially the draft and impressment of supplies for the army, but went along with them until the victory could be won. Only then would he challenge them in court to prevent the Confederacy from becoming too centralized, as had happened in the United States, and infringing upon states' rights. His constant collaboration with the Confederate authorities in unpopular measures did not sit well with his constituency. He did oppose the central government on such matters as the treatment of Union officers who incited slave revolts and Union soldiers from western Virginia. He wanted to be more severe but gave in to fears of retaliation. In order to continue his political career after the conclusion of his term, he ran, in 1863, for a seat in the Second Confederate Congress but was defeated. He returned home in early 1864, and his home was burned by federal forces in June. Impoverished by his service to the state, he resumed his law practice. He was imprisoned for six weeks at the end of the war and served briefly in the state legislature before his death. (Boney, Francis Nash, *The Life of John Letcher, Virginia's Civil War Governor*)

LEVENTHORPE, Collett (1815-1889)

A veteran of the British army's 14th Regiment of Foot, Collett Leventhorpe lent his military talents to the Confederacy but for some reason refused to accept a brigadier generalship in the final months of the Civil War. The Devonshire officer eventually settled in North Carolina. His Confederate assignments included: colonel, 34th North Carolina (November 1861); colonel, 11th North Carolina (April 2, 1862); brigadier general, North Carolina State Troops (1864); and brigadier general, CSA (February 18, 1865). He commanded one regiment from his adopted state until taking charge of what was nicknamed the "Bethel Regiment" in the spring of 1862. With this unit he served in North Carolina until joining the Army of Northern Virginia for the invasion of Pennsylvania. He was wounded on the first day at Gettysburg and was taken prisoner on July 5, 1863. Following his recovery he was confined at Fort McHenry and Point Lookout before being exchanged on or about March 10, 1864. On the 27th of April he resigned his colonelcy, citing his Gettysburg wounds. However, that same year Governor Zebulon Vance named him a state brigadier and he was assigned to duty guarding the railroad to Petersburg. The next winter, however, he declined a Confederate appointment on March 6, 1865. After the war he retired to North Carolina.

LEWIS, David Peter (ca. 1820-1884)

A confirmed Unionist, but one-time Confederate congressman and judge, David P. Lewis quit the Confederacy and after the war was the scalawag governor of Alabama. A native of Virginia, he had practiced law and run a plantation in Alabama. A Democrat and Unionist, he voted against secession but nonetheless signed the ordinance. Named to the Provisional Confederate Congress, he was admitted on February 8, 1861, but resigned on April 29 after the close of the first session, claiming inconvenience in his further attendance. During his brief tenure he served on the committees on Indian Affairs and Patents. Alabama Governor John G. Shorter appointed him a judge, but he soon fled to Union-controlled Nashville where he remained for the balance of the war. Returning to Alabama in 1865, he resumed his practice and joined the Radical Republicans in Reconstruction. From 1872 to 1874 he served as governor and became thoroughly hated by the ex-Confederate population. He was forced into private life by the return of white supremacist rule.

LEWIS, John Wood (1801-1865)

A successful Georgia businessman and farmer, John W. Lewis was appointed to the Confederate Senate by Governor Joseph E. Brown—whom Lewis had earlier loaned the money to attend Yale Law School. Born in South Carolina, Lewis practiced medicine and sat in the state legislature there before becoming a Baptist preacher and moving to Georgia where he also proved effective as a railroad superintendent, an appointment from Brown. When Robert Toombs rejected election to the Confederate Senate, Lewis was appointed. He sat on the committees on: Finance; and Post Offices and Post Roads. Allied with Brown, he proved to be an ardent states' righter doing much to hinder the central government in its ability to wage war. He opposed the draft and the establishment of a Confederate supreme court and was part of the anti-Bragg faction—he supported P.G.T. Beauregard for command in the West. Not seeking reelection to a full six-year term, he finished the war looking after Georgia's share in the salt mines at Saltville, Virginia.

LEWIS, Joseph Horace (1824-1904)

As commander of the famed Kentucky, or Orphan, Brigade, Joseph H. Lewis finished the Civil War as part of the escort for the fleeing Jefferson Davis and his party. The native Kentuckian was a lawyer and state legislator before the war. His Confederate assignments included: colonel, 6th Kentucky (November 1, 1861); commanding Helm's Brigade, Breckinridge's-Bate's Division, Hill's-Breckinridge's-Hindman's Corps, Army of Tennessee (September 20, 1863-February 28, 1864); brigadier general, CSA (September 30, 1863) commanding Kentucky Brigade, Bate's-Brown's Division, Hardee's Corps, Army of Tennessee (February 28-September 4, 1864); commanding brigade, Iverson's Division, Wheeler's Cavalry Corps, Army of Tennessee (September 4-late 1864); commanding brigade, Iverson's Division, Wheeler's Cavalry Corps, Department of South Carolina, Georgia and Florida (late 1864-March 1865); and commanding brigade, Iverson's Cavalry Division, Military District of South Carolina and Georgia, Department of South Carolina, Georgia and Florida (March-May 9, 1865). He led his regiment at Shiloh, Murfreesboro, and during the Tullahoma Campaign. On the second day at Chickamauga he succeeded the deceased Benjamin H. Helm in command of the Kentucky Brigade and was promoted to brigadier general at the end of the month. He led the brigade at Chattanooga and throughout the Atlanta Campaign at the conclusion of which the brigade was mounted. Serving out the balance of the war as cavalry, the brigade, under Lewis' direction, fought in the Savannah Campaign and in May 1865 was part of Davis' escort. Surrendering when the president was captured in Georgia, Lewis resumed his practice and again entered politics as a state legislator and U.S. congressman. He later spent nearly two decades as a judge. (Davis, William C., *The Orphan Brigade: The Kentucky Confederates Who Couldn't Go Home*)

LEWIS, Levin M. (?-?)

Serving in the Trans-Mississippi, Levin M. Lewis received an extralegal promotion to brigadier after most of the Confederate armies had surrendered. His service included: colonel, 3rd Missouri, 5th Division, Missouri State Guard (early 1861); lieutenant colonel, 7th Missouri; colonel, 16th Missouri; and brigadier general, CSA, by General E. Kirby Smith (May 16, 1865). During the first year of the war he served in the state forces. Transferring to Confederate service, he became second in command of the 7th Missouri which became the 16th when he took over as colonel. His service was principally in the District of Arkansas but he was part of the detachment sent to the District of West Louisiana to face N.P. Banks' Red River Campaign in the spring of 1864. In the final days of the war he commanded a brigade and was rewarded with a promotion to brigadier 10 days before the surrender of the Trans-Mississippi Department.

LEWIS, William Gaston (1835-1901)

Educated at a military school, former North Carolina educator William G. Lewis gave up a railroading job to enter the Confederate military where he was twice assigned to duty as a temporary brigadier general. His assignments included: ensign, 1st North Carolina (April 21, 1861); major, 33rd North Carolina, (January 17, 1862); lieutenant colonel, 43rd North Carolina (April 25, 1862); commanding Hoke's (old) Brigade, Ransom's Division, Department of North Carolina and Southern Virginia (May 1864); temporary brigadier general, CSA (May 31, 1864); commanding same brigade, Early's-Ramseur's-Pegram's Division, 2nd Corps, Army of Northern Virginia (May-June 1864 and December 1864-April 7, 1865); and commanding brigade, Ramseur's-Pegram's Division, Valley District, Department of Northern Virginia (June-August 5 and November-December 1864). Serving with his first regiment, he fought at Big Bethel before it was mustered out in the fall of 1861. He soon became a field grade officer in the 33rd North Carolina but remained only a few months before transferring to the 43rd. However, he did see action at New Bern. In his new unit, he served in the Seven Days, in the Department of North Carolina, and at 2nd Winchester before succeeding to regimental leadership upon the capture of the

colonel at Gettysburg. After serving at Bristoe Station and in the Mine Run Campaign, his regiment was temporarily detached to serve with Hoke's Brigade in North Carolina. Fighting at Plymouth, he earned temporary promotion to brigadier and the command of Hoke's brigade which he led back to Lee's army for the fighting at the North Anna and Cold Harbor and with Early at Monocacy. In August 1864 he was relieved of brigade command upon the return of newly promoted General A.C. Godwin. Following the latter's death he again served as a general through the Petersburg siege and in the retreat to Appomattox until wounded and captured at Farmville on April 7, 1865. He engaged in civil engineering for over three decades. (Freeman, Douglas S., *Lee's Lieutenants*)

LEYDEN, Austin (?-1900)

Pennsylvania-born Atlanta manufacturer Austin Leyden served with his artillery battalion throughout most of the war but mostly in the less-chronicled theaters. He entered his adopted state's service at the outbreak of hostilities and his assignments included: lieutenant, Company F, 1st Georgia (March 18, 1861); major, 9th Georgia Artillery Battalion (April 1862); commanding Artillery Battalion, Preston's Division, Buckner's Corps, Army of Tennessee (August 6-late September 1863); commanding artillery battalion, Longstreet's Corps, Army of Tennessee (September-November 1863); and commanding artillery battalion, Department of East Tennessee (November 1863-April 1864). On November 5, 1861, he resigned his infantry commission in order to raise an artillery unit with which he served in Georgia, southwest Virginia, and East Tennessee. When the forces in the Department of East Tennessee were organized into a corps and assigned to the Army of Tennessee, Leyden took part in the Chickamauga Campaign and the beginning of the Chattanooga siege. Accompanying Longstreet back into East Tennessee, he took part in the unsuccessful Knoxville siege. Moving into Virginia, he was in charge of a reserve artillery camp at Staunton in the summer of 1864. By that fall the battalion had been assigned to the fortifications around the capital where it served until the city's fall. Leyden returned to Atlanta after Appomattox and was active in local politics and as an inventor.

LIDDELL, St. John Richardson (1815-1870)

Resigning in 1838 after only one year at West Point, St. John R. Liddell settled on a Louisiana plantation until the Civil War gave him a second chance for a military career—in the Southern service. The Mississippi native's assignments included: colonel and volunteer aide-de-camp (1861); commanding 1st Brigade, 3rd Corps, Army of the Mississippi (June-July 5, 1862); commanding brigade, Buckner's Division, Army of the Mississippi (July 5-August 15, 1862); brigadier general, CSA (July 17, 1862); commanding brigade, Buckner's Division, Left Wing, Army of the Mississippi (August 15-November 20, 1862); commanding brigade, Buckner's-Cleburne's Division, Hardee's-Breckinridge's Corps, Army of Tennessee (November 20, 1862-September 1863 and September 22-November 30, 1863); commanding division, Reserve Corps, Army of

Tennessee (September 1863); commanding brigade, Cleburne's Division, Hardee's (new) Corps, Army of Tennessee (November 30-December 2, 1863); commanding Sub-District of North Louisiana, District of West Louisiana, Trans-Mississippi Department (spring 1864); and commanding in the Department of Alabama, Mississippi and East Louisiana: District of Southwest Mississippi and East Louisiana (August 2-25, 1864); brigade, District of the Gulf (August-October 1864); and division, District of the Gulf (October 1864-April 9, 1865). He held a staff position in central Kentucky with William J. Hardee early in the war and then served as a special messenger to Richmond for Albert S. Johnston. For a few weeks he commanded a brigade in Mississippi before being named a brigadier general. He led a brigade at Perryville, Murfreesboro, and during the Tullahoma Campaign. At Chickamauga he led a division in William H.T. Walker's Reserve Corps. Back with his regular brigade, he fought at Chattanooga and the next year led a sub-district in Louisiana during the Red River Campaign. Transferring back to the east of the Mississippi, he led a brigade and division around Mobile during the final stages of the war. Captured at the fall of Fort Blakely, he returned to his plantation upon his release and was killed by a fellow planter five years later. (Hughes, Nathaniel C., ed., Liddell, St. John Richardson, *Liddell's Record*)

LIGHTFOOT, Charles Edward (1834-1878)

Starting out in the Confederate infantry, Charles Edward Lightfoot ended up serving for most of the war in the artillery defenses of the capital. A graduate of the Virginia Military Institute, he was teaching at the Hillsboro Military Academy in North Carolina at the outbreak of the war. His service included: major, 6th North Carolina (May 16, 1861); lieutenant colonel, 6th North Carolina (July 11, 1861); colonel, 22nd North Carolina (March 29, 1862); lieutenant colonel, Artillery (August 18, 1862); commanding Light Artillery Battalion, Richmond Defenses, Department of Richmond (ca. April 1, 1863-ca. April 2, 1865); and commanding artillery battalion, 2nd Corps, Army of Northern Virginia (ca. April 2-9, 1865). With his first regiment he served at the battle of 1st Bull Run and was praised by his superiors. Elected to command another regiment, he was captured at Seven Pines on May 31, 1862. Upon his exchange on August 5, 1862, he found that he had been defeated for reelection upon the reorganization of the regiment on June 13. However, within two weeks he was given an appointment in the artillery. He eventually commanded an artillery battalion defending Richmond until the fall of that city. He then took command of a battalion in the retreat to Appomattox. Settling back in his native Culpeper County, Virginia, he served on the faculty of the Bethel Military Academy.

LILLEY, Robert Doak (1836-1886)

Appointed under the act authorizing Jefferson Davis to appoint temporary general officers, Robert D. Lilley did not last long in active field command. A native Virginian and a survey equipment salesman, he raised the Augusta Lee Rifles for the Con-

federate army. His assignments included: captain, Company C (D from May 1862), 25th Virginia (ca. May 1861); major, 25th Virginia (January 28, 1863); lieutenant colonel, 25th Virginia (August 20, 1863); brigadier general, CSA (May 31, 1864); commanding Pegram's Brigade, Early's-Ramseur's Division, 2nd Corps, Army of Northern Virginia (June 4-13, 1864); commanding Pegram's Brigade, Ramseur's Division, Valley District, Department of Northern Virginia (June 13-July 20, 1864); and commanding reserve forces, same district and department (November 28, 1864-April 1865). His company and regiment fought at Rich Mountain, Greenbrier River, Allegheny, McDowell, in the Shenandoah Valley Campaign, the Seven Days, at Cedar Mountain, 2nd Bull Run, Antietam (commanding the regiment), Fredericksburg, Gettysburg, Mine Run, and the Wilderness. At Spotsylvania his regiment was so mauled that it was consolidated with the other regiments of the brigade. Lilley was soon promoted to temporary brigadier and placed in charge of the wounded General Pegram's Brigade. After fighting at Cold Harbor he went with Early to the Shenandoah and fought at Monocacy and on the outskirts of Washington. While scouting near Winchester, Virginia, on July 20, 1864, he received three wounds and was captured. When federals left the area a few days later they left Lilley, who recovered to finish the war in command of the reserve forces in the Valley. After the war he was employed by Washington College. (Freeman, Douglas S., *Lee's Lieutenants*)

LINEBAUGH, John H. (?-ca. 1865)

One striking victim of the historic conflict between the press and the military was John Linebaugh. Using the pen-name "Shadow," Linebaugh was the special correspondent for the *Memphis - Grenada - Jackson - Meridian - Atlanta - Montgomery Appeal* in Chattanooga. While reporting for the refugee paper, he became very critical of General Braxton Bragg's apparent lack of willingness to fight the Union forces. Finally, in September 1863, the commander of the Army of Tennessee, who had retired from middle Tennessee into northern Georgia, abandoning Chattanooga, placed the reporter under arrest for excessive criticism. The *Appeal* struck back in behalf of its correspondent, who was being held without a trial, and obtained his release in early October. The paper blasted Bragg's actions as a "civil offense." Resuming his reportorial duties, Linebaugh was accidentally drowned in the Alabama River during one of the paper's many flights from capture.

LITTLE, Lewis Henry (1817-1862)

Baltimore native Lewis Henry Little resigned his regular army captaincy in the 7th Infantry on May 7, 1861, and ended up giving his life to the Confederate cause. He had been commissioned directly into the old army in 1839 and had won a brevet in Mexico. His Confederate assignments included: major, Artillery (ca. May 1861); colonel and assistant adjutant general (1861); commanding 1st Brigade, Missouri State Guard (Confederate volunteers), Trans-Mississippi District (Army of the West), Department #2 (ca. February-March 17, 1862);

commanding 1st Brigade, 1st Division, Trans-Mississippi District (Army of the West), Department #2 (March 17-April 1862); brigadier general, CSA (April 12, 1862); commanding 1st Brigade, Price's Division, Army of the West, Department #2 (April-June 1862); commanding the division (June-September 1862); and commanding 1st Division, Price's Corps (Army of the West), Army of West Tennessee, Department #2 (September-September 19, 1862). Attracting the attention of Sterling Price of the Missouri State Guard, on whose staff he was serving, he was given charge of a brigade which he led at Pea Ridge. Promoted to brigadier general, he led his command across the Mississippi and took part in the operations around Corinth. Then, on September 19, 1862, he was instantly killed by a bullet in the head while meeting with Price and other officers during the battle of Iuka.

LITTLE ROBE (fl. 1860s-1870s)

It was the massacre at Sand Creek which prompted Little Robe to move from being a proponent of peace with the whites, into the war camp. One of the leading Cheyenne chiefs, he had long urged accommodation with the advancing whites. In this he was allied with Black Kettle. He had been reported as killed at Sand Creek in 1864, so Coloradans were surprised to hear that he was alive and well and stirring up trouble in the war camp in early 1865. He fought actively for the next two years but then signed the Treaty of Medicine Lodge in 1867. The next year he again went on the war path but surrendered shortly after the battle of the Washita. Placed on a reservation, he again counseled peace. By this time he was the principal chief of the Cheyennes—succeeding Black Kettle who had been killed in the massacre on the Washita. Twice, in 1871 and 1873, he toured the East—meeting President Grant on the latter trip. The next year he stayed on the reservation when the Red River War broke out. (Brown, Dee, *Bury My Heart At Wounded Knee*)

LIVERMORE, Thomas Leonard (1844-1918)

Although he had been born in Illinois, Thomas L. Livermore became the most famous writer on New Hampshire's Civil War history and also authored one of the top statistical studies on that conflict, North and South. Having applied to West Point, he went to Washington in 1861 to speed up his appointment but got caught up in the war fever raging there and enlisted in a New Hampshire unit. His assignments included: private, 1st New Hampshire (spring 1861); lieutenant, 5th New Hampshire (ca. October 22, 1861); captain, 5th New Hampshire (1863); chief of Ambulance Corps, 2nd Corps, Army of the Potomac (fall 1863); major, 5th New Hampshire (1864); acting assistant inspector general, 2nd Corps, Army of the Potomac (1864-spring 1865); and colonel, 18th New Hampshire (mid 1865). He took part in Patterson's campaign in the Shenandoah in July 1861 before being mustered out on August 9, 1861. Soon becoming a line officer in a new unit, he was highly commended by his regimental commander, Edward E. Cross, at Antietam. The regiment also fought on the Peninsula and at Fredericksburg, Chancellorsville, and

Gettysburg. As a captain, he directed the 2nd Corps' ambulances at Bristoe Station. The following year, he became acting assistant inspector general on the staff of Winfield Hancock and was advanced to major. Continuing under Andrew A. Humphreys in the same position, he took part in the Petersburg and Appomattox campaigns. With hostilities at a close he was named to head the 18th New Hampshire, of which he wrote *History of the Eighteenth New Hampshire Volunteers, 1864-5*. Mustered out on July 29, 1865, he became a lawyer and was engaged in the mining and milling businesses. Entering the historical writing field, he wrote several articles. His statistical work was *Numbers and Losses in the Civil War in America, 1861-65*. His memoirs, *Days and Events, 1860-1866*, appeared two years after his death. (See also: Bibliography)

LLOYD, John M. (?-1892)

One of the key witnesses against Mary E. Surratt, John M. Lloyd did much to send her to the gallows but later declared that he had been coerced into giving testimony. When the widowed Mrs. Surratt moved into Washington, Lloyd had rented the tavern at Surrattsville in Maryland. It was here that the guns to be used in the escape of the assassins were stored for convenient use. At the conspirators' trial Lloyd claimed that it was Mrs. Surratt who brought the message from Booth telling Lloyd to have the guns handy for imminent use. Lloyd's testimony should have been somewhat suspect because he was noted for his heavy drinking and lapses of memory. He was, however, supported in his claims by a boarder at the Surratt house in the city, Louis J. Weichmann. Lloyd later claimed that he was threatened with death in the event that he did not testify against Mrs. Surratt.

LOGAN, George Washington (1815-1889)

The disatisfaction with the war in North Carolina led to the formation of the "Red Strings" and their election of George W. Logan as a peace candidate to the Second Confederate Congress. A lawyer and former Whig, he never accepted secession and held no position of importance in the first years of the war. Elected as an antiwar congressman, he served on the committees on: Printing; and Ordnance and Ordnance Supplies. Reflecting his 10th District constituents' views, he proposed the repeal of the tax-in-kind and fought arbitrary impressments. On conscription he favored a wide range of exemptions. Turning Republican at the close of the war he served as a superior court judge. Considered too friendly to the freed slaves in his decisions, he required military protection from the Ku Klux Klan to hold his court sessions. In 1874 he retired to private life and was engaged in the real estate business.

LOGAN, Thomas Muldrop (1840-1914)

A recent South Carolina College graduate, Thomas M. Logan fought throughout the war and was one of the last men in the cavalry to become a general officer. After witnessing the bombardment of Fort Sumter he joined the Confederate army. His assignments included: first lieutenant, Company A,

Hampton (S.C.) Legion (early 1861); captain, Company A, Hampton Legion (ca. July 21, 1861); major, Hampton Legion (1862); lieutenant colonel, Hampton Legion (1862); colonel, Hampton Legion (ca. May 19, 1864); brigadier general, CSA (February 15, 1865); and commanding brigade, Butler's Cavalry Division, Hampton's Cavalry Command (February-April 9, 1865); and commanding brigade, Butler's Division, Hampton's Cavalry Command, Army of Tennessee (April 9-26, 1865). He fought at 1st Bull Run and on the Peninsula until wounded at Gaines' Mill during the Seven Days. The legion went on to fight at Antietam, Fredericksburg, in southeastern Virginia, Chickamauga, and Knoxville. Having steadily risen in rank he was with the unit when it was converted into mounted infantry in early 1864 and succeeded to command it that spring. Serving with the cavalry of the Department of Richmond, he was wounded during the Richmond-Petersburg operations. Two months before the war ended he was promoted to brigadier and was transferred to his native state to join Hampton and Butler in trying to stop Sherman. Commanding a brigade, he fought at Bentonville and surrendered what was left of the division at Greensboro with Joe Johnston. He was a lawyer and highly successful railroader after the conflict.

LOMAX, Lunsford Lindsay (1835-1913)

Born to a Virginia army officer in Rhode Island, Lunsford L. Lomax followed his father's lead and opted for a career in the military. An 1856 graduate of West Point, he served in the cavalry until his April 25, 1861, resignation as first lieutenant. Originally a captain and assistant adjutant general in the state forces, he transferred to those of the Confederacy as an inspector. Serving on the staffs of Ben McCulloch, J.E. Johnston, and Earl Van Dorn, he rose from captain to lieutenant colonel. His later assignments included: colonel, 11th Virginia Cavalry (ca. February 15, 1863); brigadier general, CSA (July 23, 1863); commanding brigade, F. Lee's Division, Cavalry Corps, Army of Northern Virginia (September 9, 1863-August 10, 1864); major general, CSA (August 10, 1864); commanding Ransom's (old) Cavalry Division, Valley District, Department of Northern Virginia (August 10, 1864-April 1865); and also the district (from March 29, 1865). After serving with his new regiment in the Shenandoah Valley he fought at Brandy Station and Gettysburg. Promoted and given a brigade, he served through the Overland Campaign and in the early operations at Petersburg. Taking over Ransom's Cavalry Division in the Valley, he fought under Early at 3rd Winchester and Fisher's Hill. The day after the latter he was temporarily captured at Woodstock but escaped within hours. He then fought at Cedar Creek and took part in a number of raids in the western part of the state. In the last days he was in charge of the district and following Lee's surrender he made his way to Johnston's army in North Carolina and commanded some fragments from the former's army. He was surrendered at Greensboro and subsequently was a farmer and educator. Lomax worked on the *Official Records* for six years and sat on the commission for the Gettysburg park. (Freeman, Douglas S., *Lee's Lieutenants*)

LONG, Armistead Lindsay (1825-1891)

Veteran artilleryman Armistead L. Long was promoted from a staff position with Lee to the command of the 2nd Corps' artillery. The native Virginian and West Pointer (1850) resigned his first lieutenant's commission and a position as aide-de-camp to his father-in-law, General Edwin V. Sumner, on June 10, 1861. For the South his assignments included: major, PACS (1861); colonel, PACS (ca. March 1861); brigadier general, CSA (September 21, 1863) and commanding Artillery, 2nd Corps, Army of Northern Virginia (September 23, 1863-April 9, 1865, with frequent absences). In western Virginia he served as W.W. Loring's artillery chief and inspector before being transferred to the southern coast as chief of artillery and ordnance for Lee and Pemberton. When Lee became the advisor to the president he made Long his military secretary, with the rank of colonel. In this position Long served in all of Lee's campaigns through Gettysburg. In the fall of 1863 he was promoted and given charge of the 2nd Corps' guns. He led them at the Wilderness, Spotsylvania, and Cold Harbor. At times in charge of the Valley District's artillery during Early's campaign there, he was often off duty due to illness. Returning to the main army, he surrendered with it at Appomattox. A civil engineer after the war for five years, he subsequently wrote *Memoirs of Robert E. Lee* despite being completely blind. President Grant appointed Long's wife postmistress of Charlottesville. (Freeman, Douglas S., *R.E. Lee* and Wise, Jennings, C., *The Long Arm of Lee*)

LONGSTREET, James (1821-1904)

Corps commander James Longstreet made three mistakes that have denied him his deserved place in Southern posterity: He argued with Lee at Gettysburg, he was right, and he became a Republican. Born in South Carolina, he entered West Point from Alabama, graduated in 1842, and was wounded at Chapultepec in Mexico. With two brevets and the staff rank of major he resigned his commission on June 1, 1861, and joined the Confederacy. His assignments included: brigadier general, CSA (June 17, 1861); commanding brigade (in 1st Corps after July 20), Army of the Potomac (July 2-October 7, 1861); major general, CSA (October 7, 1861); commanding division, 1st Corps, Army of the Potomac (October 14-22, 1861); commanding division (in Potomac District until March 1862), Department of Northern Virginia (October 22, 1861-July 1862); commanding 1st Corps, Army of Northern Virginia (July 1862-February 25, 1863; May-September 9, 1863; April 12-May 6, 1864; and October 19, 1864-April 9, 1865); lieutenant general, CSA (October 9, 1862); commanding Department of Virginia and North Carolina (February 25-May 1863); commanding his corps, Army of Tennessee (September 19-November 5, 1863); and commanding Department of East Tennessee (November 5, 1863-April 12, 1864). Commanding a brigade, he fought at Blackburn's Ford and 1st Bull Run before moving up to divisional leadership for the Peninsula Campaign. There he saw further action at Yorktown, Williamsburg, Seven Pines, and the Seven Days. In the final days of the latter he also directed A.P. Hill's men. Command-

James Longstreet, Lee's "war horse." (NA)

ing what was variously styled a "wing," "command," or "corps," the latter not being legally recognized until October 1862, he proved to be a capable subordinate to Lee at 2nd Bull Run, where he delivered a crushing attack, South Mountain, Antietam, and Fredericksburg. By now promoted to be the Confederacy's senior lieutenant general, he led an independent expedition into southeastern Virginia where he displayed a lack of ability on his own. Rejoining Lee, he opposed attacking at Gettysburg in favor of maneuvering Meade out of his position. Longstreet, who had come to believe in the strategic offense and the tactical defense, was proven right when the Confederate attacks on the second and third days were repulsed. Detached to reinforce Bragg in Georgia, he commanded a wing of the army on the second day at Chickamauga. In the dispute over the follow-up of the victory he was critical of Bragg and was soon detached to operate in East Tennessee. Here again he showed an incapacity for independent operations, especially in the siege of Knoxville. Rejoining Lee at the Wilderness, he was severely wounded, in the confusion, by Confederate troops. He resumed command in October during the Petersburg operations and commanded on the north side of the James. Lee's "Old War Horse" remained with his chief through the surrender at Appomattox. After the war he befriended Grant and became a Republican. He served as Grant's minister to Turkey and as a railroad commissioner. Criticized by many former Confederates, he struck back with his book, *From Manassas to Appomattox*. He outlived most of his high-ranking postwar detractors. (Eckenrode, H.J. and Conrad, Bryan, *James*

Longstreet, Lee's War Horse and Sanger, Donald and Hay, Thomas, *James Longstreet*)

LOOMIS, John Q. (?-?)

Heavy casualties in the brigade to which he was attached twice brought John Q. Loomis to its temporary command, but he was never given permanent charge, in part because he also became a victim of enemy fire. His Confederate assignments included: lieutenant colonel, 1st Alabama Battalion (September 17, 1861); colonel, 25th Alabama (January 28, 1862); commanding Gladden's Brigade, Withers' Division, 2nd Corps, Army of the Mississippi (ca. April 8-23, 1862); and commanding Gardner's Brigade, Withers' Division, Polk's Corps, Army of Tennessee (December 1862). After initial service in the Mobile area his battalion was merged with another and he was given command of the resulting regiment. He led his command at Shiloh until superficially wounded late on the first day. Returning shortly after the battle, he took over direction of the brigade until General Gardner was assigned to replace the deceased Gladden. Loomis fought at Farmington and Bridge Creek and took part in the Kentucky Campaign but was not actively engaged. In December he again took command of the brigade and on the last day of the year was struck by a falling tree limb during the battle of Murfreesboro. He does not appear to have rejoined the regiment and resigned on September 14, 1863.

LORING, William Wing (1818-1886)

A one-armed veteran of the Mexican War, William W. Loring became one of the more troublesome of Confederate generals, frequently engaging in disputes with his superiors. The North Carolina native had been raised in Florida and served as a second lieutenant of state volunteers in the fighting against the Seminoles. He then practiced law and became a state legislator before being commissioned directly into the regular army for the Mexican War. As a captain of the Mounted Riflemen, he won two brevets in that conflict, being wounded at both Churubusco and Chapultepec and losing an arm at the latter. By the time of his May 13, 1861, resignation he was his regiment's colonel. His Confederate assignments included: brigadier general, CSA (May 20, 1861); commanding Army of the Northwest (July 20-August 3, 1861 and October 1861-February 9, 1862); commanding brigade, Army of the Northwest (August 3-October 1861); major general, CSA (February 17, 1862); commanding Department of Southwestern Virginia (May 8-October 16, 1862); commanding division, 2nd Military District, Department of Mississippi and East Louisiana (ca. January-April 1863); commanding division, Department of Mississippi and East Louisiana (April-May 16, 1863); commanding division, Department of the West (May 16-July 1863); commanding division, Department of Mississippi and East Louisiana (July 1863-January 28, 1864); commanding division, Department of Alabama, Mississippi and East Louisiana (January 28-May 4, 1864); commanding division, Polk's (Army of Mississippi)-Stewart's Corps, Army of Tennessee (May 4-June 14, July 7-July 28, 1864, September 1864-ca. March 1865, and April 9-26, 1865); and temporarily commanding the corps (June 14-July 7, 1864). While serving under Robert E. Lee in the first summer of the war, he took part in the disappointments of the campaign in western Virginia. That winter his command was placed under the overall command of Stonewall Jackson. Following the Romney Campaign, Loring opposed the stationing of his men in the exposed town during the bitter winter and obtained orders from Secretary of War Judah P. Benjamin to move to Winchester. Outraged, Jackson threatened to resign and was eventually upheld in his views of military etiquette. On February 9, 1862, Loring was removed from his post but a few days later was appeased with promotion to major general. After departmental command in southwestern Virginia, he was named to command a division in Mississippi. Frequently in conflict with department commander John C. Pemberton, he fought in the Vicksburg Campaign until cut off from the rest of Pemberton's force at Champion Hill. The two generals blamed each other for the defeat there. Loring then joined the forces under Joseph E. Johnston and took part in the defense of Jackson, Mississippi, and the Meridian Campaign. By now he was known to his men as "Old Blizzards" because of his battle cry "Give them blizzards, boys!" Transferred to Georgia, he fought in the Atlanta Campaign. When Leonidas Polk was killed at Pine Mountain, Loring briefly took charge of the corps but was succeeded the same day by Alexander P. Stewart. Returning to divisional command, he was wounded at Ezra Church and was out of action until after the fall of Atlanta. He then fought at Franklin, Nashville, and in the Carolinas. From 1869 to 1879 he was a division commander in Egypt and upon his return was called "Pasha Loring." (Loring, William Wing, *A Confederate Soldier in Egypt*)

LOVELL, Mansfield (1822-1884)

With a greatly insufficient force Mansfield Lovell was charged with the defense of the Confederacy's largest port, New Orleans, and its fall became his own. The native of the nation's capital and a West Pointer (1842) had served as an artillery officer during the Mexican War, winning a brevet and being wounded at Chapultepec. Resigning from the army as first lieutenant, 4th Artillery, in 1854, he was New York City street commissioner Gustavus W. Smith's deputy at the outbreak of the Civil War. Heading south, his assignments included: major general, CSA (October 7, 1861); commanding Department #1 (October 18, 1861-June 25, 1862); commanding 1st Division, District of the Mississippi, Department #2 (September 8-October 16, 1862); and commanding corps, Army of West Tennessee, Department #2 (October 16-December 7, 1862). Relieving David E. Twiggs from command in Texas and Louisiana, his major chore was the defense of the Crescent City. With most of his organized units called to Corinth, Mississippi, for the buildup prior to the battle of Shiloh, Lovell was left with only a handful of green troops. When the city fell in April 1862 he was blamed for the loss, but the next year a court of inquiry he had asked for absolved him of blame. In the meantime he led a division at the battle of Corinth and for a time a corps facing Grant's attempt to get at Vicksburg through central Mississippi. Relieved of duty he awaited orders until March

1865 when he was directed to join Joseph E. Johnston's forces in North Carolina. He was included in Johnston's surrender before he could be given a command. As a civil engineer he was John Newton's assistant in removing obstructions in New York's East River at Hell Gate.

LOWREY, Mark Perrin (1828-1885)

Leaving the Baptist ministry in Mississippi in order to join the Confederate army, Tennessee-born Mark P. Lowrey resigned his brigadier general's commission shortly before the fledgling nation's demise. A veteran of the Mexican War as a member of the 2nd Mississippi, his Civil War assignments included: colonel, 4th Mississippi State Troops (fall 1861); colonel, 32nd Mississippi (April 3, 1862); brigadier general, CSA (October 4, 1863); commanding brigade, Cleburne's Division, Hill's-Breckinridge's Corps, Army of Tennessee (October-November 1863); commanding brigade, Cleburne's Division, Hardee's-Cheatham's Corps, Army of Tennessee (November 1863-August 31, 1864 and September 2, 1864-ca. March 14, 1865); and temporarily commanding the division (August 31-September 2, 1864). After commanding his first 60-days unit, he took charge of a regular volunteer unit which, although participating in the Kentucky, Murfreesboro, and Chickamauga campaigns, was not present in the main battles. Given command of a brigade, with the rank of brigadier general, he fought at Chattanooga. During the Atlanta Campaign he was briefly in command of the division at the battle of Jonesboro. He later fought at Franklin and Nashville and in the early stages of the Carolinas Campaign before resigning on March 14, 1865. Thereafter he was engaged in religious and educational matters.

LOWRY, Robert (1830-1910)

South Carolina-born merchant and lawyer Robert Lowry rose to the rank of brigadier general during the final months of the Confederacy. Enlisting in the Rankin Grays, his assignments included: private, Company I, 6th Mississippi (1861); major, 6th Mississippi (August 1861); colonel, 6th Mississippi (May 23, 1862); commanding John Adams' (old) Brigade, Loring's Division, Stewart's Corps, Army of Tennessee (November 30, 1864-March 1865 and April 9-26, 1865); and brigadier general, CSA (February 4, 1865). As a field officer, he was twice wounded at Shiloh before being advanced to command of his regiment. This he led at Corinth and in the Vicksburg Campaign. During the latter he was serving in Loring's division and after the battle at Champion Hill was cut off from the rest of John C. Pemberton's army. The division then joined the forces under Joseph E. Johnston in a feeble, unsuccessful attempt to lift the siege of the city. Again joining Johnston in northern Georgia in May 1864, Lowry led his regiment through the Atlanta Campaign and then accompanied John B. Hood into middle Tennessee. When John Adams was killed at Franklin, Lowry took over the brigade and led it at Nashville. Early the next year he was advanced to brigadier general and led his brigade in the Carolinas Campaign, seeing action at Bentonville, before being included in the surrender to Johnston's forces. Thereafter he was active in politics and veterans' organizations. In the 1880s he served two four-year terms as governor of his adopted state.

LUBBOCK, Francis Richard (1815-1905)

During his two years as governor of Texas, South Carolina-born Francis R. Lubbock was primarily concerned with the raising of state funds to support the war. Having turned down a West Point appointment, he engaged in several business ventures before moving to Texas in 1836 where he was a druggist. As a militiaman, he fought Indians and Mexicans. Under the Texas Republic he was clerk of the House of Representatives, comptroller of the treasury, and a district clerk before being elected lieutenant governor of the state in 1857. He attended the Democratic national convention in 1860 and the next year was elected governor. Taking office three days later (November 7, 1861), he found the state's financial situation in a mess and attempted to remedy it. One method was the exportation of cotton through Mexico in order to bypass the Union blockade along the coast. Not seeking reelection, he left the governor's mansion on November 5, 1863, and joined the army. His assignments included: lieutenant colonel, PACS (late 1863); and colonel and aide-de-camp (1864). His entire service was on the staff of Jefferson Davis in Richmond. He fled South with his chief after the fall of Richmond and was then imprisoned for a time. He later returned to Texas as a rancher and served as a tax official. (Lubbock, Percy, *Six Decades in Texas: The Memoirs of Francis R. Lubbock*)

LUCAS, William (?-?)

A black living on the plantation of Dr. Richard H. Stewart, William Lucas was the driver of the team which took John Wilkes Booth and David Herold from Stewart's plantation to Port Conway, a ferry crossing point on the Rappahannock River. It was also Lucas who carried the insulting note and the money back to Dr. Stewart. He himself received $10 for his services.

LYNCH, William Francis (1801-1865)

A navy veteran since 1819, William F. Lynch had had a distinguished career when he resigned in 1861 to go with his native Virginia. His service included cruises to Brazil, China, in the West Indies, and around the world. In 1848 he made an historic exploration of the Jordan River and the Dead Sea. During the Mexican War he was at sea in the Gulf of Mexico. Early in 1861 he was named a captain in the Virginia naval forces and then on June 10 he was commissioned captain, CSN. As such he commanded the Aquia Creek batteries during their bombardment early in the war and then was sent to North Carolina where he commanded the mismatched Confederate fleet in the fighting at Roanoke Island and Elizabeth City. In the latter engagement he lost all his vessels. From March to October 1862 he served on the Mississippi near Vicksburg and then returned to North Carolina in charge of all naval operations on the coast of that state. He was at Smithville at the time of the fall of Fort Fisher. Settling in Baltimore he barely outlived the war, dying

on October 17, 1865. (Scharf, J. Thomas, *History of the Confederate States Navy*)

LYON, Francis Strother (1800-1882)

Having earned a reputation as a financial expert in the liquidation of Alabama's state bank in the 1840s and 1850s, Francis S. Lyon served as the chairman of the Confederate House of Representatives' Committee on Ways and Means in the Second Regular Congress. A North Carolinian by birth, he was a lawyer and served in the upper house of the Alabama legislature. While in private practice he had become a secession Democrat and took part in the walkout at the Charleston convention in 1860. He was returned to the legislature in 1861 and late that year was elected to the First Regular Confederate Congress where he sat on the Committee on Ways and Means. He chaired the committee in the next congress. His votes in Richmond indicate that he strongly favored a powerful national government supporting higher taxes and in effect the nationalization of the railroads. He lost heavily in his private investment in the cotton loan and his large plantation was devastated during the war. Returning to private practice after the war, he was active in the reclaiming of the state government for the white supremacists and served a term in the state senate.

LYON, Hylan Benton (1836-1907)

In his Confederate career Kentucky native and West Pointer (1856) Hylan B. Lyon served in all three branches of the service. Upon his graduation, he had been posted to the artillery and served on the frontier before resigning on April 30, 1861, as a first lieutenant in the 3rd Artillery in order to join the Confederacy. His assignments there included: first lieutenant, Artillery (ca. April 1861); captain, Cobb's (Ken.) Battery (late 1861); lieutenant colonel, 8th Kentucky (February 3, 1862); colonel, 8th Kentucky (September 1862); commanding brigade, Buford's Division, Forrest's Cavalry Corps, Department of Alabama, Mississippi and East Louisiana (early June 1864 and August-September 1864); brigadier general, CSA (June 14, 1864); commanding Infantry Division, Forrest's Cavalry Corps, Department of Alabama, Mississippi and East Louisiana (improvised organization July 1864); and commanding Department of Western Kentucky (September 26, 1864-spring 1865). After serving as an artillery officer he was captured at Fort Donelson while commanding an infantry regiment. Not exchanged until September 1862—having been imprisoned on Johnson's Island, Ohio—he was promoted to the permanent command of the regiment, which was converted to mounted infantry during the Vicksburg operations. Cut off from the city with William W. Loring after Champion Hill, he joined Joseph E. Johnston for the defense of Jackson, Mississippi. Following a period of detached service with Joseph Wheeler in East Tennessee, he returned to Mississippi, fighting at Brice's Crossroads. Promoted to brigadier general, he led the dismounted troopers of the infantry division under Forrest at Tupelo. In the final months of the war he commanded in western Kentucky. After a year in Mexico he took up farming in his native state.

LYONS, James (1801-1882)

The defeat of Virginia Congressman James Lyons' bid for reelection in 1863 was considered a rebuke to the Davis administration. A Whig-turned-Democrat lawyer, he was an early (1856) proponent of secession. In the 1861 congressional election he was defeated by former president John Tyler. But Tyler died before the beginning of the Regular Congress and Lyons won in a special election. Once in office he chaired the Committee on Public Buildings and sat on the Committee on Commerce. A Davis friend, he was one of the administration's staunchest supporters and fought against local interests which were tearing the states' rights-based Confederacy apart. In retaliation for the Emancipation Proclamation he favored the raising of the black flag and the payment of rewards to blacks who killed the enemy. In the fall of 1863 he was defeated by Williams C. Wickham and retired to private practice. He later served as Jefferson Davis' defense counsel.

M

MABRY, Hinchie Parham (1829-1885)

Whenever he was superseded by a senior colonel, Hinchie P. Mabry received the thanks of his superiors, but he never received promotion to brigadier. His Confederate assignments included: captain, Company G, 3rd Texas Cavalry (June 13, 1861); lieutenant colonel, 3rd Texas Cavalry (May 8, 1862); colonel, 3rd Texas Cavalry (October 8, 1862); commanding Whitfield's (old) Brigade, Jackson's Division, Lee's Cavalry Corps, Department of Mississippi and East Louisiana (fall-December 16, 1863); and commanding in the Department of Alabama, Mississippi and East Louisiana the following: brigade, Adams' Cavalry Division (ca. March 28-August 1864); brigade, District North of Homochitto (August-November 6, 1864); brigade, Northern Sub-District, District of Mississippi and East Louisiana (November 6, 1864-March 3, 1865); and Ross' Cavalry Brigade, District of Mississippi, East Louisiana and West Tennessee (March-May 4, 1865). He raised the "Dead Shot Rangers" which was assigned to the South Kansas-Texas Mounted Regiment and later designated as Company G, 3rd Texas Cavalry. He fought at Wilson's Creek, suffering a slight wound in the hand, and in the pursuit of the loyal Indians under Opothleyohola. After fighting at Pea Ridge, his regiment was dismounted and sent east of the Mississippi where he was wounded and captured at Iuka. Exchanged in October 1862, and with his regiment remounted, he served the rest of the war in the cavalry. He was on the fringes of the Vicksburg Campaign and was detached from Wirt Adams' command to join Forrest at Tupelo and in opposing A.J. Smith's August 1864 invasion of Mississippi. His brigade was broken up in early 1865 and he rejoined his regiment. Within a short time he was again an acting brigade commander. He was included in Richard Taylor's surrender in May 1865.

McANERNEY, John, Jr. (1838-1928)

A clerk in the Confederate post office in Richmond, John McAnerney, Jr., was serving as a captain of local defense troops when he earned great distinction in the repulse of the Kilpatrick-Dahlgren raid on Richmond. A native of Rhode Island, he was living in New Orleans when the Civil War began and entered the Confederate service. His assignments included: sergeant, Company F, 3rd Alabama (1861); captain, Company B, 3rd Virginia Battalion, Local Defense Troops (June 18, 1863); lieutenant colonel, 3rd Virginia Battalion, Local Defense Troops (April 20, 1864); and colonel, 3rd Virginia, Local Defense Troops (September 23, 1864). After serving as an enlisted man, he received a clerkship at the Richmond post office and became the commander of the company made up of the department's employees which was to be used only when the capital was directly threatened. In repulsing the February 1864 cavalry raid on the city, he was wounded while distinguishing himself. As the war progressed his regiment spent more and more time in the trenches. He was there for at least three months straight at the end of 1864. After the war he was in the railroad equipment and banking businesses in New York City.

McBRIDE, James H. (?-?)

A brigadier general in the Missouri State Guard, James H. McBride does not appear to have ever received a commission in the Confederate army. From the time of its formation, he commanded the Guard's 7th Division, seeing action at Wilson's Creek and in the siege of Lexington. In February 1862 he resigned his command and thus was not in the battle of Pea Ridge. However, his resignation does not appear to have been acted upon right away since he still appears as commanding a brigade as late as September 1862. At this point he disappears from the military records.

McCAUSLAND, John (1836-1927)

The next-to-last Confederate general to die, John McCausland spent most of his postwar years trying to justify his 1864 burning of Chambersburg, Pennsylvania. A graduate of the Virginia Military Institute, he had served as a professor at his alma mater during the intervening years before the Civil War. Despite being from the Unionist, western part of Virginia, he decided to join the majority of the state and not really the Confederacy proper. He had had some military field experience at the John Brown hanging. His Civil War assignments included: colonel, 36th Virginia (early 1861); commanding brigade, Floyd's Division, Army of Central Kentucky, Department #2 (January-February 1862); commanding brigade, Department of Southwestern Virginia (May 8-November 25, 1862); commanding brigade, Department of Western Virginia (November 25, 1862-May 1864); brigadier general, CSA (May 18, 1864); commanding brigade, Ransom's-Lomax's Cavalry Division, Valley District, Department of Northern Virginia (June 1864-March 1865); and commanding brigade, Rosser's Division, Cavalry Corps, Army of Northern Virginia (March-April 9, 1865). During the first year of the war he served under Generals Wise and Floyd in the western part of the state. At the beginning of 1862 the command was moved into Kentucky where McCausland directed a brigade. Part of the defending force at Fort Donelson, he managed to ferry his small brigade out of the capitulating fortification. For the next two years he was stationed in western Virginia protecting the Virginia and Tennessee Railroad and the local saltworks. After the battle of Cloyd's Mountain, in which he succeeded to overall command upon the death of General A.G. Jenkins, he was promoted to brigadier. He blamed his connection with the Donelson disaster for not having received the general's wreath earlier. Assuming command of part of Jenkins' old cavalry, he went with Early to the outskirts of the Union capital, fighting well at Monocacy on the way. After returning to the Valley, he was sent by Early to demand $100,000 in gold from the residents of Chambersburg. If not paid he was to fire the town. He did. Afterwards he served through the Valley Campaign, fighting at 3rd Winchester, Fisher's Hill, and Cedar Creek. Joining Lee before Petersburg in March 1865, he cut his way out rather than surrender his brigade at Appomattox. A few days later he disbanded his men. Returning home to what was now West Virginia, he had difficulties with his Unionist neighbors. He soon went into exile and spent several years in Canada, Europe, and Mexico. He was formally charged with arson in Pennsylvania, but President Grant intervened on his behalf. He increasingly felt mistreated by his neighbors and the press, who he felt never presented his case properly, and became something of a recluse on his farm until his death. (Freeman, Douglas, S., *Lee's Lieutenants*)

McCAW, James Brown (1823-1906)

When Richmond periodically turned into one large hospital after many of the battles of the Army of Northern Virginia, Dr. James McCaw was the director of its largest hospital—the largest in the Confederacy. A native of Richmond, McCaw received his medical training at the University of the City of New York. Returning to his home town he was a physician of some note before joining the Confederate army as a surgeon. He was assigned to the post of chief surgeon at Chimborazo Hospital on the outskirts of Richmond on October 9, 1861. He was responsible for a number of innovations in the operation of the hospital, including effective use of the hospital fund to purchase

special food stuffs, purchase of cows, rental of farm and pasture land, and the purchase of two canal boats to transport supplies. However, he was in frequent conflict with the Quartermaster's and Commissary Departments which stuck to the absolute letter of the army's regulations, often bringing to naught McCaw's efforts. During the Peninsula Campaign his hospital was filled to well over its capacity of 3,000 but muddled through. The surgical staff, although always shorthanded, managed to perform some innovative operations, preventing the loss of limbs by many a Confederate. During the latter part of the war, McCaw was also editor of the *Confederate States Medical Journal*. Based on very incomplete figures, it has been claimed that Chimborazo had a very low mortality rate. While this is questionable, the hospital was one of the most efficient of its time. McCaw returned to civilian practice after Richmond's fall and was also a college professor.

McCLANAHAN, John R. (?-ca. 1865)

A case of journalistic persistence in the face of adversity is that of the *Memphis Appeal* and its coeditors, Benjamin F. Dill and John R. McClanahan. They had succeeded to their positions in 1851 upon the death of Henry Van Pelt. Editorially, the paper was not originally a secessionist organ, and it stuck to the candidacy of Democrat Stephen A. Douglas despite the breakaway of the Southern part of the party. Finally giving up on the preservation of the Union, McClanahan and his associates threw the paper into complete support for the Confederacy. With the military fortunes of the South on the decline in early 1862, the paper and its staff fled the city just before it fell to Union forces. Setting up shop in Grenada, Mississippi, McClanahan started a three-year career as a refugee journalist. With successive Union advances, the paper subsequently published in Jackson and Meridian, Mississippi, Atlanta, and, finally, Montgomery, Alabama. Offering half-price subscriptions to soldiers in the field, McClanahan and Dill were able to keep the paper thriving, and even survived a strike. The paper was not very popular with the Union army, whose grasp it eluded in several narrow escapes, particularly at Jackson and Atlanta. With the surrender at Appomattox and Wilson's cavalry closing in on its last refuge, the *Appeal* staff fled again but was surrounded and captured at Columbus, Georgia. McClanahan managed to smuggle the press away, but Dill and the other equipment were not so lucky. Returning to Memphis, McClanahan's own luck ran out and he died in a fall from a hotel. (Baker, Thomas Harrison, *The Memphis Commercial Appeal*)

McCLELLAN, Henry Brainerd (1840-1904)

One of the most well-known memoirs dealing with the life of Jeb Stuart was written by his one-time adjutant, Henry B. McClellan. Joining the 3rd Virginia Cavalry, he had become a first lieutenant and adjutant and served through most of Jeb Stuart's early campaigns. On June 1, 1863, he was announced in orders as a member of the cavalryman's staff as a major and assistant adjutant general. In this position he played a key role in the fighting on Fleetwood Hill at Brandy Station a few days later. He took part in Stuart's ride around the Army of the Potomac during the Gettysburg Campaign. After serving in the fall campaigns, he continued with his chief in the Wilderness Campaign until the fall of Stuart at Yellow Tavern. With the death of his commander, he joined General Lee's staff as an aide for the next several months. After the war he was active in veterans' affairs and wrote his memoirs. (McClellan, Henry Brainerd, *The Life and Campaigns of Maj. Gen. J. E. B. Stuart*)

McCOMB, William (1828-1918)

Pennsylvania-born manufacturer William McComb entered Confederate service from his adopted state of Tennessee. He was elected a second lieutenant in the 14th Tennessee in May 1861. His later positions included: major, 14th Tennessee (ca. April 26, 1862); lieutenant colonel, 14th Tennessee (ca. August 15, 1862); colonel, 14th Tennessee (September 2, 1861); brigadier general, CSA (January 20, 1865); and commanding brigade, Heth's Division, A. P. Hill's Corps, Army of Northern Virginia (January 20-April 9, 1865). After service in the Cheat Mountain and Peninsula campaigns, McComb took part in the battles of Cedar Mountain, 2nd Bull Run, and Antietam where he was seriously wounded. Returning to the army he led the regiment at Chancellorsville where he was again severely wounded. Participating in the campaign from the Wilderness to Petersburg, McComb took part in the siege at the latter place and temporarily commanded Archer's Brigade during the battle of Poplar Spring Church. During the siege winter McComb was given his general's wreath and assigned to command a new brigade formed from the Tennessee regiments of Archer's and Bushrod Johnson's brigades. Leading this brigade, McComb took part in the remainder of the siege and finally surrendered at Appomattox Court House. After the war he settled in Virginia and became a farmer for nearly half a century. (Freeman, Douglas S., *Lee's Lieutenants*)

McCOWN, John Porter (1815-1879)

As a Confederate major general, West Pointer (1840) John P. McCown had a troubled career. Posted to the artillery, he had seen service in the Seminole War, on the frontier, during the Mexican War—winning a brevet—and on the expedition against the Mormons. Resigning his captaincy in the 4th Artillery on May 17, 1861, he offered his services to his native Tennessee. His Southern assignments included: lieutenant colonel, Artillery (1861); colonel, Tennessee Corps of Artillery (May 17, 1861); commanding 2nd Brigade, 1st Geographical Division, Department #2 (September 7-October 24, 1861); brigadier general, CSA (October 12, 1861); commanding 3rd Division, 1st Geographical Division, Department #2 (October 24, 1861-February 1862); commanding McCown's Command, 1st Geographical Division, Department #2 (February-April 1862); major general, CSA (March 10, 1862); commanding division, Army of the West, Department #2 (April-July 1862); also commanding the army (June 20-27 and July 20, 1862); commanding division, Department of East Tennessee (summer-December 1862); commanding the depart-

ment (September 1-19 and September 27-October 1862); commanding division, attached to Hardee's Corps, Army of Tennessee (December 1862-January 1863); and commanding division, Smith's Corps, Army of Tennessee (February-March 1863). Initially in charge of the state's artillery, he commanded a brigade and then a division at Columbus, Kentucky. He did not however cross the Mississippi for the fight at Belmont. Commanding at New Madrid and Island #10, he came in for severe criticism for his handling of the defense and withdrawal from the latter. By now a major general he led a division in the Corinth siege before being transferred to East Tennessee. On the invasion of Kentucky he fought at Richmond and then, attached to Bragg's army, fought at Murfreesboro. He then ran into trouble with the army commander who brought charges against him for disobedience of orders. Court-martialed on March 16, 1863, McCown was sentenced to six months' suspension from duty without pay. Afterwards he held only minor posts for the balance of the war. He was a teacher and farmer postwar.

McCULLOCH, Ben (1811-1862)

By the outbreak of the Civil War, Ben McCulloch had already served in two wars—the War for Texas Independence and the Mexican War. The Tennesseean had gone to Texas for the first struggle and had settled there as a surveyor and later as a U.S. marshal. With Texas' secession he offered his services to the state and his subsequent assignments included: colonel, Texas

Ben McCulloch, victor at Wilson's Creek, was later killed at Pea Ridge. (*Leslie's*)

State Troops (February 1861); brigadier general, CSA (May 11, 1861); commanding all Confederate forces in the Indian Territory (May 11-summer 1861); commanding all Confederate forces in Arkansas (summer 1861); commanding division, Department #2 (September 2, 1861-January 9, 1862); and commanding division, District of the Trans-Mississippi, Department #2 (January 9-March 7, 1862). Commanding state troops he accepted the surrender of regular army units in Texas during the first month of Texas' new status. Promoted to a general's wreath, although he never wore a uniform, he commanded a force sent to the Indian Territory (now Oklahoma) and moved with it into Arkansas and later into Missouri. Assuming command of Price's Missouri State Guard and N.B. Pearce's Arkansas state forces as well, he won a victory at Wilson's Creek, but bickering among the commanders prevented exploitation of the success. Returning to Arkansas, he commanded his division, under Earl Van Dorn, at Pea Ridge until he was almost instantly killed by a bullet in the chest on March 7, 1862. (Nunn, W. Curtis, ed., *Ten More Texans in Gray*)

McCULLOCH, Henry Eustace (1816-1895)

The younger brother of Ben McCulloch, Henry E. McCulloch also became a Confederate general, but his service was confined to the area west of the Mississippi River. Born in Tennessee, he had moved to Texas in 1837. For a time he served as a sheriff and during the Mexican War was a company commander in the 1st Texas Rifles, Bell's Regiment and Smith's Battalion. In the interwar years he was a state legislator and U.S. marshal. His Confederate assignments included: colonel, 1st Texas Mounted Rifles (April 15, 1861); commanding Department of Texas (September 4-18, 1861); commanding Military Sub-District of the Rio Grande, Department of Texas (February 25-April 24, 1862); brigadier general, CSA (March 14, 1862); and commanding in the Trans-Mississippi Department: Eastern Sub-District of Texas, District of Texas, New Mexico and Arizona (August 15-29, 1863); Northern Sub-District of Texas, District of Texas, New Mexico and Arizona (August 29, 1863-May 26, 1865); and also 8th (Texas) Cavalry Brigade, 3rd (Texas) Cavalry Division, 3rd Corps (or District of Texas, New Mexico and Arizona) (September 1864-May 26, 1865). Serving mostly in Texas he held various sub-district commands and in the final months of the war he also commanded a paper organization cavalry brigade. His one major action came in Louisiana during the Vicksburg Campaign when he took part in the attack on Milliken's Bend. Following the department's surrender on May 26, 1865, he returned to his farm for the balance of his life.

McCULLOCH, Robert (1820-1905)

Known as "Black Bob," Colonel Robert McCulloch was in command of a brigade of cavalry for the latter half of the war but without receiving promotion to the appropriate rank. His Confederate assignments included: captain, 1st Cavalry, 6th Division, Missouri State Guard (May 12, 1861); lieutenant colonel, 1st Cavalry, 6th Division, Missouri State Guard (June 1861); colonel, 1st Cavalry, 6th Division, Missouri State Guard

(October 1, 1861); commanding 6th Division, Missouri State Guard (December 28, 1861-March 4, 1862); lieutenant colonel, 4th Missouri Cavalry Battalion (April 27, 1862); colonel, 2nd Missouri Cavalry (August 1862); and in the Department of Mississippi and East Louisiana: commanding brigade, Jackson's Division, Van Dorn's Cavalry Corps (November 7, 1862-January 1863); commanding 1st Brigade, 5th Military District (May 30-June 1863); commanding brigade, Chalmers' Cavalry Division (October 18-November 1863); commanding brigade, Chalmers' Division, Lee's Cavalry Corps (November 1863-January 11, 1864); commanding brigade, Chalmers' Division, Forrest's Cavalry Corps (January 11-28, 1864); and commanding brigade, Chalmers' Division, Forrest's Cavalry Corps, Department of Alabama, Mississippi and East Louisiana (January 28-ca. August 4 and late August 1864-May 1865). With the state forces, he saw action at Booneville, Carthage, Wilson's Creek, Dry Wood, Lexington, and Pea Ridge. Transferring to Confederate service, he raised a cavalry battalion which was later increased to a regiment and was sent across the Mississippi. Serving initially dismounted, it fought at Corinth during the siege. Remounted, McCulloch and his men fought at Iuka, Corinth, Okolona, and Tupelo. He was wounded at each of the latter two. His brigade, which he had been leading under Forrest, was detached to the District of the Gulf from September 1864 to February 6, 1865. The command's horses suffered severely at Mobile and the command was sent to northern Mississippi to recuperate and gather up deserters. They finished the war in this service.

McDANIEL, Zedekiah (?-?)

One of the more mysterious of Civil War soldiers was Captain Zedekiah McDaniel, the commander of a Confederate secret service company. A Kentuckian, McDaniel worked with the torpedo service. He was responsible for the sinking of the Union gunboat *Cairo* in the Yazoo River of Mississippi on December 12, 1862. His expenses were paid by the War Department as engineering services. On February 29, 1864, he was authorized to recruit a secret service company of up to 50 men. The unit was designated as "Captain Z. McDaniel's Company, Secret Service." A shadowy organization, it appears to have operated in various theaters. One of McDaniel's agents, John Maxwell, with a civilian companion on August 9, 1864, detonated an "horological" torpedo, or time bomb, at the immense Union supply base at City Point, Virginia, where Grant maintained his headquarters. An estimated total of 169 soldiers and civilian dock workers were killed or wounded. Some $2 million was lost to the Union cause and, although General Grant survived unscathed, some members of his headquarters were among the casualties. On March 28, 1865, McDaniel was ordered to the Mississippi Valley to report to General Henry Gray. Following the Union capture of the Confederate War Department's records, Maxwell's report to McDaniel of the City Point sabotage was found. Based on this evidence General Halleck ordered McDaniel's arrest on June 3, 1865, but here the record ends and McDaniel vanishes into obscurity. (Stern, Philip Van Doren, *Secret Missions of the Civil War*)

McGLASHAN, Peter Alexander Selkirk (1831-1908)

The incompleteness of Confederate records often makes it difficult to determine who was a general officer and who was not. Such is the case of Peter A.S. McGlashan who some claim was made a brigadier general in the last days of the war but never received the actual commission. A native of Edinburgh, Scotland, he had come to America in time to take part in the California Gold Rush. An adventurer, he also went to Nicaragua with William Walker's expansionist scheme. When he entered the Confederate army in the war's second year, his assignments included: first lieutenant, Company E, 50th Georgia (March 4, 1862); captain, Company E, 50th Georgia (October 1, 1862); colonel, 50th Georgia (July 31, 1863); and commanding Bryan's (old) Brigade, Kershaw's Division, 1st Corps, Army of Northern Virginia (February-March 1865). After service on the Georgia coast, his regiment was sent to join Lee in Virginia and saw action at 2nd Bull Run, Antietam, Fredericksburg, Chancellorsville, and Gettysburg. Going west with Longstreet in September 1863, his unit arrived too late to take part in the fighting at Chickamauga. Moving to East Tennessee he commanded the regiment at Knoxville and returned with it to Virginia for the Wilderness and Petersburg campaigns. During these actions he was wounded and did not return until February 1865 when he took over command of Bryan's Brigade. By the time of the fall of Richmond and Petersburg he was back in command of the 50th and led it at Sayler's Creek where he was captured. He was not released until July 25. Active in politics and veterans' affairs, he served as mayor of Thomasville, Georgia.

McGOWAN, Samuel (1819-1897)

A quartermaster of volunteers during the Mexican War, South Carolinian Samuel McGowan had served in the state legislature and was a militia major general at the outbreak of the war. Becoming a brigadier general of state troops, he commanded a brigade at the attack on Fort Sumter. Serving as a volunteer aide to General Bonham he was present at 1st Bull Run. His later positions included: lieutenant colonel (ca. September 9, 1861) and colonel (ca. April 11, 1862), 14th South Carolina; brigadier general, CSA (April 23, 1863, to date from January 17); commanding Maxcy Gregg's old Brigade, A.P. Hill's Division, Jackson's Corps, Army of Northern Virginia (January 19-May 3, 1863); and commanding same brigade, Wilcox's Division, Hill's Corps, Army of Northern Virginia (early 1864-April 9, 1865). After service on the South Carolina coast McGowan accompanied the brigade to Virginia in the spring of 1862. He led his regiment in the Seven Days Battles at Beaver Dam Creek, Gaines' Mill, and Frayser's Farm. He remained in the field despite being wounded at Gaines' Mill. Fighting at Cedar Mountain he was later wounded at 2nd Bull Run. Returning to his command after the battle of Antietam, he took part in the battle of Fredericksburg. He was then promoted to replace the slain General Gregg in command of the brigade. Wounded again at Chancellorsville, he was out of action for the rest of 1863. He then fought at the Wilderness and was wounded at Spotsylvania. Resuming command of his brigade he led it through the siege at Petersburg and in the Appomattox Campaign. After the surrender he resumed his political career, serving in the state legislature, having been refused a seat in Congress, and as a judge on the state supreme court. (Caldwell, J.F.J., *The History of a Brigade of South Carolinians*)

McGRAW, T.G. (?-1863)

The manpower shortage in the South caused the Richmond authorities to authorize their recruiting officers to operate in territory under Union control. This was hazardous duty, with many officers like T.G. McGraw being caught. He was arrested in Pendleton County, Kentucky, on April 9, 1863, along with William F. Corbin. They were charged with being Confederates out of uniform taking enlistees to the Southern forces. Found guilty, they were taken to Johnson's Island, Ohio, and on May 15 were shot by a firing squad. This led to a series of threatened retaliatory killings. The Richmond authorities refused to accept the Union position that recruiting behind enemy lines was a form of espionage.

McGUIRE, Hunter Holmes (1835-1900)

A secessionist medical professor, Virginian Hunter H. McGuire served as the medical director for the troops under Stonewall Jackson and Richard S. Ewell. Born in Winchester, he had received his training in Virginia and Pennsylvania and taught in Louisiana. His military assignments included: major and surgeon, CSA (May 1861); medical director, Valley District, Department of Northern Virginia (spring 1862); medical director, 2nd Corps, Army of Northern Virginia (June 1862-June 1864): and medical director, Army of the Valley District, Department of Northern Virginia (1864). He was instrumental in the organization of the ambulance corps and a system of reserve hospitals. Captured in March 1865, he was held until the end of the war. Subsequently he was active in medical education. (Cunningham, Horace Herndon, *Doctors in Gray*)

McINTOSH, Chilly (?-?)

The elder brother of Daniel N. McIntosh, Chilly McIntosh was also a chief of the Creek Indians and played a leading role in the aligning of the nation with the Confederacy. He took part in the bloody pursuit of the fleeing Upper Creeks under Opothleyohola, who wanted to remain loyal to the Union. In 1861 he raised the 1st Creek Cavalry Battalion and became its lieutenant colonel. This unit was subsequently increased to a regiment and designated the 2nd Creek Cavalry with McIntosh as colonel. He served through the remainder of the war in the Indian Territory and in raids into Kansas. (Monaghan, Jay, *Civil War on the Western Border, 1854-1865*)

McINTOSH, Daniel N. (?-?)

After being instrumental in getting his tribe to join with the Confederacy, mixed-blood chief Daniel N. McIntosh of the Creeks raised and commanded the 1st Creek Mounted Rifles.

His commission was dated August 19, 1861. In November and December of that year he led his regiment in pursuit of the fleeing band of Upper Creeks under Opothleyohola. Unlike Drew's regiment of Cherokees—some of that tribe were also fleeing toward Kansas—McIntosh's men had no qualms about killing members of their own tribe. Early the following year the treaty with the Confederacy was violated by the whites when they ordered the regiment out of the Indian Territory to serve in Arkansas. Here serving under General Albert Pike, who had negotiated with the Indians, McIntosh's command fought at Pea Ridge. Following the capture of three enemy cannons, of which the Indians were greatly afraid, they celebrated by scalping a disputed number of the enemy. Subsequently returned to the Indian Territory, McIntosh finished out the war there. (Monaghan, Jay, *Civil War on the Western Border, 1854-1865*)

McINTOSH, David Gregg (1836-1916)

Without any prior artillery experience, South Carolinian David Gregg McIntosh received relatively rapid promotion in the artillery of the Army of Northern Virginia. While practicing law he had also been an officer in a local volunteer company which offered its services soon after the state's secession. His assignments included: captain, Company D, 1st South Carolina (July 29, 1861); captain, Pee Dee (S.C.) Artillery (March 1862); major, Artillery (March 2, 1863); commanding artillery battalion, Reserve Artillery, 2nd Corps, Army of Northern Virginia (April 16-June 2, 1863); commanding artillery battalion, Reserve Artillery, 3rd Corps, Army of Northern Virginia (June 2-July 1863); commanding artillery battalion, 3rd Corps, Army of Northern Virginia (July 1863-March 1865); lieutenant colonel, Artillery (February 27, 1864); and colonel, Artillery (February 18, 1865). He saw action with his infantry company at Vienna. With his company converted to a light artillery battery, he fought in the Seven Days Battles, 2nd Bull Run, Harpers Ferry, Antietam, and Fredericksburg. Promoted to battalion commander, he led his enlarged command at Gettysburg and in the Bristoe, Mine Run, and Wilderness campaigns. Taking part in the defense of Petersburg he was slightly wounded at the Crater. He was again wounded at the battle of the Weldon Railroad a couple of weeks later. He was present with his battalion until shortly before the Appomattox Campaign. After the war he settled in Towson, Maryland, and resumed the practice of law, becoming head of the state bar association. (Wise, Jennings C., *The Long Arm of Lee*)

McINTOSH, James McQueen (1828-1862)

The brother of Union General John B. McIntosh, James M. McIntosh gave his life for the Confederacy at the same rank. The Florida-born West Pointer (1849) was, by virtue of his standing at the bottom of his class, posted first to the infantry, but in 1855 he transferred to the cavalry when the mounted branch was expanded. Most of his service was spent on the frontier before resigning as a captain in the 1st Cavalry on May 7, 1861. His Confederate assignments included: captain, cavalry (May 1861); colonel, 2nd Arkansas Mounted Rifles (July 29, 1861);

commanding 1st Brigade, McCulloch's Division, Department #2 (late 1861-March 1862); brigadier general, CSA (January 24, 1862); and commanding Cavalry Brigade, McCulloch's Division, Trans-Mississippi District (or Army of the West), Department #2 (March-March 7, 1862). Taking charge of a mounted Arkansas regiment, he was soon in command of a brigade and as brigadier general he directed Ben McCulloch's mounted troops at Pea Ridge. There, while he was leading his regiment, a bullet pierced his heart on March 7, 1862.

MACKALL, William Whann (1817-1891)

The Civil War was the first war in which William W. Mackall served without being wounded. The Maryland West Pointer (1837) had served with the artillery in Florida against the Seminoles. During this tour he was ambushed and wounded at River Inlet on February 11, 1839. During the Mexican War he won two brevets and was wounded at Chapultepec. After transferring to the adjutant's branch in 1846, he later declined an appointment as a lieutenant colonel, offered on May 11, 1861, and instead resigned as a brevet major on July 3. His Confederate assignments included: lieutenant colonel and assistant adjutant general (ca. July 1861); brigadier general, CSA (March 6, 1862, to rank from February 27); commanding District of the Gulf, Department #2 (December 8-14, 1862); chief of staff, Army of Tennessee (April-fall 1863 and January-July 17, 1864); and commanding Hébert's (old) Brigade, Forney's Division, Department of Mississippi and East Louisiana (November 1863-January 1864). After serving as Albert Sidney Johnston's adjutant, he was promoted to brigadier general and was captured at Island #10 while serving as second in command. Exchanged on or about August 27, 1862, he held minor posts until he became Bragg's staff chief. After the victory at Chickamauga he asked to be relieved of staff duty and for a time commanded a brigade of paroled and exchanged prisoners from Vicksburg. Shortly after Joseph E. Johnston took over the Army of Tennessee, Mackall resumed his old staff post and held it until John B. Hood superseded Johnston. At that time Mackall again asked to be relieved and held no more assignments for the balance of the war. Thereafter he was a Virginia farmer.

McKAY Henry K. (?-?)

Although he held the rank of brigadier general during the Civil War, it appears that Henry K. McKay's only military experience was with the Georgia militia. Officers in this force were elected by the rank and file. In May 1864 he was elected lieutenant colonel, 1st Georgia Militia Battalion, and at some point during the siege of Atlanta he was elected brigadier and assigned to command the new 4th Brigade. He took part in the defense of the city and served with the forces vainly trying to slow down Sherman's advance to the coast. In this latter effort he fought in the dismal defeat at Griswoldville. His last service appears to have been in the unsuccessful defense of Savannah.

McLAWS, Lafayette (1821-1897)

A division commander early in the war, Lafayette McLaws proved capable but not brilliant enough to warrant further advancement. A graduate of West Point in 1842, he had been serving as a captain of infantry for almost 10 years when he resigned his commission to join the South on March 23, 1861. The native Georgian's assignments included: major, Infantry (May 1861); colonel, 10th Georgia (June 17, 1861); brigadier general, CSA (September 25, 1861); commanding 1st brigade, Department of the Peninsula (October 3-November 10, 1861); commanding 2nd Division, Department of the Peninsula (November 10, 1861-April 12, 1862); commanding division, Magruder's Command, Department of Northern Virginia (April 12-July 1862); major general, CSA (May 23, 1862); commanding division, 1st Corps, Army of Northern Virginia (July 1862-September 9, 1863); commanding division, Longstreet's Corps, Army of Tennessee (September 19-November 5, 1863); commanding division, Department of East Tennessee (November 5-December 17, 1863); commanding District of Georgia and 3rd Military District of South Carolina, Department of South Carolina, Georgia and Florida (May 25-July 1864); and commanding division, same department (July 1864-April 9, 1865). Serving on the Peninsula during the first year of his service, he saw action during the Seven Days. In the Maryland Campaign he fought at Harpers Ferry and Antietam and later at Fredericksburg, Chancellorsville, and Gettysburg. He did not reach Chickamauga in time to serve with the part of the division which arrived from Virginia but took part in the Knoxville Campaign. Longstreet became displeased with his cooperation and preparations for the assault at Fort Sanders and at Bean's Station. On December 17, 1863, he was relieved of command, and Longstreet brought charges against him for the Fort Sanders incident. A court found him guilty of some charges on May 4, 1864, but Jefferson Davis disapproved the findings on the 7th and ordered him back to duty with his division, now back in Virginia. It was thought better, however, to assign him other duty, and he was sent to the Southern coast where he fought at Bentonville during the Carolinas Campaign against Sherman. Following the surrender he was in insurance, a tax collector, and a postmaster. (Freeman, Douglas S., *Lee's Lieutenants*)

MACLAY, Robert Plunket (ca. 1820-1903)

Relatively little is known about the Confederate career of Robert P. Maclay despite the fact that he was a West Pointer (1840) and was appointed brigadier general extralegally by General E. Kirby Smith. He had resigned his commission as captain, 8th Infantry, on December 31, 1860, to retire to a Louisiana plantation. The veteran of the Seminole and Mexican wars—during the latter he was wounded at Resaca de la Palma—held the following assignments for the South: major, Artillery; brigadier general, CSA, by Smith (May 13, to rank from April 30, 1864); commanding brigade, District of West Louisiana, Trans-Mississippi Department (spring and summer 1864); and commanding 3rd Texas Brigade, 1st Texas Division, 1st Corps, Trans-Mississippi Department (September 1864-January 1865). He appears to have been assigned to command of a brigade from a staff position with General J.G. Walker. This move seems to have created dissension within the brigade to

which he was named, and when a leave of absence was about to expire, Smith felt obliged to grant a 60-day extension on January 31, 1865. Smith feared that Maclay's promotion, which had not been legally made by the president, would be challenged. He felt the added time would delay a test until an appointment was forthcoming from Richmond. It never came and Maclay does not appear to have rejoined the brigade.

McLEAN, James Robert (1823-1870)

The Confederate congressional career of James R. McLean was spent mostly in defending the reputation of his native North Carolina as a loyal part of the Confederacy. A lawyer and planter, he served in the state legislature and became a proponent of secession. Elected from the state's 6th District to the First Regular Confederate Congress, he served on the committees on Claims and Foreign Affairs. Generally a supporter of the war effort, he did however have some disagreements with the administration. Matters of health prompted him not to seek reelection in 1863. Entering the state reserves, his assignments included: major, Camp Stokes Light Duty Battalion (1864); and major, 7th North Carolina Senior Reserves (1864). His regiment served in the defenses of Wilmington, then took part in the operations against Sherman's invading forces, and later fought at Bentonville. After the war he tried to recoup his prewar fortune but died before he could accomplish this.

McLEAN, Wilmer (?-?)

Despite the fact that he was an elderly noncombatant, Wilmer McLean seems to have been incapable of remaining out of the war's path. At the outbreak of the conflict he was maintaining his acreage, "Yorkshire," in Prince William County, Virginia. Unfortunately for McLean, his estate bordered on Bull Run. With the formation of the Confederate Army of the Potomac and its positioning along the creek, troops began to construct defensive works on his fields. Then, on July 18, 1861, General Beauregard took over the house as his headquarters. During the battle of Blackburn's Ford, McLean aided the general with his knowledge of the area. Three days later, during the battle of 1st Bull Run, a shell ripped into his home while Beauregard was breakfasting. That was enough for McLean. He moved his family to an estate in Appomattox County. Here he was far removed from the war—for three and a half years. Then, on the morning of April 9, 1865, he was stopped by two mounted men, one in blue and one in gray. They were looking for a place to hold a meeting between Grant and Lee. After the first place McLean showed them was rejected, he took the officers to his own home, and it was here that agreement for the surrender of the Army of Northern Virginia was made. (Hanson, Joseph Mills, *Bull Run Remembers*)

McMULLEN, LaFayette (1805-1880)

Representing Virginia's 13th District (the southwest corner of the state), LaFayette McMullen became a peace man in the Second Confederate Congress but wanted terms that would not be construed as submission. A native of the state, he had sat in

The second Wilmer McLean house at Appomattox, where Lee surrendered to Grant. (NA)

the state legislature and in Congress. In 1856 he predicted that a Republican victory for president would terminate the Union. The next year he was named to the governorship of the Territory of Washington by fellow Democrat James Buchanan. After one year he returned to a Virginia farm. On his second bid he won a seat in the Confederate House of Representatives where he chaired the Committee on Public Buildings. He also sat on the committees on: Post Offices and Post Roads; and Territories and Public Lands. Generally a supporter of the war effort, he favored price controls and wanted taxes concentrated away from small farmers who predominated in his district. Despite his desire for an end to the war, he felt that congressmen who were absent from Richmond were deserters and proposed their arrest at the last meeting of Congress. After the collapse he returned to agriculture and was engaged in banking and railroading enterprises until a rail accident ended his life. He had made one last entry into politics in 1878, when he was soundly defeated for the governorship.

McNEILL, Jesse C. (ca. 1842-?)

During most of the Civil War Jesse McNeill served as first lieutenant in his father's company of partisan rangers but after his father's death he became famous for his exploit in raiding Cumberland, Maryland. While assisting his father, John Hanson McNeill, to raise a new company in Missouri, young McNeill was captured but escaped within a few days and went to Virginia where his father had been born. After his father joined him, McNeill was elected first lieutenant in his father's new Virginia company and participated in raids on Union forces and their supply lines, especially the Baltimore and Ohio Railroad. With his father's death in October 1864, McNeill took over command. In memory of his father, he decided to get revenge upon General B.F. Kelley who had been responsible for the arrest of his mother, brother, and sister. Leading his 62 men into the town of Cumberland, in the midst of large Union forces, he came out with Kelley, and General George Crook, another officer, and two privates as prisoners. This exploit muted criticism of the irregular cavalry as ineffective and possibly saved the unit from being broken up. McNeill was praised in orders by General Lee and promoted to captain. But by the time of the February 21-22, 1865, affair the war was nearly over and it was merely a bright spot in the dismal prospects of the Confederacy. (Jones, Virgil Carrington, *Gray Ghosts and Rebel Raiders*)

McNEILL, John Hanson (1815-1864)

One of the more effective partisan leaders in the western portion of Virginia was John McNeill. Born in what is now West Virginia, McNeill later moved to Kentucky and finally to Missouri where, after being a Unionist during the secession crisis, he raised a company of cavalry as part of the Missouri State Guard. He led his company in combat at Booneville, Carthage, Wilson's Creek, and Lexington. He was wounded in the last action. With the December 1861 expiration of the time of his company, McNeill returned home to raise a new unit. During this time he was captured but escaped on June 15, 1862. Making his way back to West Virginia, he was granted authority to raise a company of partisan rangers. He became captain of this new command in about September 1862. Although officially designated Company E, 18th Virginia Cavalry, McNeill's men served mainly as an independent unit. He led his men in numerous raids, especially against the Baltimore and Ohio Railroad. During this time he developed a personal grudge against General B.F. Kelley, the Union defender of the line, but he did not live long enough to get revenge for Kelley's treatment of his wife. That would be up to his son Jesse. In the fall of 1864, his command joined Early's command in the Shenandoah Valley where, in an attack at Mt. Jackson on October 3, he was mortally wounded by one of his own men, apparently by accident. (Jones, Virgil Carrington, *Gray Ghosts and Rebel Raiders*)

McQUEEN, John (1804-1867)

One of South Carolina's most ardent secessionists, John McQueen lost his seat in the Confederate Congress to an anti-Davis candidate. A native of North Carolina, he had taken up the practice of law in South Carolina and subsequently become a planter and a major general in the militia. In 1849 he took a seat in the U.S. House of Representatives where he sat until his resignation, with the rest of the delegation, on the day after the state's secession. He then served as his state's commissioner to urge Texas to secede. Unopposed for his bid to sit in the First Regular Confederate Congress, he chaired the Committee on Accounts and also served on the Committee on Foreign Affairs. On matters of taxation and the draft, he was an opponent of Confederate nationalism. However, on matters of foreign relations, peace negotiations, and presidential appointments he was a staunch supporter of the Davis administration, and this support cost him his reelection from the state's northeastern 1st District. After the Confederacy's fall he retired to private pursuits. (Cauthen, Charles Edward, *South Carolina Goes to War, 1861-1865*)

McRAE, Colin John (1812-1877)

One of the Gulf coast's most prominent businessmen, Colin J. McRae served the Confederacy as its chief financial agent in Europe and got caught up in the disastrous Erlanger Loan. Born in North Carolina, he came to settle in Mobile, Alabama, via Mississippi—including a term in the Mississippi legislature. His enterprises included coastal shipping, railroads, land, slaves, and the commission trade. With the secession of Alabama, the Democrat was named to the Provisional Confederate Congress where he sat on the committees on Buildings, Engrossment, Finance, and Naval Affairs. Naturally, on military matters he was most concerned with the defense of Mobile and keeping the port open. Thus he favored state control over large numbers of troops. He worked toward the eventual approval of privateering. Not seeking reelection, he went into the arms and munitions business with an arsenal at Selma, Alabama. His European assignment began in 1863 when he negotiated the unfavorable terms of the cotton loan. Nonetheless his record of financial dealings was about the best that could be expected for the failing South. Finally cleared of liabilities in England, for the Confederate debts, in 1867, he never returned to the United States. Instead, he settled in Belize, British Honduras. Buying some land, he resumed some of his former business activities for the remaining decade of his life. (Davis, Charles Shepard, *Colin J. McRae: Confederate Financial Agent*)

McRAE, Dandridge (1829-1899)

Before his 1864 resignation as a Confederate brigadier general, Alabama-born Arkansas lawyer Dandridge McRae had commanded a battalion, two regiments and a brigade. At the outbreak of the Civil War he was the inspector general of his adopted state. His later assignments included: lieutenant colonel, 3rd Arkansas Battalion (July 15, 1861); colonel, 21st (McRae's) Arkansas (December 3, 1861); colonel, 28th (McRae's) Arkansas (June 1862); brigadier general, CSA (November 5, 1862); and commanding brigade, Hindman's-Price's Division, District of Arkansas, Trans-Mississippi Department (January 1863-early 1864). He led his battalion at Wilson's Creek and his first regiment at Pea Ridge. However, on May 20, 1862, he declined reelection to its colonelcy. The next month he took command of a new unit with which he served mostly in Arkansas until named brigadier general that fall. Leading a brigade he fought at Helena and Little Rock. Commanding in northeastern Arkansas in the spring of 1864, he resigned and returned to his home and practice. He also held minor state offices in the postwar years.

McRAE, Duncan Kirkland (1820-1888)

Petty jealousies over rank cost the Confederacy some of its experienced officers. Such was the case with Colonel Duncan K. McRae. A state legislator in his native North Carolina and a diplomat to France before the war, he entered the Confederate army shortly after the state's secession. His assignments included: colonel, 5th North Carolina (May 16, 1861) and commanding Garland's Brigade, D.H. Hill's Division, Jackson's Command, Army of Northern Virginia (September 14-ca. November 6, 1862). After serving at Yorktown, he displayed his inexperience when he led a gallant but futile charge upon a Union battery at Williamsburg. He fought at Seven Pines until overtaken by exhaustion. During the Seven Days he led the regiment through the early battles, but then the unit was detailed to guard prisoners and gather abandoned equipment. Rejoining Lee's army in Maryland, the division was assigned to guarding the passes through South Mountain. When General Garland was killed at Fox's Gap, McRae took over brigade command and also received a wound. He remained in command however and suffered another wound at Antietam. Still retaining command after that action, he submitted his resignation on November 13, 1862, only a week after his junior, Colonel Alfred Iverson, was promoted to brigadier and given permanent command of the brigade. The resignation was accepted on December 12. He represented the Richmond government in Europe in regards to a cotton deal and subsequently returned to North Carolina as a newspaper editor during the final months of the conflict.

MacRAE, William (1834-1882)

A North Carolina civil engineer, William MacRae entered the service of the South at the head of the Monroe Light Infantry. His later assignments included: captain, Company B, 15th North Carolina (June 11, 1861); lieutenant colonel, 15th North Carolina (May 2, 1862); commanding Cobb's Brigade, McLaws' Division, 1st Corps, Army of Northern Virginia (briefly in September 1862); colonel, 15th North Carolina (February 27, 1863); temporary brigadier general, CSA (June 22, 1864); commanding Kirkland's Brigade, Heth's Division, 3rd Corps, Army of Northern Virginia (June 27, 1864-April 9, 1865); and permanent brigadier general, CSA (November 4, 1864). His regiment was initially sent to the Peninsula and fought at Yorktown and the Seven Days before moving north to 2nd Bull Run and into Maryland. At Antietam MacRae succeeded to command of the brigade after it had suffered extreme losses. He was promoted to colonel after Fredericksburg, and his regiment was sent to North Carolina and southern Virginia. During the Gettysburg Campaign it was stationed at Hanover Junction just north of Richmond. Rejoining Lee's army, MacRae took part in the futile charge at Bristoe Station. In the Overland Campaign, he led the regiment at the Wilderness, Spotsylvania, and Cold Harbor. With the wounding of General Kirkland of the other North Carolina brigade in the division, MacRae was given temporary rank as a brigadier and transferred to its direction. He led the unit through the Petersburg operations and to the surrender at Appomattox. During the siege his promotion had been made permanent. He was a railroad superintendent in his remaining years. (Freeman, Douglas S., *Lee's Lieutenants*)

MACWILLIE, Marcus H. (?-?)

Nothing is known about the Arizona Territory delegate to the Confederate Congress, Marcus H. Macwillie, before the Civil War—except that he had been a lawyer in Mesilla, New Mexico

Territory—nor after its close. He worked for the secession of the southern half of the territory to become the Confederacy's Arizona Territory. Confederate forces from Texas invaded the area in the summer of 1861 and in August John R. Baylor established a military government with Macwillie as attorney general. Then in a disputed election, Macwillie was elected as the territory's delegate to the First Regular Confederate Congress. Replacing the provisional representative Granville H. Oury, he was seated on March 11, 1862. Not entitled to sit on any committees, he seems to have taken little part in legislation other than to favor the extermination of the Indians in the territory and to support his friend Baylor. Reelected to the Second Congress, he vanished into oblivion after the South's fall.

MACHEN, Willis Benson (1810-1893)

As the representative of Kentucky's 1st District in both of the regular Confederate congresses, Willis B. Machen was, with some limitations, a staunch supporter of the Davis regime. A native Kentucky farmer he had served in both state houses before the Civil War. In the Confederate Congress he served on the committees on: Accounts (First Congress); Ways and Means (First Congress); and Quartermaster's and Commissary Departments (Second Congress). He opposed military destruction of private property in retreat, impressment without payment, and governmental control of railroads. Also part of the anti-Bragg faction, he nonetheless usually supported presidential appointees. At the close of the war he returned to his farm but served a couple of months as a Democratic U.S. Senator.

MAFFITT, John Newland (1819-1886)

The first commander of the famed Confederate commerce raider *Florida*, John N. Maffitt, was forced to relinquish command of his vessel because of the effects of yellow fever contracted in the service of the Confederacy. Born at sea, it was natural for Maffitt to enter the old navy at the age of 13. He fought against the slave trade and worked for the U.S. Coastal Survey before the Civil War. Educated in North Carolina, he resigned his lieutenant's commission on April 28, 1861. Appointed a lieutenant in the Confederate Navy on May 2, he served at Hilton Head. Promoted to captain in January 1862, he ran the blockade with a cargo of cotton to England aboard the *Cecile*. Here he took command of the steamer *Oreto*, which was soon to become the first of the British-built Confederate raiders, the *Florida*. Despite problems with the British and Spanish authorities and a yellow fever epidemic, Maffitt managed to bring his undermanned craft into Mobile to complete its outfitting. On the night of January 15, 1863, the *Florida* finally broke out onto the high seas to become a terror to Union merchant vessels. After seven months of raiding, Maffitt put his vessel into dock at Brest, France, on August 23. Weakened by the fever and the rigors of the voyage, he asked to be relieved. His record included about 55 prizes, but with a couple of brief exceptions he held no further commands. After the war he retired to his farm. (Boykin, Edward C., *Sea Devil of the Con-*

federacy: The Story of the Florida *and Her Captain, John Newland Maffitt)*

MAGEVNEY, Michael, Jr. (?-?)

Michael Magevney, Jr., commanded a regiment which greatly confused the Union authorities as to the number of regiments Tennessee had provided the Confederacy. His command, the 154th Tennessee Senior Infantry, was formed from a fraternal order of an old militia unit which kept its former numeric designation and received permission to append "Senior" to its name in order to indicate that it was in fact an older unit than those with lower numbers. But since no other Tennessee unit had a number higher than the 80s, the Union command was befuddled. Magevney's assignments included: captain, Company C, 154th Tennessee (May 14, 1861); lieutenant colonel, 154th Tennessee (1862); colonel, 154th Tennessee (to date from August 30, 1862); and commanding Vaughan's Brigade, Cheatham's Division, Hardee's Corps, Army of Tennessee (July 4-September 1864). He fought at Belmont commanding his company, the Jackson Guards, and at Shiloh. At Richmond, Kentucky, during the Perryville Campaign he succeeded to regimental command upon the death of the colonel. After leading his men at Murfreesboro, he became a supernumery in March 1863 when the regiment was consolidated with the 13th Tennessee. Returning from detached service, he commanded the consolidated unit in the Atlanta Campaign and took over the brigade upon the wounding of General Vaughan. He retained this command through the siege until General G.W. Gordon was assigned. Again in command of the 13th and 154th, Magevney took part in the Tennessee Campaign and was captured at Nashville, ending his Civil War career.

MAGOFFIN, Beriah (1815-1885)

A proslavery governor of Kentucky, Beriah Magoffin attempted to keep his state neutral at the beginning of the Civil War. The native Kentuckian had practiced law in Mississippi and Kentucky, served as a judge, been a state legislator, and served as a delegate to several Democratic conventions. An unsuccessful 1855 candidate for lieutenant governor, he was elected to the top spot four years later. Looking for a secession compromise, he supported the Crittenden proposals but insisted on a rigid enforcement of the Fugitive Slave Law. He called for a state convention but was turned down by the legislature. In response to Lincoln's call for 75,000 volunteers following the firing on Fort Sumter, he declared that the state would "furnish no troops for the wicked purpose of subduing her sister Southern states." In May he issued a proclamation of neutrality for the state and this awkward situation lasted until September 1861. With a Unionist legislature overriding his vetoes, he resigned on August 18, 1862, and returned to his law practice and his farm. Reconciled to the defeat of slavery, he urged the ratification of the 13th Amendment and the granting of civil rights to the freedmen. He later sat in the legislature and was in the real estate market. (Coulter, E. Merton, *The Civil War and Readjustment in Kentucky*)

MAGRATH, Andrew Gordon (1813-1893)

Taking office as South Carolina's last Confederate governor on December 18, 1864, Andrew G. Magrath was almost immediately faced with Sherman's invasion of the state and the resultant disruption of civil government. A native Charlestonian lawyer and Democrat, he served two terms in the state legislature and was a U.S. district judge at the outbreak of the Civil War. He had been Governor Picken's secretary of state during the secession winter in which he attended the convention which dissolved the Union. With the formation of the Confederacy he was named Confederate district judge for South Carolina. Since some of his rulings were counter to a strong central Confederate government, he became unpopular with Jefferson Davis. In 1864 he left the bench to take up his duties as governor—to which post he had been elected by a secret, closed session of the legislature. Within months the capital was occupied and his effectiveness was diminished. With the fall of Richmond he called on the other Southern governors to continue the fight. Arrested by the Union forces on May 28, 1865, he spent seven months behind bars. Following his release he resumed his practice. (Wallace, David D., *History of South Carolina*)

**South Carolina Governor Andrew G. Magrath.
(*Harper's*)**

MAGRUDER, John Bankhead (1807-1871)

The life style of Confederate General John B. Magruder, which earned him the nickname of "Prince John," did not do much for his popularity with his troops. The Virginian West Pointer (1830) had spent a year with the infantry before securing a transfer to the artillery. He won two brevets during the Mexican War, being wounded at Chapultepec. Also a veteran of Seminole fighting and frontier service, he spent most of the interwar years in various garrison assignments where he earned a reputation as a *bon vivant*. On April 20, 1861, he gave up this life when he resigned his captaincy in the 1st Artillery and offered his services to the South. His assignments included: colonel, Virginia Volunteers (May 16, 1861); commanding Department of the Peninsula (May 21, 1861-April 12, 1862); brigadier general, CSA (June 17, 1861); major general, CSA (October 7, 1861); commanding Magruder's Command, Department of Northern Virginia (April 12-July 3, 1862); commanding District of Texas, Trans-Mississippi Department (November-December 1862); commanding District of Texas, New Mexico and Arizona, Trans-Mississippi Department (December 1862-August 4, 1864 and March 31-May 26, 1865); commanding District of Arkansas, Trans-Mississippi Department (August 4, 1864-January 29, 1865, February 1-15, and ca. February-March 31, 1865); also commanding 2nd Corps (or District of Arkansas), Trans-Mississippi Department (September 1864-January 29, 1865, February 1-15, and ca. February-March 31, 1865); and also commanding 3rd Corps (or District of Texas, New Mexico and Arizona), Trans-Mississippi Department (March 31-May 26, 1865). Assigned to command on the Peninsula, he won the early fight at Big Bethel and soon rose to the rank of major general. The next spring he performed admirably in fortifying Yorktown and delaying McClellan's advance on Richmond until Joseph E. Johnston could arrive with reinforcements from northern Virginia. Magruder's command was absorbed into what became the Army of Northern Virginia. In May 1862 it was determined to place him in charge of the Trans-Mississippi West but this was put in abeyance until after the Seven Days. During that series of battles he did not enhance his reputation. He did hold most of McClellan's army in check while the initial flank attack on the other side of the Chickahominy was being launched. He failed at Savage Station, Glendale, and Malvern Hill in the later stages of the campaign. At his own request he was then reordered to the West, but charges of drunkenness and cowardice forced his recall before he could take command. Eventually cleared, he took command of only the Texas district in November 1862. At the beginning of the next year he scored a major success in Galveston Harbor, driving off portions of the blockading fleet. He spent the rest of the war in district command in Texas and Arkansas and then fled to Mexico. With a band of fellow ex-Confederates he offered his services to Emperor Maximilian but, turned down, set up a colony at Cordoba. Magruder returned to the United States as a lecturer in 1867 but failed to earn the kind of living he was used to. He died in relative poverty.

MAHONE, William (1826-1895)

Mediocre in his two years as a brigade commander, William

"Prince John" Magruder. (NA)

Mahone excelled once promoted to division command—in a reverse of the Peter Principle. A graduate of the Virginia Military Institute, he was active prewar in education and railroading in his native Virginia. His assignments for the Confederacy included: colonel, 6th Virginia (1861); commanding 2nd Brigade, Department of Norfolk (by October 2, 1861-April 12, 1862); brigadier general, CSA (November 16, 1861); commanding brigade, Huger's-Anderson's Division (in 1st Corps from July 1862 and 3rd Corps from May 30, 1863), Army of Northern Virginia (April 12-August 30 and fall 1862-May 7, 1864); commanding the division (May 7, 1864-April 9, 1865); and major general, CSA (July 30, 1864). Following the Union evacuation of the Gosport Navy Yard at Norfolk, Virginia forces under Mahone occupied it. When the South abandoned the city, he fought against the federal flotilla at Drewry's Bluff and then moved to the Peninsula. There he saw action at Seven Pines and Malvern Hill. In Longstreet's assault at 2nd Bull Run he suffered a severe wound. When his wife was told by the governor that it was only a flesh wound she knew it was serious, as she exclaimed, "the General hasn't any flesh!" Mahone weighed less than 100 pounds. He returned to duty for Fredericksburg and Chancellorsville. At Gettysburg he displayed a reluctance to commit his brigade. His record had not been outstanding to this time. Following the Wilderness, where some of his men accidentally wounded General Longstreet, he succeeded to division command when Anderson was transferred to command Longstreet's men. He fought through Spotsylvania and Cold Harbor and took his place in the Petersburg trenches. Following the explosion of the Union mine on July 30, he became the hero of the battle of the Crater. In brilliant fashion he led two of his brigades up to the edge of the gaping hole and kept up a merciless fire on the troops, white and black, milling about within until they surrendered. For this he was upped to major general. He continued to distinguish himself during the remainder of the siege and in the retreat to the Appomattox surrender. Returning to the railroads in peacetime he soon entered politics and lost much of his popularity, since he dominated the state's Republican Party affiliate. (Blake, N.M., *William Mahone of Virginia, Soldier and Political Insurgent*)

Hardhitting "Little Billy" Mahone. (NA)

MAJOR, James Patrick (1836-1877)

On his way to becoming a Confederate brigadier general, Missourian West Pointer (1856) James P. Major served mostly west of the Mississippi River. Upon his graduation he was posted to the cavalry and participated in Indian fighting in

Texas. Resigning as a second lieutenant in the 2nd Cavalry on March 21, 1861, he offered his services to his native state. His assignments included: lieutenant, Cavalry (ca. March 1861); lieutenant colonel, 1st Cavalry, 3rd Division, Missouri State Guard (1861); colonel, Cavalry Regiment, 3rd Division, Missouri State Guard (1862); chief of Artillery, District of the Mississippi, Department #2 (summer 1862); brigadier general, CSA (July 21, 1863); and commanding in the Trans-Mississippi Department: brigade, District of West Louisiana (summer 1863-March 1864); brigade, Green's-Wharton's Cavalry Division, District of West Louisiana (March-summer 1864); and 2nd (Texas) Cavalry Brigade, 1st (Texas) Cavalry Division, 2nd Corps (or District of Arkansas) (September 1864-May 26, 1865). He led a mounted battalion of the Missouri State Guard at Wilson's Creek. Crossing the Mississippi in 1862, he was Earl Van Dorn's artillery chief in the defense of Vicksburg. Promoted to brigadier general, he commanded a brigade during the Red River Campaign and later in Arkansas. Following a period of residence in France, he returned as a planter to Louisiana and Texas.

MALLET, John William (1832-1912)

This Irish-born chemist came to America in 1853 and eventually became the head of the Richmond ordnance labs. Educated in his field in Ireland and Germany, Mallet served the Alabama geological survey and taught at the state university in the 1850s. Enlisting in an Alabama unit early in the war, he became a staff officer to Robert E. Rodes. In 1862 he was given the rank of colonel of artillery and assigned to the labs where he fought against shortages to aid the Southern military effort. After the war he taught at several Southern universities, dying in retirement in Virginia.

MALLORY, Stephen Russell (1813-1873)

Secretary of the Navy Stephen R. Mallory was one of only two Confederate cabinet members to serve throughout the war in one post. Born in Trinidad, he was raised in Florida where he became familiar with naval matters. Not old enough to vote, and with only about three years of formal schooling, he was appointed customs inspector at Key West. Studying law, he was given a judgeship. During the Seminole War he served in the militia. Elected to the U.S. senate in 1851, he served for almost 10 years on the Committee on Naval Affairs, most of the time as chairman. A reluctant secessionist, he resigned in early 1861 and strived, during the lull between secession and war, to prevent the outbreak of war at Fort Pickens in Pensacola Harbor. On February 21, 1861, he was named head of the navy department by Jefferson Davis, who, not being well-informed on naval matters, left the department's running almost entirely to Mallory—who faced the problem of organizing from scratch. He made some mistakes, such as refusing to accept jurisdiction over the River Defense Fleet and leaving it in a command limbo which contributed to the defeats at New Orleans and Memphis. But he was eager to accept new technologies to counterbalance the Union's superiority, even travelling to England in his search. He remained with Davis in the flight from Richmond until shortly before they were both captured in Georgia. He was paroled in March 1866 and returned to his Florida law practice. (Durkin, Joseph T., *Stephen R. Mallory: Confederate Naval Chief*)

MANEY, George Earl (1826-1901)

Tennessee lawyer and Mexican War veteran—as a first lieutenant in the 3rd Dragoons—George E. Maney rose to the command of a Confederate division. Giving up his Nashville practice, his assignments included: captain, Company A, 11th Tennessee (May 1861); colonel, 1st Tennessee (May 9, 1861); commanding 2nd Brigade, 2nd (Cheatham's) Division, 1st (Polk's) Corps, Army of the Mississippi (April 6-July 2, 1862); brigadier general, CSA (April 16, 1862); commanding 2nd Brigade, Cheatham's Division, Army of the Mississippi (July 2-August 15, 1862); commanding 3rd Brigade, Cheatham's Division, Right Wing, Army of the Mississippi (August 15-November 20, 1862); commanding brigade, Cheatham's Division, Polk's-Cheatham's Corps, Army of Tennessee (November 20, 1862-November 12, 1863); commanding brigade, Walker's Division, Hardee's Corps, Army of Tennessee (November 12-25, 1863); commanding brigade, Cheatham's Division, Hardee's Corps, Army of Tennessee (May-early July 1864); and commanding the division (July-August 31, 1864). Sent with his regiment to western Virginia, he participated in the fizzle at Rich Mountain under Robert E. Lee and then served for a time under Stonewall Jackson before being ordered to Mississippi. Taking command of a brigade, he led it at Shiloh and was promoted to brigadier general a few days later. He then took part in the defense of Corinth, Mississippi, and fought at Perryville during the Kentucky Campaign. After seeing further action at Murfreesboro, during the Tullahoma Campaign, and at Chickamauga, he was wounded at Chattanooga. He returned to duty at the beginning of the Atlanta Campaign and took charge of Cheatham's division that summer. However, he appears to have been relieved during the action at Jonesboro. This was apparently his last command and after the war he was engaged in railroading, Republican politics, and as a diplomat in Latin America—in Colombia, Bolivia, Paraguay, and Uruguay.

MANIGAULT, Arthur Middleton (1824-1886)

South Carolina businessman and Mexican War veteran—as a first lieutenant in the Palmetto Regiment—Arthur M. Manigault reentered the military in 1860 and rose to the rank of brigadier general in the Confederate service. His assignments included: captain, North Santee Mounted Rifles (December 1860); lieutenant colonel and adjutant and inspector general (April 1861); colonel, 10th South Carolina (May 31, 1861); commanding 1st Military District of South Carolina, Department of South Carolina, Georgia and Florida (December 10, 1861-May 28, 1862); commanding 4th Brigade, Reserve Corps, Army of the Mississippi (June-July 2, 1862); commanding 4th Brigade, Withers' Division, Army of the Mississippi (July 2-August 15, 1862); commanding 4th Brigade, Withers' Division, Right Wing, Army of the Mississippi (August 15-November 20, 1862); commanding brigade, Withers'-Hindman's Division, Polk's-Cheatham's-Breckinridge's-Hardee's Corps, Army of Tennessee (November 20, 1862-January 1864); brigadier general, CSA (April 26, 1863); and commanding brigade, Hindman's-Anderson's-Johnson's Division, Hindman's-Hood's-Lee's Corps, Army of Tennessee (January-November 30, 1864). After commanding a militia company he joined Beauregard's staff in Charleston Harbor and took part in the bombardment of Fort Sumter. Shortly thereafter he took command of a regiment. For a time he was in district command in his native state before joining Beauregard's army at Corinth. He later fought at Murfreesboro as a brigade commander and was advanced to brigadier general in time for the Tullahoma Campaign. Fighting at Chickamauga and Chattanooga, he was slightly wounded at Resaca during the Atlanta Campaign. A head wound at Franklin ended his active field career. A postwar planter, he served as his state's adjutant and inspector general. (Tower, R. Lockwood, ed., *A Carolinian Goes to War: The Civil War Narrative of Arthur Middleton Manigault, Brigadier General, CSA*)

MANN, Ambrose Dudley (1796-1889)

The Confederate diplomatic career of Ambrose D. Mann was far from a success. Born in Virginia, he had attended West Point until his resignation shortly before his graduation. Following admission to the bar, he served as a diplomat in Germany, Hungary, and Switzerland. In the mid-1850s he was assistant secretary of state. A staunch Southerner, he urged that the South be made commercially independent. With secession he was appointed a commissioner to Great Britain on March 16, 1861, but despite his efforts to gain recognition and a meeting with Lord Russell he and his fellow commissioners failed. He subsequently attempted to get the friendly King Leopold of Belgium to use his influence with Queen Victoria and Napoleon III in behalf of the South. Again he was unsuccessful. His efforts with the press in both Britain and Belgium were more favorable. On September 24, 1863, he was named special agent to the Vatican and was successful in enlisting the support of the Pope in opposing the Union army's efforts to recruit Catholics in Europe, primarily Irish and German. However, this appears to have had little impact on Union manpower. Settling in Paris after Appomattox, he worked as a journalist until his death.

MANNING, Vanney Hartrog (1839-1892)

It took a year's imprisonment to put an end to Vanney H. Manning's fighting career in the Civil War. He had been born in North Carolina and educated in Tennessee before settling in Arkansas. Entering the Confederate army, he received the following assignments: captain, Company K, 3rd Arkansas (June 20, 1861); major, 3rd Arkansas (July 9, 1861); colonel, 3rd Arkansas (March 11, 1862); commanding Walker's Brigade, Holmes' Division, Army of Northern Virginia (early July 1862); commanding same brigade, Walker's Division,

Longstreet's Command, Army of Northern Virginia (August 1862-September 17, 1862); and commanding Texas Brigade, Hood's Division, Longstreet's Corps, Army of Tennessee (temporarily from September 20, 1863). Following some initial difficulty in getting his company accepted into Confederate service, he took part in the Cheat Mountain and Romney campaigns before being transferred to the Rappahannock line and then to Southside Virginia. Taking part in the Seven Days he succeeded to temporary brigade command. Wounded at Antietam, where he distinguished himself, he returned in time for a relatively inactive role at Fredericksburg. After taking part in Longstreet's Suffolk Campaign he was again wounded on the third day at Gettysburg. Moving west with the corps, he fought at Chickamauga, where he again took over command of a brigade, and at Knoxville. The corps rejoined Lee and on the second day at the Wilderness Manning was severely wounded and left upon the field. He was captured and confined until July 24, 1865. During a part of his confinement he was exposed to Confederate fire by order of the Union authorities. He was a lawyer and U.S. congressman after the war.

MARKS, Samuel F. (?-?)

One of the older regimental commanders in the Confederate army at the beginning of the Civil War, Samuel F. Marks had commanded the 3rd Louisiana during the Mexican War. His assignments in the Civil War included: colonel, 11th Louisiana (August 9, 1861); commanding 1st Brigade, 3rd Division, 1st Geographical Division, Department #2 (October 24, 1861-February 1862); and commanding brigade, McCown's Command, 1st Geographical Division, Department #2 (February-March 1862). When Grant made his attack on Belmont, Missouri, Marks led his small brigade across the Mississippi from Columbus, Kentucky, to take part in the Union general's defeat. After service at Island #10, he was wounded early on the first day of the battle of Shiloh. This effectively ended his military service.

MARMADUKE, John Sappington (1833-1887)

At the time of his promotion to major general Missourian West Pointer (1857) John S. Marmaduke was confined in Boston Harbor's Fort Warren and would not be released until well after the fall of the Confederacy. Posted to the infantry, he had been a veteran of frontier service and the expedition against the Mormons in Utah when he resigned on April 17, 1861, as a second lieutenant in the 7th Infantry. His Confederate assignments included: first lieutenant, Infantry (ca. April 1861); colonel, Missouri State Guard (1861); lieutenant colonel, 1st Arkansas Battalion (summer 1861); colonel, 18th (Marmaduke's) Arkansas (fall 1861); colonel, 3rd Confederate (designation change January 31, 1862); brigadier general, CSA (November 15, 1862); commanding 4th (Cavalry) Division, 1st Corps, Trans-Mississippi Department (ca. November 1862-January 1863); commanding cavalry division, District of Arkansas, Trans-Mississippi Department (January 1863-September 18, 1864); commanding cavalry division, Army of

Missouri, Trans-Mississippi Department (September 18-October 25, 1864); also commanding 1st (Missouri) Cavalry (November 15, 1862); commanding 4th Brigade, 3rd (Hardee's) Corps, Army of the Mississippi (April 1862); commanding 4th (Cavalry) Division, 1st Corps, Trans-Mississippi Department (ca. November 1862-January 1863); commanding cavalry division, District of Arkansas, Trans-Mississippi Department (January 1863-September 18, 1864); commanding cavalry division, Army of Missouri, Trans-Mississippi Department (September 18-October 25, 1864); also commanding 1st (Missouri) Cavalry Division, Cavalry Corps, Trans-Mississippi Department (September-October 25, 1864); and major general, CSA (March 18, 1865, to rank from the 17th). With the Missouri State Guard he fought at Booneville and then took command of an Arkansas Battalion which was subsequently increased to regimental size. The unit was later designated as a "Confederate" unit and as such fought at Shiloh and during the Corinth siege. Resigning his colonelcy on September 12, 1862, Marmaduke was named a brigadier general two months later. He led his mounted division at Prairie Grove, Helena, Little Rock, and Jenkins' Ferry. He then joined Sterling Price for the invasion of Missouri and was captured during the rearguard action at Marais des Cygnes on October 25, 1864. Not released until July 1865, he never served at the higher rank. An insurance man after the war, he eventually won the gubernatorial chair, having once been defeated as a Democrat and having held other state offices.

MARR, John Quincy (1825-1861)

In a little remembered action at Fairfax Court House, Virginia, John Q. Marr was the only fatality, becoming the first martyr of the Confederacy to die in combat. A graduate and former faculty member of the Virginia Military Institute, he had been enjoying the advantages of planter society in his native county of Fauquier, when the secession crisis broke into war. He immediately took the field with the Warrenton Rifles, which he had raised after John Brown's Raid. Colonel Richard S. Ewell stationed Captain Marr's company at Fairfax, C.H., and on June 1, 1861, at about 3:00 A.M., Company B, 2nd U.S. Cavalry, passed through town firing a few shots. After a defense was prepared and the federals driven off, it was noticed that Marr was missing. He was dead from a wound in the chest.

MARSHALL, Henry (1805-1864)

A native of South Carolina and ardent believer in states' rights, Henry Marshall was an extremely wealthy Louisiana planter at the onset of the secession crisis. At the time he sat in the state's upper legislative house and was a delegate to the secession convention. Elected to the Provisional Confederate Congress, he chaired the Committee on Public Lands and sat on those on Claims and Territories. In the First Regular Congress he was on the committees on: Patents; Quartermaster's and Commissary Departments; and Territories and Public Lands. With a portion of his wealth he equipped a regiment for his cousin, Colonel (later Brigadier General) Maxcy Gregg. His states' rights views

Charge of Company B, 2nd United States Cavalry, during which John Q. Marr became the first Confederate combat fatality. (*Leslie's*)

worked to the detriment of the Davis administration's efforts to organize a centralized government to win the war. Not seeking reelection, he retired to his plantation where he died on July 13, 1864, before the Confederacy's demise. (Bragg, Jefferson Davis, *Louisiana in the Confederacy*)

MARSHALL, Humphrey (1812-1872)

One of the leaders of the neutrality movement in Kentucky, Humphrey Marshall in the end joined the Confederacy as a brigadier general but failed to attain military distinction. The Kentucky-born West Pointer (1832) had served a year with the mounted rangers and dragoons before resigning as a brevet second lieutenant. Practicing law at the outbreak of the Mexican War, he became colonel of the 1st Kentucky Cavalry and unlike many volunteers saw heavy action south of the border. From then until the Civil War he served almost continuously in the House of Representatives, interrupted by a year as a diplomat to China. During the secession crisis he backed John C. Breckinridge for the presidency. When his native state's neutrality was finally violated in the fall of 1861, he cast his lot with the South. His assignments included: brigadier general, CSA (October 30, 1861); commanding 1st Brigade, Army of Eastern Kentucky (early 1862); commanding District of Abingdon (May 2-8, 1862); commanding District of Abingdon, Department of Southwestern Virginia (May 8,

1862-May 9, 1863); and brigadier general, CSA (reappointed June 20, 1862, to rank from October 30, 1861). He served mostly in western Virginia and in Kentucky. He was involved in Bragg's campaign in Kentucky in the fall of 1862 but was not at the battle of Perryville itself. For unexplained reasons he resigned his commission on June 16, 1862, but was reinstated four days later. He resigned a second time on June 17, 1863, and early the next year was elected to the Second Confederate Congress. Taking his seat on May 2, 1864, he was a member of the Committee on Military Affairs. With his district occupied by Union forces he was a backer of the president and believed in extreme measures for maintaining the army's strength. He also favored government control over railroads and the use of slaves in the army. However, he opposed Davis on many tax issues and the question of suspending the writ of habeas corpus. After the war he resumed his law practice.

MARTIN, James Green (1819-1878)

"Old One Wing"—he had lost an arm at Churubusco in the Mexican War—James G. Martin was popular with his men because of his bravery. Once they even tossed the West Pointer (1840) in the air on the Petersburg front. He resigned his captaincy on June 14, 1861, to tender his services to his native North Carolina. His assignments included: adjutant general, North Carolina State Troops (September 20, 1861); major general, North Carolina Militia (September 28, 1861); brigadier general, CSA (June 2, to rank from May 15, 1862); commanding brigade, Department of North Carolina (June 19-July 25, 1862); reappointed brigadier general, CSA (August 11, to rank from May 15, 1862); commanding District of North Carolina, same department (August 18-September 1862); commanding brigade, same department (May-October 1863); commanding brigade, District of the Cape Fear (October 1863-April 1864); commanding brigade, Whiting's Division, Department of North Carolina and Southern Virginia (mid-May 1864); commanding brigade, Hoke's Division, same department (May-June 28, 1864); and commanding District of Western North Carolina, Department of East Tennessee (late 1864-April 1865). A brilliant organizer, he was to a large degree responsible for North Carolina providing, some claim, the largest number and best equipped troops of any Southern state in the first year of the war. He resigned his first commission in the Confederate service because the duties conflicted with his state job. However, Lee had him reappointed from the original date and assigned to North Carolina so that he could handle both jobs. By April of 1863 Martin was looking for a more active role, and he received command of a brigade with which he served for a year in the Kinston and Wilmington areas. Sent to Virginia he assisted in bottling up Butler at Bermuda Hundred and was involved in the early fighting at Petersburg. His health soon broke down and he was forced to retire from active field service. For a while he guarded the Richmond and Danville and the Southside railroads and later in 1864 he was given command of the western part of his own state. He held this post until the close of hostilities. After the war he was admitted to the bar and practiced for his remaining years.

MARTIN, John D. (?-1862)

When his regiment was broken up, Colonel John D. Martin was kept in grade and assigned to command of a new brigade. His Confederate assignments included: colonel, 25th Mississippi (1861); commanding 1st Brigade, 4th Division, 1st Geographical Division, Department #2 (October 24-November 1861); colonel, 2nd Confederate (January 31, 1862); commanding Bowen's Brigade, Reserve Corps, Army of the Mississippi, Department #2 (April 6-May 8, 1862); and commanding 4th Brigade, Price's Corps, Army of West Tennessee, Department #2 (summer-October 3, 1862). He briefly led a brigade in western Kentucky during the first fall of the war and was in command of the regiment at Shiloh. Here, upon the wounding of the brigade commander, Martin took command of the brigade on the first day and led it through the rest of the battle. Since his regiment was made up of companies from different states, it had been designated as a "Confederate" regiment. However, on May 8, 1862, it was broken up and the companies assigned to units from their respective states. That summer Martin was given command of another brigade which he led at Iuka and Corinth. At the latter he was mortally wounded on the first day.

MARTIN, William Thompson (1823-1910)

Promotion to Confederate brigadier general brought Kentucky native William T. Martin a transfer to the western theater and service under Joseph Wheeler. A Unionist lawyer in Mississippi at the outbreak of the war, he threw in with the Confederates, raising a company. His assignments included: captain, Adams County Cavalry Company (spring 1861); major, Jeff Davis Legion (1861); lieutenant colonel, Jeff Davis Legion (February 13, 1862); brigadier general, CSA (December 2, 1862); commanding division, Wheeler's Cavalry Corps, Army of Tennessee (March 16-November 1863 and February-fall 1864); major general, CSA (November 10, 1863); commanding detachment Wheeler's Cavalry Corps, Department of East Tennessee (November 1863-February 1864); and commanding District of Mississippi and East Louisiana, Department of Alabama, Mississippi and East Louisiana (January 15-30, 1865). As a field officer in the Jeff Davis Legion, which was composed of companies from Alabama, Georgia, and Mississippi, he fought at Yorktown and Williamsburg. He took part in Jeb Stuart's ride around McClellan in June 1862 and commanded the legion and the 4th Virginia Cavalry during the Seven Days. After fighting at South Mountain and Antietam he was promoted to brigadier general and was eventually given command of a mounted division under Wheeler. With this command he took part in the Tullahoma and Chickamauga campaigns. Promoted to major general, he led that portion of the cavalry corps which went to East Tennessee for the Knoxville operations. Rejoining the main army, he led his division through the Atlanta Campaign and later briefly held a district command in Mississippi. As a Democrat, he served for over a decade in the state legislature and was also active in railroading and education.

MASON, A.P. (?-?)

From 1862 until 1865 A.P. Mason rose from captain to full colonel while serving on the staffs of several of the South's top generals. He joined the staff of General Joseph E. Johnston early in 1862 and served with that officer on the Peninsula until the general was wounded at Seven Pines on May 31, 1862. The next day, when Robert E. Lee took over what was to become known as the Army of Northern Virginia, Mason was the only one of Johnston's staff officers to elect to remain. He retained his position as assistant adjutant general with Lee until the spring of 1863. He participated in the Seven Days, 2nd Bull Run, Antietam, and Fredericksburg campaigns. He rejoined Johnston in the western theater and participated in the Vicksburg and Atlanta campaigns. When Johnston was relieved by General John B. Hood, Mason remained as assistant adjutant general of the Army of Tennessee. After the fall of Atlanta and the disastrous Tennessee invasion, he served under Lieutenant General Richard Taylor until Johnston returned to duty opposing Sherman in North Carolina. Here he finished out the war as a colonel. He was apparently named colonel of the 2nd Mississippi Cavalry at some time in the war, but this was either not accepted by him or was never confirmed.

MASON, James Murray (1798-1871)

The seizure of Confederate emissary James M. Mason and his colleague John Slidell from the British mail-steamer *Trent* probably did the Confederacy more good on the foreign affairs front than did Mason's activities in England following his release. Born in the nation's capital, he became a lawyer in Winchester, Virginia, before launching his political career. A state legislator, he was a states' righter and supporter of John C. Calhoun. He served in both houses of the national legislature, including 10 years as the chairman of the Senate Committee on Foreign Affairs. He gave up his seat on March 28, 1861—before Virginia's secession—and was formally expelled on July 11. Two weeks later, on July 24, he was admitted to the Confederacy's Provisional Congress where he may have sat on the Committee on Foreign Affairs before being tapped by Jefferson Davis to serve on a diplomatic mission to Great Britain. On the way his vessel was stopped by the USS *San Jacinto* under the command of Charles Wilkes on November 8, 1861. The violation of international law in the captives' removal to Boston brought the United States and Britain to the brink of war, but the United States backed down and released the captives. Mason tried to curry favor with the English upper classes, but his prediction that the cotton weapon would force recognition of the Confederacy proved faulty. Upon the Confederacy's collapse, he settled briefly in Canada before returning to Virginia. (Mason, Virginia, *The Public Life and Diplomatic Correspondence of James M. Mason, with Some Personal History by His Daughter*)

Diplomat James M. Mason of the *Trent* affair. (NA)

MAURY, Matthew Fontaine (1806-1873)

In actuality the founder of the science of oceanography, Matthew F. Maury has been called the "Pathfinder of the Seas." Born near Fredericksburg, Virginia, he was raised in Tennessee before becoming a midshipman in the U.S. Navy at the age of 19. Having already published his *A New Theoretical and Practical Treatise on Navigation*, he was lamed in an accident and devoted the remainder of his prewar years to studying the sea and publishing his findings. His works included: *Wind and Current Chart of the North Atlantic*, *Abstract Log for the Use of American Navigators*, *A Scheme for Rebuilding Southern Commerce*, *Sailing Directions*, and, most famously, *The Physical Geography of the Sea*. Following his adopted state out of the Union, he resigned his commander's commission in 1861. On June 10, 1861, he was appointed a commander in the Confederate navy. Following court-martial duty he became chief of river and harbor defenses and was charged with mining the James River approaches to Richmond. After inventing the electric torpedo, or mine, he was sent to Europe to further his research in this new field. During his stay abroad he was also engaged in preparing commerce raiders for service on the high seas. Following the Confederacy's fall he joined the cabinet of Emperor Maximilian in Mexico and then returned to England. His final years were spent as a professor of meteorology. (Williams, Frances Leigh, *Matthew Fontaine Maury, Scientist of the Sea* and Corbin, Diana Fontaine Maury, *A Life of Matthew Fontaine Maury*)

MAXEY, Samuel Bell (1825-1895)

Giving up a state senate seat in Texas, Kentucky-born lawyer and West Pointer (1846) Samuel B. Maxey was named a major general by E. Kirby Smith, but this was never recognized by the Richmond authorities. He had won a brevet in Mexico before resigning in 1849 as a second lieutenant in the 7th Infantry in order to study law. His Confederate assignments included: colonel, 9th Texas (1861); brigadier general, CSA (March 7, 1862, to rank from the 4th); commanding Detached Brigade, 1st Corps, Army of the Mississippi (ca. May-July 1862); commanding brigade, 1st (Cheatham's) Division, Army of the Mississippi (July-August 15, 1862); commanding brigade, District of East Louisiana, Department of Mississippi and East Louisiana (late 1862-early May 1863); commanding brigade, attached to Loring's Division, Department of the West (May-June 1863); commanding brigade, French's Division, Department of the West (June-July 1863); commanding brigade, French's Division, Department of Mississippi and East Louisiana (July-ca. December 11, 1863); commanding Indian Territory, Trans-Mississippi Department (December 11, 1863-ca. April 1864); commanding cavalry division, District of Arkansas, Trans-Mississippi Department (ca. April-summer 1864); major general, CSA (by E. Kirby Smith, April 18, 1864); commanding 2nd (Texas) Cavalry Division, 1st Corps (or District of West Louisiana), Trans-Mississippi Department (summer 1864-February 14, 1865); commanding District of the Indian Territory, Trans-Mississippi Department (February

14-21, 1865); and commanding division, District of Texas, New Mexico and Arizona, Trans-Mississippi Department (April 7-May 26, 1865). As a brigadier general, he commanded a brigade around Corinth, Mississippi, and then in East Tennessee before being ordered to Port Hudson, Louisiana. With the pressure building on Vicksburg, he led his brigade northward to join Joseph E. Johnston at Jackson. Following the fall of Vicksburg he took part in the defense of Jackson. Late in the year he was ordered back across the Mississippi to reorganize the troops in the Indian Territory. Rewarded for this by Smith with a promotion, he was given a division first in Arkansas and then in Louisiana. Early in 1865 he returned briefly to the Indian Territory but finished the war commanding a division in his adopted state. After the war he was an attorney and U.S. senator. (Horton, Louise, *Samuel Bell Maxey: A Biography*)

MAXWELL, Augustus Emmett (1820-1902)

Georgia-born and Alabama-raised Florida lawyer and Democrat, Augustus E. Maxwell proved to be one of the staunchest supporters of the Davis administration—and especially of Secretary of the Navy Stephen R. Mallory—in the Confederate Senate. He had practiced law in Alabama for two years before moving to Florida where he served as attorney general, secretary of state, state legislator, and U.S. congressman. Elected to the Confederate Senate in November 1861, he was chairman of the Committee on Patents and also served on the committees on: Commerce; Engrossment and Enrollment; Foreign Affairs (First Congress); Indian Affairs (Second Congress); and Naval Affairs (First Congress). He chaired a special investigatory committee to check on naval matters and Mallory came out of it looking good. Maxwell proved willing to support strong measures to win the war, wanting to draft speculators and concentrate on food production. After the Confederacy's fall, Maxwell served on the state supreme court before returning to private practice with Mallory. He later presided over the court and again returned to his practice.

MAXWELL, John (?-?)

The most successful confederate saboteur was John Maxwell of the shadowy organization known as "Captain Z. McDaniel's Company, Secret Service." The company was authorized by the War Department on February 29, 1864, and Maxwell would have joined some time after that date. Apparently members of company worked as individuals or in small teams in the torpedo service. Maxwell himself had devised a "horological" device, or time bomb. Under Captain McDaniel's orders, he left Richmond on July 26, 1864, headed for the Union supply depot at City Point. He was accompanied by a civilian accomplice, R.K. Dillard. Approaching the wharves, he and Maxwell went forward with a package which he induced a Negro dock worker to take upon a nearby ordnance boat, explaining that it was the captain's orders. An hour later, at just before noon on August 9, 1864, there was a tremendous explosion. Two million dollars in damage was done. Some 169 soldiers and civilians were dead or wounded. Supply buildings

and 180 feet of wharf were demolished. Grant's nearby headquarters were showered with explosives and debris. The general was unharmed but some of his orderlies and staff officers were not so lucky. Maxwell and Dillard slipped back out of the Union lines and resumed spying activities along the river. The explosion was originally ruled an accident by the Union authorities until Maxwell's report was discovered in the captured rebel archives. He survived the war and in 1872, during Grant's presidency, he visited Grant's secretary and former staff officer, Horace Porter, in an unsuccessful effort to obtain patents on some of his inventions. He even described his adventure at City Point. (Stern, Philip Van Doren, *Secret Missions of the Civil War*)

MAYO, Robert Murphy (1836-1896)

When Robert M. Mayo offered his services to the South, his status as a graduate and faculty member of the Virginia Military Institute indicated that much could be expected from him, but he never made it to general officer, perhaps due to a fondness for the bottle. The native Virginian's assignments included: major, 47th Virginia (May 8, 1861); colonel, 47th Virginia (May 1, 1862); commanding Heth's (old) Brigade, Heth's Division, 3rd Corps, Army of Northern Virginia (July 3-19, 1863); commanding Walker's and Archer's brigades, Heth's Division, 3rd Corps, Army of Northern Virginia (May 9-August 19, 1864 and October 24, 1864-January 20, 1865); and commanding Walker's (old) Brigade, Department of Richmond (January 20-February 1865). As a field officer he served at Mathias Point and in the siege at Yorktown. Promoted to command the regiment, he led it at Seven Pines, the Seven Days, 2nd Bull Run, Fredericksburg, and Chancellorsville. A wound received at 2nd Bull Run prevented him from taking part in the Maryland invasion. At Gettysburg he led the brigade, for some unexplained reason, in Pickett's Charge. Back in command of the regiment he served through the Bristoe, Mine Run, and Wilderness campaigns. Upon the wounding of General H.H. Walker at Spotsylvania, he took over command of that brigade and soon of Archer's as well. He then served at Cold Harbor and in the defense of Petersburg. In January 1865 the Virginia regiments of Walker's old command were transferred to the Department of Richmond where Mayo was soon replaced. One of the reasons he was never made a general may have been a July 8, 1863, incident in which he was charged and convicted of being drunk on duty. After the war he served in the state legislature and briefly in the U.S. Congress. (Freeman, Douglas S., *Lee's Lieutenants*)

MEADE, Richard Kidder (ca. 1836-1862)

Virginia-born West Pointer (1857) Richard Meade's divided loyalties led him to fight for both the Union and the Confederacy. A second lieutenant in the engineers, Meade found himself a newly assigned engineer in charge at Castle Pinckney in Charleston Harbor when South Carolina seceded on December 20, 1860. A few days later he joined Major Robert Anderson's two companies of artillery in the move to uncompleted Fort Sumter. When the *Star of the West* made its attempt to reprovision the garrison on January 9, 1861, Meade urged Anderson not to fire on the batteries that were in action against the vessel because, "It will bring civil war on us." The guns remained silent. When the South Carolinians made their later demand for the surrender of the fort itself, Meade, remembering his oath and his debt for his military training, voted against complying. During the bombardment of the fort, Meade was busy directing the manufacture of cartridge bags from clothing, sheets, and paper. After the surrender of the fort Meade went with the garrison to New York but then resigned, returned to his native state, and became a captain of engineers in Confederate service. In this capacity, he worked on the Confederate works on the Peninsula, at Drewry's Bluff, and in North Carolina where he was engaged in the battle of New Bern. In the spring of 1862, he was promoted to major and died of disease on July 31, 1862. (Swanberg, W.A., *First Blood*)

MEMMINGER, Christopher Gustavus (1803-1888)

As the Confederacy's first secretary of the treasury, Christopher G. Memminger faced a hopeless situation aggravated by poor relations with Congress. A native of Württemberg, in Germany, Memminger's father had been killed in the duke's army, and he was soon an orphan in South Carolina where his widowed mother had brought him. Comfortably adopted, he studied law and became a leader in education. Despite his hatred for the abolitionists he didn't favor secession until Harpers Ferry was attacked by John Brown. He signed South Carolina's secession ordinance and became chairman of the Provisional Confederate Congress' Committee on Commercial Affairs. Under the provisional constitution he was able to keep his congressional seat when he became a member of the cabinet on February 21, 1861. For three and a half years he struggled with the dismal financial situation of the South. Despite unfriendly meddling with his plans by Congress, he retained the faith of Jefferson Davis of whom he was an unwavering follower. He opposed the embargo of cotton shipments to force foreign recognition, realizing that Southern credit would evaporate. Blamed for the mess by many in and out of the Congress—which he had left at the end of the Provisional Government—he resigned on June 15, 1864. In 1867 he was pardoned; he resumed his law practice and favored the establishment of educational opportunities for the freedmen. (Capers, Henry D., *The Life and Times of C.G. Memminger*)

MERCER, Hugh Weedon (1808-1877)

Poor health forced Confederate Brigadier General Hugh W. Mercer—grandson of Revolutionary War General Hugh Mercer who was mortally wounded at Princeton—from the field. The Virginian West Pointer (1828) had served for seven years before resigning in 1835 as a first lieutenant in the 2nd Artillery. A bank cashier at the outbreak of the Civil War, he joined the Confederacy and his assignments included: colonel, 1st Georgia (early 1861); brigadier general, CSA (October 29, 1861); com-

manding brigade, District of Georgia, Department of South Carolina and Georgia (early 1862-May 28, 1862); commanding 2nd Military District of South Carolina, Department of South Carolina, Georgia and Florida (May 28, 1862); commanding 1st Military District of South Carolina, Department of South Carolina, Georgia and Florida (May 28-June 1862); commanding District of Georgia, Department of South Carolina, Georgia and Florida (June 1862-April 26, 1864); commanding brigade, Walker's Division, Hardee's Corps, Army of Tennessee (May-July 22, 1864); and commanding the division (July 22-24, 1864). Most of his early war service came in the Savannah area, with a brief stint in South Carolina. Just before the start of the Atlanta Campaign he took command of a brigade in the Army of Tennessee. When the division commander, William H.T. Walker, was killed at the battle of Atlanta, Mercer took over the larger unit. But this was broken up two days later and about this time Mercer's health broke. He soon returned to Savannah for the balance of the war and with his field career at an end. He was in banking and trade in Savannah and Baltimore after the war before moving to Baden Baden, Germany, in the early 1870s.

MERCIER, (Édouard) Henri (1816-1886)

A career foreign service officer, and the French ambassador to the United States during the first portion of the Civil War, Henri Mercier was frequently considered to be pro-Southern. He had been born in Baltimore when his father was stationed there as consul for Louis XVIII but received his education in France and Switzerland. He managed to survive the transitions in French government from monarchy to republic to monarchy while serving in diplomatic missions to Dresden, Athens, and Stockholm. He took up his Washington duties in July 1860, at the peak of the sectional crisis. Closely attuned to the policies of Napoleon III, he favored French mediation efforts and joint recognition, with Great Britain, of the Confederacy. He also proposed a common market for the United and Confederate States which would have allowed commercial unity while providing the necessary political separation. Despite his leanings toward the South—he even visited Richmond in 1862—he developed a respectful and friendly relationship with Secretary of State Seward. Seward even congratulated Mercier on a later appointment. The Frenchman had long desired a transfer and finally got it in December 1863 after it became apparent that a mediation effort would not be acceptable to Washington. He left as the problem over Mexico was developing and later served in Madrid until the collapse of France in the Franco-Prussian War. (Carroll, Daniel B., *Henri Mercier and the American Civil War*)

MILES, William Porcher (1822-1899)

While serving as South Carolina's 2nd District congressman and chairman of the Committee on Military Affairs, William P. Miles was a steady supporter of Jefferson Davis, only questioning—late in the war—his commitment to the defense of Charleston. A native of the first state to secede, he practiced law

Part of the diplomatic corps on an outing in New York. Henri Mercier is fifth from the right while Secretary of State William H. Seward sits, hat in hand. British envoy Lord Lyons stands next to Mercier and directly behind Seward. (NA)

for a time before entering education and politics. He served in Congress from 1857 until just before his state seceded. As chairman of the Committee on Foreign Relations, he was a member of the secession convention and signed the document which took South Carolina out of the Union. He sat in the Provisional and both regular congresses. During the crisis in Charleston Harbor, he was sent by Beauregard to arrange Fort Sumter's submission. During the Provisional Congress he sat on the committees on: Commercial Affairs; Flag and Seal; Military Affairs; and Printing. During the regular congresses he chaired the Committee on Military Affairs but gave up the rest of his committee assignments. On war matters he was an unwavering supporter of the president and of an all-out effort, despite being a member of the pro-Beauregard anti-Bragg faction. He did oppose the suspension of the writ of habeas corpus and other Davis-proposed issues less connected with his specialty. After the war he was president of the University of South Carolina and ran his father-in-law's Louisiana sugar plantation.

MILLER, James M. (1816-1865)

One of the most horrid aspects of warfare occurs when a commander feels that he must resort to retaliatory executions. James

M. Miller was the first victim of one such order. At the age of 48 he was captured while serving in the 3rd South Carolina Reserves Battalion opposing Sherman's march through that state. Atrocities had been occurring for previous several days, and Sherman had announced that for every Union soldier murdered he would execute one prisoner of war. On February 28, 1865, Private Robert M. Woodruff of the 30th Illinois was found with a crushed skull. On March 2 some prisoners were forced to draw lots. An hour later Miller, a father of nine, was dead. It later turned out that the Union soldier had been killed by a slave while the soldier was looting the plantation of the slave's master.

MILLER, William (1820-1909)

Florida attorney and Mexican War veteran William Miller was operating a saw mill at the outbreak of the Civil War. The New York-born Confederate's assignments included: lieutenant colonel, 3rd (also known as 1st) Florida Battalion (early 1862); colonel, 1st Florida (August 15, 1862); commanding Brown's Brigade, Anderson's Division, Left Wing, Army of the Mississippi (October 8-fall 1862); brigadier general, CSA (August 2, 1864); commanding Reserve Forces, Florida

(September 8, 1864-April 26, 1865); and also commanding District of Florida (or Miller's Brigade), Department of South Carolina, George and Florida (September 29, 1864-April 26, 1865). His battalion joined the main army in Mississippi shortly after the battle of Shiloh and was merged into the old 1st Florida. Rising to colonel, Miller led this unit at Perryville and succeeded the wounded John C. Brown in brigade command. At Murfreesboro he was in charge of the consolidated 1st and 3rd Florida and was wounded during Breckinridge's doomed assault on January 2, 1863. Following a lengthy recovery he was placed in charge of the conscription operations in Alabama and Florida. Promoted to brigadier general, he was placed in command of the Florida reserve forces and shortly thereafter of the District of Florida. Included in Johnston's surrender, he returned to his milling business and was a state legislator.

MILTON, John (1807-1865)

Although elected to the Florida governorship in October 1860, John Milton did not take office until the state was a part of the Confederacy—a nation he would not outlive. Born in Georgia, he had practiced law in Georgia, Alabama, and Louisiana and served as a captain of Alabama volunteers in the Seminole War before moving to a Florida plantation in 1846. Three years later he was elected to the state senate. Taking his seat as a Democratic governor on October 7, 1861, he was quickly involved in war work. He favored paper money and the banning of alcohol during the war. He actively supported the formation of infantry and artillery units but was opposed to the use of cavalry in the rough terrain of the state. Noted for cooperating with the central government, he was committed to the Confederate cause and just before the fall of Richmond he committed suicide, on April 1, 1865. (David, William W., *The Civil War and Reconstruction in Florida*)

MINOR, Robert Dabney (1827-1891)

A veteran of the U.S. Navy, Robert D. Minor held positions in both the Confederate naval and land forces. The Fredericksburg, Virginia, native resigned his commission and headed south where he was appointed almost immediately as a naval lieutenant. Assigned to the CSS *Virginia* early in 1862, he led the detachment which burned the USS *Congress* during the attack on the wooden blockaders in Hampton Roads. He subsequently became superintendent of the Naval Ordnance Works in Richmond. When the workers in his plant were organized into an infantry battalion for local defense he accordingly became major, 4th Virginia Battalion, Local Defense Troops, on June 30, 1863. This unit was usually referred to as the "Naval Battalion." When ordered to duty in North Carolina he resigned his army commission on February 13, 1864. Later in the year he commanded a small fleet in the Chowan River and then finished out the war with the James River Squadron. After the war he maintained his interest in maritime affairs. His papers are in the collection of the Virginia Historical Society.

MITCHEL, Charles Burton (1815-1864)

As Arkansas' Confederate senator, Charles B. Mitchel proved to be regional in his outlook on legislative issues. The Tennessee native had practiced medicine in Arkansas for a quarter of a century and served in the state legislature. Defeated for a congressional seat in 1860, he was then named to the U.S. Senate and attended the special session of that body in March 1861. Before the first regular session was held, he had joined the Confederacy with his state and was expelled by a resolution of July 11, 1861. Elected to the Confederate Senate, he chaired the Committee on Accounts in the First Congress and also sat on the committees on: Engrossment and Enrollment; and Post Offices and Post Roads. In the Second Congress he chaired the last committee and also served on the Committee on Territories. Interested primarily in the affairs of the Trans-Mississippi Department, he favored E. Kirby Smith over Thomas C. Hindman for the regional command. Between sessions he died at his Little Rock home on September 20, 1864.

MITCHELL, John K. (?-?)

Surviving a court of inquiry into his role in the fall of New Orleans, John K. Mitchell went on to a desk job and then again took command of a river borne flotilla and received a promotion to captain. During the operations along the lower Mississippi River—below Forts Jackson and St. Philip—in the spring of 1862 Mitchell was hampered by a divided command of the forces afloat. He himself commanded the Confederate States vessels while the army controlled the River Defense Fleet. In addition, two vessels belonged to the state of Louisiana. Thus, with the rank of commander, and aboard the flagship CSS *Louisiana*, he commanded only six armed vessels directly. Following the dispersal of the fleet and the eventual fall of the Crescent City, a court of inquiry was called to look into the actions of Mitchell. Cleared, he later served as chief of the Bureau of Orders and Detail. Then in 1864 he led the James River Squadron in the defense of Richmond with a subsequent promotion to captain.

MONTGOMERY, James Ed (c. 1817-?)

Displeased with the level of effectiveness of the Confederate navy in protecting the Mississippi River, Kentucky steamboatman James Ed Montgomery cajoled the Confederate Congress into adopting his defense plans. One million dollars was to be spent purchasing 14 vessels and converting them into rams carrying only one gun apiece and protected by cotton bales. The vessels were to be commanded by rivermen and not by naval officers. The Navy Department expressed no interest in the plan. So the River Defense Fleet was made part of the War Department. This division of authority led to a miserable showing of the naval forces at New Orleans and the loss of the entire lower division of the River Defense Fleet, six vessels, most of them being deserted by their inexperienced crews and officers.

Montgomery, with the eight vessels of the upper division, fought the Union fleet at the battle of Plum Run Bend. Despite the steamboatmen's inability to cooperate among themselves, they won a victory, sinking the *Mound City* and *Cincinnati* on May 10, 1862. Navy officers scoffed at the ragtag fleet, controlled by the army and officered by men who had no idea of how to fight a naval action. They felt that they should direct the vessels. Montgomery's next battle proved to be his last. On June 6, 1862, in the battle of Memphis, Montgomery lost all his vessels except the *Van Dorn*, which fled, to the Union gunboats and Colonel Ellet's rams. His flagship, the *Little Rebel*, was run aground by a Union ram and he fled into the Arkansas woods. Escaping capture, Montgomery later turned up in Mobile.

MOODY, Young Marshall (1822-1866)

Surviving four years of war, Confederate Brigadier General Young M. Moody went on a business trip to New Orleans the very next year—and succumbed to yellow fever. The Alabamian had given up a judicial clerkship to lead a company to war in 1861. His assignments included: captain, Company A, 11th Alabama (June 11, 1861); lieutenant colonel, 43rd Alabama (May 15, 1862); colonel, 43rd Alabama (November 4, 1862); commanding Gracie's (old) Brigade, Johnson's Division, Anderson's Corps, Army of Northern Virginia (December 2, 1864-April 9, 1865); and brigadier general, CSA (March 4, 1865). He served in northern Virginia with his original company but returned to the Mobile area to assist in the raising of the 43rd Alabama of which he became the second-ranking officer. This unit served in eastern Tennessee and Kentucky but its first heavy action came at Chickamauga where Moody distinguished himself at its head. He then served under Longstreet in East Tennessee and in the spring of 1864 moved to Virginia. Wounded at Drewry's Bluff in May, he returned to command his regiment in the Petersburg trenches. When Archibald Gracie was killed by a sharpshooter in December, Moody succeeded him (for the second time since Gracie had been the 43rd's first colonel). Four months later Moody was promoted officially to brigadier, but with only a month to go in the war. Following his parole at Appomattox, Moody was a Mobile businessman until his ill-fated excursion to Louisiana. (Freeman, Douglas S., *Lee's Lieutenants*)

MOORE, Andrew Barry (1807-1873)

Upon its secession on January 11, 1861, the state of Alabama was already in a good position for defense due to the actions of its governor, Andrew B. Moore. A South Carolina-born lawyer, he had entered the Alabama legislature in 1839 and served two years as the speaker of the lower house. In the 1850s he was a judge and was elected governor in 1857. A staunch Democrat, he was a long-time advocate of secession. On December 24, 1860, he ordered the seizure of all army depots in the state, gaining valuable supplies for the Confederate cause. He also offered troops to South Carolina before his own state's secession. Further aid was sent to Florida for the capture of Pensacola.

With a constitutional provision barring another term, he left office on December 2, 1861. He then became an aide to Governor John G. Shorter and, later, to Governor Thomas H. Watts. At the close of the war he was arrested by Union authorities but soon was released due to his poor health. Until his death he practiced law. (Denman, Clarence P., *The Secession Movement in Alabama*)

MOORE, John Creed (1824-1910)

Native Tennesseean West Pointer (1849) John C. Moore served the Confederacy well until his February 3, 1864, resignation as a brigadier general. As an artillery officer, he fought the Seminoles in Florida and served on the frontier before resigning as a first lieutenant in the 2nd Artillery in 1855. A college professor at the outbreak of the Civil War, he offered his services to the Confederacy. His assignments included: captain, Artillery (April 1861); colonel, Artillery (1862); commanding District of Galveston, Department of Texas (October 2-December 7, 1861); colonel, 2nd Texas (January 1862); commanding District of Houston, Department of Texas (January 3-February 25, 1862); commanding Sub-District of Houston, Department of Texas (February 25-ca. March 1862); commanding 4th Brigade, Cheatham's-Ruggles' Division, 2nd Corps, Army of the Mississippi (April-June 1862); brigadier general, CSA (May 26, 1862); commanding brigade, Maury's Division, Army of the West, Department #2 (June-October 19, 1862); commanding brigade, Maury's-Forney's Division, 2nd Military District, Department of Mississippi and East Louisiana (October 21, 1862-April 1863); commanding brigade, Forney's Division, Department of Mississippi and East Louisiana (April-July 4, 1863); and commanding brigade, Cheatham's Division, Hardee's Corps, Army of Tennessee (November-December 1863). While in district command in Texas he raised an infantry regiment with which he joined Albert Sidney Johnston's army in northern Mississippi. He fought on both days at Shiloh and on the second was placed in command of an informal demi-brigade. During the defense of Corinth, Mississippi, he was advanced to brigadier general. He led a brigade in the battle there that fall and later in the Vicksburg Campaign. Captured when that city fell, he was paroled the same day and was exchanged on September 12, 1863. Taking charge of a brigade under Bragg at Chattanooga, he fought in the battle there, although he was already under orders to report to Mobile. He reported there in December but resigned in two months and returned to Texas. He was a postwar writer and teacher.

MOORE, John Wheeler (1833-1906)

North Carolinian John W. Moore has earned himself an important page in the history of the Civil War, not so much for his rather uneventful role in the conflict as for his postwar writings. His Confederate service included: captain and assistant commissary of subsistence, 2nd North Carolina Cavalry (June 18, 1861); and major, 3rd North Carolina Light Artillery Battalion (February 24, 1862). He served in the supply department with the cavalry regiment on the North Carolina coast until transferred to the artillery in early 1862. The battalion was soon ordered to Richmond and remained to camp there until it reinforced the Army of Northern Virginia in late September 1862 after the battle of Antietam. But, the horses being in such poor condition, it was ordered back to the capital. During the battle of Fredericksburg Moore was stationed along the North Anna River to guard the railroad bridge against a cavalry raid. Subsequent service took the battalion to various points in North Carolina, mostly in the District of the Cape Fear. Near the close of the war he led the command at Bentonville and was surrendered as part of Joe Johnston's army. After the war he wrote several histories and novels. His most important work was *Roster of North Carolina Troops in the War Between the States.*

MOORE, Patrick Theodore (1821-1883)

Knocked out of action early in the war, County Galway native Patrick T. Moore spent the balance of the Civil War primarily in staff and administrative assignments. His family moved to Canada in his mid-teens and then to Boston where his father was a British diplomat. In 1850 he relocated to Richmond where he served in the militia while engaged in mercantile pursuits. Joining the Confederacy, his assignments included: colonel, 1st Virginia (May 1861); brigadier general, CSA (September 30, 1864); and commanding 1st Brigade, Virginia Reserves, Department of Richmond (December 1864-April 1865). While most accounts report him as being wounded at the head of his regiment at 1st Bull Run he was in fact wounded three days earlier at Blackburn's Ford along the same creek. Unable to lead his men, he served on Joseph E. Johnston's staff on the Peninsula, seeing action at Seven Pines. When Johnston was wounded there, Moore joined James Longstreet's staff for the Seven Days. From the summer of 1862 until the fall of 1864 he was engaged primarily on court-martial duty. Promoted to brigadier general, he assisted James L. Kemper in organizing the Virginia Reserves. He commanded a brigade of these during the final months of the war at Richmond, but it did not take part in the retreat to Appomattox. Thereafter he was in the insurance business.

MOORE, Samuel Preston (1813-1889)

Given the circumstance of a constantly low stock of supplies, the Confederacy's surgeon general, Samuel Moore, did an amazing job in keeping the medical services operating. Receiving his medical education in his native state of South Carolina, Moore had accepted an appointment in 1835 as a regular army assistant surgeon with the rank of captain and served in the Mexican War, being promoted to surgeon and major in 1849. Resigning this commission in 1861, he briefly practiced in Arkansas before being named to the top medical post that June. He organized the system of general hospitals to replace the existing confusing situation of each state having its own hospitals in the field. He also established the *Confederate States Medical Journal.* His methods of improvising medicines and other supplies saved many Confederate lives. Following the war he practiced in Richmond.

MOORE, Thomas Overton (1804-1876)

A firm believer in the power of cotton diplomacy, Louisiana Governor Thomas O. Moore banned the export of that staple on October 3, 1861, in the hope that a shortage would prompt the foreign recognition of the Confederacy. Born in North Carolina, he became a Louisiana sugar planter and served in both houses of the legislature before being elected as a Democrat to the gubernatorial chair in November 1860. Inaugurated in January 1861, he recommended the state convention which took the state out of the Union. He promptly began the organization of supply depots and packing houses to supply an army in the field. He called for an additional 5,000 volunteers over the number requested by Jefferson Davis. With the fall of New Orleans, he moved the state government from Baton Rouge to Opelousas and had to share control of the state with Union military governor George F. Shepley, who ruled in the occupied areas. Moore banned trade with the enemy and halted the export of the cotton crop. His term ended on January 25, 1864, and he fled to Cuba upon the fall of the Confederacy to avoid the arrest which had been ordered by the state senate. A year later he returned, fully pardoned, to his plantation. (Gayarre, Charles, *History of Louisiana* and Bragg, Jefferson Davis, *Louisiana in the Confederacy*)

MORGAN, John Hunt (1825-1864)

One of the leading Confederate raiders, John Hunt Morgan found it difficult to comply with the constraints placed upon his activities by his superiors. Born in Alabama, he had served in the Mexican War as a first lieutenant with the 1st Kentucky. Unlike many volunteer officers he did see action in that conflict. A Lexington merchant between the wars, he raised the Lexington Rifles in 1857. Even though his state never did secede, he did join the Confederacy and his assignments included: captain, Morgan's Kentucky Cavalry Squadron (1861); colonel, 2nd Kentucky Cavalry (to rank from April 4, 1862); commanding cavalry brigade, Army of Tennessee (November 20, 1862-February 25, 1863); brigadier general, CSA (December 11, 1862); commanding brigade, Wheeler's Cavalry Division, Army of Tennessee (February 25-March 16, 1863); commanding division, Wheeler's Cavalry Corps, Army of Tennessee (March 16-July 26, 1863); commanding cavalry brigade, Department of East Tennessee (early 1864-May 2, 1864); commanding cavalry brigade, Department of Southwestern Virginia (May 2-June 22, 1864); and commanding Departments of East Tennessee and Southwestern Virginia (June 22-August 30, 1864). He led his squadron in central Kentucky and at Shiloh and was then promoted to colonel. He led his regiment during the Corinth siege and then took two regiments on a raid through Kentucky from July 4, to August 1, 1862. This raid, together with that of Nathan Bedford Forrest, greatly hampered the advance of Don C. Buell on Chattanooga. In October 1862 shortly after the collapse of the

Southern campaign in Kentucky, he led his brigade on another raid through his adopted state. During the Murfreesboro Campaign he led a mounted division into Kentucky, from December 21, 1862, through January 1, 1863, against Rosecrans' supply lines. Having been promoted to brigadier general, he also received the thanks of the Confederate Congress for his exploits. Following the Tullahoma Campaign he again received permission to enter Kentucky. On this raid from July 2 to 26, 1863, he violated Bragg's instructions not to cross the Ohio River. Crossing over into Indiana, he moved into Ohio, skirting Cincinnati which went into a panic. Pursued by cavalry and militia, he was finally captured near New Lisbon, Ohio, on July 26th after most of his command had been taken prisoner. Confined in the Ohio State Penitentiary, he escaped on November 26, 1863. Placed in command in East Tennessee and southwestern Virginia the next year, he was surprised and killed at Greeneville, Tennessee, on September 4, 1864. (Holland, Cecil Fletcher, *Morgan and His Raiders, A Biography of the Confederate General*; Noel, Lois, *John Hunt Morgan*; and Swiggert, Howard, *Rebel Raider: A Life of John Hunt Morgan*)

Confederate raider John Hunt Morgan. (*Leslie's*)

MORGAN, John Tyler (1824-1907)

In an effort which proved to be too little too late, Confederate Brigadier General John T. Morgan was recruiting black troops when the end came for the fledgling nation. The Tennessee-born Alabama lawyer attended his adopted state's secession convention and then enlisted in the Cahaba Rifles. His assignments included: private, 5th Alabama (May 5, 1861); major, 5th Alabama (ca. May 11, 1861); lieutenant colonel, 5th Alabama (ca. November 20, 1861); colonel, 51st Alabama Partisan Rangers (September 2, 1862); brigadier general, CSA (June 6, 1863); commanding brigade, Martin's Division, Wheeler's

Cavalry Corps, Army of Tennessee (summer-November 1863 and February-ca. June 1864); reappointed brigadier general, CSA (November 17, 1863, to rank from the 16th); and commanding Martin's Division, Martin's detachment of Wheeler's Cavalry Corps, Department of East Tennessee (November 1863-February 1864). He served at 1st Bull Run as a field officer with his first unit and then resigned in 1862 to raise a regiment of partisan rangers. As a colonel, he led it at Murfreesboro and during the Tullahoma Campaign. Named a brigadier general with the idea that he would command Robert E. Rodes' old brigade in the Army of Northern Virginia, Morgan declined the appointment on July 14, 1863. Given command of a cavalry brigade under Joseph Wheeler, he was reappointed four months later. He commanded the division in the operations against Knoxville and was back in charge of his brigade during the early portion of the Atlanta Campaign. Recruiting in Mississippi at the close of the war, he resumed his practice and was a leader in the movement to end black rule in Alabama. He spent his last three decades in the U.S. Senate.

MORRIS, William S. (?-?)

The telegraph was an innovation in warfare during the Civil War, and it was William S. Morris who was the key to its use by the Confederacy. A Georgia physician and businessman before the war, he owned a large share of the American Telegraph Company at the outbreak of the Civil War. He was named to head the military telegraph operations by Confederate Postmaster General John Reagan and was the prime mover in establishing its potential for warfare in the South. He served throughout the war and then returned to private business.

MORTON, Jackson (1794-1874)

When his old political foe, Stephen R. Mallory, was named to the cabinet without the customary consultation with the Florida delegation, Jackson Morton developed a lasting dislike for Jefferson Davis. The Virginia native had established himself as a Florida merchant, lumberman, and plantation owner. Politically a Whig he served in the state's legislative and constitutional bodies before serving a term in the U.S. Senate. He tried to delay secession by making it a cooperative venture with neighboring Alabama. He was admitted to the Provisional Confederate Congress on February 6, 1861, and became chairman of the Committee on Indian Affairs. He also sat on the committees on: Commercial Affairs; and Flag and Seal. His principal activities appear to have been to protect the Florida coastline and limit the president's appointive powers in the wake of the Mallory affair. Failing in a bid for the Senate in the First Regular Congress in November 1861, he retired from public life at the conclusion of the Provisional Congress. (Davis, William W., *The Civil War and Reconstruction in Florida*)

MOSBY, John Singleton (1833-1916)

It has been claimed by some that the activities of partisan ranger bands in northern and western Virginia, especially those of John

John Singleton Mosby, master Confederate raider. (NA)

S. Mosby, may have prevented a Union victory in the summer or fall of 1864. A Virginian with a penchant for violence, Mosby had been practicing law at the outbreak of the war. His assignments included: private, 1st Virginia Cavalry (1861); first lieutenant, 1st Virginia Cavalry (February 1862); captain, PACS (March 15, 1863); major, PACS (March 26, 1863); major, 43rd Virginia Cavalry Battalion (June 10, 1863); lieutenant colonel, 43rd Virginia Cavalry Battalion (January 21, 1864); and colonel, Mosby's (Va.) Cavalry Regiment (December 7, 1864). Originally an enlisted man and officer in the 1st Virginia Cavalry, he came into conflict with that unit's colonel, "Grumble Jones," and joined Jeb Stuart's staff as a scout. During the Peninsula Campaign he paved the way for Stuart's famous ride around McClellan. After a brief period of captivity in July 1862 he rejoined Stuart and was rewarded with the authority to raise a band of partisans for service in the Loudoun Valley in northern Virginia. Originally a battalion, his command was raised to a regiment in the last months of the war. In the meantime he managed to wreak havoc among the Union supply lines, forcing field commanders to detach large numbers of troops to guard their communications. His forays took him within the lines guarding Washington, with Mosby himself often doing the advance scouting in disguise. Early in 1863, with 29 men, he rode into Fairfax Court House and roused Union General Edwin H. Stoughton from bed with a slap on the rear end. Following the capture of Generals Crook and Kelley by McNeil's partisans, Mosby complimented them, stating that he would have to ride into Washington and bring out Abraham Lincoln to top their success. On another occasion he came near

capturing the train on which Grant was travelling. The disruption of supply lines and the constant disappearance of couriers frustrated army, and lesser-group, commanders to such a degree that some took to the summary execution of guerrillas, i.e. partisan rangers. George Custer executed six of Mosby's men in 1864, and the partisan chief retaliated with seven of Custer's. A note attached to one of the bodies stated that Mosby would treat all further captives as prisoners of war unless Custer committed some new act of cruelty. The killings stopped. With the surrender of Lee, Mosby simply disbanded his command on April 20, 1865, rather than formally surrender. While the partisans were certainly a nuisance to federal commanders, it is an open question as to how effective they were in prolonging the conflict. Many Southerners were very critical of the partisans, only some Southerners excepting Mosby's command. Not pardoned until 1866, Mosby practiced law and befriended Grant. For supporting Grant, a Republican, in the 1868 and 1872 elections, he earned the emnity of many Southerners. He received an appointment as U.S. consul in Hong Kong and other government posts. (Jones, Virgil Carrington, *Ranger Mosby*)

MOUTON, Jean Jacques Alfred Alexander (1829-1864)

Confederate division commander Jean J.A.A. Mouton gave his life in the defeat of Nathanial P. Banks at Mansfield, which brought to an end the Union advance in the Red River Campaign. Better known as Alfred Mouton, the Louisiana Acadian had graduated from West Point in 1850 but was allowed to resign as a brevet second lieutenant with the 7th Infantry less than three months later since the Mexican War was over and a retrenchment was taking place in the regular army. A railroading engineer for the next decade, he also rose to the rank of brigadier general in the militia of his native state. His Confederate assignments included: brigadier general, Louisiana Militia (prewar); colonel, 18th Louisiana (October 5, 1861); brigadier general, CSA (April 16, 1862); and commanding in the District of West Louisiana, Trans-Mississippi Department: Sub-District of Lafourche (October 1862); brigade (October 1862-November 1863); and 2nd Division (November 1863-April 8, 1864). On the second day at Shiloh he was severely wounded while leading his regiment. Promoted to brigadier general that same month, he was assigned to western Louisiana upon his recovery. He led a brigade and then a division under Richard Taylor and was part of the force gathered to confront Banks in April 1864. On the 8th he was instantly killed while leading a charge. (Arceneaux, William, *The Acadian General*)

MUDD, Samuel A. (1833-1883)

Then as now the case of Dr. Samuel A. Mudd in the Lincoln assassination plot has been a subject of much debate. The Maryland physician had not practiced medicine for years and was running a farm near Bryantown. At about 4:00 A.M. on April 15, 1865, two men—John Wilkes Booth and David E. Herold—came to his door. The former was injured in the leg and Dr. Mudd invited them in and set the broken limb. Although it has been shown that Mudd had met Booth on at least two occasions, he later claimed that he did not recognize the Lincoln assassin because he was wearing a phony beard. Whatever the case, detectives soon arrested the doctor and hustled him off to join the other conspirators. Largely through the testimony of Louis J. Weichmann, he was found guilty of involvement in the conspiracy and was sentenced to life imprisonment. President Andrew Johnson determined that those conspirators not sentenced to death should be sent to Fort Jefferson in Dry Tortugas, Florida—a hellhole for guards as well as prisoners. The place suffered from frequent yellow fever outbreaks and one of Mudd's fellow prisoners, Michael O'Laughlin (convicted in the Lincoln Plot), succumbed to the epidemic. Ironically, after having been treated inhumanely by the prison staff, Dr. Mudd volunteered to treat guards, officials, and prisoners alike after the army surgeons had died in 1867. News of this got out and there was a campaign to gain Mudd's freedom, spurred on by his wife. One of Johnson's last acts as president was the release of Mudd and his fellow conspiracy convicts, Edward Spangler and Samuel Arnold. Dr. Mudd lived out his life in Maryland and has been the subject of controversy ever since. Led by members of his family, there have been repeated movements to gain a pardon. While these movements have gained the support of many political leaders, including former president Jimmy Carter, there are also a number of experts on the assassination who believe that Mudd was involved in the plots to kidnap the president, if not also the murder scheme. (Mudd, Nettie, *Life of Samuel A. Mudd*)

MUMFORD, William B. (ca. 1820-1862)

One of the actions of Benjamin F. Butler in New Orleans that earned him the nickname of "Beast Butler" was the hanging of William B. Mumford. When the New Orleans gambler had spied a U.S. flag flying over the Mint, he climbed to the roof and tore it down. It was still prior to the official surrender of the Crescent City and the flag had been raised without Farragut's knowledge. Thus it could not properly be considered an act of treason. Nonetheless Butler had him arrested and tried on that charge. On June 7, 1862, Mumford was hanged in front of the U.S. Mint. In retaliation Jefferson Davis declared Butler to be a common felon deserving of capital punishment and ordered that any Confederate officer capturing the Union general immediately execute him by hanging. He further ordered that no Union officers be paroled before being formally exchanged.

MUNDY, Sue

See: *Clarke, Marcellus Jerome*

MUNFORD, Thomas Taylor (1831-1918)

Despite the recommendations of most of his superiors, Thomas T. Munford never appears to have made it to the rank of general. A native of Virginia and a graduate of the Virginia Military Institute, he was a planter before the Civil War. His Confederate assignments included: lieutenant colonel, 2nd Virginia Cavalry

(May 8, 1861); colonel, 2nd Virginia Cavalry (April 25, 1862); commanding Cavalry Brigade, Valley District, Department of Northern Virginia (June 6-26, 1862); commanding Cavalry, Jackson's Command, Army of Northern Virginia (June 26-July 1862); commanding Robertson's Brigade, Cavalry Division, Army of Northern Virginia (early September-ca. November 10, 1862); commanding Wickham's (old) Brigade, Fitz Lee's Division, Cavalry Corps, Army of Northern Virginia (ca. November 9, 1864-March 1865); and commanding the division (March-April 9, 1865). After distinguished service at 1st Bull Run, he commanded the regiment in the Shenandoah Valley until the

MURDAUGH, William H. (?-?)

A veteran of almost two decades of service to the old navy, Virginian William H. Murdaugh is an example of how some Southern officers were treated by the U.S. Navy Department. Although intending to resign his lieutenant's commission in the event that his native state seceded, he loyally followed orders to land a force of troops in Fort Pickens in violation of an agreement with the Confederate forces at Pensacola. When, on April 25, 1861, Murdaugh received notice of the secession of Virginia, he submitted his resignation to his captain. The captain refused to allow Murdaugh to quit the vessel until Washington had accepted the resignation. So for six weeks Murdaugh performed faithful but distasteful service. He was then retroactively dismissed from the service. In June he was assigned to duty obstructing the James River for the Southern navy. Sent to North Carolina, he was wounded at Fort Hatteras in August. Assigned to ordnance duty at Norfolk, he witnessed the fight at Hampton Roads from aboard the tug *Harmony*. Setting up ordnance operations at Charlotte, North Carolina, Murdaugh remained there until ordered to the command of the *Beaufort* in the James River Squadron. Shortly thereafter he was sent to Europe to purchase ordnance supplies. He was praised for his tact and judgment by his superior, Commander Bulloch. Before he could be assigned to an ironclad built in Europe the war came to an end. (Scharf, J. Thomas, *History of the Confederate States Navy*)

MURRAH, Pendleton (1824-1865)

The last Confederate governor of Texas, Pendleton Murrah was forced to flee to Mexico during the confusion rampant in the state following the death of the Confederacy. Born in South Carolina, he had been a lawyer in Alabama before moving to Texas where he was also in the legal business. Defeated for a congressional seat in the mid-1850s, he won a seat in the legislature in 1857. A Democrat, he took a favorable view of secession and served in the Quartermaster's Department in Texas early in the war. In 1863 he was elected governor and three days later—November 5—was sworn in. The increasingly harsh measures of the Richmond authorities in trying to preserve the Confederate States brought Murrah into conflict with their representatives, especially the military. He resented impressments and the draft which was robbing the state of manpower to maintain law and order and guard the frontier.

Trying to maintain order after the final collapse, he worked for the state's early reentry into the Union. He called a constitutional convention but was labelled a traitor by the Union authorities and was forced to flee before it could be held as scheduled on June 11, 1865. He was succeeded by the lieutenant governor, Fletcher S. Stockdale. Within two months Murrah was dead in Mexico. (DeShields, James T., *They Sat in High Places: The Presidents and Governors of Texas, 1835-1939*)

MYERS, Abraham Charles (1811-1889)

South Carolinian by birth and Louisianan by adoption, Abraham Myers had a long record of service in the Quartermaster's Department when he resigned on January 28, 1861, and offered his services to the Confederacy. On March 25, he was appointed the first quartermaster general, with the rank of lieutenant colonel. The West Pointer's (1833) duties included the supply of the armies in the field with everything that was not either eaten or fired by the troops. His efforts to keep the field forces clothed, shod, and mobile with thousands of wagons and teams was a losing battle. Naturally, he was a prime target for the wrath of the soldiers, possibly more so because he was Jewish. Promoted colonel on February 15, 1862, he had to compete with other supply departments for the limited resources of the South. Superseded by General Lawton, Myers resigned from the army on August 10, 1863. At least in part, his removal was not due to his failures, but rather to the activities of his gossipy wife in criticizing Mrs. Davis and describing her as a squaw. Myers, bitter toward Davis, lived for the rest of the war in poor circumstances in Georgia. He died in Washington in 1889.

N

NAPOLEON, Louis (1808-1873)

French Emperor Napoleon III wanted to recognize the Confederacy early in the war and offered an effort to mediate the conflict but wished that Britain and Russia would go along with the proposal. Not gaining such an agreement, he never went ahead with the idea, but the North always feared his possible actions in the New World. Having granted the South the status of a belligerent, he criticized the North for the seizure of Mason and Slidell from the British steamer *Trent* and refused suggestions that he mediate that dispute. Expansionist in his policies, he had his forces remain in Mexico after a joint operation with the British and Spanish to force repayment of debts. He established Archduke Maximilian of Austria on a throne in Mexico City. Lincoln's fears of the French designs in Mexico prompted him to postpone Grant's projected movement against Mobile, after the fall of Vicksburg and Port Hudson. Instead, he ordered a large portion of the forces sent to Texas. The South often toyed with the idea of an alliance with Napoleon, and there were even suggestions that the Confederacy become a French protectorate. Napoleon was deposed after the Franco-Prussian War of 1870-71.

NEELY, James Jackson (1827-?)

A grudge over being superseded in command of a brigade of cavalry led to James J. Neely being cashiered from the Confederate army and charged with inciting a mutiny. A native of Tennessee, he joined the Confederate army where his service included: captain, Company B, 6th Tennessee Cavalry Battalion (ca. June 1861); colonel, 14th Tennessee Cavalry (July 1, 1863); and commanding Richardson's Brigade, Chalmers' Division, Forrest's Cavalry Corps, Department of Alabama, Mississippi and East Louisiana (May 10-August 30, 1864). With his original company, the "Hardeman Avengers," he took part in the battle of Belmont. In April 1862 the battalion was merged with other companies to form a regiment. However, in the consolidation he became a supernumerary without a command. In

the spring of the next year he was granted authority to raise a regiment behind Union lines in West Tennessee. He completed the assignment in August and took part in numerous raids in the enemy's country. Ordered to northern Mississippi, he joined the regular cavalry forces operating there and fought under Forrest at Okolona and against A. J. Smith the next year. In the spring of 1864 he assumed command of the brigade but was relieved by Colonel E. W. Rucker in late August. Resenting the outsider taking over the command, the regimental commanders refused to obey Rucker's orders and even wrote him requesting that he not take command. They were arrested and suspended from command. That is, all except Neely who was kicked out of the army on October 18, 1864.

NEFF, John Francis (1834-1862)

The famed Stonewall Brigade often suffered from dissension among its officer corps. This was the case for one regimental commander, John Neff, and the brigade commander, General Charles S. Winder. Neff, born into a Shenandoah Valley Dunkard-sect family, felt it necessary to slip away from home, with $200 of his father's money, after being refused permission to attend the Virginia Military Institute. Eventually gaining admission, he graduated in 1858 and then studied law and was admitted to the bar. With the outbreak of the war he went to Richmond and was ordered to Harpers Ferry to help drill the volunteers. With the formation of the 33rd Virginia in July 1861 he was appointed a first lieutenant and regimental adjutant. With the brigade under General Thomas J. Jackson, the regiment moved to Manassas Junction and took part in the battle of 1st Bull Run, earning the sobriquet "Stonewall." Several months later the command returned to the Valley, fought at Kernstown, and on April 22, 1862, the regiment was reorganized with Neff as its colonel. He led the regiment through the Valley Campaign (1st Winchester and Port Republic) and the Seven Days (Gaines' Mill, White Oak Swamp, and Malvern Hill). After a brief rest the command moved to Gordonsville where Neff was highly critical of

Winder's harsh treatment of some of the men. Word got back to Winder, and Neff, repeating the offending remarks to Winder's face, was placed under arrest. Despite his disqualification, Neff led his men at Cedar Mountain where Winder was killed. The charges dropped, Neff resumed formal command and was killed less than three weeks later at Groveton, the opening of the battle of 2nd Bull Run. Had he lived, his calm demeanor in battle would have probably earned him a promotion and the leadership of the Stonewall Brigade, which never kept a commander for very long. (Robertson, James I., Jr., *The Stonewall Brigade*)

NELSON, Allison (1822-1862)

For Allison Nelson the Civil War was but another in a series of adventures. The Georgia-born local politician had always been more interested in things military. He took part in the Mexican War as captain of an independent Georgia company, the Cuban independence movement as a general, and in the agony of "Bleeding Kansas." Having moved to Texas in 1856 and favoring secession at the Texas convention, he helped raise the 10th Texas. Becoming the regiment's first colonel, he was stationed initially at Galveston and along the coast. Moving his regiment to Arkansas in June 1862, his later commands included: commanding a brigade, Trans-Mississippi Department (late June-August 20, 1862); commanding a brigade and a division, District of Arkansas, Trans-Mississippi Department (August 20-September 28, 1862); brigadier general, CSA (September 12, 1862); and commanding 1st Brigade, 2nd Division, 1st Corps, Army of the West, Trans-Mississippi Department and the division (September 28-October 11, 1862). After seeing only limited campaigning he died of fever on October 11, 1862. His most important contribution was in stemming organized desertion by the strict punishment of ringleaders.

NEWSOM, Ella King (ca. 1830s-post 1913)

A wealthy Arkansas widow, Ella K. Newsom became "The Florence Nightingale of the Southern Army." The Mississippi-born widow of a doctor, she joined the Confederate army as a nurse upon the outbreak of the war and afterwards served in hospitals at Memphis, Nashville, Chattanooga, Bowling Green, Atlanta, Corinth (Mississippi), and Abingdon (Virginia). Much of her time was spent in the training of other nurses. After the war she was married for a time to an ex-Confederate Arkansas officer. While working for the Washington pension office she wrote *Reminiscences of War Time*. She died in the nation's capital. (Richard, J. Fraise, *The Florence Nightingale of the Southern Army*)

NICHOLLS, Francis Reddin Tillou (1834-1912)

In a rather limited combat career Francis R.T. Nicholls suffered two amputations and was retired to post and conscript duty. A West Pointer (1855), he had served one year in the artillery before resigning to study law. Giving up his practice, he raised the Phoenix Guards and offered them to the Confederacy. His assignments included: captain, Company K, 8th Louisiana (spr-

ing 1861); lieutenant colonel, 8th Louisiana (June 9, 1861); colonel, 15th Louisiana (June 24, 1862); brigadier general, CSA (October 14, 1862); commanding 2nd Louisiana Brigade, Jackson's (old) Division, 2nd Corps, Army of Northern Virginia (January 16-May 2, 1863); and commanding post at Lynchburg, Va. (August 11, 1863-June 1864). He fought at 1st Bull Run and joined Jackson for the Shenandoah Valley Campaign in which he was captured and lost his left arm at 1st Winchester. During his convalescence after an exchange he was transferred to a new regiment and twice promoted. Finally returning to duty in January 1863, he led a brigade at Chancellorsville until again wounded, this time in the foot by a shell. Amputation completed the projectile's work. Three months later he was assigned to post duty at Lynchburg, holding the position until June 1864. The next month he was ordered to the Trans-Mississippi Department to head the volunteer and conscript service. He finished the war there. Back in Louisiana he served two separate terms as governor, supressed the Louisiana Lottery, and headed the state supreme court. (Freeman, Doublas S., *Lee's Lieutenants*)

NICHOLSON, Alfred Osborn Pope (1808-1876)

In a manner highly typical of the nineteenth century, Alfred O.P. Nicholson mixed the fields of law, politics, and journalism in his career. The native Tennessean was admitted to the bar in 1831 and the next year became the editor of the *Columbia* (Tenn.) *Western Mercury*. Sent to the state legislature in 1833, he gave up his editorship two years later. He remained in the legislative post until named to fill a vacancy in the U.S. Senate in 1839. He took his seat as a Democrat in 1840 and held it until 1842 when his appointment lapsed. The next year he was elected to the upper house of the state legislature and served there until 1845. From 1844 until 1846 he edited the *Nashville Union* and then went into banking. Having turned down a cabinet post in 1853, he became the editor of the *Washington Union* until 1856. He was again named to the U.S. Senate and served from 1859 until March 3, 1861. He did not return for the next congress and was formally expelled by a resolution on July 11, 1861. After the war he was the chief justice of the Tennessee Supreme Court from 1870 until his death.

NISBET, Eugenius Aristides (1803-1871)

As the culmination of a political career which spanned the Whig, Know-Nothing, and Democratic parties, Eugenius A. Nisbet chaired the convention committee which drafted Georgia's secession ordinance. The Georgia native had practiced law, served in both houses of the state legislture, served a term in the U.S. Congress, and been an associate justice of the state supreme court before returning to private practice in 1853. Always a states' righter, he nonetheless supported Stephen A. Douglas in the 1860 election and was elected to the secession convention as a staunch Unionist. Named to the Provisional Confederate Congress after his shift to secession, he sat on the committees on: Foreign Affairs; and Territories. He backed

Alexander H. Stephens for vice president and favored a single eight-year presidential term. Although generally a supporter of the central government, he wished to maintain state control over volunteers. For reasons of health he resigned on December 10, 1861, and returned to private life.

NORTHROP, Lucius Bellinger (1811-1894)

One of the most hated men in any army is the commissary, and Lucius B. Northrop was no exception. Born in Charleston, South Carolina, he had graduated from West Point in 1831 and been posted to the infantry but two years later secured his transfer to the dragoons. Severely wounded fighting the Seminoles in Florida, he went on an apparently permanent sick leave. (Actually, the knee wound was inflicted by his own pistol when it accidentally discharged). He studied at the Jefferson Medical College in Philadelphia and then entered upon private practice in Charleston. In 1848 he was dropped from the army rolls for practicing his profession but was reinstated at the behest of his old army comrade, Jefferson Davis, who then sat in the U.S. Senate. On January 8, 1861, he resigned his commission as a captain in the 1st Dragoons and joined the South. There his assignments included: lieutenant colonel and acting commissary general of subsistence (March 27, 1861); colonel and commissary general of subsistence (June 21, 1831, to rank from March 16); and brigadier general, CSA (November 26, 1864). He almost immediately ran into problems with field commanders when, after 1st Bull Run, Joseph E. Johnston and Beauregard blamed their inability to follow up the victory with a drive on Washington on the commissary department. Northrop was forced to deal with an inadequate transportation system and did the best anyone probably could. But that was not good enough for the Confederate cause, and he was too dedicated to red tape to come up with the miracles required. Lee was also displeased with Northrop but did not insist upon his removal until early 1865. In the meantime Northrop had survived a number of congressional investigations, and his friend Davis was even afraid to submit his appointment of Northrop to brigadier general to the Senate for confirmation. In the end even Davis despaired of the wisdom of retaining Northrop and the latter was finally relieved on February 16, 1865. After the fall of the Confederacy, he was arrested by the Federals, on June 30, 1865, on the charge of having deliberately starved Union war prisoners. The charges were never pressed and he was released in October. He then retired to a Virginia farm. (Dufour, Charles L., *Nine Men in Gray*)

O

OATES, William Calvin (1833-1910)

It was not until the Spanish-American War that William C. Oates got to wear the stars of a general. A native of Alabama, he had entered the Confederate army where his assignments included: captain, Company G, 15th Alabama (July 1861); colonel, 15th Alabama (April 28, 1863); major, 15th Alabama (in 1864, to date from April 28, 1863); and lieutenant colonel, 15th Alabama (December 7, 1864). With his company he served in the Shenandoah Valley Campaign, the Seven Days, Cedar Mountain, Antietam, and Fredericksburg. While taking part in Longstreet's campaign in southeastern Virginia he was named colonel, but it was never confirmed and he officially became a major from that date at some time in early 1864. He became a bitter enemy of the man who became colonel in his stead, Alexander A. Lowther, and charged him with incompetence and cowardice. In the meantime, he had commanded the regiment at Gettysburg where he led his command to the top of Big Round Top. Realizing that this point was the key to the Union's southern flank, he wanted to hold the position and bring up some artillery. His orders were to advance against Little Round Top and this was confirmed by a staff officer. Advancing down the hill and up the next, he took part in the attack on the 20th Maine. He never forgot the lost opportunity, when he actually saw the enemy supply trains in their rear. Oates went on to command the 15th at Chickamauga and Knoxville. He served in his reduced capacity through the rest of the war in Virginia. After the war he was a governor and congressman and in the war with Spain donned the blue uniform of a U.S. brigadier general. He wrote an excellent war memoir. (Oates, William C., *The War Between the Union and the Confederacy and Its Lost Opportunities*)

O'LAUGHLIN, Michael (1840-1867).

He was the only one of the four Lincoln assassination conspirators sent to Dry Tortugas not to benefit from Andrew Johnson's 1869 releases; Michael O'Laughlin had died there in a yellow fever epidemic two years earlier. Like Samuel B. Arnold, he had been a childhood friend of John Wilkes Booth in Baltimore and had been in the Confederate army for a time. He was working as a clerk in Baltimore when he was summoned by Booth. When he heard the plan to kidnap Lincoln and cart him off to Richmond for a possible prisoner exchange, he was shocked. However, the well-known magnetism of the actor won him over and he was involved in the planning and attempts. But when the plan turned to murder, O'Laughlin did not play an active role, but neither did he report what he knew. After hearing of the assassination he turned himself in on April 17, 1865, in Baltimore. Tried with seven other plotters, in a proceeding in which there was little if any concern for the rights of the

Michael O'Laughlin, Lincoln conspirator. (NA)

defendants, he was found guilty on June 30, 1865, and was sentenced to life imprisonment. During the epidemic at Dry Tortugas in which Dr. Samuel A. Mudd so distinguished himself, O'Laughlin succumbed.

OLDHAM, Williamson Simpson (1813-1868)

A deeply disappointed secessionist, Williamson S. Oldham refused to take the oath of allegiance upon his return to his adopted Texas from Canada. A Tennessee native, he was a teacher and lawyer before moving to Arkansas where he served as speaker of the lower house of the legislature and as a state supreme court justice. Defeated in bids for both houses of the national legislature he moved to Texas in 1849. A Democrat, he edited the *Texas State Gazette* and became an ardent secessionist. He attended the secession convention and sat in the Confederate Congress from March 2, 1861, to the end of the Confederacy. During the Provisional Congress he sat on the committees on: Engrossment; Judiciary; Naval Affairs; and Territories. Named to the Senate, his committee assignments included those on: Claims (Second Congress); Commerce (both congresses; chairman in Second Congress); Finance (Second Congress); Indian Affairs; Judiciary (Second Congress); Naval Affairs (First Congress); and Post Offices and Post Roads (chairman in both congresses). A firm believer in states' rights, he wanted many limitations on the national administration but in some fields was willing to grant predominate power to the Richmond authorities. He favored the fight against inflation, heavy taxes, and the recruiting of black troops. He also fought for better protection for his state. When the end came he fled via Mexico to Canada and became a photographer and wrote *The Last Days of the Confederacy*. He returned to Texas in 1866, embittered, and soon died of typhoid fever.

OLMSTEAD, Charles Hart (1837-1926)

Although he served through some of the heavy campaigns of the Army of Tennessee in the last year of the war, Charles H. Olmstead was fortunate enough to be on detached service during the disasters under Hood in Tennessee. His assignments included: major, 1st Georgia (1861); colonel, 1st Georgia (December 26, 1861); commanding Mercer's-Smith's Brigade, Cleburne's Division, 1st Corps, Army of Tennessee (August-fall and November 30, 1864-early 1865); and colonel, 1st Georgia Consolidated (April 9, 1865). Initially serving in the Savannah area, he surrendered Fort Pulaski after a two-day bombardment. Exchanged, he continued to serve on the Georgia coast until sent to the defense of Charleston in the summer of 1863. He then returned to the Savannah region until ordered to report to the Army of Tennessee on May 24, 1864. He served through the remainder of the Atlanta Campaign and during the siege took over command of the brigade. Relinquishing command to newly assigned General J.A. Smith after the fall of the city, he led his regiment into Tennessee with Hood. Smith took over the division after General Cleburne had been killed at Franklin and Olmstead was again in command of the brigade, which had been detached guarding a supply train during the fight. The

brigade was again absent when the army was all but destroyed at Nashville. The army was then sent to North Carolina in the spring of 1865 to stop Sherman and on April 9, 1865, Olmstead took command of the 1st Georgia Consolidated which was composed of the old 1st, 57th, and 63rd regiments. He surrendered the command as a part of Johnston's army a few weeks later.

O'NEAL, Edward Asbury (1818-1890)

A poor performance at Gettysburg caused the appointment of Edward A. O'Neal as a brigadier general to be revoked. A lawyer and secessionist politician in his native Alabama, he entered the Confederate army at the head of the Calhoun Guards. His later assignments included: captain, Company I, 9th Alabama (June 1861); lieutenant colonel, 9th Alabama (October 21, 1861); colonel, 26th Alabama (April 2, 1862); commanding Rodes' (old) Brigade, D.H. Hill's-Rodes' Division, 2nd Corps, Army of Northern Virginia (ca. January 14-May 3 and June-July 1863); brigadier general, CSA (June 6, 1863; revoked); and commanding Cantey's Brigade, Walthall's Division, Polk's-Lee's Corps (known as Army of Mississippi until July), Army of Tennessee (ca. June-fall 1864). On the Peninsula he fought at Yorktown and Seven Pines where he suffered a wound. Back on duty he fought in the Seven Days only to be hit again at South Mountain. In command of the brigade, he was wounded yet again at Chancellorsville. By the time of the battle of Gettysburg, General Lee had already received O'Neal's appointment to brigadier general but had not yet delivered it to him. Then disaster struck the recipient on the first day of the battle. He proved unable to control his five Alabama regiments which became scattered. Then Lee sent the commission back to the War Department, and President Davis canceled the appointment and recalled the request for Senate confirmation. Cullen A. Battle was assigned in his stead. In early 1864, O'Neal and the 26th were sent to Georgia and he commanded a brigade in the Atlanta Campaign. That fall he was relieved and he served out the war gathering up deserters in northern Alabama. A post-war lawyer he reentered politics and served two terms as governor. (Freeman, Douglas S., *Lee's Lieutenants*)

ORR, James Lawrence (1822-1873)

The dilemma of the Confederacy, with its need for a strong central government in order to win it's independence and its inability to achieve that independence because of its own birth from a states' rights philosophy, is demonstrated in the Confederate career of James L. Orr. A native South Carolina lawyer, he had also edited the *Anderson Gazette* for two years before serving in the state legislature. He then served for five terms in the U.S. Congress--the last of which, 1857 to 1859, he served as speaker of the house--and was a supporter of Stephen A. Douglas. A Democrat, he was nonetheless a moderate on the question of secession and opposed the theory of nullification as it had been presented by John C. Calhoun. A believer in states' rights, he attended the 1851 Southern convention in Charleston and the Democratic conventions in 1856 and 1860. In December 1860 he attended the state secession convention and was sent to Washington, with two other commissioners, to negotiate the surrender of the national forts and other property in Charleston Harbor. After the fall of Fort Sumter he organized a regiment and was commissioned colonel, 1st South Carolina Rifles (July 20, 1861). He served with the regiment in the harbor area until February 1, 1862, when he resigned, having been elected to the Senate in the First Regular Confederate Congress. He was specially seated in the Provisional Congress on February 17, 1862, the day of its final adjournment. The next day he was formally seated in the Senate where he served for the remainder of the war. He was chairman of the Committee on Foreign Affairs throughout and of the Committee on Rules in the Second Congress. He also served on the First Congress committees on Commerce, Flag and Seal, and Pay and Mileage and the Second Congress committees on Finance and Printing. Initially supporting the required war measures, his states' rights philosophy caused him to revolt at increasing infringements on that philosophy. He opposed the draft and demanded full payment for impressed goods. He was a member of the group opposed to Jefferson Davis' friend General Braxton Bragg and opposed the suspension of the writ of habeas corpus. Late in the war he was the leader of the Senate peace block. The states' righters were denying the Confederacy the means to gain its independence. With the collapse of the Confederacy he went to Andrew Johnson to set up a provisional government for the state. Successful, he was elected governor in October 1865 and proved to be a moderate. He served until 1868 and then was a circuit judge. Becoming a Republican and a supporter of Grant's anti-KKK measures, he was named minister to Russia in late 1872. He died within a matter of months at St. Petersburg. (Leembuis, Roger, *James L. Orr and the Sectional Conflict*)

ORTON, Lawrence W.

See: *Williams, William Orton*

OSBORN, James M. (fl. 1861)

The high prices caused by the Union blockade ensured the virtual anonymity of Charleston photographer James M. Osborn despite his excellent work. Together with his partner, F.E. Durbec, he was operating "Osborn & Durbec's Photographic Mart" at 223 King Street at the outbreak of the Civil War. Within days of the firing upon Fort Sumter the pair took their stereo camera to the scene of the action and compiled an extraordinary record of the fort and the batteries which had compelled its submission. However, the blockade which was soon in place prevented them from acquiring the supplies they needed to market their prints in any large quantities. This may have led to the disruption of their partnership before the close of the war, but not before they had made a valuable contribution to the photographic coverage of the conflict.

OULD, Robert (1820-1881)

A prominent attorney in his native District of Columbia, Robert Ould was a Southern partisan and left his post as U.S.

district attorney to join the Confederacy. During the first three months of 1862 he was the assistant secretary of war but later that year became the chief of the Bureau of Exchange of Prisoners. It was in this post that he made his mark in the history of the Confederacy. Paying great attention to details, he represented the Richmond authorities in their dealings with Washington over the formal parole and exchange of prisoners of war. Thousands of officers and men on both sides benefitted from this cartel until its collapse in early 1864. Ould subsequently held a judicial post in the military. At the war's close he was confined for eight weeks until cleared of charges that he had misappropriated the funds of captured Federal prisoners. After his release he resumed the practice of law, this time in Richmond.

OURY, Granville Henderson (1825-1891)

In a disputed election, Granville H. Oury lost his seat as Arizona Territory's nonvoting delegate to the Confederate Congress and spent the remainder of the war in the military. Born in Virginia, he had become a Missouri lawyer before moving to Texas and participating in the California gold rush. In 1856 he moved to Tucson, New Mexico Territory, and five years later was sent to Richmond by a convention of voters to represent them before the Confederate Congress and push for a new territory, Arizona, to be formed from the southern half of the then-New Mexico Territory. This was done and he was admitted as a nonvoting delegate to the Provisional Congress on January 18, 1862. Meanwhile, the military governor, John R. Baylor, called an election in which Oury's supporters refused to take part on the grounds of insufficient notice, with the result that Marcus H. Macwillie was elected. Leaving Richmond, Oury joined the army where his assignments included: captain, Herbert's (Ariz.) Cavalry Battalion (1862); and colonel (ca. 1863). In the latter part of the war he served as a staff officer to General Henry H. Sibley. After the war he served in the new Arizona's territorial legislature and as its congressional delegate—again nonvoting.

OWEN, William Miller (1840-1893)

The historian of the famed Washington Artillery of New Orleans, William Miller Owen was for much of the war the unit's adjutant. A native of Ohio, he had relocated to Louisiana three years before the outbreak of the conflict. His assignments included: first lieutenant and adjutant, Washington (La.) Artillery Battalion (May 26, 1861); major, Artillery (August 10, 1863); executive officer, King's Artillery Battalion, Departments of Western Virginia and East Tennessee (1863-64); commanding Artillery Battalion, Colquitt's Division, Department of North Carolina and Southern Virginia (May-June 1864); commanding Gibbes' Artillery Battalion, 3rd Corps, Army of Northern Virginia (July 20, 1864-spring 1865); lieutenant colonel, Artillery (early 1865); and commanding McIntosh's Artillery Battalion, 3rd Corps, Army of Northern Virginia (spring-April 9, 1865). As a battalion staff officer, he served at 1st Bull Run, Yorktown, the Seven Days, 2nd Bull Run, Antietam, and on Marye's Heights at both

Fredericksburg and Chancellorsville. After serving at Gettysburg, he was promoted to major and transferred to duty with King's Battalion in southwestern Virginia. The next spring he returned east and commanded a battalion in the hastily gathered forces defending Petersburg. His command was soon absorbed into the Army of Northern Virginia. Despite a wound received at the Crater he commanded a battalion through most of the siege and was in command of a different battalion during the final campaign to Appomattox. He returned to Louisiana after the war and wrote his memoirs. (Owen, William Miller, *In Camp and Battle with the Washington Artillery of New Orleans*)

OWENS, James Byeram (1816-1889)

As one of Florida's representatives to the Provisional Confederate Congress, James B. Owens proved to be a doctrinaire states' righter and an opponent of Jefferson Davis. He had been a Baptist minister in his native South Carolina before moving to Florida where he became a wealthy cotton and citrus planter, and was something of a pioneer in the latter field. A signer of the secession ordinance, he was chairman of the Committee on Accounts and also sat on the Committee on Naval Affairs in Congress. He refused to grant the central government much in the way of emergency powers. Not seeking election to the First Regular Congress, he returned to his plantation and did some preaching. Having nothing further to do with the conflict and with this area virtually untouched by the war, he was able to reestablish his lifestyle, with many of his former slaves working for him.

P

PAGE, Richard Lucian (1807-1901)

Due to the Confederacy's policy of issuing army ranks to naval officers serving with troops defending land positions, Richard L. Page was an officer in both branches of the service. Resigning his commander's commission in the old navy, in which he had served since 1824, Page became an aide-de-camp to Virginia's Governor Letcher. He was charged with organizing the state navy. His later assignments included: commander, CSN (June 10, 1862); captain, CSN (spring 1862); brigadier general, CSA (March 1, 1864); and commanding Page's Brigade, District of the Gulf, Department of Alabama, Mississippi, and East Louisiana (March 1-August 23, 1864). After working on the fortifications of the James and Nansemond Rivers, Page was assigned to ordnance duty at the Norfolk Navy Yard until it was abandoned. During the *Virginia*'s battles in Hampton Roads, he served a gun in the Sewell's Point battery. After the abandonment of Norfolk, he transferred his ordnance operations to Charlotte, North Carolina, where he remained in charge until early 1864, except for one brief period in command at Savannah during which he saw action at Port Royal. On March 1, 1864, he was appointed to a brigadier general's rank in the army so that he could command the outer defenses of Mobile Bay. With headquarters in Fort Morgan, he worked on strengthening the defenses until he surrendered after two days of attack by the Union Fleet. He was not released from captivity until July 24, 1865. Settling in Norfolk, he was public school superintendent there for eight years.

PAINE, Lewis

See: *Powell, Lewis Thornton*

PALMER, John B. (?-?)

The consolidation of regiments due to heavy casualties resulted in Colonel John B. Palmer being detached from his command as a supernumerary and assigned elsewhere. His Confederate assignments included: lieutenant colonel, 5th North Carolina Partisan Rangers Battalion (1862); colonel, 58th North Carolina (July 29, 1862); commanding brigade, Department of East Tennessee (fall 1862-ca. May 19, 1863); commanding District of Western North Carolina, Department of East Tennessee (November 18, 1863-December 1864); and commanding brigade, District of Western North Carolina, Department of East Tennessee (December 1864-May 10, 1865). After his battalion was increased to regimental size, he served initially in eastern Tennessee. His command became part of the Southern buildup for the victory at Chickamauga where he was wounded on the second day. On November 18, 1863, he was assigned to command the District of Western North Carolina but he may not have left the Army of Tennessee until after the defeat at Chattanooga. Shortly after his detachment from his regiment it was consolidated with the 60th North Carolina. In the mountains of North Carolina he was responsible for rounding up deserters and draft evaders and fighting off Union raids. He continued on this duty until he was included in the surrender of his successor as district commander, on May 10, 1865.

PALMER, Joseph Benjamin (1825-1890)

Despite being a prewar Unionist, Tennessee lawyer, and politician, Joseph B. Palmer entered the Confederate army and rose to the rank of brigadier general. His prewar career had included service in the state legislature and as mayor of Murfreesboro. His military assignments included: captain, Company C, 18th Tennessee (May 1861); colonel, 18th Tennessee (June 11, 1861); commanding 2nd Brigade, Army of Middle Tennessee, Department #2 (October 28-November 7, 1862); commanding 2nd Brigade, Breckinridge's Division, Right Wing, Army of the Mississippi (November 7-20, 1862); commanding 2nd Brigade, Breckinridge's Division, Polk's Corps, Army of Tennessee (November 20, 1862-January 2, 1863); commanding Western District of North Carolina, Department of East Tennessee (November 18-December 4, 1863); commanding Brown's (old) Brigade, Stevenson's Division, Hood's-Lee's Corps, Army of Tennessee (early July-

September 1864); commanding Brown's and Reynolds' Brigades (consolidated), Stevenson's Division, Lee's Corps, Army of Tennessee (September 1864-April 9, 1865); brigadier general, CSA (November 15, 1864); and commanding brigade, Cheatham's Division, Hardee's Corps, Army of Tennessee (April 9-26, 1865). Captured at Fort Donelson, he was confined in Boston Harbor's Fort Warren until his exchange on September 26, 1862. Commanding a brigade, he fought at Murfreesboro until relieved by Gideon J. Pillow on the last day of the fight. Leading his regiment that same day in the disastrous assault of Breckinridge's division on the Union left, Palmer suffered three wounds. Returning to duty in the spring, he resumed command of the regiment for the Tullahoma Campaign. Still in regimental command at Chickamauga he sustained another wound. Recovering, he served for a time in North Carolina and then took command of a brigade during the Atlanta Campaign. Wounded at Jonesboro, he remained to lead two consolidated brigades in the Franklin-Nashville Campaign. Detached during both battles, his brigade did take part in covering the retreat from the latter. Moving back to North Carolina, Palmer led his command in the Carolinas Campaign against Sherman. In the final reorganization he was given charge of a brigade composed of the remnants of 38 Tennessee regiments and two battalions which were consolidated into four regiments. Surrendered at Durham Station, he resumed his law practice but stayed aloof from politics.

PALMERSTON, Henry John Temple, 3rd Viscount (1784-1865)

A veteran of over a half century in British politics, Lord Palmerston served as prime minister throughout the American Civil War. Although personally inclined toward the South, he enforced the Queen's neutrality proclamations, opposing moves in Parliament to get involved in the struggle. During the *Trent* affair his government presented an ultimatum, softened somewhat by Prince Albert, to the United States demanding the release of Confederate diplomats Mason and Slidell. To back up his demands he dispatched a naval squadron with 8,000 troops and munitions to Canada. It is also reported that immediately following the seizure he actually discussed joint military operations with Confederate operatives. However, once the dust had settled he returned to his policy of maintaining a general neutrality. He died the year the war ended. (Ridley, Jasper, *Lord Palmerston*)

PARHAM, William Allen (?-?)

Severely injured at the Battle of Malvern Hill, Colonel William A. Parham was, successively, forced out of field service, forced to retire from the army, and finally died from the effects of the wound after the close of the war. His Confederate assignments included: lieutenant, Company A, 41st Virginia (May 24, 1861); captain, Company A, 41st Virginia (early 1862); lieutenant colonel, 41st Virginia (May 3, 1862); colonel, 41st Virginia (July 25, 1862); and commanding Mahone's Brigade, Anderson's Division, Longstreet's Corps, Army of Northern Virginia (August-September 1862). Originally stationed at

Norfolk, he moved to the Peninsula when the former was abandoned. He saw action at Seven Pines and during the Seven Days, being severely wounded in the last action at Malvern Hill. He recovered in time to receive a promotion and to be in temporary command of the brigade at South Mountain. Here he made a gallant defense at Crampton's Gap. He also led the brigade at Antietam and the regiment at Chancellorsville and Gettysburg. However, by the fall of 1864 his wound was giving him so much trouble that he was assigned to provost duty along the Blackwater River and soon thereafter was made post commandant at Hicksford. Finally he retired from the service on March 31, 1865, and eventually succumbed to his wound.

PARKER, William Harwar (1826-1896)

Graduating first in his class at Annapolis in 1848, New York City native William H. Parker later organized and superintended the Confederate States Naval Academy. In the prewar years he had served afloat during the Mexican War and as an instructor at his alma mater before resigning as a lieutenant in 1861. His Confederate assignments included: lieutenant commander, CSN (1861); commanding CSS *Beaufort* (February 1862); executive officer, *Palmetto State* (winter 1862-63); captain, CSN (1863); and Superintendent, Confederate State Naval Academy (1863-65). He fought at Roanoke Island and in South Carolina waters before organizing the naval school. During the retreat from Richmond he escorted the national archives and the remaining treasures of the Confederacy. In the postwar years he was a mail steamer captain and served as a diplomat to Korea. He also wrote a number of technical works.

PARSONS, Mosby Monroe (1822-1865)

A lawyer, Mexican War veteran, and Missouri politician, Mosby M. Parsons survived some heavy fighting in the Civil War only to die a few months later in Mexico's internal conflict. The Virginia-born politician had offered his services to his adopted state and his assignments included: brigadier general, Missouri State Guard (spring 1861); commanding 6th Division, Missouri State Guard (spring 1861-April 9, 1862); commanding Missouri State Guard (April 9-summer 1862); commanding brigade, District of Arkansas, Trans-Mississippi Department (summer and fall 1862); brigadier general, CSA (November 5, 1865); commanding brigade, Hindman's-Price's Division, District of Arkansas, Trans-Mississippi Department (winter 1862-63-March 24, 1864); commanding the division (March 24, 1864-January 29, 1865 and February 1-15 and to May 26, 1865); and commanding the district (January 29-February 1 and briefly from February 15, 1865). While in the command of state troops he fought at Carthage and Wilson's Creek but missed the fighting at Pea Ridge. Moving to the east side of the Mississippi he arrived too late for the battle of Shiloh and three months later was ordered to take his men who had not joined Confederate service back to Arkansas. Commissioned into the Confederate army shortly thereafter, he held a series of commands in the Trans-Mississippi Department, seeing action at Helena and near Little Rock. Sent in early 1864 to western

Louisiana he helped repulse Banks' Red River Campaign before returning to Arkansas to face Steele's Union column. Later that year he took part in Price's invasion of Missouri. Following the department's surrender he went to Mexico. Accounts differ on his motives, some saying he intended to join one side or the other and others claiming he was trying to flee to Europe, and differ as to who was responsible for his death—near the village of China about August 15, 1865.

PATE, Henry Clay (1832-1864)

During the battle of Yellow Tavern, Henry C. Pate and Jeb Stuart ended their longstanding feud. Within a matter of hours both had suffered mortal wounds. Pate was a native Virginian who had moved to Missouri by way of Kentucky and Ohio. Living close to the Kansas border, he led a Missouri militia force against John Brown in 1856. By the outbreak of the Civil War he was back in Virginia editing the *Petersburg Bulletin*. Enlisting in the Confederate army, he received the following assignments: captain, Petersburg Rangers (June 5, 1861); lieutenant colonel, 2nd Virginia Cavalry Battalion (May 1862); lieutenant colonel, 5th Virginia Cavalry (June 24, 1862); and colonel, 5th Virginia Cavalry (September 28, 1863). After seeing service during the Seven Days, 2nd Bull Run, Antietam, and Fredericksburg, he was hauled before a court-martial in March 1863. It was from this hearing that Jeb Stuart and John Pelham set out for Kelly's Ford where Pelham was killed. Pate soon rejoined his regiment and took part in countering Stoneman's Raid during the Chancellorsville Campaign and at Gettysburg. Receiving a promotion to colonel, he led the regiment in the Bristoe and Mine Run campaigns and at the Wilderness. Then on May 11, 1864, at Yellow Tavern, Stuart directed that Pate make a desperate stand against the Union cavalry. He promised to hold them off. Stuart complimented his attitude and Pate offered his hand. With the two reconciled, Pate rode to his assignment which he accomplished at the cost of his life. Stuart was mortally wounded later in the fight. From his death bed he told a staff officer of the reconciliation and praised Pate's services, stopping now and then from the pain of his mortal wound. (Freeman, Douglas S., *Lee's Lieutenants*)

PATTERSON, Josiah (1837-1903)

Because he commanded an unofficial brigade, Colonel Josiah Patterson was not considered to be eligible for promotion. His Confederate assignments included: first lieutenant, 1st Alabama Cavalry (September 1861); captain, 1st Alabama Cavalry (1862); colonel, 5th Alabama Cavalry (December 1862); and commanding brigade, Roddey's Cavalry Division, Department of Alabama, Mississippi and East Louisiana (April-September 24, 1864). The Alabama lawyer adapted quickly to military life, distinguishing himself in the battle of Shiloh for which he was promoted to captain. Detached from his company, he saw action at Iuka and Corinth before being given command of a newly organized regiment which he led under General P.D. Roddey in Northern Alabama. A part of the buildup in northern Georgia, Roddey and Patterson participated in the victory at Chickamauga. Serving back in northern Alabama,

Patterson was given a brigade when Roddey divided his command. Joining Forrest in Mississippi, he fought at Tupelo. Again joining with Forrest, Roddey and Patterson were active in the campaign to stop Wilson's Raid through Alabama in the final months of the war. Although much of his command surrendered at Selma, Patterson was still at liberty with a sizable force in late April 1865 when he declared his opposition to the idea of a guerrilla war.

PATTON, George Smith (1833-1864)

Following graduation from the Virginia Military Institute in 1852, the grandfather of the famous World War II General George S. Patton III, George S. Patton became a lawyer and captain of a local militia company which entered Confederate service. Patton's assignments included: captain, Company H, 22nd Virginia (May 22, 1961); lieutenant colonel, 22nd Virginia (July 1861); colonel, 22nd Virginia (January 1863, to rank from November 23, 1861); and in 1863-64 frequently commanding a brigade, Department of Western Virginia, which sometimes served with the Army of Northern Virginia or in the Valley District. In his first engagement, at Scary Creek, Patton was wounded and captured but shortly exchanged. Serving mainly in western Virginia and the Shenandoah Valley, he saw further action in the Kanawha Valley in September 1862, on Imboden's June 1863 expedition, combating Averell's August 1863 raid, and during the Lewisburg Expedition in November 1863. Moving to the Shenandoah, he participated in the Confederate victory at New Market and then joined the Army of Northern Virginia at the battle of Cold Harbor where he commanded Echols' Brigade. Moving to Lynchburg, Patton then participated in General Early's invasion of Maryland in July 1864. After being driven back from the outskirts of Washington, Patton's brigade faced Sheridan's advance on Winchester and in the third battle at that place Colonel Patton was severely wounded in the leg. Refusing an amputation, he died a few days later from loss of blood.

PATTON, John Mercer, Jr. (1826-1898)

This ancestor of World War II's General Patton, John M. Patton, Jr., did not have a career as glorious as those of his two brothers or of his great nephew, but he did survive the Civil War. A graduate of the Virginia Military Institute and a Richmond lawyer, he entered the Confederate service where his assignments included: lieutenant colonel, 21st Virginia (ca. June 1861); and colonel, 21st Virginia (April 21, 1862). After leading the regiment at the battle of Kernstown, he was elected colonel of the regiment at the spring 1862 reorganization of the unit and led it through part of Stonewall Jackson's Shenandoah Valley Campaign. Having missed the Seven Days Battles due to ill health, he resigned on August 8, 1862. He was a leading postwar legal authority.

PATTON, Waller Tazewell (1835-1863)

Brother of George Smith Patton, Waller Patton graduated from the Virginia Military Institute and was serving as a Latin instructor at that school at the outbreak of the Civil War. A lawyer in his community, Patton became captain of a local militia company and took it to Harpers Ferry when the state seceded. His later commissions included: major, 7th Virginia (July 1, 1861); lieutenant colonel, 7th Virginia (April 27, 1862); and colonel, 7th Virginia (June 3, 1863). Patton saw action at 1st Bull Run, Williamsburg, Seven Pines, the Seven Days, and at 2nd Bull Run where he was severely wounded. Returning to his regiment in the spring of 1863, he commanded it in the Suffolk and Gettysburg campaigns. Exactly one month after being promoted to the three stars of a colonel, Patton took part in Pickett's famous charge at Gettysburg, as a part of General Kemper's brigade. He was struck down by Union artillery fire as he approached the stone wall in front of the Yankee lines. With his lower jaw nearly removed, Patton lingered until July 21, 1863, in extreme agony. His great-nephew was General George S. Patton, III, of World War II fame.

PAUL, Franc M. (ca. 1832-?)

When the advance of the Union forces upon his city forced *Chattanooga Daily Rebel* editor Franc M. Paul to move his paper to Georgia and later Alabama, it was dubbed "The Chattanooga Rebel-on-Wheels." The North Carolina native had been serving as the clerk of the Tennessee state senate when Federal forces occupied the capital. He then moved to Chattanooga where, on August 1, 1862, he published the first issue of his paper. It enjoyed a wide circulation in the Confederate Army of Tennessee and the vicinity. Unfortunately the editorial line of the paper was noted for its harsh criticism of that army's commander, Braxton Bragg. At least twice the paper was banned from his lines, and Paul was forced to demand the resignation of his editor, Henry Watterson, late in 1863. With the fall of the city Paul took his equipment to Marietta and later to Atlanta. But further Union advances forced its removal to Selma, Alabama, where the press and equipment were finally destroyed by Union forces in April 1865. From the rubble, Paul was able to publish a series of one-page flyers for a few days following his release after being captured while serving in the militia defending the town. (Andrews, J. Cutler, *The South Reports the Civil War*)

PAXTON, Elisha Franklin (1828-1863)

The promotion of E. Frank Paxton from a staff position and over the heads of the regimental commanders of the Stonewall Brigade prompted one of their number, A.J. Grigsby, to resign in disgust. A graduate of Yale, he had practiced law until 1859 when eye problems forced him to give it up. At the outbreak of the war he joined the Rockbridge Rifles. His assignments included: first lieutenant, Company B, 5th Virginia (April 1861); major, 27th Virginia (October 14, 1861); major and assistant adjutant general (spring 1862); brigadier general, CSA (November 1, 1862); and commanding Stonewall Brigade, Jackson's (old) Division, 2nd Corps, Army of Northern Virginia (November 6, 1862-May 3, 1863). He fought at 1st Bull Run and was promoted to major in October. Having served through the Romney Campaign, he failed to gain reelection in the May 1862 reorganization of the regiment. He then was

named to Jackson's staff and remained with him through the fall when he was promoted three grades to command his old brigade. He fought at Fredericksburg and was present at Chancellorsville when Jackson made his famous attack. However, the brigade did not take part, being assigned to guard a flank. The next day he led the brigade into action and soon fell dead. (Paxton, Dick, ed., *Civil War Letters of General Frank "Bull" Paxton*)

PAYNE, Lewis

See: *Powell, Lewis Thornton*

PEARCE, Nicholas Bartlett (ca. 1816-1894)

West Pointer (1850) and frontier veteran Nicholas Bartlett, a farmer and merchant at the outbreak of the war, was made a brigadier general in the Arkansas state forces and assigned to command the western part of the state. Assuming command at Fort Smith on May 20, Pearce organized his forces which he led into southwestern Missouri in the summer of 1861. Joining forces with Price's Missouri State Guard and McCulloch's Confederate troops, Pearce's Arkansans took part in the Southern victory at Wilson's Creek after being surprised at the start of the battle. At the beginning of September 1861, the troops under Pearce's command unanimously voted not to enter Confederate service, because they would be transferred to the command of General Hardee instead of remaining under General McCulloch, their victorious leader at Wilson's Creek. Pearce promptly marched them back to Arkansas and disbanded them, a move for which he was severely criticized and his potential general's appointment in the Confederate army was scuttled. Pearce was appointed a major in the commissary department of the rebel army and assigned as chief commissary for the Indian Territory and western Arkansas on December 20, 1861. He served in various locations in the Trans-Mississippi Department and at one point in 1862 was post commandant at Fort Smith. There were also accusations that he was too closely linked with speculators who were making large profits while he was chief commissary of the District of Texas, New Mexico and Arizona.

PEARSON, Richmond Mumford (1805-1878)

As chief justice of North Carolina's supreme judicial body, Richmond M. Pearson exemplified the difficulties faced in administering the national draft in a country founded on the basis of states' rights. A native of the state, he had begun the practice of law in 1826 and after several terms in the state legislature began his judicial career in 1836. A dozen years later he was named to the state supreme court and in 1858 became its presiding officer. An opponent of secession, his opinions releasing numerous individuals from military service greatly annoyed the Richmond authorities. He was destined to remain a thorn in their side through the end of the war. In the reorganization of the state under Reconstruction he was continued in office until his death. He became a Republican and supporter of Governor William W. Holden three years after the close of the war.

(Mitchell, Memory F., *Legal Aspects of Conscription and Exemption in North Carolina 1861-1865*)

PECK, William Raine (1818-1871)

Serving with the Louisiana troops in the Army of Northern Virginia, Louisiana planter William R. Peck rose to the rank of brigadier general in the final months of the war. The Tennessee-born soldier's assignments included: private, 9th Louisiana (July 7, 1861); lieutenant colonel, 9th Louisiana (ca. July 4, 1863); colonel, 9th Louisiana (October 8, 1863); commanding Consolidated Louisiana Brigade, Gordon's Division, 2nd Corps, Army of Northern Virginia (January-February 1865); and brigadier general, CSA (February 18, 1865). Rising through the grades from private to colonel of his regiment, he was present during most of the campaigns of the unit, which included the Shenandoah Valley Campaign of 1862, the Seven Days, 2nd Bull Run, Antietam, Fredericksburg, Chancellorsville, and Gettysburg. He commanded the regiment in the Bristoe and Mine Run operations. The regiment then served in opposing Grant's Overland Campaign until sent to the Shenandoah Valley to threaten Washington. During the fight at Monocacy he was in charge of half of the Consolidated Louisiana Brigade. He served later in the Shenandoah Valley under Jubal A. Early. Returning to the main army, he took command of the brigade in the Petersburg trenches and was promoted to brigadier general. He apparently went on leave before the final debacle at Appomattox and was paroled in Mississippi. Thereafter he resumed the now-altered life of a planter.

PEGRAM, John (1832-1865)

Marrying one of the belles of the Confederacy, General John Pegram's wedded life is symptomatic of the collapse of the South. Three weeks after his wedding, which was the social high point of the dismal last winter of the war in Richmond, the guests were back in the same church for his funeral. A Virginia-born West Pointer (1854), he had resigned as a first lieutenant of dragoons on May 10, 1861, to join the South. His assignments included: lieutenant colonel, PACS (early 1861); colonel, PACS (ca. April 1862); commanding cavalry brigade, Department of East Tennessee (ca. October 31, 1862-August 1863); brigadier general, CSA (November 7, 1862); commanding division, Forrest's Cavalry Corps, Army of Tennessee (August-September 1863); commanding Smith's (old) Brigade, Early's Division, 2nd Corps, Army of Northern Virginia (October 11, 1863-May 5, 1864); commanding brigade, Early's-Ramseur's Division, Valley District, Department of Northern Virginia (July-September 20, 1864); commanding the division (September 20-December 1864); and commanding division, 2nd Corps, Army of Northern Virginia (December 1864-February 6, 1865). Serving under General Garnett, he was captured at Rich Mountain early in the war. Upon his exchange he went west and was Beauregard's and Bragg's chief engineer and chief of staff to E.K. Smith before being given a cavalry brigade with which he was detached to serve at Murfreesboro. He later led the command in a raid into Kentucky and joined Forrest in command of the cavalry from

the Department of East Tennessee for Chickamauga. Transferred to Virginia for reasons of the heart, he led an infantry brigade at Mine Run and was wounded at the Wilderness. Returning to duty while the unit was in the Shenandoah, he fought at 3rd Winchester and the next day took over command of the division when General Ramseur transferred to the deceased Rodes' Division. Although never promoted to major general, Pegram led the division at Fisher's Hill, Cedar Creek, and in the Petersburg trenches until killed at Hatcher's Run shortly after his marriage to Hetty Cary. (Freeman, Douglas, S., *Lee's Lieutenants*)

PEGRAM, William Johnson (1841-1865)

After serving throughout the entire Civil War and rising from private to colonel, artillerist Willie Pegram was killed a few days before Lee's surrender. His Confederate assignments included: private, 21st Virginia (April 1861); lieutenant, Richmond "Purcell" Artillery (May 1861); captain, Richmond "Purcell" Artillery (April 1862); major, Artillery (from March 2, 1863); executive officer, Walker's Artillery Battalion, A.P. Hill's Division, 2nd Corps, Army of Northern Virginia (April 16-June 2, 1863); executive officer, Walker's Battalion, Reserve Artillery, 3rd Corps, Army of Northern Virginia (June 2-4, 1863); commanding battalion, Reserve Artillery, 3rd Corps, Army of Northern Virginia (June 4-July 1863); and commanding same battalion, 3rd Corps, Army of Northern Virginia (July 1863-April 1, 1865). After seeing some initial service along the Potomac, he commanded his battery at the Seven Days, Cedar Mountain, 2nd Bull Run, Harpers Ferry,

Confederate artillerist Willie Pegram. (NA)

Antietam, and Fredericksburg. At Antietam he suffered his first wound. Promoted to major, he served as second in command of A.P. Hill's artillery at Chancellorsville. When R. Lindsay Walker moved up to command of the new 3rd Corps' artillery, Pegram took over the battalion. He served through the remaining campaigns of the Army of Northern Virginia, rising rapidly to the rank of colonel despite the normally slow promotions common in the artillery. Less than two months after the death of his brother, General John Pegram, Willie Pegram was himself killed at the battle of Five Forks. His loss was mourned throughout the army, which itself had only about a week of life left. (Freeman, Douglas S., *Lee's Lieutenants* and Wise, Jennings, C., *The Long Arm of Lee*)

PEGUES, Christopher Claudius (1823-1862)

Lee's first action in command of the Army of Northern Virginia, the Seven Days Battles, cost the Confederacy many regimental commanders who, had they survived, might well have grown into solid brigade commanders. One of these was a native of South Carolina, Christopher C. Pegues. By the time of the secession crisis he was a lawyer in Alabama, and he entered the military two days before Fort Sumter was fired upon. His assignments included: captain, Company G, 5th Alabama (April 10, 1861); and colonel, 5th Alabama (April 27, 1862). After service at 1st Bull Run and on the Manassas and Yorktown lines, he was elected to command the regiment upon its reorganization in the spring of 1862. He then served through the actions at Williamsburg and Seven Pines. In his first action during the Seven Days, Gaines' Mill, he fell mortally wounded. He died on July 15.

PELHAM, John (1838-1863)

Although "The Gallant Pelham" served the entire war with the artillery, he was destined to fall while moonlighting in a cavalry charge. A native Alabamian, he withdrew from West Point upon the outbreak of hostilities and joined the Confederate army. His assignments included: lieutenant, Wise (Va.) Artillery (early 1861); captain, Stuart Horse Artillery (March 23, 1862); major, Artillery (August 9, 1862); lieutenant colonel, Artillery (April 4, 1863, to rank from March 2); and commanding Horse Artillery Battalion, Cavalry Division, Army of Northern Virginia (August 1862-March 17, 1863). After fighting at 1st Bull Run, he became the captain of the first horse artillery battery that served with Jeb Stuart, becoming close friends with the general. Commanding his unit, he saw action at Yorktown and during the Seven Days. Promoted, he commanded all of Stuart's horse batteries at 2nd Bull Run and Antietam. At Fredericksburg he held up the advance of a Union division against the Confederate right with only two guns. With only one gun left, he continued to shift positions despite the fact that 24 enemy guns were now concentrating their fire on him. Disobeying repeated orders to withdraw, he only did so upon running out of ammunition. General Lee observed and said, "It is glorious to see such courage in one so young!" Known as the "Boy Major," he heard of an impending action at Kelly's

Ford on March 17, 1863. Away from his battalion at the time, he joined the fray with the cavalry. He fell victim to a shell fragment while directing a column past a fence. Thought to be dead, he was thrown over a horse and led from the field. Quite a while later he was lowered to the ground and found to be still alive. He died shortly thereafter. Some believed that prompt attention might have saved his life. (Hassler, William Woods, *Colonel John Pelham, Lee's Boy Artillerist*)

PEMBER, Phoebe Yates (1823-1913)

While serving as the chief matron of Chimborazo Hospital's second division, Phoebe Yates Pember gathered the material for *A Southern Woman's Story*, the best first person account of Confederate hospitals. Born into a wealthy Jewish Charleston family, she was widowed during the early months of the war when her husband died of tuberculosis. Through her friendship with the wife of the Confederate Secretary of War George W. Randolph, she was offered the hospital post in late 1862. Her account relates the activities of the next two and a half years with a mixture of realism and humor. She recounts the sufferings and the spirit of the wounded, criticizes many of the surgeons, and bemoans the shortages of supplies. Her combativeness appears in her efforts to define her status, especially in dealing with the thorny question of the rationed whiskey for which she was held accountable. Her fall 1864 trip to visit her refugeed family in Georgia provides glimpses of the difficulties of travel. But it is the stories of individual patients which provide the most interesting reading. After the fall of Richmond she remained with her charges until the transition to Federal control was completed. She devoted the rest of her life to travel.

PEMBERTON, John Clifford (1814-1881)

In an unusual case of self-sacrifice for the Civil War officer corps, Northern-born John C. Pemberton resigned his lieutenant general's commission in order to serve as a private when it became obvious that his loss of Vicksburg made him unacceptable with the army and the South for high command. The Philadelphian West Pointer (1837) had served his entire old army tour with the artillery. He saw service in the Seminole War, Mexican War (winning two brevets) on the frontier, and on the Utah expedition against the Mormons. Having married a Virginian, he resigned as a captain in the 4th Artillery on April 29, 1861, and joined that state's forces. His Southern assignments included: lieutenant colonel, Virginia Volunteers (April 28, 1861); colonel, Virginia Volunteers (May 8, 1861); major, Artillery (June 15, 1861); brigadier general, CSA (June 17, 1861); commanding brigade, Department of Norfolk (summer-November 1861); commanding 4th Military District of South Carolina, Department of South Carolina, Georgia and Florida (December 10, 1861-March 4, 1862); major general, CSA (January 14, 1862); commanding the department (March 4-September 24, 1862); lieutenant general, CSA (October 13, 1862); commanding Department of Mississippi and East Louisiana (October 17, 1862-July 4, 1863); lieutenant colonel, Artillery (May 1864); and commanding Richmond Defenses, Department of Richmond (May 1864-February 1865). Following service at Norfolk he commanded along the Atlantic coast. Promoted to lieutenant general, he was sent to Mississippi with the assignment to guard Vicksburg and Port Hudson. When Grant crossed the river below Vicksburg, Pemberton sent portions of his command. After fighting at Port Gibson, Raymond, Jackson, Champion Hill, and Big Black River Bridge, Pemberton was forced back into the Vicksburg defenses and was compelled to undergo a siege. With his command starving, he determined to surrender on the Fourth of July in the hopes of gaining a more favorable agreement. This coupled with his Northern birth led to charges of treason in the press and among the public. Once declared exchanged, it became obvious that it would be difficult to find a place for Pemberton at his high rank. The possibility of a corps command with the Army of Tennessee evaporated when even Jefferson Davis realized that he would not be acceptable to the soldiers. Finally on May 18, 1864, he resigned and offered to serve as a private. However, Davis would not allow that and recommissioned him as a lieutenant colonel of artillery. For nine months he commanded the artillery defenses of the Confederate capital and then went on inspection duty. Having loyally served his adopted country, he lived on a Virginia farm after the war. (Pemberton, John C., III, *Pemberton: Defender of Vicksburg*)

PENDER, William Dorsey (1834-1863)

A career soldier, North Carolinian William Dorsey Pender gave his life to the Confederacy. A West Pointer (1854), he had served the intervening years, mostly on the West Coast, in the artillery and dragoons before resigning on March 21, 1861. His Southern assignments included: captain, Artillery (spring 1861); colonel, 3rd North Carolina Volunteers (May 16, 1861); colonel, 6th North Carolina (August 17, 1861); brigadier general, CSA (June 3, 1862); commanding brigade, A.P. Hill's Division, (in 1st Corps June 29 and in 2nd Corps from July 27), Army of Northern Virginia (June-December 13, 1862 and early 1863-May 3, 1863); commanding the division (May 3, 1863); major general, CSA (May 27, 1863); and commanding division, 3rd Corps, Army of Northern Virginia (May 30-July 2, 1863). Having distinguished himself at Seven Pines he was promoted to brigadier a few days later and assigned to Hill's Light Division. With that famous command he fought through the Seven Days, suffering a wound at Malvern Hill, and Cedar Mountain, 2nd Bull Run, Harpers Ferry, and Antietam. Wounded at Fredericksburg, he returned for Chancellorsville and was in command of the division when wounded. Promoted to major general, he was assigned to command a division of four of the six brigades from Hill's former command and attached to Hill's new 3rd Corps. The North Carolinian led this unit on the first day at Gettysburg and on the second was hit by a shell fragment. Following the amputation of his leg back in Virginia he died on July 18. (Freeman, Douglas S., *Lee's Lieutenants*)

PENDLETON, William Nelson (1809-1883)

An accomplished administrator, William N. Pendleton was less than effective as a battlefield tactician while serving as chief artillerist in Lee's army. The Virginian was a West Pointer

(1830) who had resigned, after three years in the artillery and as a faculty member at his alma mater, to become an educator and Episcopal minister. He reentered the military upon the secession of his state. His assignments included: captain, Rockbridge (Va.) Artillery (May 1, 1861); colonel, Artillery (July 13, 1861); chief of artillery, Army of the Shenandoah (July 1861); chief of artillery, Army of the Potomac (July-October 22, 1861); chief of artillery, Department (later Army) of Northern Virginia (October 22, 1861-April 9, 1865); and brigadier general, CSA (March 26, 1862). Not forgetting his religious training in his first battle, he shouted "May the Lord have mercy on their poor souls—Fire!" as his four guns, "Matthew," "Mark," "Luke," and "John" roared into action. As Johnston's artillery chief he fought at 1st Bull Run and served on the Peninsula. Under Lee, he failed to mass his guns before the assault at Malvern Hill. Another failure came at the end of the Maryland invasion when he reported, incorrectly, that the entire reserve artillery of the army has been captured; only four pieces had been lost. However, his administrative talents proved his value. He developed the system of artillery battalions assigned to the infantry divisions which allowed for a more rapid concentration of firepower. His skill was also apparent to Lee in the supplying, officering, and equipping of the long arm. Following the Chancellorsville reorganization, the last reserve battalions were assigned to the corps and he was confined to administrative work. In March 1864 President Davis dispatched Pendleton to Johnston's Army of Tennessee to report on its internal artillery organization and suggest improvements. His recommendations did the impossible in pleasing the everfeuding Davis and Johnston. Rejoining Lee he served for the remainder of the war as nominal chief artillerist. At one point Davis considered naming Pendleton to an infantry corps command in the West, but Lee refused to endorse the idea. After the war he returned to his preaching in Lexington and was closely linked with Lee during his years at Washington College. There was a striking facial resemblance between them. (Wise, Jennings C., *The Long Arm of Lee* and Freeman, Douglas S., *R.E. Lee*)

PERKINS, John, Jr. (1819-1885)

Confederate Congressman John Perkins, Jr., was planning beyond victory and the permanent establishment of the new nation when he called for the creation of a tariff specifically adverse to the United States after the war. The Mississippi native and former lawyer had been a marginal Louisiana cotton planter, a judge, and a U.S. congressman before the Civil War. He chaired the state's secession convention and then was named to the Provisional Congress. Remaining throughout the life of the Confederacy, he rose to be the chairman of the Committee on Rules and Officers; he had sat on that panel in the previous Confederate congress as well. Representing Louisiana's northeastern 6th District, his constituents were fully under Union control by the end of 1864. He also sat on the committees on: Commerce (Second Congress); Foreign Affairs; Military Affairs (Provisional Congress); Printing (Provisional Congress); and Ways and Means (First Congress). Although often linked with the Davis administration, he opposed the draft, blacks in the army, and many presidential appointees. Viewing a negotiated settlement to be possible, he based economic planning on that premise. After the war he went into exile in Mexico and Europe until 1878; a venture in the cultivation of coffee in Spain failed, and he then returned to Louisiana.

PERRIN, Abner Monroe (1827-1864)

Having served as a regular army first lieutenant in the Mexican War, Abner Perrin was made a captain in the 14th South Carolina in the summer of 1861. His later assignments in the Army of Northern Virginia, included: colonel, 14th South Carolina (February 20, 1863); commanding McGowan's Brigade, A.P. Hill's Division, Jackson's Corps (May 3, 1863); commanding same brigade, Pender's-Wilcox's Division, A.P.· Hill's Corps (May 30, 1863-early 1864); brigadier general, CSA (September 10, 1863); and commanding Wilcox's old Brigade, Anderson's Division, Hill's Corps (early 1864-May 12, 1864). After service on the South Carolina coast, including its first fight at Port Royal Ferry on New Year's Day 1862, the regiment was ordered to Virginia in the spring. Serving in Maxcy Gregg's Brigade of A.P. Hill's Division, Perrin participated with his regiment in the fighting in the Seven Days, Cedar Mountain, 2nd Bull Run, the capture of Harpers Ferry, Antietam, and Fredericksburg. Promoted to colonel he led the regiment in Jackson's famous flank attack on the Union 11th Corps at Chancellorsville until, following the wounding of McGowan and Colonel Edwards, he took over command of the brigade. Perrin directed the brigade during all three days at Gettysburg. Perrin's promotion to brigadier general over the more senior Colonel D.H. Hamilton caused that officer's resignation in disgust two months later. Perrin continued in temporary command of the brigade, during the Bristoe and Mine Run campaigns, until McGowan's return when Perrin was given command of Wilcox's Alabama Brigade which had been without a general since that officer had been given a division. Perrin led this brigade at the Wilderness and in the fighting at Spotsylvania Court House where he led a counterattack against the Union breakthrough at the Bloody Angle on May 12, when he was struck by seven bullets and fell dead. (Freeman, Douglas S., *Lee's Lieutenants*)

PERRY, Edward Aylesworth (1831-1889)

Born and raised in New England, Edward A. Perry taught school and practiced law in Alabama and Florida before the war in which he was to rise to brigade command. At the head of the Rifle Rangers he entered the Confederate service where his assignments included: captain, Company A, 2nd Florida (July 13, 1861); colonel, 2nd Florida (May 11, 1862); brigadier general, CSA (August 28, 1862); and commanding Florida Brigade, Anderson's-Mahone's Division, 1st (after May 30, 1863, 3rd) Corps, Army of Northern Virginia (November 10, 1862-May 1864). After fighting at Williamsburg he was elected colonel to replace Colonel Ward who had been killed. He led his men at Seven Pines and was severely wounded at Frayser's Farm during the Seven Days. Promoted during his absence, he commanded the Florida troops of Lee's army at

Fredericksburg and Chancellorsville. Felled by typhoid he was out of action for an undetermined period of time, including the Gettysburg Campaign. He was back on duty by the time of the Wilderness but was wounded there. Later that month his three regiments were merged into another brigade of Florida troops recently arrived. Upon his recovery, he was ordered, on September 28, 1864, to duty with the Alabama reserve forces. The war ended while he was performing these duties. A postwar lawyer, he was active in politics and served a term as governor of Florida. (Freeman, Douglas S., *Lee's Lieutenants*)

PERRY, Madison Stark (1814-1865)

As a South Carolina-born governor of Florida, Madison S. Perry steered his state into becoming the third state to secede from the Union. A plantation owner in Florida, he entered politics as a Democratic member of the lower state house in 1849 and the next year moved on to the upper house. In October 1856 he was elected governor but did not take his seat until the following October. A leading force in the secession crisis within the state, he recommended a state convention as early as November 27, 1860, and with legislative approval called for an election of delegates on December 22. By January 10, 1861, the secession ordinance had passed and he affixed his signature the next day. During the next few months he was busy in preparing the state for war. His term expired and he left office on October 7, 1861. He was commissioned colonel, 7th Florida (April 26, 1862), and served in East Tennessee. Ill health forced his resignation the next year and he returned to his plantation where he died the month before Lee's surrender. (David, William W., *The Civil War and Reconstruction in Florida*)

PERRY, William Flank (1823-1901)

By the time that William F. Perry received his well-deserved promotion to brigadier he had already been in command of the wounded General Law's Brigade for some eight months. Born in Georgia and self-educated he had been a non-practicing attorney active in public education in his adopted Alabama. Enlisting as a private in the 44th Alabama in early 1862, he rose rapidly in the Confederate army. His assignments included: major, 44th Alabama (May 1862); lieutenant colonel, 44th Alabama (September 1, 1862); colonel, 44th Alabama (September 17, 1862); commanding Law's Brigade, Hood's-Field's Division, Department of East Tennessee (December 19, 1863-April 1864); commanding Law's Brigade, Field's Division, 1st Corps, Army of Northern Virginia (June 3, 1864-April 9, 1865); and brigadier general, CSA (February 21, 1865). He served in the Seven Days and at 2nd Bull Run before receiving the colonelcy upon the death of the regimental commander at Antietam. After service with Longstreet around Suffolk, Virginia, he fought at Little Round Top at Gettysburg. Ordered west with Longstreet, he saw action in the victory at Chickamauga and around Knoxville. As a result of the Law-Jenkins feud, he was in brigade command that winter. He commanded the regiment at the Wilderness, Spotsylvania, and the North Anna. Upon the wounding of General Law at Cold Harbor, he again assumed charge of the brigade, a position he held until the surrender at Appomattox. It was not until the winter of the Petersburg and Richmond siege that he received the general's wreath. He was an Alabama planter and Kentucky educator after the war. (Freeman, Douglas S., *Lee's Lieutenants*)

PETER, Walter G. (?-1863)

Although he was hanged as a spy, Walter G. Peter was probably on some other kind of secret mission. A lieutenant in the Confederate army, he accompanied his cousin, William Orton Williams, on a mission behind enemy lines on June 8, 1863. Posing as Union inspectors they visisted Fort Granger where Peter was identified as one "Major George Dunlop." After showing their papers and borrowing some money, they were quickly on their way. Suspicions having arisen, they were brought back and their true identities were revealed. At 3:00 A.M. a court-martial was convened. Found guilty, they were executed the same morning. It now appears that Williams was on a mission to Europe and Peter was escorting him at least to Canada.

PETERS, William Elisha (1829-1906)

Virginia-born and Berlin-educated William E. Peters was arrested for refusing to make war on civilians. He had entered the Confederate army in the war's first year. His assignments included: lieutenant colonel, 45th Virginia (November 14, 1861); colonel, 45th Virginia (January 6, 1862); colonel, 2nd Virginia State Line (fall 1862); and colonel, 21st Virginia Cavalry (August 31, 1863). After service in western Virginia and East Tennessee, he failed to gain reelection at the Spring 1862 reorganization of the 45th. Given command of a mixed infantry and cavalry regiment of the Virginia State Line, he served in western Virginia and Kentucky. With his regiment transferred to Confederate service as a cavalry unit, he served in those areas and in the Knoxville Campaign. Later serving in the Shenandoah Valley he joined McCausland's raid on Chambersburg, Pennsylvania. When the general revealed his orders to burn the city in the event of non-payment of tribute, Peters refused to comply, threatening to break his sword in two or in effect resign in protest on the spot. He was immediately placed under arrest. Following the burning he was restored to duty. He later served in the Valley under General Early. After the war he was a university professor.

PETTIGREW, James Johnston (1828-1863)

Lacking combat experience, J. Johnston Pettigrew was loath to accept a brigadier generalship and actually sent the commission back to the Confederate War Department. The North Carolinian had taught at the Washington Naval Observatory and studied law in the United States and Germany. Practicing in Charleston, he was involved in the militia and became an officer. His military assignments included: colonel, 1st South Carolina Rifles (November 1860); private, Hampton (S.C.) Legion (1861); colonel, 12th North Carolina Volunteers (July 11, 1861); colonel, 22nd North Carolina (designation change

on November 14, 1861); brigadier general, CSA (February 26, 1862); commanding French's (old) Brigade, Aquia District, Department of Northern Virginia (March 12-mid April 1862); commanding brigade, Whiting's-G.W. Smith's Division, same department (April-May 31, 1862); commanding Martin's (old) Brigade, Department of North Carolina (September 1862-February and April 1-May, 1863); commanding brigade, Hill's Command, Department of Virginia and North Carolina (February-April 1, 1863); commanding brigade, Heth's Division, 3rd Corps, Army of Northern Virginia (May 30-July 1 and July-July 14, 1863); and commanding the division (July 1-mid July 1863). After commanding his rifles at Fort Sumter, he went to Virginia as a private but was appointed to the colonelcy of the North Carolina regiment before 1st Bull Run. He served that winter in the Fredericksburg area and the next spring moved to the Peninsula. After the Yorktown siege he was wounded and captured at Seven Pines. Exchanged in late August 1862, he commanded a brigade in southern Virginia and North Carolina until May 1863 when it was ordered to Lee's army. At Gettysburg he succeeded the wounded Heth in charge of the division and led it in Pickett's Charge two days later. During the retreat he was mortally wounded on July 14 at Falling Waters while commanding his brigade. Carried back to Virginia, he died three days later. (Freeman, Douglas S., *Lee's Lieutenants*)

PETTUS, Edmund Winston (1821-1907)

Serving throughout the Civil War in the western theater, Alabama-born lawyer and judge Edmund W. Pettus rose to brigade command and the rank of brigadier general in the Confederate service. His assignments included: major, 20th Alabama (September 16, 1861); lieutenant colonel, 20th Alabama (October 8, 1861); colonel, 20th Alabama (May 28, 1863); brigadier general, CSA (September 18, 1863); commanding brigade, Breckinridge's Division, Breckinridge's Corps, Army of Tennessee (November 3-12, 1863); commanding brigade, Stevenson's Division, Hardee's Corps, Army of Tennessee (November 12, 1863-February 20, 1864); and commanding brigade, Stevenson's Division, Hood's-Lee's Corps, Army of Tennessee (February 20, 1864-January 1865 and April 9-26, 1865). Stationed in East Tennessee during the early part of the war, he did take part in E. Kirby Smith's drive into Kentucky in the summer and fall of 1862. He was then transferred with Stevenson's division to the Vicksburg area in late 1862. He was briefly captured at Port Gibson, during the early stages of the Vicksburg Campaign proper but, escaping, rejoined his command. He fought at Champion Hill and rose to regimental command during the siege of the city. Paroled upon the surrender of Vicksburg, he was exchanged on September 12, 1863, and was promoted to brigadier general six days later. Commanding a brigade, he fought at Chattanooga and throughout the Atlanta Campaign. His command was not engaged at Franklin but did fight at Nashville. Wounded during the Carolinas Campaign, he was back in brigade command at the final surrender of Joseph E. Johnston's forces. Resuming his law practice, he also became active in Democratic politics and died during his second term in the U.S. Senate.

PETTUS, John Jones (1813-1867)

After previously serving as Mississippi's governor for five days, John J. Pettus was again in that position at the time of the state's secession, which he had been active in achieving. A native of Tennessee, he had settled in Mississippi and become active in Democratic politics. He served in both houses of the state legislature before succeeding Governor Henry S. Foote in 1854, since Pettus was then president of the state senate. The term expired in less than a week. He was elected in his own right in October 1859 and took up his duties the next month. After the secession of the state he was reelected to a second term. He was active in supporting the Confederacy and in preparing the defense of the state. However, he had to move the capital from Jackson to Meridian and finally to Macon. His second term expired on November 16, 1863, and after the war he moved to Arkansas. (Dubay, Robert W., *John Jones Pettus, Mississippi Fire-Eater: His Life and Times 1813-1867*)

PEYTON, Robert Ludwell Yates (1822-1863)

Virginia-born and Ohio-raised lawyer Robert L.Y. Peyton survived a number of battles only to die while representing the rival, secessionist government of Missouri in the Confederate Senate. At the outset of the war he was in the state senate and served as colonel, 3rd Cavalry, 8th Division, Missouri State Guard. Under Price he fought at Carthage, Wilson's Creek, Big Dry Wood, and Lexington. Named to the Confederate Senate for the First Regular Congress, he arrived early enough to be seated on January 22, 1862, in the Provisional Congress. He was not, however, assigned any committee duties. Once in the Senate he served on the committees on: Claims; Commerce; Engrossment and Enrollment; Indian Affairs; and Post Offices and Post Roads. He was a supporter of strong war measures but was protective of local interests on most matters. He died of malaria in Alabama on September 3, 1863, either while returning home or as a result of the Vicksburg siege.

PHELAN, James (1821-1873)

Mississippi's Confederate Senator James Phelan may well have written off his reelection chances when he proposed the government's impressment of all cotton—to build up the Confederacy's foreign credit—and the death penalty for violations. The Alabama native had been, successively, an editor, state printer, lawyer, and, in 1860, state senator. Named to the First Regular Confederate Congress in the fall of 1861, he only received a two-year term. He sat on the committees on: Engrossment and Enrollment; Indian Affairs; Judiciary; and Printing. He was critical of the system of military exemptions which favored the upper classes and the use of substitutes in the army. In an 1863 rematch he was defeated for a full six-year term by John W.C. Watson. After finishing the war as a judge advocate in the army he was a Memphis attorney.

PHIFER, Charles W. (?-?)

Appointed by General Earl Van Dorn, Charles W. Phifer served as a brigadier general for five months before he was rejected by President Davis. A native of Tennessee, he had entered the regular army from Mississippi in 1855 as a lieutenant of cavalry. He resigned his commission on April 1, 1861, to offer his services to the South. His assignments included: first lieutenant, Cavalry (April 1861); major, 6th (sometimes called 1st) Arkansas Cavalry Battalion (ca. June 1861); acting brigadier by Van Dorn (May 25, 1862); commanding 3rd Brigade, 3rd Division, Army of the West, Department #2 (June-summer 1862); and commanding brigade, Maury's Division, Price's Corps, Army of West Tennessee, Department #2 (summer-October 16, 1862). He was initially assigned to recruiting duty in New Orleans until he took command of a battalion of cavalry composed of companies from Louisiana and Arkansas. He led this unit in central Kentucky and northern Mississippi until it was merged into a new regiment on May 15, 1862. Shortly thereafter he was appointed a brigadier, extralegally, and assigned to command a brigade of dismounted cavalry in Price's Army of the West. He led the brigade at Corinth but a couple of weeks later, on October 16, 1862, was relieved of duty due to the fact that Jefferson Davis refused to appoint him officially. He later served, with the rank of major, on the staff of Colonel A.W. Reynolds as an assistant adjutant general and was captured at Vicksburg.

PHILLIPS, Eugenia Levy (1819-?)

The sister of Chimborazo Hospital matron Phoebe Yates Pember and wife of former Alabama congressman Philip Phillips, Eugenia Levy Phillips became a target of what many would term Ben Butler's tyranny in New Orleans. An open Rebel sympathizer in the occupied city, she was charged with laughing as the funeral procession of a Union officer passed her home. Allegedly, she was at a children's party in her residence and was not laughing at the events outside. Giving this explanation, she refused to apologize and Butler banished her to Ship Island, which at that time was a yellow fever station in the Gulf of Mexico, as "a vulgar woman of the town." Told that she would only be allowed to communicate with Butler and her own maid she retorted, "It has one advantage over the city, sir; you will not be there." She further stated that "It is fortunate that neither the fever nor General Butler is contagious." The incident received international attention.

PHILLIPS, Pleasant J. (ca. 1824-1876)

A longtime militia officer, Georgian Pleasant J. Phillips spent very little time in the Confederate army, and most of his combat action was while serving with the state forces. His assignments included: colonel, 31st Georgia (November 19, 1861); brigadier general, Georgia Militia; and commanding 2nd Brigade, 1st Division, Georgia Militia serving with the Army of Tennessee and in the Department of South Carolina, Georgia and Florida. With his first command he went to Virginia but resigned on May 13, 1862, even before Robert E. Lee took over command of what was to be the Army of Northern Virginia. Returning to the militia, he commanded a brigade in the Atlanta Campaign and remained behind when Hood headed his army to Tennessee and disaster. In Georgia he commanded the forces in the wasteful battle of Griswoldville while opposing Sherman's march through the state. He served in later operations against Sherman while the latter was still in Georgia.

PHILLIPS, William (1824-1908)

A Georgia attorney, William Phillips became the organizer and first commander of one of the handful of Confederate "legions," a mixed force of infantry, cavalry, and sometimes artillery, to serve throughout the war. Having attended the University of Georgia, the North Carolina-born lawyer was a respected member of the Marietta community. Thus, although he had no military training, it is no surprise that his friend, Governor Joseph Brown, placed him in charge of the recruiting and training of the area's volunteer forces. On August 2, 1861, he was appointed colonel of a portion of the recruits which became known as Phillips' Georgia Legion. Moving to western Virginia, the command took part in the campaigning in the Kanawha Valley, where Phillips was wounded and lost an eye. In December 1861, the legion was transferred to the Department of South Carolina, Georgia and Florida where it was assigned to duty protecting the rail lines near Hardeeville, South Carolina. Ordered to reinforce the Army of Northern Virginia in late 1862, the infantry and cavalry battalions (the artillery having previously been detached) were separated and assigned to different brigades. While the cavalry served on the right, the infantry battalion fought on Marye's Heights at Fredericksburg. On February 13, 1863, Phillips was forced to resign due to "paralysis." However, later in the war he served as major of a local unit, the 9th Georgia Cavalry Battalion, State Guard. He subsequently resumed his Marietta law practice.

PICKENS, Francis Wilkinson (1805-1869)

At the beginning of the war the governor of the first seceding state, South Carolina, was Francis Pickens. Although admitted to the bar, he had never practiced law and, having inherited great wealth, he spent his time on his plantation or in politics. After a term in the state legislature, he was elected to Congress in 1834. A Democrat, he supported Calhoun's nullification policies during his tenure in Washington. In 1844 he left Washington to become a state senator. A secessionist at heart, he did support efforts to settle the sectional dispute. He attended the 1850 Nashville convention. He was appointed minister to Russia in 1858 and returned to become governor in December 1860 just as the secession crisis was coming to a head. It was under Pickens' direction that the preliminary efforts were made to force the capitulation of the Fort Sumter garrison before Confederate authorities took over. Early in the war he was responsible for organizing the state forces; he preferred enlistments "for the war" rather than for 12 months. Privately, he was critical of Southern generals for their lack of dash. With no military experience he was a behind-the-lines commander. In 1862 he retired to his plantation and after the war he favored compliance with federal reconstruction policies. (Cauthen, Charles Edward, *South Carolina Goes to War, 1861-1865*)

PICKETT, George Edward (1825-1875)

The "leader" of the famous doomed charge at Gettysburg, George E. Pickett, never forgave Lee ("that old man . . . had my division massacred") for it. Graduating at the bottom of the 1846 West Point class, he earned two brevets for fighting Indians and Mexicans. He resigned an infantry captaincy on June 25, 1861, to join the Confederacy where his assignments included: major, Artillery, and colonel, PACS (summer 1861); commanding on lower Rappahannock, in the Department of Fredericksburg (September 23-October 22, 1861) and in the Aquia District, Department of Northern Virginia (October 22, 1861-February 28, 1862); brigadier general, CSA (February 13, to rank from January 14, 1862); commanding Cocke's (old) Brigade, Longstreet's Division, same department (February 28-June 27, 1862); commanding division, 1st Corps, Army of Northern Virginia (late September 1862-February 25, 1863, May-September 23, 1863, and May 1864-April 8, 1865); major general, CSA (October 10, 1862); commanding division, Department of Virginia and North Carolina (February 25-April 1, 1863); commanding division, Department of Southern Virginia (April 1-May 1863): and commanding department of North Carolina (September 26, 1863-May 19, 1864). After serving on the Rappahannock, he joined the main army for actions at Williamsburg, Seven Pines, and Gaines' Mill. Wounded at the latter he returned to a division and a major generalcy after Antietam. Only lightly engaged at Fredericksburg, he next served in Longstreet's campaign in southeastern Virginia. At Gettysburg he became linked with

South Carolina Governor Francis W. Pickens. (*Harper's*)

the futile charge on the third day despite commanding only a third of the troops. When Longstreet went west, Pickett was sent to North Carolina where he directed operations against New Bern. He distinguished himself in the defense of Drewry's Bluff and then rejoined Lee for Cold Harbor. During the siege of Petersburg and Richmond his men were often used as a mobile reserve, seeing action throughout the lines. As such they were defeated by Sheridan at Five Forks, necessitating the evacuation. Pickett was relieved by Lee the day before the surrender and ordered home to await orders, his division having been all but destroyed at Five Forks and at Sayler's Creek. However, he surrendered with the army the next day. A postwar meeting with the dying Lee was an icy affair as reported by witness John S. Mosby to whom Pickett made the massacre comment. (Pickett, LaSalle Corbell, *Pickett and His Men* and Freeman, Douglas S., *Lee's Lieutenants*)

PICKETT, John T. (ca. 1820s-1890s)

The most important Civil War role played by Confederate diplomat John T. Pickett was his postwar sale to the U.S. government of the largest batch of Confederate diplomatic papers. A native of Kentucky, he had been educated there and briefly at West Point before studying law. A filibusterer and adventurer, he took part in the Cuban operations of Lopez and served in the Hungarian army. A diplomat at the outbreak of the Civil War, he resigned to join the Confederacy and served two stints as a diplomat in Mexico. In between he served as a staff officer to John C. Breckinridge. Returning to Washington at the close of the war, he netted $75,000 from the sale of the "Pickett Papers."

PIERCE, Franklin (1804-1869)

One of the five living ex-presidents in 1861 Franklin Pierce actually believed that he would be arrested for his opposition to the prosecution of the war. The New Hampshire native had succeeded to the presidency upon the death of Zachary Taylor in 1850 and during the next three years was noted for his Southern leanings. Calling the war "suicidal madness," he was known for his antiwar stance from the very beginning. In December 1861 he actually received a communication from the State Department inquiring whether he was "a member of a secret league, the object of which is to overthrow the Government." In a Fourth of July speech in 1863 he was harshly critical of the Republicans and the war and expressed his fear that he would be a victim "of unconstitutional, arbitrary, irresponsible power." At about the same time a letter of his to Jefferson Davis written in 1860 came to light. Being a very friendly letter it lost for Pierce much of his dwindling respect in the North. He survived the war by four years. (Nichols, Roy F., *Franklin Pierce: Young Hickory of the Granite Hills*)

PIERSON, Scipio Francis (?-?)

Artillery battalion commander S.F. Pierson seems to be one of those early officers in the Army of Northern Virginia who did not survive the shakedown period. His Confederate assignments included: lieutenant, Orleans (La.) Artillery (April 9, 1861); major, Artillery (March 27, 1862); chief of artillery, D.H. Hill's Division, Army of Northern Virginia (March-July 1862); commanding Artillery Battalion, D.H. Hill's Division, 1st Corps, Army of Northern Virginia (July-September 1862); and commanding Artillery Battalion, D.H. Hill's Division, 2nd Corps, Army of Northern Virginia (September-fall 1862). After serving with his battery, as heavy artillery, on the Peninsula in Virginia, he was promoted to battalion level and fought at Seven Pines, the Seven Days, and Antietam. Relieved from duty with the army he was sent to Europe in 1863 to purchase ordnance. Returning in the middle of 1864 he was assigned to duty with the Virginia Reserves on July 21 but four days later was ordered to report to General E. Kirby Smith in Texas. He served out the war in the Trans-Mississippi Department.

PIKE, Albert (1809-1891)

A prominent Arkansas lawyer, Albert Pike had earned a position of trust in representing the Creeks, one of the Five Civilized Tribes, in a victorious lawsuit before the war. A native Bostonian, he was opposed to secession but went along with the South because of his friends and extensive property and became the Confederate commissioner to the Indians. Using large cash subsidies and gifts he eventually brought over to the Con-

Albert Pike, commander of Confederate Indians. (NA)

federate side portions of the Creeks, Chickasaws, Choctaws, Cherokees, and Seminoles. A former captain of Arkansas volunteers in the Mexican War, he was appointed brigadier general, CSA, on August 15, 1861, and on November 22, 1861, he was given command of the newly created Department of Indian Territory. He led a brigade of Indians at Pea Ridge the following winter where they proved of dubious value. He came into conflict with his superiors and charged that the Indians had been promised that they would only be used in their home territory. On July 12, 1862, he submitted his resignation which was accepted on November 5. He returned home and resumed his activities as a teacher, journalist, writer, poet, and Freemason. After the war he was indicted but never tried. Living in Memphis and Washington after the war he became something of a legal scholar. (Duncan, Robert Lipscomb, *Reluctant General, The Life and Times of Albert Pike*)

PILLOW, Gideon Johnson (1806-1878)

One of the most reprehensible men ever to wear the three stars and wreath of a Confederate general was certainly Gideon J. Pillow. The Tennessee native lawyer had been appointed a brigadier general of volunteers by his former law partner, President James K. Polk, during the Mexican War. His performance south of the border was less than outstanding, but he had friends in high places. He was twice wounded in that war and was rewarded with promotion to major general. Mustered out at the conclusion of the peace treaty, he resumed his legal career and engaged in national politics as a conservative on secession. However, when push came to shove, he followed his state out of the Union. His Tennessee and Confederate assignments included: major general, Provisional Army of Tennessee (May 9, 1861); brigadier general, CSA (July 9, 1861); commanding 1st Geographical Division, Department #2 (September 7-late September 1861); commanding 1st Division, 1st Geographical Division, Department #2 (October 24, 1861-February 1862); commanding Fort Donelson, Army of Central Kentucky, Department #2 (ca. February 9-13 and 15, 1862); commanding 2nd Brigade, 1st (Breckinridge's) Division, Hardee's Corps, Army of Tennessee (January 2, 1863); and commissary general of prisoners (February 14-April 1865). Named the senior major general in the Tennessee forces, he took a leading role in their organization and was then named a brigadier general in the Confederate service. Serving at Columbus, Kentucky, he fought across the Mississippi at Belmont and several months later took command at Fort Donelson on the Cumberland River. While the post was being invested he was superseded by John B. Floyd. Following an unsuccessful breakout attempt Floyd turned over command again to Pillow who followed his chief's lead and also fled the post, leaving the surrender to Simon B. Buckner. He was then relieved of field duty and was eventually assigned to conscript duty in his native state. He was very briefly in the field again when he was given charge of a brigade during the battle of Murfreesboro on January 2, 1863. When Breckinridge's division made its futile assault on the Union left it was reported that Pillow hid behind a tree rather than lead his men foward into the holocaust. In any event he never again held field command.

After performing conscript duties for almost two years he was placed in charge of the Union prisoners in the final months of the war. Bankrupted by the war, he managed to scrape together a living by returning to his law practice.

POAGUE, William Thomas (1835-1914)

One of the most effective of the Army of Northern Virginia's battalion level artillery commanders, William Thomas Poague saw heavy fighting in all the campaigns of that army. A native of Virginia, he was practicing law in Missouri when the secession crisis came to a head. He returned to the state of his birth in order to be of service to it. As soon as the state seceded, he entered the military where his assignments included: second lieutenant, Rockbridge (Va.) Artillery (April 1861); first lieutenant, Rockbridge (Va.) Artillery (1861); captain, Rockbridge (Va.) Artillery (April 22, 1862); major, Artillery (March 2, 1863); executive officer, McIntosh's Artillery Battalion, Reserve Artillery, 2nd Corps, Army of Northern Virginia (April 16-June 2, 1863); commanding Artillery Battalion, Pender's Division, 3rd Corps, Army of Northern Virginia (June 2-July 1863); commanding artillery battalion, 3rd Corps, Army of Northern Virginia (July 1863-April 9, 1865); and lieutenant colonel, Artillery (February 27, 1864). As a battery officer he fought at 1st Bull Run, Romney, Kernstown, McDowell, in the Shenandoah Valley Campaign of 1862, the Seven Days, Cedar Mountain, 2nd Bull Run, Harpers Ferry, Antietam, and Fredericksburg. Then came the well-deserved promotion to field grade. He served as deputy to McIntosh at Chancellorsville, but with the creation of a third corps, he was assigned to command a new battalion before Gettysburg. After that battle he went on to fight at Mine Run, the Wilderness, Spotsylvania, the North Anna, and Cold Harbor. In the latter he was twice wounded. He took part in the defense of Petersburg and finally surrendered at Appomattox. After the war he was a farmer, teacher, state legislator, and treasurer of the Virginia Military Institute. (Poague, William T., *Gunner With Stonewall, Reminiscences of William T. Poague*)

POLIGNAC, Camille Armand Jules Marie, Prince de (1832-1913)

The only person still owing allegiance to a foreign power to rise to the rank of major general in the service of either the Union or the Confederacy was French Prince de Polignac who served the South. He was a veteran of six years with the French army in the 3rd Chasseurs, 4th Hussars, and 4th Chasseurs before resigning as a lieutenant in 1859. Sailing for America in 1861 he secured a commission through his acquaintance with Pierre G.T. Beauregard. His assignments included: lieutenant colonel, Infantry (July 16, 1861); brigadier general, CSA (January 10, 1863); commanding brigade, District of West Louisiana, Trans-Mississippi Department (summer-November 1863); commanding brigade, 2nd (Mouton's) Division, District of West Louisiana, Trans-Mississippi Department (November 1863-April 8, 1864); commanding the division (April 8, 1864-February 1865); and major general, CSA (June 13, 1864, to rank from April 8). Assigned to inspection duty with Beauregard, he found himself chafing for action and advancement. After taking part in the Corinth siege, he fought at Richmond, Kentucky, before being named a brigadier general early in 1863. Transferred to western Louisiana, he was given a brigade which he led into the Red River Campaign. At Mansfield or Sabine Crossroads on April 8, 1864, the division commander, Jean J.A.A. Mouton, was killed and Prince de Polignac took over the unit with a subsequent promotion to major general. He served through the rest of the campaign and in March 1865 he sailed to France, through the blockade, on a diplomatic mission which proved to be too late. Remaining in Europe, he became a mathematician and economist.

POLK, Leonidas (1806-1864)

Soldier-turned-bishop Leonidas Polk finally complied with the request of his friend Jefferson Davis, reentered the military as a Confederate general, and gave his life to the cause. The North Carolina native and West Pointer (1827) had served only a few months in the artillery before his resignation as a brevet second lieutenant was accepted. Becoming an Episcopal minister, he rose to become Missionary Bishop of the Southwest in 1838 and Bishop of Louisiana three years later. Finally agreeing to join the Confederate army, his assignments included: major general, CSA (June 25, 1861); commanding Department #2 (July 13-September 15, 1861 and October 24-November 3, 1862); commanding 1st Geographical Division, Department #2 (September 15, 1861-March 5, 1862) commanding 1st Grand Division, Army of the Mississippi (March 5-29, 1862); commanding 1st Corps, Army of the Mississippi (March 29-July 2, 1862); second in command, Department #2 (July 2-October 24, 1862); also commanding Right Wing, Army of the Mississippi (August 15-September 28, 1862); commanding Army of the Mississippi (September 28-November 20, 1862); lieutenant general, CSA (October 10, 1862); commanding corps, Army of Tennessee (November 20, 1862-October 23, 1863); commanding the army (August and December 23-27, 1863); commanding Department of Mississippi and East Louisiana (December 23, 1863-January 28, 1864); commanding Department of Alabama, Mississippi and East Louisiana (January 28-May 4, 1864); and commanding corps (or "Army of Mississippi"), Army of Tennessee (May 4-June 14, 1864). Davis assigned Polk the duty of fortifying the Mississippi Valley, and the general occupied Columbus, Kentucky, ending that state's neutrality. From that post he ferried troops across the river to repulse Grant at Belmont. He commanded a corps under Albert Sidney Johnston at Shiloh and under Beauregard in the defense of Corinth. At Perryville he was in charge of the Army of the Mississippi while Braxton Bragg headed the department. He fought at Murfreesboro and during the Tullahoma Campaign. At Chickamauga he came in for much criticism from Bragg for his slow performance on the second day while in command of the army's right. In fact there had long been trouble between the two officers, Polk having urged Davis to remove Bragg. Bragg retaliated by relieving his subordinate and ordering a court-martial. Davis reversed this move and then sent Polk to Mississippi. At the beginning of the Atlanta Campaign Polk led

a corps, styled an "army" to join Joseph E. Johnston in northern Georgia. While consulting with Johnston and William J. Hardee at Pine Mountain he was struck by an artillery round and instantly killed on June 14, 1864. He was not considered to be one of the shining lights of the Confederacy's high command. (Parks, Joseph H., *General Leonidas Polk, C.S.A.*)

POLK, Lucius Eugene (1833-1892)

The nephew of the "Bishop General"—Leonidas Polk—Lucius E. Polk also received the three stars and wreath of a Confederate general but later proved to be an opponent of the Ku Klux Klan. The North Carolina-born and Tennessee-raised officer had been a planter in Arkansas in 1861. Joining Patrick R. Cleburne's Yell Rifles, his assignments included: private, Company F, 1st Arkansas State Troops (1861); second lieutenant, Company B, 1st Arkansas (July 23, 1861); second lieutenant, Company C, 15th Arkansas (designation change December 31, 1861); colonel, 15th Arkansas (April 12, 1862); brigadier general, CSA (December 13, 1862); commanding Cleburne's (old) brigade, Cleburne's Division, Hardee's-Hill's-Breckinridge's Corps, Army of Tennessee (December 1862-November 1863); and commanding brigade, Cleburne's Division, Hardee's Corps, Army of Tennessee (November 1863-June 27, 1864). Serving mostly under Cleburne, he was in central Kentucky and was wounded in the face at Shiloh. Named colonel a week later, he was again wounded at Richmond, Kentucky, but went on to fight at Perryville. Promoted to brigadier general, he led his brigade at Murfreesboro, during the Tullahoma Campaign, at Chickamauga, and Chattanooga. During the Atlanta Campaign he was severely wounded at Kennesaw Mountain on June 27, 1864, so that he was unable to again take the field. His brigade was accordingly broken up the next month. Active in Democratic politics, he sat in the state legislature. When one of his black employees was being whipped by the K.K.K., Polk, in an act of bravery uncommon at that place and time, faced them down.

POLLARD, Edward Alfred (1831-1872)

Law school graduate and journalist Edward Pollard became editor of the *Richmond Examiner* in 1861 just as the war was beginning. During his tenure with the newspaper in the Confederate capital he was one of the harshest journalist critics of Jefferson Davis. His commentary on the progress of the war gave the *Examiner* a shrill voice that made it one of the more interesting papers in the city. In installments from 1862 to 1866, Pollard wrote his *Southern History of the War*. In 1866 he published *The Lost Cause*. The thrust of both books was to point out the failures of the Confederate president which led to the collapse of the fledgling nation. He also lamented the fact that the Confederate Congress did not measure up to the standards needed for a revolutionary cause. Although Pollard left the *Examiner* in 1867, he continued in the journalism profession until his death in 1872, and is more remembered for his anti-Davis rhetoric than as a journalist-historian.

POND, Preston, Jr. (?-?)

A brigade commander at Shiloh, Preston Pond, Jr., appears to have had a great deal of difficulty in serving the Confederacy. On September 29, 1861, he was mustered in as colonel of the 16th Louisiana. Joining in the Confederate buildup of forces in northern Mississippi in early 1862, he commanded the 3rd Brigade, Ruggles' 1st Division, 2nd Grand Division or Corps, Army of the Mississippi (March 9-May 8, 1862). Leading this brigade at Shiloh, he did not receive the order at the end of the first day to retire slightly. The next morning he found his command in an untenable position. After extricating the brigade he received too many orders and his brigade kept going from one area to another in the confusion. When the regiment was reorganized the next month he was not reelected to the colonelcy. Retiring to his home near Clinton, Louisiana, he sent letters of advice to the War Department. In August 1862 he appears to have commanded an irregular unit known as the 1st Louisiana Partisan Rangers during the fighting at Baton Rouge. As late as mid-1864 he still wished to take the field again but in a letter to the governor he stated that President Davis would consider it to be undue favoritism. There is no record of his receiving another command.

PORCHER, Francis Peyre (1825-1895)

A Confederate surgeon, Francis P. Porcher wrote one of the leading medical manuals prepared by the Confederate government. A native of South Carolina, he had recieved his medical training in South Carolina and France. Until the Civil War he was in private practice and medical education. Early in the Civil War he became the surgeon for the state's Holcombe Legion and served at Norfolk and Petersburg. In 1863 his *Resources of the Southern Fields and Forests* was published by the Surgeon General's Department. He then returned to the classroom and edited the *Charleston Medical Journal and Review*.

PORTER, George Camp (?-1919)

Upon the secession of Tennessee, George C. Porter raised the "Haywood Blues," and entered the service of the state. His later assignments included: captain, Company A, 6th Tennessee (May 1861); major, 6th Tennessee (May 23, 1861); colonel, 6th Tennessee (May 6, 1862); and commanding Maney's Brigade, Cheatham's Division, 1st Corps, Army of Tennessee (early 1864-May 1864 and July 22-fall 1864). He was at Columbus, Kentucky, while the battle of Belmont took place across the Mississippi. After fighting at Shiloh, he was elected colonel upon the reorganization of the regiment. He led the regiment at Perryville in the Kentucky Campaign, after which the regiment was consolidated with the 9th Tennessee. Porter assumed command after Murfreesboro and led the consolidated unit at Chickamauga and Chattanooga. At times during the Atlanta Campaign he was in command of the brigade. He left the regiment after Franklin and appears to have never returned.

PORTERFIELD, George Alexander (1822-1919)

A graduate of the Virginia Military Institute and a veteran of the Mexican War, George A. Porterfield was appointed colonel of Virginia Volunteers and assigned to staff duty at Harpers Ferry on April 24, 1861. Sent to western Virginia in early May to raise troops there, he destroyed two bridges on the Baltimore and Ohio Railroad before retiring to Philippi. In one of the Confederacy's first military defeats, Porterfield and his 800 men were surprised and routed by a part of McClellan's command on June 3. The victory was celebrated in the North as "The Philippi Races," and in disgrace Porterfield was superseded by Brigadier General Robert S. Garnett. A subsequent Court of Inquiry praised his actions during the fighting itself but censured him for a "want of forethought and vigilance." He was relegated to staff positions until May 1862, when he was not reelected colonel of the 25th Virginia under the Reorganization Act. The next month he was captured and paroled by the Federals, ending his military career. He was a successful Charlestown banker after the war.

POSEY, Carnot (1813-1863)

Mississippi lawyer and planter Carnot Posey was promoted to brigadier to succeed an ill officer only to find himself without a command when that general resumed his post even before Posey reported. Posey had been wounded at Buena Vista during the Mexican War while serving as a first lieutenant in Jefferson Davis' 1st Mississippi Rifles. He entered the Southern army at the head of the Wilkinson Rifles and his later assignments included: captain, Company K, 16th Mississippi (spring 1861); colonel, 16th Mississippi (June 1861); commanding Featherston's Brigade, Wilcox's Division, 1st Corps, Army of Northern Virginia (August 30 and September-November 1862); brigadier general, CSA (November 1, 1862); and commanding Featherston's (old) Brigade, Anderson's Division, 1st (3rd after May 30) Corps, same army (January 19-October 14, 1863). His regiment was not at 1st Bull Run and Ball's Bluff, as commonly indicated, but he did see action under Ewell in Jackson's Valley Campaign where he was wounded. After being engaged in the Seven Days, he directed the brigade during part of 2nd Bull Run and at Antietam. Promoted to brigadier, he was displaced by Featherston's return and was without a brigade until that officer, at his own request but probably with some hints, transferred to Mississippi. Posey then led the brigade at Chancellorsville and Gettysburg. In covering the assault at Bristoe Station on October 14, 1863, he was struck by an artillery projectile. The wound was not assumed to be mortal but he died on November 13, from infection. (Freeman, Douglas S., *Lee's Lieutenants*)

POWEL, Samuel (1821-1902)

In the summer of 1861, Samuel Powel raised a company for the Confederate army. In his brief career, he held the following assignments: captain, Company A, 29th Tennessee (summer 1861); colonel, 29th Tennessee (September 30, 1861); commanding 3rd Brigade, Anderson's Division, Left Wing, Army of the Mississippi (fall-November 20, 1862); and commanding 3rd Brigade, Anderson's Division, Hardee's Corps, Army of Tennessee (November 1862). In his first battle, Mill Springs, Powel suffered a severe wound. During the battle of Shiloh, the regiment was stationed at Iuka, Mississippi. Powel and his command then joined the Army of the Mississippi and by the fall of 1862 he was in command of the brigade, replacing General Marmaduke. He led the brigade at Perryville where it suffered heavily. Powel resigned near the end of November 1862.

POWELL, Lewis Thornton (1844-1865)

When John Wilkes Booth was making his attack on Lincoln at Ford's Theater, Lewis T. Powell was making the only other attack—on Secretary of State William H. Seward. Known to his fellow conspirators as Lewis Paine, or Payne, he was a large-framed Floridian who had been captured at Gettysburg, made good his escape, and served for a time with John S. Mosby. As a Confederate courier, he was known as Wood, and was so introduced to his fellow plotters in the beginning. Because of his size it was assumed that he would be able to overpower Lincoln in the original kidnapping scheme. When the plan was changed to assassination his assigned target was Seward. The secretary was bedridden from a carriage accident. Powell smashed the skull of Frederick Seward with his pistol butt and forced his way into the bedroom where, after wounding others, he set upon the cabinet official. Stabbed several times around the face and neck, Seward was at first thought to be dead but his neck brace had saved him. Powell fled from the scene but lost his way and was not able to join in the general flight. He was arrested on April 17, 1865, when he arrived at the Surratt boardinghouse. During the trial he professed the innocence of Mary Surratt. Found guilty on June 30, 1865, he was hanged on July 7. His bravery impressed Christian Rath, the hangman.

Lewis Powell, Seward's would-be assassin. (NA)

POWER, John Logan (1834-1901)

As the editor of the *Jackson* (Miss.) *Daily News*, John L. Power was an active supporter of the Confederacy. A native of Ireland, he had been raised in poverty in the United States and became a printer on a number of New Orleans newspapers. Moving to Jackson, Mississippi, he became co-owner of the *Mississippian* in 1855. A year before the state's secession he commenced the publication of the *News*. He was the official reporter of the proceedings at the state secession convention. Active in support of the war effort, he was rewarded in 1864 with the clerkship of the lower house of the state legislature. At the same time he was made superintendent of the state's military records. After Appomattox he ran the *Mississippi Standard* and served as state printer and secretary of state.

PRENTICE, George D. (?-?)

A prominent Kentucky Unionist, George D. Prentice turned his newspaper into a "noosepaper" for guerrilla Marcellus J. Clarke in a political feud with the Union commander in the Louisville area, Stephen G. Burbridge. Angered by Burbridge's political activities in behalf of the Republican Party, Prentice decided to launch a campaign against the general in his *Louisville Courier* over his inability to effectively deal with the guerrilla warfare that was being waged throughout the state in the later part of the Civil War. He picked a minor guerrilla leader who was small enough to be confused for a woman and developed a major military problem for Burbridge. He renamed the bandit Sue Mundy after a disreputable black woman of the city and charged that Burbridge could not deal with him or her. He quipped that his paper would be a "noosepaper" for the young Confederate and it turned out to be so when Clarke-Mundy was captured and hanged by Burbridge's successor John M. Palmer in March 1865.

PRESTON, John Smith (1809-1881)

A leading secessionist in his adopted South Carolina, John S. Preston became a Confederate general but saw only limited action. The Virginia native had practiced law there and in South Carolina. He also was a Louisiana planter for a time. He attended the Charleston convention of 1860 and with South Carolina already out of the Union was sent the next year to Virginia to urge his native state to follow suit. Joining the military his assignments included: lieutenant colonel and assistant adjutant general (August 31, 1861); commanding prisoner of war camp, Columbia, S.C. (January 28, 1862-July 30, 1863); colonel and assistant adjutant general (April 23, 1863); superintendent, Bureau of Conscription (July 30, 1863-March 17, 1865); and brigadier general, CSA (June 10, 1864). After serving on Beauregard's staff at Fort Sumter and 1st Bull Run he was placed in charge of a prison camp until named to the Conscription Bureau. While engaged in the neverending search for more men he was promoted to brigadier general. He held the post until the bureau was abolished in the final months of the war. After three years in England after the collapse of the Confederacy, he continued to speak out on the justification for succession.

PRESTON, William (1816-1887)

Harvard-educated lawyer William Preston served his native Kentucky before and after the Civil War, in which he rose to the rank of Confederate brigadier general. During the Mexican War he had held the position of lieutenant colonel in the 4th Kentucky and in the interwar period sat in both houses of the state legislature and in the U.S. Congress. In the years just before the Civil War, he was James Buchanan's representative in Spain. During the secession crisis he urged his state to withdraw from the Union but was unsuccessful. Joining the Confederate army, his assignments included: colonel (September 1861); brigadier general, CSA (April 14, 1862); commanding 2nd (Kentucky) Brigade, Reserve Corps, Army of the Mississippi (May-June 1862); commanding 3rd Brigade, Breckinridge's Division, Hardee's Corps, Army of Tennessee (December 1862-May 9, 1863); commanding the division (January 1863); commanding District of Abingdon, Department of Western Virginia (May 9, 1863-January 7, 1864); also commanding Department of East Tennessee (June 26-July 4, 1863); and commanding division, Buckner's Corps, Army of Tennessee (September 1864). At Shiloh he served on the staff of Albert Sidney Johnston and was promoted to brigadier general later in the month. He took part in the Siege of Corinth, Mississippi, and at the end of the year led a brigade at Murfreesboro. After service in western Virginia and East Tennessee he led a division from there to reinforce Bragg before Chickamauga. On January 7, 1864, he was named as minister to the court of Maximilian but found it impossible to reach Mexico City. Returning to the Confederacy, he was in the Trans-Mississippi Department at the close of the war. He did not return to Kentucky until 1866, having traveled via Mexico, England, and Canada. He then resumed his political career as a Democrat sitting in the state legislature.

PRESTON, William Ballard (1805-1862)

A veteran of both houses of the state legislature and of the U.S. Congress—as an antislavery Whig—William B. Preston was a long-standing opponent of secession. The Virginia native had practiced law before his entry into politics and served as Zachary Taylor's secretary of the navy. It was not until Lincoln's call for 75,000, after the firing on Fort Sumter, that Preston became a secessionist. At that time, in a move to gain support from former Unionists, he was tapped to present the ordinance of secession to the state convention—unexpected for a man who had favored the admission of California as a free state. Named to the Provisional Confederate Congress from his western Virginia district, he was admitted on July 20, 1861, and sat on the Committee on Military Affairs. Named to the Senate in the First Regular Congress he sat on the corresponding committee and on those on: Flag and Seal; and Foreign Affairs. He wanted strict limits on the national government's war-making ability that would favor state and local control. He also wanted to keep the

economy free from government regulations. Between the second and third congressional sessions, he died at his Montgomery County home on November 16, 1862.

PRICE, Sterling (1809-1867)

As the leader of the Missouri State Guard, Virginia-born Sterling Price became one of the principal forces in Confederate Missouri at the beginning of the Civil War. A lawyer and farmer in his adopted state, he had gradually entered politics as a state legislator and U.S. congressman. During the Mexican War he was colonel of the 2nd Missouri and a brigadier general of volunteers. In the interwar years he served as governor and, as the secession crisis approached, he opposed separation but gradually altered his views. Accepting command of the Missouri State Guard, his assignments included: major general, Missouri State Guard (May 1861); commanding Missouri State Guard (May 1861-March 17, 1862); major general, CSA (March 6, 1862); commanding 1st Division, Trans-Mississippi District, Department #2 (March 17-April 1862); commanding division, Army of the West, Department #2 (April-May 1862); commanding the army (July 3-September 26, 1862); also commanding District of the Tennessee, Department #2 (July 1862); commanding corps (Army of the West), Army of West Tennessee, Department #2 (October-December 1862); commanding corps, Department of Mississippi and East Louisiana (ca. December 1862-February 27, 1863); commanding division, District of Arkansas, Trans-Mississippi Department (March 30-July 24, 1863 and September 25, 1863-March 16, 1864); commanding the district (July 24-September 25, 1863 and March 16-early August 1864); commanding Army of Missouri, Trans-Mississippi Department (September 18-December 1864); and also commanding Cavalry Corps, Trans-Mississippi Department (September 1864-early 1865). Meeting in June 1861 with Francis P. Blair and Nathaniel Lyon at the Planter's Hotel in St. Louis, he felt himself pushed into the Confederate camp. Leading the Missouri State Guard under Ben McCulloch, he fought at Wilson's Creek and then captured the Union garrison at Lexington. Unable to cooperate with McCulloch, he agreed to the idea of both of them serving under Earl Van Dorn and in such a setup fought in the Southern defeat at Pea Ridge. Appointed to a major generalcy in the regular Confederate forces from the date of the opening of the battle, he worked to transfer his men to that service. Transferred to the east of the Mississippi River, his forces arrived too late for the battle of Shiloh but took part in the defense of Corinth, Mississippi. He lost the fight at Iuka and again under Van Dorn took part in the unsuccessful attacks on Corinth. He maneuvered against Grant during that officer's drive into central Mississippi and then transferred back west of the Mississippi where he led the unsuccessful attack on Helena in an effort to relieve the pressure on Vicksburg which, ironically, fell the same day. Commanding the District of Arkansas, he failed to hold Little Rock but the next year campaigned successfully against Steele's drive on Camden, taking part in the victory at Jenkins' Ferry. Placed in charge of a large force of cavalry, he was dispatched on a raid into Missouri in the late summer and fall of

1864. Deterred from an attack on St. Louis by Union reinforcements, he moved to the West and was finally defeated at Westport. After fighting a rear-guard action at Marais des Cygnes, Kansas, he continued his retreat back into Arkansas by a roundabout route. While the campaign had thrown a fright into the Union high command, which felt this to be a dormant sector, it had not achieved any significant lasting result and had decimated Price's command. In the final months of the war there was a Confederate inquiry into the causes of the failure. At the war's close he moved into Mexico where he remained until the fall of Maximilian. The final year of his life was spent in St. Louis. To the end he had been popular with his Missourians who dubbed him "Old Pap." (Castel, Albert, *General Sterling Price and the Civil War in the West* and Stalhope, Robert E., *Sterling Price, Portrait of a Southerner*)

Sterling Price (center), Missouri State Guard commander, with fellow exiles in Mexico after the war. Clockwise from Price: Cadmus M. Wilcox, John B. Magruder, William P. Hardeman, and Thomas C. Hindman. (NA)

PRYOR, Roger Atkinson (1828-1919)

Twice Roger A. Pryor found himself a brigadier without a brigade and finished out the war, in effect, as a private. He had had a distinguished career before the war as a lawyer, journalist, and politician. He resigned from the U.S. Congress on March 3, 1861, and witnessed the shelling of Fort Sumter. On July 24, 1861, he took a seat in the Provisional Congress and was later reelected to the First Regular Congress. During both congresses he served on the Committee on Military Affairs but resigned on April 5, 1862, to devote his full energies to his military career. His assignments included: colonel, 3rd Virginia (1861); brigadier general, CSA (April 16, 1862); commanding brigade, Longstreet's Division (in 1st Corps from July), Army of Northern Virginia (May-August 1862), commanding brigade, Wilcox's Division, same corps and army (August-early September 1862); commanding brigade, Anderson's Division, same corps and army (September 1862); commanding the division (September 17, 1862); commanding brigade, Pickett's Division, same corps and army (September-November 10, 1862); and commanding brigade, Department of Virginia and North Carolina (December 1862-March 1863). He led his men at Williamsburg, Seven Pines, the Seven Days, and 2nd Bull Run. At Antietam he succeeded to division command. Apparently having displeased both Lee and Longstreet, he was sent to southern Virginia and his brigade was divided up. With Longstreet sent to command in this area later, the process was repeated in March with Pryor's new command being broken up. In disgust, he resigned and served after that as a special courier with the cavalry until captured on November 27, 1864, near Petersburg. Not released until near the war's close, he moved to New York as a journalist and lawyer, eventually becoming a judge. (Holzman, Robert, *Adapt or Perish, The Life of General Roger Pryor, C.S.A.*)

Q

QUANTRILL, William Clarke (1837-1865)

While there are other contenders for the title of "The Bloodiest Man in American History"—Civil War leaders "Bloody Bill" Anderson and John M. Chivington quickly come to mind—William C. Quantrill earned his share of the sobriquet for his depredations in the Trans-Mississippi area. An Ohio native, he had earned a prewar reputation as an outlaw while living under the name of Charley Hart in Kansas. After some regular service at Wilson's Creek he became a guerrilla leader and was soon branded an outlaw by the Union authorities. His band attracted some of their most notorious names in Missouri's Civil War, and Wild West, history—including Anderson, the Youngers, and Frank James. Officially made a captain in the Confederate army, he claimed a shadowy commission as colonel. In August 1862 he took Independence, but his most famous exploit came the next year when he returned to Lawrence, Kansas, destroying much of the community and killing all the male inhabitants he could find—about 150, young and old. In 1864 his command broke up when he quarreled with his principal lieutenants, but he soon organized another, smaller group, which now included Jesse James, and moved his operations to Kentucky. He continued his pillaging, which most Rebel leaders considered counterproductive, until May 10, 1865, when he was paralyzed by a Union bullet at Bloomfield. He died a prisoner on June 6. (Castel, Albert E., *William Clarke Quantrill: His Life and Times*)

QUARLES, William Andrew (1825-1893)

Captured for the second time at Franklin, William A. Quarles ended his career as a Confederate brigadier general. The Virginia-born Tennessee lawyer and judge had also been involved in politics, railroading, and banking before the outbreak of sectional warfare. His Confederate assignments included: colonel, 42nd Tennessee (November 28, 1861); brigadier general, CSA (August 25, 1863); commanding brigade, Department of the Gulf (fall 1863); commanding brigade, Breckinridge's Division, Breckinridge's-Hindman's Corps, Army of Tennessee (December 1863-early 1864); commanding brigade, Department of Mississippi and East Louisiana (early 1864); commanding brigade, District of the Gulf (April 6-May 1864); and commanding brigade, Cantey's-Walthall's Division, Polk's (Army of Mississippi)-Stewart's Corps, Army of Tennessee (May-November 30, 1864). Leading his regiment, he was taken prisoner at Fort Donelson. Exchanged on September 21, 1862, he for a time commanded a consolidated regiment composed of the remnants of five Tennessee regiments and a battalion which had been captured at Fort Donelson. With this unit he served at Port Hudson. Promoted to brigadier general, he led a brigade through the Atlanta Campaign and then embarked on Hood's ill-fated invasion of middle Tennessee. Wounded at Franklin, he was taken prisoner and not released until May 25, 1865. Thereafter he practiced law and later sat in the state legislature.

QUINTARD, Charles Todd (1824-1898)

Despite his Northern birth, Charles T. Quintard became one of the more popular of Confederate regimental chaplains. A native of Connecticut, he had studied law in New York and taken up practice in Georgia. In the 1850s he became a medical professor in Tennessee where he eventually joined the ministry as an Episcopalian rector. His long residence in the South affected his political views and in 1861 he was appointed the chaplain of the 1st Tennessee. As such he was present at Cheat Mountain, Perryville, Murfreesboro, Chickamauga, Chattanooga, the Atlanta Campaign, and Franklin and Nashville. During much of his service he also doubled as a regimental surgeon, for which the men were highly grateful. Settling in Nashville after the war, he became the second bishop of the state and helped refound the University of the South. (Noll, Arthur Howard, *Doctor Quintard*)

QUINTERO, Juan (?-?)

Juan Quintero was a native of Havana, Cuba, and served the Confederacy well as a diplomat to its Southern neighbor, Mexico. A U.S. citizen since 1853, he had been a lawyer, apparently in New Orleans. Offering his services to the Confederate government, he was dispatched to Mexico where he befriended the Vidaurri government and ensured the neutrality of Juarez in the American Civil War. He was also involved in the smuggling of cotton southwards, out of the Confederacy. He was a government official in Texas after the war.

R

RAINS, Gabriel James (1803-1881)

A tinkerer at heart rather than a field commander, Gabriel J. Rains was involved in a line of war work that raised grave questions about the ethical conduct of military operations among his fellow Confederates—as well as the enemy. Graduating in 1827 from West Point, he had risen to the rank of lieutenant colonel, 5th Infantry, by the time his native North Carolina withdrew from the Union. Pre-secession he had been wounded while fighting Seminoles near Fort King, Florida, and had gained a reputation for experimenting with explosives. Resigning on July 31, 1861, he entered the Southern army and his assignments included: brigadier general, CSA (September 23, 1861); commanding division, Department of the Peninsula (October 3, 1861-April 12, 1862); and commanding brigade, D.H. Hill's Division, Army of Northern Virginia (April 12-June 16, 1862). Following long service in the defenses of Yorktown, his forces were merged into D.H. Hill's Division. He fought at Williamsburg but was roundly criticized by Hill for his failures in the fighting at Seven Pines on May 31. On June 18, Rains was removed from field duty and received an appointment better fitted to his capabilities. He was to direct the submarine defenses of the James and Appomattox Rivers. His use of hidden explosive devices caused a debate within the Confederate hierarchy, and in December 1862 he was assigned as chief of the Bureau of Conscription. But from May 25, 1863, he was back at work, placing his weapons around Richmond, Mobile, and Charleston. After the war he briefly held a government clerkship. (Freeman, Douglas S., *Lee's Lieutenants*)

RAINS, George Washington (1817-1898)

The brother of the Confederate general—Gabriel J. Rains—who was so deeply involved in the development of mine warfare, George W. Rains rose to the rank of colonel in the Ordinance Department while in charge of the powder works at Augusta, Georgia. The North Carolinian had received his West Point appointment from Alabama. Upon his 1842 graduation, he was posted to the engineers but the next year transferred to the artillery. He won two brevets in Mexico and then fought the Seminoles in Florida. Resigning as a captain in the 4th Artillery in 1856, he spent the next five years in the iron business in New York. Joining the Confederacy, his assignments included: major, Artillery (July 10, 1861); lieutenant colonel, Artillery (May 22, 1862); and colonel, Artillery (July 12, 1863). Working under Josiah Gorgas, he was assigned to the Augusta works and was responsible for providing the Confederate armies with some 2,750,000 pounds of gunpowder. In addition he was in charge of the post there until it was threatened by Sherman's Union forces. During the war he published a manual entitled *Notes on Making Saltpetre from the Earth of the Caves*. Following the war he engaged in business in New York and was a college professor. He also authored *History of the Confederate States Powder Works*.

RAINS, James Edwards (1833-1862)

Tennessee lawyer, journalist, and district attorney, James E. Rains gave his life for the Confederacy—a brigadier general for less than two months. His Confederate assignments included: captain, Company A, 11th Tennessee (May 2, 1861); colonel, 11th Tennessee (May 10, 1861); commanding Cumberland Gap, District of East Tennessee, Department #2 (January-ca. March 1862); commanding 2nd Brigade, 1st (Stevenson's) Division, Department of East Tennessee (ca. March-June and July-December 1862); brigadier general, CSA (November 4, 1862); and commanding 2nd Brigade, McCown's Division (detached from Department of East Tennessee), Hardee's Corps, Army of Tennessee (December-December 31, 1862). Originally the head of the Hermitage Guards, he rose to regimental command and was stationed in East Tennessee. For a time he commanded at Cumberland Gap and then took part in driving the Union forces under George W. Morgan from the region during the Kentucky Campaign. Rewarded with promotion to brigadier general, he commanded a brigade at Murfreesboro and led his men on the extreme Confederate left during the initial assaults on the first day of the battle—the last day of the year. In these attacks he was killed.

RAINS, James S. (?-?)

An active politician before the war, James S. Rains was made a brigadier general in the Missouri State Guard at the beginning of the Civil War but appears to have preferred to remain in state service when most of his command was enlisted in the Confederate army. At Dug Springs he commanded the Guard's 8th Division. Commanding the 2nd Division, he fought at Wilson's Creek before resuming command of his own division in the actions at Lexington and Pea Ridge. Returning to Missouri when most of his command was absorbed into the Confederate army, he remained active in recruiting for the Southern army and commanded small forces when General Price invaded Missouri in 1864.

RAMSEUR, Stephen Dodson (1837-1864)

Three days after receiving word that he was a father, West Pointer (1860) Stephen D. Ramseur was mortally wounded; he died surrounded by former fellow cadets from the other side. He had served less than a year in the artillery when he resigned on April 6, 1861, to aid the South. His assignments included: first lieutenant, Artillery (to rank from March 16, 1861); captain, Battery A, 1st North Carolina Artillery (April 16, 1861); major, 1st North Carolina Artillery (May 8, 1861); colonel, 49th North Carolina (April 12, 1862); brigadier general, CSA (November 1, 1862); commanding G.B. Anderson's (old) Brigade, Rodes' Division, 2nd Corps, Army of Northern Virginia (April 1863-June 4, 1864); commanding the division (May 2, 1863); also commanding Iverson's (old) Brigade (July 1-September 8, 1863); major general, CSA (June 1, 1864); commanding Early's (old) Division, same corps and army (June 4-13, 1864); commanding same division, Valley District, Department of Northern Virginia (June 13-September 20, 1864); and commanding Rodes' (old) Division, same district and department (September 20-October 19, 1864). After serving in the artillery in North Carolina and on the Peninsula, he was elected to command an infantry regiment. Leading his men he fell wounded at Malvern Hill, the last of the Seven Days Battles. During his long recovery, he was promoted and assigned to command a brigade in the fall of 1862. Taking up his assignment the next spring, he distinguished himself in a charge on May 3 at Chancellorsville. Wounded in the battle he remained on duty. At Gettysburg he led the brigade and that of Iverson, after that general suffered a breakdown on the first day. During a leave that fall, he was married. During the battle of the Wilderness, his brigade was not engaged but at Spotsylvania it played a leading role in plugging the holes in the Southern lines on May 12. Three weeks later he was rewarded with promotion to major general and command of Early's Division. Taking charge at Cold Harbor, he then went on the raid through the Shenandoah Valley to Monocacy and the outskirts of Washington. Retiring into the Valley, his division was routed on July 20 in a small action at Winchester. He was severely

censured for his failures in the independent action. He went on to fight at 3rd Winchester and was then transferred to the division of the deceased General Rodes. He fought at Fisher's Hill and in the early defeat of two Union corps at Cedar Creek. In the Union counterattack he fell mortally wounded. Visited by friends from the military academy still in the old service, he died the next day in the hands of the enemy. (Freeman, Douglas S., *Lee's Lieutenants* and Gallagher, Gary W., *Stephen Dobson Rauseur: Lee's Gallant General*)

RANDAL, Horace (1831-1864)

Horace Randal, one of E. Kirby Smith's extralegal appointees as a general, did not live long enough to find out if Richmond would approve of Smith's action. Graduating from West Point in 1854, he had served in both the infantry and the dragoons before resigning his second lieutenant's commission on February 27, 1861. Offering his services to the Confederacy he was soon commissioned colonel, 28th Texas Cavalry. When this regiment reached Arkansas it was dismounted and served the entire war as infantry. His entire service being in the Trans-Mississippi Department, he held the following commands: brigade, District of West Louisiana (spring-fall 1863); brigade, Walker's Division, District of West Louisiana (early 1864); and a brigade, Walker's Division, District of Arkansas (April 1864). Serving in Louisiana, he fought at Milliken's Bend during the Vicksburg Campaign and at Mansfield in the Red River Campaign. For the latter action, General Smith promoted him to brigadier general on April 13, 1864, to rank from the day of the battle. A November 1863 request to Jefferson Davis for Randal's promotion had received no action, so Smith acted on his own, claiming his distance from the government required this unorthodox action. On April 30, 1864, Randal was mortally wounded in the battle of Jenkins' Ferry, Arkansas, in the action against Union General Steele's expedition.

RANDALL, James Ryder (1839-1908)

The first clash of arms—between Massachusetts troops and pro-Southern citizens of Baltimore—of the Civil War in Maryland resulted in James R. Randall writing the memorable lyrics for "Maryland, My Maryland." The resident of that city, then a college professor in Louisiana, was mourning the death of a former classmate in the melee. Believing the South the aggrieved party, he tried to enlist in the army but was turned down for medical reasons. Meanwhile his poem gained popularity after his reading of it before his English class and its publication in the *New Orleans Delta*. The Cary sisters further popularized it by putting it to the tune "Lauriger Horatius." But it achieved its immortality when it was put to the music of "Tannenbaum, O Tannenbaum." Following the battle of Antietam and the failure of the campaign in western Maryland—where Southern sentiment was weak—many Confederate soldiers did not want to hear the song again. After the war Randall was active in journalism and continued to write poetry. (Andrews, M.P., *The Poems of James Ryder Randall*)

RANDOLPH, George Wythe (1818-1867)

Tuberculosis deprived the Confederacy of the services of Virginia lawyer George W. Randolph who had served it as a general and cabinet officer early in the Civil War. The Virginia native had served six years at sea by the time he was 19 and two years later resigned as a midshipman to enter upon the practice of law. He was engaged in this profession in Richmond when John Brown's Harpers Ferry raid occurred. As a response he founded the Richmond Howitzers which were absorbed into the Confederate army shortly after Virginia formed its military bonds with the Confederacy. His assignments included: major, Richmond Howitzers (spring 1861); colonel, 1st Virginia Artillery (September 1861); commanding Artillery, Department of the Peninsula (fall 1861-early 1862); and brigadier general, CSA (February 12, 1862). Two companies from his three-company battalion joined John B. Magruder and fought at Big Bethel in one of the earliest actions of the war. As colonel of an artillery regiment, he continued to serve on the Peninsula and took command of that arm under Magruder. Promoted to brigadier general in February 1862, he was named secretary of war the next month, on March 18, 1862. He served in this position only until November 15, 1862, and then with his illness diagnosed he set off for France in a doomed attempt to regain his health. While still overseas, he resigned his general's commission on December 18, 1864; he returned to his native state shortly after the fall of the Confederacy. He died less than two years after Appomattox.

RANSOM, Matthew Whitaker (1826-1904)

When his younger brother Robert was promoted to other duties, Matthew W. Ransom, a lawyer and state legislator in his native North Carolina, was made a brigadier to succeed him. Before the secession of the state Ransom had served as a commissioner to the fledgling Confederacy. Entering the army as a private early in the war, his later assignments included: lieutenant colonel, 1st North Carolina State Troops (May 16, 1861); colonel, 35th North Carolina (April 21, 1862); brigadier general, CSA (June 13, 1863); commanding R. Ransom's Brigade, Department of North Carolina (June-July and October 1863-May 1864); commanding brigade, R. Ransom's Division, Department of Richmond (July-September 1863); commanding brigade, Colquitt's Division, Department of North Carolina and Southern Virginia (mid-1864); commanding brigade, Johnson's Division, Anderson's Corps, Army of Northern Virginia (October-December 1864 and February-April 9, 1865). Sent to join Lee's army on the Peninsula, the elder Ransom was twice wounded at Malvern Hill during the Seven Days. He returned to command the regiment at Antietam before being transferred back to North Carolina. During the course of the next year he fought at Plymouth and Weldon and at Suffolk in southeastern Virginia and rose to brigade level. In May of 1864 he was wounded during the fighting at Drewry's Bluff and did not rejoin his unit until his command had been absorbed into Lee's army. He served through parts of the Petersburg siege and surrendered at Appomattox at the head of a unit shattered at Five Forks and Sayler's Creek. Law, politics,

and farming filled his later years. (Freeman, Douglas S., *Lee's Lieutenants*)

RANSOM, Robert, Jr. (1828-1892)

The younger brother of M.W. Ransom, Robert Ransom, Jr., rose one grade higher in the Confederate service until felled by illness. The North Carolinian was a West Pointer (1850) and veteran of a decade in the mounted service when he resigned from the Old Army on January 31, 1861. His Southern assignments included: captain, Cavalry (spring 1861); colonel, 1st North Carolina Cavalry (October 13, 1861); brigadier general, CSA (March 1, 1862); commanding brigade, Department of North Carolina (April-July 1862); commanding brigade, Walker's-Ransom's Division, 1st Corps, Army of Northern Virginia (August 1862-January 3, 1863); also commanding the division (November 7, 1862-January 3, 1863); commanding brigade, Department of Virginia and North Carolina (January-April 1, 1863); commanding brigade, Department of North Carolina (April 1-May 1863); major general, CSA (May 26, 1863); commanding division, Department of Richmond (July 1863); commanding division, Department of West Virginia and East Tennessee (October 1863-January 1864); temporarily commanding the department (January 1864); commanding Cavalry, Department of East Tennessee (March-April 1864); commanding Department of Richmond (April 25-June 13, 1864); and commanding Cavalry Division, Valley District, Department of Northern Virginia

Confederate brigade commander Matthew W. Ransom. (NA)

(June-August 10, 1864). Serving with his cavalry regiment in Northern Virginia, he commanded the forces in the skirmish at Vienna on November 26, 1861, before being returned to North Carolina. Soon promoted to brigadier he fought at the Seven Days attached to Huger's Division although his brigade properly belonged to Holmes'. In the Maryland invasion, he led his North Carolinians at the capture of Harpers Ferry and in the action at Antietam. In the victory at Fredericksburg he commanded the division on Marye's Heights. The next month his command was sent back to North Carolina and he was soon promoted. He then performed duty at Richmond and in western Virginia and East Tennessee. Returning to Richmond, he led a field division under Beauregard in the defense at Drewry's Bluff in May 1864. Sent to command the cavalry in the Valley, he participated in the raid on Washington, including action at Monocacy. Too ill for active duty, he was relieved on August 10, 1864. After military court duty and the end of the war, he became a civil engineer. (Freeman, Douglas S., *Lee's Lieutenants*)

READ, Charles William (1840-1892)

Having earned the sobriquet of "Savez" for the one word of French he had mastered on his way to graduating at the bottom of the 1860 class at Annapolis, no one would have thought that the Mississippian Charles W. Read would develop into one of the Civil War's more daring naval commanders. Joining the Southern forces in 1861, he was assigned to duty in August, assisting in the construction of batteries along the Potomac River near Quantico Creek. Following this service he was transferred to the West and with the rank of lieutenant served as the executive officer aboard the *McRae*, part of Commander George N. Hollins' fleet on the upper Mississippi, where he participated in operations around Island #10. Moving downriver, the fleet made a poor showing in the naval actions below New Orleans. One of the few exceptions was the behavior of Lieutenant Read who took command of the *McRae* when her commander, Lieutenant Thomas B. Huger, was mortally wounded. Involved in the preparation of the ram CSS *Arkansas*, Read served as a lieutenant aboard her during her summer of spreading consternation among the Union's Mississippi fleet. However, faulty engines caused her to break down on the way to join the Confederate land attack on Baton Rouge. Shortly thereafter she was destroyed by her crew when attacked. Next serving aboard the commerce raider CSS. *Florida*, from November 4, 1862, Read suggested in May 1863 that the captured brig *Clarence* be converted into a raider as well and he himself placed in command. His request granted, he found his new command sluggish and spent the next few weeks in fruitless search of prey. Then on June 6 he secured his first prize and his luck turned and he captured several more vessels. On June 12 Read transferred his crew aboard the *Tacony*, one of three vessels taken that day. The *Clarence* was burned. His new command made its first capture that very afternoon and his subsequent cruise, capturing 14 more vessels, led to a massive search by the Union navy. But Read burned the *Tacony* on June 25 and took over the captured *Archer*. The next night the *Archer* entered the harbor at Portland, Maine, in an effort to seize the revenue cutter *Caleb Cushing*. However, the cutter's new commander, arriving to assume command, reported the unexpected sailing of his vessel and soon a scratch fleet was in pursuit of the Confederates. After running out of ammunition Read abandoned the vessel and he and his men became prisoners. After 16 months of imprisonment, Read was exchanged. Made a lieutenant commander, Read took part in one more adventure, the attempted escape of the ram *Webb* from the Red River to the Gulf of Mexico as a cruiser. The effort was made following Lee's surrender and Read was forced to run his vessel ashore below New Orleans where he was captured. After the war he was a harbor master in New Orleans. (Read, Charles W., "Reminiscences of the C.S. Navy," *Southern Historical Society Papers*, Vol. I. No. 5. May 1876)

READE, Edwin Godwin (1812-1894)

A former Know-Nothing congressman and Unionist, Edwin G. Reade was appointed by Governor Zebulon Vance to complete the Confederate Senate term of the resigned George Davis. He quickly became identified with the growing North Carolina peace movement. A native North Carolina lawyer, he had served only one term in the U.S. legislature where his most notable act was to be the only Southerner to vote for the censure of Congressman Lawrence M. Keitt in the Brooks-Sumner beatings. In 1861 Reade turned down both a Lincoln offer of a cabinet position and a seat at the state secession convention. Elected to a judgeship, he was named to the Senate on January 22, 1864, before he could be sworn into the judicial post. He was soon threatening separate peace negotiations on the part of his state and was a thorn in the Davis administration's side. As a peace candidate, he was defeated for reelection and so retired to private practice. During Reconstruction he supported Andrew Johnson and chaired the convention held at the end of the war. As a Republican, he sat on the state supreme court until he went into banking. (Hamilton, Joseph Gregoire de Roulhac, *Reconstruction in North Carolina*)

REAGAN, John Henninger (1818-1905)

As the Confederacy's only postmaster general, John Reagan struggled to keep his department functioning in the black as mandated by the constitution. Born in Tennessee, Reagan moved to Texas when 21 and became an Indian fighter, farmer, lawyer, judge, and state legislator. With the secession crisis in Texas, he was a participant in the state convention as a moderate and, giving up his seat in congress which he had held since 1857, was appointed to the Provisional Confederate Congress. Before receiving any committee assignments, he was appointed to the cabinet on March 6, 1861. Realizing the difficulties of the post, he twice turned it down, not wanting to become a martyr, before finally accepting. He had flattered Jefferson Davis by opposing his naming as president, preferring to place Davis in military command. Becoming a close and trusted advisor, he remained with his chief until the final capture. Through a combination of high rates, consolidation of post offices, low pay, and equipment and supplies taken from the

U.S. Post Office, Reagan was able to keep the department running, albeit slowly, without being a drain on the treasury. During the final days of the Confederacy he advised Davis on acceptable peace terms. Captured with Davis in Georgia, Reagan spent several months imprisoned in Boston Harbor during which he wrote his fellow Texans advising compliance with Reconstruction. After a period of enmity from his constituents for this, he was elected to the U.S. House of Representatives and later served in the Senate and on the state railroad commission. (Procter, Benjamin H., *Not Without Honor, the Life of John H. Reagan*)

RECTOR, Henry Massey (1816-1899)

A reluctant secessionist, Henry M. Rector was forced out of the Arkansas governorship for his opposition to the central Confederate government. Born in Kentucky, he had relocated to Arkansas where he was, successively, a bank teller, farmer, U.S. marshal, state legislator, and surveyor. He had been admitted to the bar in 1854 and again sat in the legislature before becoming a judge. Inaugurated as governor in 1860, he refused Lincoln's call for 75,000 volunteers and pushed the state toward secession. But he soon came into conflict with the Confederate authorities and began to prevent state troops from leaving the state. When a new state constitution was approved, it effectively eliminated him from office and he resigned on November 4, 1862. A postwar planter, he attended two constitutional conventions but never again held public office.

REDWOOD, Allen Christian (1844-1922)

After a career in the Confederate army—being thrice wounded and twice captured—Allen C. Redwood went on to become one of the premier artists in depicting the Southern soldier, earning the praise of former General Bradley Johnson as "the best drawer of the Confederate soldier who has ever lived." His military service included: private, Middlesex Southrons (July 24, 1861); private, Company C, 55th Virginia (September 1861); detailed to Commissary Department (December 1862); sergeant major, Commissary Department (March 1, 1863); rejoined company (April 1863); and private, Company C, 1st Maryland Cavalry (January 12, 1864). He saw action at Mechanicsville (slightly wounded by a shell), 2nd Bull Run (captured and paroled the next month), Chancellorsville (wounded by a shell), and Gettysburg (wounded in Pickett's Charge). Transferring to the cavalry, he took part in the drive to the outskirts of Washington and in the Valley Campaign of 1864. He later served on the staff of General Lomax as a clerk and courier. While trying to locate a remount in southeastern Virginia he was captured two days before Lee's surrender. Released in July, the Virginia-born, New York-educated veteran converted his prewar art hobby into a career. His concentration was upon the Southern soldier in battle and camp. Many of his realistic works were produced especially for numerous soldiers' reminiscences. His crowning achievement was his illustration of *Battles and Leaders*, originally published serially by the *Century Magazine*. Many of the scenes he sketched were first-hand accounts. He died in North Carolina more than a half century after the war.

REMINGTON, Frederic Sackrider (1861-1909)

Although his painting career was after the Civil War and he is best known for his works dealing with the American West,

"The Washington Artillery on Marye's Hill Firing Upon the Union Columns Forming for the Assault" by Allen C. Redwood. (*B&L*)

Frederic Remington did execute a number of works depicting the sectional conflict. A native of New York he had travelled widely gathering material for his work—even being deported from Russia. But the West was his primary artistic interest. He became known for his action scenes and his ability to faithfully portray man and horse. His characters included Indians, cowboys, and soldiers. He covered the war with Spain but for some of his military works he dug back into recent history to depict the Civil War. He died suddenly of appendicitis. (Vail, R.W.G., *Frederic Remington, Chronicler of the Vanished West*)

REYNOLDS, Alexander Welch (1816-1876)

A veteran of Seminole fighting, Virginia West Pointer (1838) Alexander W. Reynolds served as a Confederate brigadier general and later joined the Egyptian army. Posted to the infantry upon his graduation, he had transferred to the quartermaster's branch in 1847 but was dismissed in 1855 in a dispute over his accounts. Reinstated three years later, he was dropped, as a captain, on October 4, 1861, having joined the Confederacy seven months earlier. His assignments in the latter service included: captain, Infantry (March 1861); colonel, 50th Virginia (July 10, 1861); commanding brigade, Department of East Tennessee (May-July 3, 1862); commanding brigade, 1st (Stevenson's) Division, Department of East Tennessee (July 3-October 31, 1862); commanding brigade, Heth's Division, Department of East Tennessee (October 31-December 1862); commanding 4th Brigade, Stevenson's Division, 2nd Military District, Department of Mississippi and East Louisiana (December 1862-April 1863); commanding 4th Brigade, Stevenson's Division, Department of Mississippi and East Louisiana (April-July 4, 1863); brigadier general, CSA (September 14, 1863); commanding brigade, Buckner's Division, Army of Tennessee (October-November 30, 1863); commanding brigade, Stevenson's Division, Hardee's Corps, Army of Tennessee (November 30, 1863-February 20, 1864); and commanding brigade, Stevenson's Division, Hood's Corps, Army of Tennessee (February 20-May 27, 1864). Following service as a regimental commander in western Virginia and at Cumberland Gap he was transferred with Stevenson's division to Mississippi where he took part in the unsuccessful defense of Vicksburg. Paroled on the day of the river city's surrender, he was formally exchanged in September 1863 in time to fight in command of a brigade, with the increased rank of brigadier general, at Chattanooga. He led his brigade in the early stages of the Atlanta Campaign. Wounded at New Hope Church, his active field career was ended. In Egypt he served with the rank of colonel on the staff of William W. Loring, and he died there.

REYNOLDS, Daniel Harris (1832-1902)

Rising from the rank of captain to a brigadier generalship, Ohio-born Arkansas lawyer Daniel H. Reynolds fought across the breadth of the map for the Confederacy. His assignments included: captain, Company A, 1st Arkansas Mounted Rifles (June 14, 1861); major, 1st Arkansas Mounted Rifles (April 14, 1862); lieutenant colonel, 1st Arkansas Mounted Rifles (May 1,

1862); colonel, 1st Arkansas Mounted Rifles (September 20, 1863); brigadier general, CSA (March 5, 1864); commanding brigade, Department of the Gulf (April 1-6, 1864); commanding brigade, District of the Gulf, Department of Alabama, Mississippi and East Louisiana (April 6-May 1864); and commanding brigade, Cantey's-Walthall's Division, Polk's (Army of Mississippi)-Stewart's Corps, Army of Tennessee (May 1864-March 19, 1865). He fought at Wilson's Creek and Pea Ridge before his regiment was transferred east of the Mississippi. He served in the Kentucky and Tullahoma campaigns. Promoted to the unit's colonelcy following Chickamauga, he soon became part of the Mobile garrison where he led a brigade as a brigadier general. Joining the main western army in Georgia, he served throughout the Atlanta Campaign and then embarked on Hood's disastrous invasion of middle Tennessee. He took part in the assault at Franklin and the defeat at Nashville. During the Carolinas Campaign he was wounded at Bentonville, losing a leg, and was effectively put out of the war. He subsequently practiced law and sat in the Arkansas legislature. It should be noted that during much of the conflict his original regiment served dismounted as infantry.

REYNOLDS, Jim (?-1864) and John (?-1871)

As the heads of a band of allegedly Confederate irregulars in Colorado, Jim and John Reynolds ended up on the wrong side of Colonel John M. Chivington of subsequent Sand Creek fame. Suspected of being highwaymen in 1863, and being from Texas, it was considered expedient to simply place the brothers in the local internment center for southern sympathizers in Denver. Making their escape to Texas, the pair returned to Colorado at the head of a band of Confederate irregulars who allegedly were to turn over their loot to the Confederacy. Until the spring of 1864 the gang was highly successful, supposedly burying much of the loot for the cause. Then the gang got into a gunfight in which one man was killed. Jim and four others were captured while John and one other got away. The five were tried in a civilian court and sentenced to life imprisonment. Reacting to fears that sympathizers might stage a breakout attempt, Chivington stepped in and tried the prisoners as conspirators against the United States, sentencing them to hang. Sending them to Leavenworth, Kansas, for review of the case, Chivington entrusted them to Captain George Cree of the Colorado Cavalry. A few days after his departure on August 19, 1864, the captain returned, reporting the prisoners shot while attempting to escape. However, their bodies were soon found tied to trees and full of bullet holes. Cree claimed that he merely followed Chivington's verbal orders, but no one believed him—until after the Sand Creek massacre. Meanwhile John Reynolds returned in 1871, allegedly to look for the buried treasure. Instead he committed a few more holdups until mortally wounded.

REYNOLDS, Thomas C. (1821-1887)

A native of South Carolina, Missouri Lieutenant Governor Thomas C. Reynolds was an outspoken secessionist. After studying at Heidelberg, he had served as a diplomat in Spain. Settling in St. Louis in the early 1850s, he soon became embroiled in the violent politics of the day, including a duel with B. Gratz Brown. Entering the state's number two office at the beginning of 1861, he was active in the preparations for war. Out of state when the capital was abandoned, he sought the aid of the Confederate government in the liberation of his state and later joined Governor Claiborne F. Jackson in a government in exile which declared Missouri to be out of the Union and part of the Confederacy. With the December 1862 death of Jackson, Reynolds took over the governor's chair with the backing of Confederate Missouri troops. But with the state under Union control and with a new Union governor, he was unable to exercise most of his duties. He served as a volunteer aide in the 1864 invasion of the state by General Sterling Price. Fleeing the United States at the war's conclusion, he served Emperor Maximilian in Mexico. Returning three years later, he was subsequently elected to the state legislature and in 1887 committed suicide. (Snead, Thomas L., *The Fight for Missouri*)

RHETT, Robert Barnwell (1800-1876)

Lawyer, plantation owner, but, most importantly, politician Robert Barnwell Rhett was one of the earliest secession advocates in South Carolina. A supporter of Nullification during the Jackson administration, he spent decades working for an independent South. In 1860, he drafted South Carolina's Ordinance of Secession and the next year took part in the writing of the Confederate Constitution, gaining for himself the title of the "Father of Secession." He was considered too extreme for the presidency, though. As owner-editor of the *Charleston Mercury* he became a harsh critic of the Davis administration. By 1863, his brand of fire-eater secessionism had been sufficiently discredited so that he was defeated in a race for a seat in the Confederate Congress. After the war he refused to apply for a pardon. He died in 1876, with his dream of a new nation crushed. (White, Laura A., *Robert Barnwell Rhett: Father of Secession*)

RHETT, Thomas Smith (1827-1893)

A West Pointer (1848), Thomas S. Rhett of South Carolina had resigned his commission as a first lieutenant in the 2nd Artillery in 1855 and then left his job as a Baltimore bank clerk to offer his services to the South. His assignments included: captain, Artillery (November 19, 1861); colonel, Artillery (May 10, 1862); commanding the artillery defenses of Richmond (August 30, 1862-April 1, 1863); and commanding Richmond Defenses, Department of Richmond (April 1-October 28, 1863). After service in South Carolina training artillery batteries in 1861 he was assigned to duty with the Ordnance Department in Richmond. Placed in command of the guns defending the capital, he directed them until the fall of 1863 when he was ordered to Europe to purchase arms. His principal activities were in France. Ordered back across the Atlantic on October 16, 1864, he finished out the war in the Ordnance Department. After the surrender he resettled in Baltimore.

RICHARDSON, Robert Winkler (1820-1870)

Questions of recruiting authority, discipline, and effectiveness prompted Jefferson Davis to request that the nomination of Robert W. Richardson as a Confederate brigadier general be returned by the Senate, despite the fact that Richardson had actually been confirmed at that rank. A North Carolina-born Tennessee lawyer, he had served in a minor military capacity in the early part of the Civil War before receiving permission to raise units behind enemy lines. In the meantime he had fought at Shiloh and in the defense of Corinth, Mississippi. His later assignments included: colonel, 12th Tennessee Cavalry (February 14, 1863); brigadier general, CSA (December 3, 1863, to rank from the first); commanding brigade, Chalmers' Cavalry Division, Department of Mississippi and East Louisiana (October 18-December 1863); commanding brigade, Forrest's Cavalry Corps, Department of Mississippi and East Louisiana (January 25-28, 1864); and commanding brigade, Chalmers' Division, Forrest's Cavalry Corps, Department of Alabama, Mississippi and East Louisiana (January 28-March 20, 1864). His regiment was also known as the 1st Tennessee Partisan Rangers and served in western Tennessee. Richardson was then authorized to raise more units in occupied areas and was named a brigadier general. But after a series of recruiting controversies and battlefield misfortunes he was ordered to join Nathan Bedford Forrest. On February 9, 1864, his nomination was returned to the president and he performed little service thereafter. Engaged in railroading after the war, he was murdered for obscure reasons five years after the Confederacy's fall.

RION, James Henry (1828-1866)

The case of James H. Rion demonstrates the poor state of command that existed under Brigadier General Nathan G. Evans during his service in South Carolina. Rion, a native of Canada, was a colonel of the South Carolina militia at the outbreak of the Civil War. His war assignments included: colonel, 6th South Carolina (early 1861); captain, Company B, 7th South Carolina Battalion (November 13, 1861); major, 7th South Carolina Battalion (March 5, 1863); temporarily commanding 22nd South Carolina (early 1863); and lieutenant colonel, 7th South Carolina Battalion (June 24, 1864). He led part of his regiment to Charleston Harbor just after the fall of Fort Sumter but failed to gain reelection to his post when the command went into Confederate service that summer. Organizing the Lyle Rifles, he became their captain but was placed under arrest on February 5, 1862, along with all three of his lieutenants for refusing to obey Evans' orders. He was finally released on May 21, 1862. He fought at Battery Wagner and through much of the siege of Charleston until the spring of 1864 when his command moved to Virginia. Here the unit was engaged at Bermuda Hundred and during the sieges of Richmond and Petersburg. Moving to North Carolina, it was engaged in the defense of Wilmington and surrendered with Johnston's army. Rion went back to the practice of law.

RIPLEY, Roswell Sabine (1823-1887)

West Pointer (1843) and 10-year artilleryman Roswell S. Ripley became a brigadier general during the first year of the war but never rose any higher, in part due to an inability to get along with his superiors. An Ohio native, he had resigned his commission, having earned two brevets in Mexico, in 1853 to become a businessman in his wife's state, South Carolina. He cast his lot with the South, his services including: lieutenant colonel, 1st South Carolina Artillery Battalion Regulars (January 1861); brigadier general, CSA (August 15, 1861); commanding Department of South Carolina (August 21-November 5, 1861); commanding 2nd Military District of South Carolina, Department of South Carolina, Georgia and Florida (December 10, 1861-May 28, 1862); commanding brigade, D.H. Hill's Division (in 2nd Corps in September), Army of Northern Virginia (June-September 17, 1862); commanding the division (August 1862); commanding 1st Military District of South Carolina, Department of South Carolina, Georgia and Florida (October 17, 1862-October 17, 1864); commanding Sub-district No. 2, District of South Carolina, same department (October 17-late 1864); also commanding brigade, same department (July-late 1864); and commanding Brown's Division, Cheatham's Corps, Army of Tennessee (March 19-April 9, 1865). During the bombardment of Fort Sumter Ripley commanded some artillery on Sullivan's Island. After some more service on the coast, and having problems with the departmental commander, he transferred to Lee's army for the Seven Days. Severely wounded at Antietam, he was again assigned to Charleston where he served until the last few months of the war. After Bentonville he commanded Brown's Division but lost his post during the reorganization of Johnston's forces on April 9, 1865. After the South's collapse he was in business in England, Charleston, and New York.

RIVES, Alfred Landon (1830-1903)

Colonel Alfred L. Rives served for almost half of the war as chief of the Confederate War Department's Engineer Bureau, but only in an acting capacity. After receiving his engineering training at the Virginia Military Institute, the University of Virginia, and in France, he had been active in railroad engineering before the war. He had also been secretary of the interior under Franklin Pierce. Entering the Confederate engineers, he served successively at the ranks of captain, lieutenant colonel, and colonel. He was acting chief of the bureau at three periods during the war: November 13, 1861-September 24, 1862; August 18, 1863-March 1864; and April-June 1864. His position in Richmond naturally led him to work closely with the Army of Northern Virginia. Resuming his railroad engineering career, he was active in the United States and Panama. (Nichols, James L., *Confederate Engineers*)

ROANE, John Selden (1817-1867)

Mexican War veteran John S. Roane spent his entire service as a Confederate brigadier general in the Trans-Mississippi West. As second in command of Yell's Arkansas Regiment in the fighting south of the Rio Grande, he succeeded to its colonelcy upon the death of his superior. The Tennessee native had entered politics in his adopted state, sitting in the legislature and serving as Arkansas' governor. Opposed to secession he did not join the Confederate service until almost a year after the firing on Fort Sumter. His assignments included: brigadier general, CSA (March 20, 1862); commanding Trans-Mississippi District, Department #2 (May 11-31, 1862); commanding brigade, Shoup's Division, 1st Corps, Trans-Mississippi Department (December 1862); and commanding 1st (Arkansas) Brigade, 1st (Arkansas) Division, 2nd Corps (or District of Arkansas), Trans-Mississippi Department (September 1864-May 26, 1865). He briefly commanded all Southern forces in Arkansas but was soon succeeded by Thomas C. Hindman. He led a brigade at Prairie Grove and in the final half year of the war but spent most of his career in post and special assignments throughout the Trans-Mississippi West. He lived less than two years longer than the Confederacy.

ROBERTS, William Paul (1841-1910)

Holding every lower commissioned rank but two, William P. Roberts rose to be the Confederacy's youngest general officer. Enlisting at the beginning of the war, he held the following assignments: third lieutenant, 2nd North Carolina Cavalry (August 30, 1861); first lieutenant, 2nd North Carolina Cavalry (September 13, 1862); captain, Company C, 2nd North Carolina Cavalry (November 19, 1863); major, 2nd North Carolina Cavalry (February 18, 1863); colonel, 2nd North Carolina Cavalry (August 19, to rank from June 23, 1864); brigadier general, CSA (February 23, to rank from February 21, 1865); and commanding Dearing's (old) Brigade, W.H.F. Lee's Division, Cavalry Corps, Army of Northern Virginia (March-April 9, 1865). The regiment, with Roberts as a junior officer, served at New Bern, Fredericksburg, Brandy Station, Gettysburg, and in the Overland Campaign. At Black and Whites on June 23, 1864, the colonel was killed and Roberts succeeded to command the regiment. He served through the Petersburg siege, including distinguished action at Ream's Station. When General Dearing was assigned to a different brigade in March 1865, Roberts, who had recently been promoted, was transferred to replace him. At Five Forks his command, only one regiment and a battalion, was decimated and he surrendered with the fragments at Appomattox a week later. After the war he served as a legislator in his native North Carolina and was state auditor for eight years. (Freeman, Douglas S., *Lee's Lieutenants*)

ROBERTSON, Beverly Holcombe (1826-1910)

Somehow Beverly H. Robertson never fit into the cavalry command of Jeb Stuart, having irritated that officer as early as October 1861. A West Pointer (1849), he had been dismissed as a captain, 5th Cavalry (late 2nd Dragoons), on August 8, 1861, for having accepted an appointment from the Confederate War Department. His Southern assignments included: captain and assistant adjutant general (1861); colonel, 4th Virginia Cavalry

(November 19, 1861); brigadier general, CSA (June 9, 1862); commanding Cavalry Brigade, Valley District, Department of Northern Virginia (June-August 1862); commanding brigade, Cavalry Division, Army of Northern Virginia (August-September 5, 1862); commanding Cavalry Brigade, Department of North Carolina (October 1862-May 1863); commanding brigade, Cavalry Division, Army of Northern Virginia (May-August 1863); commanding 2nd Military District of South Carolina, Department of South Carolina, Georgia and Florida (October 15, 1863-October 17, 1864); commanding 4th Sub-District of South Carolina, District of South Carolina, same department (October 17-late 1864); and also commanding brigade, same department (from July 1864). After initial service under Stuart in northern Virginia and on the Peninsula he was transferred to the command of Ashby's old cavalry in the Valley after the close of the campaign there. He joined Jackson at Cedar Mountain and was at 2nd Bull Run under Stuart. A few days later he was dispatched to organize the cavalry in North Carolina. In May 1863 he rejoined Lee and Stuart with two North Carolina regiments from his new brigade. Left with Lee during Stuart's ride around the Union army in the Gettysburg Campaign, he put in a poor performance, not complying promptly enough with Lee's orders to join him in Pennsylvania. In August he was again transferred out of Stuart's command and spent a year or more commanding a district in South Carolina. There is no record of his service after November 20, 1864. He was in the insurance business in the reunited nation's capital after the war. (Freeman, Douglas S., *Lee's Lieutenants*)

ROBERTSON, Felix Huston (1839-1928)

Starting the Civil War as a staff officer, native Texan Felix H. Robertson transferred to the artillery and finally the cavalry, as a Confederate brigadier general, before his field career was ended by wounds. Appointed to West Point in 1857, he had resigned on January 29, 1861, within months of his planned graduation, to offer his services to the South. His assignments there included: second lieutenant, Artillery (March 9, 1861); captain and assistant adjutant general (October 1861); captain, Robertson's Florida Battery (January 1, 1862); major, Artillery (July 1, 1863); commanding Reserve Artillery, Army of Tennessee (September-November 1863); commanding battalion, Reserve Artillery, Army of Tennessee (November 1863-April 3, 1864); lieutenant colonel, Artillery (January 1864); commanding Artillery, Wheeler's Cavalry Corps, Army of Tennessee (April 3-July 1864); commanding battalion, Artillery, Wheeler's Cavalry Corps, Army of Tennessee (July-August 6, 1864); brigadier general, CSA (July 26, 1864); chief of staff, Wheeler's Cavalry Corps, Army of Tennessee (summer 1864); and commanding brigade, Wheeler's Cavalry Division, Army of Tennessee (fall 1864). He served at Fort Sumter and then as a staff officer with Adley H. Gladden at Pensacola before taking command of an artillery battery which he led at Shiloh and Murfreesboro. After serving in the Tullahoma Campaign he became an artillery field officer. He led a reserve battalion at Chickamauga and Chattanooga and Wheeler's artillery in the early part of the Atlanta Campaign. After a stint as the cavalry chieftain's staff chief he was promoted to brigadier general and

assigned command of a mounted brigade. Opposing Sherman's March to the Sea, he was wounded on November 29, 1864, at Buckhead Creek, Georgia. Removed from active field duty, his nomination as brigadier general was rejected by the Senate on February 29, 1865. However, he was assigned the task of surrendering the city of Macon and was paroled at his highest rank. After the war he returned to his home state and became a practicing attorney. At the time of his death he was the sole surviving Confederate general officer.

ROBERTSON, Jerome Bonaparte (1815-1891)

John B. Hood's successor in command of the famed Texas Brigade, Jerome B. Robertson, was found to be a poor officer. A Kentucky native and physician, he had relocated to Texas in the 1830s where he had gained some military experience in serving the republic and as an Indian fighter. Also active in politics he sat in both houses of the state legislature and in the secession convention. For the Confederacy, his assignments included: captain, 5th Texas (1861); lieutenant colonel, 5th Texas (November 1861); colonel, 5th Texas (June 1, 1862); brigadier general, CSA (November 1, 1862); and commanding Texas Brigade, Hood's Division, in 1st Corps, Army of Northern Virginia (November 6, 1862-February 25 and May-September 9, 1863), in Department of Virginia and North Carolina (February 25-April 1, 1863), in Department of Southern Virginia (April 1-May 1863), in Longstreet's Corps, Army of Tennessee (September 19-October 1863), and in Department of East Tennessee (November 1863-January 26, 1864). He saw early action at West Point, Seven Pines, and in the Seven Days. At 2nd Bull Run he was wounded and at South Mountain he had to be taken from the field after collapsing from exhaustion and the effects of the recent wound. Promoted, he led the Texans at Fredericksburg, in southeastern Virginia, and at Gettysburg where he was slightly wounded. Sent west he fought at Chickamauga but was removed as incompetent by Longstreet after the battle of Wauhatchie. Reinstated by Bragg, he was again relieved after Bean's Station. Never tried, he was sent to command the reserve forces of Texas in June 1864 and finished the war there. After the war he practiced medicine, was a state official, and was in railroading. (Freeman, Douglas S., *Lee's Lieutenants*)

ROBINSON, George Foster (?-?)

For his actions on the bloody Washington night of April 14, 1865, Private George F. Robinson of Company B, 8th Maine, was awarded a gold medal by a joint resolution of Congress in 1871. The Maine native had enlisted on August 15, 1863, and after that time his regiment served on the South Carolina coast, at Bermuda Hundred, Cold Harbor, and in the operations against Petersburg and Richmond. By the night of Lincoln's murder, he had been detailed as a nurse for Secretary of State William H. Seward who had been severely injured in a carriage accident. On that fatal night he opened the door to the secretary's room to find the would-be assassin Lewis Paine who promptly cut him with a knife in the forehead. Recovering, he assisted in grabbing Paine after Paine had inflicted several wounds upon the statesman. But Paine caught Robinson around the neck and then knocked him down with a blow to the head, making good his escape. After receiving his medal Robinson in 1879 became a major and paymaster in the regular army; he had been discharged from the volunteers on May 19, 1865. He finally retired in 1896. (Weichmann, Louis J., *A True History of the Assassination of Abraham Lincoln and of the Conspiracy of 1865*)

ROCHELLE, James Henry (?-?)

In almost two decades in the old navy, James H. Rochelle had seen action in the Mexican War and risen from master to lieutenant before he resigned his commission on April 17, 1861, while serving aboard the USS *Cumberland*. Finally allowed to leave his vessel before the acceptance of his resignation, he was appointed a lieutenant in the Virginia service on May 2, 1861. On the 29th he was assigned to command the *Teaser*. Transferred to the Confederate Navy on June 6, he commanded the *Jackson* on the Mississippi River until the 27th. He was then appointed executive officer of the *Patrick Henry* back at Richmond, with which he took part in the fight at Hampton Roads in March 1862, and the subsequent defense of Drewry's Bluff. He was shortly given command of the *Nansemond*, a gunboat in the James River which he commanded until September 6, 1863, with the exception of a brief period in command of the blockade runner *Stono* which was destroyed on June 5, 1863. Relinquishing command of the *Nansemond*, Rochelle was next engaged in the assembly of guard boats in Charleston Harbor. From April 24, 1864, to the fall of Charleston he commanded the ironclad *Palmetto State*. He later took part in the defense of Wilmington, North Carolina, and as commander served in the final stages of the war as commandant of cadets and executive officer at the South's naval school. During the retreat of the Treasury Department from Richmond he guarded the specie shipments. For a time after the war he was employed by the Peruvian Hydrographical Society. (Scharf, J. Thomas, *History of the Confederate States Navy*)

RODDEY, Philip Dale (1826-1897)

In his scouting and raiding operations—mostly in northern Alabama—Alabama tailor, sheriff, and riverman Philip D. Roddey proved highly successful and rose to the command of a Confederate cavalry division. His assignments included: captain, Roddey's Alabama Cavalry Company (spring 1861); colonel, 4th (Roddey's) Alabama Cavalry (October 1, 1862); commanding brigade, 2nd Division, Cavalry Corps, Department of Mississippi and East Louisiana (January-February 1863); commanding brigade, Martin's Division, Cavalry Corps, Department of Mississippi and East Louisiana (February-April 1863); commanding District of Northern Alabama, Department of Tennessee (July 1863); brigadier general, CSA (August 3, 1863); commanding cavalry brigade, Army of Tennessee (August 1863); commanding brigade, Martin's Division, Wheeler's Cavalry Corps, Army of Tennessee (September 1863); commanding cavalry brigade, Army of Tennessee

(October 1863-July 1864); commanding cavalry division, Department of Alabama, Mississippi and East Louisiana (July 1864); and commanding District of North Alabama (also called Roddey's Brigade), Department of Alabama, Mississippi and East Louisiana (September 24, 1864-May 4, 1865). He served as Bragg's escort at Shiloh and then led forces in northern Alabama where he raised several regiments. Sometimes cooperating with larger forces in Georgia, Tennessee, and Mississippi, he usually operated independently in his home region. He did however fight at Tupelo. His command was engaged in the unsuccessful resistance to Wilson's raid through Alabama in the final days of the war. He was later a New York City businessman.

RODES, Robert Emmett (1829-1864)

Distinguishing himself early in the war, Virginian Robert E. Rodes had risen to be the senior division commander in Stonewall's old 2nd Corps by the time of his death at 3rd Winchester. A Virginia Military Institute student and professor, Rodes had been a railroad engineer at the commencement of the war. At the head of the Warrior Guards, he joined the Southern war effort. His assignments included: captain, Company H, 5th Alabama (May 1861); colonel, 5th Alabama (May 11, 1861); brigadier general, CSA (October 21, 1861); commanding Ewell's (old) Brigade, Van Dorn's-D.H. Hill's Division (in Potomac District until March), Department of Northern Virginia (October 22, 1861-May 31 and June 1862); commanding brigade, D.H. Hill's Division (in 2nd Corps from September), Army of Northern Virginia (ca. August 1862-January 14, 1863); commanding the division (January 14-May 2 and May 3, 1863-June 13, 1864); major general, CSA (May 7, 1863); temporarily commanding the corps (May 2, 1863); and commanding division, Valley District, Department of Northern Virginia (June 13-September 19, 1864). Basically not engaged at 1st Bull Run, Rodes was promoted to brigade command three months later and led the unit at Yorktown and Williamsburg. At Seven Pines the brigadier led his men in a series of attacks and continued at their head even though himself wounded. He relinquished command that evening but was soon back on duty and fought at Gaines' Mill in the Seven Days. He was still suffering from his wound and had to again give up his post before the fight at Malvern Hill. Next action for Rodes came at South Mountain and Antietam where he was slightly injured. The brigade was not directly engaged at Fredericksburg but the next month he replaced Hill in charge of the division when that officer was sent to North Carolina. At Chancellorsville Rodes earned his promotion to major general and briefly led the corps on the evening of May 2, following the wounding of Generals Jackson and A.P. Hill. Heavily engaged on the first day at Gettysburg, he went on to serve at Kelly's Ford, the Wilderness, Spotsylvania, and Cold Harbor. Accompanying Early to the Valley, he was at Monocacy, in the suburbs of Washington, and at 2nd Kernstown. In covering the Confederate withdrawal at 3rd Winchester he was hit by a shell fragment. He was dead in minutes. (Freeman, Douglas S., *Lee's Lieutenants*)

ROGERS, William P. (1817-1862)

The colonel of the 2nd Texas, William Rogers, entered the service of the Confederacy as lieutenant colonel of the 2nd in October 1861 and served initially in his home state. The regiment left Houston on March 12 and arrived at Corinth, Mississippi, on April 1, 1862, in time to participate in the Confederate successes on the first day at Shiloh. On the second day he led the regiment while Colonel J.C. Moore commanded an informal brigade. After the ultimate defeat, the rebels retired to and were eventually driven out of their base at Corinth. About May 26, 1862, Rogers became colonel when Moore was promoted brigadier general. During the September fight at Iuka, Rogers led his men in skirmishing, away from the battlefield, to prevent a Union column from aiding the forces in the main battle. At Corinth, after the Confederates had driven the Union forces back to the outskirts of town on the first day, Rogers led the regiment in an assault on Battery Robinett. Just as his command entered the work, and he had grabbed a Union flag, an enemy flanking column appeared. In the resulting volley, Rogers fell dead with 11 wounds.

RONALD, Charles A. (1827-1898)

A Virginia lawyer and Mexican War veteran, Charles A. Ronald entered the Confederate army as soon as his state seceded and rose to the command of one of the regiments of the prestigious Stonewall Brigade. His assignments included: captain, Company E, 4th Virginia (April 18, 1861); colonel, 4th Virginia (April 23, 1862); and commanding Stonewall Brigade, Jackson's (old) Division, Jackson's Corps, Army of Northern Virginia (August 7-8 and 9, 1862). Leading his company, the Montgomery Highlanders, he fought at 1st Bull Run and in the early stages of the Shenandoah Valley Campaign of 1862 before being promoted to regimental command upon the spring reorganization of the unit. He then commanded the 4th through the rest of the current campaign and in the Seven Days battles around Richmond. Taking part in the campaign against Union General Pope, he was in temporary command of the brigade at Cedar Mountain where his men broke in the face of the enemy. Missing the remainder of the campaign and the invasion of Maryland, Ronald was severely wounded in the thigh by a piece of shell in a skirmish at Kearneysville, West Virginia, on October 16, 1862. The wound and complications forced his resignation on September 11, 1863. With the Confederacy about to collapse in March 1865, he petitioned the War Department to be recommissioned at his old grade. It was too late for any action to be taken. (Robertson, James I., Jr., *The Stonewall Brigade*)

ROSS, John (1790-1866)

Although only one-eighth Cherokee, John Ross was the principal chief of the tribe both before and after its forced transplantation from Georgia to what is now Oklahoma. A well-educated planter, he dreamed of statehood for the Cherokee Nation under the U.S. Constitution. He was able to maintain a state of neutrality at the outbreak of the Civil War

Cherokee chief John Ross switched sides in the midst of the Civil War. (SI)

but after the Confederate victory at Wilson's Creek, the pressure became too great and he entered into an alliance with the Confederacy. However, much of the tribe refused to agree to the treaty and joined with the Upper Creeks under Opothleyohola in a flight to Union-occupied Kansas. Ross took part in the bloody pursuit. He also took part in the battle of Pea Ridge in March 1862. In June 1862 a Union force of loyal Indians and whites invaded the Cherokee country and Ross gave up without a fight, with many of his people switching sides to join with the Union. The split in the nation widened as Colonel Stand Watie's regiment remained with the Confederacy and eventually burned Ross' home in retaliation for his defection. Ross died a year after the war ended, while on a mission to Washington. (Eaton, Rachel C., *John Ross and the Cherokee Indians*)

ROSS, Leonard Fulton (1823-1901)

Financially ruined by his service as a Confederate brigadier general, Iowa native and noted Indian fighter Lawrence S. Ross returned to his adopted Texas where he became one of the state's most popular private citizens. Raised on the Texas frontier he had fought against the Comanches, killing chief Peta Necona, and becoming a captain in the Texas Rangers. His Civil War assignments included: private, 6th Texas Cavalry (1861); major, 6th Texas Cavalry (September 1861); colonel, 6th Texas Cavalry (May 14, 1862); commanding brigade, Jackson's Cavalry Division, Department of Mississippi and East Louisiana (September 1863-May 1864); brigadier general, CSA (December 21, 1863); commanding brigade, Jackson's Cavalry Division, Polk's (Army of Mississippi)-Stewart's Corps, Army of Tennessee (May-July 26, 1864); commanding brigade, Jackson's Cavalry Division, Army of Tennessee (July 26-31, 1864 and August 1864-February 13, 1865); and commanding brigade, Jackson's Division, Forrest's Cavalry Corps, Department of Alabama, Mississippi and East Louisiana (February 13-May 4, 1865). He led his regiment dismounted at Corinth before it was reconverted into cavalry. After taking part in the efforts to relieve the pressure on Vicksburg he was promoted to brigadier general and led his brigade through the Atlanta and Franklin-Nashville campaigns. In the final months of the war he served under Nathan Bedford Forrest. He was subsequently a farmer, sheriff, state legislator, governor, and president of Texas A. & M. (Benner, Judith Ann, *Sul Ross: Soldier, Statesman, Educator*)

ROSSER, Thomas Lafayette (1836-1910)

Resigning from the United States Military Academy on April 22, 1861, only two weeks before graduation, Thomas L. Rosser was nonetheless able to don the stars of a general in both the Confederate and U.S. armies. A native of Virginia and a former resident of Texas, he joined the Confederacy where his assignments included: first lieutenant, Washington (La.) Artillery Battalion (May 1861); captain, Washington (La.) Artillery Battalion (summer 1861); lieutenant colonel, Artillery (June 1862); colonel, 5th Virginia Cavalry (ca. June 25, 1862); brigadier general, CSA (September 28, 1863); commanding Laurel Brigade, Hampton's-Butler's Division, Cavalry Corps, Army of Northern Virginia (October 1863-October 5, 1864); commanding same brigade, F. Lee's Division, Army of the Valley District, Department of Northern Virginia (October 1864); commanding the division (October 1864-January 1865); major general, CSA (November 1, 1864); and commanding his own division, in the Valley District (January-March 1865) and in the Army of Northern Virginia (March-May 2, 1865). Serving in the artillery initially as an instructor, he commanded a battery at Blackburn's Ford, 1st Bull Run, and Yorktown. Transferred to the cavalry, he commanded a regiment at the Seven Days (wounded at Mechanicsville), 2nd Bull Run, South Mountain, Antietam, Kelly's Ford (wounded), Chancellorsville, and Gettysburg. Promoted to brigade command, he fought in the campaign from the Rapidan to the James, before being sent to the Shenandoah Valley in the fall of 1864. Here he quickly became known as the "Saviour of the Valley." However, he was bested by his old classmate and friend, George Custer, at Woodstock. He later fought at Cedar Creek in temporary divisional command. In the next few months Rosser led three successful raids into West Virginia. Returning to the Petersburg front in March 1865 he was hosting a shad-bake for Pickett and Fitzhugh Lee when their lines were broken at Five Forks. Retreating with the army, he fought his way out with much of his command but was himself captured a month later. Active in farming and railroading after the war, he again donned a blue uniform as a brigadier general for the Spanish-American War and for a time commanded a training camp on the old battlefield of Chickamauga. (Bushong, Millard K., *Fightin' Tom Rosser, C.S.A.*)

RUCKER, Edmund Winchester (1835-?)

A self-educated surveyor and engineer, Edmund W. Rucker started his Confederate service in that field before transferring to the cavalry. His assignments included: private and second lieutenant, Pickett's (Tenn.) Company Sappers and Miners (May 1861); captain, Stewart Invincibles (Tenn.) Heavy Artillery Company (fall 1861); captain, Company E, 1st Tennessee Heavy Artillery (May 10, 1862); major, 16th Tennessee Cavalry Battalion (October 1862); colonel, Cavalry (February 1863); colonel, Rucker's Legion (ca. June 1, 1863); and commanding in Forrest's Cavalry Corps, Department of Alabama, Mississippi and East Louisiana: 6th Brigade, Buford's Division (spring 1864); 6th Brigade, Chalmers' Division (June-July 14, 1864); and 1st Brigade, Chalmer's Division (September 1864-February 13, 1865). After serving in the engineers at Columbus, Kentucky, he was given command of a group of Illinoisans who wanted to join the Confederacy. Serving as heavy artillery, he commanded them at Island #10 and escaped with part of his unit upon the fall of the place. After some service at Fort Pillow, he was transferred to the cavalry in East Tennessee and was assigned to rounding up conscripts, a duty which he detested. He also took part in Pegram's Kentucky raid. He led a field organization of the 12th and 16th Cavalry Battalions, known as Rucker's Legion, from June 1863 to February 1864, including fighting at Chickamauga. At Forrest's request he was transferred to Mississippi and given command of a brigade, which he led at Brice's Crossroads and Tupelo until wounded. Returning to duty, he was given command of another brigade, causing great dissatisfaction among the regimental commanders. One of them, James J. Neely, was cashiered for disobedience of orders. With Chalmers' Division, he was temporarily assigned to duty with the Army of Tennessee and fought at Nashville. In the February 1865 reorganization of Forrest's cavalry, Rucker lost his brigade.

RUFF, Solon Zackery (1837-1863)

A graduate and former faculty member of the Georgia Military Institute, Solon Z. Ruff had a promising career in the Confederate army until he was cut down in the disastrous assault on Fort Sanders at Knoxville. His assignments included: lieutenant colonel, 18th Georgia (April 25, 1861); colonel, 18th Georgia (fall 1863, to rank from January 17, 1863); and commanding Wofford's Brigade, McLaws' Division, Longstreet's Corps, Department of East Tennessee (early November-November 29, 1863). Initially assigned to the Texas Brigade, Ruff and the 18th saw action at Seven Pines, in the Seven Days, 2nd Bull Run, and Antietam. In all but the first-named battle Ruff was in command of the regiment. In the fall of 1862 the 18th was transferred to Cobb's, later Wofford's, Brigade and Ruff continued in regimental command at Fredericksburg, in the Suffolk Campaign, and at Gettysburg. The brigade arriving too late, he missed the battle of Chickamauga when Longstreet went west. Shortly after this, Ruff finally received his colonel's commission, backdated to the start of the year. In the Knoxville Campaign he was in temporary command of the brigade until he was killed on November 29, 1863, directing its assault on Fort Sanders.

RUFFIN, Edmund (1794-1865)

Having argued so long and so hard for the establishment of the Confederacy, Edmund Ruffin was unable to bear the thought of living in a reunited nation. Born into the Virginia plantation society, Ruffin had attended William and Mary. Entering the life of a gentleman farmer, he was dissatisfied and became what can best be described as a scientific farmer, the preeminent leader of Virginia agriculture, urging others to follow his system of crop rotation and the use of marl as fertilizer. As editor of the *Farmer's Register* and president of the Virginia Agricultural Society, he was able to foster a recovery of the industry in the Upper South. Retired from farming in 1856, he visited throughout the South and wrote articles for various publications, urging and campaigning for the region's secession and the formation of an independent country. He also wrote *Slavery and Free Labor Described and Compared*. He was present at the hanging of John Brown, whose raid added fuel to his arguments. He also attended three state secession con-

Edmund Ruffin, secession fanatic and suicide. (NA)

ventions and, disgusted with the failure of Virginia to take the final step, went to South Carolina where he was given the honor, as a member of the Palmetto Guards, to fire one of the first shots at Fort Sumter (the 1812 veteran claimed it was the first). At 1st Bull Run it has been alleged that he fired the artillery shot which blocked the Cub Run Bridge, leading to the Union rout and abandonment of much of its equipment. Too old for military service, he retired from the field but continued to write in his diary which he had started in 1856. With the collapse of the South he committed suicide on June 15, 1865, rather than live under the American flag. (Mitchell, Betty L., *Edmund Ruffin: A Biography*)

RUGGLES, Daniel (1810-1897)

Although a Confederate brigadier general, Daniel Ruggles fought in only one major action and appears to have displeased his superiors to such an extent that he could not get another command. The Massachusetts-born West Pointer (1833) had served in the Seminole War with the infantry and won two brevets in Mexico. Marriage into a Virginia family linked him with the South and he resigned as a captain in the 5th Infantry on May 7, 1861. His Confederate assignments included: brigadier general, Virginia Volunteers (April 1861); commanding Department of Fredericksburg (April 22-June 5, 1861); brigadier general, CSA (August 9, 1861); commanding District of North Alabama, Department of Alabama and West Florida (February 23-ca. February 1862); commanding 1st Corps, 2nd Grand Division, Army of the Mississippi (March 5-29, 1862); commanding 1st Division, 2nd Corps, Army of the Mississippi (March 29-April 1862); commanding 1st District, Department of Southern Mississippi and East Louisiana (June 26-July 2, 1862); and temporarily commanding District of Mississippi, Department #2 (September 5-October 3, 1862). As a Virginia officer he commanded along the Rappahannock in the early months of the war before being named a Confederate brigadier general. Ordered to New Orleans, he proved too ill for a time to command troops. Eventually he commanded a brigade at Shiloh where he is credited with gathering a large number of guns to fire on the Union position at the Hornet's Nest. However, he lost that command the same month and then held minor district-level commands. In the final days of the Confederacy he was appointed commissary general of prisoners. He was subsequently a Virginia resident, Texas planter, and member of the West Point board of visitors.

RUSSELL, Alfred A. (?-?)

Although he was not in many of the great battles of the western theater, Alfred A. Russell did see a great deal of action on the fringes of the larger campaigns, on raids and in fighting enemy raids. His Confederate services included: major, 7th Alabama (May 18, 1861); lieutenant colonel, 15th Tennessee Cavalry Battalion (1862); colonel, 4th (Russell's) Alabama Cavalry (November 23, 1862); commanding brigade, Martin's Division, Wheeler's Cavalry Corps, Army of Tennessee (July-fall

1863); and commanding Morgan's Brigade, Martin's Division, Wheeler's Cavalry Corps, Army of Tennessee (December 1863-February 1864). His first regiment was only a 12-months unit, but he did see action with it in the bombardment of Pensacola in October 1861. Following its muster out, he was given command of a cavalry battalion which was soon raised to a regiment. With this unit he took part in Forrest's December 1862 West Tennessee raid. He then fought at Chickamauga and took part in Wheeler's Sequatchie raid. He was with the Army of Tennessee throughout the Atlanta Campaign, after having been with Longstreet in East Tennessee. He took part in the defeat of Stoneman's raid. When Hood invaded Tennessee in the fall of 1864 Russell served in the Tennessee Valley, joining up with General Roddey and later with Forrest. He took part in the unsuccessful defense against Wilson's raid through Alabama and surrendered with Forrest. He survived two wartime wounds.

RUSSELL, Lord John (1792-1878)

The British foreign secretary during the Civil War, Lord Russell was quick to explain that the granting of belligerent status to both sides during the conflict was not to be followed by recognition of the Confederate States. Nevertheless, in retaliation the United States refused to accept the Declaration of Paris on the rights of neutrals in time of war, due to the clause outlawing privateers if private property was not respected. Russell was outraged, since the United States had pushed for neutral's rights ever since the Revolution. In 1862 Russell almost came to the point of offering mediation services to resolve the crisis. His neutrality pleased neither side. He failed to stop the sailing of the vessel which became the Confederate raider *Alabama*, a lack of decision which in 1872 cost Britain £3,000,000 in settlements, but, in contrast, he was also considered rude to the Confederate commissioner Mason when approached on British recognition. After the war he succeeded Palmerston as prime minister. (Walpole, Spencer, *The Life of John Russell*)

RUSSELL, Robert Milton (1826-1894)

A West Pointer (1848) and veteran of two years in the infantry of the old army, Robert M. Russell commanded a Confederate brigade in the early part of the Civil War but commanded only his own regiment for most of the conflict. The native Tennessean held the following positions: colonel, 12th Tennessee (May 1861); commanding 3rd Brigade, 1st Geographical Division, Department #2 (September 7-October 24, 1861); commanding 2nd Brigade, 1st Division, 1st Geographical Division, Department #2 (October 24, 1861-March 5, 1862); commanding 3rd Brigade, 1st Grand Division, Army of the Mississippi, Department #2 (March 5-29, 1862); commanding 1st Brigade, 1st Division, 1st Corps, Army of the Mississippi, Department #2 (March 29-May 1862); colonel, 20th (sometimes called 15th) Tennessee Cavalry (February 5, 1864); and colonel, 19th and 20th Consolidated Tennessee Cavalry (February 13, 1865). He led an infantry brigade at Belmont, where he was among the first engaged, and at Shiloh before he failed to gain reelection at the May 1862 reorganization of the regiment. A year and a half later

he was given command of a cavalry regiment which was formed from various units raised behind enemy lines. Serving under Nathan Bedford Forrest, he saw action at Okolona, Paducah, Fort Pillow, Brice's Crossroads, and Tupelo. Wounded at the latter, he returned to participate in Hood's Tennessee Campaign. After being given command of the consolidated regiment he helped oppose Wilson's raid through Alabama. He was surrendered with Forrest at Gainesville.

RUST, Albert (1818-1870)

Born in Virginia, Arkansas Congressman Albert Rust was a reluctant secessionist when he resigned his seat to join his state. With the admission of Arkansas to the Confederacy he was named as a representative to the Provisional Congress, where he served on the Postal Affairs Committee through February 17, 1862. However, in the spring and early summer of 1861 Rust raised the 3rd Arkansas and was named its colonel on July 5, 1861. Sent to western Virginia, Rust's regiment was assigned to General H.R. Jackson's Brigade in General Loring's Army of the Northwest. Taking part in General Lee's Cheat Mountain Campaign, Rust discovered a route to outflank the Union forces. Given command of this movement, which would signal the start of the action, Rust for some reason failed to act and the attack never materialized. Subsequently Rust was commended for his actions during the Romney Campaign and was promoted to brigadier general on March 6, 1862, to rank from two days earlier. Transferred back to Arkansas he was directed on March 13 to gather up scattered Confederate forces and reinforce General Van Dorn. With the organization complete he was given command of the brigade on April 8 and directed later that month to move to Corinth, Mississippi. He commanded this brigade as part of Jones' Division, Army of the West (April 29-May 27, 1862), before being ordered back to the Trans-Mississippi District. His later commands included: 4th Brigade, Breckinridge's-Lovell's Division, District of the Mississippi (September 8-October 1862); commanding brigade, Department of Mississippi and East Louisiana (October 1862-early 1863); and commanding same brigade, District of East Louisiana, Department of Mississippi and East Louisiana (early 1863-April 15, 1863). On October 3 and 4, 1862, he took part in the battle of Corinth. Transferred again to the Trans-Mississippi in April 1863, he was shifted frequently from one post to another. He was ordered to the District of Texas, New Mexico and Arizona on January 19, 1864. By March 16, 1865, the commander of the Trans-Mississippi Department, General E.K. Smith, reported that Rust was "without command and not on duty." It appears that he was removed from duty for unionist sentiments and his criticism of the rebel government. After the war he returned to the U.S. Congress and eventually became a Republican in 1869. He died the next year.

RYAN, Abram Joseph (1838-1886)

A Catholic priest and chaplain in the Confederate army, who lost a brother in battle, became one of the most famous poets of the "Lost Cause." Born in Hagerstown, Maryland, and ordained into the priesthood in 1856, Ryan was a mystical character who appeared and disappeared throughout the conflict. Unreconciled to the collapse of the South, he wrote a series of poems that achieved great popularity throughout the old Confederacy. His works included: "Land without Ruins," "The Sword of Robert E. Lee," "March of the Deathless Dead," and his most famous "The Conquered Banner." About 15 years after the war, he retired to a monastery. Following his death, Southern children contributed to a monument over his grave. (Weaver, Gordon, ed., *Selected Poems of Father Ryan*)

RYAN, Jonathan George (?-?)

Lincoln's assassination sparked a wave of terror which transcended all bounds imposed by the Constitution, and one of its unfortunate victims was Confederate Captain Jonathan Ryan. Canadian-born Ryan was traveling through the South from late 1859 until the Civil War began. The Toronto printer finally caught the war fever and joined an Arkansas regiment in early 1862. Initially he was detailed as a clerk in the medical service but joined his regiment for the battle of Corinth, where he was wounded and captured. He made good his escape while recuperating from his wounds. After serving again with his unit, he was directed to raise a company which served in the Volunteer and Conscript Bureau rounding up draft dodgers. Early in 1864 the company became Company B, 12th Mississippi Cavalry, and Ryan was detailed in charge of a horse depot at Talladega, Alabama. In September he was demoted to second lieutenant in Captain Johnson's Company of special service troops operating along the Mississippi River, often behind Union lines. At the close of the year he was directed to raise a similar company of his own and was restored to the rank of captain. However, he never raised the unit, being on sick leave for most of the remainder of the war. On May 4, 1865, General Richard Taylor surrendered his department, which included Ryan, who was paroled on May 12 upon condition that he not again serve the Confederacy until exchanged. However, Ryan's troubles started with an angry letter to the editor of a Jackson, Mississippi, newspaper praising the assassination of Lincoln. He penned the letter on April 26, 1865, before he was surrendered. In the crazy times following the president's death facts such as these were often ignored. On the basis of an anonymous letter, Ryan was arrested on July 22, 1865, in Memphis, where he was trying to make arrangements to get home to Canada. He was held four months without a trial or even being told why he was being confined, much of the time with ball and chain. Letters from Union officers, stating that Ryan had written the letter to the editor prior to his parole, were of no avail. On November 5, 1865, following a letter to President Johnson and imprisonment in Memphis, Washington, and Vicksburg, Ryan was freed without an explanation of the cause of his incarceration. Becoming a lawyer in Chicago, he petitioned the authorities for 20 years before finding out that it was his letter to the editor that had caused him so much trouble. He never received his personal belongings seized at the time of his arrest. During his imprisonment, the press wondered about the mysterious prisoner, speculating that it was John Surratt. But it was just an unfortunate soldier who was a little too free with his pen.

S

ST. JOHN, Isaac Munroe (1827-1880)

Early in the Civil War it became apparent that the South was desperately lacking in the raw materials to manufacture gunpowder, and therefore Isaac M. St. John was named superintendent of the newly created Niter (soon to be Niter and Mining) Bureau in the Confederate War Department. A native of Georgia, he was raised in New York and studied law but instead took journalism and then civil engineering in Baltimore. His Civil War military assignments included: private, Fort Hill (S.C.) Guards (1861); private, Engineers (1861); captain, Engineers (February 1862); major, Artillery (ca. May 1862); superintendent, Niter (and Mining) Bureau (ca. May 1862-February 16, 1865); lieutenant colonel, Artillery (May 28, 1863); colonel, Artillery (June 15, 1864); brigadier general, CSA (February 16, 1865); and commissary general of subsistence (February 16-April 1865); He first served as an engineering officer under Magruder on the Peninsula. As the bureau's superintendent he oversaw the necessarily improvised methods to produce the required raw materials. After his successful performance in this field he was named to replace the highly unpopular Commissary General Lucius B. Northrop near the end of the war. In this post he was responsible for some major innovations, but they came too late.

SANDERS, Christopher Columbus (1840-1908)

Georgian Christopher Columbus Sanders graduated from the Georgia Military Institute in the spring of 1861 and immediately entered the service of the Confederacy. His assignments included: lieutenant colonel, 24th Georgia (August 30, 1861); commanding Cobb's Brigade, McLaws' Division, Longstreet's Command, Army of Northern Virginia (September 17, 1862); colonel, 24th Georgia (January 9, 1864); and commanding DuBose's Brigade, Kershaw's Division, 1st Corps, Army of Northern Virginia (October-December 1864). As a field-grade officer he saw action at

Yorktown, in the Seven Days, and at South Mountain. At Antietam he was in temporary command of the brigade and directed its actions until forced to leave the field, exhausted. He had been unwell for a time. The regiment then fought at Fredericksburg and Chancellorsville before taking part in the invasion of Pennsylvania. He led the regiment at Gettysburg. Going west, the brigade arrived too late for Chickamauga, and Sanders was not present during the operations against Knoxville. He did, however, participate in the Overland and Petersburg campaigns back in Virginia. After service in the Shenandoah, the 24th returned to the siege lines at Petersburg, with Sanders commanding the brigade during the latter part of 1864. Taking part in the Appomattox retreat, he was captured at Sayler's Creek. Paroled in July 1865, he became active in the banking business after the war.

SANDERS, John Caldwell Calhoun (1840-1864)

A student at the Alabama state university, John Sanders left his classes to join the Confederate army and was elected captain of the Confederate Guards, or Company E, 11th Alabama, on June 11, 1861. Ordered to Virginia the 11th was assigned to Colonel Forney's 5th Brigade, Army of the Shenandoah, on July 21, 1861. At this time most of the army had left for Manassas and was engaged in the battle of 1st Bull Run but the brigade was still in the Valley. Eventually the brigade, now under General C.M. Wilcox, joined Johnston's army. Captain Sanders led his company in its first action at Seven Pines May 31 and June 1, 1862, on the Peninsula. During the Seven Days Battles Sanders saw action at Gaines' Mill and Frayser's Farm where he was wounded. He rejoined his company on August 11, 1862, and assumed command of the regiment as the senior officer present. In this position he saw action at 2nd Bull Run and Antietam where he was again wounded. Having been promoted to major in the late summer he was promoted to colonel of his regiment to date from September 11, 1862, shortly after Antietam. Sanders led his regiment at Fredericksburg, Chancellorsville, and Gettysburg where on the second day he was severely wounded. With General Wilcox promoted to command a division, Sanders took over the brigade on August 15, 1863. He commanded the brigade in R.H. Anderson's Division, A.P. Hill's Corps, Army of Northern Virginia, in the Bristoe and Mine Run campaigns. In early 1864, he resumed command of his regiment when General Perrin was assigned to command of the brigade. Sanders saw action at the Wilderness and Spotsylvania where Perrin was killed. Sanders again took command and was promoted brigadier general on a temporary basis from May 31, 1864. He commanded the brigade at Cold Harbor and Petersburg, including the fight at the Crater. On August 21, 1864, Sanders was killed in the battle of Globe Tavern, near Petersburg. (Freeman, Douglas S., *Lee's Lieutenants*)

SAULSBURY, Gove (1815-1881)

The elevation of Democrat Gove Saulsbury to the Delaware governorship upon the death of his Republican predecessor doomed each of the Civil War-era constitutional amendments to defeat in the border slave state. A Delaware doctor for 20 years, he was elected as a Democrat to the state senate in 1862 and the next session rose to be its speaker. Under the state constitution, there being no lieutenant governor, he succeeded Unionist William Cannon in the gubernatorial seat upon the latter's death on March 1, 1865. An outspoken critic of Reconstruction, he opposed the amendments abolishing slavery and each of them was defeated by the state legislature. Elected to a full term in 1866, he served until 1871. Although he did not hold further office, he was a delegate to the 1876 and 1880 Democratic conventions. (Conrad, Henry Clay, *History of the State of Delaware*)

SAVAGE, John Houston (1815-1904)

Colonel John H. Savage was able to bluff himself into the single-handed capture of an entire Union company. During the Mexican War he had served as major, 14th Infantry, and lieutenant colonel, 11th Infantry, both of which were regular army regiments raised especially for the war. Entering the Confederate service, he held the following assignments: colonel, 16th Tennessee (June 1861), and commanding Donelson's Brigade, Cheatham's Division, Right Wing, Army of the Mississippi. His regiment was sent to western Virginia in the late summer of 1861 and it was here that Savage made his capture. Accompanied only by a guide on September 21, 1861, he suddenly came upon an enemy company with both parties being greatly surprised. Calling upon them to surrender, he warned that his men would open fire. They gave up to a force that was not there. He then participated in the Cheat Mountain fizzle before the regiment was transferred to South Carolina. After the winter on the coast, the regiment went to northern Mississippi and took part in the defense of Corinth. In command of the brigade, he fought at Munfordville and Perryville during the Kentucky Campaign. Falling back into Tennessee, he resumed command of the 16th which he led at Murfreesboro. He resigned his commission on February 20, 1863. (Head, Thomas A., *Campaigns and Battles of the Sixteenth Tennessee Volunteers*)

SCALES, Alfred Moore (1827-1892)

The Confederate career of Alfred M. Scales seems to march in step with that of William D. Pender, with Scales succeeding Pender in the chain of command and the pair even riding in the same ambulance in the retreat from Gettysburg. Only Scales lived. Prewar he had been a lawyer and state legislator and sat one term in the U.S. House of Representatives. Entering the Southern military as a private, his later assignments included: captain, Company H, 3rd North Carolina Volunteers (May 27, 1861); colonel, 3rd North Carolina Volunteers (October 12, 1861); colonel, 13th North Carolina (designation change on November 14, 1861); commanding Pender's Brigade, A.P. Hill's Division, 2nd Corps, Army of Northern Virginia (December 13, 1862); brigadier general, CSA (June 13, 1863); and commanding Pender's (old) Brigade, Pender's-Wilcox's Division, 3rd Corps, same army (June 20-July 1 and August 1863-February 1865). After service in the Norfolk area, his regiment, formerly Pender's, was transferred to the Peninsula where it saw action at Yorktown, Williamsburg, Seven Pines, and in the Seven Days. At Fredericksburg he succeeded Pender in brigade command for an unspecified period. Returning from a Chancellorsville wound, he was given permanent charge of the brigade but suffered another wound on the first day at Gettysburg. Rejoining his unit, he saw further action in the Overland and Petersburg campaigns but was on sick leave at the time of Lee's surrender. He returned to the legal and political professions, as congressman and governor, and also went into banking. (Freeman, Douglas S., *Lee's Lieutenants*)

SCHARF, John Thomas (1843-1898)

As a midshipman in the Confederate navy, J. Thomas Scharf took part in some of the more daring exploits of the war. A native of Maryland, he left his father's lumber business to enter the Confederate service and apparently served originally in the army. As a naval officer, he took part in the February 1864 raid led by John Taylor Wood which destroyed the USS *Underwriter*. Shortly after that success he served in the failed expedition of Lieutenant George W. Gift to destroy two Union blockaders guarding the mouth of the Appalachicola River. He succeeded Gift in command of the one surviving boat, which was sailed 15 miles to St. George's Island where the crew ate alligators to survive. After his rescue he returned to his previous duty station, the Charleston Naval Station. In December 1864 he served on the *Sampson* on the Savannah River. Near the close of the war he was captured on a mission to Canada. His varied postwar career included the lumber business, law, journalism, and service as an immigration official in New York. Throughout this time he devoted much time to historical writing, mostly on his native state. His works include *History of Maryland* and *History of the Confederate States Navy*.

SCOTT, Dred (ca. 1800-1858)

Although he lost his Supreme Court fight for his freedom from slavery, Dred Scott furthered the movement toward the abolition of the "peculiar institution." Born into slavery in Virginia at about the turn of the century, he had been moved with his owner to Alabama and then Missouri before being sold in 1833 to an army assistant surgeon from Pennsylvania, John Emerson, who took him into the free areas of Illinois, Iowa, and Minnesota before returning to Missouri. Following the doctor's death he twice attempted to purchase his freedom but was refused by the widow. In 1846 Scott launched his legal battle in the Missouri courts, citing his family's travels in free territory as justification for his freedom. The decision of the Supreme Court was finally tendered in 1857. It stated that slaves were not citizens of the United States or Missouri and thus could not sue in the courts, that he was still a slave due to his being returned to Missouri, and that the Missouri Compromise—which prohibited slavery in certain territories—was unconstitutional. The following year Scott and his family achieved their freedom through a private manumission. The freed slave had only a year to live and died before he could realize the impact of his case upon history. The outrage against the decision furthered the cause of the Republicans and contributed to the election of Lincoln in 1860. (Fehrenbacher, Don E., *The Dred Scott Case: Its Significance in American Law & Politics*)

SCOTT, John S. (?-?)

A brigade and district commander during much of the war, John S. Scott never received promotion to brigadier general, perhaps because he earned the displeasure of General Forrest. His assignments for the Confederacy included: colonel, 1st Louisiana Cavalry (May 4, 1861); commanding 3rd Cavalry Brigade, Department of East Tennessee (October 31-December 1862); commanding 2nd Cavalry Brigade, Department of East Tennessee (spring-August 6, 1863); commanding brigade, Pegram's Division, Forrest's Cavalry Corps, Army of Tennessee (August 6-October 1863); and in the Department of Alabama, Mississippi and East Louisiana: commanding District of Southwest Mississippi and East Louisiana (April 5-June 1864); commanding brigade, Adams' Cavalry Division (June-August 1864); commanding Cavalry Brigade, District South of Homochitto (August-October 6, 1864); and commanding brigade, Forrest's Cavalry Corps (early 1865). After service in central Kentucky he served under Forrest in East Tennessee. After the battle of Murfreesboro, Scott led his regiment in Pegram's raid into Kentucky in the spring of 1863. The forces in East Tennessee joined Bragg's army for the Chickamauga Campaign during which Scott commanded the brigade. Sent to Mississippi in early 1864, he commanded a district and later a brigade serving in the southern part of the state and in eastern Louisiana. It was during this time that Forrest expressed displeasure with Scott's performance in controlling deserters and conscripts in his vicinity. He even suggested dismounting the command. In the final days of the war Scott was ordered to join Forrest with his brigade to face Wilson's raid in Alabama and was surrendered with him.

SCOTT, Thomas Moore (1829-1876)

Until severely wounded at Franklin in late 1864, Georgia-born

Louisiana farmer Thomas M. Scott served as a Confederate regimental and brigade commander in some of the most important actions of the western theater. His assignments included: colonel, 12th Louisiana (August 13, 1861); commanding Buford's (old) Brigade, Loring's Division, Department of Alabama, Mississippi and East Louisiana (early March-May 1864); brigadier general, CSA (May 10, 1864); and commanding brigade, Loring's Division, Polk's (Army of the Mississippi)-Stewart's Corps, Army of Tennessee (May-November 20, 1864). His regiment was apparently present at Columbus, Kentucky, during the battle of Belmont but did not cross the river. He fought at Island #10 and then was stationed for a time at Fort Pillow and Port Hudson. During the Vicksburg Campaign he served in Loring's division and was cut off with it after the fight at Champion Hill. Joining Joseph E. Johnston's forces trying to lift the siege against the river city, he was later engaged in the Jackson and Meridian campaigns. He led a brigade, as a newly appointed brigadier general, in the Atlanta Campaign and then accompanied Hood into middle Tennessee. There he was severely wounded by a shell at Franklin and held no further field positions. He returned to planting in Louisiana.

SCOTT, William Campbell (1809-1865)

A prominent Virginia lawyer and state legislator, William C. Scott was already active in the state militia by the outbreak of the Civil War. His assignments for the South included: colonel, 112th Virginia Militia (early 1861); brigadier general, Virginia Militia (early 1861); colonel, 44th Virginia (June 14, 1861); commanding 2nd Brigade, Army of the Northwest (early May-May 17, 1862); and commanding 2nd Brigade, Ewell's Division, Valley District, Department of Northern Virginia (May 17-June 4 and June 8-9, 1862). He saw action at Rich Mountain and in the Cheat Mountain and Romney campaigns, and he commanded a brigade at McDowell and in the Shenandoah Valley Campaign. Relieved of command of the brigade for four days during the latter, he was again in charge at the campaign's close. With his health failing, he was apparently absent from any further actions with the regiment. On January 14, 1863, he resigned. Returning home to Powhatan County, he died on the day Lee surrendered.

SCURRY, William Read (1821-1864)

A highly competent Confederate officer, as shown by his performance at Glorieta Pass, the Tennessee-born Mexican War veteran William R. Scurry gave his life for the South later in the Civil War. During the earlier part of the war he had fought as a private in the 2nd Texas Mounted Volunteers. In the late 1850s he had been a boundary commissioner and upon the outbreak of the Civil War joined the Confederate army. His assignments included: lieutenant colonel, 4th Texas Cavalry (1861); brigadier general, CSA (September 12, 1862); commanding Eastern Sub-District of Texas, District of Texas, New Mexico and Arizona, Trans-Mississippi Department (February 13-June 10, and ca. August-September 17, 1863); and commanding brigade, 1st (Walker's) Division, District of West Louisiana, Trans-Mississippi Department (fall 1863-April 30, 1864).

Accompanying Henry H. Sibley into the New Mexico-Arizona area, he fought at Valverde. At Glorieta pass he directed the forces in the pass itself—and was highly successful. Only the capture and destruction of the Confederate supply train by a Union flanking column under John M. Chivington forced the Southerners to withdraw from the territory. The balance of Scurry's service came in the Trans-Mississippi West. He fought at Galveston and in the Red River Campaign. Moving north to face Steele's drive on Camden, Arkansas, he was mortally wounded at Jenkins' Ferry and bled to death on the field.

SEARS, Claudius Wistar (1817-1891)

Marriage into a Texas family overrode the northern birth and military academy appointment of Claudius W. Sears and led him to a Confederate brigadier generalship. The Massachusetts-born West Pointer (1841) had received his appointment from New York. He served only a year before resigning as a second lieutenant in the 8th Infantry. A college professor before the war, he was a school president in 1861 when he offered his military services to the Confederacy. His assignments included: captain, Company G, 17th Mississippi (spring 1861); colonel, 46th Mississippi (December 11, 1862); brigadier general, CSA (March 1, 1864); and commanding brigade, French's Division, Polk's (Army of Mississippi)-Stewart's Corps, Army of Tennessee (May-December 15, 1864). Named to command the Magnolia Guards early in the war, he became part of the 17th Mississippi. Before his promotion to colonel of a new regiment this unit fought at 1st Bull Run, Ball's Bluff, Yorktown, Seven Pines, in the Seven Days, and at Antietam. His new regiment fought at Chickasaw Bayou against Sherman in the defense of Vicksburg, and Sears was captured while commanding at Vicksburg. Paroled on the day of the surrender, he was eventually exchanged. Despite illness, he served through most of the Atlanta Campaign. Heading north, he fought at Allatoona, Franklin and Nashville. In the latter he was wounded and a few days later was taken captive. Having lost a leg, he was paroled until June 23, 1865. He served as a college professor until two years before his death.

SEDDON, James Alexander (1815-1880)

The longest-lasting of the Confederate secretaries of war, James A. Seddon was nonetheless highly criticized by both the Confederate Congress and the public for his unquestioning support of Jefferson Davis. A native Virginia lawyer, he had served two nonconsecutive terms in the U.S. Congress. He came out of retirement during the secession winter to attend the Washington Peace Conference. After one unsuccessful bid for a seat in the Provisional Confederate Congress, he was seated on July 20, 1861, but was given no committee assignments. He did not seek reelection but later changed his mind and ran for a vacant seat in April 1862, finishing third. On November 21, 1862, Jefferson Davis, seeking a loyal supporter for his cabinet, appointed Seddon secretary of war in place of the resigned George W. Randolph. Once in office he was virtually a total yes-man—and was condemned for it. His complicity in the removal of Joseph E. Johnston in front of Atlanta lowered his stock in the eyes of the public as well as the already hostile Congress. Faced with a demand from the Virginia congressional delegation for a cabinet reshuffle, Davis accepted Seddon's resignation on February 6, 1865, but not without a harsh condemnation of the legislative branch. Following a brief internment at the end of the war, Seddon returned to his retirement.

SEIBELS, Emmett (1821-1899)

One in the seemingly endless stream of duels between Confederate officers was that between Major Emmett Seibels and Captain Elbert Bland of the 7th South Carolina. Seibels had been a lawyer before the war and his later military assignments included: major, 7th South Carolina (April 15, 1861) and lieutenant colonel, 7th South Carolina (May 9, 1862). Having enlisted shortly after the firing on Fort Sumter, he took part in the battle of 1st Bull Run. That winter he became embroiled in a dispute with one of the company commanders, Bland. The result was a duel in which neither party was fatally hurt. It is, however, interesting to note that in the elections held upon the May 1862 reorganization of the regiment, while Bland won a lieutenant colonelcy, Seibels failed in his attempt to become a colonel. After the duel both officers went on to fight at the battle of Williamsburg. Displaced in the elections, Seibels tried for the rest of the war to gain another appointment but failed. He did serve for a while as a volunteer aide to General M.C. Butler.

SEMMES, Paul Jones (1815-1863)

For a decade and a half Georgia banker and plantation owner Paul J. Semmes had been an officer in the militia of Columbus, Georgia. Upon the outbreak of the Civil War he put this experience to use for the confederacy. His assignments included: colonel, 2nd Georgia (ca. June 1, 1861); brigadier general, CSA (to rank from March 11, 1862); commanding McLaws' (old) Brigade, McLaws' Division, Magruder's Command, Department of Northern Virginia (early May-July 1862); and commanding brigade, McLaws' Division, 1st Corps, Army of Northern Virginia (July 1862-July 2, 1863). After serving at Yorktown, he was given command of a brigade which he was to command for the remainder of his career. He led it at Williamsburg and in the Seven Days on the Peninsula. In the Maryland Campaign he fought at Crampton's Gap on South Mountain and at Antietam. He was on Marye's Heights at Fredericksburg and at Salem Church at Chancellorsville. In the Confederate attack on the Union left on the second day at Gettysburg he fell mortally wounded. Carried back with the retreating army, he died on the 10th at Martinsburg, in what had officially become West Virginia three weeks earlier. (Freeman, Douglas S., *Lee's Lieutenants*)

SEMMES, Raphael (1809-1877)

The second-ranking Confederate naval officer, Marylander Raphael Semmes, along with his most famous command, CSS *Alabama*, became the most renowned of the Southern commerce raiders. Having entered the Old Navy in 1826, Semmes had risen to the rank of commander by the time of the secession crisis. In between assignments he had also studied law and been admitted to the bar in 1834. His Mexican War command, the brig *Somers*, sank off Vera Cruz, and Semmes and 38 of his crew went down with her. Semmes and two others were rescued by the *Somers'* sole lifeboat, returning after landing its first load. A court of inquiry praised Semmes' actions during the crisis. He later served as a naval observer/adviser on the march to Mexico City. In the interwar period Semmes frequently made use of his legal skills in defending other officers against the "system." Having come to consider Mobile his home, Semmes resigned his commission on February 15, 1861, just over a month after Alabama's secession. Offering his services to Jefferson Davis, he was sent north to obtain naval supplies before the outbreak of actual hostilities. After much success he returned south and on April 4, 1861, found a commission as commander, CSN, awaiting him in Montgomery. For two weeks he served as chief of the Lighthouse Bureau, before gaining permission to convert a former packet steamer, the *Havana*, into a commerce raider. This first of the Confederate raiders, renamed the *Sumter*, hit the open seas on June 30, 1861. Three days later Semmes made his first capture. After cruising on both sides of the Atlantic and capturing some 18 prizes, the *Sumter*, in desperate need of repairs, was blockaded at Gibraltar by three Union vessels, including the USS *Kearsarge*. Leaving the vessel there (it was sold in December 1862), Semmes started on his return to the Confederacy but was promoted to captain and ordered to England to take command of the *290*, soon to become infamous as the *Alabama*. From September 1862 to June 1864, Semmes sailed his new command from the Atlantic to the China Sea, taking some 69 prizes including the Union gunboat *Hatteras* which he sank in a naval battle in the Gulf of Mexico. Finally, on June 11, 1864, the *Alabama* put into Cherbourg, France, for much-needed repairs. But soon her old nemesis, the *Kearsarge*, set up a blockade outside the harbor. Semmes decided to fight and after an hour's conflict and with his vessel sinking, on June 19 was forced to strike his colors. Picked up by the *Deerhound*, an English yacht, he and several of his officers were feted in England before returning to the Confederacy. At home he was promoted to rear admiral and in February 1865 was given command of the James River Squadron. With the fall of the Confederate capital, he was forced to destroy his vessels and form his men into an infantry unit. He finally surrendered with Johnston's army, signing his parole as rear admiral and brigadier general. He had been appointed to the army grade by Jefferson Davis after he scuttled his fleet, but with the fall of the country it could not be confirmed by the Senate. In December 1865 he was imprisoned for four months while the Union authorities tried to find a way to try him for treason and piracy. Returning to Mobile, he was elected to a judgeship, but the authorities removed him from office. He was also driven from employment in education and journalism. Resuming the practice of law, he later published *Memoirs of Service Afloat, During the War Between the States*. During the periods between his numerous captures, Semmes was noted for passing the time by walking the decks, supervising the crew, and at the same time engaging in an endless battle with his unruly mustache. His crew dubbed him "Old Beeswax." (Roberts, W.A., *Semmes of the Alabama*)

SEMMES, Thomas Jenkins (1824-1899)

The cousin of the famed commander of the CSS *Alabama*, Raphael Semmes, Thomas J. Semmes served the Confederacy as a senator from Louisiana. The native of the nation's capital had practiced law first in Washington and then in New Orleans. He was a one-term state legislator and, as district attorney, prosecuted filibuster William Walker. At the outbreak of the Civil War he was serving as the state's attorney general. Elected to the Confederate Senate, he was admitted on February 19, 1862. In the First Regular Congress he sat on the committees on: Finance; Flag and Seal; and Judiciary. In the next Congress he substituted the Committee on Rules for that on the Flag and Seal. In his support for the war effort he had a mixed record. For example, he supported conscription but opposed the suspension of the writ of habeas corpus and its uncontrolled use. A defender of the president's right to make military appointments, he was part of the Beauregard-bloc but a critic of Joseph E. Johnston. In a pragmatic manner, he favored the recruiting of slaves to preserve a part of the "peculiar institution." After the war he retired to private practice and legal instruction. Except for his leadership role in the 1879 constitutional convention he withdrew from the political arena.

SEYMOUR, Isaac Gurdon (1804-1862)

Receiving his first chance to direct a brigade in combat, Isaac G. Seymour lost his life after only one day in temporary command. A one-time mayor of Macon, Georgia, he had served in the early Indian wars and in Mexico as a lieutenant colonel of Georgia volunteers. At the outbreak of the Civil War he was editing the *New Orleans Bulletin*. His Confederate assignments included: colonel, 6th Louisiana (June 4, 1861); and commanding Taylor's Brigade, Ewell's Division, Jackson's Command, Army of Northern Virginia (June 26-27, 1862). He led his regiment at 1st Bull Run and in Jackson's Valley Campaign. Moving to the defense of Richmond, he took over brigade command when General Richard Taylor became too ill to remain on duty the day before the battle of Gaines' Mill. In the struggle the next day, Seymour was shot and killed. The demoralized Louisiana brigade broke shortly afterwards. The publication of an obituary for Seymour in occupied New Orleans angered General Benjamin F. Butler who sent Seymour's son to jail.

SHADOW

See: *Linebaugh, John H.*

SHANKS, John T. (1832-?)

Fighting in Arkansas and Tennessee and rising from private to captain, Texas-born bookkeeper John Shanks lost his company when it was consolidated with another. Joining John Hunt Morgan's Confederate cavalry as a scout in 1863, Shanks was captured at Buffington Island, Ohio, on July 19, 1863, during Morgan's famous Indiana and Ohio raid. Confined at Camp Douglas, Shanks became a spokesman for the enlisted prisoners and, because of his clerical abilities, became a clerk in the office of the commandant, Colonel Benjamin J. Sweet. Shanks' ingratiation with the commandant made him the natural choice to work under cover when word was received that rebel agents planned to attack the camp on November 8, 1864, free the prisoners, and capture Chicago. After a staged escape, Shanks was to contact the conspirators and identify them to Sweet. Not totally trusted, he was followed everywhere. With the conspiracy broken up, Shanks was the key witness in convicting one of the conspirators, Colonel George St. Leger Grenfell, a British soldier-of-fortune. After the trial, Shanks received a commission on April 6, 1865, as captain, Company I, 6th United States Volunteers, a regiment composed of ex-prisoners, which he commanded on the plains until October 11, 1866. (Brown, D. Alexander, *Galvanized Yankees*)

SHANNON, Alexander May (?-?)

When John Bell Hood moved the Army of Tennessee off to middle Tennessee in late 1864 and let Sherman's army march through Georgia, there was not much to stop the enemy. But one force, under Alexander M. Shannon, was active on the fringes of Sherman's army. Shannon was the captain of Company C, 8th Texas Cavalry. While his regiment had participated in such battles as Shiloh, Perryville, Murfreesboro, Chickamauga, and Atlanta, he had become known for his activities behind enemy lines, often in Union uniform. During the March to the Sea he led a detachment of 30 men in gathering information on troop movements. However, they also became involved in attacks on stragglers and foraging parties. Following the fall of Savannah Shannon served through the Carolinas Campaign, reporting to Joe Wheeler. After the war he was a business partner of John B. Hood.

SHARP, Jacob Hunter (1833-1907)

Succeeding the wounded William F. Tucker in command of a brigade during the Atlanta Campaign, Alabamian lawyer Jacob H. Sharp was promoted to brigadier general and commanded the unit for the balance of the war. His assignments included: private, 1st (Blythe's) Mississippi Battalion (early 1861); captain, 44th (Blythe's) Mississippi (1861); colonel, 44th Mississippi (1863); commanding Anderson's Brigade, Hindman's Division, Polk's Corps, Army of Tennessee (September 20, 1863); commanding Tucker's (old) Brigade, Hindman's-Johnson's Division, Hood's-Lee's Corps, Army of Tennessee (May 14, 1864-March 1865); brigadier general, CSA (July 26, 1864); and commanding brigade, Hill's Division, Lee's Corps, Army of Tennessee (April 9-26, 1865). He fought as a company commander at Shiloh and in the campaigns of Perryville, Murfreesboro, and Tullahoma. Promoted to colonel, he took command of the brigade when J. Patton Anderson took over the division upon the wounding of Thomas C. Hindman at Chickamauga. His regiment fought at Chattanooga and then embarked upon the Atlanta Campaign. When Tucker was

wounded at Resaca, Sharp took command of the brigade and was promoted to brigadier general and its permanent command two months later. Accompanying Hood into middle Tennessee, he fought at Franklin and Nashville. He later commanded a brigade during parts of the Carolinas Campaign. Resuming his law practice, he was active in restoring white government to Mississippi and engaged in journalism.

SHEADS, Carrie (?-?)

When the great Civil War armies invaded the peaceful Adams County countryside in the summer of 1863 the principal of the young ladies' Oakridge Seminary, Carrie Sheads, found herself at the head of a corps of nurses. During the first day of the battle of Gettysburg the school was taken over by the Union forces as a field hospital. The principal, staff, and students were soon at work tending the wounded, but the Union forces were quickly forced to fall back to the south and east of town. The occupying Confederate troops allowed the nurses' operations to continue until the close of the battle, and the Southern withdrawal allowed the Union army to retake control. Shortly after the battle the care of the wounded was transferred to the appropriate authorities and the school began to pick up the pieces.

SHEATS, Charles Christopher (1839-1904)

The idea of secession was not at all popular in some of the mountainous regions of the Confederacy, and in one such area, the county of Winston in Alabama, the opposition, under the leadership of Charles Sheats, was especially vehement. Sheats, a school teacher before the war, had been elected as a "cooperationist," or Unionist, delegate to the state secession convention. Refusing all attempts at coercion in Montgomery, he and two other delegates refused to sign the Ordinance of Secession. He was promptly seized by an angered mob and thrown in jail, where he remained until the close of the convention. Returning home, he was greeted as a hero and that summer was elected to the state legislature where he voted against war measures and tried to concentrate on financial affairs, realizing that he alone could not stop the war. Then in early April 1862 he was the principal organizier of a Unionist gathering of mountaineers at Bill Looney's Tavern back in Winston. Over 2,500 were present, including some from other states. Although the county did not actually secede from the state, it did reserve that right—since Alabama felt it could secede from the Union. The county was dubbed "The Free State of Winston" by one secessionist. Many Winston men went to the Union Army and others resisted officers who tried to enforce the Confederate draft. In September the area was occupied by Southern troops, and Sheats was ordered to Montgomery where he was imprisoned until sent into the Union lines in 1864. During this time the area became a haven for rebel deserters, and Winston had a vicious civil war of its own. After the war Sheats was a delegate to the 1865 state constitutional convention, editor of *The North Alabamian*, a presidential elector for Grant, U.S. consul in Denmark, one-term U.S. congressman, and federal appointee.

SHEFFIELD, James Lawrence (1819-1892)

While many Confederate officers sacrificed their blood for the infant nation, James L. Sheffield also donated a sizable fortune to the cause. A sheriff and state legislator in his native Alabama before the war, he had served in the secession convention. Deciding to take the field, he raised the 48th Alabama, equipping it himself at a cost of $60,000. He was commissioned colonel on May 13, 1862. During the war he held the following brigade commands: Taliaferro's Brigade, Jackson's (old) Division, Jackson's Command, Army of Northern Virginia (September 17, 1862); Law's Brigade, Hood's Division, 1st Corps, Army of Northern Virginia (July 2-September 1863); and Law's Brigade, Hood's Division, Longstreet's Corps, Army of Tennessee (September 20-October 1863). In his first action at Cedar Mountain he was wounded. He recovered in time to fight later that month at 2nd Bull Run. At Antietam he succeeded to brigade command and held it until the end of the battle. After serving with Longstreet in southeastern Virginia, he fought at Gettysburg on Little Round Top, again taking over command of the brigade. Accompanying Longstreet's Corps to the West, he fought at Chickamauga and Knoxville. At the former he was for the last time in brigade command. Missing the battle of the Wilderness, he resigned his commission on May 31, 1864.

SHELBY, Joseph Orville (1830-1897)

One of the Confederacy's most effective cavalry leaders, Joseph O. Shelby served entirely in the Trans-Mississippi West. A planter and rope manufacturer, he had had investments in both his native Kentucky and Missouri. During the Bleeding Kansas episode he led a company of Kentuckians on the slavery side. Early in the Civil War he entered the Missouri State Guard and his assignments included: captain, Shelby's Ranger Company, Missouri State Guard (spring 1861); colonel, 5th Missouri Cavalry (1862); commanding brigade, Marmaduke's Cavalry Division, 1st Corps, Trans-Mississippi Department (summer-December 1862); commanding brigade, Marmaduke's Cavalry Division, District of Arkansas, Trans-Mississippi Department (January-July 4, 1863 and late 1863-September 1864); brigadier general, CSA (December 15, 1863); commanding division, Army of Missouri, Trans-Mississippi Department (September 18-September 1864); and commanding 1st (Missouri) Cavalry Brigade, 1st (Missouri) Cavalry Division, Cavalry Corps, Trans-Mississippi Department (September 1864-May 26, 1865). As a company commander he fought at Carthage, Wilson's Creek, and Pea Ridge before being sent back to Missouri to raise a regiment. As a colonel in charge of a brigade in John S. Marmaduke's mounted division, he fought at Prairie Grove and was wounded at Helena. Upon his recovery he was promoted to brigadier general and led a brigade at Jenkins' Ferry. During Price's invasion of Missouri in the late summer and fall of 1864 he led a cavalry division. When the Confederacy's collapse came he refused to surrender and led part of his force to Mexico where they unsuccessfully offered their services to either side. He then returned to his business interests in Missouri. (O'Flaherty, Daniel, *General Jo Shelby, Undefeated Rebel*)

SHELLEY, Charles Miller (1833-1907)

Distinguishing himself in one of the first actions of the Civil War—Blackburn's Ford—Tennessee-born Alabama architect Charles M. Shelley rose to become a Confederate brigadier general. His assignments included: lieutenant, Alabama Militia Artillery (February 1861); captain, 1st Company E, 5th Alabama (May 11, 1861); colonel, 30th Alabama (January 31, 1862); commanding Cumming's (old) Brigade, Stevenson's Divison, Hood's-Lee's Corps, Army of Tennessee (August 31-October 2, 1864); brigadier general, CSA (September 17, 1864); commanding Cantey's Brigade, Walthall's Division, Stewart's Corps, Army of Tennessee (October 2, 1864-April 9, 1865); and commanding brigade, Loring's Division, Stewart's Corps, Army of Tennessee (April 9-26, 1865). After serving in the defenses of Mobile, his company was converted to infantry and dispatched to Virginia. As a captain he was highly commended for his role in repulsing the Union forces at Blackburn's Ford along Bull Run a few days before the main battle. His regiment then fought at 1st Bull Run and Shelley subsequently raised a new regiment which he led in the western theater. He served in the Kentucky Campaign and was captured at Port Gibson at the beginning of the Vicksburg Campaign. Exchanged, he again led his men at Chattanooga and during the Atlanta Campaign, succeeding to command of a brigade at Jonesboro. He led a different brigade as a brigadier general at Franklin and Nashville and in the Carolinas. Following the surrender he was a sheriff, congressman, and treasury official.

SHEPHERD, Haywood (?-1859)

It is certainly ironic that in John Brown's famous raid upon Harpers Ferry, Virginia—to initiate an uprising among Virginia's slave population and put an end to the "peculiar institution" of the South—the first fatality was a free black, Haywood Shepherd. The stationmaster for the Baltimore and Ohio Railroad, he had gone to investigate the gunfire coming from the armory and was cut down in a fusillade of bullets. He died several hours later from his wounds, probably unaware of the cause in which he died.

SHEPPARD, William Ludwell (1833-1912)

Serving in the Confederate artillery, William Sheppard had ample opportunity to produce his sketches of army life. Born in Richmond, Sheppard displayed an early aptitude for art but at first was unable to make it his career. As a sideline to his mercantile business, he designed labels for tobacco products. His talent discovered, he went to New York for artistic training. With the outbreak of the war, he became a second lieutenant in the Richmond Howitzers. His unit fought through all the campaigns of the Army of Northern Virginia, and he depicted life in camp and battle. After the war his sketches appeared in several magazines and he provided illustrations for numerous books. But he considered his masterpiece to be the sculpting of the monument to the Richmond Howitzers which stands in the Confederacy's former capital. In the postwar period he studied in London and Paris and was active in the Richmond Art Club.

He was also a landscape artist and portrait painter. Sheppard remained active in artistic pursuits until the final long illness that claimed his life in 1912.

SHIPP, Scott (1839-1917)

An 1859 graduate of the Virginia Military Institute, Scott Shipp served as the commandant of cadets at his alma mater during the latter part of the Civil War and as such led the cadet battalion in the field when called. With the outbreak of hostilities he had left his position on the faculty and joined the Confederate army as major, 21st Virginia, in June 1861. With this unit he took part in early operations in western Virginia. On January 20, 1862, he was detached from his regiment and assigned to duty at VMI with the rank of lieutenant colonel. In this position he led the cadet battalion in the field during part of the Shenandoah Valley Campaign of 1862, but they saw no action. During the summer of 1863, while the school was out of session he served as a private in Company H, 4th Virginia Cavalry. Resuming his duties at the academy, he again led the cadet battalion at the battle of New Market where they suffered heavy casualties. For the remainder of the war the cadets divided their time between their studies and service in the field. Shipp was in the field and in the trenches around Petersburg and Richmond and also tried to intercept Union cavalry raids in the Shenandoah region. At the time of the fall of Richmond, Shipp was commanding a mixed force of cadets, regular troops, and convalescents. On April 3, 1865, the battalion was disbanded. With the reopening of the school Shipp resumed his duties and became a lawyer. Late in the century he became superintendent of the institute. (Wise, Jennings C., *The Military History of the Virginia Military Institute from 1839 to 1865*)

SHORTER, John Gill (1818-1872)

At first extremely popular as governor of Alabama, John G. Shorter fell in the public esteem along with the Davis administration with which he was closely associated. Born in Georgia, he had taken up the practice of law in Alabama in 1838, sat in the state legislature, and served as a judge. Giving up his judgeship in early 1861, he became a commissioner from Alabama to the Georgia secession convention. He was then named to the Provisional Confederate Congress where he was appointed chairman of the Committee on Engrossment. He also sat on the committees on: Buildings; Executive Departments; and Flag and Seal. Elected governor in August 1861, he resigned his congressional seat in November. Sworn in on December 2, 1861, he was active in preparing the state, especially Mobile, for defense and organizing troops for the field armies. However, his pro-Davis stance rapidly made him unpopular and he was handily beaten by Thomas H. Watts in 1863. Dropping out of politics, he resumed the practice of law. (Denman, Clarence P., *The Secession Movement in Alabama*)

SHOUP, Francis Asbury (1834-1896)

When John B. Hood relieved Joseph E. Johnston of command of the Army of Tennessee before Atlanta, Francis A. Shoup be- came the army's chief of staff. The native Indianan West Pointer (1855) had become a career artillerist, seeing action against the Seminoles before resigning as a first lieutenant in the 1st Artillery on January 10, 1860. He took up the practice of law in Florida and despite his northern birth joined the Confederacy. His assignments included: major, Artillery (October 1861); lieutenant colonel, Artillery (1861); brigadier general, CSA (September 12, 1862); commanding 3rd Brigade, Smith's Division, Department of Mississippi and East Louisiana (May-July 4, 1863); chief of artillery, Army of Tennessee (early 1864-July 24, 1864); and chief of staff, Army of Tennessee (July 24-ca. December 1864). During the Battle of Shiloh he served as chief artillerist with William J. Hardee's 3rd Corps and then fought at Prairie Grove as adjutant to Thomas C. Hindman. During the siege of Vicksburg he directed a brigade and was paroled with the garrison on July 4, 1863. Exchanged a few months later, he joined Johnston for the Atlanta Campaign as chief artillerist and then became Hood's staff chief until the latter's resignation after the disastrous battles at Franklin and Nashville. Thereafter he was involved in education and the Episcopal ministry.

SIBLEY, Henry Hopkins (1816-1886)

Although he designed the conical Sibley field tent, used by both armies during the Civil War, Henry Hopkins Sibley suffered from an excessive fondness for the bottle which to a large extent denied the Confederacy the full advantages of his West Point (1838) training. The native Louisianian had been posted to the dragoons and won a brevet during the Mexican War. On May 13, 1861, the same date as his commission as major, 1st Dragoons, he resigned from the regular army to join the South. His Confederate assignments included: colonel, Cavalry (May 16, 1861); brigadier general, CSA (June 17, 1861); and commanding Army of New Mexico (December 14, 1861-December 1, 1862). In the summer of 1861 he was sent to Texas to take command of the forces operating on the upper Rio Grande. Invading what is now New Mexico, he commanded during the campaign and was in command at the Confederate victory at Valverde. However, the next month a portion of his forces, under William R. Scurry, was forced to break off an action at Pigeon's Ranch in Glorieta Pass when a force under John M. Chivington, then a major, destroyed virtually its entire supply train and herd of horses and mules. This soon committed Sibley to evacuate Santa Fe and fall back into Texas. For the balance of the war—during which time it was common knowledge that he was a heavy drinker—he served in the Trans-Mississippi Department but was often without a command. He later spent four years as an Egyptian artillery general and upon his return to the United States joined the lecture circuit, which did not provide him with a large income.

SIMMS, James Phillip (1837-1887)

A Georgia lawyer, James P. Simms does not appear to have entered the Confederate army until a year after Fort Sumter. His assignments included: major, 53rd Georgia (September 24, 1862); colonel, 53rd Georgia (October 8, 1862); commanding

Bryan's (old) Brigade, Kershaw's Division, 1st Corps, Army of Northern Virginia (June 2, 1864-April 6, 1865, except for the early part of 1865); and brigadier general, CSA (December 8, 1864). After indicating service in the Seven Days Battles, the records are silent on whether he took part in the Maryland and Fredericksburg campaigns. He was however present for the fighting at Salem Church in the battle of Chancellorsville and in the heavy fighting on the second day at Gettysburg. Going to the West with Longstreet, the brigade arrived too late for Chickamauga, but Simms led the regiment at Knoxville and back in Virginia at the Wilderness, Spotsylvania, and Cold Harbor. During the latter action he assumed command of the brigade when General Goode Bryan relinquished it. He led the brigade at Petersburg and then went with the division to reinforce Early in the Shenandoah, seeing action at Cedar Creek. Returning to the trenches around Richmond and Petersburg, he led the brigade in the retreat toward Appomattox but was captured in the debacle at Sayler's Creek on April 6, 1865.

SIMMS, William Elliott (1822-1898)

Despite the fact that his state never seceded from the Union, William E. Simms represented Kentucky as a senator in both of the Regular Confederate congresses. A Mexican War veteran, he had served in the state legislature, practiced law, and edited the *Kentucky State Flag*. A Democrat in the U.S. Congress, he condemned the Republicans and became known as an extreme states' righter—for Kentucky. At the outbreak of the Civil War he joined the Confederacy and as lieutenant colonel, 1st Kentucky Cavalry Battalion, he served with General Humphrey Marshall in Kentucky and western Virginia in the first months of the war. In November of the first year of the war he was appointed a commissioner of the provisional government of the state in order to treat with the Confederate government in Richmond. There he was appointed one of the state's senators in the First, and later the Second, Regular Confederate Congress. He sat on the committees on: Accounts; Foreign Affairs (Second Congress); Indian Affairs (First Congress); Naval Affairs; and Public Buildings (Second Congress). On the floor itself he appears to have been a proponent of total war and favored the idea that Jefferson Davis himself command the armies in the field. With the failing of the war effort, he supported major command changes. After a year's exile he returned to his Kentucky agricultural pursuits and gave up politics.

SINCLAIR, James (ca. 1823-1877)

Late in the war desertion was a major problem for the Confederate armies, requiring the detachment of line troops to round up deserters. The case of James Sinclair indicates that the problem was limited to neither the latter part of the war nor to the enlisted ranks. A clergyman in the Presbyterian church in North Carolina he had entered the Confederate army. His assignments were: chaplain, 5th North Carolina (May 15, 1861); and colonel, 35th North Carolina (November 8, 1861). Taking part in the March 1862 battle of New Bern in command of his regiment, he ordered it back before it had suffered any casualties. The next month he was replaced by a new colonel in the reorganization. Going over to the enemy, he served as a chaplain for the Union army. A scalawag after the war, he was a Republican member of the state legislature during Reconstruction.

SINGLETON, Otho Robards (1814-1889)

Elected to both of the Confederate regular congresses from his central Mississippi 5th District, Otho Robards Singleton failed to attend the second, and final, session of the Second Congress, having become disenchanted with the war. Born in Kentucky, he had taken up the practice of law in Canton, Mississippi. He served in both houses of the state legislature and withdrew from the U.S. Congress with the rest of the Mississippi delegation during the secession winter. As a private in the army, he ran for the Confederate Congress and won. He chaired the Committee on Indian Affairs in both congresses and sat on that on Pay and Mileage in the First Congress. He was a solid supporter of a strong central government to win the war and believed in the use of force to keep the states in line. He was also opposed to the use of substitutes for military service. On leave after the first session of the Second Congress, he was active in reestablishing conservative rule in the state in the latter stages of Reconstruction and served six terms in the U.S. Congress.

Otho R. Singleton, Confederate administration supporter. (*Harper's*)

SLACK, William Yarnel (1816-1862)

Lawyer and Mexican War captain, William Slack was made a brigadier general in the Missouri State Guard, the pro-Southern state forces serving under Sterling Price. On July 4, 1861, General Slack was directed to assemble the units of the 5th District of Missouri together and a week later the command was designated the 4th Division, Missouri State Guard. Actually a brigade, Slack's command took part in the fighting at Carthage and Wilson's Creek where he was severely wounded in the hip. Considered to be Price's best brigadier, Slack was given command of the 2nd Brigade, Confederate Volunteers, of the Missouri State Guard on January 23, 1862. This command was composed of those members of the organization who had decided to enlist in Confederate service while others remained in state ranks. At the battle of Pea Ridge, on March 7, Slack was again wounded. Moved to avoid capture, he died exactly two weeks later. Possibly without knowing of his demise, the Richmond authorities appointed him a brigadier in the Confederate army on April 17, to rank from April 12.

SLAUGHTER, James Edwin (1827-1901)

Although he spent most of his Confederate career in staff positions, General James E. Slaughter commanded the troops engaged in the last land engagement of the Civil War. The native Virginian had been commissioned directly into the regular army during the Mexican War. Initially posted to the infantry, he then served with the Regiment of Voltigeurs and Foot Riflemen until that unit was discontinued at the close of the war. Transferred to the artillery, he was dismissed as a first lieutenant in the 1st Artillery on May 14, 1861. His Southern assignments included: captain, Artillery (spring 1861); major, Artillery (November 1861); brigadier general, CSA (March 8, 1862); commanding brigade, District of the Gulf, Department #2 (1862-63); and commanding in the Trans-Mississippi Department: division, District of Texas, New Mexico and Arizona (December 15, 1863-January 1864); Eastern Sub-District, District of Texas, New Mexico and Arizona (January 1864); 7th (Texas) Cavalry Brigade, 3rd (Texas) Cavalry Division, 3rd Corps (September 1864-May 26, 1865); and also Western Sub-District, District of Texas, New Mexico and Arizona (October 1864-May 26, 1865). He was on Bragg's staff at Pensacola and fought at Shiloh as an inspector with Albert S. Johnston. He held the same post with Beauregard during the Corinth siege and with Bragg during the Kentucky Campaign. In the spring of 1863 he became Magruder's chief artillerist at Galveston. Remaining in Texas for the balance of the war, he was mostly engaged in district commands but also led a mounted brigade. Ironically, his Confederates won the last battle of the war, on May 12, 1865, at Brownsville. For a time after the war he lived in Mexico and upon his return he was a civil engineer and postmaster.

SLIDELL, John (1793-1871)

His capture aboard the British mail steamer *Trent* did the cause of Confederate diplomacy more good than all of John Slidell's years of subsequent effort in Paris. A New York-born lawyer and merchant, he had been ruined by the War of 1812 and relocated to New Orleans following a duel. There he practiced commercial law and served in the state legislature, losing several races for both houses of the U.S. Congress. He finally took a seat in the House of Representatives in 1843, for one term as a Democrat. Ten years later he was admitted to the Senate, where he sat until 1861. Having become a proponent of slavery, he backed the Lecompton Constitution for Kansas and opposed Stephen A. Douglas. Appointed ambassador to France from the Confederacy shortly after the outset of the war, he was seized along with James M. Mason, the minister to England, in November 1861 by Captain Charles Wilkes of the USS *San Jacinto*. Questionable under international law, this capture aroused great resentment in Britain and brought the two countries to the verge of armed conflict. Fortunately the Washington authorities backed down and released the captives on January 1, 1862. Slidell eventually arrived in Paris but was unable to gain the active support, let alone the recognition, of Napoleon III. He did play a major role in the negotiation of the disastrous Erlanger cotton loan. After the war he never returned to the United States, remaining in France until the fall of Napoleon III, and he died under the British crown. (Sears, Louis Martin, *John Slidell* and Willson, B., *John Slidell and the Confederates in Paris*)

SMITH, Caraway (?-?)

As a part of the relatively small Confederate forces left in Florida, Caraway Smith was usually involved in small-unit actions rather than the larger fights common in the Virginia and western theaters. His assignments included: captain, Ancilla Troop Florida Cavalry (early 1862); colonel, 2nd Florida Cavalry (December 4, 1862); commanding sub-district, District of Middle Florida, Department of South Carolina, Georgia and Florida (December 1863); and commanding Cavalry, District of East Florida, Department of South Carolina, Georgia and Florida (February 1864). Serving the entire war in his home state, he was often in command of a geographical area, directing the operations of semi-independent companies of cavalry, partisan rangers, and infantry. One exception was the fight at Olustee when forces from all over the state and from Georgia concentrated to defeat a Union expedition. He commanded the equivalent of a brigade of cavalry in this Confederate victory. Small-scale operations continued until the district was surrendered on May 17, 1865.

SMITH, Charles Henry (1826-1903)

A Georgia lawyer and Confederate staff officer, Charles H. Smith wrote a series of four satirical letters to "Mr. Lincoln, sir," which appeared, during 1861 and 1862, in the Rome (Ga.) *Southern Confederacy*. Signing as "Bill Arp," Smith utilized satire, and good-natured humor to ridicule the Lincoln administration and the entire North. Complaining that "It is utterly impossible for us to disperse in twenty days" in compliance with a Lincoln proclamation, Bill Arp asked for an extension of time. Using his quaint dialect he explained that, "I tried my darn'dst yesterday to disperse and retire, but it was no go." Smith trumpeted the Confederate fighting ability in a later letter: "The Lee side of any shore is unhealthy to your population; keep away from those Virginia watercourses, go around them or under them, but for the sake of economy don't try to cross them. It is too hard upon your burial squads and ambulance horses." Following the war, Smith returned to the practice of law, dabbled in politics, and took up farming.

SMITH, Edmund Kirby (1824-1893)

Following the fall of Vicksburg and Port Hudson and the closing of the Mississippi, Confederate General E. Kirby Smith was confronted with the command of a virtually independent area of the Confederacy and with all of its inherent administrative problems. The Floridian West Pointer (1845)—nicknamed "Seminole" at the academy—had been posted to the infantry upon his graduation and won two brevets in the Mexican War. In 1855 he transferred to the cavalry and served until his resignation as major in the 2nd Cavalry on April 6, 1861. In the meantime he had taught mathematics at his alma mater and been wounded in 1859 fighting Indians in the Nescutunga Valley of Texas. When Texas seceded, Smith refused to surrender his command to the state forces under Ben McCulloch. Joining the Confederacy, his assignments included: lieutenant colonel, Cavalry (spring 1861); chief of staff, Army of the Shenandoah (spring-summer 1861); brigadier general, CSA (June 17, 1861); commanding 4th Brigade, Army of the Shenandoah (ca. June-July 20, 1861); commanding 4th Brigade, 2nd Corps, Army of the Potomac (July 20-21, 1861); major general, CSA (October 11, 1861); commanding 4th Division, Potomac District, Department of Northern Virginia (October 22, 1861-February 21, 1862); commanding Department of East Tennessee (March 8-August 25, ca. October 31-December 1862, and December 23, 1862-January 1863); commanding Army of Kentucky, Department #2 (August 25-November 20, 1862); lieutenant general, CSA (October 9, 1862); also commanding corps, Army of Tennessee (November 20-December 1862); commanding Southwestern Army (January 14-March 7, 1863); commanding Trans-Mississippi Department (March 7, 1863-April 19, 1865 and April 22-May 26, 1865); and general, PACS (February 19, 1864). After serving as Joseph E. Johnston's staff head in the Shenandoah Valley he was promoted to brigadier general and given command of a brigade which he led at 1st Bull Run. Wounded severely in that action, he returned to duty as a major general and division commander in northern Virginia. Early in 1862 he was dispatched to command in East Tennessee. Cooperating with Braxton Bragg in the invasion of Kentucky, he scored a victory at Richmond and was soon named to the newly created grade of lieutenant general. Early in 1863 he was transferred to the Trans-Mississippi West where he remained for the balance of the war. With the fall of the Mississippi River to the Union forces he was virtually cut off from Richmond. He was forced to deal himself with such matters as impressment of supplies, destruction of cotton to prevent capture, and blockade-running through Mexico, in addition to his normal military duties. He also, in an irregular fashion, promoted officers to general's rank, sometimes making his actions subject to the president's approval and sometimes not. Davis approved some and never acted on others. Smith could be forgiven for exceeding his authority in such matters due to the situation of his command as an almost separate country. In the spring of 1864 he soundly defeated Nathanial P. Banks' Red River Campaign and then dispatched reinforcements northward to defeat Steele's cooperating column in Arkansas. With the pressure relieved, Smith attempted to send reinforcements east of the Mississippi but, as in the case of his earlier attempts to relieve Vicksburg, it proved impracticable due to Union naval control of the river. Instead he dispatched Sterling Price, with all available cavalry, on an unsuccessful invasion of Missouri. Thereafter the war west of the river was principally one of small raids and guerrilla activity. By now a full general, he surrendered his department—the only significant Confederate army left—on May 26, 1865. After the war he was active in the telegraph business and education. At the time of his death he was the last of the full Confederate ex-generals. (Parkes, Joseph H., *General Kirby Smith C.S.A.*)

SMITH, Gerrit (1797-1874)

Although for the rest of his life Gerrit Smith denied vigorously any foreknowledge of John Brown's raid on Harpers Ferry, the evidence is now quite clear that he was involved. A wealthy New Yorker, he had been well known for his interest in charities, making large contributions. Involved in many of the reform movements of the day, he concentrated upon the antislavery issue. He aided runaways and was a member of the Kansas Aid Society and was also connected with the New England Emigrant Aid Company. John Brown visited his home in early 1858, with his plan for freeing Virginia's slaves, and sought financial as well as moral support. Both were given, it now appears, after a second visit in early 1859. Following the disaster at Harpers Ferry, Smith went into a state of temporary insanity. A believer in political action, he was closely linked with the Liberty Party and was its candidate for a number of offices. As an independent he did sit in Congress and during the Civil War he worked hard for the war effort, becoming a Republican. A moderate on Reconstruction, he signed the papers which freed Jefferson Davis. (Hammond, C.A., *Gerrit Smith*)

SMITH, Gustavus Woodson (1821-1896)

Considerations of rank prompted a senior Confederate major general, Gustavus W. Smith, to resign his commission. The Kentucky-born West Pointer (1842) had served with the engineers in Mexico, winning two brevets, and taught at his alma mater before resigning as a first lieutenant in 1854. As a civil engineer he became New York City's street commissioner. Joining the Confederacy, his assignments included: major general, CSA (September 19, 1861); commanding 2nd Corps, Army of the Potomac (September-October 22, 1861); commanding 2nd Division, Potomac District, Department of Northern Virginia (October 22, 1861-March 23 1862); commanding Aquia District, Department of Northern Virginia (March 23-April 18, 1862); commanding Reserve, Department of Northern Virginia (April 18-early May 1862); commanding

1st Division, Department of Northern Virginia (early May-May 31 and June 1-2, 1862); commanding the department (May 31-June 1, 1862); commanding Department of North Carolina and Southern Virginia (September 19, 1862-February 17, 1863); acting secretary of war (November 17-21, 1862); major general, Georgia Militia (June 1864); commanding 1st Division, Georgia Militia, Army of Tennessee (June-October 1864); and commanding 1st Division, Georgia Militia, Department of South Carolina, Georgia and Florida (October 1864-April 20, 1865). In the first fall and winter of the war he was the senior major general operating in northern Virginia and, going to the Peninsula, commanded the reserves at Yorktown. At Seven Pines he led a division until the wounding of Joseph E. Johnston put him in charge of the army. Within a few hours, however, he was relieved by Robert E. Lee. Smith then suffered an attack of paralysis which made him miss the rest of the Peninsula Campaign. Upon his recovery, he was assigned to command all forces operating to the South of Lee's army. However, in the fall of 1862 the new grade of lieutenant general was created; and while Smith did not gain one of the promotions, several major generals junior to him did. Smith resigned his Confederate commission on February 17, 1863, having served four days as the acting head of the War Department. The next year he was appointed to the same rank in the Georgia Militia by Governor Joseph E. Brown. During the Atlanta and Savannah campaigns Smith led a division of these troops with the Army of Tennessee and the forces along the coast. He commanded during the largest action of the March to the Sea—Griswoldville. After surrendering on April 20, 1865, at Macon, he was engaged in the iron and insurance businesses. Active in historical writing, he wrote a work on the controversial and confused battle at Seven Pines, *The Battle of Seven Pines*. He also wrote on other aspects of the Civil War as well as the Mexican War.

SMITH, Hiram (?-1862)

Missouri resident Hiram Smith was told at 11:00 A.M. that he was to die at 1:00 P.M. for the disappearance of Andrew Allsman. The story began when Andrew Allsman, a resident of the strongly pro-Southern town of Palmyra, Missouri, vanished after having been paroled by Confederate troops. He had served in the 3rd Missouri Cavalry in the Union army until discharged on account of his advanced age. Unpopular at home, he was accused of spying on his neighbors for the Union. Captured when the Confederates raided the town, he was sentenced to death but then paroled. His body was never found. John McNeil, a Union general, then declared that 10 men would die if Allsman was not returned. One of the doomed men was William T. Humphrey, whose wife pleaded for his release. Since there was evidence that Humphrey had not belonged to a Confederate band, he was spared and Hiram Smith was the substitute victim. He died with the other nine men on October 18, 1862.

SMITH, James Argyle (1831-1901)

Transferring from the staff to the line, the Tennessee West Pointer (1853) James A. Smith rose to the rank of brigadier general in the Confederate service while serving in the western theater. Posted to the infantry upon his graduation, he had resigned as a first lieutenant in the 6th Infantry on May 9, 1861, following frontier duty. His Southern assignments included: captain, Infantry (spring (1861); major and assistant adjutant general (March 1862); lieutenant colonel, 2nd Tennessee (spring 1862); colonel, 5th (AKA 9th) Confederate (July 21, 1862); brigadier general, CSA (September 30, 1863); and commanding in the Army of Tennessee: brigade Cleburne's Division, Hill's-Breckinridge's Corps (ca. October-November 30, 1863); brigade, Cleburne's Division, Hardee's Corps (November 30, 1863-spring 1864 and June-July 22, 1864); Mercer's (old) Brigade, Cleburne's Division, Hardee's-Cheatham's Corps (fall-November 30, 1864); the division (November 30, 1864-April 9, 1865); and brigade, Brown's Division, Hardee's Corps (April 9-26, 1865). After serving as Leonidas Polk's adjutant he took command of a Tennessee regiment shortly before Shiloh and later led a unit designated as a "Confederate" unit at Perryville and Murfreesboro and in the Tullahoma Campaign. At Chickamauga he commanded the 3rd and 5th Confederate. Promoted to brigadier general later that month, he fought through the Atlanta Campaign until wounded at the battle of Atlanta proper. Returning to duty, he led another brigade in the invasion of middle Tennessee. Guarding the trains during the fight at Franklin, he then succeeded Patrick R. Cleburne in division command. He fought at Nashville and in the Carolinas. In the final reorganization of the Army of Tennessee, he was reduced to command of a brigade with which he surrendered at Durham Station. He was subsequently a farmer and engaged as an education official in Mississippi.

SMITH, Martin Luther (1819-1866)

Although an engineer by training, New Yorker Martin L. Smith did command Confederate line troops in battle. The West Pointer (1842) had served his entire tour in the old army with the topographical engineers. Service in the South led to his resignation, as a captain, on April 1, 1861, and his joining the Confederacy. His assignments included: major, Engineers (March 16, 1861); colonel, 21st Louisiana (February 1862); brigadier general, CSA (April 11, 1862); commanding 3rd District, Department of Southern Mississippi and East Louisiana (June 26-ca. October 1862); commanding 2nd Military District, Department of Mississippi and East Louisiana (October 21-late December 1862); major general, CSA (November 4, 1862); commanding division, 2nd Military District, Department of Mississippi and East Louisiana (late December 1862-April 1863); commanding division, Department of Mississippi and East Louisiana (April-July 4, 1863); chief engineer, Army of Northern Virginia (April-July 1864); chief engineer, Army of Tennessee (July 20-October 1864); and chief engineer, Military Division of the West (October 1864-early 1865). Despite the fact that he was given charge of a volunteer regiment of infantry, he worked early in the war on the defenses of New Orleans and Vicksburg. At Chickasaw Bayou he led a division in the repulse of Sherman and was later captured at Vicksburg. Although paroled on July 4, 1863, he was not exchanged until about February 1864. He then served successively as the chief engineer to Robert E. Lee, John B. Hood, and Pierre G.T. Beauregard. During the later period he worked on the defenses at Mobile. He died a little more than a year after the fall of the Confederacy.

SMITH, Maurice Thompson (1828-1863)

A graduate of the University of North Carolina, Maurice Smith entered Confederate service and proved to be an example of the changing values of the "Old South." Smith left his planting and became captain, Company K, 55th North Carolina, on May 30, 1862. Early the next year he was promoted to lieutenant colonel. In the action at Fort Huger on April 19, 1863, during Longstreet's siege of Suffolk, the 55th and other units were surprised by a Union force and five guns and over 130 men were captured. There were recriminations between the North Carolinians and the Alabamians supporting them, with each blaming the other for the debacle. A report by Captains Terrell and Cussons of the staff of the Alabamians' commander, General Law, outraged the officers of the 55th. The regimental commander, Colonel Connally, resenting the charge of cowardice and having determined who the originators of the charge were, suggested that officers of the regiment challenge the two staff officers to duels with all field and company officers taking part until each was killed or satisfaction had been given. Smith, the second in command, was the only man to declare that he was morally opposed to the "code duello" and would not participate. The proceedings continued without him. A little over two months later Lieutenant Colonel Smith was mortally wounded on the first day at Gettysburg and called "a gallant and efficient officer" by his brigade commander, General Davis, proving that he had made his earlier decision on moral grounds. (Freeman, Douglas S., *Lee's Lieutenants*)

SMITH, Preston (1823-1863)

Native Tennessee lawyer Preston Smith gave his life to the Confederacy—not leading his men but, rather, when he accidentally rode into the enemy lines. The Memphis resident's Confederate assignments included: colonel, 154th Tennessee Senior (May 14, 1861); commanding 1st Brigade, 2nd Division, 1st Geographical Division, Department #2 (October 24, 1861-March 5, 1862); commanding 1st Brigade, 1st Grand Division, Army of the Mississippi (March 5-12, 1862); commanding 1st Brigade, 2nd Division, 1st Grand Division, Army of the Mississippi (March 12-mid-March 1862); commanding 1st (Johnson's) Brigade, 2nd Division, 1st Corps, Army of the Mississippi (April 6-7, 1862); commanding brigade, Cheatham's Division, Army of the Mississippi (July 2-August 15, 1862); commanding brigade, Cheatham's Division, Right Wing, Army of the Mississippi (August 15-late August 1862 and October-November 20, 1862); commanding brigade, Cleburne's Division, Left Wing, Army of the Mississippi (August-October 1862); brigadier general, CSA (October 27, 1862); and commanding brigade, Cheatham's Division, Polk's Corps, Army of Tennessee (November 20-December 1862 and January-September 19, 1863). His regiment kept its old militia numerical designation but was authorized to append the word "Senior" to its title in order to indicate its seniority to other Tennessee regiments. During the battle of Belmont, Smith commanded a brigade which was part of the reinforcements sent from Columbus, Kentucky, to the Missouri side of the Mississippi River. On the first day at Shiloh he succeeded the wounded Bushrod R. Johnson in brigade command but himself fell wounded the next day. He recovered to take part in the Tullahoma Campaign and was also in the Kentucky and Murfreesboro campaigns but not in the main battles. He went on to Chickamauga, and while reconnoitering on the evening of the first day at that battle and planning an attack, he rode into the enemy and was mortally wounded. Within the hour he was dead.

SMITH, Robert Benjamin

See: *Hilton, Robert Benjamin*

SMITH, Thomas Benton (1838-1923)

As with any war, the Civil War had its cases of cruelty against prisoners of war. Tennessee native Thomas B. Smith was one of those cases. Educated at the Nashville Military Institute, he had been a railroad employee at the outbreak of the Civil War. Joining the Confederacy, his assignments included: second lieutenant, Company C (later B), 20th Tennessee (June 12, 1861); captain, Company B, 20th Tennessee (1861); colonel, 20th Tennessee (May 8, 1862); commanding 4th Brigade, 1st (Clark's) Division, Breckinridge's Command, District of the Mississippi, Department #2 (August-August 5, 1862); commanding the division (August 5, 1862); commanding Tyler's (old) Brigade, Bate's Division, Hardee's-Cheatham's Corps, Army of Tennessee (early 1864-December 16, 1864); and brigadier general, CSA (July 29, 1864). As a company officer he fought at Mill Springs and Shiloh and then at the reorganization of the regiment was elected colonel. Due to illness within his regiment, it was consolidated with three others into a depleted battalion. Smith himself was given charge of the brigade and at Baton Rouge succeeded Charles Clark, Jr., in command of the division when the latter was wounded and captured. Rejoining the main army, Smith was wounded at Murfreesboro but recovered in time to be again wounded at Chickamauga. Missing Chattanooga, he fought through the Atlanta Campaign as a brigade commander and in the course of it was promoted to brigadier general. He fought at Franklin and was taken prisoner at Nashville. While a prisoner and being herded to the rear with much of his command, he was repeatedly struck by Colonel William L. McMillan around the head with a sword. The injuries were so serious that Smith was expected to die but he survived—with permanent damage—and returned to railroad work. However, he was forced by his injuries to enter the asylum at Nashville in 1876. He died there nearly half a century later.

SMITH, Walter W. (?-?)

In the early months of the Civil War there were many questions concerning the legality of the use of privateers. Walter W. Smith got caught up in the dispute. The Confederate sailor was a member of the crew of the *Jeff Davis*, which had been fitted out at Charleston on June 28, 1861. On July 16 the privateer captured the schooner *Enchantress*, and Smith was made the head of the prize crew sent to take the vessel into port. Six days later the prize was retaken by the Union fleet and Smith was charged with piracy. Convicted in October, he faced the hangman's noose. But the Confederate government retaliated by the selection of Colonel Michael Corcoran as a hostage. Soon 13 more hostages were selected to guarantee the treatment of additional captured privateers as prisoners of war. The crisis was resolved when the courts ruled that the men were in fact not pirates but regularly enlisted soldiers. From then on Smith was treated as a prisoner of war. His case is treated in detail in the *Official Records*, Series II, Volume III.

SMITH, William (1796-1887)

With no militia experience, ex-Virginia governor William Smith was one of the oldest men to seek an active field commission, and he became one of the more colorful officers of Lee's army. He had earned the nickname "Extra Billy" for some questionable charges made while running a postal route. Returning from a brief residence in California, Smith was serving out a fourth term in the U.S. Congress when the war began. Happening to be at Fairfax Court House when a detachment of regular cavalry charged through the town, killing the Confederate commander, Captain J.Q. Marr, Smith directed the defense. After this first blood the 64-year-old politician sought and received the colonelcy of the 49th Virginia. His later assignments included: commanding Early's Brigade, Ewell's-Early's Division, 2nd Corps, Army of Northern Virginia (September 17, 1862 and ca. April 4-July 10, 1863); brigadier general, CSA (April 23, to rank from January 31, 1863); and major general, CSA (August 12, 1863). He fought at 1st Bull Run and in November 1861 was elected to the First Regular Congress where he sat on the committee on Claims and Naval Affairs. Returning to the field when action was imminent, he fought at Williamsburg and was wounded at Seven Pines. He returned to fight during the Seven Days and the 2nd Bull Run Campaign in which he was teased for carrying an umbrella during the rainstorm at Chantilly. He had gained a reputation for despising West Point and its tactics, finding that neither he nor his men understood them and that common sense was more useful in battle. At Antietam he took over the brigade and suffered three wounds. However, he remained in control until the action was over. After recovering and receiving a generalship, he resigned his congressional seat and returned to the field in time for Chancellorsville. Although elected to another term as governor he participated in the invasion of Pennsylvania and fought at Gettysburg. A few days later he left the field and then received a second promotion, being assigned to duty encouraging recruiting in Virginia. He was inaugurated on January 1, 1864, and served until the war's close. Remaining active in Virginia politics, Smith sat in the legislature into his 80s. (Freeman, Douglas S., *Lee's Lieutenants*)

SMITH, William Duncan (1825-1862)

Yellow fever cut short the promising career of Confederate Brigadier General William D. Smith. The native Georgian West Pointer (1846) had been wounded at Molino del Rey during the Mexican War while serving with the 2nd Dragoons. Resigning as a captain on January 28, 1861, he offered his services to the Confederacy. His assignments included: captain, Cavalry (March 16, 1861); colonel, 20th Georgia (July 14, 1861); brigadier general, CSA (March 14, 1862, to rank from the 7th); and commanding 1st Military District of South Carolina, Department of South Carolina, Georgia and Florida (July 8-October 4, 1862). Taking charge of a volunteer regiment, he led it in northern Virginia until promoted to brigadier general and ordered to South Carolina. There he fought at Secessionville and commanded a district until his death. Highly respected, he was repeatedly recommended for promotion and a larger command. His death came on October 4, 1862.

SMITH, William Nathan Harrell (1812-1889)

For the entire time that North Carolina was represented in the Confederate Congress, William N.H. Smith was there for the northeastern 1st District. He proved to be a loyal supporter of the war effort despite being a former Unionist and coming from an often troublesome state. A native of North Carolina, he had practiced law and become a Whig politician in the state legislature. As a Democrat, he sat in the 36th Congress and narrowly missed being elected its speaker of the house. He left office on March 3, 1861, and was still a Unionist until Lincoln called for 75,000 volunteers after the surrender of Fort Sumter. Taking his seat in the Provisional Confederate Congress on July 20, 1861, he held no committee assignments in that body. In the First Regular Congress he chaired the Committee on Elections and sat on those on: the Medical Department; and Rules and Officers. In the Second Congress he chaired the Committee on Claims and remained on the Committee on Rules and Officers. Granting the central government broad powers for the war effort—over volunteers, transportation, and commerce—he was also a protector of local and states' rights and wanted the Confederacy to pay claims against it quickly. In the postwar years he backed Andrew Johnson and was a leader in the restoration of a conservative state government. For the final 11 years of his life he was the state supreme court's presiding judge.

SNEAD, Thomas Lowndes (1828-1890)

While serving as a staff officer, Thomas L. Snead was elected to the Second Confederate Congress from Missouri's 1st District (St. Louis) by the soldier vote. A native of Virginia, he had practiced law there before moving to St. Louis where he also published the *St. Louis Bulletin*. While the Union was being disrupted, he was serving as aide-de-camp and military secretary to Missouri's secessionist governor, Claiborne F. Jackson. Joining the army, his assignments included: colonel and adjutant general, Missouri State Guard (1861); and major and assistant adjutant general, CSA (1862). On the staff of General Sterling Price, he fought at Booneville, Carthage,

Wilson's Creek, and Lexington and later accompanied Price to Mississippi with the Army of the West. In a May 1864 special election in which only soldiers and refugees could vote, since St. Louis was behind Union lines, he was elected to the Second Confederate Congress. Resigning his commission in the army, he was seated at the beginning of the second session on November 7, 1864. With his district occupied and his being a soldier, he voted for a vigorous prosecution of the war but was wary of Jefferson Davis' leadership. Moving to New York after the war—the atmosphere in St. Louis was strongly anti-Confederate—he edited the *New York Daily News* and practiced law. He wrote *The Fight for Missouri* and numerous articles for *Battles and Leaders of the Civil War*.

SORREL, Gilbert Moxley (1838-1901)

Although he served through most of the war on the staff of James Longstreet, G. Moxley Sorrel did hold a field command for about four months late in the conflict. A clerk and militia private before the war in Savannah, he participated in the capture of Fort Pulaski and was an observer at the bombardment in Charleston Harbor. Going to Virginia he served as a volunteer aide-de-camp to Longstreet at 1st Bull Run. He remained with the South Carolinian through the general's wounding at the Wilderness. He participated in all of "Old Pete's" campaigns, gaining advancement from captain to lieutenant colonel as his chief received his own promotions. Sorrel directed a flanking movement in the Wilderness which marked him for higher responsibilities. During the Petersburg fighting he was wounded in the leg. Then he was appointed brigadier general, CSA (October 27, 1864) and commanded Wright's (old) Brigade, Mahone's Division, 3rd Corps, Army of Northern Virginia (October 31, 1864-February 7, 1865). Suffering a severe chest wound on the latter date, he was returning to duty when the army surrendered. A Savannah merchant in his postwar years, he also wrote *Recollections of a Confederate Officer*.

SOULÉ, Pierre (1801-1870)

Exiled from his native France, Pierre Soulé always managed to keep in the middle of trouble. Fleeing by a circuitous route to New Orleans, he eventually became a lawyer and rose to represent Louisiana in the Senate. While serving as minister to Spain he became involved with the Ostend Manifesto calling for the annexation of Cuba, with or without Spain's consent. When this was rejected, he resigned. In the intervening years until the Civil War he practiced law. Although opposed to secession he backed Louisiana's decision and once the Crescent City was captured earned the wrath of Union General Benjamin F. Butler. In June 1862 he was arrested and confined in Fort Lafayette until he fled while on parole in Boston. Running the blockade into the Confederacy, he became part of the Beauregard bloc and for a time served on his staff as an honorary brigadier. Since Jefferson Davis was a foe of Beauregard, there was no action to make his position official. Again running the blockade in 1864, he attempted to raise a foreign legion to fill

the Confederate ranks. After the war he was busy with efforts to establish a Confederate veterans' colony in Sonora.

SPANGLER, Edward (?-1875)

A scene shifter in Ford's Theater, Edward (sometimes Edmund or Edman) Spangler was befriended by the actor John Wilkes Booth and as a result was sentenced to six years imprisonment. The Maryland native was arrested with the other conspirators and was accused of having built the stables where Booth kept his horse behind the theater and of holding his horse while the assassination was under way. For his role he was sent to Dry Tortugas and, having survived a yellow fever epidemic there, was released in 1869 after serving only two-thirds of his sentence.

SPARROW, Edward (1810-1882)

As the Confederate Senate's chairman of the Committee on Military Affairs, Louisiana's Edward Sparrow believed that the unlimited war powers rested in the hands of Congress. A Dublin, Ireland, native, he had been raised in Ohio before he took up law in Louisiana. He was a court clerk and sheriff before becoming a planter. Favoring the immediate disruption of the Union, he attended the secession convention. Named to the Provisional Confederate Congress—he was to serve throughout the war—he sat on the committees on: Flag and Seal; Indian Affairs; and Military Affairs. Elected to the Senate in November 1861, he chaired the Committee on Military Affairs for the rest of the conflict. His one reluctance in granting the central

Edward Spangler, Booth horse holder. (NA)

government adequate warmaking powers came on the matter of exemptions from military service. He felt this should be left in the hands of the several states. Part of the anti-Bragg faction, he supported both Joseph E. Johnston and P.G.T. Beauregard. He returned to his relatively untouched plantation at the close of the war.

SQUIER

See: *Bras Coupe*

STAFFORD, Leroy Augustus (1822-1864)

A successful Louisiana planter, Leroy A. Stafford had started his military career in the Mexican War as an enlisted man and in the Civil War rose to be a Confederate brigadier. His assignments included: captain, Company B, 9th Louisiana (July 1861), and lieutenant colonel, 9th Louisiana (late 1861); colonel, 9th Louisiana (April 24, 1862); commanding 1st Louisiana Brigade, Ewell's Division, Jackson's Command, Army of Northern Virginia (June 27-July 1862); commanding 2nd Louisiana Brigade, McLaws Division, 1st Corps, same army (July 26-27, 1862); commanding 2nd Louisiana Brigade, Jackson's-Johnson's Division, 2nd Corps, same army (July 27-mid-August, August 28-September 7, September 17, 1862, and October 1863-May 5, 1864); and brigadier general, CSA (October 8, 1863). After serving in the Shenandoah Valley Campaign, Stafford led the brigade in the latter part of the Seven Days Battles and a newly created brigade at Cedar Mountain. He resumed command at 2nd Bull Run when his successor was hit. Again at Antietam he succeeded to brigade command only to be wounded in the foot. Returning to duty, he led his regiment at Gettysburg and was promoted to general that fall. He directed his brigade at Mine Run and on the first day of the Wilderness he was mortally wounded. Three days later, on May 8, he was dead. (Freeman, Douglas S., *Lee's Lieutenants*)

STANLEY, Henry Morton (1841-1904)

John Rowlands renamed himself Henry Morton Stanley after leaving Wales at age 15 as a cabin boy enroute to New Orleans. There he jumped ship and embarked on a most extraordinary career in the Civil War and beyond. Having adopted the name of his New Orleans benefactor, young Stanley was sent to study plantation management in Arkansas, but in July 1861 he ran off and joined the "Dixie Grays," later Company E, 6th Arkansas. Taking part in the rebel attack on the first day at Shiloh, his unit was at a disadvantage, being armed with outmoded steel flintlock muskets. Captured on the second day and confined at Camp Douglas, Chicago, Stanley accepted the unauthorized offer of the commandant, Colonel James A. Mulligan, to take the oath of allegiance and join the Union army. Assigned to an artillery unit he was sent to Harpers Ferry where he promptly fell ill and, on June 22, 1862, was discharged. Stanley went to Cuba in search of his benefactor, discovered he had died, and returned to New York where he enlisted in the Union navy.

Serving aboard the USS *Minnesota* he took part in both attacks on Fort Fisher, North Carolina. On February 10, 1865, Stanley, probably the only man to serve in the Union and Confederate armies and the Union navy, ended his military career by deserting in Portsmouth, New Hampshire. Stanley went on to more adventures as a noted journalist and explorer, famed for his Lake Tanganyika greeting "Dr. Livingstone, I presume." (Stanley, Henry Morton, *Autobiography*)

STARKE, Peter Burwell (1815-1888)

Leaving the Mississippi Senate in 1862, Virginia native Peter B. Starke rose to the rank of brigadier general with the cavalry under Nathan Bedford Forrest. His Confederate assignments included: colonel, 28th Mississippi Cavalry (February 24, 1862); brigadier general, CSA (November 4, 1864); commanding brigade, Jackson's Cavalry Division, Army of Tennessee (ca. November 4, 1864-February 18, 1865); and commanding brigade, Chalmers' Division, Forrest's Cavalry Corps, Department of Alabama, Mississippi and East Louisiana (February 18-May 4, 1865). Commanding his mounted regiment he served in the vicinity of Vicksburg until its fall, at which time he was with the forces under Joseph E. Johnston trying to relieve the city. He then took part in the unsuccessful defense of Jackson, Mississippi, against Sherman. Joining the Army of Tennessee in Georgia in the spring of 1864, he fought through the Atlanta Campaign and was promoted to brigadier general during the Franklin-Nashville Campaign. Joining Forrest, he opposed Wilson's Raid through Alabama and Georgia. He held several minor offices in Mississippi before returning to Virginia for his remaining years.

STARKE, William Edwin (1814-1862)

When a second brigade of Louisiana troops in Lee's army was formed in the summer of 1862, Virginian William E. Starke was considered a good choice for its brigadier since he had lived in New Orleans for a number of years. Giving up his cotton broker business he entered the military as a colonel and served as an aide-de-camp to General R.S. Garnett until that general's death. His later assignments included: colonel, 60th Virginia (1861); brigadier general, CSA (August 6, 1862); commanding 2nd Louisiana Brigade, Jackson's (old) Division, 2nd Corps, Army of Northern Virginia (mid-August-August 28 and September 7-17, 1862); and commanding the division (August 28-September 7 and September 17, 1862). After serving in western Virginia and North Carolina, Starke joined what was to become the Army of Northern Virginia as a part of A.P. Hill's Division. In the first action of the Seven Days Battles, Mechanicsville, he received a severe wound but insisted upon resuming command for the fighting three days later at Frayser's Farm. A month after the close of the fighting he was promoted and transferred to command the Louisianans assigned to Jackson's former division. Fighting at 2nd Bull Run, he succeeded to command of the division and led it creditably. The same thing happened three weeks later at Antietam but this time General Starke was killed. (Freeman, Douglas S., *Lee's Lieutenants*)

STEELE, William (1819-1885)

Marriage into a Texas family explains why native New Yorker William Steele became a Confederate brigadier general. A West Pointer (1840), he had been posted to the dragoons, then fought the Seminoles and won a brevet in Mexico. Most of his remaining old army service—until his May 30, 1861, resignation as a captain in the 2nd Dragoons—was spent on the Texas frontier. His Southern assignments included: colonel, 7th Texas Cavalry (1861); brigadier general, CSA (September 12, 1862); and commanding the Trans-Mississippi Department: division, District of Arkansas (spring 1863); Indian Territory (ca. October 3-December 11, 1863); cavalry division, District of West Louisiana (April 12-21, 1864); division, Wharton's Cavalry Corps (April-June 1864); cavalry brigade, District of Texas, New Mexico and Arizona (June-summer 1864); 1st (Texas) Cavalry Brigade, 1st (Texas) Cavalry Division, 2nd Corps (September 1864-March 1865); and division, Wharton's Cavalry Corps (March-May 26, 1865). He took part in Henry H. Sibley's campaign in New Mexico before becoming a brigadier general. Thereafter he led various mounted brigades and divisions in Texas, Louisiana, and Arkansas. In 1863 he commanded in the Indian Territory—now Oklahoma—and later at Galveston. In the Red River Campaign he succeeded Thomas Green in command of the cavalry division. After the Confederacy's collapse he was a commission merchant and adjutant general of Texas.

STEEN, Alexander Early (?-1862)

A brigadier general in the Missouri State Guard, Alexander E. Steen is frequently and erroneously listed as a general in the Confederate army. His actual assignments for the South included: brigadier general, Missouri State Guard (early 1861); commanding 5th Military District, Missouri State Guard (to July 11, 1861); commanding 5th Division, Missouri State Guard (July 11, 1861-March 1862); commanding 3rd Brigade, 1st Division, Army of the West, Department #2 (March 1862); and colonel, 10th Missouri (November 10, 1862). He had served in the regular army during the Mexican War in one of the infantry regiments raised for the duration of that conflict and again during the period 1852 to 1861. During this time he had suffered a wound in 1857 on the Gila River in what is now New Mexico. He resigned as first lieutenant, 3rd Infantry, on May 10, 1861. Commanding his division of the state forces, the native Missourian took part in the final stages of the Lexington Siege. In the spring of 1862 he was transferred with the Guard to the east side of the Mississippi. Returning to Missouri he raised a regiment for Confederate service, which was designated the 10th Missouri after his death, and was commissioned its colonel. In the battle of Prairie Grove he was shot in the head and killed while leading his regiment.

STEPHENS, Alexander Hamilton (1812-1883)

Although he had been a strong unionist until the last moment, Alexander Stephens, called "Little Ellick" in reference to his 90 pounds, became the Confederacy's vice president and a thorn in the side of President Davis. A Georgia lawyer, Stephens served in the state legislature and, from 1843 to 1859, in the U.S. House of Representatives where he quickly became a leader of the Whigs. Despite his strong belief in states' rights he remained a firm believer in the Union and supported Stephen Douglas in 1860. With the defection of other Georgia unionists, he followed his state in secession, attending the secession convention as a unionist delegate but signing the resulting secession document. In February 1861 he took his seat in the Provisional Congress in Montgomery, Alabama, where he chaired the Rules Committee and the Committee on the Executive Departments. His hopes to become provisional president were dashed and he accepted the vice presidency. Under the provisional government this office held no specific responsibilities, so he retained his seat in Congress until the implementation of the permanent Confederate Constitution in February 1862. Almost immediately there was friction between the chief executive and his deputy. Stephens, finding his advice often ignored, became an obstructionist when faced with the president's proposals. After refusing to go on a couple of earlier missions, he had to be ordered to proceed to Virginia as the Confederacy's commissioner to the then-independent state. He soon joined forces with three other Georgians: his brother Linton, Robert Toombs, and Governor Joe Brown. Davis' support for the draft and the right to suspend the writ of habeas corpus provided the malcontents with ammunition in their

Alexander H. Stephens, troublesome vice president of the Confederacy. (NA)

defense of state sovereignty. Stephens was delighted with the governor's efforts to scuttle conscription by exempting large number of Georgians as being vital to the operation of state government or by placing them in the state militia, which was dubbed "Joe Brown's pets." The vice president was an outspoken proponent of a negotiated peace. It was this position which gave Davis an opportunity to defuse the vice president's attacks. He summoned Stephens from his Liberty Hall estate, to which he retired, often for months at a time, to sulk about the political situation, and assigned him a mission to Washington to deal in public on an exchange of prisoners but also, if the opportunity arose, to discuss a peaceful settlement of the war. Although originally his own idea, Stephens became lukewarm when the mission was set to coincide with the Gettysburg Campaign. The Lincoln administration refused to receive Stephens on the grounds that there were military channels to discuss exchanges. Stephens returned to his sulking and a long and heated correspondence with the president. Again, in February 1865, Davis sent Stephens, along with Senator Robert Hunter and Judge John A. Campbell, to meet with Lincoln. This time, on the 3rd, the meeting took place, on the *River Queen* in Hampton Roads, but was a complete failure. Stephens realized that Davis had outsmarted him, knowing the conference was doomed, and was forced to make a formal report to Congress acknowledging the disaster and thus refuting his previous claims of a possible settlement. Returning to Georgia, he saw Davis when they were both captives of the Federal authorities. They never met again. After five months imprisonment in Boston's Fort Warren, Stephens was released, but the next year he was denied the right to sit in the Senate seat to which he had been elected. In 1871 he purchased the *Atlanta Southern Sun*. His publication of *A Constitutional View of the Late War Between the States* was financially highly successful. He returned to the U.S. House of Representatives from 1873 to 1882 before being elected governor of Georgia. He died a few months after taking office. (Von Abele, Rudolph Radama, *Alexander H. Stephens, A Biography*)

STEPHENS, Linton (1823-1872)

Half-brother of the Confederate vice president, Linton Stephens was part of the group of Georgia politicians who were constantly on the alert to protect their native state from the encroachment upon its sovereignty represented by Jefferson Davis. Admitted to the bar, he had served in the state legislature from 1849 to 1855, was an unsuccessful congressional candidate in 1855 and 1857, and was appointed to the state supreme court in 1859. While his half-brother, Alexander, was serving in Washington, Linton served as his Georgia spokesman and shared his views opposing secession. With the outbreak of the war, however, he became the lieutenant colonel of the 15th Georgia, on July 15, 1861. He was forced to resign due to ill health on December 19, 1861. Reelected the same year to the legislature, he served there for the rest of the war as an advocate of a peace settlement and, along with Governor Joe Brown, Robert Toombs, and his half-brother, he was opposed to the policies of the Davis administration and tried to throw numerous obstacles in its path. His home often served as the locale for the group's strategy sessions.

Opposed to the central government's direct conscription of troops, he favored the recruitment of troops by the states and supported the governor's policy of granting mass exemptions to the state militia and the padded state payrolls. He even commanded the 7th Georgia State Guard Cavalry Battalion subject to the governor's orders. Following the Confederacy's fall he resumed the practice of law. (Waddell, James D., *Biographical Sketch of Linton Stephens*)

STEPHENS, William H. (?-?)

Entering the Confederate service at the head of the "Jackson Grays," William H. Stephens rose from captain to colonel on May 23, 1861, when the company became Company G, 6th Tennessee. His commands in Department #2 included: 4th Brigade, 1st Geographical Division (September 7-October 24, 1861); 2nd Brigade, 2nd Division, 1st Geographical Division (October 24, 1861-March 5, 1862); 2nd Brigade, 1st Grand Division, Army of the Mississippi (March 5-29, 1862); and 2nd Brigade, 2nd Division, 1st Corps, Army of the Mississippi (March 29-April 6, 1862). After transferring from state to Confederate service on August 12, 1861, he was soon given command of a brigade which he commanded at Columbus, Kentucky, during the battle of Belmont across the Mississippi River. He commanded the brigade during the first half of the first day at Shiloh until relieved by Colonel George Maney. Stephens led the regiment during the remainder of the fight but a month later he failed to gain reelection to the colonelcy upon the May 8, 1862, reorganization of the regiment, and his military career ended.

STEUART, George Hume (1828-1903)

Although their state did not secede, a number of Maryland West Pointers joined the Confederacy, among them George H. Steuart of the class of 1848. A veteran of 13 years in the mounted service, he resigned his captaincy on April 22, 1861. His assignments for the Confederacy included: captain, Cavalry (early 1861); lieutenant colonel, 1st Maryland (ca. May 1861); colonel, 1st Maryland (July 21, 1861); brigadier general, CSA (March 6, 1862); commanding in Ewell's Division, Valley District, Department of Northern Virginia: Maryland Line (ca. April-May 24, 1862), Cavalry (May 24-June 2, 1862), and 2nd Brigade (June 4-8, 1862); commanding brigade, Johnson's Division, 2nd Corps, Army of Northern Virginia (May 28, 1863-May 12, 1864); and commanding Barton's (old) Brigade, Pickett's Division, 1st Corps, Army of Northern Virginia (September 1864-April 9, 1865). Distinguished at 1st Bull Run, he succeeded to regimental command there. He held a series of commands in the Shenandoah Valley Campaign of 1862 until wounded at Cross Keys. After a long recovery he was given command of a brigade which he led at Culp's Hill at Gettysburg. He led it in the fall campaigns of 1863 and at the Wilderness. During the massive Union assault at Spotsylvania's Bloody Angle he was captured along with much of his unit. Exchanged that summer, he commanded a brigade in Pickett's Division for the war's final campaigns. He saw action during the Petersburg fighting and at Five Forks and Sayler's Creek before surrendering at Appomattox. Known as "Maryland" Steuart to distinguish him from the more famous cavalryman, he returned home as a farmer and was active in veterans' organizations. (Freeman, Douglas S., *Lee's Lieutenants*)

STEVENS, Clement Hoffman (1821-1864)

A volunteer aide at the beginning of the Civil War, Connecticut-born Clement H. Stevens rose to the rank of brigadier general in the Confederate service before giving up his life. After serving as a secretary at sea, he had been a South Carolina banker at the outbreak of the Civil War. His Confederate assignments included: volunteer aide-de-camp (summer 1861); colonel, 24th South Carolina (ca. April 1, 1862); brigadier general, CSA (January 20, 1864); and commanding Wilson's (old) Brigade, Walker's Division, Hardee's Corps, Army of Tennessee (ca. February 20-July 20, 1864). During the encirclement of Fort Sumter in Charleston Harbor, Stevens designed an ironclad battery which played a leading role in the reduction of the Federal fort, and the idea was later adapted to the CSS *Virginia*. He then served as a volunteer aide to Bernard E. Bee who was killed at 1st Bull Run. Commissioned colonel of a new regiment, Stevens commanded it at Secessionville and was then sent to Mississippi to aide Joseph E. Johnston in his unsuccessful attempt to lift the siege of Vicksburg. Thereafter he served in the Army of Tennessee. Under Bragg, he fought at Chickamauga and Chattanooga. Wounded at the former, he was named a brigadier general early the next year. Nicknamed "Rock" for his performance at Chickamauga, he led his brigade through the Atlanta Campaign until mortally wounded in the battle of Peach Tree Creek on July 20, 1864. He died on the 25th, in the beleaguered city.

STEVENS, Walter Husted (1827-1867)

Despite his New York birth and appointment to West Point, Walter H. Stevens developed an attachment to the South through his service there and his marriage into a Louisiana family and so joined the Confederate army, rising to brigadier general. Graduating from the U.S. Military Academy in 1848, he had been posted to the engineers and served with that branch until he was dismissed on May 2, 1861, as a first lieutenant. In fairness to him it must be stated that his resignation had been refused by the War Department, and he was then ousted. His Confederate assignments included: captain, Engineers, (spring 1861); major, Engineers (1861); colonel, Engineers (1862); commanding Richmond Defenses, Department of Richmond (fall 1863-July 1864); chief engineer, Army of Northern Virginia (July 1864-April 9, 1865); and brigadier general, CSA (August 28, 1864). At 1st Bull Run he served as an engineer on the staff of Pierre G.T. Beauregard and then with Joseph E. Johnston in northern Virginia and at Seven Pines. He was then assigned to the construction and command of the defenses of the Confederate capital. Rejoining the main army in Virginia in the summer of 1864, he became its chief engineer and after serving in the Petersburg and Appomattox campaigns was surrendered at the latter place. While working in Mexico on a railroad organized by Emperor Maximilian he died of disease.

STEVENSON, Carter Littlepage (1817-1888)

A veteran of much hard campaigning in the old army, Virginian West Pointer (1838) Carter L. Stevenson became one of the fighting division commanders of the Confederate army of the West. Posted to the infantry, he had fought in the Second Seminole War and in the Mexican War. In the interwar years he campaigned against the Indians on the frontier and participated in the campaign against the Mormons in Utah. When his June 6, 1861, resignation was not forwarded by his superiors, he was dismissed from the regular army as a captain in the 5th Infantry on June 25, 1861. He was charged with having "expressed treasonable designs against" the United States. Joining the Confederacy, his assignments included: major, Infantry (spring 1861); colonel, 53rd Virginia (July 1861); brigadier general, CSA (March 6, 1862, to rank from February 27); commanding 2nd Brigade, Department of East Tennessee (spring-June 1862); commanding 1st Division, Department of East Tennessee (mid-June-December 18, 1862); major general, CSA (October 13, 1862, to rank from the 10th); commanding Defenses of Vicksburg, Department of Mississippi and East Louisiana (December 1862-January 1863); commanding division, 2nd Military District, Department of Mississippi and East Louisiana (January-April 1863); also commanding the district (January-April 1863); commanding division, Department of Mississippi and East Louisiana (April-July 4, 1863); and commanding in the Army of Tennessee: division (early October 1863); division, Hill's-Breckinridge's Corps (October 18-November 1863); division, Hardee's Corps (November 1863-February 20, 1864); division, Hood's-Lee's Corps (February 20, 1864-April 26, 1865); and also the corps (July 18-19, 1864). As a regimental commander, he served in western Virginia. Promoted to brigadier general, he served at Cumberland Gap and in the Kentucky Campaign. Transferred at the end of 1862 to Mississippi, he fought at Chickasaw Bayou and in the defense of Vicksburg. Captured upon the fall of the city, he and his division were exchanged in time to fight at Chattanooga. Long a major general, he led his division in the Atlanta Campaign and then embarked on Hood's invasion of middle Tennessee. At the time of the fight at Franklin his division was still on the south side of Duck River. He did however fight at Nashville and then went on to the Carolinas. Following Joseph E. Johnston's surrender, he was a civil engineer in his native state.

STEWART, Alexander Peter (1821-1908)

Known to his men as "Old Straight," Alexander P. Stewart rose to the temporary command of the infantry and artillery of the Army of Tennessee in the final stages of the Civil War. The Tennessean West Pointer (1842) had served in the artillery until his 1845 resignation as a second lieutenant in the 3rd Artillery. For the next decade and a half he was a professor at Cumberland University in his native state. Upon the outbreak of the Civil War he joined the Confederacy, where his assignments included: major, Artillery (1861); brigadier general, CSA (November 8, 1861); commanding brigade, 1st Geographical Division, Department #2 (December 1861-February 1862);

commanding brigade, McCowan's Command, 1st Geographical Division, Department #2 (February-April 1862); commanding 2nd Brigade, 1st (Clark's) Division, 1st Corps, Army of the Mississippi (early April-April 6 and April 14-July 2, 1862); commanding the division (April 6-14, 1862); commanding 2nd Brigade, 1st (Cheatham's) Division, Army of the Mississippi (July 2-August 1862); commanding 2nd Brigade, Cheatham's Division, Right Wing, Army of the Mississippi (August-November 20, 1862); commanding 2nd Brigade, Cheatham's Division, Polk's Corps, Army of Tennessee (November 20, 1862-February 27, 1863); commanding McCown's (old) Division, Polk's Corps, Army of Tennessee (February 27-June 6, 1863); major general, CSA (June 5, 1863); commanding division, Hardee's-Hill's-Breckinridge's-Hindman's-Hood's Corps, Army of Tennessee (June 6-September 1, 1863 and October 1, 1863-July 7, 1864); commanding division, Buckner's Corps, Army of Tennessee (September 1-October 1, 1863); lieutenant general, CSA (June 23, 1864); commanding Army of Mississippi (Polk's Corps), Army of Tennessee (July 7-26, 1864); commanding corps, Army of Tennessee (July 26-29, 1864, August 1864-March 1865, and April 9-26, 1865); and commanding the army (March-April 9, 1865). As an artillery officer, he commanded the guns stationed at Columbus, Kentucky, and thus witnessed the fight across the river at Belmont. The next day he was named a brigadier general and he led his brigade at Island #10. At Shiloh he succeeded to command of the division when Charles Clark was wounded. Again in charge of a brigade he participated in the defense of Corinth, Mississippi, and fought at Perryville and Murfreesboro. He led a division as a major general, in the Tullahoma Campaign and at Chickamauga and Chattanooga. During the Atlanta Campaign he was promoted to lieutenant general and assigned to replace Leonidas Polk in command of what was still styled the "Army of Mississippi" but was in actuality a corps of the Army of Tennessee. Wounded at Ezra Church, he recovered to take part in the final stages of the Atlanta fighting and then went on Hood's ill-fated expedition into middle Tennessee. There he fought at Franklin and Nashville before moving into the Carolinas. When Joseph E. Johnston took charge of the varied forces in North Carolina, Stewart took command of the infantry and artillery of the Army of Tennessee proper until the final reorganization on April 9, 1865. From then until the end he was again in corps command. He was later an educator, businessman, and commissioner of the Chickamauga and Chattanooga National Military Park. (Wingfield, Marshall, *General A.P. Stewart, His Life and Letters*)

STEWART, Richard H. (?-?)

John Wilkes Booth was so outraged by the treatment he had received at the farm of Dr. Richard H. Stewart that he sent back a highly insulting note and $2.50 as a further insult for the food that he and David Herold had received. Stewart was the richest man in Virginia's King George County and was a staunch Confederate. His place was the first stopping point for the fugitives since crossing the Potomac, but the doctor was outraged to find

the assassin of Lincoln at his door. Not inviting the pair into the house—it was full of relatives and others returning from the war—he made them stay outside. He did, however, provide them with food. Whether or not it was by Stewart's arrangement, the fleeing men were able to get a wagon and team driven by William Lucas, a black living on the farm, to take them to Port Conway on the Rappahannock River. When detectives came to question him later, Dr. Stewart readily admitted that two men had come to his door and that one was lame. Explaining that he was not a surgeon, he declared that he had not provided medical treatment. Despite seeing the insulting note from Booth, the detectives were skeptical and took him into custody. He was later freed.

STOREY, Wilbur Fisk (1819-1884)

With his sharp editorial criticism of the administration's war aims, Wilbur Storey managed to bring down the wrath of the Union army on his newspaper. At the outbreak of the Civil War, Vermont-born Storey was the publisher of the *Detroit Free Press*, one of the leading Democratic organs in the West. During the first year of the conflict, Storey purchased the *Chicago Times* from Cyrus McCormick and continued to support the prosecution of the war until Lincoln issued the Emancipation Proclamation in September 1862. He felt that the administration had deceived the country as to its goals for the war. He launched blistering attacks on the government and the *Times* became a copperhead paper. Describing Storey's attacks as "incendiary," the commander of the Department of the Ohio, General Ambrose Burnside, ordered the suppression of the *Times* on June 3, 1863. The army's occupation of the premises brought angry mobs into the streets of Chicago as Peace Democrats and Republicans faced each other. The Copperheads threatened to burn the plant of the pro-Union *Tribune* in retaliation for the closure. To prevent rioting, Lincoln was wired to revoke the general's order. It was revoked the next day. The *Times* resumed its attacks but with a bit less venom. Following the war, Storey continued with his view of journalism as "raising hell" by campaigning against political corruption. He continued his crusading journalism until he suffered a stroke in 1878.

STOVALL, Marcellus Augustus (1818-1895)

After fighting the Seminoles in Florida, Georgia native Marcellus A. Stovall studied for a year at West Point before resigning due to ill health in 1837, but he went on to become a Confederate brigadier general. His assignments included: captain, Cherokee (Ga.) Artillery (1861); colonel, Georgia Artillery (1861); lieutenant colonel, 3rd Georgia Battalion (October 8, 1861); brigadier general, CSA (January 20, 1863); commanding brigade, Breckinridge's Division, Department of the West (June 6-August 25, 1863); commanding brigade, Breckinridge's Division, Hill's-Breckinridge's Corps, Army of Tennessee (August 28-November 12, 1863); and commanding brigade, Stewart's-Clayton's Division, Breckinridge's-Hindman's-Hood's-Lee's Corps, Army of Tennessee (November 12, 1863-early 1865). His initial service came in East Tennessee and during the Kentucky Campaign. He commanded his battalion at Murfreesboro before being named a brigadier general. He led a brigade under Joseph E. Johnston trying to relieve the Vicksburg garrison. He later fought at Chickamauga, Chattanooga, during the Atlanta Campaign, and at Franklin and Nashville. His final service came in the Carolinas Campaign in which he served in the early stages. After the war he engaged in the cotton, fertilizer, and chemical businesses.

STRAHL, Otho French (1831-1864)

At the age of 34, Ohio native Otho F. Strahl became one of six Confederate generals to be killed at Franklin. The Tennessee lawyer's assignments included: captain, 4th Tennessee (May 1861); lieutenant colonel, 4th Tennessee (May 15, 1861); colonel, 4th Tennessee (ca. May 1862); commanding Stewart's (old) Brigade, Cheatham's Division, Polk's Corps, Army of Tennessee (July-November 1863); brigadier general, CSA (July 28, 1863); commanding brigade, Stewart's Division, Breckinridge's-Hindman's Corps, Army of Tennessee (November 1863-February 20, 1864); and commanding brigade, Cheatham's-Brown's Division, Hardee's-Cheatham's Corps, Army of Tennessee (February 20-November 30, 1864). At Shiloh he succeeded to command of the regiment and was soon promoted to colonel. He then served in the Corinth siege and fought at Perryville. At Murfreesboro he commanded the consolidated 4th and 5th Tennessee. After serving in the Tullahoma Campaign he was promoted to brigadier general, and he led a brigade at Chickamauga, Chattanooga, and during the Atlanta Campaign. Accompanying John B. Hood into middle Tennessee, he died in front of the Union works at Franklin during the suicidal attack ordered by Hood.

STRONG, Henry B. (ca. 1821-1862)

After having been in temporary command of the brigade, Henry B. Strong had only resumed command of his regiment that morning when he was struck down at the battle of Antietam. He had been an Irish-born clerk working in New Orleans when the Civil War began. Joining the army, his assignments included: captain, Company B, 6th Louisiana (June 5, 1861); lieutenant colonel, 6th Louisiana (May 9, 1862); colonel, 6th Louisiana (ca. June 27, 1862); and commanding Taylor's (old) Brigade, Ewell's Division, Jackson's Corps, Army of Northern Virginia (August 29-September 17, 1862). He served in action at 1st Bull Run, in the Shenandoah Valley Campaign and at Cedar Mountain before assuming command of the brigade when Colonel Henry Forno was wounded at 2nd Bull Run. He led the brigade through the capture of Harpers Ferry and on the morning of the battle of Antietam he was relieved by General Harry T. Hays and resumed command of the 6th. In the fighting near the Dunkard Church he was fatally shot.

STUART, James Ewell Brown (1833-1864)

Known as "Jeb," Stuart was probably the most famous cavalryman of the Civil War. A Virginia-born West Pointer (1854), Stuart was already a veteran of Indian fighting on the plains and of Bleeding Kansas when, as a first lieutenant in the 1st Cavalry, he carried orders for Robert E. Lee to proceed to Harpers Ferry to crush John Brown's raid. Stuart, volunteering as aide-de-camp, went along and read the ultimatum to Brown before the assault in which he distinguished himself. Promoted to captain on April 22, 1861, Stuart resigned on May 14, 1861, having arrived on the 6th in Richmond and been made a lieutenant colonel of Virginia infantry. His later appointments included: captain of Cavalry, CSA (May 24, 1861); colonel, 1st Virginia Cavalry (July 16, 1861); brigadier general, CSA (September 24, 1861); and major general, CSA (July 25, 1862). His commands in the Army of Northern Virginia included: Cavalry Brigade (October 22, 1861-July 28, 1862); Cavalry Division (July 28, 1862-September 9, 1863); temporarily Jackson's 2nd Corps (May 3-6, 1863); and Cavalry Corps (September 9, 1863-May 11, 1864). After early service in the Shenandoah Valley, Stuart led his regiment in the battle of 1st Bull Run and participated in the pursuit of the routed Federals. He then directed the army's outposts until given command of the cavalry brigade. Besides leading the cavalry in the Army of Northern Virginia's fights at the Seven Days, 2nd Bull Run, Antietam, Fredericksburg, Chancellorsville, Gettysburg, and the Wilderness, Stuart was also a raider. Twice he led his command around McClellan's army, once in the Peninsula Campaign and once after the battle of Antietam. While these exploits were not that important militarily, they provided a boost to the Southern morale. During the 2nd Bull Run Campaign, he lost his famed plumed hat and cloak to pursuing Federals. In a later Confederate raid, Stuart managed to overrun Union army commander Pope's headquarters and capture his full uniform and orders that provided Lee with much valuable intelligence. At the end of 1862, Stuart led a raid north of the Rappahannock River, inflicting some 230 casualties while losing only 27 of his own men. At Chancellorsville he took over command of his friend Stonewall Jackson's Corps after that officer had been mortally wounded by his own men. Returning to the cavalry shortly after, he commanded the Southern horsemen in the largest cavalry engagement ever fought on the American continent, Brandy Station, on June 9, 1863. Although the battle was a draw, the Confederates did hold the field. However, the fight represented the rise of the Union cavalry and foreshadowed the decline of the formerly invincible Southern mounted arm. During the Gettysburg Campaign, Stuart, acting under ambiguous orders, again circled the Union army, but in the process deprived Lee of his eyes and ears while in enemy territory. Arriving late on the second day of the battle, Stuart failed the next day to get into the enemy's rear flank, being defeated by Generals Gregg and Custer. During Grant's drive on Richmond in the spring of 1864, Stuart halted Sheridan's cavalry at Yellow Tavern on the outskirts of Richmond on May 11. In the fight he was mortally wounded and died the next day in the rebel capital. (Davis, Burke, *Jeb Stuart: The Last Cavalier*)

SULLY, Alfred (1821-1879)

Philadelphia native Alfred Sully spent more of his Civil War career fighting Indians than Confederates. The West Pointer (1841) had been posted to the infantry with which he took part in actions against the Seminoles in Florida. He fought in Mexico and was then on the frontier fighting the Cheyenne at the outbreak of the Civil War. His assignments in that conflict included: captain, 2nd Infantry (since February 23, 1852); colonel, 1st Minnesota (March 4, 1862); major, 8th Infantry (March 15, 1862); commanding 1st Brigade, 2nd Division, 2nd Corps, Army of the Potomac (June-July, October 29-December 19, 1862, and March 10-May 1, 1863); brigadier general, USV (September 26, 1862); commanding 3rd Division, 2nd Corps, Army of the Potomac (December 20, 1862-January 10, 1863); commanding District of Dakota, Department of the Northwest (May-December 4, 1863); commanding District of Iowa (included Dakota Territory), Department of the Northwest (December 4, 1863-June 27, 1865); and temporarily commanding the department (November 24-December 1864). Initially he served in his regular army capacity in northern Missouri and the Washington defenses before being named commander of a volunteer regiment. This he led to the Peninsula where he fought at Yorktown and was brevetted for Seven Pines. While commanding the brigade during the Seven Days he was brevetted for Malvern Hill. He led his regiment at Antietam and was shortly thereafter awarded a brigadier's star. He took part in the assaults at Fredericksburg and was preparing to move his brigade for the Chancellorsville Campaign when he was relieved by his division commander, John Gibbon. The problem stemmed from the refusal of the 34th New York to perform its duty. Apparently Sully was unsure of his right to use the amount of force called for by regular army regulations against volunteers. Following his removal he asked for a court of inquiry. That panel cleared him of the charges on May 16, 1863, but he was nonetheless shunted off to the Northwest. For his campaigns against the Sioux during the war he was brevetted brigadier general in the regular army and was also brevetted major general of volunteers. Mustered out of the latter on April 30, 1866, he remained in the army and saw extensive frontier service. He died as colonel, 21st Infantry, while commanding Fort Vancouver, Washington Territory. (Sully, Langdon, *No Tears for the General: The Life of Alfred Sully, 1821-1879*)

SURRATT, John Harrison (1844-1916)

The one member of the Lincoln conspirators to escape punishment was the former Confederate courier John H. Surratt. The Maryland native had been involved with the early plots to kidnap the president and carry him off to Richmond. There is much controversy as to whether or not he was involved in the assassination plot. He later claimed that he had been in Canada on the day of the murder and could not have been involved. However, there was testimony that it was he who had prepared the hole in the president's box door and arranged the wooden obstruction to prevent John Wilkes Booth from being interrupted in his preparations for the killing. Union soldiers later claimed that it was Surratt who repeatedly announced the time in front of Ford's Theater in order to alert the other conspirators

that the moment was close at hand. Some claim that Booth assigned Surratt to the killing of General Grant. While his friends were being rounded up, Surratt showed up in Canada and remained there until September 1865 when he sailed for Europe, eventually joining the guards at the Vatican. Spotted by an old schoolmate, he fled to Egypt where he was finally apprehended. A trial was held in 1867, but the jury could not come to a decision and he was released. This may have been out of a sense of guilt over Mary Surratt's execution. His remaining years were spent as a clerk and on the lecture circuit. (Campbell, Helen Jones, *Confederate Courier*)

SURRATT, Mary E. (1820-1865)

To this day the guilt or innocence of Mary E. Surratt in the Lincoln assassination conspiracy is a matter of intense debate. The Maryland widow had leased out her tavern in Surrattsville to a John M. Lloyd, who was destined to be a star witness against her. In the meantime Mrs. Surratt ran a boarding house on Washington's H Street. Her son, John H. Surratt, was an

Mary E. Surratt went to the gallows, but her guilt is still questioned today. (LC)

active member in the plots of John Wilkes Booth to kidnap Lincoln and hustle him off to the South. And it was in her boarding house that much of the planning was done. Whether she knew it or not is an open question. Shortly after the assassination she was arrested and was put on trial with the other conspirators—John Surratt had escaped to Canada—and was given little resembling a fair trial by the military commission. Along with three others she was sentenced to hang. Many believed that she would not actually go to the gallows, and General Winfield S. Hancock, the military commander in the capital, set up a relay of horses to carry any reprieve order from the White House to the arsenal grounds where the execution was to take place. On July 7, 1865, she was hanged.

SWANN, Oswald (?-?)

Although Oswald Swann had aided in the flight of John Wilkes Booth and David Herold, he provided vital information to detectives which kept them on the trail of the assassination conspirators. After leaving the home of Dr. Samuel A. Mudd, Booth and Herold found themselves lost when they emerged from the Zekiah Swamp near Brice's Chapel, Maryland. Herold then located Swann, a black, who agreed to lead them to their next stopping place, the home of a "Captain" Samuel Cox. Having completed his mission, Swann later told the authorities that he had noticed a whispered conversation before the pair had been ordered from the house. He further reported that he then saw them returning to the Cox place.

T

TALCOTT, Thomas Mann Randolph (1838-1920)

It was not until the final full year of war that the Confederate War Department completed the formal organization of engineer regiments. To the command of the first of these was appointed Thomas M.R. Talcott, a civil engineer and the son of an old army friend of Robert E. Lee. His Confederate assignments included: captain, Engineers (1861); major, Engineers (April 26, 1862); lieutenant colonel, Engineers, (July 25, 1863); and colonel, 1st Confederate Engineers (April 1, 1864). After general engineering duties he was assigned as an aide to General Lee when that officer was serving as an advisor to the president in the spring of 1862. Becoming part of Lee's personal staff with the Army of Northern Virginia, he was generally assigned to engineering projects. In the winter of 1863-64 he was detailed to begin organization of an engineer regiment and was made its commander upon its completion. He served through the surrender at Appomattox and returned to civil engineering in Richmond. (Freeman, Douglas S., *R.E. Lee*)

TALIAFERRO, Alexander Galt (1808-1884)

As a regimental, and briefly as a brigade, commander, Alexander G. Taliaferro fought through much of the heavy campaigning of Jackson's command in 1862, until he was disabled for further field service. A lawyer in his native Virginia, he had also been a field-grade officer in the state militia at the beginning of hostilities. Volunteering for active service, his assignments included: captain, Company G, 13th Virginia (May 28, 1861); lieutenant colonel, 23rd Virginia (September 12, 1861); colonel, 23rd Virginia (April 15, 1862); commanding 3rd Brigade, Jackson's (old) Division, Jackson's Corps, Army of Northern Virginia (August 9-ca. 28, 1862); and commanding post at Charlottesville (September 1863-March 18, 1865). During the battle of 1st Bull Run his regiment was left behind to guard Manassas Junction. Transferring to another regiment, he saw action at Cheat Mountain, in the Romney

Campaign, and in command of the regiment at Kernstown, McDowell, in the Shenandoah Valley Campaign, and at Cedar Mountain. He was wounded at both Kernstown and Port Republic during the Shenandoah Valley Campaign. At Cedar Mountain he succeeded to brigade command when General William B. Taliaferro took over the division. He led the brigade at 2nd Bull Run until he was again wounded. Unfit to rejoin his unit, he was assigned to post duty until his resignation for health reasons on March 18, 1865.

TALIAFERRO, William Booth (1822-1898)

Stonewall Jackson never forgot that William B. Taliaferro had sided with General Loring in the feud over the Romney Campaign. A Virginia lawyer and politician, Taliaferro had served as a captain and major in two of the regular army regiments raised for the Mexican War. As a major general of militia he was present during a part of the John Brown crisis at Harpers Ferry. As a militia officer he was assigned to duty in the Norfolk area and later to volunteer service on the Peninsula. His later assignments included: colonel, 23rd Virginia (spring 1861); commanding brigade, Army of the Northwest (summer 1861-ca. March 1862); brigadier general, CSA (March 4, 1862); commanding brigade, Valley District, Department of Northern Virginia (March 1862); commanding brigade, Jackson's Division, same district and department (May and June 1862); commanding brigade, Jackson's Division, 2nd Corps, Army of Northern Virginia (July-August 9, 1862); commanding the division (August 9-28 and fall 1862-February 20, 1863); commanding brigade, District of Georgia, Department of South Carolina, Georgia and Florida (March 6-July 1863); commanding 1st Subdivision, 1st Military District of South Carolina, same department (July-October 22, 1863); commanding 7th Military District of South Carolina, same department (October 22, 1863-October 17, 1864); commanding 3rd Sub-district of South Carolina, District of South Carolina, same department (from October 17, 1864); and also commanding brigade (after December 28 a division), same department or (from March) Hardee's Corps (July 1864-April 9, 1865). Sent to western Virginia, he participated in the Romney Campaign and fought at McDowell and in the Valley Campaign. He took command of Jackson's Division, over Stonewall's protest, at Cedar Mountain and was wounded at Groveton. After Fredericksburg he was shunted off to the coast where he served in the defense of Charleston. He commanded a division of coast defenders in opposing Sherman's march through the Carolinas and saw action at Bentonville. In the April 9, 1865, reorganization of Johnston's forces it appears that Taliaferro lost his position, but he was still paroled with that army. He was a legislator and judge back in Virginia after the war. (Robertson, James I., Jr., *The Stonewall Brigade*)

TANEY, Roger Brooke (1777-1864)

When Supreme Court Chief Justice Roger B. Taney died on October 12, 1864, some of the comments included: "The Hon. old Roger B. Taney has earned the gratitude of the country by dying at last," "Providence has given us a victory," and "Better late than never." The Maryland native had practiced law, sat in the state legislature, and served as state attorney general, U.S. attorney general, acting secretary of war, and secretary of the treasury. During this period he supported the War of 1812 and opposed the second national bank. As a reward for his political support, Andrew Jackson appointed him as an associate justice of the Supreme Court, but Senate confirmation was postponed.

Roger B. Taney of Maryland, chief justice of the Supreme Court at the time of the *Dred Scott* decision. (NA)

In the meantime Chief Justice John Marshall died and Jackson named Taney to the post on December 28, 1835. he was finally confirmed on March 15, 1836, and began his highly controversial 28 years as presiding judge. His ruling in the *Dred Scott* case ignited outrage throughout large sectors of the country. He held that since the slave had returned to slave territory he was still a slave and therefore could not sue. Additionally, he declared that even if a black were not a slave he was still not a citizen and therefore was to be denied the right to appeal to the courts. Early in the Civil War he clashed with Lincoln over the presidential right to suspend *habeas corpus* without the consent of Congress. In 1863 he also voted, in the minority, against the president's right to declare a blockade without a declaration of war or authorization by Congress. Many Unionists were greatly encouraged in the cause when he died. (Swisher, Carl B., *Roger B. Taney*)

TAPPAN, James Camp (1825-1906)

Arkansas lawyer and judge James C. Tappan served the Confederacy on both sides of the Mississippi River and rose to the rank of brigadier general. Born of northern stock in Tennessee, he practiced his profession in Mississippi before settling in Arkansas. His military assignments included: colonel, 13th Arkansas (May 11, 1861); brigadier general, CSA (November 5, 1862); and commanding in the Trans-Mississippi Department: brigade, Price's Division, District of Arkansas (spring 1863-March 24, 1864); Churchill's (Arkansas) Division, Detachment District of Arkansas, District of West Louisiana (March 24-April 1864); brigade, Churchill's (Arkansas) Division, District of Arkansas (April-ca. August 1864); the division (ca. August-September 1864); and 3rd (Arkansas) Brigade, 1st (Arkansas) Division, 2nd Corps (September 1864-May 26, 1865). His regiment was part of the Confederate force already on the west bank of the Mississippi when Grant attacked at Belmont, and Tappan was praised for his handling of his unit. Transferred to the east side of the river, he fought at Shiloh, in the Corinth siege, and at Richmond and Perryville. Promoted to brigadier general shortly thereafter, he was transferred to the Trans-Mississippi Department. He led a brigade in the unsuccessful defense of Little Rock and a division during the repulse of Banks' Red River Campaign. Heading north, he was again in charge of his brigade at Jenkins' Ferry. After the war—he saw little action after the repulse of Frederick Steele's column—he resumed his practice and returned to the state legislature.

TATTNALL, Josiah (1795-1871)

A veteran of the War of 1812, the campaign against the Barbary pirates, and the Mexican War, Josiah Tattnall was eventually found by the Confederacy to be too old for service afloat. The Georgia-born, English-educated Tattnall had been in the U.S. Navy since 1812, but, although he was not a secessionist, he resigned his commission as a captain on February 20, 1861. Eight days later he was named Georgia's senior naval officer. The next month he was appointed captain, CSN, and assigned to command of the naval defenses of Georgia and South Carolina. He led his vessels in an attack upon the Union fleet at Port Royal in November 1861. The following March, Tattnall was ordered to Virginia to replace the wounded Buchanan in command of the defenses there. In this position he made the decision to scuttle the ironclad *Virginia* when the army evacuated Norfolk. Censured by a court of inquiry, Tattnall requested a court-martial which cleared him of blame. In July 1862 he returned to duty on the Georgia coast but on April 2, 1863, he was relieved as too old for sea duty and assigned to shore duty in Savannah. For the remainder of the war, he busied himself with construction and supply matters. After surrendering with Johnston's command, he moved to Nova Scotia before returning, broke, to Savannah in 1870. The post of Inspector of the Port was created for him by a grateful city. (Jones, Charles C., *Life and Services of Commodore Josiah Tattnall*)

TAYLOR, Richard (1826-1879)

Brother-in-law of Jefferson Davis and son of President Zachary Taylor, Richard Taylor served as a Confederate lieutenant general and department commander. Born in Kentucky and educated at Harvard and Yale, he had served as his father's military secretary during the Mexican War. A Louisiana plantation owner, he was active in state politics and supported secession at the convention. His military assignments included: colonel, 9th Louisiana (July 7, 1861); brigadier general, CSA (October 21, 1861); commanding 1st Louisiana Brigade, E.K. Smith's-Ewell's Division, Potomac District (Valley District from April), Department of Northern Virginia (October 22, 1861-June 26, 1862); commanding same brigade, Ewell's Division, Jackson's Corps, Army of Northern Virginia (June 26 and July 1862); major general, CSA (July 28, 1862); commanding District of West Louisiana, Trans-Mississippi Department (August 20, 1862-June 10, 1864); lieutenant general, CSA (May 16, to rank from April 8, 1864); commanding Department of Alabama, Mississippi and East Louisiana (September 23-November 22, 1864 and December 12, 1864-May 4, 1865); and also commanding Army of Tennessee (January 23-February 22, 1865). Too late for the fighting at 1st Bull Run, he commanded a brigade in the Shenandoah Valley Campaign and, until taken ill, in the Seven Days. Transferred west of the Mississippi he commanded in western Louisiana and directed the forces which defeated Banks at Mansfield and Pleasant Hill. Critical of department commander E.K. Smith for not letting him follow up the victories, he was relieved at his own request. Promoted, he was given command in the Deep South and was in overall control of the forces defeated at Mobile and Selma. He surrendered the last major force east of the Mississippi. After the war he was active in trying to alleviate the effects of Reconstruction upon the South. (Taylor, Richard, *Destruction and Reconstruction*)

TAYLOR, Thomas Hart (1825-1901)

A veteran of the Mexican War as a first lieutenant of the 3rd Kentucky, businessman Thomas H. Taylor joined the Confederate service and rose to the rank of brigadier general. The native Kentuckian's assignments included: captain, Infantry (1861); lieutenant colonel, 1st Kentucky (summer 1861); colonel, 1st Kentucky (October 14, 1861); commanding 1st Brigade, Department of East Tennessee (ca. June-July 1862); commanding brigade, 1st (Stevenson's) Division, Department of East Tennessee (early July-December 18, 1862); brigadier general, CSA (November 4, 1862); commanding brigade, Stevenson's Division, 2nd Military District, Department of Mississippi and East Louisiana (January-April 1863); provost marshal general, Department of Mississippi and East Louisiana (April-July 4, 1863); commanding District of Southern Mississippi and East Louisiana, Department of Alabama, Mississippi and East Louisiana (March 5-April 5, 1864); provost marshal general, Department of Alabama, Mississippi and East Louisiana (mid-1864); and commanding Taylor's Command (Post of Mobile), District of the Gulf, Department of Alabama, Mississippi and East Louisiana (fall 1864-April 12, 1865). He served in northern Virginia and on the Peninsula with a 12-months regiment which was mustered out in May 1862. He was then assigned to East Tennessee where he commanded a brigade and took part in the Kentucky Campaign of the summer and fall of 1862. Transferred to Mississippi, he was the provost marshal during the Vicksburg siege and was paroled upon the capture of the city. He then performed district and provost marshal duty (as a brigadier general since the fall of 1862). However, his appointment was never forwarded to the Senate for confirmation and he reverted to his rank of colonel. During the final winter and spring of the war he was in charge of the Post of Mobile until its evacuation. After engaging in business in Mobile, he became a law officer in his native state.

TAYLOR, Walter H. (ca. 1838-?)

The youngest member of Robert E. Lee's personal staff was Walter H. Taylor who served the entire war with Lee. He had attended the Virginia Military Institute in the mid 1850s and was in banking when the secession crisis broke. Offering his services, they included: lieutenant, Virginia Militia (early 1861); lieutenant colonel, Virginia Forces (May 1861); captain and aide-de-camp, CSA (November 8, 1861); major and aide-de-camp, CSA (March 27, 1862); and lieutenant colonel and assistant adjutant general, CSA (November 4, 1864). Joining Lee's staff in May 1861, he assisted in the organization of the Virginia forces and their transfer to the Confederacy. He was one of only two staff officers, and the only one to survive, who accompanied his chief to western Virginia. He served with Lee on the South Carolina coast before the general was made the personal advisor of the president. Here Taylor's position was upgraded to that of a major and he was promoted. In June of 1862 he began his connection with the Army of Northern Virginia which was destined to last until Appomattox. A young man wishing for action, Taylor on at least three occasions joined in the fighting. Upset by the idea of surrender, he was not present during Lee's meeting with Grant in the McLean House. After the war he wrote two works based upon his experiences, *Four Years with General Lee* and *General Lee*. (Freeman, Douglas S., *R.E. Lee*)

TERRELL, Alexander Watkins (1827-1912)

Serving in the cut-off Trans-Mississippi Department, Alexander W. Terrell was promoted extralegally by General E. Kirby Smith when the collapse of the Confederacy was already nearly complete. His assignments included: major, 1st Texas Cavalry, Arizona Brigade (1861); captain and volunteer aide-de-camp (June 12, 1862); lieutenant colonel, Terrell's (Tex.) Cavalry Battalion; colonel, Terrell's (Tex.) Cavalry Regiment (1863); commanding 4th Texas Cavalry Brigade, 4th Texas Cavalry Division, 1st Corps, Trans-Mississippi Department (September and November 1864 and early 1865); and brigadier general, CSA, by Smith (May 16, 1865). After initially serving in the District of Texas, New Mexico and Arizona, Terrell and his regiment were part of the force sent to the District of West Louisiana to help defeat Banks' Red River Campaign in the spring of 1864. He continued to serve in the western portion of Louisiana for the remainder of the war, much of the time in command of a cavalry brigade. In recognition of this fact, Smith promoted him to brigadier in orders 10 days before the department was surrendered. After the collapse Terrell went to Mexico with other ex-Confederates. (Spencer, John, *Terrell's Texas Cavalry*)

TERRELL, Leigh Richmond (1835-1864)

Early in the war Leigh Terrell was made a lieutenant in the 4th Alabama, and when the regimental commander, Colonel E.M. Law, was given command of Whiting's Brigade, Terrell was assigned to his staff as assistant adjutant general. As such he saw action and was commended for his part in the battles of 2nd Bull Run and Antietam. Promoted to captain in the adjutant general's department, he saw further action at Fredericksburg. In April 1863, still on Law's staff, he filed a report on the fall of Fort Huger—on the 19th during Longstreet's siege of Suffolk—that was not flattering of the role of the 55th North Carolina. That regiment's commander, Colonel John K. Connally, and Major Alfred H. Belo demanded satisfaction from Terrell and Captain John Cussons, another officer on the staff. When this was not forthcoming they challenged the two captains to a pair of duels. While Cussons and Belo fired two rounds at each other in a display of rather poor marksmanship, Terrell and Connally resolved the matter verbally. Everyone agreed to go back to killing Yankees. Captain Terrell continued on Law's staff, seeing action at Wauhatchie, the Wilderness, Spotsylvania, and Cold Harbor, until promoted to lieutenant colonel and assigned to the 47th Alabama on June 15, 1864. Three days later he was wounded in the shoulder and on October 13 he was mortally wounded in the siege lines around Richmond and Petersburg. He died nine days later. (Freeman, Douglas S., *Lee's Lieutenants*)

TERRILL, James Barbour (1838-1864)

Both James and his brother William Barbour died in the Civil War, but they fought on opposite sides. An 1858 graduate of the Virginia Military Institute, James Terrill was practicing law in Warm Springs, Virginia, at the time of the firing on Fort Sumter. Unlike his brother, James decided to go with his native state and became the major in A.P. Hill's 13th Virginia in May 1861. His later assignments included: lieutenant colonel, 13th Virginia (ca. October 30, 1862); colonel, 13th Virginia (May 15, 1863); and brigadier general, CSA (May 31, 1864). Terrill's regiment was left behind at Manassas Junction when the brigade went forward into the battle of 1st Bull Run and did not participate in the fight. However, in September 1861 Terrill led the infantry under Colonel Jeb Stuart in the skirmish at Lewinsville, Virginia. Terrill's later battles included the Shenandoah Valley Campaign, Gaines' Mill, White Oak Swamp, Malvern Hill, Cedar Mountain, and, in command of the regiment, Fredericksburg. During the Gettysburg Campaign, the regiment was left behind in Winchester. He then led the regiment in the fighting at the Wilderness and Spotsylvania, and on May 30, 1864, he was nominated by Davis to the Senate as a temporary brigadier to take over the command of the wounded General Pegram. But on the same day, at Bethesda Church, he was killed in action and his body was left to the enemy. His appointment was confirmed the next day. (Freeman, Douglas S., *Lee's Lieutenants*)

TERRY, William (1824-1888)

The least-known commander in the Stonewall Brigade, William Terry did not take it over until it had ceased to exist officially as a unit. A lawyer and journalist in the Upper Shenandoah Valley, he had been an officer in the militia for a number of years before the Civil War and was present for part of the John Brown crisis at Harpers Ferry. Upon the outbreak of the war he went with his company back to the ferry, where the company became part of what was to be the Stonewall Brigade. His assignments included: first lieutenant, Company A, 4th Virginia (ca. May 1861); major, 4th Virginia (April 23, 1862); colonel, 4th Virginia (September 11, 1863); brigadier general, CSA (May 19, 1864); commanding brigade, Johnson's-Gordon's Division, 2nd Corps, Army of Northern Virginia (May 14-June 13 and December 1864-March 25, 1865); and commanding brigade, Gordon's Division, Valley District, Department of Northern Virginia (June 13-December 1864). He fought at 1st Bull Run as a company officer before being elected to field grade upon the reorganization of the regiment. He fought in the Shenandoah, the Seven Days, and at 2nd Bull Run where he was wounded. He returned in time to fight at Fredericksburg where he succeeded to regimental command. He was at the regiment's head at Chancellorsville, Gettysburg, the Wilderness, and at Spotsylvania when the greater part of Johnson's Division was captured. Two days later, 14 Virginia regiments, five from the Stonewall Brigade, were consolidated into one brigade, and Terry was soon promoted to brigadier and given command. He then fought at Cold Harbor, 3rd Winchester, where he was again wounded, Fisher's Hill, and Cedar Creek. Taking up position in the Petersburg trenches, he was wounded in the assault on Fort Stedman on March 25, 1865, and was put out of the war. After the war he resumed the practice of law and served as a U.S. congressman. He drowned during a storm. (Robertson, James I., Jr., *The Stonewall Brigade*)

TERRY, William Richard (1827-1897)

It is claimed that William R. Terry suffered seven wounds during the Civil War. A graduate of the Virginia Military Institute, he had been a merchant in 1861. He raised a cavalry company in his home county, Bedford, and joined the Confederate army where his assignments included: captain, Company A, 2nd Virginia Cavalry (spring 1861); colonel, 24th Virginia (September 1861); commanding Kemper's Brigade, Kemper's Division, 1st Corps, Army of Northern Virginia (August 30-September 1862); commanding Kemper's Brigade, Department of Richmond (September 1863-January 1864); commanding Kemper's Brigade, Department of North Carolina (January-May 1864); commanding Kemper's Brigade, Ransom's Division, Department of Richmond (May 1864); commanding Kemper's (old) Brigade, Pickett's Division, 1st Corps, Army of Northern Virginia (May 1864-March 31, 1865); and brigadier general, CSA (May 30, 1864). After leading his cavalry at 1st Bull Run, he was rewarded by being promoted to colonel and assigned to the 24th Virginia. Leading a charge at Williamsburg, he was wounded but returned to duty in time for 2nd Bull Run. Here he relieved the wounded Colonel Corse in command of the brigade. At the head of the 24th, he fought at Antietam before serving in southeastern Virginia with Longstreet early the next year. Rejoining Lee's army, he was wounded in Pickett's Charge at Gettysburg. With the division again detached he served in Richmond and North Carolina, with fighting at New Bern and Drewry's Bluff. Back with Lee, he was promoted to brigadier and saw more action at Cold Harbor and Petersburg. On March 31, 1865, he received his final wound, at Dinwiddie Court House in a minor Confederate triumph the day before the Five Forks disaster which necessitated the evacuation of the Richmond and Petersburg lines. After the war he served as a state legislator, prison superintendent, and in charge of a soldiers' home. He is often confused with Brigadier General William Terry, also of Virginia.

TEW, Charles Courtenay (1827-1862)

Well qualified for military service, Charles Tew did not live long enough to become a brigadier general in the Confederacy. In 1846 Tew had graduated at the head of his class at the South Carolina Military Academy, or the Citadel. After serving for over a decade as an instructor at his alma mater, Tew moved to North Carolina and founded the Hillsboro Military Academy in 1858. With the outbreak of the Civil War, Tew was assigned to duty drilling troops and commanding Fort Macon. On June 5, 1861, he succeeded General T.H. Holmes in command of the Southern Department Coast Defenses of North Carolina. Having been appointed colonel, 2nd North Carolina State Troops, on May 8, 1861, Tew assumed command of his regiment on June 20. After service in Virginia's Aquia District and back in North Carolina, the 2nd moved to the Peninsula of Virginia in time to participate in the Seven Days Battles where Tew saw action at Gaines' Mill and Malvern Hill. Taking part in the Maryland invasion, Tew saw action at Fox's Gap on South Mountain, and at Antietam he assumed command of the brigade after the mortal wounding of General G.B. Anderson

and was himself killed shortly thereafter while fighting in the Bloody Lane. Tew's division commander, General D.H. Hill, described him as "one of the most finished scholars on the continent, and [Tew] had no superior as a soldier on the field." Had Tew survived the Maryland Campaign he probably would have been promoted to permanent command of Anderson's Brigade. (Freeman, Douglas S., *Lee's Lieutenants*)

THOMAS, Allen (1830-1907)

Captured at the fall of Vicksburg, Maryland-born Louisiana planter Allen Thomas was exchanged and transferred to the Trans-Mississippi Department where he was assigned to reorganizing the paroled and exchanged prisoners and became a brigadier general. The former attorney's Confederate assignments included: major, Thomas' Louisiana Battalion (1861); colonel, 29th (also known as 28th) Louisiana (October 1862, to rank from May 3); commanding brigade, Provisional Division, Department of Mississippi and East Louisiana (December 1862-January 1863); brigadier general, CSA (February 4, 1864); commanding 1st (Louisiana) Brigade, Polignac's Division, 1st Corps (or District of West Louisiana), Trans-Mississippi Department (September 1864-February 1865); and commanding the division (February-May 26, 1865). Serving in defense of Vicksburg, he was in charge of a brigade at Chickasaw Bayou and his regiment in the siege proper. Taken prisoner, he was exchanged and sent into western Louisiana where he came under the command of his brother-in-law, Richard Taylor. About this time he carried John C. Pemberton's report of the campaign to the authorities in Richmond. Late in 1864 he took charge of a brigade of Louisianans in the division of Prince Polignac. When that officer sailed for Europe on a diplomatic mission, Thomas succeeded him in divisional command. After the Confederacy's fall General Thomas was a planter, politician, educator, diplomat, and public official.

THOMAS, Bryan Morel (1836-1905)

Beginning the war as a staff officer, recent graduate of West Point (1858) Bryan M. Thomas rose to the rank of brigadier general and command of a brigade in the later stages of the conflict. The Georgia native had resigned his first lieutenant's commission in the infantry on April 6, 1861, and offered his services to the Confederacy. The veteran of Indian fighting and the Utah expedition saw the following assignments: lieutenant, Infantry (spring 1861); major, Infantry (late 1861); colonel, Thomas' Alabama Reserves Cavalry Regiment (1864); brigadier general, CSA (August 4, 1864); and commanding brigade, District of the Gulf, Department of Alabama, Mississippi and East Louisiana (August 1864-April 9, 1865). At Shiloh, Perryville, and Murfreesboro he served as Jones M. Withers' ordnance and artillery chief. Named to organized Alabama reserve units, he took command of a mounted regiment and in the summer of 1864 was appointed a brigadier general. The balance of his service was spent in the defenses of Mobile where he commanded a brigade. Captured at the fall of Fort Blakely on April 9, 1865, he was a planter, law officer, and educator after the war.

THOMAS, Edward Lloyd (1825-1898)

Capitalizing upon his Mexican War experience, as a lieutenant of Georgia cavalry, plantation owner Edward L. Thomas was granted permission to raise a regiment for the Confederacy. His assignments included: colonel, 35th Georgia (October 15, 1861); commanding Pettigrew's Brigade, G.W. Smith's-Whiting's Division, Department of Northern Virginia (May 31-June 1862); commanding J.R. Anderson's Brigade, A.P. Hill's Division (in 1st Corps from June 29 and in 2nd Corps from July 27), Army of Northern Virginia (June 30, 1862-May 30, 1863); brigadier general, CSA (November 1, 1862); and commanding brigade, Pender's-Wilcox's Division, 3rd Corps, same army (May 30, 1863-January 1865 and February-April 9, 1865). Sent to the Peninsula in Virginia, Thomas was involved in the Yorktown operations and at the battle of Seven Pines succeeded to the brigade command of the wounded and captured Pettigrew. He reverted to regimental leadership when the brigade was broken up in June. The 35th was assigned to J.R. Anderson's Brigade, and when this officer was wounded at Glendale, Thomas was in charge of the brigade that he would direct until Appomattox. His wound, received a few days earlier at Mechanicsville, did not alter this. He led his fellow Georgians at Cedar Mountain, 2nd Bull Run, and Harpers Ferry but was still paroling the prisoners when the fight at Antietam occurred. Promoted six weeks later, he went on to fight at Fredericksburg, Chancellorsville, Gettysburg, and in the Overland, Petersburg, and Appamattox campaigns. After the surrender he went back to his land and held a number of government appointments. (Freeman, Douglas S., *Lee's Lieutanants*)

THOMAS, William Holland (1805-1893)

One of the unique units of the Civil War was a legion of Cherokees and white North Carolinian mountain men commanded by William H. Thomas. A friend of the Indians in western North Carolina, Thomas gained the permission of Andrew Jackson for a number of them to remain in the area—while the majority was deported west of the Mississippi in 1838—and was made one of their chiefs. The state legislator determined to raise an Indian company for the local defense of their area at the outbreak of the war. His assignments included: captain, North Carolina Cherokee company (April 9, 1862); major, Cherokee battalion (July 19, 1862); and colonel, Thomas' (N.C.) Legion (September 27, 1862). With the success of his recruiting activities he kept enlarging his force until it was composed of infantry, cavalry, artillery, and sappers and organized into a regiment and a battalion. His force was used in the mountains of western North Carolina and East Tennessee. However, he was eventually detached from his command—with his two Cherokee companies—after a feud with his brigade commander, Brigadier General Alfred E. Jackson, and sent to round up deserters in their home district. The white portion of the unit fought in East Tennessee and the Shenandoah Valley under Early before rejoining Thomas. By the time that they returned the war was almost over. However, a company of the legion fired the last shot of the war in North Carolina on

May 9, 1865, near Waynesville. The next day they surrendered, but the Union commander was so intimidated by the Cherokees that he allowed them to keep their arms and to leave the area. This "surrender" marked the end of Thomas' Legion. Thomas himself had surrendered two days earlier. (Crow, Vernon, *Storm in the Mountains: Thomas' Confederate Legion of Cherokee Indians and Mountaineers*)

THOMPSON, Albert P. (?-1864)

In the same month that he joined Forrest's cavalry, Kentuckian Albert P. Thompson died within sight of his home in one of the great cavalryman's raids. His Confederate assignments included: lieutenant colonel, 3rd Kentucky (July 5, 1861); colonel, 3rd Kentucky (October 25, 1861); commanding 1st Brigade, 2nd Division, Breckinridge's Command, District of the Mississippi Department #2 (July 28-August 5, 1862); and commanding 3rd Brigade, 2nd Division, Forrest's Cavalry Corps, Department of Alabama, Mississippi and East Louisiana (March 7-25, 1864). After service in central Kentucky and northern Mississippi, he led a brigade until wounded in the failed Confederate attack on Baton Rouge. Returning to duty, he served in Buford's Brigade at Jackson, Mississippi and Port Hudson, Louisiana. Ordered to Middle Tennessee, the brigade had its orders changed so that it could face Grierson's raid through Mississippi in April 1863. Then, with Grant's army threatening Vicksburg, Thompson and the brigade fought at Champion Hill where, with the rest of Loring's Division, they were cut off from Pemberton's army and subsequently joined Joe Johnston. During this campaign, Thompson was detached with six of his companies to serve as mounted infantry. With the fall of the river fortress, Thompson continued to serve in the Mississippi area until March 1864 when his regiment was mounted and he was given command of a brigade of cavalry under Forrest. A few weeks later, on Forrest's raid to the Ohio River, he was killed in the attack on Paducah, Kentucky.

THOMPSON, Jacob (1810-1885)

Involved in the Confederacy's activities in Canada, Jacob Thompson managed to get himself indicted in the investigation of the Lincoln assassination. When he fled to Europe, it now appears from recently uncovered evidence, he converted a Confederate fortune to his personal use. Born in North Carolina, he had practiced law before moving to Mississippi. He served in the House of Representatives for over a decade and in 1857 he became secretary of the interior under Buchanan. Charged in the embezzlement of funds from the Indian Trust Fund, he was later cleared. A firm believer in secession, he left the cabinet in protest against the Fort Sumter relief expedition by the *Star of the West* but not until after he had notified the South Carolina authorities of her coming. He served as a lieutenant colonel on the staffs of Beauregard and Pemberton before entering the state legislature in 1863. The next year Jefferson Davis sent him to Canada as a commissioner. He was given large sums of money, for which, given the nature of his service, he was not required to fully account. He was involved in the Northwest Conspiracy to free rebel prisoners and stage a general uprising. He also spent money to gain political and journalistic support for the South and in an attempt to cause a financial panic by speculating in gold. To a lesser extent he was involved in the St. Albans Raid and the plot to burn New York. Although he had known John Wilkes Booth in Canada, he was acquitted for complicity in the assassination but by then had already fled to Europe. Unlike other agents in exile he failed to account for his funds to top ex-Confederate officials in Europe and was investigated by ex-Secretary of War Breckinridge and ex-Secretary of State Benjamin. Failing to account for £35,000, Thompson agreed to a compromise: he paid £12,000 to the former Confederates and the rest was forgotten about. Benjamin agreed to this because he feared a scandal and knew he could not press the claim legally since the Confederacy was defunct. During the next few years, Thompson lived the high-life in Europe, making extensive tours. His windfall of £23,000, or US$113,780, offset much of the wartime losses to his extensive holdings. However, other ex-Confederates charged that his total haul exceeded $300,000, and events show this to be quite likely. Returning to the United States in 1869, he parlayed his holdings into an estate estimated at $500,000 by the time of his death. Thompson had proved that crime against a defunct government does pay. (Davis, William C., "The Conduct of 'Mr. Thompson,'" *CWTI*, May 1970)

THOMPSON, John Reuben (1823-1873)

A staunch secessionist, Virginian John R. Thompson supported the movement and the Confederacy through his editing, poems, and propaganda abroad. After briefly practicing law his father bought him the *Southern Literary Messenger*, with which he was connected through 1860. His publication was the literary periodical of the South in the pre-secession days. During the Civil War he served as assistant secretary to Virginia governor John Letcher and was an editor for the *Richmond Record* and *The Southern Illustrated News*. In July 1864, due to ill-health he went to England where he wrote for the *Index*, a pro-Confederate organ for which he had already contributed from Richmond. His wartime poems included: "Music in Camp," "The Burial of Latané," "Lee to the Rear," and "Ashby." After the war he worked for the *London Standard* and *New York Evening Post.*" He also assisted in the writing of Heros von Borcke's *Memoirs of the Confederate War for Independence.*

THOMPSON, Meriwether Jefferson (1826-1876)

Better known as M. Jeff. Thompson, the Virginia-born former mayor of St. Joseph, Missouri, was one of the more shadowy characters of the Civil War. Highly successful in just about everything he attempted, he was known for his penchant for weapons. With the secession crisis in Missouri, the professional engineer entered the service of his adopted state and became lieutenant colonel, 3rd Infantry, 1st Division, Missouri State Guard. By the fall of Fort Sumter he was a colonel and inspector in the Guard's 4th Military District and on April 15, 1861, he wrote offering his services to Jefferson Davis. By that summer

he was brigadier general in the Guard, but, although he often served in command of Confederate troops, he was never mustered into that service. His small force was active in raiding in southeastern Missouri during the war's first season, but in December his force was disbanded preparatory to reorganizing for Confederate service. In the spring of 1862 he was assigned to duty with several of his new volunteer companies, to serve as gunners and marines aboard J.E. Montgomery's River Defense Fleet. However, there was much ill blood between Thompson's men and Montgomery's river steamboatmen and Thompson had to request a transfer of his command. That summer he served with Confederate troops in the vicinity of Lake Pontchartrain, threatening New Orleans. The next summer, 1863, he was serving back in his old haunts, where his men had become known as the "Swamp Rats," in northeastern Arkansas and southeastern Missouri. On August 22, 1863, he was captured in Randolph County, Arkansas, and confined at Johnson's Island and Fort Delaware. "Beast" Butler of New Orleans ill-fame, had developed a great deal of respect for Thompson due to the latter's kind treatment of prisoners and requested that Thompson be released on his parole. This, for Butler, unusual request was denied by the U.S. War Department because of the Sawyer-Flinn dispute. In about August 1864 he was exchanged after having been sent to Charleston Harbor to be placed under Confederate fire—although this was, according to Thompson, never done. On August 9 he was ordered to report to the Trans-Mississippi Department. During part of Price's invasion of Missouri, he commanded Shelby's Brigade, Shelby's Division, Army of Missouri, Trans-Mississippi Department (October 7-December 1864) and the division (December 1864). Falling back into Arkansas, he surrendered the Northern Sub-District of Arkansas, District of Arkansas and West Louisiana, Trans-Mississippi Department, on May 11, 1865. (Monaghan, James, *Swamp Fox of the Confederacy; the Life and Military Services of M. Jeff. Thompson*)

THOUVENEL, Édouard (?-?)

Although French Emperor Napoleon III was strongly in favor of an interventionist course in the American Civil War, his foreign minister during the early part of that conflict, Édouard Thouvenel, was not convinced that such would be the wisest path for France to follow. Many claim that this led to his forced resignation from the government on October 15, 1862. News of the seizure of two Confederate commissioners, Mason and Slidell, from on board the British vessel *Trent* by the U.S. Navy, had much of Europe in a state of outrage when Thouvenel was approached by American diplomats. They sought his views on the situation. True to his abstentionist views, he declared that France considered the action to be a gross violation of international law. But when questioned upon the course France would follow in the dispute, he stated that France would place the moral force of its opinion behind the British, but he seemed to rule out any military action. The minister was worried about the growth of German power at a time when France was preoccupied with events in Mexico and Italy. Earning the displeasure of his sovereign, Thouvenel was forced out in favor of Édouard Drouyn de L'Huys.

THRUSTON, Henry C. (?-1909)

Towering over the Union's biggest Yankee—David Van Buskirk at 6 feet 10 1/2 inches—the Confederacy's was Henry C. Thruston. He enlisted with four of his brothers, all 6 1/2 feet or taller, in the Morgan County (Texas) Rangers. At mustering in he measured 7 feet 7 1/2 inches. He fought at Pea Ridge and then transferred to Company I, 4th Missouri Cavalry. Serving under Earl Van Dorn and Sterling Price, he fought in Arkansas and Missouri. In the spring of 1864 he was wounded at Poison Springs, Arkansas. In the invasion of Missouri later that year he was lightly wounded in the top of the head. A smaller man would have been spared. Surrendered and paroled on June 7, 1865, he settled in Texas for his remaining years.

THULSTRUP, Bror Thure (1848-1930)

A graduate of the National Military Academy in his native Sweden and a veteran of the French Foreign Legion, including service in the Franco-Prussian War, Bror T. Thulstrup—known in the United States as Thure de Thulstrup—naturally turned to military subjects when he decided to enter the field of creative art. His interest in topographical engineering led him into drawing and eventually he moved toward paint and canvas. Pursuing this field he moved to Canada and then the United States. Studying in the post-Civil War years, he was naturally drawn to the subject, and one of his more famous works is of Pickett's Charge at Gettysburg. A military man himself, he was strict in his devotion to accuracy in uniforms and equipment. As a free-lance artist he worked for both *Harper's Weekly* and *Frank Leslie's Illustrated Newspaper*. A collection of his work was published in 1898 as *Drawings by Thulstrup and Others*.

TILGHMAN, Lloyd (1816-1863)

In two separate efforts to keep Southern rivers blocked to the Union forces, Maryland West Pointer (1836) Lloyd Tilghman was captured in the first and later in the second, killed. He had resigned his commission as a second lieutenant in the 1st Dragoons less than three months after his graduation, then engaged in railroad engineering until the outbreak of the Civil War, except for reentering the service as an artillery captain with the Maryland and District of Columbia volunteers during the Mexican War. Residing in Kentucky when Fort Sumter was fired upon, he offered his services to the Confederacy and his assignments included: brigadier general, CSA (October 18, 1861); commanding Fort Henry, Department #2 (January-February 6, 1862); commanding brigade, Lovell's Division, District of the Mississippi, Army of West Tennessee (October 6-16, 1862); commanding brigade, Lovell's Corps, Army of West Tennessee (October 16-December 7, 1862); commanding brigade, 1st Corps, Department of Mississippi and East Louisiana (December 7, 1862-January 2, 1863); commanding brigade, 1st Loring's Division, 2nd Military District, Department of Mississippi and East Louisiana (January 2-April 1863); and commanding brigade, Loring's Division, 2nd Military District, Department of Mississippi and East Louisiana (January 2-April 1863); and commanding brigade, Loring's Division,

Department of Mississippi and East Louisiana (April-May 16, 1863). Inspecting the forts on the Tennessee and Cumberland rivers, he felt that the positioning of Fort Henry on the former was highly defective. Nonetheless he did make a brave stand with a handful of men against the Union gunboats, having dispatched the greater part of his command to Fort Donelson. Forced to capitulate, he was not exchanged until August 27, 1862, for John F. Reynolds. Assigned to command of a brigade, he spent the balance of his life in the defense of Vicksburg. Initially, he was in charge of the camp of paroled and exchanged prisoners at the river city. When Grant crossed the river south of the city Tilghman's brigade served as a part of John C. Pemberton's field force. On May 16, 1863, he was killed by a shell while supervising his own artillery.

TIMROD, Henry (1828-1867)

A college dropout, a failure as a law student, Henry Timrod throughout his life turned to the meager income that his poetry could provide him. His verse was published by the *Southern Literary Messenger* and in an 1859 collection, and his reputation grew beyond his native Charleston. A southern patriot, he celebrated the formation of the Confederacy with "Ethnogenesis" and predicted a stout defense if invaded. His poems show a rise and fall of optimism which matches the military fortunes of the Confederacy. In the winter of 1861-62, Timrod served as a private in the 13th South Carolina. In the spring he became secretary to Colonel Keitt of the 20th South Carolina. He shortly thereafter went west to cover General Beauregard's army in Northern Mississippi for the *Charleston Mercury*. Because journalists were expelled from the army's lines (prior to the retreat from Corinth), Timrod returned to his regiment in South Carolina. Discharged due to tuberculosis in December 1862 he continued to praise in verse the defenders of Charleston, General Ripley, and, in "Carmen Triumphale," victory at Chancellorsville. As associate editor of the *South Carolinian* in 1864 his prospects improved. However, illness curtailed his writing. In late 1866, he wrote his most famous piece, "Ode," mourning the lost cause of the Confederacy. He died the next year. (Parks, Edd W., *Henry Timrod*)

TODD, George (?-1864)

One of bushwhacker William C. Quantrill's principal deputies, George Todd, succeeded to the command of most of the cutthroat's band after embarrassing Quantrill in front of the rest of the men. Todd had long ridden with Quantrill, and when the latter had been named a captain, Todd was made a lieutenant. Participating in most of the bloody guerrilla actions in Missouri, Todd and Quantrill eventually came into conflict—at one point they even exchanged shots—until Todd placed a gun in Quantrill's face and forced him to back down. Quantrill rode off with a few of his men. Todd, now called captain since Quantrill had styled himself a colonel, was left in charge. He led his men in the Centralia massacre and had a running feud with another former Quantrill lieutenant, Bloody Bill Anderson. Finally, in late October 1864 he was killed outside Independence, Missouri, while scouting for Price's army.

TOMPKINS, Sally Louisa (1833-1916)

In order to retain her services to the Confederacy when all military hospitals were put under military control, Jefferson Davis had Sally L. Tompkins commissioned a captain of cavalry on September 9, 1861. She was thus the only woman to officially become an officer in the armies of the Confederacy. A resident of Richmond, she had long been active in charity work, and when the call went out after 1st Bull Run for Richmonders to open their homes for the wounded and sick, she used the home of Judge John Robertson as a hospital. Despite being sent some of the most serious cases, her Robertson Hospital maintained an enviable record. From August 1, 1861, to April 2, 1865, there occurred only 73 deaths out of 1,333 admissions. Refusing to accept any pay for her work, she made good use of her rank in running her operations. Her hospital was in operation until June 13, 1865, under the Union occupation. After the war she was active in philanthropic work through the Protestant Episcopal Church. She was buried with military honors, and two chapters of the United Daughters of the Confederacy were named for her.

TOOMBS, Robert Augustus (1810-1885)

During his career as a lawyer and politician, serving in both houses in his native Georgia and in the U.S. Senate, Robert A.

Robert A. Toombs, Confederate congressman and general. (*Harper's*)

Toombs gradually became a secessionist. After attending the state's secession convention, he was named to the Provisional Confederate Congress where he served on the Committee on Finance. An aspirant for the presidency, he instead became the first secretary of state on February 21, 1861. Bored, he stepped down in July and, capitalizing upon his experience as a captain of volunteers during the Creek War, entered the military service. His assignments included: brigadier general, CSA (July 19, 1861); commanding brigade, 2nd Corps, Army of the Potomac (summer-October 22, 1861); commanding brigade, G.W. Smith's Division, (in Potomac District until March), Department of Northern Virginia (October 22, 1861-April 1862); commanding brigade, D.R. Jones' Division, Magruder's Command, same department (April-July 3, 1862); temporarily commanding the division (April 1862); and commanding brigade, Jones' Division, 1st Corps, Army of Northern Virginia (July and August 30-September 17, 1862). Seeing action in the Seven Days, he was criticized by D.H. Hill for the behavior of his brigade at Malvern Hill. His demand for satisfaction went unanswered. Still retaining a seat in congress, he was absent for part of the summer but rejoined his command at 2nd Bull Run. At Antietam his brigade performed creditably and he suffered a hand wound. At about the time that congress adjourned he submitted his resignation, which took effect on March 4, 1863. He was disgruntled about being passed over for promotion. He lost a race for the Senate but was named adjutant and inspector general for the Georgia Militia in the Atlanta Campaign. Fleeing the country to avoid arrest at the war's close, he returned and resumed his law practice. Late in life he suffered from blindness and alcoholism. (Thompson, William Y., *Robert Toombs of Georgia*)

TOON, Thomas Fentress (1840-1902)

A Wake Forest College student at the outbreak of the war, Thomas F. Toon enlisted on April 24, 1861, but then returned to complete his studies. Once finished he rejoined his company in time for mustering in. His assignments included: first lieutenant, Company K, 20th North Carolina (June 18, 1861); captain, Company K, 20th North Carolina (July 19, 1861); colonel, 20th North Carolina (February 26, 1863); commanding Johnston's Brigade, Ramseur's Division, 2nd Corps, Army of Northern Virginia (May 12-June 13, 1864); temporary brigadier general, CSA (May 31, 1864); and commanding Johnston's Brigade, Ramseur's Division, Valley District, Department of Northern Virginia (June 13-August 1864). As a company officer, he was so distinguished at Seven Pines, the Seven Days, South Mountain, and Fredericksburg that the following winter he was promoted three grades to command the regiment. He returned in time to fight at Mine Run, the Wilderness, and Spotsylvania. With General Johnston wounded in the latter, Toon took over the brigade and was appointed a temporary brigadier. As such he served in Early's campaign to the outskirts of Washington, including fighting at Monocacy. In August Johnston resumed command, and Toon reverted to colonel in charge of the 20th. Toon then fought at 3rd Winchester, Fisher's Hill, and Cedar Creek. Moving to the Petersburg trenches, he was severely wounded in the Confederate assault on Fort Stedman. He served in education and railroading after the war and also sat in the legislature.

TRACY, Edward Dorr (1833-1863)

Georgia-born Alabama lawyer Edward D. Tracy gave his life for the Confederacy in the first stages of Grant's final drive against Vicksburg. His assignments included: captain, Company I, 4th Alabama (May 7, 1861); major, 4th Alabama (July 25, 1861); lieutenant colonel, 19th Alabama (October 12, 1861); brigadier general, CSA (August 16, 1862); commanding brigade, McCown's Division, Department of East Tennessee (October 31-December 1862); commanding brigade, Stevenson's Division, 2nd Military District, Department of Mississippi and East Louisiana (January-April 1863); and commanding brigade, Stevenson's Division, Department of Mississippi and East Louisiana (April-May 1, 1863). He commanded his company at 1st Bull Run and was shortly afterwards made a field officer. That fall he was named second in command of another regiment in the western theater, and he had a horse killed under him at Shiloh. He then served in East Tennessee. Promoted to brigadier general, he and his brigade were transferred to Stevenson's division and ordered to Mississippi. After Grant had crossed the Mississippi the first significant action came at Port Gibson on May 1, 1863. It was in this fight that Tracy fell.

TRAPIER, James Heyward (1815-1865)

Despite his West Point (1838) education, South Carolinian James H. Trapier was found wanting as a field commander and was relegated to district command in his native state for the balance of the war. He had served a week in the artillery after his graduation before being assigned to the engineers. In 1848 he resigned as a first lieutenant to return to his plantation. Also active in the militia, he offered his services to his state in 1861 and his assignments included: captain, South Carolina Engineers (early 1861); major, South Carolina Engineers (spring 1861); brigadier general, CSA (October 21, 1861); commanding Department of Middle and Eastern Florida (October 22, 1861-early 1862 and March 14-19, 1862); commanding brigade, Withers' Division, 2nd Corps, Army of the Mississippi (late April-June 1862); commanding 4th Military District of South Carolina, Department of South Carolina, Georgia and Florida (November 6, 1862-March 14, 1863 and June 16, 1863-October 17, 1864); commanding Sub-District #2, 1st Military District of South Carolina, Department of South Carolina, Georgia and Florida (March 14-May 10, 1863); commanding 2nd Military District of South Carolina, Department of South Carolina, Georgia and Florida (May 10-28, 1863); commanding 1st Sub-District of South Carolina, Department of South Carolina, Georgia and Florida (October 17, 1864-ca. April 1865); and also commanding brigade, Department of South Carolina, Georgia and Florida (October 17, 1864-ca. April 1865). During the bombardment of Fort Sumter he was present as an engineering officer. Promoted to brigadier general, he commanded in Florida and was then sent to Beauregard's army in Mississippi. Failing to make the grade,

he was returned to district command in South Carolina after participating in the Corinth siege. During the Carolinas Campaign his sub-district, now styled a brigade, was not part of Hardee's Corps of Joseph E. Johnston's army but was presumably included in the surrender of April 26, 1865. He died on December 21st of the same year.

TRENHOLM, George Alfred (1807-1876)

The Confederacy's last secretary of the treasury, George Trenholm, presided over the dwindling of his nation's resources and of his own personal fortune. A highly successful businessman in foreign trade, Trenholm had served four years in the South Carolina legislature before retiring from politics in 1856. Having supported the principle of nullification as propounded by Calhoun, he was an early secessionist. Throwing himself fully behind the new Confederacy, he ran a successful fleet of blockade runners early in the war. He maintained branches of his company in Liverpool, Nassau, and Bermuda. The English office served as the headquarters for the Confederate purchasing agents, Caleb Huse and James Bulloch, as well as a depository for Confederate funds. His firm was also involved in the securing of the Erlanger loan for the Confederacy. He served as an advisor to his predecessor in the treasury post, Christopher Memminger, until the latter's resignation. On July 18, 1864, he succeeded to the cabinet position. To the regret of the Confederate Congress, he continued Memminger's policies and called on the legislators to crack down on inflation by imposing heavy taxes rather than just issuing more notes. By the time Congress acted the war was just about over. In the retreat of the rebel cabinet, Trenholm had to be left behind because of ill health and Postmaster General John Reagan took over his duties on a temporary basis. The war cost Trenholm most of his fortune and he spent several months in jail. The Federal authorities sold his company's assets to retrieve duties which had not been collected on imports it had made during the war. With a small amount of money saved from the debacle he recouped a portion of his former wealth and served his last two years back in the state legislature. (Nepveux, Ethel S., *George Alfred Trenholm and the Company That Went to War 1861-1865*)

TRIGG, Robert Craig (1830-1872)

A lawyer and graduate of the Virginia Military Institute, Robert C. Trigg commanded one of the handful of Virginia units to serve in the western theater. Entering the army, he was commissioned colonel, 54th Virginia, on September 4, 1861. His other assignments included: commanding brigade, Department of East Tennessee (summer-August 6, 1863); commanding brigade, Preston's Division, Buckner's Corps, Army of Tennessee (August 6-September 1863); commanding brigade, Buckner's Corps, Army of Tennessee (August 6-September 1863); commanding brigade, Buckner's Division, 1st Corps, Army of Tennessee (September-November 1863); and commanding Reynolds' Brigade, Stevenson's Division, 2nd Corps, Army of Tennessee (May 27-June 1864). After initial service in western Virginia, eastern Kentucky, and East Tennessee, his command became part of Bragg's army and he led a brigade at Chickamauga. Taking part in the Atlanta Campaign, he succeeded to brigade command upon the wounding of General A.W. Reynolds at New Hope Church. But with the heavy losses suffered in that campaign, the brigade was consolidated with another and Trigg was no longer a brigade commander. He spent the latter part of the war rounding up deserters. His detachment was in Virginia when the regiment surrendered in North Carolina. Trigg disbanded his men at that time.

TRIMBLE, Isaac Ridgeway (1802-1888)

A West Pointer (1822) and veteran of 10 years' artillery service, Isaac R. Trimble left railroad engineering to aid the Confederacy. He started by burning railroad bridges north of Baltimore. After obstructing the route for Washington-bound troops, he left his adopted state, Maryland, and went to the state of his birth, Virginia, to offer his services in a more orthodox manner. His assignments included: colonel, Virginia Engineers (May 1861); brigadier general, CSA (August 9, 1861); commanding Crittenden's (old) Brigade, E.K. Smith's-Ewell's Division, Potomac District (Valley District after April), Department of Northern Virginia (November 22, 1861-June 26, 1862); commanding brigade, Ewell's Division, 2nd Corps, Army of Northern Virginia (June 26-August 29, 1862); major general, CSA (April 23, to date from January 17, 1863); commanding Valley District, Department of Northern Virginia (May 28-late June 1863); and commanding Pender's Division, 3rd Corps, Army of Northern Virginia (July 3, 1863). After constructing batteries along the Potomac at Evansport, in the Department of Fredericksburg, and later in the Aquia District, he was given a brigade in what became Ewell's Division. He fought under Jackson in the Shenandoah and in the Seven Days. Moving north, his actions included Cedar Mountain, Hazel Run, Manassas Junction, and 2nd Bull Run where he was severely wounded. In early 1863 he was promoted with the expectation that he would command Jackson's former division but was found too feeble. Instead he was given charge of the Valley District, an assignment of which he soon tired. He accompanied the army into Pennsylvania without a command, serving as a volunteer aide to Ewell. On July 3 he took over command of the wounded Pender's Division for Pickett's Charge. Wounded, he lost a leg and was captured. Exchanged in February 1865, he was unable to rejoin Lee before Appomattox. He returned to Baltimore as an engineer. (Freeman, Douglas S., *Lee's Lieutenants*)

TUCKER, John Randolph (1812-1883)

With the secession of his native Virginia, John R. Tucker resigned his commodore's commission in the U.S. Navy in order to join the second of three navies he was to serve—the Confederacy's. A veteran of 35 years at sea and of the Mexican War, Tucker was appointed a commander in the Southern fleet. After briefly commanding the *Yorktown*, he was given command of the *Patrick Henry* with which he took part in the famous action in Hampton Roads, including the duel between the *Monitor* and the *Merrimac*. At the battle of Drewry's Bluff,

his crew and guns, mounted on the bluff, played a prominent role in the repulse of the Union naval expedition up the James River against Richmond. Promoted to captain he was transferred to Charleston, where he was placed in charge of all naval forces. With the fall of that city in early 1865, Tucker returned to Drewry's Bluff and joined in the retreat from the Richmond-Petersburg lines. In the rearguard action at Sayler's Creek on April 6, 1865, he was captured along with most of his command. As a rear admiral in the Peruvian navy, Tucker commanded the joint Peruvian-Chilean fleets in the 1866 war with Spain. As president of the Peruvian Hydrographic Commission he led a surveying expedition to the upper Amazon. Returning to Virginia, he died there in 1883. (Scharf, J. Thomas, *History of the Confederate States Navy*)

TUCKER, Julius G. (?-?)

As the Confederacy grew ever poorer in manpower, the War Department began authorizing officers to recruit and organize prisoners of war for the Confederate army. One of these officers was Julius G. Tucker. His Confederate assignments included: lieutenant, Cavalry (1861); captain, 13th Virginia Cavalry (1862); lieutenant colonel, 1st Confederate Foreign Battalion (October 16, 1864); and colonel, Tucker's Regiment Confederate Infantry (February 25, 1865). As a cavalry officer he served through most of the campaigns of the Army of Northern Virginia, while some of the time his company was detached from the regiment to serve as part of the provost guard for the Second Corps. Here he gained some experience in dealing with prisoners of war. In the fall of 1864 he went to work recruiting foreign-born Union prisoners at the prison camps in Richmond, Salisbury, and Florence. He got into a feud with General York over who would get the lion's share of the recruits, and the War Department decided in favor of Tucker. With his battalion organized, he took command and eventually raised it to a regiment following the spring. The unit was assigned to duty with the remnants of the Army of Tennessee in North Carolina. Serving as pioneer [engineer] troops, Tucker and his command surrendered along with Johnston's army.

TUCKER, William Feimster (1827-1881)

Surviving the Civil War, Confederate General William F. Tucker was assassinated by hired gunmen a decade and a half after the close of the conflict. The North Carolinian had been a judge and lawyer in Mississippi before the secession crisis. His military assignments included: captain, Company K, 11th Mississippi (May 1861); colonel, 41st Mississippi (May 8, 1862); commanding Anderson's Brigade, Hindman's Division, Breckinridge's Corps, Army of Tennessee (November 1863); brigadier general, CSA (March 1, 1864); commanding Anderson's (old) Brigade, Hindman's Division, Hood's Corps, Army of Tennessee (March-May 14, 1864); and commanding District of South Mississippi and East Louisiana, Department of Alabama, Mississippi and East Louisiana (ca. April-May 1865). As a company commander he fought at 1st Bull Run and continued to serve in northern Virginia until his company was ordered back to Mississippi to become part of a new regiment of which Tucker became colonel. This unit he commanded at Perryville, Murfreesboro, during the Tullahoma Campaign, at Chickamauga, and Chattanooga. Shortly before the beginning of the Atlanta Campaign he was advanced to brigadier general and given charge of a brigade. This he led in the campaign until severely wounded at Resaca. Incapacitated for further field duty, he was in district command in Mississippi and Louisiana during the last days of the Confederacy. A lawyer and state legislator after the war, he was shot apparently as a result of a fraud case he was prosecuting.

TURNER, Joseph Addison (1826-1868)

As a Georgia journalist, Joseph A. Turner was a supporter of the national ideas of Jefferson Davis and an opponent of Governor Joseph Brown and his states' rights philosophy. A native of the state, he had been a teacher and lawyer before entering the journalistic profession. He met with mixed success in this field and that of politics. A state senator before he Civil War, he was not an out-and-out secessionist, but neither did he wish to bow down to the Washington authorities. Once the Confederacy was established he began publication of *The Countryman*, which was pro-Davis and anti-Brown and was well received by the troops in the field. In return Governor Brown accused him of being a war profiteer—he was engaged in the sale of hats to the army. At the war's close his paper was suppressed by the occupation forces, and he was, as a result, financially ruined. He then wrote his *Autobiography of "The Countryman."* Two years after an unsuccessful bid for a judgeship he died. (Andrews, J. Cutler, *The South Reports the Civil War*)

TURNER, Nat (1800-1831)

A religious and literate slave foreman in Southampton County, Virginia, Nat Turner had not shown any predilection for revenge, yet he became the leader of the bloodiest slave insurrection in U.S. history. Turner had considered his master kind and was even allowed to serve as a preacher for the slave community on the plantation. The revolt against slavery in general had originally been planned for the Fourth of July, 1831, but had to be postponed due to Turner's illness. On the night of August 21-22, Nat Turner and six fellow slaves launched the attack by entering the bedroom of his owners, Mr. and Mrs. Joseph Travis. Turner failed in his attempt to kill his master; one of the others did it for him. In fact, Turner himself only killed one of the 57 victims of the insurrection, Mrs. Margaret Whitehead, whom he finally killed with a blow to her head with a fence post after repeatedly striking her with a dull sword. For 48 hours the bloodletting continued, with the rebels numbering between 60 and 80, some mounted and serving as cavalry to prevent the inhabitants of the plantations from escaping and warning others. Moving on the town of Jerusalem, the marauding band was met by 18 whites, and the slaves drove them back until more whites appeared. The rebellious slaves then withdrew. There followed a reign of terror as 2,800 militia and federal troops swept through the county, killing an estimated 100 to 200 blacks. Some two months later Turner was captured by a single white man and was subsequently hanged along with 16

others. The bloody revolt influenced the South to adopt a policy of not questioning the system of slavery since it feared such a discussion would encourage further revolts. (Johnson, F. Roy, *The Nat Turner Slave Insurrection*)

TWAIN, Mark

See: *Clemens, Samuel Langhorne*

TWIGGS, David Emanuel (1790-1862)

Of all the officers of the Old Army who went over to the Confederacy, only one, Brevet Major General David E. Twiggs, committed an act of treason at the time. He was a veteran of virtually half a century of service, including action in the War of 1812 and the Black Hawk, Seminole, and Mexican wars. Having risen to the rank of brigadier general, he was commanding the Department of Texas during the secession crisis. Most departing officers submitted their resignations, and many of the commanders among them actually waited for the arrival of their successors before leaving their stations. Twiggs instead surrendered his trust to Colonel Ben McCulloch of the state forces on February 18, 1861. On March 1 he was dismissed from the army. His Confederate assignments included: major general, CSA (March 22, 1861); commanding Military District of Louisiana (April 17-May 27, 1861); and commanding Department #1 (May 27-October 18, 1861). His command comprised Louisiana, southern Mississippi, and southern Alabama, but he was no longer fit for active duty and retired. He died the following July, having provided the Confederacy his greatest service while still wearing a blue uniform.

TYLER, John (1790-1862)

Of the five ex-presidents alive at the start of the Civil War only one, John Tyler, was from a Southern state, Virginia, and thus the only one to join the Confederacy. The first vice president to succeed to the presidency upon the death of his predecessor—and sometimes called "His Accidency"—he considered the annexation of Texas to be his most important accomplishment during his 1841 to 1845 term. Throughout a career as National Republican, Democrat, Whig, and Democrat again, he stuck to his belief in a strict interpretation of the constitution. Before his presidency he had served as governor, congressman, senator, and state legislator, and afterwards he went into retirement but became involved in the secession crisis. He had always believed in the right of a state to secede but rightly predicted that war would follow and the North would win. Trying to find a peaceful formula for the crisis, he attended the Washington Peace Conference of which he was elected president. After its collapse he attended the state secession convention as an advocate of secession. On August 1, 1861, he was admitted to the Provisional Confederate Congress where he was a relatively inactive legislator although he did tend to support Davis. Elected to a seat in the First Regular Congress, he died on January 18, 1862, before he could take his seat. (Seager, Robert, *And Tyler Too* and Morgan, Robert, *A Whig Embattled: The Presidency Under John Tyler*)

TYLER, Robert Charles (ca. 1833-1865)

Little is known of the prewar career of one of the Confederacy's most obscure general officers, Robert C. Tyler. Apparently born and raised in Baltimore, he appears to have served as a first lieutenant in the 1856 filibustering expedition of William Walker to Nicaragua. Returning to Baltimore, he eventually moved to Memphis where he joined the Confederate army. His assignments included: private, Company D, 15th Tennessee (April 18, 1861); captain and quartermaster, 15th Tennessee (1861); lieutenant colonel, 15th Tennessee (December 26, 1861); colonel, 15th Tennessee (May 1862); commanding brigade, Breckinridge's Division, Breckinridge's Corps, Army of Tennessee (November-November 25, 1863); and brigadier general, CSA (February 23, 1864). As a supply officer, he was present at Belmont. Promoted to lieutenant colonel, he com-manded his unit at Shiloh where he was wounded. Assigned to provost duty, he served in the Kentucky Campaign but took charge of the regiment again in time for Perryville. Following the Tullahoma Campaign he led the regiment—he had become its colonel at the spring 1862 reorganization—at Chickamauga and was again wounded. Returning to duty, he led a brigade at Chattanooga where he lost a leg on Missionary Ridge. Promoted to brigadier general early the next year, he never rejoined the main army and appears to have spent the next year and a half in the hospital at West Point, Georgia. He may have engaged in some light duty there, as a local fortification was named for him. It was at Fort Tyler that he was killed on April 16, 1865, while trying to defend it against James H. Wilson's Union raiders.

U

UNKNOWN

The death of a young Georgia soldier early in the Civil War illustrates many of the ironies of that conflict. Serving in the campaign in western Virginia during the first spring of the Civil War, he was probably a member of the 1st Georgia. Confederate forces under Brigadier General Robert S. Garnett were forced from their positions on Laurel Hill. The command made a fighting retirement in the face of the rapid Union pursuit. Garnett leapfrogged his regiments in the retreat, with each taking its turn as the rear guard. Finally, at Carrick's Ford, Garnett remained behind with 10 men from a Virginia regiment. Why the Georgian was there is unknown. Then Garnett sent away the Virginians and was about to leave when he was struck and killed. At the same instant the Georgia private reeled and fell next to his general. Many Union soldiers had witnessed his bravery, and this early in the war could afford an unusual concern. They knew that Garnett's body—he was the first general to die in the Civil War—would be returned to his family for burial. But what would be the fate of his brave companion? They formally buried their late opponent and inscribed on the marker, "Name Unknown. A brave fellow, who shared his general's fate, and fell fighting at his side, while his companions fled." (Jones, Virgil Carrington, *Gray Ghosts and Rebel Raiders*)

V

VANCE, Robert Frank (1828-1899)

North Carolinian Robert B. Vance spent the last year of the Civil War as a prisoner. The brother of the state governor, Zebulon Vance, this court clerk had raised a company for the Confederacy, and his later assignments included: colonel, 29th North Carolina (September 11, 1861); commanding 2nd (Rains' old) Brigade, McCown's Division, Hardee's Corps, Army of Tennessee (December 31, 1862-ca. February 1863); brigadier general, CSA (March 16, 1863); and commanding Western District of North Carolina, Department of East Tennessee (September 16-November 18, 1863 and December 4, 1863-January 14, 1864). As a regimental commander, he served at Cumberland Gap in East Tennessee and succeeded to command of a brigade at Murfreesboro. Forced from the field by a bout with typhoid fever, he was nonetheless promoted to brigadier general. Upon his return to duty he was assigned to command in the mountains of western Virginia where he had to deal with deserters and draft resisters as well as the Union troops. In a minor action at Cosby Creek, across the border in Tennessee, he was captured on January 14, 1864. It was not until March 10, 1865, that his confinement in Fort Delaware came to an end. By then the war was all but over, and he does not appear to have held any further commands. After the war he served in both the state and national legislatures and as an assistant patent commissioner.

VANCE, Zebulon Baird (1830-1894)

As the governor of a state which had already provided so many troops to the Confederate cause, North Carolinian Zebulon B. Vance came into conflict with Jefferson Davis' ideas over conscription. A lawyer by training, he sat in the state and national legislatures and was a Unionist supporting John Bell for the presidency in 1860. Nevertheless he joined the Confederate army where his assignments included: captain, Company F, 4th North Carolina Volunteers (May 3, 1861); and colonel, 26th North Carolina (August 27, 1861). He fought at New Bern and

during the Seven Days on the Peninsula. Elected governor, he resigned his commission on August 12, 1862. This was accepted on August 29th and he was sworn in at the state capitol on September 8th. As governor he engaged the state in blockade-running and pardoned the state's deserters. An opponent of a separate surrender by the state, he won reelection in 1864 and was arrested on May 13, 1865, by the Union authorities. Released on July 6, 1865, he resumed his practice and was again governor in the late 1870s. (Tucker, Glenn, *Zeb Vance: Champion of Personal Freedom*)

VAN DORN, Earl (1820-1863)

One of the Confederacy's most promising general officers early in the Civil War, Mississippian West Pointer (1842) Earl Van Dorn proved to be a disappointment and died, not at the hands of the enemy but at those of a jealous husband. Posted to the infantry, he had won two brevets in the Mexican War, being wounded at the City of Mexico. Transferring to the cavalry in 1855, he was wounded in Indian fighting in 1858 near Wichita Village, Indian Territory (now Oklahoma). Resigning as a major in the 2nd Cavalry on January 31, 1861, he offered his services to his native state. His assignments included: brigadier general, Mississippi State Troops (ca. January 1861); major general, Mississippi State Troops (ca. February 1861); colonel, Cavalry (March 16, 1861); commanding Department of Texas (April 21-September 4, 1861); brigadier general, CSA (June 5, 1861); major general, CSA (September 19, 1861); commanding division, 1st Corps, Army of the Potomac (October 4-22, 1861); commanding 1st Division, Potomac District, Department of Northern Virginia (October 22, 1861-January 10, 1862); commanding Trans-Mississippi District, Department #2 (March 4-June 20, 1862); commanding Department of Southern Mississippi and East Louisiana (June 20-July 2, 1862); commanding District of the Mississippi, Department #2 (July 2-October 1, 1862); commanding Army of West Tennessee, Department of Mississippi and East Louisiana (October 1862); commanding 1st Corps, Army of the Depart-

Earl Van Dorn, victim of a personal dispute. (AC)

ment of Mississippi and East Louisiana (December 1862); commanding cavalry division, Army of the Department of Mississippi and East Louisiana (January 13-20, 1863); commanding Cavalry Corps, Department of Mississippi and East Louisiana (January 20-February 1863); and commanding cavalry division, Army of Tennessee (February 25-May 7, 1863). Early in the war he commanded in Texas where he seized U.S. property and received the surrender of regular army detachments. Promoted rapidly to brigadier and major general, he was ordered to Virginia where he led a division near Manassas. Early in 1862 he was sent to command in Arkansas in order to get Ben McCulloch and Sterling Price to cooperate. Launching an attack at Pea Ridge, he was repulsed after two days of fighting. Ordered east of the Mississippi, he arrived too late to take part in the fighting at Shiloh but participated in the unsuccessful defense of Corinth, Mississippi. In the summer of 1862 he successfully defended Vicksburg but failed in his designs on Baton Rouge when the attack under John C. Breckinridge failed. Another failure occurred when he attempted to retake Corinth in October 1862. By this time many Southerners were disenchanted with him, and he was placed in charge of the mounted troops under Pemberton. His raid on Holly Springs, Mississippi, was a major factor in ending Grant's campaign in central Mississippi. Moving his division into middle Tennessee, he was killed on May 7, 1863, by Dr. George B. Peters for attentions paid by the general upon the physician's wife in Spring Hill. (Hartje, Robert G., *Van Dorn, The Life and Times of a Confederate General*)

VAUGHAN, Alfred Jefferson, Jr. (1830-1899)

Virginia Military Institute graduate Alfred J. Vaughan, Jr., rose to the rank of brigadier general in the Confederate army while fighting in most of the major actions in the western theater until wounded during the Atlanta Campaign. The Virginia-born civil engineer and farmer had entered the Confederate service from Tennessee. His assignments included: captain, Company F, 13th Tennessee (spring 1861); lieutenant colonel, 13th Tennessee (June 4, 1861); colonel, 13th Tennessee (ca. November 1861); commanding Preston Smith's Brigade, Cleburne's Division, Left Wing, Army of the Mississippi (August 30-September 1862); commanding Smith's Brigade, Cheatham's Division, Polk's Corps, Army of Tennessee (December 1862-ca. January 1863 and September 19-November 1863); colonel, 13th and 154th Senior Tennessee Consolidated (March 1863); brigadier general, CSA (November 18, 1863); commanding brigade, Hindman's Division, Breckinridge's-Hindman's Corps, Army of Tennessee (November 1863-February 20, 1864); and commanding brigade, Cheatham's Division, Hardee's Corps, Army of Tennessee (February 20-July 4, 1864). After briefly commanding the Dixie Rifles he was named a field officer and as a colonel led his regiment across the Mississippi during the fight at Belmont. He was at its head at Shiloh and during the operations around Corinth. During the Kentucky Campaign he succeeded to the command of the brigade at Richmond and led it again at Murfreesboro. After serving in the Tullahoma Campaign he took command of the brigade when Preston Smith was killed. Named a brigadier general, he fought at Chattanooga and then during the Atlanta Campaign. In a small action at Vining's Station his leg was torn off by a shell on July 4, 1864. This effectively ended his field career. Active in veterans' organizations after the war, he was a farmer and political activist in Mississippi. He was subsequently a court clerk in Memphis.

VAUGHN, John Crawford (1824-1875)

Although at one point his command was deemed little more than a band of marauders, Tennesseean John C. Vaughn led his brigade as part of the escort for Jefferson Davis during the president's flight. A merchant by profession, he had served as a company commander in the 5th Tennessee during the Mexican War. After witnessing the firing on Fort Sumter he returned home and raised a regiment for the Confederacy. His assignments included: colonel, 3rd Tennessee PACS (June 6, 1861); brigadier general, CSA (September 22, 1862); commanding brigade, Defenses of Vicksburg, Department of Mississippi and East Louisiana (December 1862-January 1863); commanding brigade, Smith's Division, 2nd Military District, Department of Mississippi and East Louisiana (January-April 1863); commanding brigade, Smith's Division, Department of Mississippi and East Louisiana (April-July 4, 1863); commanding brigade, Stevenson's Division, Hill's-Breckinridge's Corps, Army of Tennessee (fall 1863); commanding brigade, Buckner's Division, Department of East Tennessee (November 1863-

January 1864); commanding cavalry brigade, Department of East Tennessee (January-March and April-June 1864); commanding division, Cavalry Corps, Department of East Tennessee (March-April 1864); commanding cavalry brigade, Valley District, Army of Northern Virginia (June-summer 1864); and commanding cavalry brigade, Department of Western Virginia and East Tennessee (fall 1864-April 1865). He led his regiment in western Virginia and at 1st Bull Run before being ordered to East Tennessee. Promoted to brigadier general, he was ordered to the Vicksburg area and commanded a brigade at Chickasaw Bayou. Captured upon the fall of Vicksburg, he was exchanged on September 12, 1863, and then managed to have his command converted into mounted infantry. As such it served under James Longstreet in East Tennessee and then moved into Virginia. He fought at Piedmont and in the defense of Lynchburg. Accompanying Jubal A. Early northward he was wounded at Martinsburg, West Virginia. Upon his recovery, he resumed command of his brigade and led it until after the fall of Richmond when he joined the fleeing government officials. He surrendered in Georgia and later served in the Tennessee legislature.

VELAZQUEZ, Loreta Janeta (1838-?)

If there has ever been a case of exaggeration with a hidden element of truth, it is likely to be in the claims put forward by Loreta J. Velazquez in her book, *The Woman in Battle: A Narrative of the Exploits, Adventures, and Travels of Madame Loreta Janeta Velazquez, Otherwise Known as Lieutenant Harry T. Buford, Confederate States Army.* In this work published in 1876, she claims to have fought at 1st Bull Run, Fort Donelson, and Shiloh—being wounded at the latter two—to have been a blockade runner and spy, and to have had several wartime marriages and access to the presidents and secretaries of war of both the United and Confederate States, as well as to high-ranking generals on both sides, while passing as a man. Little in her work can be even circumstantially supported. Yet there may be an element of truth. She may have done some of the things she claimed, but this will never be definitely known due to her penchant for exaggeration. It must be realized that she may have written the work solely to provide an income for herself and her infant daughter. One of her harshest critics was none other than ex-Confederate General Jubal A. Early.

VENABLE, Charles Scott (1827-1900)

As an aide-de-camp to General Lee, Charles Venable served throughout the campaigns of the Army of Northern Virginia. Born in Virginia, he graduated from Hampden-Sidney College at the age of 15 and was, for several years, a tutor in mathematics at the school. Receiving further education at the University of Virginia and in Berlin and Bonn, he became a mathematics professor at various schools in Virginia and South Carolina as well as an astronomer. He served as a lieutenant during the firing on Fort Sumter and later fought at 1st Bull Run as a private in Company A, 2nd South Carolina. He joined Lee's staff as a major, when that general was the military advisor to Jefferson Davis. When Lee was given command of the Department, soon to be the Army, of Northern Virginia, Venable continued as his aide-de-camp. Serving from the Peninsula Campaign to Appomattox, he was promoted to lieutenant colonel. Following the surrender, he resumed his career as an educator. During a visit to Prussia, he was received at the castle of General Stuart's former aide-de-camp, Heros von Borcke, with Prussian and Confederate flags flying.

VESEY, Denmark (1767-1822)

At the turn of the century, after purchasing his freedom from his master with $600 he had won in a lottery, Denmark Vesey, a free black carpenter, began plotting with other blacks for an uprising of the slaves in Charleston, South Carolina. But the group of conspirators grew very large, and it was impossible to keep the plan a secret. Word leaked out a month before the planned July 2, 1822, revolt, and Vesey and coconspirator Peter Poyas were arrested. They denied everything and were eventually released. With the date of the uprising moved up to June 16, excessive black activity the night before led the authorities to believe that a revolt was imminent and they rearrested Vesey, Poyas, and many slaves. Thirty-five blacks, including the two free blacks, were hanged for their part in the threatened insurrection, and an additional 43 slaves were banished. The fear of such a plot to kill slaveholders was to remain a part of southern life until the Civil War, almost four decades later. (Lofton, John, *Denmark Vesey's Revolt*)

VEST, George Graham (1830-1904)

The record is unclear, but for either a public or private matter—whether from a bill requesting the ages of government clerks or an affair of the heart—Missouri's George G. Vest was the only Confederate congressman to be publicly whipped (by a woman in an impromptu punishment). Appointed to the Provisional Confederate Congress, the Kentucky-born Democratic lawyer automatically became a member of the First Regular Congress, since no elections could be held in his occupied 5th District. In the Provisional Congress he sat on the Committee on the Judiciary and in the First Congress on the Committee on Elections. He supported the government's war policies in the hope that there would be a reconquest of his constituency in central Missouri. Nonetheless, by the war's end he was highly critical of the Davis administration and supported calls for its reorganization, both in the cabinet and in the field. As an administration supporter he had been reelected by the soldier and refugee vote in a special election organized by the Congress. In the Second Congress he sat on the Committee on the Judiciary before being named to the Senate on January 12, 1865, where he held no committee assignments. Returning to the legal profession at the war's close—and after submitting to Missouri's test oath—he later served four terms in the U.S. Senate. He was always considered an effective legislator, even gaining the respect of opposing Republican newspapers. (French, Edwin Malcolm Chase, *Senator George G. Vest*)

VICTORIA, Queen (1819-1901)

The United Kingdom of Great Britain and Ireland was ruled during the Civil War years by Queen Victoria. Raised for the throne, she acceded to it at age 18. With internal warfare breaking out in the United States, she issued a proclamation of neutrality on May 13, 1861. This policy, which granted the Confederacy belligerent's status, was unsatisfactory to both sides. Outraged by the United States' seizure of Confederate commissioners Mason and Slidell from the British mail steamer *Trent*, she did allow her husband, Prince Albert, to modify the foreign secretary's ultimatum to Washington. This, together with the eventual release of the prisoners, alleviated the crisis. On December 4, 1861, she banned all munitions exports to either side but lifted the ban the next February. Even after the December 1861 death of her husband, she fought against any effort to bring her country into the conflict. The prime minister, Lord Palmerston, was openly sympathetic to the South. Neutrality irritated many Northerners since they expected Britain, which had recently abolished slavery throughout its empire, to back the Union's war against slavery. The Confederacy, on the other hand, thought that Britain, in need of cotton, would come to her assistance. Both were wrong and both were unhappy with the situation. Queen Victoria ruled into the next century. (Warren, Gordon H., *Fountain of Discontent: The Trent Affair and Freedom of the Seas*)

VILLEPIGUE, John Bordenave (1830-1862)

The death from fever of talented General John B. Villepigue was a severe blow to the Confederate cause. The South Carolinian West Pointer (1854) had served on the frontier with the 2nd Dragoons before resigning as a first lieutenant on March 31, 1861. Joining the Confederacy, his assignments included: captain, Artillery (spring 1861); colonel, 36th Georgia (1861); commanding Army of Mobile, Department of Alabama and West Florida (February 28-March 15, 1862); brigadier general, CSA (March 13, 1862); commanding Fort Pillow, Department #2 (April-June 4, 1862); commanding brigade at Grenada, Miss., Department #2 (June 4-July 1862); commanding 3rd Sub-District, District of the Mississippi, Department #2 (July-ca. August 1862); and commanding brigade, 1st Division, District of the Mississippi, Department #2 (October 1862). Wounded at Fort McRae in Pensacola Harbor on November 22, 1861, he later commanded the forces at Mobile and was promoted to brigadier general. He then served as Braxton Bragg's artillery and engineering chief. Placed in charge of Fort Pillow on the Mississippi River, he ably defended it against Union gunboats. Ordered to withdraw, he destroyed his works and moved his command to Grenada, Mississippi. He then led his men around Vicksburg and led a brigade at Corinth. However, the next month he died of fever, on November 9, 1862, at Port Hudson.

VILLERÉ, Charles Jacques (ca. 1828-1899)

Although a supporter of a strong central government for the Confederacy, Congressman—and brother-in-law of General P.G.T. Beauregard—Charles J. Villeré was an opponent of the Davis administration. Born on the battlefield of New Orleans, he became a Louisiana lawyer and planter. A Democrat and secessionist, he was defeated for the U.S. Congress in 1860. Before the cavalry company which he organized at the outbreak of the war could get into action he was elected to represent the state's 1st District in the First Regular Confederate Congress, where he sat on the committees on: Claims; Commerce; and Military Affairs. In the Second Congress he was only a member of the Committee on Military Affairs. He used this latter post for his attacks on Davis and his defense of Beauregard. Following the war he went into retirement but supervised the Louisiana Lottery in the 1890s.

VON BORCKE, Heros (ca. 1836-1895)

The American Civil War attracted many European military men as observers and participants to both sides. One of the latter, for the South, was a Prussian lieutenant, Heros von Borcke. Taking a leave of absence from Prussia and barely avoiding capture on a blockade runner, he arrived in the Confederacy in the spring of 1862. With a letter of introduction to the secretary of war from the German consul in Charleston, von Borcke obtained a commission as a lieutenant and assignment to the staff of General J.E.B. Stuart. Quickly becoming a favorite of the rebel cavalry leader, he was rapidly promoted to major. He participated in the battles of Seven Pines, the Seven Days, Verdiersville, Fredericksburg, Chancellorsville, and Brandy Station. He was chosen to present the fancy gift uniform from Stuart to Stonewall Jackson. In the early stages of the Gettysburg Campaign von Borcke was wounded in a fight at Middleburg, Virginia. Narrowly avoiding capture while recovering, he found his Confederate military career was over. Given the Thanks of the Confederate Congress, he was sent on a diplomatic mission to Britain with the new rank of lieutenant colonel. He returned in time to rush to the bedside of his beloved, dying commander, Stuart. When the Confederacy fell, he was again on a foreign mission. Von Borcke distinguished himself in the Franco-Prussian War but never forgot the Confederacy. When Lee's former aide-de-camp, Charles Venable, visited Prussia, both the Prussian and Confederate flags flew over his castle. He visited the Virginia battlefields in 1884 and was feted by his former comrades. He also wrote *Memoirs of the Confederate War for Independence* and *Die grosse Reiterschlacht bei Brandy Station*.

VON CLAUSEWITZ, Karl

See: *Clausewitz, Karl von*

WADDELL, James Iredell (1824-1886)

The time it took for James I. Waddell to finally join the Confederate cause may well have been a record, but he made up for it by surrendering the last Confederate fighting command—almost seven months after Lee's surrender. At the outbreak of the Civil War Waddell, after decades in the navy, had been a lieutenant serving in the East Indies Squadron. Being a North Carolinian, he resigned his commission, explaining that he did not wish to fight against the home of his father and relatives and only wished he could fight for the United States against a foreign foe. He had no hostility toward the U.S. Constitution. In December 1861 he married into a secessionist family, and the Navy Department acted upon his letter of resignation by dismissing him. So in February 1862 he slipped into the Confederacy and was commissioned a first lieutenant on March 27, 1862. After duty at Drewry's Bluff and in Charleston Harbor, he was assigned to "special service." He was next ordered to run the blockade and convert the *Sea King* into the last of the Confederate cruisers, the *Shenandoah*. Waddell commissioned the vessel in the Confederate navy on October 19, 1864. On a cruise to Australia, he began the capture of an eventual total of 36 prizes. After repairing in Melbourne in January and February 1865, Waddell sailed through the Pacific, rounding up more prizes, and moved on to the American whaling fleet in the Bering Sea and the Arctic Ocean. Virtually destroying the fleet, he scored his last victories on June 28 against 11 whalers. On August 2, 1865, it was finally learned from a British vessel that the war was over. Dismounting his guns, Waddell decided the best thing to do was to turn over the vessel to the British authorities at Liverpool where the *Sea King* had been constructed. The *Shenandoah* finally lowered its flag, the last to fly over a Confederate combat unit, on November 6, 1865. (Waddell, James T., *C.S.S. Shenandoah: The Memoirs of Lieutenant Commanding James I. Waddell*)

WADLEY, William Morrill (1812-1882)

With the Confederacy founded on the basis of states' rights and the free enterprise of the capitalistic system, it was inevitable that the appointment of William M. Wadley to oversee the South's railroads in a military capacity would run into trouble with the Congress. A native of New Hampshire, he had began working for Georgia railroads in 1835 and became one of the leading managers of transportation in the South. A secessionist, he was a quartermaster at the outbreak of the war and in 1862 he was appointed the military superintendent of Confederate rail operations. Favoring a form of nationalization, he was rejected by the legislative branch and served the rest of the war as a member of the iron commission. He then retired to New Orleans. (Catherwood, T.B., ed., *Life of William M. Wadley*)

WALKER, Francis Marion (?-1864)

A veteran of the Mexican War, as a second lieutenant in the 5th Tennessee, Francis Marion Walker entered the Confederate service at the head of the "Marsh Blues" in the spring of 1861. His assignments included: captain, Company A, 19th Tennessee (June 1861); lieutenant colonel, 19th Tennessee (June 11, 1861); colonel, 19th Tennessee (May 8, 1862); commanding brigade, District of the Mississippi, Department #2 (September 1862); commanding 3rd Brigade, Breckinridge's Division, 1st Corps, Army of Tennessee (November 20-December 19, 1862); and commanding Maney's Brigade, Cheatham's Division, 1st Corps, Army of Tennessee (June-July 22, 1864). In his first significant action, Mill Springs in early 1862, he succeeded to regimental command when the colonel took over the brigade following the death of General Zollicoffer. Following the battle of Shiloh, he was elected to command the regiment upon its reorganization. He led a brigade in the fall of 1862 when it was transferred from the District of the Mississippi to Bragg's army in Tennessee. But he was only in command of his regiment at Murfreesboro. He led the 19th at Chickamauga and Chattanooga. Taking part in the Atlanta Campaign, he distinguished himself at Kennesaw Mountain in June and was given command of a brigade. He insisted that the 19th be transferred to his new brigade. He was killed on July

22, 1864, during Hood's attack at the battle of Atlanta.

WALKER, Henry Harrison (1832-1912)

A veteran of "Bleeding Kansas," West Pointer (1853) Henry Walker resigned his commission as a first lieutenant in the regular army on May 3, 1861. He was shortly appointed an infantry captain in Confederate service. His later assignments included: lieutenant colonel, 40th Virginia (spring 1861); brigadier general, CSA (July 1, 1863); and commanding Field's-Heth's old Brigade, Heth's Division, A.P. Hill's Corps, Army of Northern Virginia (July 19, 1863-May 10, 1864); also commanding Archer's Brigade, same division (July 1863-early 1864). During the Seven Days, Walker was twice wounded at Gaines' Mill. He was described by his brigade commander Charles W. Field as a "most gallant and meritorious officer." Following a slow recovery he commanded a battalion of guard forces in Richmond and while that city was relatively un-protected during the Gettysburg Campaign he armed several hundred convalescents in the Department of Henrico. Promoted to a general's wreath he was given a Virginia brigade in Lee's army. Leading his own and Archer's brigades he was engaged in the battle of Bristoe Station and the Mine Run Campaign. During the winter of 1863-64 his command served in the Valley District. Returning to the main army he took part in the battle of the Wilderness and was severely wounded at Spotsylvania where he lost a foot. He subsequently served on court-martial duty and in guarding the line of the Richmond and Danville Railroad. Following Lee's surrender, he failed to join Johnston's army in time and was paroled on May 7, 1865, in Richmond. After the war he was a New Jersey broker. (Freeman, Douglas S., *Lee's Lieutenants*)

WALKER, James Alexander (1832-1901)

Before the war, Virginian James A. Walker had been expelled from the Virginia Military Institute upon the recommendation of Thomas J. Jackson and had challenged him to a duel, but during the war, Walker earned Jackson's respect in the field. Following his expulsion, Walker had worked for a railroad and then studied law. Raising the Pulaski Guard he joined Jackson's command at Harpers Ferry. His assignments included: captain, Company C, 4th Virginia (April 1861); lieutenant colonel, 13th Virginia (June 1861); colonel, 13th Virginia (February 26, 1862); commanding Elzey's Brigade, Ewell's Division, in the Valley District, Department of Northern Virginia (June 8-mid-June 1862) and in Jackson's Command, Army of Northern Virginia (June 27-July 1, 1862); commanding Trimble's Brigade (early September-September 17, 1862) and Early's Brigade (fall 1862-ca. April 4, 1863), Ewell's-Early's Division, 2nd Corps, Army of Northern Virginia; brigadier general, CSA (May 15, 1863); commanding Stonewall Brigade, Johnson's Division, same corps and army (May 19, 1863-May 12, 1864); and commanding Ramseur's-Pegram's (old) Division, same corps and army (February-April 9, 1865). After serving briefly in what was to become the Stonewall Brigade, Walker trans-ferred to A.P. Hill's regiment and succeeded him in its com-mand. He fought in the Shenandoah and during the Seven Days

in which he commanded the brigade for a while. At Cedar Mountain and 2nd Bull Run he led the 13th and was again in command of a brigade, Trimble's, at Antietam until wounded. Returning in time for Fredericksburg, he directed Early's Brigade there. After Chancellorsville he was promoted to brigadier, upon the recommendation of his former enemy Jackson, and assigned to command the famed Stonewall Brigade. He led it at Gettysburg and the Wilderness until severely wounded at Spotsylvania's Bloody Angle where the command ceased to exist. Although still suffering from his wound, he returned to command a division in February 1865 and surrendered at Appomattox. After the war he was active in politics until he was wounded in a duel with the lawyer for a victorious opponent. (Robertson, James I., Jr., *The Stonewall Brigade*)

WALKER, John George (1822-1893)

Following service in Virginia and North Carolina, Missouri veteran of the regular army John G. Walker was transferred west and finished out his service as a Confederate general in the Trans-Mississippi Department. He had been commissioned directly as a first lieutenant in the Regiment of Mounted Riflemen at the outbreak of the Mexican War. During that con-flict he won a brevet and was wounded at Molino del Rey. Resigning as a captain on July 31, 1861, he joined the Con-federacy. There his assignments included: major, Cavalry (December 21, 1861, to rank from March 16); lieutenant colonel, 8th Texas Cavalry (1861); brigadier general, CSA (January 9, 1862); commanding 4th Brigade, Department of North Carolina (early 1862-June 1862); commanding 4th Brigade, Holmes' Division, Army of Northern Virginia (June-August 1862); commanding division, 1st Corps, Army of Northern Virginia (August-November 7, 1862); major general, CSA (November 8, 1862); commanding division, District of West Louisiana, Trans-Mississippi Department (November 1863-June 10, 1864); commanding the district (June 10-August 4, 1864); commanding district of Texas, New Mexico and Arizona, Trans-Mississippi Department (August 4, 1864-March 31, 1865); and also commanding 3rd Corps, Trans-Mississippi Department (September 1864-March 31, 1865). He led a brigade in North Carolina and then accompanied Theophilus H. Holmes to the Peninsula in Virginia where he played a minor role in the Seven Days. Left in southeastern Virginia during the 2nd Bull Run Campaign, he rejoined Lee as commander of a small division for the invasion of Maryland. He led one of the three columns under Stonewall Jackson which converged on the garrison of Harpers Ferry and then fought at Antietam. Promoted to major general, he was transferred to Louisiana where he eventually led a division. After fighting in the Red River Campaign, he commanded the western part of the state for a while and then took command of the Confederates in Texas and farther west. Fleeing to Mexico upon the Con-federacy's collapse, he returned to become a U.S. diplomat in Colombia. (Freeman, Douglas S., *Lee's Lieutenants*)

WALKER, Joseph (1835-1902)

A South Carolina merchant, Joseph Walker entered the Confederate service on the day Fort Sumter surrendered. His assignments included: captain, Company K, 5th South Carolina (April 13, 1861); lieutenant colonel, Palmetto (S.C.) Sharpshooters (April 15, 1862); colonel, Palmetto (S.C.) Sharpshooters (July 22, 1862); and commanding Jenkins' Brigade, Jones' Division, Longstreet's Command, Army of Northern Virginia (August 30-fall 1862). With his company soon ordered to Virginia, he served at 1st Bull Run and on the Manassas and Yorktown lines. When a new regiment, the Palmetto Sharpshooters, was formed from the 5th and other units, Walker became its second in command. As such he directed the regiment at Williamsburg and during a part of the Seven Days Battles while Colonel Michah Jenkins exercised brigade command. After being promoted, he took over the brigade at 2nd Bull Run when the new General Jenkins was wounded. The brigade was under his leadership at South Mountain and Antietam. The unit served at Fredericksburg, in southeastern Virginia, and the Department of Richmond before accompanying Longstreet to the West. There Walker led the regiment at Chickamauga and Knoxville. He served in the Wilderness Campaign and then took a seat in the state legislature. It is unclear whether he subsequently served with the regiment.

WALKER, Joseph Knox (1818-1863)

Devastated by the fighting at Shiloh, the 2nd Tennessee was consolidated into four companies the next month and three days later its colonel, J. Knox Walker, resigned. He had been commissioned on May 11, 1861, and commanded the 1st Brigade, 1st Division, 1st Geographical Division, Department No. 2 (October 24, 1861-March 5, 1862). He led the brigade across the Mississippi River during the battle of Belmont and played a key role in Grant's defeat. Joining the Army of the Mississippi early in 1862, he led the regiment at Shiloh where it suffered heavily. When the regiment was reorganized as a battalion he gave up his commission on May 14. He died the next year.

WALKER, Leroy Pope (1817-1884)

Following his resignation as the Confederacy's first war secretary, Alabamian Leroy P. Walker served briefly as a general officer. Admitted to the bar in 1837, he had entered politics and become a state legislator and judge. Attending the Nashville Southern convention of 1850 and both Democratic conventions in 1860, he became known for his support of the rights of his region. Tapped by Jefferson Davis, he took charge of the War Department on February 21, 1861, and held it until he resigned, in part due to his weakened health, on September 16, 1861. His tenure was not a sparkling success. His post was somewhat perfunctory since the military-minded Davis directed much of the department's operations himself. The day after his resignation the president named him a brigadier general, and he was assigned to the Department of Alabama and West Florida. Disgusted at not getting a more active command, he resigned his commission on March 31, 1862. On April 6, 1864, he was commissioned a colonel and was assigned to court-martial duty in Alabama. After the war he returned to his practice and remained active in political matters. (Harris, William Charles, *Leroy Pope Walker: Confederate Secretary of War*)

WALKER, Lucius Marshall (1829-1863)

Confederate Brigadier General Lucius M. Walker lost his life during the war, not facing the enemy but in a duel with a fellow division commander. The Tennessee native and West Pointer (1850) had resigned as a second lieutenant of dragoons in 1852 to become a Memphis merchant. His Confederate assignments included: lieutenant colonel, 40th Tennessee (October 5, 1861); commanding Post of Memphis, 1st Geographical Division, Department #2 (October-November 1861); colonel, 40th Tennessee (November 11, 1861); brigadier general, CSA (March 11, 1862); commanding brigade, McCown's Command, Department #2 (March-April 1862); commanding 3rd Brigade, 2nd (Anderson's) Division, 2nd Corps, Army of the Mississippi (June-July 2, 1862); commanding brigade, Jones'-Anderson's Division, Army of the Mississippi (July 2-August 15, 1862); commanding brigade, Anderson's Division, Left Wing, Army of the Mississippi (August 15-fall 1862); and commanding cavalry division, District of Arkansas, Trans-Mississippi Department (ca. March-September 6, 1863). He became the commander of a regiment which, although designated as a Tennessee unit, was really composed of companies from Alabama, Arkansas, Florida, and Kentucky. In order to solve the confusion it had wrought, the Confederate War Department decided to name it the 5th Confederate. But this only made matters worse since there already was a unit of this name under James A. Smith. Walker, however, was promoted to brigadier general in early 1862 and commanded a brigade at New Madrid and Island #10. Being ill, he missed the fight at Shiloh but commanded a brigade during the Corinth siege. That spring and summer, he aroused the displeasure of Braxton Bragg who declared him to be unfit for any command and was more than happy to approve his transfer west of the Mississippi. There Walker commanded a cavalry division in Arkansas and saw action at Helena and in the Little Rock vicinity. During the operations in that area fellow cavalry division commander John S. Marmaduke impugned his courage and a duel resulted, on September 6, 1863, in which Walker fell mortally wounded. He died the next day.

WALKER, Reuben Lindsay (1827-1890)

Free of a single wound from his four years with the artillery in Virginia, Brigadier General R. Lindsay Walker felt that he had to apologize for his invulnerability and deny being at fault. A Virginia engineer, he had drawn upon his education at the Virginia Military Institute to organize an artillery battery for the Confederacy and become its commander. His assignments included: captain, Richmond Purcell Artillery (spring 1861); major, Artillery (March 31, 1862); commanding Artillery Battalion, A.P. Hill's Division (in 1st Corps from June 29 and in 2nd Corps from July 27), Army of Northern Virginia (May-June and July 1862-May 30, 1863); lieutenant colonel, Artillery (ca. July 1862); colonel, Artillery (early 1863); commanding Artillery, 3rd Corps, Army of Northern Virginia (June 4 1863-April 1865); and brigadier general, CSA (February 18, 1865). Serving initially in the Fredericksburg area with his battery, he was detached briefly to fight at 1st Bull Run. The next spring he was named as A.P. Hill's artillery chief and held that position until after the latter's death. Walker missed only the Seven Days Battles, because of illness, and was in all the rest of the actions of the division and later of the corps. Two months before the surrender he was promoted to be a brigadier. The other two corps artillery chiefs had held that rank for some time. During the retreat to Appomattox, he was detached with the excess artillery and was attacked by Custer's cavalry. He engaged in farming and engineering after the war. (Wise, Jennings C., *The Long Arm of Lee*)

WALKER, Richard Wilde (1823-1874)

The man who administered the oath of office to Jefferson Davis, Richard W. Walker, later turned against him as a senator in the Second Confederate Congress. An Alabama-born lawyer, he was the brother of the Confederacy's first secretary of war. After having served as the speaker of the state legislature, he was serving on the state supreme court at the outset of the war. Elected to the Provisional Confederate Congress, he took part in the drafting of both the provisional and regular constitutions and served on the Committee on Foreign Affairs. An administration supporter during this term, he did not seek reelection. It was not until the Second Congress that he returned to Richmond, as a senator. There he served on the committees on: Commerce; Engrossment and Enrollment; the Judiciary; Post Offices and Post Roads; and Public Buildings. By this time he was concerned over the growth of the central government and favored limitations. He supported strong measures for manning and supplying the field armies and endorsed the freedom of slaves in return for military service. Retiring from politics at the war's close, he returned to the private practice of law.

WALKER, William (1824-1860)

The epitome of the filibustering era was Nashville native William Walker, who was executed some three months before South Carolina's secession. He had studied medicine and law but was unsuccessful in the latter as well as in journalism. In 1853 he led a filibustering expedition in Mexico. In 1855 he installed himself as leader of the government in Nicaragua but was forced out in 1857. His efforts to reintroduce slavery in Central America continued later in the year when he attempted to reenter Nicaragua but was arrested by U.S. naval forces under Commodore Hiram Paulding. In 1860 he attempted to enter Honduras but was caught by the British who handed him over to the local authorities by whom he was tried and shot on September 12, 1860. His nickname, which became something of a title, was "The Grey-Eyed Man of Destiny."

WALKER, William Henry Talbot (1816-1864)

Along with Patrick R. Cleburne, William H.T. Walker proposed the arming and freeing of the slaves in an effort to achieve the South's independence; but within the year both generals would be dead, as would the Confederacy, before the plan could be effectively implemented. The native Georgian West Pointer (1837) had resigned from the army as a first lieutenant in the 6th Infantry in 1838 after being wounded and brevetted during Seminole fighting in Florida. Reinstated two years later, he was again wounded at Molino del Rey during the Mexican War. During that conflict he was twice brevetted. With the secession crisis reaching its peak, he again resigned, on December 20, 1860, with the rank of captain, 6th Infantry. His Southern assignments included: major general, Georgia Volunteers (April 25, 1861); brigadier general, CSA (May 25, 1861); assigned to command 1st Brigade, 4th Division, Potomac District, Department of Northern Virginia (October 22-29, 1861); major general, Georgia State Troops (December 1861); brigadier general, CSA (February 9, 1863) commanding brigade, Department of the West (May-June 1863); major general, CSA (May 23, 1863); commanding division, Department of the West (June-July 1863); commanding division, Department of the West (June-July 1863); commanding division, Hill's Corps, Army of Tennessee (August 25-September 1863); commanding Reserve Corps, Army of Tennessee (September 1863); commanding division, Polk's Corps, Army of Tennessee (September-September 26, 1863); commanding division, Longstreet's Corps, Army of Tennessee (September 26-November 12, 1863); and commanding division, Hardee's Corps, Army of Tennessee (November 12-November 1863 and December 1863-July 22, 1864). As a brigadier general in the Confederate army, he served in northern Virginia until his resignation on October 29, 1861. Within two months he was a major general of state troops and served as such for over a year. Reappointed in the Confederate service early in 1863, he was assigned to the forces under Joseph E. Johnston attempting to relieve the pressure on Vicksburg. Promoted to major general during that campaign, he fought twice at Jackson and then commanded the Reserve Corps at Chickamauga. Missing the battle of Chattanooga, he then engaged in the movement with Cleburne for the recruiting of black troops. On January 1, 1864, the plan was approved by the Army of Tennessee's corps and division commanders. Forwarded to the authorities it was not acted upon until it was too late. Walker then commanded his division through the Atlanta Campaign until killed in the battle of Atlanta proper on July 22, 1864.

WALKER, William Stephen (1822-1899)

Having served most of the Civil War on the Atlantic seaboard, Confederate General William S. Walker was wounded and captured in his first major action. The Pittsburgh native joined the regular army during the Mexican War as the first lieutenant and adjutant of the Regiment of Voltiguers and Foot Riflemen. Winning a brevet he was mustered out in 1848. With the enlargement of the regular establishment in 1855, he was recommissioned as a company commander in the 1st Cavalry. Raised in Mississippi, he resigned on May 1, 1861, to join the Confederacy. His assignments included: captain, Infantry (from March 16, 1861); colonel and assistant inspector general

(1862); assistant inspector general, Department of South Carolina and Georgia (1862); brigadier general, CSA (October 30, 1862); commanding 4th and 5th Military Districts of South Carolina, Department of South Carolina, Georgia and Florida (May 6-28, 1862); and commanding 3rd Military District of South Carolina, Department of South Carolina, Georgia and Florida (May 28, 1862-May 1864). Assigned initially to mustering duty, he served as a staff officer on the South Carolina coast during 1862 and then transferred to the line, commanding a number of districts and being promoted to brigadier general. In the spring of 1864 he was ordered to reinforce Beauregard in southern Virginia and was engaged in the defense of Petersburg when wounded and captured on May 20. He was exchanged that fall, having lost a foot, and was assigned to post duty for the balance of the war. He then retired in Georgia.

WALLACE, William Henry (1827-1905)

Appointed as a temporary brigadier, William Henry Wallace finished the war before the regular brigade commander was able to return. A South Carolina planter, he had tinkered in journalism, the law, and politics. As a state legislator in 1860 he voted for the calling of a convention to decide on the issue of secession. Instead of seeking reelection he enlisted in the Confederate service. His assignments included: private, Company A, 18th South Carolina (ca. November 18, 1861); first lieutenant and adjutant, 18th South Carolina (ca. January 2, 1862); lieutenant colonel, 18th South Carolina (May 1862); colonel, 18th South Carolina (August 30, 1862); brigadier general, CSA (September 20, 1864); commanding Elliott's Brigade, Johnson's Division, Department of North Carolina and Southern Virginia (September-October 19, 1864); and commanding Elliott's Brigade, Johnson's Division, Anderson's Corps, Army of Northern Virginia (October 19, 1864-April 9, 1865). In the spring 1862 reorganization he became a field officer and as a part of Evans' Brigade went to Virginia. Under Lee he fought at 2nd Bull Run where he assumed command of the regiment and in Maryland at South Mountain and Antietam before returning to his native state with the brigade. After over a year in the Charleston vicinity, Wallace again went to Virginia and took a position in the Petersburg lines. On July 30, 1864, four of his companies were blown up in the mine explosion and the brigade commander was wounded preparing a counterstroke. Shortly thereafter Wallace took over and led the brigade through to Appomattox. Following the same civilian pursuits after the war, he also became a judge. (Freeman, Douglas S., *Lee's Lieutenants*)

WALTHALL, Edward Cary (1831-1898)

Entering the Confederate service as a lieutenant in the Yalobusha Rifles, Virginia-born and Mississippi-raised lawyer and district attorney Edward C. Walthall rose to the rank of major general. His assignments included: first lieutenant, Company H, 15th Mississippi (1861); lieutenant colonel, 15th Mississippi (1861); colonel, 29th Mississippi (April 11, 1862); brigadier general, CSA (December 13, 1862); commanding brigade, Withers'-Hindman's Division, Polk's-Cheatham's-

Hardee's Corps, Army of Tennessee (June 2-August 21 and September 22-November 1863); commanding brigade, Liddell's Division, Reserve Corps, Army of Tennessee (August 21-September 22, 1863); commanding brigade, Cheatham's Division, Hardee's Corps, Army of Tennessee (November-November 25, 1863 and early 1864-February 20, 1864); commanding brigade, Hindman's Division, Hindman's-Hood's Corps, Army of Tennessee (February 20-ca. July 6, 1864); major general, CSA (July 6, 1864); and commanding in the Army of Tennessee: Cantey's (old) Division, Polk's (Army of Mississippi)-Stewart's Corps (ca. July 6, 1864-March 1865); the corps (March-April 9, 1865); and McLaws' Division, Stewart's Corps (April 9-26, 1865). Almost immediately named a field officer, he fought at Mill Springs and was then made colonel of another regiment. This he led in the defense of Corinth and in the Kentucky Campaign. He led a brigade in the Tullahoma Campaign and at Chickamauga. At Chattanooga he defended Lookout Mountain and was wounded the next day on Missionary Ridge. Recovering, he led his brigade in the Atlanta Campaign until tapped to command a division, with the appropriate advancement to major general. He led his division at Franklin and was in charge of covering the retreat after the defeat at Nashville. During the Carolinas Campaign he commanded the corps for a time while Alexander P. Stewart led the infantry and artillery of the Army of Tennessee. In the final reorganization and consolidation of the forces in North Carolina, Walthall was placed in charge of a division of troops formerly assigned to guarding the Atlantic seaboard. Surrendered with Joseph E. Johnston, he returned to his practice, entered politics, and eventually sat in the U.S. Senate.

WALTON, James Burdge (1813-1885)

Although he had served for over two decades in the famed Washington Artillery of New Orleans, James B. Walton was gradually eased out of his position as commander of the First Corps' artillery. A prominent New Orleans merchant, the New Jersey-born Walton had joined the Washington Artillery as adjutant upon its organization in 1839. In the Mexican War he commanded the 1st Louisiana and had risen to command of the battery by the outbreak of the Civil War, when the unit offered its services to the Confederacy. It sent four batteries to Virginia and one was organized later, serving in the West. Walton's assignments included: major, Washington Artillery Battalion (May 26, 1861); colonel, Washington Artillery Battalion (March 26, 1862); and nominal chief of artillery, 1st Corps, Army of Northern Virginia (June 4-early September 1863). After serving at 1st Bull Run, Walton and his command were assigned to Longstreet's forces and served in the Seven Days, 2nd Bull Run, and Antietam. At both Fredericksburg and Chancellorsville, Walton directed his guns on Marye's Heights, earning much distinction. In the battle of Gettysburg, he was humiliated by, in effect, being superseded by one of his subordinates, E. Porter Alexander. When the First Corps was sent to Georgia only part of the artillery went along, and Walton held various commands in southern Virginia. When the battalion was ordered back to the First Corps, Walton resigned on July 18, 1864, rather than serve under Alexander who was now officially the corps' artillery chief. There had been an effort to ease Walton out the previous month by assigning him to inspection duties. He returned to his business interests. (Owen, William M., *In Camp and Battle With the Washington Artillery of New Orleans*)

WARD, George Taliaferro (1810-1862)

A Transylvania University graduate, wealthy planter and banker, George Ward was one of those early, promising Confederate officers who didn't live long enough to earn a general's wreath. Ward had long been involved in politics when the secession crisis came to his native Florida. In the state convention, Ward tried to delay the rush to independence. However, with the action taken, he was appointed to the Provisional Confederate Congress on May 2, 1861, where he served on the Claims, Military Affairs, and Public Lands committees. On July 13 he was appointed colonel of the 2nd Florida, the first regiment from the state sent to Virginia. That fall the regiment joined Magruder's army on the Peninsula. He resigned from Congress on February 5, 1862. In the spring of 1862, Ward was commanding a demi-brigade composed of his own regiment and the 2nd Mississippi Battalion, in D.H. Hill's Division. During the siege at Yorktown, Ward's command made a charge upon some Union sharpshooters near Fort Magruder, a charge which General Magruder described as "quick and reckless." At the battle of Williamsburg, a short time later, Colonel Ward was killed, a fact much lamented as a tragedy for the fledgling nation. (Evans, Clement A., ed., *Confederate Military History*)

WARREN, Edward (1828-1893)

A North Carolina native, Edward Warren had been active in the medical profession in Maryland when he joined the Confederacy and wrote one of the leading medical manuals for that service. He received his training both in Pennsylvania and France and upon the outbreak of the Civil War was a professor at the University of Maryland and the editor of the *Baltimore Journal of Medicine*. Returning to North Carolina, he became its surgeon general and also an inspector in the Confederate medical service. A member of the medical examining board, he favored tough standards and an increase in the department's manpower. In 1863 his *An Epitome of Practical Surgery for Field and Hospital* was published. After the war he was active in the medical field in the United States, Europe, and the Middle East. He wrote *A Doctor's Experiences in Three Continents* and died in Paris. (Cunningham, Horace Herndon, *Doctors in Gray*)

WARREN, Edward Tiffin Harrison (1829-1864)

When Edward T.H. Warren was killed at the battle of the Wilderness, it was found unnecessary to secure a replacement for him as colonel of his regiment—since most of the command was captured a few days later at Spotsylvania. A native Virginia, he had been practicing law in Harrisonburg at the outbreak of the Civil War. His assignments included: lieutenant colonel,

10th Virginia (July 1, 1861); colonel, 10th Virginia (August 16, 1862); and commanding 3rd Brigade, Jackson's (old) Division, Jackson's Corps, Army of Northern Virginia (June 27-28, ca. September 5-17, and fall 1862-May 2, 1863). After serving in northern Virginia, including action at 1st Bull Run, Warren and his regiment were transferred to the Shenandoah Valley. At the battle of McDowell he succeeded to command of the regiment upon the death of the colonel. He fought through the rest of the Valley Campaign and the Seven Days, where he briefly commanded the brigade. He was again in charge of the brigade at Harpers Ferry, Antietam, Fredericksburg, and Chancellorsville. Wounded in the latter, he returned in time for Gettysburg but commanded only the 10th. Serving through the Bristoe and Mine Run campaigns, he was killed the following May in the battle of the Wilderness.

WASHINGTON, John A. (?-1861)

The custodian of Mount Vernon, John A. Washington was the first member of Robert E. Lee's military family to die in the conflict. On May 13, 1861, Washington was appointed aide-de-camp to General Lee, with the rank of lieutenant colonel in the Virginia volunteers. At this time Lee was serving as the commander of the Virginia forces and arranging for their transfer into Confederate service. Serving on the undermanned staff, Washington soon became an acting assistant adjutant general and was subsequently promoted to colonel. On July 28 Lee, Washington, and Lieutenant Colonel W.H. Taylor, another staff officer, left Richmond for western Virginia in an effort to recover the sagging fortunes of the Confederacy in that area. With the failure of Lee's overcomplicated plan of attack at Cheat Mountain the previous day, Washington begged for permission to accompany Lee's son, W.H.F. Lee, and his cavalry in a reconnaissance expedition to see if the plan could be revived. The patrol ran into Union pickets and Washington was left dead on the field. (Freeman, Douglas S., *R.E. Lee*)

WASHINGTON, Thornton Augustin (?-1894)

West Pointer (1849) Thornton A. Washington resigned his commission as first lieutenant, 1st Infantry, on April 8, 1861. His experience had included service as regimental adjutant and quartermaster, so he requested appointment in one of those departments in the Confederate service. On November 8, 1861, already a captain in the Adjutant General's Department, he was assigned as assistant adjutant general to Robert E. Lee on the coast of South Carolina. After the general was transferred to Richmond as an advisor to the president, Lee decided that he needed the services of his fellow Virginian, by now a major, and had him assigned again to his staff, in March 1862. Washington left this assignment in the latter part of April and the next year was serving as a quartermaster in charge of all departmental purchasing in Texas, with headquarters at San Antonio.

WATERHOUSE, Richard (1832-1876)

Serving in the Trans-Mississippi West, Richard Waterhouse was one of several Confederate officers promoted to general by

E. Kirby Smith in an extralegal fashion—but his promotion was finally sanctioned by Jefferson Davis, nearly a year later. As a youth he had fought in the Mexican War and then moved with his family from his native Tennessee to Texas. Engaged in trade before the war, he threw in his lot with the Confederacy. His assignments included: colonel, 19th Texas (May 13, 1862); brigadier general, CSA (per Edmund Kirby Smith, May 13, 1864, to rank from April 30); commanding 2nd (Texas) Brigade, 1st (Texas) Division, 1st Corps (or District of West Louisiana), Trans-Mississippi Department (September 1864-May 26, 1865); and brigadier general, CSA (per Jefferson Davis, March 17, 1865). Serving entirely west of the Mississippi River, he fought in Arkansas and at Milliken's Bend in Louisiana during the Vicksburg Campaign. For his abilities in leading his regiment at Mansfield and Pleasant Hill during the Red River Campaign, he was named a brigadier general, but by his department commander because the area was cut off from the authorities in Richmond. After Waterhouse had commanded a brigade for several months, Davis made the appointment legal. Until his death in an accident, he was a land speculator.

WATIE, Stand (1806-1871)

The highest-ranking Indian in the Confederate army was a three-quarter Cherokee named Degataga, better known as Brigadier General Stand Watie. He was in large part responsible for swinging the Cherokee from a neutralist position into an alliance with the Confederacy. Connecticut-educated, he was part of the pro-treaty faction which had accepted the tribe's eviction to Indian Territory. He became a leading planter and journalist among his people and fought at Wilson's Creek in command of a company. His later assignments included: colonel, 1st Cherokee Mounted Volunteers or 2nd Mounted Rifles (July 12, 1861); brigadier general, CSA (May 6, 1864); and commanding 1st Brigade, Cooper's Indian Division, Cavalry Corps, Trans-Mississippi Department (fall 1864-May 1865). In the pursuit of the fleeing band of Upper Creeks under Opothleyohola, which included some Cherokees and Seminoles as well, Watie's staunch Confederate Indians did not suffer from the same qualms as Colonel John Drew's Cherokee regiment over killing fellow Cherokees. After fighting at Pea Ridge he fought mostly in the Indian Territory but did take part in Price's invasion of Missouri in 1864. He did not surrender his command until June 23, 1865. After that he was a planter and businessman in what is now Oklahoma. (Franks, Kenny A., *Stand Watie and the Agony of the Cherokee Nation*)

WATSON, John William Clark (1808-1890)

A former Whig and an opponent of secession, John W.C. Watson reluctantly went along with his state and was elected to the Confederate Senate in the Second Regular Congress. A Virginia-born lawyer, he had moved to Mississippi in 1845. He failed in a bid to sit in the state convention which eventually took the state out of the Union. Elected in 1863, he sat on the committees on: Claims; Engrossment and Enrollment; the Judiciary; and Printing. He felt that the conscription laws were

adequate if properly enforced and wanted a reorganization of the army's high command as well as Davis' cabinet. But for the prosecution of the war he favored the suspension of the writ of habeas corpus and the use of black troops. He also urged the opening of peace negotiations. Willing to cooperate with the victorious Union forces at the war's close, he refused to aid in the defense of Jefferson Davis. Nonetheless he was active in the redemption of the state government from black and Republican control. After the war he served six years as a judge and was active in the prohibitionist movement.

WATTERSON, Henry (1840-1921)

It was his violent antipathy for Confederate General Braxton Bragg which cost Henry Watterson his editorship of the *Chattanooga Daily Rebel*. A native of Washington, D.C., he had worked on the family plantation in Tennessee until joining the reportorial staff of the *New York Times* in 1858. Although initially opposed to secession, he was serving on the staff of Rebel cavalryman Nathan Bedford Forrest when called upon to rejoin the journalistic profession late in 1862. He immediately gained a reputation for his harsh criticism of Bragg's failures—and the enmity of the general. The failures at Murfreesboro added fuel to the fire. During the dismal Tullahoma Campaign Bragg banned the *Rebel* from his army's lines but Watterson had this ban lifted by allowing the army's intelligence network to plant false stories in his paper to fool the enemy. At a party shortly thereafter he was strongly critical of Bragg in a discussion with a Rebel officer who turned out to be the general himself. Watterson kept the paper running until the fall of Chattanooga. Chickamauga launched the editor on another tirade against Bragg who again ordered a ban upon the paper's circulation. The paper's publisher, Franc M. Paul, was forced to accept Watterson's resignation in order to rebuild his circulation. Watterson then joined the *Atlanta Southern Confederacy* and later the *Montgomery Mail*. After a stint as a prisoner, he worked for a paper in Ohio before becoming the editor of the *Louisville Courier-Journal* for half a century. He served a term in Congress and was in the Wilson administration. (Wall, Joseph Frazier, *Henry Watterson, Reconstructed Rebel*)

WATTS, Thomas Hill (1819-1892)

In a varied Confederate career, Thomas H. Watts served as a member of the Alabama secession convention, colonel of infantry, attorney general, and governor. Born when his state was still a territory, he became a lawyer in 1841 and later served in both houses of the state legislature but failed in a bid for a seat in Congress. A Unionist, he supported Bell's Constitutional Union ticket in 1860 but, following Lincoln's election, came around to the secessionist cause. In August 1861 he was defeated by John G. Shorter for the governorship and shortly afterwards raised and was commissioned colonel of the 17th Alabama. He served at Pensacola and Corinth before being named Davis' attorney general on March 18, 1862. Then in an August 1863 rematch with Shorter he was elected governor. He continued as attorney general until October 1, 1863. He took office in the state capital in December 1863 and was engaged in a futile attempt to promote resistance to the Federal invasion. He was removed from office by the Federal military in April 1865 and subsequently arrested. Resuming his law practice after his release, he joined the Democratic Party, served again as a state legislator, and was president of the state bar association. (Denman, Clarence P., *The Secession Movement in Alabama*)

WAUL, Thomas Neville (1813-1903)

Having lost a bid for reelection to the Provisional Confederate Congress, this Texas planter and lawyer returned home, raised a legion for the Confederate army, and rose to the rank of brigadier general. The South Carolina native served in the Congress from February 4, 1861, to February 17, 1862 (the end of the provisional government), and sat on the committees on: Commercial Affairs and Indian Affairs. His military assignments following his November 1861 election loss included: colonel, Waul's Texas Legion (May 17, 1862); brigadier general, CSA (September 18, 1863); commanding brigade, Walker's Division, District of West Tennessee, Trans-Mississippi Department (February-April and May-summer 1864); commanding brigade, Walker's Division, District of Arkansas, Trans-Mississippi Department (April-May 1864); and commanding 1st (Texas) Brigade, 1st (Texas) Division, 1st Corps (or District of West Louisiana), Trans-Mississippi Department (summer 1864-May 26, 1865). Captured at Vicksburg, he was transferred to the west side of the Mississippi and promoted to brigadier general upon his exchange. After serving in various minor posts in Texas he was ordered to Arkansas and West Louisiana where he fought at Mansfield and Pleasant Hill during the Red River Campaign. Moving north to intercept Steele's expedition against Camden, Arkansas, he fought at Jenkins' Ferry. Following the surrender of E. Kirby Smith's department he resumed his legal practice and was active in reconstruction politics.

WAYNE, Henry Constantine (1815-1883)

One of the briefest careers of a Confederate general was that of Georgian Henry C. Wayne. The West Pointer (1838) had served in the quartermaster's department. He served in Mexico and earned a brevet to major. In 1855 he was involved in the army's experiment in using camels to transport supplies in the West. He resigned his commission on December 31, 1860, to go with his state. Governor Brown named him adjutant and inspector general of the state forces. As such he played a leading role in raising troops. He became brigadier general, CSA, on December 16, 1861, but resigned on January 11, 1862, four days after being assigned to duty in northern Virginia. Again working under the governor's authority he was responsible for the state's militia which governor Joseph Brown kept jealously from Confederate control. After the fall of the South he was in the lumber business in Savannah.

WAYNE, James Moore (ca. 1790-1867)

When his state seceded, Georgian James M. Wayne elected to retain his seat on the U.S. Supreme Court. He was considered a traitor by many in the South. Born in Savannah, he had fought as an officer of the Chatham Light Dragoons during the War of 1812 and then entered the state legislature. He later served as his hometown's mayor and a judge on local and state courts. At the time of his appointment by Andrew Jackson to the high bench on January 7, 1835, he was the chairman of the Committee on Foreign Relations in the U.S. House of Representatives. He was confirmed by a voice vote two days later. In the infamous *Dred Scott* decision Wayne held that Dred Scott was still a slave, and even if he were not a slave a black could never be a citizen and be entitled to sue in state or federal courts. This view was shared by the chief justice, Roger B. Taney. During the Civil War he was a strong backer of the Union cause and was described as an enemy alien in the South. During Reconstruction he favored a moderate approach and refused to perform his circuit duties in states that were under military rule. (Lawrence, Alexander A., *James Moore Wayne, Southern Unionist*)

WEBB, William A. (?-?)

By early 1863 the Confederate Navy Department realized that it needed to shake up its officer corps and bring the more daring younger officers to important commands. In its choice of William A. Webb for the command of the Savannah Squadron it got more than it had bargained for—recklessness. As a lieutenant, Webb had commanded the one-gun *Teaser*, and as a consort to the CSS *Virginia* he had thrown his wooden vessel into action against the wooden blockading fleet in Hampton Roads. Next, Webb organized a fleet of torpedo boats, of various types of craft, equipped with 20-foot poles mounting 60-pound explosive charges. Before he could place them into action, he was promoted to commander in the provisional navy and assigned to command the squadron at Savannah, including the ironclad *Atlanta*, formerly the blockade runner *Fingal*. His assignment was to take some action with what was believed to be the most powerful vessel afloat. Delayed by mechanical problems and betrayed by deserters from his crew, Webb was forced to alter his well-laid plans. His new plan called for an attack on the two Union ironclads guarding his escape route to the sea. It would have been much better to have tried to slip by the formidable vessels in order to wreak havoc among the wooden blockaders on the South Atlantic coast. As it turned out, Webb attacked the *Weehawken* and *Nahant* on June 17, 1863. After only 35 minutes, and without the *Nahant* really getting into the fray, Webb surrendered his craft. He and his officers were vilified by the Southern public for the loss of the vessel upon which so much hope had been placed. Webb's naval career had ended. (Scharf, J. Thomas, *History of the Confederate States Navy*)

William A. Webb's former command, the Ironclad *Atlanta*, as a Union blockader on the James River. (NA)

WEICHMANN, Louis J. (1842-1902)

A boarder at the Washington boardinghouse of Mrs. Mary E. Surratt, Louis J. Weichmann was arrested the morning after the assassination of Lincoln but instead became a star witness in the trial of the conspirators. Of German heritage, he had been born in Baltimore and raised in Washington and Philadelphia. Having flunked out when preparing for the Catholic priesthood, he worked during the Civil War in a clerical position in the War Department. He resided in the boardinghouse of the mother of a former classmate, John H. Surratt. This was where much of the planning was done to kidnap Lincoln and spirit him off to Richmond. There have been charges that Weichmann may actually have been a member of the group but, following his release, he provided extensive testimony against the members of the conspiracy, all of whom he knew to one degree or another. His testimony, and that of John M. Lloyd, is credited with having sent Mrs. Surratt to the gallows. Following her execution—many had thought that it would not be carried out—large segments of the public blamed Weichmann, and he spent much of the rest of his life defending his testimony. When John H. Surratt was finally apprehended, Weichmann was again in the witness box but this time the trial ended in a deadlocked jury. To defend himself against the charges of the younger Surratt and the public at large, he wrote his own account of the tragedy but it was not published until seven decades after his death. (Weichmann, Louis J., ed. by Floyd E.

Risvold, *A True History of the Assassination of Abraham Lincoln and of the Conspiracy of 1865*)

WEISIGER, David Addison (1818-1899)

The friction between Confederate brigadier David A. Weisiger and his division commander, William Mahone, did not affect their ability to work together in the last year of the war during which their division was considered by many to be the best in Lee's army. A Petersburg businessman and veteran of the Mexican War, as a second lieutenant in the 1st Virginia, Weisiger had been active in the militia. As a captain he was present at the John Brown hanging and took the field at the head of the 4th Militia Battalion in April 1861. His later assignments included: colonel, 12th Virginia (May 9, 1861); commanding Mahone's Brigade, Anderson's-Mahone's Division, 1st (3rd after May 30, 1863) Corps, Army of Northern Virginia (August 30, 1862 and May 7, 1864-April 9, 1865); and brigadier general, CSA (November 1, to rank from July 30, 1864). After occupying Norfolk in the first months of the conflict, he moved with his regiment to the Peninsula and battled at Seven Pines and the Seven Days. Succeeding to command of the brigade when Mahone was wounded in Longstreet's assault at 2nd Bull Run, Weisiger was also hit. Unable to return to duty until mid-1863, he fought at Gettysburg and in the fall campaigns. The day after the Wilderness he again took over brigade leadership and held it for the balance of the conflict.

After Spotsylvania and Cold Harbor the brigade took up its duties in the Petersburg trenches. It was one of Mahone's two brigades which played the key role at the Crater on July 30. Two months later, Weisiger was promoted to brigadier to rank from the date of this victory. After the city's fall he surrendered at Appomattox and was a banker and businessman for the remainder of his life. (Freeman, Douglas S., *Lee's Lieutenants*)

WELLS, James Madison (1808-1899)

Condemned by his family and friends for his opposition to secession, Louisiana native James M. Wells became the Unionist governor of the state upon the resignation of Michael Hahn on March 4, 1865. He had studied law, run a plantation, and served as a sheriff before the Civil War. In February 1864 he was elected lieutenant governor, under Hahn, and took up his duties the next month. Upon the governor's resignation to claim a U.S. Senate seat, Wells was inaugurated in his place. Elected himself in November 1865 on the Citizen Party ticket, he served until removed on June 3, 1867, following a long feud with General Philip H. Sheridan over politics. Wells had favored the granting of suffrage to blacks. He retired to his plantation but held a number of government appointments. (Fortier, Alcee, *A History of Louisiana*)

WHARTON, A.D. (?-?)

When Tennessean A.D. Wharton's vessel returned to the United States at the outbreak of the Civil War, the veteran of over four years in the old navy tendered his resignation. Since it was realized that he planned to join the Confederate forces, he was imprisoned at Forts Lafayette and Warren. Exchanged early in 1862, he became a lieutenant in the Southern navy on February 8, 1862. Assigned to the CSS *Arkansas*, he commanded two of that ship's guns during its run down the Mississippi to Vicksburg. Before the *Arkansas* was scuttled near Baton Rouge in August, Wharton had been transferred to the *Harriet Lane* which had recently been captured. It was hoped to turn her into a cruiser. This being found impracticable, he spent the year 1863 in command of the *Webb* while awaiting the completion of the *Missouri*. At the end of the year he suggested using the *Webb* for running the blockade. However, before receiving approval he was assigned to the ironclad *Tennessee* at Mobile. On August 5, 1864, in the famous battle of Mobile Bay, Wharton commanded the ironclad's forward gun division and personally fired a shot which nearly sank Farragut's flagship, the *Hartford*. He later lamented not having ricocheted the shot to strike along the water line. In the end the *Tennessee* was forced to surrender and Lieutenant Wharton again became a prisoner. Shortly exchanged, he was named executive officer aboard the ironclad *Richmond* in the James River Squadron. In January 1865 he led an expedition of his own design to destroy the bridges on the Tennessee River in East Tennessee. The mission was a failure and Wharton became a prisoner for the third and final time. Released at the close of the war, he became an official in the Nashville school system and a member of the Board of Visitors

at Annapolis. (Scharf, J. Thomas, *History of the Confederate States Navy*)

WHARTON, Gabriel Colvin (1824-1906)

Escaping from surrounded Fort Donelson with John B. Floyd, Virginian Gabriel C. Wharton returned to western Virginia where he rose to the rank of brigadier general in the Confederate service. A graduate of the Virginia Military Institute, he had been a civil engineer when Fort Sumter was fired upon. His Confederate assignments included: major, 45th Virginia (ca. June 17, 1861); colonel, 51st Virginia (ca. July 17, 1861); commanding 1st Brigade, Floyd's Division, Central Army of Kentucky, Department #2 (February 9-16, 1862); commanding 3rd Brigade, Department of Western Virginia (early 1863-July 1863); brigadier general, CSA (September 25, 1863, to rank from July 8); commanding Valley District, Department of Northern Virginia (July 1863); commanding brigade, Ransom's Division, Department of Southwestern Virginia and East Tennessee (fall 1863-January 1864); commanding brigade, Department of Southwestern Virginia and East Tennessee (January 1864); commanding Ransom's Division, Department of East Tennessee (January-February 1864); commanding brigade, Department of East Tennessee (February-March 1864); commanding brigade, Department of Western Virginia (April-May 1864); commanding brigade, Breckinridge's Division, Valley District, Department of Northern Virginia (May-June and June-summer 1864); commanding brigade, Breckinridge's Division, Army of Northern Virginia (June 1864); and commanding division, Valley District, Department of Northern Virginia (summer 1864-March 2, 1865). Following the confused campaigning in western Virginia during the first part of the war, Wharton and his regiment were ordered to the West where they took part in the defense of Fort Donelson. When surrender became imminent Wharton escaped with most of the division. For the next two years he served in southwestern Virginia and East Tennessee and received promotion to brigadier general. He commanded a brigade in the victory at New Market against Franz Sigel and then joined Lee's army at Cold Harbor. His brigade was part of the relief force that arrived in time to save Lynchburg. Returning to the Shenandoah Valley, he advanced into Maryland with Jubal A. Early and fought at Monocacy and on the outskirts of Washington. He led a division at 3rd Winchester, Fisher's Hill, and Cedar Creek. In Early's final disaster at Waynesboro, Wharton's division disintegrated. In the postwar years he was active in mining and served in the state legislature. (Freeman, Douglas S., *Lee's Lieutenants*)

WHARTON, John Austin (1828-1865)

Having survived one wound and fought through the entire war, John A. Wharton was destined to die in a personal altercation—three days before Lee surrendered. Tennessee-born and Texas-educated, he had become a lawyer by the time of the secession crisis during which he attended the convention that took the state out of the Union. After falling ill on the way to fight at 1st Bull Run as an independent volunteer, he returned to Texas and formally joined the Confederate army. His assignments included: captain, 8th Texas Cavalry (mid 1861); colonel, 8th Texas Cavalry (early 1862); commanding Cavalry Brigade, Right Wing, Army of the Mississippi (September 27-November 20, 1862); brigadier general, CSA (November 18, 1862); commanding Cavalry Brigade, Polk's Corps, Army of Tennessee (November 22-ca. December 28, 1862); commanding brigade, Wheeler's Cavalry Division, Army of Tennessee (ca. December 28, 1862-January 22, 1863); commanding division, Wheeler's Cavalry Corps, Army of Tennessee (January 22-April 1864); major general, CSA (November 10, 1863); commanding Cavalry Division, District of West Louisiana, Trans-Mississippi Department (from April 21, 1864); commanding Cavalry Division, District of Arkansas, Trans-Mississippi Department (fall 1864); and commanding Cavalry Corps, Trans-Mississippi Department (various times from the spring of 1864 to April 1865). In command of his regiment he was wounded at Shiloh but returned to lead a brigade at Perryville and Murfreesboro. He took over the division and led it at Chickamauga and in Wheeler's Raid during the Chattanooga Campaign. In the spring of 1864 he was granted leave to visit Texas for reasons of health. However, upon crossing the Mississippi, he joined Taylor's troops fighting Banks' Red River Campaign and commanded the cavalry. With frequent leaves he continued to serve in the Trans-Mississippi Department until April 6, 1865, when he was shot and killed by a former subordinate, George W. Baylor, apparently in a dispute over the junior's failure to gain promotion. During the war, Wharton's mother, proud of her son's distinguished combat record, refused to allow his friends to run him for a seat in the Confederate Congress.

WHEAT, Chatham Roberdeau (1826-1862)

An adventurer, Chatham Roberdeau Wheat, was found to be the only officer capable of keeping his battalion of New Orleans toughs under any sort of discipline. The Virginia-born Wheat had become a New Orleans lawyer and served as a state legislator. But he was also a military adventurer, having served in Latin America with Lopez, Caravajal, Walker, and Alvarez, and in Italy with Garibaldi. Returning home at the outbreak of the Civil War, he was commissioned major, 1st Louisiana Special Battalion. One of the unit's companies had given its nickname, "Tigers," to the entire battalion. Wheat needed every inch of his 6-foot-4-inch frame to keep the rowdy toughs from the city's wharves and alleys in line. Moving to Virginia, Wheat led his men at the battle of 1st Bull Run where they were one of the first two units to face the Union flank attack. In the defense Wheat was wounded through both lungs. He defied the medical experts and recovered. The next summer, after taking part in the Shenandoah Valley Campaign, he was killed at the battle of Gaines' Mill during the Seven Days. The Tigers proved to be too unruly without him and were shortly thereafter broken up. (Dufour, Charles L., *Gentle Tiger, The Gallant Life of Roberdeau Wheat*)

WHEELER, Joseph (1836-1906)

One of only a handful of Confederates to be buried in Arlington National Cemetary, Joseph Wheeler qualified on the basis of his later service as a major general of volunteers in the Spanish-American War. The Georgia-born West Pointer (1859) had resigned his commission as a second lieutenant in the Regiment of Mounted Riflemen—he had briefly been posted to the dragoons in 1859—and, joining the South, had a meteoric rise. The cavalryman's assignments included: first lieutenant, Artillery (1861); colonel, 19th Alabama (September 4, 1861); commanding Cavalry Brigade, Left Wing, Army of the Mississippi (September 14-November 20, 1862); brigadier general, CSA (October 30, 1862); commanding Cavalry Brigade, Polk's Corps, Army of Tennessee (November 20-22, 1862); commanding Cavalry Brigade, Hardee's Corps, Army of Tennessee (November 22-December 1862); commanding cavalry division, Army of Tennessee (December 1862-March 16, 1863); major general, CSA (January 30, 1863); commanding cavalry corps, Army of Tennessee (March 16, 1863-fall 1864); commanding Cavalry Corps, Department of South Carolina, Georgia and Florida (fall 1864-March 1865); lieutenant general, CSA (February 28, 1865); and commanding corps, Hampton's Cavalry Command, Army of Tennessee (March-April 26, 1865). He led an infantry regiment at Shiloh and during the operations around Corinth, Mississippi, but was then assigned in the summer of 1862 to be chief of cavalry for Bragg's Army of the Mississippi. He led a mounted brigade at Perryville and a division at Murfreesboro. Given command of a corps of mounted troopers, he led it in the Tullahoma Campaign and at Chickamauga was in charge of one of the two cavalry corps (the other was under Nathan Bedford Forrest). However, soon after the battle conflicts between Forrest and Wheeler and Forrest and Bragg led to the reassignment of Forrest. Thus Wheeler was again in charge of all the mounted troops with the Army of Tennessee. He fought thus at Chattanooga and led his men in the Atlanta Campaign. During these last two campaigns he was noted for his raids on the Union supply lines. Following the fall of Atlanta, Wheeler's corps was left behind to deal with Sherman while Hood launched his invasion of middle Tennessee. With the small force at hand Wheeler proved unsuccessful in hindering Sherman's March to the Sea. During the course of the campaign in the Carolinas, Wheeler was placed under the orders of Wade Hampton who had been transferred from Virginia. Taken prisoner in Georgia in May 1865, Wheeler was held at Fort Delaware until June 8th. A longtime congressman from Alabama in the postwar years, he donned the blue as a major general of volunteers in the war with Spain. In 1900 he was retired with the regular army rank of brigadier general. His Confederate career had earned him the sobriquet "Fightin' Joe." (Dyer, John Percy, *"Fightin' Joe" Wheeler* and *From Shiloh to San Juan*)

WHITE, Elijah Viers (1832-1907)

A hard fighter, Elijah V. White was nonetheless a problem for his superiors. A Maryland native and veteran of the Kansas troubles, he had been farming in Loudoun County, Virginia, at the outbreak of the Civil War. Since John Brown's raid he had been a member of the Loudoun Cavalry. His later assignments included: private, Company G, 7th Virginia Cavalry (early

1861); captain, White's (Va.) Rebels (January 11, 1862); lieutenant colonel, 35th Virginia Cavalry Battalion (February 4, 1863); and commanding Dearing's Brigade, Rosser's Division, Cavalry Corps, Army of Northern Virginia (April 7-8, 1865). After distinguishing himself at Ball's Bluff as a volunteer aide, he was authorized to raise an independent company for border service. Assigned to Ewell's divisional headquarters, White and his men fought in the Valley Campaign, the Seven Days, and at Cedar Mountain; White was wounded in the Valley. Finally returning to Loudoun County during the 2nd Bull Run campaign, his unit was highly successful. The command joined the Maryland invasion but was ordered back to Virginia by Jeb Stuart when he became displeased with its lack of discipline. This was not one of White's strong points; lax in filing reports, he was notorious for disliking drill and saber-grinding. White was again wounded in a fight at Leesburg. In October 1862 his command was increased to a battalion, which nearly mutinied upon assignment to a regular cavalry brigade. The command, by now nicknamed "The Comanches," was given frequent opportunity for separate forays, but did fight in regular service at Brandy Station, Gettysburg, Mine Run, the Wilderness, Trevilian Station, in the Shenandoah Valley, and Petersburg. White briefly took over brigade command upon the death of General Dearing at High Bridge. White and many of his men slipped out of the trap at Appomattox only to surrender later. After the war White resumed farming and served as a banker and sheriff. (Myers, Frank M., *The Comanches: A History of White's Battalion, Virginia Cavalry, Laurel Brigade, Hampton Division, ANVa., C.S.A.*)

WHITFIELD, John Wilkins (1818-1879)

Within a period of only a few months after receiving his commission as a Confederate brigadier general, John W. Whitfield appears to have lost his command. The Tennessee native had been an Indian agent, territorial delegate from Kansas to the U.S. Congress, and land office official before settling in Texas. His Confederate assignments included: major, 4th Texas Cavalry Battalion (1861); colonel, 27th Texas Cavalry (spring 1862); brigadier general, CSA (May 9, 1863); commanding brigade, Jackson's Cavalry Division, Department of the West (June 9-July 1863); and commanding brigade, Jackson's Cavalry Division, Department of Mississippi and East Louisiana (July-fall 1863). Considering his Mexican War service—he had been a captain in the 1st Tennessee and lieutenant colonel of the 2nd Tennessee—he took a step down when he took command of the battalion. He served in the Indian Territory early in the war and then led his battalion at Pea Ridge and across the Mississippi. At about this time his unit was increased to a regiment which was often styled "Whitfield's Legion." Leading this he was severely wounded at Iuka. Returning to duty the following spring, he was commissioned a brigadier general and assigned to a brigade which he led during the siege of Jackson. That fall he disappears from the extant records, until he was paroled back in Texas on June 29, 1865. After the war he was a state legislator.

WHITING, William Henry Chase (1824-1865)

One of the generals who failed to make the grade while serving under Lee, William H.C. Whiting was quietly moved aside to make room for the promotion of John Bell Hood. Having graduated at the top of the 1845 West Point class, Whiting had served in the engineers until he resigned as a captain on February 20, 1861. The native Mississippian held the following assignments in Confederate service: major, Engineers (early 1861); brigadier general, CSA (August 28, 1861); commanding division (known as Forces near Dumfries and in the Potomac District until March), Department of Northern Virginia (late 1861-June 1862); commanding division, Valley District, same department (June 1862); commanding division, in 2nd Corps (June 26-July 1862); major general, CSA (April 12, 1863); and in 1st Corps (July 1862), Army of Northern Virginia; commanding District of the Cape Fear (an independent department September 26, 1863-April 18, 1864), Department of North Carolina (November 8, 1862-July 14, 1863 and September 26, 1863-January 15, 1865); and commanding the Department (July 14-September 26, 1863). As Joe Johnston's engineering officer, he served in the Shenandoah and at 1st Bull Run where he so impressed Jefferson Davis that he was promised promotion three grades to brigadier. He commanded what was in effect a division on the Manassas line and was the center of a controversy between Johnston and Davis, who wanted Whiting to command a brigade of Mississippi troops. Johnston felt that to move troops many miles in the face of the enemy was suicidal. Whiting served through the Peninsula Campaign, seeing action at Yorktown, Seven Pines, and in the Seven Days. During this time he moved to reinforce Jackson to fool the Union. Ill for several months, he was supplanted by Hood and sent to North Carolina, where his engineering skills could be used to advantage. With the exception of a brief time in command of the department and in command of a field division in May 1864 around Petersburg, he served in the Cape Fear area until his capture. When Fort Fisher was threatened by a joint navy-army Union attack he moved into the fort where he was mortally wounded and captured on January 15, 1865. He died in New York, a prisoner, on March 10.

WICKHAM, Williams Carter (1820-1888)

Despite the fact that he had opposed secession, Virginia planter, lawyer, and state legislator Williams C. Wickham served in either the cavalry or the Confederate Congress throughout the war. His military assignments included: captain, Hanover (Va.) Dragoons (ca. April 1861); lieutenant colonel, 4th Virginia Cavalry (September 1861); colonel, 4th Virginia Cavalry (August 1862); brigadier general, CSA (September 1, 1863); commanding brigade, F. Lee's Division, Cavalry Corps, Army of Northern Virginia (September 9, 1863-August 1864); commanding brigade, F. Lee's Cavalry Division, Valley District, Department of Northern Virginia (August-September 19, 1864); and commanding the division (September 1864). He

Confederate cavalryman Williams C. Wickham. (NA)

fought at 1st Bull Run and was wounded at Williamsburg. While recuperating at home he was captured and not exchanged until August 1862. Promoted to colonel, he led the regiment at 2nd Bull Run, South Mountain, and Antietam. That fall he suffered another wound but was back on duty in time for Fredericksburg. He then fought at Chancellorsville, Gettysburg, and in the Mine Run operations. He opposed Kilpatrick's raid on Richmond in February 1864. After serving through the Overland and part of the Petersburg Campaign he was sent with the division to the Shenandoah to reinforce Early. At 3rd Winchester he succeeded the wounded Fitz Lee in command of the division but soon resigned to take his seat in the Second Confederate Congress. He had been elected the previous year but had missed the first session due to his active campaigning in the field. He was admitted on the opening day of the second session, November 7, and his resignation from the army was accepted two days later. Sitting on the Committee on Military Affairs, he soon became known as a friend of the military and an opponent of the president. He supported the Hampton Roads Peace Conference which ended in failure. Almost immediately after Lee's Appomattox surrender, Wickham embraced the Republican Party, being much reviled for it. He was on his county board and active in railroading before sitting in the state legislature. (Freeman, Douglas S., *Lee's Lieutenants*)

WIECHMANN, Louis J.

See: *Weichmann, Louis J.*

WIGFALL, Louis Trezevant (1816-1874)

Although also a brigadier, Louis T. Wigfall gave his principal service, if such it can be called, in the Confederate Senate. Born in South Carolina, he had been an early secessionist there and in Texas which he represented in the U.S. Senate. He was admitted to the Provisional Confederate Congress on April 29, 1861, where he served on the Committee on Foreign Affairs. Earlier that month he had played a leading role in arranging Fort Sumter's surrender, and he soon decided to return to the military. His brief service was limited to northern Virginia where his assignments included: colonel, 1st Texas (August 28, 1861); brigadier general, CSA (October 21, 1861); and commanding Texas Brigade, Forces Near Dumfries, Potomac District, Department of Northern Virginia (November 12, 1861-February 20, 1862). Resigning on the latter date, he took a seat in the First Regular Congress and served throughout the war. He sat on the committees on: Foreign Affairs; Military Affairs; Territories; and Flag and Seal. A cantankerous soul who had fought two prewar duels, Wigfall soon came into conflict with President Davis. After the chief executive vetoed Wigfall's bill to upgrade staff positions in the army and limit presidential selections, the Texan carried his fight into social circles, refusing to stand when Davis entered. A friend of the military and the generals, he was especially supportive of Joe Johnston and Beauregard. However, he was also an obstructionist in opposing Davis' nominations. He spent six years in self-imposed exile in England before returning via Baltimore to Texas, never adjusting to defeat. (King, A.L., *Louis Wigfall: Southern Fire-Eater*)

WILCOX, Cadmus Marcellus (1824-1890)

An experienced officer, West Pointer (1846), Mexican War brevet winner, and author of a rifle manual, Cadmus M. Wilcox proved to be a steady and competent divisional leader in the Army of Northern Virginia. He resigned his infantry captain's commission on June 8, 1861, to cast his lot with his native South. The North Carolina-born and Tennessee-raised officer entered the Confederate service in an Alabama unit. His assignments included: colonel, 9th Alabama (May 1861); brigadier general, CSA (October 21, 1861); commanding brigade, G.W. Smith's Division (in the Potomac District until March), Department of Northern Virginia (October 22, 1861-ca. March 1862); commanding brigade, Longstreet's Division (in 1st Corps from July), Army of Northern Virginia (ca. March-August 1862); commanding brigade and division, 1st Corps, same army (August-September 1862); commanding Anderson's Division, same corps and army (September-November 1862); commanding brigade, same division, corps and army (December 1862-May 30, 1862); commanding brigade, Anderson's Division, 3rd Corps, Army of Northern Virginia (May 30-August 1863); major general, CSA (to rank from August 3, 1863); and commanding the division (August 1863-February 1865 and March-April 9, 1865). After serving in the Shenandoah and northern Virginia, he led his brigade on the Peninsula, including fighting at Williamsburg, Seven

Pines, and the Seven Days. At 2nd Bull Run he was in charge of a provisional division composed of three brigades from Longstreet's former command. This force was later assigned to Anderson's Division, and Wilcox was in temporary command of the division after Antietam. He led his brigade at Fredericksburg and made crucial independent decisions that aided in the victory. After fighting at Gettysburg he was promoted to major general and transferred to command Pender's former division. In this position he served out the war fighting at the Wilderness, Spotsylvania, Cold Harbor, and Petersburg and surrendered at Appomattox. When the lines around Petersburg were crumbling, it was his men who held firm and allowed sufficient time for the evacuation. Settling in the reunited nation's capital, he held a number of government appointments. His eight pallbearers were a bi-partisan group of generals. (Freeman, Douglas S., *Lee's Lieutenants*)

WILCOX, John Allen (1819-1864)

When Confederate Congressman John A. Wilcox died of apoplexy on February 7, 1864, the Davis administration lost an unwavering friend in the legislative branch. A native of North Carolina, he was the brother of Confederate General Cadmus M. Wilcox. Raised apparently in Tennessee, he had practiced law in Mississippi and served as the lieutenant colonel of the 2nd Mississippi during the Mexican War. Defeated in a bid for a second U.S. congressional term, he moved to Texas. His political career had spanned the Whig, Know-Nothing, and Democratic parties. He helped draft the Texas secession ordinance and was elected to the First Regular Confederate Congress that November. There he sat on the committees on: Enrolled Bills; Military Affairs; and Territories and Public Lands; he chaired the latter. Deferring to executive authority during the emergency posed by the war, he never introduced a bill which did not have administration backing and always voted for the president's program. In between the sessions in Richmond he returned to Texas where he served on the staff of General John B. Magruder as a volunteer aide with the honorary rank of colonel. In late 1863 he was reelected by his southernmost, 1st District constituents, but he died before the expiration of the First Congress.

WILDES, Thomas Francis (1834-1883)

Canadian-born editor and teacher Thomas Wildes was honored by a Virginia town for saving it from the torch of General Sheridan. Wildes had been named lieutenant colonel of the 116th Ohio upon its organization on August 18, 1862. His later military assignments included: commanding 1st Brigade, 1st Infantry Division, Army of West Virginia (October 19-December 24, 1864); commanding 1st Brigade, Independent Division, 24th Corps, Army of the James (December 24, 1864-February 3, 1865); and colonel, 186th Ohio (February 28, 1865). He served in West Virginia and in the Shenandoah Valley from 1862 to 1864. At the battle of Piedmont he was wounded by the concussion from a shell and in the 3rd Battle of Winchester he was thrown from his horse. On October 3, 1864, Lieutenant John R. Meigs, the only son of the Union

quartermaster general, was killed in a controversial encounter with some rebel scouts. In retaliation, General Sheridan ordered the nearby town of Dayton put to the torch. Seeing the distress of the townspeople, Wildes dissuaded the general from destroying the town and only a few scattered buildings outside of town were burned. After the war the townspeople erected a tablet in Wildes' honor. At the battle of Cedar Creek, Wildes succeeded to the command of the brigade upon the death of Colonel George D. Wells and led it through the rest of the Valley Campaign of 1864, then joined the forces facing Petersburg and Richmond at the end of the year. Given command of a new regiment in March 1865, he commanded it in garrison duty in Tennessee until the end of the war. He was brevetted brigadier general of volunteers the next month and after the war he studied and practiced law. (Wildes, Thomas F., *Record of the One Hundred and Sixteenth Regiment, Ohio Infantry Volunteers*)

WILKES, Charles (1798-1877)

During the 19th century naval commanders on the high seas had a far greater degree of independence than is the case today. This was due to the lack of rapid communications. One of these officers was destined to commit an act that brought international law into question and caused grave diplomatic problems for the United States. Charles Wilkes had entered the navy as a midshipman in 1818 and acquired a reputation for violating orders. Unpopular with his subordinate officers, he was much harsher with the enlisted men and was once publicly reprimanded for illegally punishing a seaman. At the beginning of hostilities he was a captain, in command of the *San Jacinto*. With this vessel he stopped the British mail steamer *Trent*, seizing two of its passengers, Confederate commissioners James

Charles Wilkes of the *Trent* affair. (*Leslie's*)

M. Mason and John Slidell. For this action he was feted in the North and reviled in the South. In the end, however, the captives had to be freed. While commanding the West India Squadron in early 1863 he seized another British vessel, the *Peterhoff*, bound for Mexico, on the grounds that much of its cargo was destined for transfer to the Confederacy. The courts later ruled against his interpretation. He had been promoted to commodore on July 16, 1862, while commanding the James River Flotilla and on June 25, 1864, was retired. Two years later he was promoted on the retired list to rear admiral. (Warren, Gordon H., *Fountain of Discontent: The* Trent *Affair and Freedom of the Seas*)

WILKINSON, John (1821-1891)

One of the lesser known Confederate naval leaders, John Wilkinson had one of the most varied of oceangoing careers. A veteran of two dozen years in the old navy, with more than the usual amount of sea duty, Wilkinson resigned his commission on April 6, 1861, and offered his services to his native state of Virginia. Appointed a lieutenant in the Virginia navy, he served at Fort Powhatan and on Aquia Creek. Transferred to the Confederate navy on June 10, he was subsequently sent to the Mississippi where he briefly commanded the *Jackson* before being named executive officer of the *Louisiana*. Assuming command during the Union capture of New Orleans, Wilkinson was forced to destroy his craft. Captured shortly thereafter, he was exchanged and sent to England where he bought a ship, which was renamed *R.E. Lee*, and ran the blockade. After directing the failed conspiracy to free the prisoners at Johnson's Island, he returned to Bermuda and took command of the blockade runner *Whisper*. After briefly commanding the ironclad *Roanoke*, he was for a time involved in another plot to free Confederate prisoners—this time at Point Lookout. Then he directed blockade-running operations at Wilmington, North Carolina. Given command of the raider *Chickamauga*, he made a short but successful cruise along the Atlantic coast before anchoring under Fort Fisher. After participating in the defense of that fort, he took command of another blockade runner, the *Chameleon*, which failed in several attempts to make its return voyage to Wilmington. With the Confederacy collapsing, he went to Liverpool and turned over his government funds to Captain Bulloch. He was engaged in business in Nova Scotia before returning to Virginia in 1874. (Wilkinson, John, *Narrative of a Blockade Runner*)

WILLIAMS, James (1796-1869)

While a U.S. diplomat, James Williams was opposed to secession, but once it became an established fact he readily joined the Confederacy. A Tennessee native, he had been active in journalism, riverboats, railroads, mining, and manufacturing before being appointed a minister to Turkey in 1857. He had also been elected to the state legislature as a Whig for one term. By the time of the Civil War, he was a Democrat and returned to the United States as a Unionist, but soon changed his colors. Sent as an agent to Great Britain, he wrote propagandistic articles for the *London Times* and the *Index*, a Confederate

organ. He also wrote *Letters on Slavery from the Old World*, *The South Vindicated*, and *The Rise and Fall of the Model Republic*. He was instrumental in opening diplomatic channels with Mexico in 1863 but was a failure in attempts to gain recognition from France and Germany. Remaining in Europe after the war, he died in Graz, Austria. (Cullop, Charles P., *Confederate Propaganda in Europe*)

WILLIAMS, Jesse Milton (1831-1864)

Although he led his brigade in several major battles of the Army of Northern Virginia, Jesse M. Williams never received the right to wear the wreathed stars of a general officer. He had enlisted early in the war and his assignments included: captain, Company D, 2nd Louisiana (May 11, 1861); colonel, 2nd Louisiana (ca. July 1, 1862); and commanding Starke's-Nicholls' Brigade, Jackson's-Trimble's-Johnson's Division, 2nd Corps, Army of Northern Virginia (September 17, 1862 and May 2-July 19, 1863). As a company officer, he fought at Yorktown and in the Seven Days Battles. In the summer of 1862 he was promoted to regimental command, and he led the 2nd at Cedar Mountain and 2nd Bull Run. At Antietam he took over command of the brigade until he was wounded out of action. At Chancellorsville he again succeeded to brigade command and led it through the rest of the battle and in the Gettysburg Campaign. Returning to the direction of the 2nd, he served through the Bristoe and Mine Run campaigns and fought at the Wilderness. On May 12, 1864, in the heavy fighting at Spotsylvania's "Bloody Angle," he was killed.

WILLIAMS, John Stuart (1818-1898)

Despite his opposition to the idea of secession, native Kentuckian John S. Williams joined the Confederacy and became a brigadier general. The lawyer and state legislator had served in the Mexican War as captain of an independent Kentucky company and later as colonel of the 4th Kentucky. In one of his political races he was derisively dubbed "Cerro Gordo" Williams by his opponent, Roger W. Hanson, over Williams' disputed actions in that Mexican War battle. Williams won the election and retained the nickname as a mark of honor. Reluctantly, he finally entered the Confederate army where his assignments included: colonel, 5th Kentucky (November 16, 1861); brigadier general, CSA (April 16, 1862); commanding Department of Southwestern Virginia (November 19-25, 1862); commanding Department of Western Virginia (November 25-December 10, 1862); commanding 2nd Brigade, Department of Western Virginia (ca. December 10, 1862-mid 1863); commanding cavalry brigade, Department of Western Virginia and East Tennessee (fall 1863-ca. December 1863); commanding Kentucky Brigade, Humes' Division, Wheeler's Cavalry Corps, Army of Tennessee (ca. June-July 1864); and commanding Kentucky Brigade, Kelly's Division, Wheeler's Cavalry Corps, Army of Tennessee (July-September 1864). Early in the war he commanded his regiment in the Kentucky-Virginia border area, under Humphrey Marshall, and was for a time in departmental command. He won a battle for the defense of the Abingdon, Virginia, salt works while in command of a brigade. During the Atlanta Campaign he was assigned to command a Kentucky brigade under Wheeler but became separated on a raid into Tennessee, for which he was roundly criticized by the famed cavalryman. He finished out the war in the mountains of southwestern Virginia and was a farmer and state national legislator after the war.

WILLIAMS, Lawrence Orton

See: *Williams, William Orton*

WILLIAMS, R.S. (?-?)

The inventor of the first Confederate machine gun to actually be fired in combat was Kentuckian R.S. Williams. At the beginning of the war he offered his creation to the Confederate War Department whose Bureau of Ordnance secretly adopted it. It was capable of firing 65 rounds a minute from its single 1.57-caliber barrel while being crank-operated. One battery of these novel weapons saw action at Seven Pines, and on January 14, 1863, Williams was given the authority to raise a battery of Kentuckians to be equipped with his invention. Apparently, this unit saw some action with Williams as its captain.

WILLIAMS, Thomas Henry (1822-1904)

In order to improve the medical treatment of wounded Confederate soldiers, Thomas H. Williams made the sensible, but not always practical, request that there be more coordination between the medical department and the high command in regard to troop movements. The native Marylander had received his medical education in that state and in 1849 joined the regular army as an assistant surgeon. Resigning on June 1, 1861, he offered his services to the South and was appointed a full surgeon. He was a director and inspector during the first year of the war in Virginia and served as an assistant to the surgeon general. As such he was responsible for many of the hospitals and the medical staffs themselves in their organization. In 1863 he served for a time as the medical director of the Army of Northern Virginia, where he found that even the high command did not always have an early enough warning of impending battles to alert the surgeons and so facilitate the accumulation and transport of medical equipment and supplies. After the war he retired to private practice in Virginia and then Maryland. (Cunningham, Horace Herndon, *Doctors in Gray*)

WILLIAMS, William Orton (?-1863)

One of the mysteries of the Civil War is what was William Orton Williams up to when he was captured and executed as a spy by the Union authorities. Born in New York, the son of a Virginian army officer who was killed in the war with Mexico, William Orton Williams had been a lieutenant in the 2nd Cavalry when the Civil War began. When Virginia seceded, he resigned his position on the staff of General Scott and offered his services to the Confederacy. As a lieutenant he served on the staff of General Leonidas Polk in western Tennessee. At the battle of

Shiloh and in the subsequent siege at Corinth he was assistant artillery chief to General Braxton Bragg, with the rank of captain. On April 2, 1863, he was appointed a colonel, under the assumed name Lawrence W. Orton, and ordered to report to General Joseph Wheeler. Then, on June 8, 1863, he and a cousin, Walter G. Peter, went behind Union lines posing as Union inspectors. Posing as "Colonel Lawrence W. Auton" and "Major George Dunlop," they visited Fort Granger, told their story, and even borrowed $50 from the commander before going on their way. However, suspicions were aroused and they were brought back for further questioning. Their identities revealed, they were tried as spies at three in the morning and hanged a few hours later. Williams, sometimes identified as Lawrence Orton Williams, is now believed to have been on his way to Canada to take ship for Europe on a diplomatic or ordnance purchasing mission. After the war, Robert E. Lee, whose wife was related to Williams, was still outraged by the hanging. (Freeman, Douglas S., *R.E. Lee*)

WILLIS, Edward S. (1840-1864)

When Grant began his relentless drive on Richmond in May 1864, the effect on the Confederate general officers' corps was devastating. This opened the way for the promotion of younger officers, such as Edward S. Willis, many of whom did not last long enough in their new positions to actually receive their new commissions. A native of Georgia, Willis had been attending classes at West Point when the war began. He promptly resigned his commission and offered his services to the Confederacy. His assignments included: first lieutenant and adjutant, 12th Georgia (July 5, 1861); lieutenant colonel, 12th Georgia (December 13, 1862); colonel, 12th Georgia (January 22, 1863); and commanding Pegram's Brigade, Early's-Gordon's Division, 2nd Corps, Army of Northern Virginia (ca. May 5-30, 1864). After serving in western Virginia, including actions at Greenbrier and Alleghany, he was detailed to Stonewall Jackson's staff, part of the time serving as assistant chief of artillery. During the Shenandoah Valley Campaign he was briefly captured at Port Republic while trying to rally a Union cavalry unit he mistook for Confederates. Feigning illness, he later made good his escape. Serving with Jackson, he participated in the Seven Days Battles, Cedar Mountain, and 2nd Bull Run. With the death of the 12th's lieutenant colonel at Fredericksburg and the resignation of its colonel the next month, Willis became a colonel. He distinguished himself at Chancellorsville and was heavily engaged on the first day at Gettysburg. After a stint of detached service with his regiment in the Valley in the winter of 1863-64, he rejoined Lee to face Grant in the spring. After General John Pegram was wounded at the Wilderness, Willis was transferred to temporary command of the Virginia brigade. He saw action at Spotsylvania and the North Anna. On May 30, 1864, in a futile charge at Bethesda Church, he fell mortally wounded. He died the next day after having been visited by men from his old command. (Thomas, Henry W., *The History of the Doles-Cook Brigade, Army of Northern Virginia, 1861-1865*)

WILSON, Claudius Charles (1831-1863)

Native Georgia lawyer Claudius C. Wilson served only 11 days as a Confederate brigadier general before succumbing to disease. His assignments included: captain, Company I, 25th Georgia (summer 1861); colonel, 25th Georgia (September 2, 1861); commanding brigade, Walker's Division, Department of the West (June-July 1863); commanding brigade, Walker's Division, Department of Mississippi and East Louisiana (July-August 23, 1863); commanding brigade, Walker's Division, Hill's Corps, Army of Tennessee (August 25-September 1863); commanding brigade, Walker's Division, Reserve Corps, Army of Tennessee (September 1863); commanding brigade, Walker's Division, Longstreet's Corps, Army of Tennessee (September 26-November 12, 1863); commanding brigade, Walker's Division, Hardee's Corps, Army of Tennessee (November 12-27, 1863); and brigadier general, CSA (November 16, 1863). Elected colonel of his regiment upon its organization, he served on the Georgia and South Carolina coasts until ordered to join Joseph E. Johnston in his efforts to relieve the pressure on Vicksburg in the spring and summer of 1863. In Mississippi he led a brigade during these operations and the subsequent defense of Jackson. Joining the Army of Tennessee, he fought at Chickamauga. Promoted to brigadier general, he fought at Chattanooga but died a couple of days later, on November 27, of camp fever.

WINDER, Charles Sidney (1829-1862)

A harsh disciplinarian, Charles S. Winder was not one of the more popular commanders of the Stonewall Brigade. Winder was a West Pointer (1850) from Maryland who had served in the artillery until his April 1, 1861, resignation. His assignments for the South included: major, Artillery (to rank from March 16, 1861); colonel, 6th South Carolina (July 8, 1861); brigadier general, CSA (March 1, 1862); commanding G.B. Anderson's (old) Brigade (the old garrison at Manassas), D.H. Hill's Division, Department of Northern Virginia (March 25-April 2, 1862); commanding Stonewall Brigade (in Jackson's Division from May), Valley District, same department (April 2-June 26, 1862); commanding Stonewall Brigade, Jackson's Division, 2nd Corps, Army of Northern Virginia (June 26-August 9, 1862); and commanding the division (August 9, 1862). He held a staff position during the bombardment of Fort Sumter and then headed the 6th South Carolina on the Manassas lines. He held a brigade command there for a few days before being sent to the Valley. Unpopular as an outsider with the brigade, his regular army ways offended even Jackson when he had 30 men bucked and gagged; a very cruel but common punishment. Some men promised that Winder would not survive his next battle. Winder proved a mediator in the problems between Jackson and Turner Ashby. He fought throughout the Valley Campaign and with Lee during the Seven Days. At Cedar Mountain he led the division when the senior brigadier A.R. Lawton, had conveniently been left behind to guard the wagon trains. The Confederacy lost his services when he was mortally wounded by a shell that day. (Robertson, James I., Jr., *The Stonewall Brigade*)

WINDER, John Henry (1800-1865)

If Marylander John H. Winder had survived the Civil War, he, rather than Henry Wirz, would probably have been hanged for the treatment of Union prisoners of war. The West Pointer (1820) had served with the artillery and riflemen before resigning as a second lieutenant in 1823. Four years later he was reinstated with his previous rank. During the Mexican War he won two brevets, and during times of peace he was a professor of tactics at his alma mater. Resigning as a major in the 3rd Artillery on April 27, 1861, he joined the Confederacy. His Southern assignments included: brigadier general, CSA (June 21, 1861); commanding Department of Henrico (October 21, 1861-May 5, 1864); and commanding 2nd Military District, Department of North Carolina and Southern Virginia (May 25-June 9, 1864). Assigned to duty as provost marshal in Richmond, his duties included guarding prisoners of war on Belle Isle and at Libby Prison. Eventually placed in military command of the capital's vicinity, his powers over the lives of the inhabitants were expanded, with the normal resentment developing. In the spring of 1864 he took command in the area around Goldsboro, North Carolina, but in June was assigned to command the prisoner of war camp at Andersonville. A month later his powers were expanded over all such camps in Alabama as well as Georgia. On November 21, 1864, he was placed in charge of all camps east of the Mississippi. Already despised in the South, he now aroused a similar feeling in the North. There were accusations that he was deliberately attempting to starve the Union captives, but in actuality it was the extreme shortage of supplies and the lack of an effective distribution network that was responsible. The strenuous nature of his work proved too much for him and he died at Florence, South Carolina, on February 7, 1865.

WIRZ, Henry (1823-1865)

If Confederate General John H. Winder, had not died in February 1865, the victorious Union would probably have hanged him instead of Andersonville commandant Henry Wirz, and would probably have granted Wirz's request to return to his native Zürich, Switzerland. But the North needed a scapegoat. Educated in Zürich, Paris, and Berlin, Wirz had immigrated to Kentucky in 1849 and was practicing medicine in Louisiana at the outbreak of the Civil War. His Confederate assignments included: private, Company D, 4th Louisiana Battalion (June 16, 1861); lieutenant, 4th Louisiana Battalion (1861); captain and assistant adjutant general (August 1862); and major and assistant adjutant general (ca. 1863). Severely wounded at Seven Pines, his right arm was virtually paralyzed for life. Named as a staff officer, he was assigned to duty at the Tuscaloosa military prison in Alabama but was granted leave to visit Europe. Upon his return he served as a dispatch bearer until ordered to direct the interior of the Andersonville prison. He took command in March 1864 and held it until the end of the war. After awaiting capture at the camp, he was at first given a safe-conduct but was then sent to Washington for trial by a military tribunal. All his objections were overruled, and the trial proceeded with contradictory evidence of his having taken part in the killing of prisoners. It was clear, however, that he had felt no need to exceed his orders in order to improve conditions. Convicted, he was sentenced to hang. With four companies chanting ''Remember Andersonville,'' and 250 other curiosity seekers, the sentence was carried out in a bungled manner. (McElroy, John, *Andersonville: A Story of Rebel Military Prisons*)

WISE, Henry Alexander (1806-1876)

Virginia governor at the time that John Brown went to the gallows, Henry A. Wise had no military experience but became one of the more colorful brigadiers in Lee's army. His prewar career had included the practice of law in Tennessee and Virginia, sitting as a states' rights member of congress, a post as diplomatic representative to Brazil, as well as chief executive of the Old Dominion. Entering the Confederate military, he held the following assignments: brigadier general, CSA (June 5, 1861); commanding District of the Albemarle, Department of Norfolk (December 21, 1861-February 23, 1862); commanding Wise's Command, Army of Northern Virginia (June-July 1862); commanding brigade, D.H. Hill's Division, Army of Northern Virginia (July 1862); commanding brigade, Department of Virginia and North Carolina (August-December 1862); commanding brigade, Elzey's Command, same department (December 1862-April 1, 1863); commanding brigade,

Department of Richmond (April 1-September 1863); commanding 6th Military District of South Carolina, Department of South Carolina, Georgia and Florida (October 22, 1863-May 1864); commanding brigade, Whiting's Division, Department of North Carolina and Southern Virginia (mid-May 1864); commanding brigade, Johnson's Division, same department (May-June 1, 1864); commanding 1st Military District, same department (June 1-December 1864); and commanding brigade, Johnson's Division, Anderson's Corps, Army of Northern Virginia (December 1864-April 9, 1865). After service at the head of the Wise Legion in the Kanawha Valley of western Virginia, he was transferred to eastern North Carolina because of difficulties with another commander in the region, John B. Floyd. He was in command when Union General Burnside captured Roanoke Island in February 1862. His son was mortally wounded in this action. Subsequently he served in the Seven Days and for about a year in the Richmond Defenses. Once requested to report at his commander's headquarters as early in the morning as possible, he showed up before six. In the fall of 1863 he was transferred to South Carolina and remained there until the following spring. He fought at Drewry's Bluff and then commanded a district in the Petersburg area during the siege. In the retreat to Appomattox, he proved that he had learned something of the art of war by keeping his command together and bringing it out of the debacle at Sayler's Creek as a unit. In the last days before Appomattox he wore what looked

Henry Wirz's domain: the prison at Andersonville. (AC)

like war paint. Actually, he had washed in a muddy stream and his face was streaked. He died without ever accepting amnesty. (Wise, Barton H., *The Life of Henry A. Wise of Virginia*)

WITHERS, Jones Mitchell (1814-1890)

Having twice resigned from the old army, native Alabamian West Pointer (1835) Jones M. Withers rose to the rank of major general in the Confederate service. Posted to the 1st Dragoons, he had resigned as a brevet second lieutenant the very year of his graduation. The Mexican War brought him a commission as lieutenant colonel in the specially authorized 13th Infantry; this he resigned in 1848. A merchant and state legislator in Mobile, he was that city's mayor in the immediate pre-Civil War years. Offering his military talents to the South, his assignments included: colonel, 3rd Alabama (April 28, 1861); brigadier general, CSA (July 10, 1861); commanding District of Alabama, Department of Alabama and West Florida (October 14, 1861-January 27, 1862); commanding Army of Mobile (January 27-February 28, 1862); commanding division, 2nd Corps, Army of the Mississippi (ca. March 29-June 1862); commanding Reserve Corps, Army of the Mississippi (June-July 2, 1862); commanding Reserve Division, Army of the Mississippi (July 2-August 15, 1862); commanding division, Right Wing, Army of the Mississippi (August 15-November 20, 1862); major general, CSA (August 16, 1862, to rank from April 6); commanding division, Polk's Corps, Army of Tennessee (November 20, 1862-August 13, 1863); commanding District of Northern Alabama, Department of Alabama, Mississippi and East Florida (February 6-July 27, 1864); and commanding Alabama Reserve Forces (July 27, 1864-May 1865). Promoted to brigadier general early in the war, he commanded in the vicinity of his hometown. Given command of a division under Albert S. Johnston, he fought at Shiloh and during the Union advance on Corinth, Mississippi. Named a major general, he served in the Perryville and Tullahoma campaigns before being succeeded by Thomas C. Hindman. For the balance of the war he was stationed in Alabama either in district or reserve commands. A postwar merchant and journalist, he again served as mayor and was a federal official.

WOFFORD, William Tatum (1824-1884)

A Georgia lawyer, state legislator, and editor, William T. Wofford voted against secession but nonetheless entered the Confederate army and became a department commander in the final months of the war. He had been a captain in the Mexican War. His assignments included: colonel, 18th Georgia (early 1861); commanding Texas Brigade, Hood's Division, 1st Corps, Army of Northern Virginia (September 1862); brigadier general, CSA (April 23, to date from January 17, 1863); commanding Cobb's (old) Brigade, McLaws'-Kershaw's Division, 1st Corps, same army (ca. January-September 1863 and spring-summer 1864); commanding brigade, McLaws' Division, Longstreet's Corps, Army of Tennessee (fall 1863); and commanding Department of Northern Georgia (January 23-May 2, 1865). After serving in North Carolina and northern Virginia, Wofford joined Hood's Texas Brigade and saw action at

Yorktown, West Point, Seven Pines, 2nd Bull Run and Antietam. In the latter action he commanded a brigade. Given charge of Cobb's former command, he led it at Chancellorsville and Gettysburg but arrived too late to participate in the victory at Chickamauga. Apparently not present for the Knoxville Campaign, he next fought at the Wilderness and Spotsylvania. His brigade later served around Richmond and Petersburg and in the Shenandoah, but he was apparently absent. For the last few months of the war he was in command in northern Georgia, principally charged with rounding up deserters and conscripts. After the surrender he was active in railroading, politics, and education. (Freeman, Douglas S., *Lee's Lieutenants*)

WOOD

See: *Powell, Lewis Thornton*

WOOD, John Taylor (1830-1904)

Perhaps the most unorthodox of Confederate naval commanders was the grandson of President Zachary Taylor, John Taylor Wood. The Louisiana veteran of the Mexican War had been serving as an assistant professor of seamanship and gunnery at the Naval Academy when he resigned on April 21, 1861, to offer his services to the South. Serving at first with the Virginia forces, he took part in the blockading of the Potomac River. Commissioned a lieutenant in the Confederate Navy on October 4, 1861, he was assigned to the CSS *Virginia* at the beginning of the next year. During the fight with the *Monitor* he commanded the aft gun. After the scuttling of his vessel, Wood took command of a company of sharpshooters which fought at Drewry's Bluff. Given the rank of colonel of cavalry, he was assigned to Jefferson Davis' staff as an aide-de-camp. Chaffing for action, he frequently received permission to launch commando-style raids against the Union fleet. His small boat expeditions had by early 1864 captured two Union gunboats and five other vessels. Then on February 2, during a raid in conjunction with an advance by General Pickett on New Bern, North Carolina, Wood captured the gunboat *Underwriter*. However, he was forced to destroy the prize. By August he was a commander and was given command of the raider *Tallahassee* with which, in less than a month before docking at Fort Fisher, he captured 31 prizes. He declined command of the James River Squadron during the last winter of the war and notified President Davis of Lee's plans to abandon Richmond and Petersburg. Accompanying the fleeing government, he was briefly captured with Davis in Georgia before making his escape to Cuba. he settled in Nova Scotia and was engaged in the insurance business. (Shingleton, Royce Gordon, *John Taylor Wood: Sea Ghost of the Confederacy*)

WOOD, Sterling Alexander Martin (1823-1891)

There is only a hint of military failure to explain the resignation of Alabamian Sterling A.M. Wood as a Confederate brigadier general. A lawyer, state legislator, and journalist before the

Civil War, he was a supporter of the secession movement and the candidacy of John C. Breckinridge for president in 1860. Entering the Confederate army, his assignments included: colonel, 7th Alabama (May 18, 1861); brigadier general, CSA (January 7, 1862); commanding 3rd Brigade, 3rd Corps, Army of the Mississippi (spring-April 6 and April 6-July 2, 1862); commanding brigade, Buckner's Division, Army of the Mississippi (July 2-August 15, 1862); commanding brigade, Buckner's Division, Left Wing, Army of the Mississippi (August 15-October 8 and fall-November 20, 1862); and commanding brigade, Buckner's-Cleburne's Division, Hardee's-Hill's-Breckinridge's Corps, Army of Tennessee (November 20, 1862-October 17, 1863). Initially stationed at Pensacola, he was promoted to brigadier general and became part of the Confederate buildup at Corinth, Mississippi, just prior to Shiloh. There he ably led his brigade and was temporarily disabled by the fall of his mount. Following the defense of Corinth, he embarked upon Bragg's invasion of Kentucky and was severely wounded by a shell at Perryville. He recovered in time to fight at Murfreesboro and then went on to serve in the Tullahoma Campaign. The battle of Chickamauga proved to be his last. His division commander, Patrick R. Cleburne, failed to praise him in his battle report. Less than a month later he resigned, on October 17, 1863. He resumed his law practice and in the 1880s sat in the state legislature again.

WORK, Phillip Alexander (1832-1911)

Surviving the slaughter of 82 percent of his regiment in the infamous Cornfield at Antietam, Phillip Work was forced out of the Confederate army by a different kind of wound—syphilis. A member of the Texas convention that removed the state from the Union, Work had been appointed captain, Company F, 1st Texas, on May 28, 1861, and sent to Virginia. He became a lieutenant colonel on May 19, 1862. After serving through the Peninsular Campaign, Work took command of the regiment for the battles of Groveton, 2nd Bull Run, and Antietam, where it was mowed down. He was not present at Fredericksburg but again commanded the regiment at Gettysburg. His resignation for medical reasons was accepted effective from January 5, 1864. Back in Texas he raised a company and became its captain, and they served together in the District of Texas, New Mexico and Arizona, Trans-Mississippi Department, until the close of the war.

WRIGHT, Ambrose Ransom (1826-1872)

A Georgia lawyer and frequently unsuccessful political aspirant, "Rans" Wright was a hard-fighting brigadier under Lee for much of the war. His assignments included: colonel, 3rd Georgia (May 8, 1861); brigadier general, CSA (June 3, 1862); commanding Blanchard's (old) Brigade, Huger's Division, Army of Northern Virginia (June-July 1862); commanding brigade, Anderson's-Mahone's Division, 1st (3rd after May 30, 1863) Corps, same army (July-September 17 and fall 1862-July 1, and July 2, 1863-August 1864); major general, CSA (November 26, 1864); and commanding division, Department of South Carolina, Georgia and Florida (November 1864-

February 1865). After service in the Norfolk area, including action at South Mills, North Carolina, he led his regiment to the Peninsula. Following Seven Pines he was given charge of the brigade, supervising its movements through the Seven Days, 2nd Bull Run, and Antietam. Wounded in the latter, he returned to fight at Fredericksburg, Chancellorsville, and Gettysburg where he temporarily relinquished command due to illness. He fought through the Overland Campaign and at the Crater. Ordered to the Army of Tennessee in August 1864, he does not appear to have joined, possibly because of illness and perhaps for political reasons—he had been elected president of the Georgia senate the previous year. Promoted to major general, he served in the Savannah and Carolinas campaigns. He was a lawyer, journalist, and politician postwar and died before he could be sworn in as a congressman. (Freeman, Douglas S., *Lee's Lieutenants*)

WRIGHT, Marcus Joseph (1831-1922)

Civil War historians would rate Marcus J. Wright's postwar, yeoman service in the compilation of the *Official Records* as more important than his services in the field as a Confederate brigadier general. The Tennessee native had been a lawyer and court clerk prior to the secession of his state and was also active in the militia. When his regiment joined the Southern cause he went with it as second in command. His assignments included: lieutenant colonel, 154th Tennessee Senior (May 14, 1861); brigadier general, CSA (December 20, 1862, to rank from the 13th); commanding brigade, Cheatham's Division, Polk's-Hardee's Corps, Army of Tennessee (early 1863-early 1864); and commanding District of North Mississippi and West Tennessee, Department of Alabama, Mississippi and East Louisiana (February 3-May 1865). Keeping its old regimental number, his regiment was specially authorized to attach the word "Senior" to its designation. Wright commanded the regiment at Belmont and again succeeded to that position at Shiloh where he was severely wounded. Recovering, he was at Perryville on Benjamin F. Cheatham's staff. Promoted to brigadier general, he led a Tennessee brigade during the Tullahoma, Chickamauga, and Chattanooga campaigns. During the Atlanta Campaign he was in post command in Georgia and in the final months of the war led a district in northern Mississippi. A lawyer and naval official after the surrender, he was chosen by the War Department to supervise the collection of Confederate records in 1878. Given the widely scattered collections and the reluctance of many ex-Confederates to cooperate with a project they thought would be a vindication of the Northern cause, his was a difficult task. Nonetheless he was able to prove to many that the work would be an unbiased historical record and was successful in gaining access to some large and valuable stores of papers. Wright also engaged in historical writing of his own.

WYATT, Henry L. (?-1861)

Although John Q. Marr, a Virginia volunteer, had been killed in action nine days previously, Henry L. Wyatt became the first

Confederate soldier to die in action—since Marr was not in Confederate service. At the war's outbreak Wyatt had enlisted as a private in the Southern Stars, which became Company K, 1st North Carolina, and was mustered into service on May 13, 1861. Less than a month later, on June 10, at the battle of Big Bethel, Wyatt and four others volunteered to advance beyond the Confederate lines to burn a house that was a potential haven for enemy sharpshooters. A bullet in the forehead made him the first non-Virginian to be killed in the Old Dominion.

Y

YANCEY, William Lowndes (1814-1863)

One of the most extreme of states' righters, William L. Yancey wrote the Alabama secession ordinance and even feuded with Jefferson Davis when he persisted in views in favor of local rights during his tenure in the Confederate Senate. In the 1830s he had edited the Unionist *Greenville (S.C.) Mountaineer* and practiced law. In 1836 he moved to Alabama and rented a plantation. He also edited the *Cahaba Democrat* and the *Cahaba Gazette*. He served in the state legislature in the early 1840s and sat in the U.S. Congress until his first debate—which resulted in a duel with future Confederate General Thomas L. Clingman—prompted him to resign. Over the years his belief in the inalienable rights of the states grew. He proposed a Southern confederacy as early as 1858 and was a leading figure in the splitting of the Democratic Party in 1860. Following his work at the Alabama secession convention he was sent to England and France by Jefferson Davis to seek recognition for the fledgling country. While abroad he was elected to the Confederate Senate, and he returned to take his seat on March 27, 1862. He served on the committees on: Foreign Affairs; Naval Affairs; Public Lands and Territories. Remembering his states' rights views, it is easy to see how he came into conflict with Davis' idea of a strong central government. He constantly wanted to limit the president's powers, especially in the field of appointments, and wanted to require the payment of market prices for impressed goods. Between congressional sessions he died at his home on July 23, 1863. (DuBose, John Witherspoon, *The Life and Times of William Lowndes Yancey*)

YANDELL, David Wendel (1826-1898)

Although only a medical officer, David W. Yandell became involved in the intricate politics of the Confederacy's Western command. A Tennessee native, he had received his medical training in Kentucky, England, Ireland, and France. By the outbreak of the Civil War he was a professor of medicine in Kentucky. He joined the Confederate medical service, and as a military medical officer, his assignments included: medical director, Central Geographical Division of Kentucky, Department #2 (September-October 1861); Medical Director, Central Army of Kentucky, Department #2 (October 1861-March 1862); medical director, Department #2 (March 1862-July 1863); and medical director, Army of Tennessee (July 1863-April 1865). He served under Generals Simon B Buckner, Albert Sidney Johnston, Braxton Bragg, and Joseph E. Johnston and became part of the anti-Bragg faction and a staunch supporter of Joe Johnston. After the surrender in North Carolina—he had been present at such battles as Shiloh, Murfreesboro, and Chickamauga—he returned to medical education and was surgeon general for the Kentucky militia. (Cunningham, Horace Herndon, *Doctors in Gray*)

YORK, Zebulon (1819-1900)

A transplanted Maine Yankee, Zebulon York lost an arm and the co-ownership of some 1,700 slaves during the Civil War. A Louisiana attorney, he had been the state's largest realty tax payer at the outbreak of hostilities, sharing ownership of six cotton plantations. He organized a company for Confederate service and his later assignments included: major and lieutenant colonel, 14th Louisiana (1861); colonel, 14th Louisiana (spring 1862); brigadier general, CSA (May 31, 1864); and commanding Consolidated Louisiana Brigade, Gordon's Division, 2nd Corps (Valley District after June 13), Army of Northern Virginia (June 4-September 19, 1864). Distinguishing himself in the battle of Williamsburg, he went on to command the regiment in the Seven Days. In the summer of 1862 he was sent with General Richard Taylor to Louisiana to gather recruits for the two Louisiana brigades in Virginia. He was on this duty into 1864, and following the disaster at Spotsylvania he was given command of the consolidated Louisiana brigades. Sent to the Shenandoah Valley, he led this unit at Lynchburg, Monocacy, and on the outskirts of Washington. At 3rd Winchester he was wounded by a shell, costing him an arm. Upon his recovery he was again assigned to duty recruiting for the Louisiana troops, this time in North Carolina from among foreign-born Union prisoners. The war ended before he could rejoin the army in the field. Ruined by the war, he ran a hotel in Mississippi. (Freeman, Douglas S., *Lee's Lieutenants*)

YOUNG, Bennett H. (1843-1919)

The raid of Lieutenant Bennett H. Young on St. Albans, Vermont, led to a major international incident with Great Britain. The Kentucky-born Confederate officer had been authorized on June 16, 1864, to recruit a force of no more than 20 men from escaped Confederate prisoners in Canada. The so-styled 5th Company, Confederate States Retributors, was intended to launch raids against prisoner of war camps near the border. Having himself escaped from Camp Douglas near Chicago—where he had been confined after raiding with John Hunt Morgan in Ohio—Young planned to hit the prison on Johnson's Island, Ohio. Forced to change his plans due to a leak, he led his 20 men on a raid against St. Albans. With perfect planning they looted three banks of a total of $201,522, while others gathered up any stray passers-by to prevent an alarm. However, a Union officer on leave managed to alert the town. In the action that followed one civilian and one raider were killed. In addition another four raiders were wounded; the balance then raced for the Canadian line with the citizens in hot pursuit. Violating international law, the posse crossed onto foreign soil and arrested the Confederate unit. On their return they were stopped by the Canadian authorities and forced to relinquish their 14 prisoners, including Young. Following two trials the Confederates were ruled to be belligerents engaged in legal military operations and released. This raised a howl of protest, especially since only $86,000 from the October 19, 1864 raid had been recovered. Young subsequently returned to Kentucky and took up the practice of law. (Kinchen, Oscar A., *General Bennett H. Young*)

YOUNG, Pierce Manning Butler (1836-1896)

Resigning his cadetship at West Point in March 1861, three months before his scheduled graduation, P.M.B. Young joined the Confederacy and rose to be a major general. His services included: second lieutenant, Artillery (March 16, 1861); first lieutenant and aide-de-camp (July 1861); first lieutenant and adjutant, Cobb's (Ga.) Legion (July 1861); lieutenant colonel, Cobb's Legion (November 1861); colonel, Cobb's Legion (November 1, 1862); brigadier general, CSA (September 28, 1863); commanding Butler's (old) Brigade, Hampton's-Butler's Division, Cavalry Corps, Army of Northern Virginia (October 1863-November 1864); major general, CSA (December 30, 1864); commanding Iverson's (old) Division, Hampton's Cavalry Command, Department of South Carolina, Georgia and Florida (February 1865); and commanding Military District of Georgia and South Carolina, same department (March-April 1865). After service at Pensacola and on W.H.T. Walker's staff, the South Carolina-born and Georgia-raised Young went to Virginia with the legion, eventually commanding the cavalry of the mixed branch unit. He fought at the Seven Days and was wounded at South Mountain. Recovering, he was at Fredericksburg, Brandy Station, and Gettysburg before being given a brigade. This he directed through the Overland and half of the Petersburg campaigns. Sent in November 1864 to secure remounts for his command, he was active against Sherman in the Augusta-Savannah area. After the war he was a planter, congressman, and diplomatic representative to Russia, Guatemala, and Honduras. (Freeman, Douglas S., *Lee's Lieutenants*)

YOUNG, William Hugh (1838-1901)

Less than two months after being named a brigadier general William H. Young's Confederate career came to an end when he was wounded and captured at Allatoona. Missouri-born and Texas-raised, he had been a student at the University of Virginia when the Civil War broke out. Recruiting a company, his later assignments included: captain, 9th Texas (September 1861); colonel, 9th Texas (ca. May 1862); commanding Ector's (old) Brigade, French's Division, Polk's-Stewart's Corps, Army of Tennessee (July-October 5, 1864); and brigadier general, CSA (August 15, 1864). He led his company at Shiloh and in the reorganization that spring he became the regiment's colonel. As such he served in the defense of Corinth, Mississippi, and in the Kentucky Campaign. Wounded at Murfreesboro, he recovered in time to lead his regiment under Joseph E. Johnston in the unsuccessful efforts to relieve the pressure on Vicksburg. He was again wounded at Jackson and at Chickamauga. Leading his regiment in the Atlanta Campaign, he was twice wounded at Kenesaw Mountain. Remaining in the field, he took over command of the brigade in July and the next month was named a brigadier general. In Hood's raids against Sherman's supply lines, Young was wounded and captured on October 5, 1864, at Allatoona, Georgia. He was confined on Johnson's Island, Ohio, until July 24, 1865. Thereafter he engaged in the practice of law and the real estate business.

YOUNGER, Cole (1844-1916)

Many of the famed outlaws of the Wild West were spawned in the sectional fighting of the Civil War. The Younger Brothers, of whom Cole was the eldest, were a case in point. Already a Southern partisan, he had joined with the brutal Missouri guerrilla William C. Quantrill in 1862 following the murder of his father by Unionists. He was with Quantrill at the massacre at Lawrence and Baxter Springs, but by March 1864 he had drifted out of the group. During that time he had ridden with Frank James and the year after the Civil War ended met Jesse James. This was the beginning of the James-Younger gang that rode until the disastrous Northfield, Minnesota, bank raid. Here Cole Younger was wounded and two weeks later captured, having suffered another 11 wounds. Sentenced to life, he was freed in 1901 and went into the tombstone business. Later he appeared in a Wild West extravaganza with Frank James. (Younger, Cole, *The Story of Cole Younger*)

Three of the notorious Younger brothers, with sister Rhetta. Left to right: James, Robert, and Cole. (NA)

YOUNGER, James (1848-1902)

Part of the famed James-Younger gang in the Wild West, Jim Younger and his brothers had received their education in crime as members of Quantrill's guerrillas in Missouri during the Civil War. When their father was killed by Missouri Unionists in 1862 four of the eight sons joined up with the brutal killer and took part in the sacking of Lawrence, Kansas, and the massacre at Baxter Springs. Meeting Frank James in this service—and his brother Jesse just after the war—the four Youngers became part of the infamous James-Younger gang of train, stage, and bank robbers. Jim took part in the crimes, killing a number of persons, including lawmen, until the 1876 raid on the Northfield, Minnesota, bank. Here Jim was severely wounded. In the getaway the Jameses wanted to put him out of his misery so they could travel faster. Faced down by two of Younger's brothers, the Jameses rode off. Two weeks later the Youngers were badly shot up and captured. Serving a life sentence, James was freed in 1901 but committed suicide the next year.

YOUNGER, John (1851-1874)

Only 10 years old when he launched his career of killing in the Civil War, John Younger went into the business fulltime when his father was killed by Unionist irregulars. He and his elder brother James killed four Union soldiers early in the war and later joined up with the notorious guerrilla William C. Quantrill, in 1862. In all, four of the eight Younger Brothers took part in the slaughter at Lawrence, Kansas, and later at Baxter Springs. Having in this service met Frank James—and after the war his brother Jesse—the four Youngers became part of the James-Younger train, bank, and stage robbing team in 1866. They were a terror to banks and transport companies throughout Missouri and the surrounding area. Then in 1874 Jim and John ran into three lawmen—two of whom they killed—but Jim was wounded and John was dead.

YOUNGER, Robert (1853-1889)

The youngest of the criminal Younger Brothers, Bob Younger was only 12 when he served under the brutal guerrilla William C. Quantrill in the raid on Lawrence, Kansas. The death of his father in 1862 at the hands of Missouri Unionists had launched four of the eight brothers into a life of crime. In 1866 they joined up with the Jameses—they had met Frank James in Quantrill's band—and they terrorized railroads and banks in the Missouri area for the next 10 years. In the 1876 raid on a bank in Northfield, Minnesota, Bob received two wounds. Two weeks later he was further shot up when the three surviving brothers were captured. Given a life sentence, he died in prison of tuberculosis.

Z

Blundering Confederate General Felix K. Zollicoffer dies at Mill Springs. (*Leslie's*)

ZOGBAUM, Rufus Fairchild (1849-1925)

Although too young to have participated in the Civil War, Rufus F. Zogbaum painted many scenes of that and other conflicts in the latter part of the 19th and the early part of the 20th century. Born in Charleston, he and his family had moved to New York around the beginning of the war. He gained his art education at Heidelberg, New York, and Paris and then launched his career in the United States, depicting historic action scenes both on land and sea. His Civil War subjects included the fighting at Hampton Roads, Lee's Surrender, and the "First Minnesota Regiment at the Battle of Gettysburg." Covering other historic events, he benefited from first-hand observation of many Spanish-American War actions. His art publications included: *Horse, Foot, and Dragoons*; *"All Hands"*; and *The Junior Officer of the Watch*. He died in New York after almost a half a century of work.

ZOLLICOFFER, Felix Kirk (1812-1862)

A veteran of the Seminole War as a first lieutenant, then a newspaperman and Whig Congressman, Felix Zollicoffer was made a brigadier general in the Tennessee state forces following the fall of Fort Sumter. He was transferred into Confederate service, with the same rank, on July 9, 1861, and given command of the District of East Tennessee, Department #2, on August 1, with the assignment to "preserve peace, protect the railroad, and repel invasion." This was a difficult task since eastern Tennessee was generally not aslaveholding area and was unsympathetic to the Confederate cause. Zollicoffer moved his forces into southeastern Kentucky in late 1861 before being superseded by General G.B. Crittenden on December 8. Zollicoffer was then given command of the 1st Brigade of the district. His rash move across the Cumberland River forced the rebels to give battle, at a disadvantage, at Mill Springs on January 18, 1862. While studying the field he came across another officer on the same mission. He told that officer not to fire on his own men. But the other man was Colonel Speed S. Fry of the 4th Kentucky, a Union regiment. After riding away and being fired upon, Fry, realizing his mistake, turned and shot the Confederate. Also fired upon by some other Federals, Zollicoffer fell dead. (Myers, Raymond E., *The Zollie Tree*)

APPENDIX
CHRONOLOGY

NOVEMBER 1860

6—Lincoln elected.

DECEMBER 1860

20—South Carolina secedes.

26—Garrison transferred from Fort Moultrie to Fort Sumter.

JANUARY 1861

9—Mississippi secedes; *Star of the West* fired upon.

10—Florida secedes.

11—Alabama secedes.

19—Georgia secedes.

21—Withdrawal of five Southern members of the U.S. Senate: Yulee and Mallory of Florida, Clay and Fitzpatrick of Alabama, and Davis of Mississippi.

26—Louisiana secedes.

29—Kansas admitted to the Union as a free state.

FEBRUARY 1861

1—Texas convention votes for secession.

4—1st Session, Provisional Confederate Congress, convenes as a convention.

9—Jefferson Davis elected provisional Confederate president.

18—Jefferson Davis inaugurated.

23—Texas voters approve secession.

MARCH 1861

4—Lincoln inaugurated; Special Senate Session of 37th Congress convenes.

16—1st Session, Provisional Confederate Congress, adjourns.

28—Special Senate Session of 37th Congress adjourns.

APRIL 1861

12—Bombardment of Fort Sumter begins.

13—Fort Sumter surrenders to Southern forces.

17—Virginia secedes.

19—6th Massachusetts attacked by Baltimore mob; Lincoln declares blockade of Southern coast.

20—Norfolk, Virginia, Navy Yard evacuated.

29—2nd Session, Provisional Confederate Congress, convenes; Maryland rejects secession.

MAY 1861

6—Arkansas secedes; Tennessee legislature calls for popular vote on secession.

10—Union forces capture Camp Jackson, and a riot follows in St. Louis.

13—Baltimore occupied by U.S. troops.

20—North Carolina secedes.

21—2nd Session, Provisional Confederate Congress, adjourns.

23—Virginia voters approve secession.

24—Union troops sieze Alexandria, Virginia.

JUNE 1861

1—Skirmish at Fairfax Courthouse, Virginia.

3—Battle of Philippi (western Virginia).

8—Tennessee voters approve secession.

10—Battle of Big Bethel (Virginia).

17—Battle of Booneville (Missouri).

JULY 1861

4—1st Session, 37th Congress, convenes.

5—Battle of Carthage (Missouri).

11—Battle of Rich Mountain (western Virginia).

13—Battle of Carrick's Ford (western Virginia).

18—Battle of Blackburn's Ford (Virginia).

20—3rd Session, Provincial Confederate Congress, convenes.

21—Battle of 1st Bull Run (Virginia).

AUGUST 1861

6—1st Session, 37th Congress adjourns.

10—Battle of Wilson's Creek.

27—Fort Clark, North Carolina, captured by Union.

28—Fort Hatteras, North Carolina, surrenders to Union.

31—3rd Session, Provisional Confederate Congress, adjourns.

SEPTEMBER 1861

3—4th (called) Session, Provisional Confederate Congress, convenes and adjourns; Confederate troops enter Kentucky, ending the state's neutrality.

6—Union troops capture Paducah, Kentucky.

10—Battle of Carnifax Ferry (Virginia).

11—Cheat Mountain Campaign (to the 15th).

12—Siege of Lexington, Missouri (to the 20th).

20—Lexington, Missouri, surrenders to Confederates.

OCTOBER 1861

21—Battle of Ball's Bluff (Virginia).

NOVEMBER 1861

6—Jefferson Davis elected regular president of the Confederacy.

7—Belmont, Missouri, and Port Royal, South Carolina, fall to Union.

8—Seizure of Confederates Mason and Slidell from aboard the British *Trent* by the USS *San Jacinto*.

18—5th Session, Provisional Confederate Congress, convenes.

28—Missouri admitted to Confederacy despite its not having seceded.

DECEMBER 1861

2—2nd Session, 37th Congress, convenes.

13—Battle of Camp Alleghany (western Virginia).

20—Battle of Dranesville (Virginia).

JANUARY 1862

19—Battle of Mill Springs (or Fishing Creek, Logan's Crossroads) (Kentucky).

FEBRUARY 1862

6—Battle of Fort Henry (Tennessee).

8—Battle of Roanoke Island (North Carolina).

12—Battle of Fort Donelson (Tennessee) (to the 16th).

16—Fort Donelson surrenders to Union.

17—5th (final) Session, Provisional Confederate Congress, adjourns.

18—1st Session, 1st Confederate Congress, convenes.

21—Battle of Valverde (New Mexico Territory).

22—Jefferson Davis inaugurated as regular president.

MARCH 1862

6—Battle of Pea Ridge (Arkansas) (to the 8th).

8—Hampton Roads Naval Actions (Virginia) (to the 9th).

9—*Monitor* vs. *Virginia* at Hampton Roads.

14—Capture of New Madrid, Missouri, and New Bern, North Carolina, by Union.

23—Battle of Kernstown (Virginia).

26—Battle of Apache Canyon (New Mexico Territory).

28—Battle of Glorieta (or Pigeon's Ranch) (New Mexico Territory).

APRIL 1862

5—Siege of Yorktown, Virginia (to May 4).

6—Battle of Shiloh (Tennessee) (to the 7th).

7—Island # 10 (Missouri) falls to Union.

11—Fort Pulaski (Georgia) captured by Union.

18—Bombardment of Forts Jackson and St. Philip, Louisiana (to the 24th).

21—1st Session, 1st Confederate Congress, adjourns.

24—Federal naval forces pass Forts Jackson and St. Philip below New Orleans.

25—Fort Macon, North Carolina, captured and New Orleans falls to Union.

MAY 1862

4—Yorktown, Virginia, occupied by Union.

5—Battle of Williamsburg (Virginia).

8—Battle of McDowell (West Virginia).

10—Norfolk, Virginia, occupied by Union; battle of Plum Bend (Tennessee).

15—Battle of Drewry's Bluff (Virginia).

23—Battle of Front Royal (Virginia).

25—Battle of 1st Winchester (Virginia).

30—Corinth, Mississippi, taken by Union.

31—Battle of Seven Pines or Fair Oaks (Virginia) (to June 1st).

JUNE 1862

5—Fort Pillow, Tennessee, abandoned by Confederates.

6—Battle of Memphis (Tennessee).

8—Battle of Cross Keys (Virginia).

9—Battle of Port Republic (Virginia).

16—Battle of Secessionville (South Carolina).

25—Battles of the Seven Days (Virginia) (to July 1; includes those marked with *).

26—Beaver Dam Creek*.

27—Gaines' Mill*.

29—Savage Station*.

30—Frayser's Farm*; White Oak Swamp*.

JULY 1862

1—Malvern Hill*.

17—2nd Session, 37th Congress, adjourns.

AUGUST 1862

5—Battle of Baton Rouge (Louisiana).

9—Battle of Cedar (or Slaughter) Mountain (Virginia).

17—Sioux uprising (to September 23) in Minnesota.

18—2nd Session, 1st Confederate Congress, convenes.

28—Battle of 2nd Bull Run (Virginia) (to the 30th).

30—Battle of Richmond (Kentucky).

SEPTEMBER 1862

1—Battle of Chantilly (Virginia).

14—Battles of South Mountain (Maryland) and Crampton's Gap (Maryland).

15—Fall of Harpers Ferry, West Virginia, to Confederates.

17—Battles of Antietam (Maryland) and Munfordville (Kentucky).

19—Battle of Iuka (Mississippi).

22—Emancipation Proclamation issued.

OCTOBER 1862

3—Battle of Corinth (Mississippi) (to the 4th).

8—Battle of Perryville (Kentucky).

13—2nd Session, 1st Confederate Congress, convenes.

DECEMBER 1862

1—3rd Session, 37th Congress, convenes.

7—Battle of Prairie Grove (Arkansas).

13—Battle of Fredericksburg (Virginia).

20—Holly Springs, Mississippi, raided by Southerners.

29—Battle of Chickasaw Bayou (Mississippi).

31—Battle of Murfreesboro (Tennessee) (to January 2, 1863).

JANUARY 1863

1—Emancipation Proclamation takes effect; battle of Galveston Harbor (Texas).

11—Arkansas Post, Arkansas, captured by Union forces.

12—3rd Session, 1st Confederate Congress, convenes.

19—"Mud March" (to the 22nd) by Army of the Potomac from Rappahannock River.

31—Charleston blockade disrupted (South Carolina).

MARCH 1863

3—3rd (final) Session, 37th Congress, adjourns.

4—Special Senate Session, 38th Congress, convenes.

11—Yazoo Pass Expedition blocked at Fort Pemberton, Mississippi.

14—Special Senate Session, 38th Congress, adjourns.

17—Battle of Kelly's Ford (Virginia).

APRIL 1863

7—Charleston naval attack by Union ironclads.

17—Grierson's Raid begins from La Grange, Tennessee.

MAY 1863

1—3rd Session, 1st Confederate Congress, adjourns; battle of Port Gibson (Mississippi) (Vicksburg Campaign); battle of Chancellorsville (Virginia) (to the 4th).

12—Battle of Raymond (Mississippi) (Vicksburg Campaign).

14—Battle of Jackson (Mississippi) (Vicksburg Campaign).

16—Battle of Champion Hill (Mississippi) (Vicksburg Campaign).

17—Battle of Big Black River Bridge (Mississippi) (Vicksburg Campaign).

18—Vicksburg, Mississippi, siege begins (to July 4).

19—1st Vicksburg assault by Union.

21—Port Hudson, Louisiana, siege begins (to July 8).

22—2nd Union assault at Vicksburg, Mississippi.

27—1st Union assault at Port Hudson, Louisiana.

JUNE 1863

7—Battle of Milliken's Bend (Louisiana).

9—Battle of Brandy Station (Virginia).

14—2nd Union assault at Port Hudson; battle of 2nd Winchester (Virginia).

15—Stephenson's Depot (Virginia).

23—Tullahoma Campaign begun by Union (Tennessee) (to July 7).

JULY 1863

1—Battle of Gettysburg (Pennsylvania) (to the 3rd).

4—Vicksburg, Mississippi, surrenders to Union.

8—Port Hudson, Louisiana, surrenders to Union; Morgan's raid north of the Ohio begins in Indiana (to the 26th).

10—Union siege of Battery Wagner in Charleston Harbor, South Carolina, begins (to September 6).

11—1st Union assault on Battery Wagner in Charleston Harbor.

13—New York City draft riots begin (to the 15th).

18—2nd Union assault on Battery Wagner in Charleston Harbor.

26—John Hunt Morgan captured at New Lisbon, Ohio.

AUGUST 1863

17—Fort Sumter, South Carolina, bombarded by Union.

21—Lawrence, Kansas, sacked by Quantrill's Confederate raiders.

SEPTEMBER 1863

6—Battery Wagner in Charleston Harbor abandoned by Confederates.

10—Little Rock, Arkansas, captured by Union.

19—Battle of Chickamauga (Georgia) (to the 20th).

OCTOBER 1863

9—Bristoe Campaign begins in Virginia (to the 22nd).

14—Battle of Bristoe Station (Virginia).

NOVEMBER 1863

7—Battle of Rappahannock Station (Virginia).

23—Battle of Chattanooga (Tennessee) (to the 25th).

26—Mine Run Campaign begins in Virginia (to December 2).

29—Battle of Fort Sanders (Knoxville, Tennessee).

DECEMBER 1863

7—4th Session, 1st Confederate Congress, convenes; 1st Session, 38th Congress, convenes.

FEBRUARY 1864

3—Meridian Campaign begins in Mississippi (to the 14th).

17—4th (final) Session, 1st Confederate Congress, adjourns.

20—Battle of Olustee (Florida).

22—Battle of Okolona (Mississippi).

MARCH 1864

12—Red River Campaign begins (Louisiana).

APRIL 1864

8—Battle of Mansfield (Louisiana).

9—Battle of Pleasant Hill (Louisiana).

12—Fort Pillow, Tennessee, massacre; battle of Blair's Landing (Louisiana) (to the 13th).

17—Battle of Plymouth (North Carolina) (to the 20th).

30—Battle of Jenkins' Ferry (Arkansas).

MAY 1864

2—1st Session, 2nd Confederate Congress, convenes.

5—Battle of the Wilderness (Virginia) (to the 6th).

6—Battle of Port Walthall Junction (Virginia) (to the 7th).

7—Atlanta Campaign (to September 2) begins from Chattanooga, Tennessee.

8—Battle of Spotsylvania (Virginia) (to the 21st).

9—Battles of Snake Creek Gap and Dalton (Georgia) (latter to the 13th).

11—Battle of Yellow Tavern (Virginia).

14—Battle of Resaca (Georgia) to the 15th.

15—Battle of New Market (Virginia).

16—Battle of Drewry's Bluff (Virginia).

23—Battle of the North Anna (Virginia) (to the 26th).

25—Battle of New Hope Church (Georgia) (to June 4).

30—Bethesda Church (Virginia) (to June 3).

JUNE 1864

1—Battle of Cold Harbor (Virginia) (to the 3rd).

10—Battle of Brice's Crossroads (Mississippi).

11—Battle of Trevilian Station (Virginia).

14—1st Session, 2nd Confederate Congress, adjourns; battle of Pine Mountain (Georgia).

15—Petersburg, Virginia, assaults (to the 18th) by Union.

18—Petersburg, Virginia, siege begun by Union (to April 2, 1865).

27—Battle of Kennesaw Mountain (Georgia).

JULY 1864

4—1st Session, 38th Congress, adjourns.

9—Battle of Monocacy (Maryland).

11—Battle of Fort Stevens (Maryland).

14—Battle of Tupelo (Mississippi).

20—Battle of Peachtree Creek (Georgia).

22—Battle of Atlanta (Georgia).

28—Battle of Ezra Church (Georgia).

30—Petersburg Mine exploded by Union sappers and battle of the Crater follows (Virginia).

AUGUST 1864

5—Battle of Mobile Bay (Alabama).

18—Battle of the Weldon Railroad (Virginia) (to the 19th).

25—Battle of Reams' Station (Virginia).

31—Battle of Jonesboro (Georgia) (to September 1).

SEPTEMBER 1864

2—Atlanta occupied by Union troops (Georgia).

19—3rd Battle of Winchester (Virginia).

22—Battle of Fisher's Hill (Virginia).

29—Battle of Peebles' Farm (to October 2) and Chaffin's Farm/Fort Harrison (to October 1) (Virginia).

OCTOBER 1864

5—Battle of Allatoona (Georgia).

9—Battle of Tom's Brook (Virginia).

19—Battle of Cedar Creek (Virginia).

23—Battle of Westport (Missouri).

27—Battle of Burgess' Mill/Boydton Plank Road (Virginia).

NOVEMBER 1864

7—2nd Session, 2nd Confederate Congress, convenes.

8—Lincoln reelected.

16—March to the Sea (to December 21) begins from Atlanta, Georgia.

29—Battles of Spring Hill (Tennessee) and Sand Creek (Colorado Territory).

30—Battle of Franklin (Tennessee).

DECEMBER 1864

5—2nd Session, 38th Congress, convenes.

15—Battle of Nashville (Tennessee) (to the 16th).

21—Savannah, Georgia, occupied by Union.

24—1st Union attack on Fort Fisher, North Carolina (to the 25th).

JANUARY 1865

13—2nd Union attack on Fort Fisher (to the 15th).

15—Fort Fisher, North Carolina, falls to Union naval and land forces.

19—Carolinas Campaign begins at Savannah, Georgia (to April 26).

FEBRUARY 1865

5—Battle of Hatcher's Run (Virginia) (to the 7th).

MARCH 1865

2—Battle of Waynesboro (Virginia).

3—2nd (final) Session, 38th Congress, adjourns.

4—Lincoln reinaugurated.

8—Battle of Kinston (North Carolina) (to the 10th).

16—Battle of Averysboro (North Carolina).

18—2nd (final) Session 2nd Confederate Congress, adjourns.

19—Battle of Bentonville (North Carolina) (to the 21st).

22—Wilson's raid (to April 24) south into Alabama.

25—Battle of Fort Stedman (Virginia); siege of Mobile, Alabama (to April 12).

31—Battle of Dinwiddie Court House (Virginia).

APRIL 1865

1—Battle of Five Forks (Virginia).

2—Selma, Alabama, falls; final Union assault on Petersburg, Virginia.

3—Richmond and Petersburg occupied by Union forces.

6—Battle of Sayler's Creek (Virginia).

7—Battle of High Bridge (Virginia).

9—Battles of Appomattox (Virginia) and Fort Blakely (Alabama); Lee surrenders at Appomattox.

12—Mobile, Alabama, surrenders to Union forces.
14—Lincoln shot by John Wilkes Booth.
15—Lincoln dies.
26—Johnston surrenders to Sherman in North Carolina.

MAY 1865

4—Taylor surrenders to Canby in Alabama.
26—Smith surrenders to Canby in Trans—Mississippi.

JUNE 1865

28—CSS *Shenandoah* ends operations in Bering Sea, having taken 11 whalers that day.

AUGUST 1865

2—CSS *Shenandoah* learns of end of the war.

NOVEMBER 1865

6—CSS *Shenandoah* surrenders to British at Liverpool.

SELECTED BIBLIOGRAPHY

Amann, William. *Personnel of the Civil War*. Thomas Yoseloff: New York, 1961. Provides valuable information on local unit designations, general officer assignments, and organizational data on geographical commands.

Boatner, Mark Mayo III. *The Civil War Dictionary*. David McKay Company: New York, 1959. Provides thumbnail sketches of leaders, battles, campaigns, events, units, weapons, etc. While generally an excellent work, there is a lack of coverage of naval figures and of Confederates below the rank of general. Also, for some of the Union officers, included because of their brevets to the rank of brigadier general, there is little indication of what they did to earn them. There is also little coverage of congressmen. Some of author's statements as to the presence of certain officers at certain battles can be contradicted in the *Official Records*.

Bowman, John S., ed. *The Civil War Almanac*. Facts On File, Inc: New York, 1982. Basically a chronology of events, it is also valuable for its sections on naval matters and weapons and its approximately 130 biographical sketches of civilian and military personalities.

Cullum, George W. *Biographical Register of the Officers and Graduates of the United States Military Academy*, 2 vols. J.F. Throw: New York, 1891. Especially valuable for providing information upon the stations of officers in the pre- and postwar years.

Cyclopedia of American Bibliography, 7 vols. Appleton & Co.: New York, 1891. A general biographical work that provides some information, albeit limited, on the Civil War careers of those covered in its seven volumes.

Dictionary of American Biography, 20 vols. Charles Scribner's Sons: New York, 1928. Being a more general work, it provides only limited information on the Civil War careers of the personalities which it covers. However, it is a starting point.

Dyer, Frederick H. *A Compendium of the War of the Rebellion*, 3 vols. Dyer Publishing Co.: Des Moines, 1908; National Historical Society: Dayton, 1979 (reprints in 2 vols). Provides histories of all Union regiments and smaller units, indexes of battles by state, and tables of organization for larger units, including the dates for their commanders.

Evans, Clement A., ed. *Confederate Military History*, 13 vols. Confederate Publishing Co.: Atlanta, 1899. The volumes of this work are primarily concerned with providing histories of one or two states in each book. Each state military account was written by a different participant in the war, and they vary in quality. All accounts, however, include biographies of the generals from their state. The Alabama chapter, by Joseph Wheeler, also has histories of the state's regiments. There are also volumes on secession, naval matters, and reconstruction. The major drawback is the lack of a comprehensive index.

Freeman, Douglas Southall. *Lee's Lieutenants: A Study in Command*, 3 vols. Charles Scribner's Sons: New York, 1941-1946. An excellent narrative history of the command structure of the Army of Northern Virginia. The author's *R.E. Lee: A Biography* also proved highly valuable.

Heitman, Francis B. *Historical Register and Dictionary of the United States Army From Its Organization, September 29, 1789, to March 2, 1903*, 2 vols. Government Printing Office: Washington, 1903. For my purposes, the most important of the compilations in this work was that listing the enlistment, assignments, and separation of all regular army officers plus those Civil War volunteers who achieved the grade of general, whether by full grade or brevet. These entries provide information on brevets. Other useful, but briefer, lists cover: wounds suffered by regular army officers, Mexican War volunteer officers, and field-grade volunteer officers in the Civil War.

Johnson, Robert Underwood and Buel, Clarence Clough, eds. *Battles and Leaders of the Civil War*, 4 vols. The Century Co: New York, 1887. Reprint 1956. Exceptionally valuable for its tables of organization for major battles as well as for its first-person accounts.

Krick, Robert K. *Lee's Colonel's: A Biographical Register of the Field Officers of the Army of Northern Virginia*, 2nd ed. Press of Morningside Bookshop: Dayton, 1984. Brief sketches of the 1,965 field-grade officers who at one time or another served with the Army of Northern Virginia but never achieved the rank of brigadier general. Sketches include, as available, dates and places of birth and death, pre- and postwar careers, height, unit, promotions, wounds, and end of military service. Also included in the 2nd edition is a listing by name and unit of those field-grade officers who never served with Lee.

Long, E.B. and Barbara. *The Civil War Day By Day: An Almanac 1861-1865*. Doubleday: Garden City, 1971. An excellent chronology of the conflict, with much information on organizational changes and assignments of commanders.

Lonn, Ella. *Foreigners in the Confederacy*. University of North Carolina Press: Chapel Hill, 1940; and *Foreigners in the Union Army and Navy*. Louisiana State University Press: Baton Rouge, 1951. Accounts of the foreign-born contribution to the Civil War.

Scharf, J. Thomas. *History of the Confederate States Navy: From Its Organization to the Surrender of Its Last Vessels*. Joseph McDonough: Albany, 1887. A rather disjointed narrative of Confederate naval operations, but it does provide thumbnail sketches of some officers. The prime defect of this book, as with most from its period, is the lack of an adequate index. It was written by an ex-Confederate midshipman.

Sifakis, Carl. *The Dictionary of Historical Nicknames: A Treasury of More than 7,500 Famous and Infamous Nicknames From World History*. Facts On File: New York, 1984. Provides the origins of nicknames of Civil War personalities.

U.S. Navy Department. *Official Records of the Union and Confederate Navies in the War of Rebellion*, 31 vols. Government Printing Office: Washington, 1894-1927. U.S. War Department. *The War of Rebellion: A Compilation of the Official Records of the Union and Confederate Armies*, 70 vols. in 128 books divided into four series, plus Atlas. Government Printing Office: Washington, 1881-1901. The two most important of primary sources on the military aspects of the Civil War. While difficult to use they provide a goldmine of information. Organized by campaigns in specified geographic regions, they are subdivided into post-action reports and correspondence. In the War Department series special volumes deal with prisoners of war and correspondence between the two governments. For my book's purpose the information contained in the hundreds of organizational tables and the orders assigning officers to duty proved exceedingly valuable.

Wakelyn, Jon L. *Biographical Dictionary of the Confederacy*. Greenwood Press: Westport, Connecticut, 1977. Short biographies of 651 leaders of the Confederacy, including congressmen, cabinet members, governors, bureaucrats, clergy, surgeons, and military leaders. However, the selection criteria in the latter category is somewhat confusing.

Warner, Ezra. *Generals in Gray: Lives of the Confederate Commanders*. Louisiana State University Press: Baton Rouge, 1959; and *Generals in Blue: Lives of the Union Commanders*. Louisiana State University Press: Baton Rouge, 1964. Sketches of the 583 Union and 425 Southern generals. Good coverage of pre- and postwar careers. The wartime portion of the entries tends to be far more complete for the Northern generals.

Warner, Ezra J. and Yearns, W. Buck. *Biographical Register of the Confederate Congress*. Louisiana State University Press: Baton Rouge, 1975. Biographical sketches of the 267 Southern congressmen, providing coverage of pre- and postwar careers, committee assignments, policy concerns, and electoral opponents. Maps of the congressional districts are also included.

Wise, Jennings Cropper. *The Long Arm of Lee: The History of the Artillery of the Army of Northern Virginia*. J.P. Bell Co.: Lynchburg, Virginia, 1915 (reprint 1959). An excellent study of Lee's artillery, providing valuable information on the artillery commanders.

Wright, Marcus J. *General Officers of the Confederate Army*. Neale Publishing Co.: New York, 1911. Long the definitive work on the Southern command structure, it was superseded by Ezra J. Warner's work.

PERIODICALS

Civil War Times Illustrated, its predecessor *Civil War Times, American History Illustrated*, and *Civil War History* all provide articles on Civil War personalities. In addition, the *Southern Historical Society Papers* (47 vols., 1876-1930) are a goldmine of information on Confederate units and leaders.